PassPorter's
Walt Disney World®
For Your
Special Needs

The take-along travel guide and planner

PassPorter Travel Press

An imprint of MediaMarx, Inc.
P.O. Box 3880, Ann Arbor, Michigan 48106
877-WAYFARER
http://www.passporter.com

PassPorter's® Walt Disney World® For Your Special Needs

by Deb Wills and Debra Martin Koma

© 2005 by PassPorter Travel Press, an imprint of MediaMarx, Inc.

P.O. Box 3880, Ann Arbor, Michigan 48106
877-WAYFARER or 877-929-3273 (toll-free)
Visit us on the World Wide Web at http://www.passporter.com

PassPorter® is a registered trademark of MediaMarx, Inc.
Photographs on page 12 © Donna Jagodzinski; pages 43 and 48 © Dotti Saroufim; page 98 Nikki Shenk; and page 311 Elizabeth Shorten. All other photographs© MediaMarx, Inc., Deb Wills, or Debra Martin Koma
Vegebility ratings and orange symbol © Susan Shumaker and Than Saffel

PassPorter's® Walt Disney World® For Your Special Needs is not affiliated with, authorized or endorsed by, or in any way officially connected with The Walt Disney Company, Disney Enterprises, Inc., or any of their affiliates.

While every care has been taken to ensure the accuracy of the information in this travel guide, the passage of time will always bring changes, and consequently, the publisher cannot accept responsibility for errors that may occur. All prices and operating schedules quoted herein are based on information available to us at press time. Operating hours, maps, resort policies, future attractions, admission fees, and other costs may change, and we advise vacationers to call ahead and verify these facts and any others that are subject to change. The authors and publishers of this book shall not be held liable for any information (valid or invalid) presented here and do not represent The Walt Disney Company.

Walt Disney World® is a registered trademark of The Walt Disney Company. This guide makes reference to various Disney copyrighted characters, trademarks, marks, and registered marks owned by The Walt Disney Company, Disney Enterprises, Inc., and other trademark owners. The use in this guide of trademarked names and images is strictly for editorial purposes, and no commercial claim to their use, or suggestion of sponsorship or endorsement, is made by the authors or publisher. Those words or terms that the authors and publishers have reason to believe are trademarks are designated as such by the use of initial capitalization, where appropriate. However, no attempt has been made to identify or designate all words or terms to which trademark or other proprietary rights may exist. Nothing contained herein is intended to express a judgment on, or affect the validity of legal status of, any word or term as a trademark, service mark, or other proprietary mark.

PassPorter's® Walt Disney World® For Your Special Needs is authored by Deb Wills and Debra Martin Koma and edited by Jennifer Marx and Dave Marx. The information presented is for your personal vacation planning. Any stated opinions are ours alone, unless otherwise noted, and do not represent The Walt Disney Company or anyone else. Materials submitted by and credited to persons other than ourselves are here with their permission and any associated rights belong to them.

Any and all written messages, suggestions, ideas, or other information shared with the authors in response to this guide shall be deemed and shall remain the property of PassPorter Travel Press.

Special Sales: PassPorter Travel Press publications are available at special discounts for bulk purchases for sales premiums or promotions. Special editions, including personalized covers and excerpts of existing guides, can be created in large quantities. For information, write to Special Sales, P.O. Box 3880, Ann Arbor, Michigan, 48106.

ISBN-13: 978-1-58771-018-6
ISBN-10: 1-58771-018-8

10 9 8 7 6 5 4 3 2 1

Printed and bound in U.S.A.

About the Authors

Deb Wills saw Walt Disney hosting his Sunday evening "Wonderful World of Color" television show and promptly fell under the spell of the Disney magic. As a child, she visited the 1964-65 World's Fair in New York and enjoyed the original debuts of attractions like It's a Small World and the GE Carousel of Progress. Her first visit to the Magic Kingdom in 1972 signaled the start of a life-long relationship with the popular vacation resort. After she graduated from college, Deb made many repeat visits to Walt Disney World and the Fort Wilderness Campground in her capacity as a rehabilitation assistant with a vacation travel program for special needs adults. Since then, Deb has paid countless visits to the "World" and has sailed on the Disney Cruise Line seven times. More than nine years ago, she began the unofficial Walt Disney World Information Guide web site now known as AllEarsNet.com, and in 1999, began publishing ALL EARS®, a weekly electronic newsletter that goes to more than 60,000 subscribers. When PassPorter publishers Jennifer and Dave Marx approached her with the idea of co-authoring a book about traveling to Walt Disney World with special needs, Deb jumped at the opportunity, realizing that it was the perfect link between her past and present interests. Deb has been a peer reviewer of the *PassPorter Walt Disney World Resort* guidebook series since 2000 and recently joined the review group for *PassPorter's Field Guide to the Disney Cruise Line*. As a breast cancer survivor, she is active in raising funds and awareness through the Avon Breast Cancer Crusade and Susan B. Komen Foundation. A native of New Jersey, Deb now resides in the Washington, D.C., suburbs.

Debra Martin Koma, a freelance writer and editor, fell in love with Walt Disney World on her first visit there—as an adult. She's returned to her Laughing Place more than 30 times in the ensuing years, enjoying new and exciting experiences with every visit. For the past six years, she has enthusiastically shared her passion with others as Senior Editor of Deb Wills' Web site AllEarsNet.com and the weekly electronic newsletter ALL EARS®, writing in-depth reports on a variety of subjects, including the Epcot International Food and Wine Festival, Disney restaurants and resorts, and overlooked attractions in

the theme parks. Debra, who has written for many local and national publications, has also been a peer reviewer of the *PassPorter Walt Disney World Resort* guidebook since 2001. Through her work with PassPorter and AllEarsNet.com, Debra has helped "share the magic" with hundreds of thousands of people. Having grown up with siblings who had a variety of health issues, Debra eagerly signed on when Jennifer and Dave approached her about writing this book, seeing it as a chance to spread a little pixie dust to people who face special challenges when traveling. A native of Pittsburgh, Debra currently resides in Northern Virginia, just outside Washington, D.C., with husband Brian, teenage son Alex, and furry, four-legged son, Dexter.

PassPorter Peer Reviewer Team

Our Expert Peer Reviewers—These experts—each with their own experience with special needs—painstakingly checked our text to ensure PassPorter's accuracy, readability, and thoroughness. Thank you for helping to make PassPorter the best it can be!

 Carrie Bass is a special education teacher from Texas who has made five trips to Disney since 1996. She has psoriatic arthritis and is the mother of Hayley and Austin, who has an autism spectrum disorder, seizures, and mobility issues.

Linda Briel has ADD, asthma, and fibromyalgia. She first visited Disney World in 1995 and has made more than 30 visits since. She is a wife, mother, and grandma of one, a precious 9-year-old with difficulties, including bipolar disorder.

mom friend

 Kelly DeBardelaben is a message board moderator for Disney Echo's special needs forum. She is an experienced caregiver of children and adults with special needs, and has worked for Kids Nite Out in-room childcare.

Sara Drews is a stay-at-home mom who enjoys traveling to Disney with her family. They have visited Disney more than 12 times in the last four years. She has two children with asthma, various allergies, and an immune deficiency.

grandmom family

 Lydia Economou has loved Walt Disney World since her first trip with roommates after college. She is married with three children: Nicholas, Andrew, and Sophia. Her son, Andrew, is lactose intolerant and has asthma.

doesn't know

Melanie Emmons has struggled with obesity all her life, and has recently had lapband surgery. Her first trip to Walt Disney World was her honeymoon in 1989; she stopped counting the number of return trips after 20.

 Joanne and Tim Ernest are veterans of more than 20 trips to Walt Disney World and three Disney cruises and are PassPorter moderators. For the past 3 1/2 years, Joanne has suffered from acute peripheral neuropathy.

Robert Feder is a columnist for the Chicago Sun-Times. His wife and daughter think he goes to Walt Disney World too often. They're right.

austin family

 Colleen Gaudette is a physical therapist and mother of two toddlers who has found ways to make traveling with small kids as light and convenient as possible. She fell in love with Disney on her first trip with her kids in December 2004.

mom law Baby daddy family

Sandra Givens, who learned to spell "encyclopedia" from Jiminy Cricket, is a librarian and a member of disabilities advisory committees in Virginia. She has visited Disney World nine times. Her teenage son Nikolaus has autism.

 Susan Heck is an avid Disney World passholder, a native Floridian, and a vegetarian. She has been to Walt Disney World 100+ times since the resort opened. She brings her 4-year-old daughter, Christina, who has spina bifida.

Donna Jagodzinski has been going to Disney World since she was a teen (almost 30 years). Donna is happily married. She has multiple sclerosis and is always accompanied by her service dog and best friend, Gracie.

Peter Johnson took his autistic 10-year-old son Alec to Walt Disney World for the first time in 1999. They both fell in love with the place and have been back every year since—sometimes twice a year.

[handwritten: Brother family]

Lori Jones is a plus-size woman, married to a very plus-size man (Randy). They have traveled 5 times to Disney World, plus 3 Disney cruises. Together with children Winston and Maria, they look forward to many more years of magic!

Masayo Kano is an international traveler from Japan who has loved Disney since her first trips to Tokyo Disneyland in '91 and to Disney World in '93. She's been 10+ times since. She's married to Mamoru, who also loves Disney.

Deb Kendall has had fibromyalgia for 14 years. She resides in Texas and has visited Disney World 6 times and Disneyland 100+ times growing up in California. She's learned a new way to enjoy Disney because of fibromyalgia.

Lori Kloman Williamson is a long-time Walt Disney World fan who has made multiple trips since 1971. She has spent a great deal of time traveling to Disney World with her visually impaired husband and best friend.

Susan Koppel vacationed at Disney before becoming a mom to Alex and Mikie. Her family has experienced Disney with food allergies, GERD, Crohns, mobility issues, sensory issues, fears, motion sickness, autism, and size issues.

Cathy McConnell is a Disney fan and travel agent who has been on countless trips to Disney World and more than 10 Disney cruises. She is the mother of a teen son who is profoundly deaf and is active in deaf advocacy groups.

Chet McDoniel is an Accredited Cruise Counselor with the Cruising Co. Etc. He has no arms and shortened legs. He travels in an electric wheelchair and absolutely loves Walt Disney World and Disney Cruise Line!

[handwritten: Brother Law Family]
Bruce Metcalf works at a major Central Florida theme park where his job includes making life easier for those with challenges. An accident that put him in a wheelchair for three months helped focus his attention.
[handwritten: family cousin]

Sue Mickelson, a nurse and mom of a child with multiple disabilities, has been on 20+ "Purple Wheelchair Tours" of Disney since 1987. Sue is the moderator of a popular Internet forum for people with disabilities planning Disney travel.

Jean Miller, a senior citizen, began her love of Disney while living near Disneyland for a year in the early '60s. A regular visitor to Disney World since its opening, she now spends several weeks each winter at Ft. Wilderness.

Yvonne Mitchell has fibromyalgia and is also a plus-sized person. She's been to Disneyland and Walt Disney World 25+ times and is taking her new husband and 13-year-old daughter to Disney World soon.

Josh Olive is a 6'6", 380-lb. man whose inner child is bigger yet. He's been a BIG fan of Walt Disney World since his first visit in 1979 and he's now a 15-trip veteran.

Kelly Pankey was born with spina bifida and gets around using a wheelchair. She's been to Walt Disney World twice as a child. Kelly is also an elementary special education teacher to kids with physical and other health impairments.

PassPorter Peer Reviewer Team
(continued)

 Pam Passwater has accompanied groups of challenged adults to Disney World and has vacationed there 20+ times. As travel coordinator for St. Louis Dream Factory, she helps seriously ill children plan their dream trips to Florida.

Leanne Phelps has been enjoying Disney World since college. She and her husband especially enjoy dining at Disney. After being diagnosed with celiac disease, she discovered that the "World" is a great place for gluten-free dining.

 Beth Shorten, self-proclaimed Queen of Allergies, is a lifelong Disney fan. Disney World is one of the few places in which she feels relaxed and comfortable dining. Beth is a member of the Food Allergy & Anaphylaxis Network.

Kitty Smith is a vegan who's made 10 trips to Disney World (so far). While quite "bashful," she can often be found lurking in her favorite Disney newsgroup, rec.arts.disney.parks, or dishing out veggie dining advice at AllEarsNet.com.

 Michelle Spurrier is an Early Childhood Special Education teacher. Walt Disney World became the favorite family vacation spot in 1997 for Michelle, her husband, and two sons. Michelle has made 9 trips to Walt Disney World.

Michelle Steiner fell in love with the "magic" on her first visit to Disney World. Now she enjoys sharing that same magic with her two sons, Jordan and Brandon. Both her boys are ADHD or "Attention Different," as she likes to think of it!

 Alissa Tschetter-Siedschlaw is a confessed Disney junkie! She and her husband Sean have four children whose special needs include autism spectrum disorder, mild cerebral palsy, behavioral issues, and one on G-tube feeds.

Amy Warren Stoll has been to Walt Disney World more than 15 times since her first trip in 1996. She hasn't let epilepsy keep her from enjoying her favorite "me, me, all for me" solo trips!

 Blossom Zell is a special education teacher, working with students of many disabilities, including autism, PDD, mental retardation, Tourette Syndrome, and ADHD, to name a few. She is the parent of two boys with special needs.

A special thanks to these important folks "behind the scenes" at PassPorter Travel Press:

Senior Editor and Project Manager: Jennifer Marx
Publishing Vision: Dave Marx
Printer: Malloy, Inc.
Visibility Specialists: Kate and Doug Bandos, KSB Promotions
Online Promotions and Newsletter Editor: Sara Varney
Office and Research Assistants: Nicole Larner and Chad Larner
Layout Assistant: Kim Larner
Proofreader: Sandy Zilka
Sorcerers' Apprentices: Carolyn Tody and Tom Anderson

From left to right: Tom Anderson, Dave Marx, Nikki Larner, Chad Larner, Jennifer Marx, Kim Larner, and Carolyn Tody

© DMediaMarx, Inc.

Acknowledgments

While you see only the authors' names on the front cover, the book you hold in your hands would not be possible without the countless people who have been there for us during this incredible adventure.

All of you gave us the inspiration and motivation to produce the best guidebook for special needs travelers that we possibly could.

A "world" of thanks to PassPorter's readers, who've contributed hundreds of tips and stories since PassPorter's debut. A special thanks to those who generously allowed us to include their contributions in this edition: Angela Robinson, Andrea Fey, Becky Sheehan (page 6); Ann Berry, April Higgins (page 18); Alissa Tschetter-Siedschlaw (page 27); Carrie Bass (page 28); Robert Feder (pages 32 and 35) Joanne Ernest (page 66); Kitty Smith (page 67); Lori Kloman Williamson (page 88); Deb Kendall, Joshua Olive (page 89); Carrie Bass, Penny de Geer (page 90); Michelle Steiner (page 92); Leanne Phelps (page 94); Robert Feder (page 99); Eileen Lloyd, Joshua Olive, Lorraine Ivester, Susan Heck (page 102); Sue Mickelson (page 126); Pam Passwater (page 174); Joanne Ernest (page 179); Amy Warren Stoll (page 182); Lori Jones (page 191); Ann Berry, Cheryl Giffear, Karen Sears, Lori Kloman Williamson, Michelle Suit, Michelle S. (page 192); Donna Jagodzinski (page 269); J.A. Anderson, John Marrinson, Kalli Mulchi, Lydia Economou (page 309); Bradley Smith, Frances McCarthy, Sally Brush (page 310); Kitty Smith (page 315); Leanne Phelps (page 322); Peter Johnson (page 365); Chet McDoniel (page 366); Erica Freeman, Jennifer Aist, Kitty Smith, Ricke Zeidman, Teresa Pitman (page 367); Beth Shorten, Lorraine Ivester, Melanie Emmons, Susie Koppel, Tracy Arabian (page 368); Cathy McConnell, Jean Miller, Joshua Olive, Michelle Rigney (page 386). May each of you receive a new magical memory for every reader your words touch.

To everyone who shared their stories, tips, and experiences, and to those who filled out our survey, we want you to know that we read each and every word and, while we are unable to name all of you here, please know that you had an impact on the writing of this book.

To our incredible review team for all their superb ideas, suggestions, and insightful comments, we can't thank you enough. We were so lucky to find you.

To our friends who provided all manner of support, from information-gathering to photo-taking to providing insight to just plain encouraging us to carry on, we owe you all so much: Cathy Bock, Mary Brennan, Craig Canady, Kenny Cottrell, Jennifer Edwards, Beth Ann Floro, Meli Emmons, Erica Freeman, Laura Gilbreath, Deb Grandon, Chet Hall, Gloria Konsler, Jack Marshall, Andrea McKenna, Linda MacLeod, Tim and Dan, Dotti Saroufim, Di and Marc Schwartz, Laura Scribellito, Patt Sheahan, Jack Spence, Donna Staffanson, Pam Teixeira, and Nancy Tynes.

Our deep appreciation to our publishers, Jennifer and Dave Marx, for having the faith in us to write a book that would meet their standard of excellence.

We also owe a huge debt of gratitude to Walt Disney, for his dreams, and to Disney cast members everywhere, who continue to make his dreams a reality, especially for those travelers who have special needs.

Debra Martin Koma would also like to thank:

Appreciations and Dedication

♥ My husband and son, who have been patient and understanding (well, most of the time), while I went on numerous "fact-finding missions" to Orlando and spent countless hours huddled in front of my computer: Brian and Alex, you are simply the best. I thank you first of all, because everything starts with you.

♥ My mother, father, and sister: Mom, Dad, and Jackie, thanks for teaching me to be compassionate and for helping to shape the person I am today. You have always had faith in me—for that, I will never be able to thank you enough.

♥ My dear friend and co-author Deb Wills, my other sister: Your warmth, generosity, and kindness, not to mention your boundless energy, are an inspiration to me.

♥ My many teachers, editors, friends, and family members, who encouraged, challenged, and supported me along the way, especially: Dr. Myron Taube, Virginia Phillips, Suzanne Martinson, and Mark Collins. I feel your influence still.

Deb Wills would also like to thank:

♥ Debbie Koma: Thank you for your friendship, dedication, motivation, and ability to keep me focused when I scattered in a hundred directions! You have been a great partner throughout this journey. When two dear friends can spend a year writing a book together and come out smiling, I'd say they have something incredibly special!

♥ Linda Eckwerth, for her love, patience, and unending belief that my dream would become a reality, "really it will!"

♥ The staff and clients at the facility where I volunteered in Lynchburg, Virginia, during my college years.

♥ The staff and clients at Centers for the Handicapped in Maryland—who taught me what it meant to have a "special need" and with whom I shared the Magic Kingdom and Fort Wilderness in the 1970s.

♥ My dad, for teaching me what's really important in life and instilling in me the values I have today.

♥ My mom, who passed on her love of Walt Disney to me in the late '50s and who experienced my first Disney attraction with me at the New York World's Fair in 1964. Mom, you weren't with us long enough to see Florida's Magic Kingdom, but I think of you every time I see the Castle and I know you are smiling down on me. I dedicate this book to you!

Contents

*List of
Maps and Charts*

Contents
(continued)

A Letter From the Publishers

We've often said, "Eventually, everyone goes to Walt Disney World." And over the years we've been writing our PassPorter Walt Disney World guidebook, it's become quite obvious that *everyone* does go to Walt Disney World. Time after time, readers write us to ask, "I have/my family member has (insert any and every condition/impairment known to humanity). How can we get the most out of our Disney vacation?" That Disney is the destination is surely no accident, thanks to Disney's sterling approach to hospitality, established a half-century ago by Walt Disney himself. Everyone is Disney's honored guest, and every Disney employee ("cast member") who interacts with guests is schooled in how to treat every one of those guests with respect and to make their Disney experience the best it can be. While you could find other institutions that may outdo Disney hospitality and accessibility in some regards, they exist in a world where attention to an individual's special needs is spotty at best. Only at Walt Disney World can you visit for a day, a week, or even longer and experience the same high level of respect and accessibility no matter where you go—at the hotel, the theme park, on amusement rides, in the theater, waiting for a parade, at the water park, on the buses, and in the restaurants. Disney "gets it," and knowing that, families that rarely venture from home will make the pilgrimage to Orlando to share in the magic. And we're honored to help!

The book you're holding in your hands is the result of countless hours of work by a team of amazing writers, editors, and expert peer reviewers. Special Needs is a huge topic—even bigger the way we've defined it—and we've needed far more help than usual. Our thanks go to many people, starting, naturally, with Deb Wills and Debra Martin Koma for deciding to take on this Herculean task, and to their families for being so supportive of their efforts. Arrayed behind "The Debs" are dozens of people who read and reread every word, contributed advice, knowledge, vacation tips, and favorite memories to a project that reflects their experience, love, and compassion. Last but not least, there is the hard-working PassPorter team behind the scenes: Proofreader Sandy Zilka, who makes sure every "i" is dotted and "t" is crossed; our phenomenal office staff, the brother-and-sister team of Chad and Nicole Larner, who really do play well together; and our amazing message board moderators. Many thanks to all!

Finally, like Walt Disney World and the Disney Cruise Line, this book is also a permanent work-in-progress. It will never be perfected or completed as long as our readers keep sharing their advice and encouragement and as long as Disney keeps growing and changing. Be sure to let us know how we can serve you better—you're our guests!

Jennifer & Dave

Planning Your Special Adventure

The book you're holding is unlike any other travel guide you may have encountered—but then again, you're just as unique. Oh sure, it's corny and it's been said before: Everybody's special. But you are not just any traveler. You have special requirements that set you apart—needs that, if they're not met, can turn the vacation of a lifetime into an ordeal you'll want to forget.

We're sure a lot of people would like to have a hotel room near a bus stop, or a room that's smoke-free. And we know that many would like to sit in the front row of the show, or have foods prepared especially for them. But while many people *prefer* this special treatment, for you and your family it is *not* a matter of preference. It's a matter of necessity.

You are special needs travelers. And you are why this book was written.

The phrase "special needs at Disney," may conjure an image of children in wheelchairs for some, but our goal is to be more inclusive. We believe that almost every traveling party has at least one member with at least one special need. It could be a dietary requirement, an age factor (infant or senior), a physical limitation, medical issue, or something else entirely. We do not discriminate on the severity of the special need.

As we've visited this wildly popular vacation destination, one of the things that's struck us is how inclusive it is. Not only does it have features that appeal to young and old alike, but there seems to be a general willingness among the people who work there to go the extra mile ... for everyone, not just the average visitor. If something doesn't work well, chances are good they'll figure out a way to make it work. If there's an inconvenience, there's bound to be someone who will try to make it less so.

Maybe you've always dreamed of taking a vacation to Walt Disney World or cruising with Disney but were reluctant, thinking that once you got there, your special situation would not be accommodated. We'd like to show you how you, too, can enjoy a vacation at this 47-square-mile playground, no matter what special need or requirement you might have.

Planning

Your Special Need

Getting There

Staying in Style

Touring

Feasting

Resources

Index

Planning

Your Special Need

Getting There

Staying in Style

Touring

Feasting

Resources

Index

The Disney Parks and Disney Cruise Line

If you've never been to the Walt Disney World Resort, you may not realize **just how much ground it actually covers**. We're always amazed when we hear someone say they want to go to "Disney World" when they really mean the Magic Kingdom, the first Disney theme park in Orlando (opened in 1971), the one with the highly recognizable icon, Cinderella Castle.

While Magic Kingdom is undeniably a major piece of this beautiful Disney puzzle, there is **so much more.** There are four major theme parks: Magic Kingdom, Epcot, Disney-MGM Studios, and Disney's Animal Kingdom. There are more than 20 resort hotels with recreation facilities that run the gamut from tame (bicycles) to wild (parasailing). There are also scores of restaurants of every style and cuisine. In addition, there are two water parks, Blizzard Beach and Typhoon Lagoon. There's a shopping and nighttime entertainment complex, called Downtown Disney, which has three components—the Marketplace, Pleasure Island, and the West Side. There are four miniature golf courses, and for the more grown up among us, five 18-hole professional-quality golf courses. And that's just for starters!

There is so much to see and do at Walt Disney World that even a full week wouldn't be enough time to cover it thoroughly. That's why as you use this book, you'll notice that we emphasize again and again to pace yourself, know your limitations, take your time, and take plenty of breaks—**do not try to do it all**. Don't bite off more than you can chew! Instead, research and plan ahead so that you can be as well prepared as possible for your vacation.

If you've never cruised with the **Disney Cruise Line**, you may not realize that you have a number of choices here, too. First of all, there are two nearly identical ships: the Disney Wonder and the Disney Magic. You have the choice of 3-, 4-, or 7-night cruises, with a variety of ports of call and land excursions. Again, reading up on the subject is the best way to prepare. The more you become familiar with the choices available to you, the better trip you will have.

Our Coverage of the Disney Cruise Line

For the most part, we integrate our coverage of the Disney Cruise Line throughout this book rather than give it a separate chapter because most vacationers taking a Disney cruise also visit Walt Disney World. If your focus is solely on cruising and you want to read just the relevant sections, flip to the index and look up Disney Cruise Line—you can use it like a mini table of contents!

Should You Go?

We're sure that's the real question you've been asking yourself: **Should I go to Walt Disney World and/or take a Disney cruise?** What if I get there and I find they won't help me? What if I have a horrible time? Or worse, what if my health is compromised as a result?

Rest assured that you **couldn't find a more accommodating spot** for special needs travelers than Walt Disney World and the Disney Cruise Line. Hopefully, as you read through this book and find the basic information you need—what's available, what's not—we'll allay your fears and concerns. To give you some insight on how others have managed a successful trip to Walt Disney World and cruised aboard Disney, we've included first-hand tips from people who have made the trip, as well as stories and anecdotes about how a Disney vacation brought a little magic into their lives.

So why should you, as a special needs traveler, go to Walt Disney World and/or take a Disney cruise? There are probably **two main reasons**:

1. **You deserve a vacation.** You struggle with day-to-day challenges, just like everybody does. And maybe your challenges are little more, well, challenging. Why not take a much-needed break at one of the most popular vacation destinations in the world?

2. Disney has been in the vacation business for 50 years. Perhaps in your day-to-day living, you find many people who haven't encountered a special need like yours. With the hundreds of millions of guests who have passed through their gates over the years, Disney has seen almost everything and likely **has a procedure or special accommodation** in place for your requirements.

Of the more than 700 special needs travelers who took a recent survey we conducted, 96.6% had made a trip to Walt Disney World within the past three years. Of these, 46.5% had or traveled with someone who had mobility issues, 22.5% allergies or asthma, and 17.7% autism spectrum disorders. And there were more than 130 travelers who vacationed at Walt Disney World with a variety of special needs ranging from multiple sclerosis to cerebral palsy to spina bifida to broken bones. Walt Disney World is a **welcoming spot** for almost anyone, no matter their ability or disability.

Planning

Your Special Need

Getting There

Staying in Style

Touring

Feasting

Resources

Index

Finding Special Needs Information

While we hope this book will be your **primary source of information** for your Walt Disney World vacation, there are certainly plenty of other resources available to you.

For a **good general guidebook**, we obviously recommend our parent publication, PassPorter Walt Disney World Resort. It packs a lot of information in a compact package and supplements the information you find in this book. See page 402 for details.

Special needs travelers to Walt Disney World will also want to avail themselves of **Disney's publications**—there's a small "Guidebook for Guests With Disabilities" printed for each of the four major theme parks. You can request them from Disney in advance by calling Walt Disney World Resort Special Reservations at 407-939-7807 and selecting option 1 (TTY Line: 407-939-7670), or you can pick them up at the theme parks' Guest Relations offices. (Versions of these guides are also available on Disney World's Web site at http://www.disneyworld.com—look for the link called "Guests with Disabilities" toward the bottom left of the page.)

Walt Disney World Resort Special Reservations is also a good source of information for planning a special needs trip, and they will assist you in making reservations, explaining what types of accommodations are available that meet your requirements. (See phone number above.)

The World Wide Web is another rich source of information for the special needs traveler. Co-author Deb Wills' well-known unofficial Disney Web site, **AllEarsNet** (http://www.allearsnet.com) is comprehensive and current, with thousands of photos from all around the resort, as well as a nearly complete collection of menus from the Disney restaurants.

Another source of information is **online discussion groups**. PassPorter has its own set of active message boards at http://www.passporterboards.com, including one especially for special needs travelers. Another great source for the special needs traveler is Pete Werner's Unofficial Disney Information Station message boards at http://www.disboards.com. His disABILITIES message board is frequented by travelers who have special health requirements and are willing to share the benefit of their Disney experiences.

Finally we've included some **relevant Web site links** within the following chapters, as well as a hefty collection of Web site links in chapter 7.

Planning With Your PassPorter

Your PassPorter is most useful when you keep it handy before and during your vacation. It fits compactly into backpacks and shoulder bags. Or, tuck your PassPorter into a **waist pack** (at least 5.5" x 9" or 14 x 23 cm).

Your PassPorter loves to go on rides and cruise with you, but do try to **keep it dry**. A simple resealable plastic bag (gallon size) is a big help.

Personalize your PassPorter! **Write your name** on the inside front cover, along with other information you feel comfortable listing. Your hotel name, trip dates, and phone number help if you misplace your PassPorter. Inside back cover are calendars and important phone numbers, too.

Two tools you may find helpful for planning are a **highlighter** (to mark "must-sees") and those sticky **page flags** (to mark favorite pages).

If you're familiar with other PassPorter titles, you may be wondering about our famous **organizer PassPockets**. Alas, due to the vast amount of information in this guidebook, we simply couldn't fit in pockets as well—the book would have required a forklift to carry! And, again due to its size, we're unable to offer a deluxe edition in a binder with pockets either. But if you just love using PassPockets to plan your vacation, you can purchase a binder and a set of pockets separately. Or you may just want to get a copy of PassPorter Walt Disney World Resort, which comes with 14 PassPockets and a wealth of general information we simply couldn't squeeze into this book. For details, see page 402.

🛈 The Scope of This Guidebook

Unlike a general guidebook for Walt Disney World or the Disney Cruise Line, this guidebook gives less attention to the basic logistics of travel so it can go into really deep detail on your special needs and requirements. Based on our own experience and that of our fellow vacationers, we've tried to cover every special need that may arise on a Disney vacation. In fact, we devote an entire chapter to describing each of these special needs, along with tips, notes, and important information you should know. We then proceed to cover traveling, lodging, touring, and dining, all with a focus on your special needs. You'll still find general, descriptive information, but not quite as much as you'll find in our more general guidebooks. You also won't encounter duplicate descriptions. If you decide to supplement this guidebook with another PassPorter, you may rest assured that it adds completely new information.

And while this guidebook is highly detailed, it's impossible for us to cover everything. When you have an unanswered question, we refer you to the PassPorter Message Boards, where you can post your question and read answers and comments from other special needs vacationers.

Planning · Your Special Need · Getting There · Staying in Style · Touring · Feasting · Resources · Index

Planning
Your Special Need
Getting There
Staying in Style
Touring
Feasting
Resources
Index

Your Planning Tips and Stories

My daughter has cerebral palsy, and her dream was to go to Disney. So in 1997, we made the trip. She was in awe as soon as we walked in the park and Pluto came up to her and "licked" her face. Usually people look and whisper but here, we truly felt special. She sat in her wheelchair and felt like a princess. All the cast members and characters alike went out of their way to help in any way they could. One day, she was having a bad afternoon and was upset. Chip and Dale were walking by and stopped and patted her head and got down to her level and spent time with her until she smiled. We truly felt blessed. The parks were awesome in all aspects. We had no problem getting around. We have been back twice since then and are trying to save for a third time. Thanks to all who work there for putting a smile on my child's face that still hasn't gone away when she remembers her first Disney trip.

—contributed by Angela Robinson

Our middle child, 10-year-old Ryan, has autism, which greatly affects his social and communicating abilities. It also makes it nearly impossible for him to wait for anything for more than a few minutes without a tantrum. He is also the biggest Disney enthusiast I know. Since he was only a few months old he was glued to Disney videos. And now, ten years later, he knows every Disney movie by heart, every word of dialogue, every song. So our first trip to Walt Disney World was going to be a memorable one. Either he would be so overwhelmed that he wouldn't know what to do and probably tantrum at every chance or he would bask in the wonder that is Walt Disney World. Most of our research on children with autism at Walt Disney World was done online. We got a great deal of information from http://www.allearsnet.com, which consequently led us to purchasing a copy of PassPorter Walt Disney World. I was afraid that too much planning would be hard to stick to, not really knowing how Ryan would be once we got there, so I didn't go overboard. After I got the book, I immediately went to the PassPorter Web site and spent hours there, starting with the tips for disabilities and venturing everywhere else. Ryan had the best time at Walt Disney World thanks to all the research! My best tip for people with children on the autism spectrum who visit Disney is to get the Guest Assistance Card (see pages 10–11).

—contributed by Becky Sheehan

My mom has an egg allergy and dining can be a problem. We love to do the character breakfast, but my mom is limited in her food choices. Most outside property restaurants are very unwilling to check ingredients for her and consider it a hassle. At Walt Disney World eateries this was not the case. The Cape May Cafe chef actually came out to talk with her and whipped up her very own special Mickey waffles made with applesauce and other ingredients, serving her right at our table. At Chef Mickey's the chef came out again, consulted with her, and made her pancakes. It was so great for her to be able to have breakfast food without feeling like she was a "problem." She was treated like royalty and they made her experience great.

—contributed by Andrea Fay

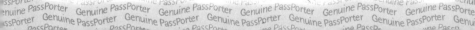

Your Special Need

It's true that everybody's special in one way or another, but some of us have unique requirements based on our physical or psychological challenges. Perhaps we're wheelchair users, or perhaps we are recovering from surgery. Perhaps we're new moms taking care of our infants, or we have children who are physically or emotionally challenged. Maybe we have a hearing or vision loss, or we're on a special diet, or we have fears or other health concerns that require special attention. No matter your special need, Walt Disney World is able to accommodate you ... in most cases.

In this chapter, we discuss the various special needs that many of us have, the general services that Disney makes available, and coping strategies for a visit to "The World."

A good way to begin planning your Disney vacation is by contacting Walt Disney World Special (Medical) Reservations at 407-939-7807 (TTY 407-939-7670). Disney's special reservations cast members are trained in the facilities and services available to Disney guests with special needs and can advise you on many aspects of your trip. They will also send you copies of Disney's "Guidebook for Guests With Disabilities" for each of the theme parks.

Even so, Disney's materials only cover certain aspects of the most obvious special needs—they don't thoroughly address all issues. The requirements of parents traveling with infants, for example, or of children and adults with less-than-obvious special needs, such as the autism spectrum disorders or even seniors, are not discussed in Disney's material.

That's where the information in this guidebook proves helpful. We have researched a wide variety of special needs and have tried to identify the services and accommodations at your disposal while you're vacationing at Walt Disney World. We have also talked extensively with people who have vacationed at Disney or have traveled with family members and/or friends who have required special considerations and can share their tips and accumulated wisdom.

Planning · Your Special Need · Getting There · Staying in Style · Touring · Feasting · Resources · Index

What's Your Special Need?

Special Need	Icon	Page
ADHD (Attention Deficit Hyperactivity Disorder)	*A*	14
Addiction Recovery	*R*	19
Allergies (Food and Other) and Asthma	*G*	21
Autism Spectrum Disorders (ASD)	*U*	24
Chronic Fatigue Syndrome	*C*	29
Cognitive Disabilities	*I*	35
Diet	*D*	31
Down Syndrome	*I*	35
Fears	*F*	37
Fertility	*E*	73
Fibromyalgia	*C*	29
Foreign Language	*Ö*	42
Fragile X	*I*	35
Hearing	*H*	46
Heart Health	♥	49
Infants	*B*	52
Medical Treatment	*T*	58
Mental Health	*T*	13
Mobility	*M*	62
Motion Sensitivity	*Q*	67
Physical Therapy	*P*	70
Pregnancy	*E*	73
Rehabilitation	*P*	70
Religion	*W*	76
Seniors	*S*	78
Service Animals	*HMTV*	12
Size	*L*	82
Vision	*V*	85

Is your special need missing? Go to the next page to find out how we developed this list.

Planning | Your Special Need | Getting There | Staying in Style | Touring | Feasting | Resources | Index

Our Special Needs Coverage

As you glance down our list of special needs on the previous page, you may be wondering, "**But what about me? Why is my special need not listed?**" It was not our intention to exclude anyone. Space and time constraints prevent us from listing each and every type of traveler who might have a condition that warrants some special attention.

Based on our extensive research (see our sidebar below), including conversations we had with hundreds of travelers, we've addressed the **most common special needs** experienced by vacationers to Walt Disney World and the Disney Cruise Line. We've therefore included sections on autism spectrum disorders, attention deficit hyperactivity disorder, size issues, hearing and vision impairments, and mobility disabilities.

We have also tried to **group together related special needs**, where appropriate. For example, allergies and asthma often go hand-in-hand, as do chronic fatigue and fibromyalgia. In many cases there's overlap, in that various special needs share similar characteristics or, more precisely, can be accommodated by the same methods. Vacationers with rheumatoid arthritis, multiple sclerosis, cerebral palsy, muscular dystrophy, and even broken legs all most likely experience some limitations on their mobility—so we hope they will all read the section on Mobility. We understand that those with these conditions may also have *other* special needs, and we expect that you know which other sections of the book will apply to you, such as the section on special diets and/or physical therapy.

We hope that, rather than feeling left out, you'll be able to find ample information that applies to you and your specific situation in these pages. We realize that in the real world, one size does *not* fit all ... and we hope we help you see how **a Disney vacation can fit you to a T**!

Our Special Needs Survey

Late in 2004, as we began our research for this book, we conducted an online survey (hosted by http://www.websurveyor.com) of vacationers with special needs who had visited Walt Disney World Resort within the last three years. The survey presented a series of questions about how the individual felt Walt Disney World accommodated the special need in question. The survey also asked the reader to rate the Disney attractions, resorts, cast members, and transportation, keeping their special need in mind. More than 700 readers took the survey, supplying us with a wealth of information that we have tried to share in these pages with you.

Side tabs: Planning · Your Special Need · Getting There · Staying in Style · Touring · Feasting · Resources · Index

Guest Assistance Card (GAC)

Many visitors to the Walt Disney World Resort have conditions that may not be **readily apparent** to the casual observer. Those with Autism Spectrum Disorders, Attention Deficit Hyperactivity Disorder (ADHD), and heart conditions are just some of the vacationers who may require special consideration for their "invisible ailments." Walt Disney World will often issue a Guest Assistance Card (see next page on how to obtain one) that provides certain accommodations for those who carry it. These accommodations may include the following, based on your special need:

✔ Use of an auxiliary entrance if you cannot wait in line due to health problems, cognitive disabilities, autism, ADHD, and related fears. You'll likely still wait, possibly even longer than if you'd waited in the queue—you'll just wait in a different location.

✔ Waiting in a shaded spot out of the sun if the attraction's queue has you standing in the sun for an excessive amount of time.

✔ Using your stroller as a wheelchair in queues and through the same auxiliary entrances that wheelchairs and ECVs are allowed to use.

✔ Sitting up front at shows if you have visual impairments.

Important Note: The GAC is not a "front of the line" pass and you will probably be asked to obtain a FASTPASS if applicable and available.

Wheelchair/ECV users don't need a GAC—your wheelchair/ECV is enough to alert the cast members at attractions to your special needs. If you encounter a cast member who insists that you need a GAC to access the wheelchair loading area, just politely ask that they call Guest Relations. But if you intend to park your wheelchair/ECV at an attraction and walk inside on your own, you may need a GAC to allow you to use the accessible seating and/or boarding areas.

Talk to the cast member stationed outside an attraction to request special assistance. The auxiliary entrance may be the FASTPASS entrance (when it exists). Be aware that many of the auxiliary entrances skip the theming found in the regular attraction queue and may even skip the attraction's pre-show.

Bright Idea: If you have more than one special needs traveler in your party, be sure that each person who needs a GAC gets his or her own individual card. This way, if your party splits up, each of the travelers still has their own GAC.

To obtain a **Guest Assistance Card**, visit Guest Relations when you enter a theme park, armed with a letter from your doctor. We've provided a sample letter below.

To Whom It May Concern:

John has been diagnosed with an Autism Spectrum Disorder. Because of this, it is difficult for him to wait in long, noisy lines with many other people close by. If there is any special consideration that you can offer to help him and his family avoid these situations, it would be to everyone's benefit.

Sincerely, thick gravey

Dr. Soandso

While **this letter is not mandatory**, it can make the process go much more smoothly. Also, if you find an occasional cast member who does not want to issue you a GAC, ask to speak to a supervisor. It's rare, but we have heard an occasional report of this happening. For special needs children, remember to request a GAC that allows you to use your stroller as a wheelchair. This means you won't have to leave the stroller behind at stroller parking, so you can use it right up to the point of entering the ride vehicle or theater. Note that the GAC will be valid in all four major theme parks—Disney's Animal Kingdom, Disney-MGM Studios, the Magic Kingdom, and Epcot. Once you obtain a GAC, it will be valid for the duration of your visit. Keep in mind, though, that even with a GAC, a particular accommodation may not be available to you at every attraction. If you want to guarantee that you have a seat while you wait, you will have to use a wheelchair/ECV.

Bright Idea: If it is difficult and/or awkward for you to discuss your special needs or the needs of your special traveler, write a brief letter explaining the situation to go along with the doctor's note.

Front of Guest Assistance Card
(text intentionally blurred)

Planning | Your Special Need | Getting There | Staying in Style | Touring | Feasting | Resources | Index

Service Animals

We understand that **several special needs**, including hearing, mobility, medical treatment, and vision, may use a service animal—therefore we use the icons for these four special needs (**[H][M][T][V]**) when referring to service animals through this book.

If you use a **service animal**, you are able to take him/her around most of Walt Disney World and on the Disney Cruise, as long as your animal is on a leash or a harness. This includes the parks, hotels, and restaurants.

If you are unsure how your service animal will react to **characters**, inquire at Guest Relations upon entering the park.

When you're approaching theme park attractions, follow the same boarding procedures as those given for wheelchair/ECV users. You may need to use an auxiliary entrance when traveling with a service animal. There are, of course, some rides or shows that service animals can't go on or into—**consult with a cast member** if you're unsure. Someone else in your party must stay with the animal. We note these locations in chapter 5, too.

When you're at the water parks, you should also follow the same entrance procedures as described for wheelchair/ECV users. Service animals are not permitted to ride any of the water attractions or enter any of the water areas for **health and safety reasons**. A member of your party must remain with the animal at all times.

If your service animal needs to make a pit stop, there are designated areas. Cast members can direct you to the proper location, but it's probably better to check on their whereabouts **in advance**. We note these locations in our individual attraction descriptions in chapter 5, too.

You and your service animal are also welcome in the **First Aid Stations** if you need a place to rest or cool off.

For details on bringing your animal on the **Disney Cruise**, see page 189.

© Donna Jagodzinski

Bright Idea: Ask cast members for water for your animal. Remember they can get dehydrated in the Florida sun, too!

Here's a **packing list** for your service animal: Food, water, bowls, special toys, medications, immunization records, and veterinary information.

Peer reviewer Donna Jagodzinski and her service dog, Gracie

Mental Health Disorders

Bipolar disorder, oppositional defiant disorder, anxiety, depression, Tourette Syndrome, obsessive-compulsive disorder, and Alzheimer's disease are just a few of the mental health disorders that a traveler may have. These disorders **may not fit neatly into any of the main categories** we address in this chapter, though some aspects are discussed in Medical Treatment (**[T]**) starting on page 58. We know that these conditions can have an effect on your Walt Disney World and/or Disney Cruise Line vacation. Based on discussions with those who deal with these disorders routinely, here are some tips that can help you enjoy your trip:

✔ Be sure to **bring all your medications**, doctors' names and numbers, and a summary of your medical history. You may be exposed to the sun more than usual during your stay in Florida, so check before you travel whether your medications increase your sun sensitivity.

✔ Talk with your doctor to see if he/she can **recommend a physician** or hospital in the Orlando area, should the need arise.

✔ **Don't overdo it.** Vacations are for relaxing. Have a general plan and be sure to leave time to "chill out."

✔ If you're concerned about **anxiety or troubles while waiting in line** for an attraction, try one of our fun things to do in the sidebar below.

✔ Remember that taking anyone out of his or her **normal routine** and environment can easily trigger the resurfacing of issues that were thought to have been put to rest. Be on guard for this possibility.

✔ Be aware of **warning signs** or potential triggers to behaviors. If you feel comfortable, discuss these with the people you are traveling with so they can help you if necessary.

⏻ Fun Things to Do While Waiting in Line

☑ Hidden Mickey searches
☑ Pin trading
☑ Game Boy or other handheld games from home
☑ Snack time!
☑ Engage in conversation! For example, "What is your favorite thing about this ride?" or "What is the funniest part?" or "Does anything scare you?"
☑ Play a game of "I Spy" to find an item of a particular color or someone engaged in a particular activity (such as reading a map).

Planning | Your Special Need | Getting There | Staying in Style | Touring | Feasting | Resources | Index

Attention Deficit Hyperactivity Disorder (ADHD)

Vacationing with individuals who have Attention Deficit Hyperactivity Disorder (ADHD) can be challenging, but it's certainly doable. Since most of those with ADHD have no visible disability, dealing with the situation can sometimes be difficult. To the average onlooker, a child who has ADHD may appear to be out of control, with unfit parents. These assumptions couldn't be farther from the truth.

In this book, we use ADHD to represent Attention Deficit Disorder (ADD), Attention Deficit/Hyperactivity Disorder (AD/HD), and Attention Deficit Hyperactivity Disorder (ADHD).

Your Icon:

A

(A=Attention)
Look for this symbol in the book for more details on your special need

Planning

"Plan but be flexible" is the mantra for your trip to Disney, but this isn't new to you if you live with someone who has ADHD. This is how you go about each day—with structure but also with the flexibility to change at the last minute, if needed. This is how to vacation at Disney with a child (or adult) who has ADHD. Research before you go, develop a plan, plan some more, and have a backup (include rain-out options)! Set realistic goals. If possible, plan to take your trip during cooler months for fewer crowds.

Involve your ADHD traveler in the plans for the trip. Watch the Disney planning videos (available from http://www.disneyworld.com or by calling 407-934-7639). Look at photos from past trips, on the Internet, or in books. Give your child one of the kid-oriented Walt Disney World books so they can read about the attractions and decide which ones to try.

If the traveler takes medication, be sure to **bring along more doses than you think you'll need** on your trip. In addition, bring a copy of the prescription with you in the event you need to refill it.

Give consideration to **transportation**. If flying, notify the airline of any special needs. Also request bulkhead seats (no one in front to kick). Be sure to let the attendant know when you board. Once you arrive in Florida, consider a rental car. While Disney transportation works great, there are times you will be waiting for a bus, boat, or monorail. There will be much less waiting involved if you don't have to rely on Disney transportation and can just walk to your car. If you don't rent a car, consider a private car service (see page 99) to take you to Disney instead of the shuttle. You will have a much quieter environment with little or no wait time. Shuttles will often wait for a minimum number of passengers and make several stops.

Disney transportation is efficient but not perfect—during peak times of the year and at park opening and closing times, there will be lines and crowds waiting for buses. If this poses a potential problem, rent a car or take a taxi (your bell services desk can assist with taxis). If you rent a car, remember that Disney resort guests get free parking at the theme parks. For the Magic Kingdom, consider riding the Disney bus as the drop-off is very close to the turnstiles. If you drive to the Magic Kingdom, you'll be much farther away and also have to take a monorail or ferry to reach the entrance.

Always have **water** with you, no matter what the mode of transportation—it's important to stay hydrated.

Know the **check-in time** for your hotel and plan your arrival accordingly. Disney resort hotels allow check-in at 3:00 pm and 4:00 pm, depending on the resort (see chapter 4). If you need to unwind in your room upon arrival, factor in these late afternoon times. If you arrive before the official check-in time, be sure to preregister anyway. This is a great time to restate your special requests. During slow times, your room might even be ready early.

As much as possible during your vacation, **keep your regular routine** regarding wake and sleep times, medication, and eating.

Try to **keep all belongings in one place** while you are away from home. A knapsack works well for this.

Bring travel games, word puzzles, activity books, and books on tape. Develop a **list of activities** for those times you do need to wait in lines. We have some suggestions to get you started in the sidebar on page 13.

Check restaurant menus in advance. (Many menus are available online at http://www.allearsnet.com/menu/menus.htm.) Make advance reservations for any table-service restaurants you plan to visit (see page 313). Scheduling early meals helps to minimize your wait time. You can always call and cancel if you change your mind. If you have special dietary requests, have this noted on your advance reservation. See also Diet on pages 31–34.

Important Note: You may be seated with strangers at the Biergarten in Epcot's Germany pavilion, Teppanyaki at Epcot's Japan pavilion, the Spirit of Aloha dinner show at the Polynesian resort, and on the Disney Cruise Line. On the Disney Cruise Line, if you wish to be seated by yourselves, be sure to request this when you make your reservations.

Remember to get a **letter from your physician** so you can obtain a Guest Assistance Card if you think it will help you (see pages 10–11).

Planning | Your Special Need | Getting There | Staying in Style | Touring | Feasting | Resources | Index

[A] ADHD (continued)

Once You Arrive

The **issues and questions** we hear most from parents traveling with children with ADHD include waiting in line for attractions/characters/shows, special effects in attractions, places where kids can let off some steam, and stimulation overload. Here are our tips for overcoming these issues and making a bit of magic along the way:

Post your itinerary in your resort room so the traveler can look at it when they want. Each day before venturing out, review the rules, expectations, and plans for the day. Point out the attractions or restaurants on the itinerary that they chose, to give them a feeling of empowerment.

Give your traveler with ADHD a **park map** so they can help get to the next attraction, let you know what's coming up, the time of the next show, etc. This gives them something to focus on and minimizes sensory overload.

Bright Idea: Offer a disposable camera to take photos of their special memories! (Be sure to put your name and address on it.)

Try to dress with **brightly colored clothes** so you can find your traveler who has ADHD if they get separated from you. Take a digital picture each morning to aid with identification (if necessary). Rehearse what to do if you are separated.

Maintain **healthy eating** and any special diets (see Diet on pages 31–34). Use caution with sweets and snacks; bring some favorites from home. Stay hydrated (yes, we've already noted this, but it bears repeating)!

Create a **"time-out plan"** for those times your child may become over-stimulated. We note places where kids can let off steam, as well as quiet spots, in chapter 4 and chapter 5.

When touring the parks, note that even though **flash photography** is not allowed in many attractions, sometimes vacationers ignore the warnings. If your ADHD traveler is sensitive to sudden flashes, be prepared.

Spend time at the resort. Some families will spend one day at the parks and the next day at the resort to break up touring and to minimize the overload factor. Others make sure they spend the afternoons at their resorts and only tour parks in the morning and evening. Still others suggest you take a break in a quiet place after each attraction, then move onto the next activity. NO commando touring!

Character meals (see chapter 6) offer plenty of positive character interactions—more than you get by waiting in line to meet Mickey, especially during crowded times. At character meals, when the character visits, it's for your table alone. Keep in mind, however, that character meals can be quite loud and boisterous, like Chef Mickey's at the Contemporary. If your child does not like to be touched, be sure to let the character and/or the escort know before they approach your child.

Some restaurants also have **special effects** that may be overly stimulating, such as the Rainforest Café (Disney's Animal Kingdom and Downtown Disney). We've noted these in chapter 6 starting on page 311

Downtown Disney is not the best place to visit with a child who has ADHD, unless the experience is specifically catered to them. There are simply too many distractions. Bring activities for them to do if needed.

Bright Idea: Cell phones or walkie-talkies can help you stay in touch.

DisneyQuest is a game lover's paradise, but it can also cause problems. It is very noisy, the floor plan is confusing, and there's a lot of visual stimulation. There are multiple levels, and it can be hard to find the elevators and stairs to move from area to area. Be sure to bring a guide map with you. Don't bring in backpacks or cameras that can be easily left behind and lost. Some parents have reported that their children with ADHD loved DisneyQuest, while others termed it a "nightmare." (See pages 295–300 for more details on DisneyQuest.)

At the **Cirque du Soleil** show (see page 293), keep in mind that there is no intermission and no talking. Also, we highly recommend you go to an early show since it's harder to pay attention when everyone's overly tired. Cirque du Soleil is a great show, but tickets are expensive and not refundable, so be sure it's something everyone can enjoy.

Thinking of the **water parks**? Typhoon Lagoon is more laid back, but Blizzard Beach has more activities for youngsters. In either park, use caution when going on the lazy river tube ride, where it is easy to get separated. The ride has multiple exits, and it's very hard to keep track of where you entered (making exiting and finding your way back a little tricky). (See chapter 5 starting on page 281 for more details.)

Blizzard Beach's Melt Away Bay

Planning
Your Special Need
Getting There
Staying in Style
Touring
Feasting
Resources
Index

[A] ADHD (continued)

PassPorter Picks

✔ Stay on Disney property for better access to your resort for breaks and at the end of the day.

✔ Rent a car to avoid bus lines, especially at theme park closing times.

✔ Use FASTPASS whenever possible to avoid long waits in line at theme park attractions (see page 206).

✔ Take advantage of Extra Magic Hour—fewer crowds and shorter lines for the hour before of a few hours after normal hours (see page 109).

✔ Make advance dining reservations and eat at off-peak times to avoid long waits for meals (see page 313).

✔ Visit the Kidcot Fun Stops at Disney's Animal Kingdom and Epcot, which offer brief hands-on activities for kids with little waiting.

What Is ADHD?

Attention Deficit Hyperactivity Disorder is one of the more common neurological disorders that develops in children and can last into adulthood. Symptoms may include impulsiveness (acting quickly without thinking), hyperactivity (can't sit still and/or talks when others are talking), and inattention (daydreams or is in "another world"). It is difficult for those with ADHD to control their behavior and/or pay attention. Children can have impaired functioning at home and school, while adults have difficulties at work and home.

Those with ADHD have sensory issues; they may be ultra-sensitive to smells, lights, loud noises, and/or tactile objects. When their nervous system overloads, it triggers behaviors like "meltdowns." For the individual who has ADHD, sitting still during meals, in an attraction, or waiting in line can be extremely difficult. Sometimes, the impulsive person will blurt out inappropriate comments or display emotions without restraint. The inattentive may become easily distracted, lose or forget things, or become slow and lethargic. They have difficulty processing information as quickly and as accurately as others.

As parent April Higgins told us: "Our son (almost 8 now) is classified as 'ADHD-Wired,' meaning he is not necessarily hyperactive in appearance, it's just that his brain doesn't take a rest. He is constantly thinking, thinking, thinking to a point of confusing himself, demanding completely fulfilled answers to many questions."

Reader Tip: "Children can quickly take over a vacation with whining and demands. When you enter a park, be armed with a plan. We tell our son, 'We are starting in Adventureland and working our way around the park.' A map is very helpful as well. We also have a list of the rides that we all want to see, and we put them in order."—contributed by Ann Berry

Addiction Recovery

Although Walt Disney World is a happy, fun-filled vacation destination, there are several aspects of the place that could prove to be danger zones for folks recovering from a variety of addictions.

Recovering From Alcoholism

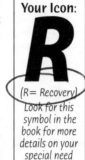

Your Icon:

R

(R= Recovery)

Look for this symbol in the book for more details on your special need

Recovery

In the theme parks: If you're looking for an alcohol-free paradise, the Magic Kingdom is the place to be. No alcohol is served there at any time during public operating hours, not even at the Magic Kingdom restaurants. The remaining theme parks—Epcot, Disney-MGM Studios, and Disney's Animal Kingdom—serve alcoholic beverages at numerous locations—in counter-service and table-service restaurants, lounges, and at various carts and stands. While these locations are difficult to avoid altogether, you might especially want to stay away from a few of the shops in Epcot's World Showcase (in Italy, Germany, and France), which often feature wine tastings. It also might be wise to avoid World Showcase during Epcot's annual International Food & Wine Festival held every fall—there are many events centered around alcohol, with free beer and wine tastings and many stands selling drinks by the glass.

At Downtown Disney/BoardWalk: Downtown Disney's Pleasure Island is brimming with nightclubs encouraging the consumption of alcohol—alcohol is even sold on the streets. You can, however, get two free soft drinks if you tell the cast member when you're entering Pleasure Island that you are a "designated driver." You'll be given a specially colored wristband (the signal to all the bartenders that they should not serve you alcohol), as well as coupons for two free soft drinks. Like Pleasure Island, the BoardWalk area has a number of nightclubs, particularly the popular Jellyrolls dueling piano bar, which might encourage alcohol overindulgence.

At the resort hotels and water parks: Walt Disney World's resort hotel table-service restaurants serve liquor, as do the lounges. There are poolside bars located at all the resorts and the water parks as well.

Aboard the Disney Cruise Line: Alcohol is everywhere—at deck parties, shows, meals, and clubs. You can avoid it at the areas geared towards families, such as the movie theater, Studio Sea, and deck 9 aft. The Beverage Station on deck 9 aft offers free coffee, tea, lemonade, punch, and soda.

[R] Addiction Recovery (continued)

Recovering From Other Addictions

For those recovering from an addiction to **narcotics**, there are meetings of Narcotics Anonymous in the area. For current meeting information, visit the group's Web site at: http://na.org or call the Orlando-area 24-hour helpline at 407-425-5157 (Florida Relay for the Deaf at 800-955-8771).

With hundreds of eateries on Disney property alone, Walt Disney World is a dining extravaganza. If, however, you have or are recovering from an **eating disorder**, you might want to avoid some of the all-you-care-to-eat meals, such as those at 'Ohana at the Polynesian Resort, the Cape May buffet at the Beach Club, or the Whispering Canyon Café at the Wilderness Lodge (see also "Feasting & Snacking"). The organization Overeaters Anonymous has support group meetings in the area. Visit the Web site for current information at http://overeatersanonymous.org, or call the Central Florida Intergroup at 800-522-2792 or 407-327-7346.

Those recovering from a **gambling addiction** won't find any slot machines or gaming tables in Orlando, although there are some carnival-style games of chance located around the resort, most notably the Fossil Fun Games in Disney's Animal Kingdom's DinoLand USA. If you're taking a Disney cruise, you'll be glad to know that there is no onboard casino. The only gambling onboard is daily bingo, with cash and merchandise prizes. However, be aware that many of the ports in the Bahamas and Caribbean do have casinos. Disney does not offer gambling-oriented excursions, although some excursions do visit casino hotels. For support, there are meetings of Gamblers Anonymous in the Orlando/Kissimmee area. For information, visit: http://gamblersanonymous.org, or call 800-397-9843.

🛑 Friends of Bill W.

As of this writing, meetings of **Alcoholics Anonymous** (Friends of Bill W.) are held daily at 3:00 pm and Sunday at 9:00 am at the Doubletree Guest Suites Resort at Downtown Disney (407-934-1000). There are also meetings held in Celebration on Wednesdays at 8:00 am at the Countryside Presbyterian Church. For more information on other area meetings, call the A.A. 24-hour hotlines: Osceola County, 407-870-8282; Orange County, 407-260-5408; Spanish-speakers, 407-240-1181; or visit their Web site: http://www.osceolaintergroup.org.

There are Friends of Bill W. meetings on board the **Disney Cruise Line**. The 7-night cruise has meetings every day except boarding and debarkation day. The 4-night cruise has meetings on day 2 and 3 (again, not on boarding or debarkation day). The 3-night cruise has meetings on the second day (again, not on boarding or debarkation day). For meeting details, check your daily Navigator (schedule) for times and locations, or contact Guest Services.

Allergies (Food and Other) and Asthma

Allegies
Your Icon:

G

(G=AllerGies)
Look for this
symbol in the
book for more
details on your
special need

Aaaachooo! Are you beset by allergies? Whether you're reacting to the dust and pollen in the air or the milk in your main dish, allergies or asthma can be a worry. And yet, with planning, allergies needn't get in your way!

Food allergies: For the most part, Walt Disney World has an excellent reputation for meeting the needs of its guests who have special dietary requirements. The key to coping here is in planning and preparation. If you alert the Disney restaurants to your particular allergens, both when you make your advance reservations and 72 hours before you dine, the chefs have a chance to prepare for your needs. Even if you have forgotten to call ahead, all you need to do in most dining situations is talk with your server. Most times, the server will send a chef out to consult with you as to how your foods will be prepared. If you need your dishes to be lactose- or gluten-free, for example, the chef can suggest tasty alternatives—in fact, many seem to enjoy the challenge of preparing something special for a guest. For more details on dealing with most food allergies, refer to our section on Diet (see pages 31–34).

Bright Idea: Call Disney table-service restaurants 72 hours in advance to allow the chefs time to accommodate your requests. Call 407-WDW-DINE (407-939-3463) to obtain restaurant contact details.

Other allergies: If your allergy/asthma is triggered by inhalants, such as pollen, molds, dust, and grasses, consider the timing of your visit to Central Florida. Obviously, the spring and summer months, when everything is in full bloom, are going to be worse for you than the cooler late autumn and winter months. Keep in mind, though, that Florida is farther south than much of the country, its "spring" starts early—things heat up and start blooming as early as late March! And the growing season lasts a lot longer. To get the daily pollen counts, consult the local newspaper, TV weather broadcasts, or visit http://www.pollen.com. If you're allergic to bee stings or other insect bites, remember to bring the appropriate treatment with you—Florida has lots of bugs! If necessary, don't forget to carry your epinephrine in case of a severe allergic reaction. To prevent bites, it's a good idea to have insect repellent, long sleeves, and long pants, especially in the evenings. If you do get bitten, Benadryl or some other antihistamine would come in handy.

Bright Idea: If your allergy is severe, wear a medical alert bracelet or necklace that identifies the allergen and treatment. These are available at many pharmacies, through your doctor's office, or from http://www.medicalert.org.

[G] Allergies and Asthma (continued)

Asthmatics and those with a sensitivity to smoke will be happy to note that the Florida Clean Indoor Air Act requires all enclosed indoor workplaces—including resort lobbies, convention spaces, common areas, dining locations, and enclosed backstage areas—to be nonsmoking. There are designated outdoor smoking areas in the theme parks indicated on the guide maps, though, that you may wish to avoid—do they ever get smoky! There are also lounge areas, as well as some closed-in spaces in queues or ride waiting areas, where you may find yourself in close quarters with other vacationers who are wearing strong scents or smoking despite the smoking restrictions. In addition, some attractions use special effects that have strong odors, including dry ice and smoke. We note these potential problem areas in the following chapters of this guidebook.

Planning Ahead

At the resort hotels: Whether you're staying on Disney property or off, remember to request a nonsmoking room when making your reservations. If you tell the Disney representative that you require a smoke-free room for medical needs, they'll help ensure that you get one.

Disney offers special cleaning services to its guests with allergies and sensitivities. If requested, Disney resort hotel housekeeping will clean your room without using harsh chemicals. They can also perform an "**allergy cleaning**," taking special care to make sure the linens, draperies, etc., are as dust-free as possible. When making your room reservation, be sure to request these services so your needs are noted. Also reiterate your requests upon check-in.

While all Disney dining establishments are smoke-free by law, a few of the **lounges**, which don't serve food, are not required to follow suit. These include the bar or lounge areas of the Lobby Court Lounge and Shula's Lounge at the Dolphin.

In the theme parks: Each theme park has a First Aid Station, staffed with a nurse. See our sidebar on First Aid Stations on page 196 for details on the services they provide. In addition, many stores in each theme park (the Emporium in the Magic Kingdom or MouseGear in Epcot, for example) also have over-the-counter medications, such as Benadryl, Tylenol, etc., in an under-the-counter location. Just ask a cast member in the store to point you to the right cashier.

At the water parks: First Aid Stations at Typhoon Lagoon (near Leaning Palms) and Blizzard Beach (near the entrance) help with minor first aid.

At Downtown Disney/BoardWalk: While the clubs and restaurants at Downtown Disney are smoke-free by law, a few of the lounges, which don't serve food, are not required to follow suit. These include the bar or lounge areas of Planet Hollywood, House of Blues, Bongo's Cuban Café, Fulton's Crab House, Rainforest Café, Portobello Yacht Club, and Captain Jack's. Jellyrolls on the BoardWalk also allows smoking.

Bright Idea: If your asthma or allergy requires you to take prescription medication, be sure to bring copies of your prescriptions with you.

PassPorter Picks

✔ Consider staying at resorts that are newer and those that are more self-contained, such as the Yacht and Beach Club or the BoardWalk.

✔ If you have food allergies, try a "Disney Vacation Club" resort, such as the Beach Club Villas or the Boardwalk Villas—these resorts feature kitchenettes or full kitchens so that you can prepare meals.

PassPorter Pans

✔ Avoid resorts that are spread out, forcing you to walk great distances in wooded areas, such as Port Orleans, Fort Wilderness, and Caribbean Beach. Also be aware that the Wilderness Lodge pipes a faux fire smoke smell into the lobby, and it and the Animal Kingdom Lodge have lobby gas fireplaces. If you have a sensitivity to smoke smell, avoid them.

✔ Avoid the outdoor areas of Disney's Animal Kingdom Lodge if you have sensitivity to animals or grasses and pollens. Avoid many of the outdoor areas around Disney's Animal Kingdom park for the same reasons.

✔ Avoid the perfume shops in Epcot's France and Norway pavilions and the Queen's Table shop in the United Kingdom pavilion if you're sensitive to heavy scents. You'll also want to avoid Basin in Downtown Disney.

✔ Limit your visits to the stables and petting zoo at Fort Wilderness resort. You might also want to steer clear of the Affection Section petting zoo in Rafiki's Planet Watch in Disney's Animal Kingdom park.

✔ Be aware that most of the restaurants featuring Asian cuisine use peanut oil in their cooking.

✔ Note that even if you are staying in a nonsmoking room or cabin, some people will smoke outside the building or on their balconies.

✔ Avoid the new "Heavenly Beds" at the Swan and Dolphin hotels, which may cause problems for those with down or feather allergies. Request hypoallergenic bedding prior to check-in or from housekeeping.

Autism Spectrum Disorders (ASD)

Having a special need that is invisible to the casual observer can be difficult, to say the least. How can you convince folks that you deserve some special considerations, when they can't *see* your problem? That's the challenge facing folks traveling with someone who has autism or one of its associated disorders. The good news is your trip to Walt Disney World can be a very magical and rewarding experience for everyone.

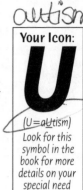

autism

Your Icon:

U

(U=aUtism)
Look for this symbol in the book for more details on your special need

Planning Ahead

Remember to **plan, but be flexible**. Have some structure to your days, but also retain the flexibility to change at the last minute if needed. Read and learn about Walt Disney World and develop a plan before your trip.

Much of what you do (or don't do) **depends on the traveler** who has ASD, their schedule, and needs. Is the traveler sensory-seeking or sensory defensive? Verbal?

As you begin to plan your vacation, **watch Disney movies** and the Disney planning videos/DVDs. These help slowly introduce your traveler with ASD to Disney characters, parks, and resorts. Remember, the characters are large and can be imposing in the parks. Introduce your ASD traveler from a distance. Prepare them with social stories, talk about the parks, and show pictures.

If at all possible, **travel in the off-season**, as there will be fewer crowds and cooler temperatures. Also, during the summer months, thunderstorms are the norm each afternoon. If the loud noise will adversely affect your traveler who has ASD, avoid June through August.

There are several things to bring with you to help make the vacation go more smoothly:

✔ **Letter from your physician** for help with obtaining a Guest Assistance Card (see pages 10-11).

✔ **Handicapped Parking Permit/Tag**—If you plan to rent/drive a car in Florida, be sure to bring your permit from home. Not only will this grant you access to closer parking spaces at the theme parks and resorts, but you can also valet park for free at participating Disney resort hotels (but don't forget the gratuity).

✔ **Earplugs**—The sounds in some attractions and fireworks shows can be quite loud and scary, as can the automatic toilets found in most Disney restrooms. Earplugs or headphones can muffle the noise. Some folks even suggest the ear protectors/sound reducers worn by construction workers.

Bright Idea: Bring a few pairs of earplugs from home. They are available from variety, grocery, or other stores and are fairly inexpensive. Disney resort stores do sell them, but they are not cheap!

✔ **Electrical outlet covers**—Some hotels will provide these upon request. Phone ahead and ask to speak to Housekeeping.

✔ **Favorite snacks and foods**—Avoid potential problems when waiting for food or with a picky eater—be sure to have favorite snacks and foods with you. If necessary, make a grocery stop on your way to Disney. (We list nearby grocery stores on page 384.)

✔ **Favorite comfort "toy"** or item from home to ground the traveler who has ASD. Don't wash it before you leave unless absolutely necessary—it's good for it to smell like home.

✔ **A sensory "grab bag"** filled with inexpensive, new toys that stimulate your child. A trip to the dollar store with $20 will do the trick.

✔ **A picture itinerary** with stickers that can be placed on things you've done. Share it with your traveler so they know what they will do each day. They can fill in the sections once you've gone on the attraction or dined at the restaurant.

✔ **Personal identification**—In the event the ASD traveler gets separated from you, be sure they are carrying identification and information as to where you are staying and how you can be contacted (see page 92). If you have a digital camera, take a photo each morning before you go out; it will be easier to remember clothing and appearance.

✔ **A collapsible stroller**, if the ASD traveler is small enough. You can rent a stroller at the parks, but then you still have to walk to your car or the bus stop and then to your room. Guest Relations can even issue a Guest Assistance Card (see pages 10-11) to allow you to use a stroller as a wheelchair. This means the stroller won't have to be parked outside the attraction and your child won't have to walk as much. Many travelers with ASD find a stroller a safe haven that helps them cope with all the stimulation at Disney. Families also report that travelers with ASD particularly liked the firm pressure provided by the plastic seats in the park strollers at Disney's Animal Kingdom, Epcot, and the Magic Kingdom.

Bright Idea: Review our section on traveling with Fears on pages 37-41.

Planning | Your Special Need | Getting There | Staying in Style | Touring | Feasting | Resources | Index

[U] Autism Spectrum Disorders (continued)

Will you drive or fly? If flying, notify the airline of any special needs well in advance of your journey. Also, request bulkhead seats (no one in front to kick). Be sure to let the attendant know your needs when you board. Bring extra facial wipes and keep up with medicine dosages and toilet routines. Once you arrive in Florida, consider a rental car. While Disney transportation works great, there are times you will be waiting for a bus, boat, or monorail. There will be much less waiting involved if you don't have to rely on Disney transportation and can just walk to your car. If you don't rent a car, consider a private car service (see page 99) to take you to Walt Disney World instead of the shuttle. You will have a much quieter environment with little or no wait time. Shuttles will often wait for a minimum number of passengers before they depart and make several stops before you reach your destination.

Bright Idea: Use airplane picture books to acquaint first-time flyers with air travel. Consider making a test run to the airport, too.

Know the **check-in time** for your resort and plan your arrival accordingly. Disney resorts allow check-in at 3:00 pm and 4:00 pm. If you will want to unwind in your room upon arrival, but not wait for it to be ready, factor in these late afternoon times. If you arrive before check-in time, be sure to let the Front Desk you're there anyway, as a sort of "pre-check-in." This is a good time to restate your special requests. During slow seasons, your room might be ready early.

When it comes to **choosing accommodations**, the deluxe resorts have less ambient noise to deal with. That said, you still need to travel within your means. When you make your hotel reservation, have the representative note that you need a room "away from all the activity" or "away from the themed pool." This will probably mean a long walk from the main check-in area, though. You might want to consider Pop Century (value resort), Port Orleans French Quarter (moderate resort), or one of the Epcot area resorts (Beach Club, Yacht Club, Swan, or Dolphin) for relatively subdued surroundings. Disney Vacation Club resorts are nice because even the studios offer kitchenettes with microwave, toaster, coffeemaker, and refrigerator, for those times when a quiet meal would be beneficial. Request a ground floor room (rather than one with a balcony), if appropriate. Consider bringing bells for the door to alert you when it's opened.

Check **restaurant menus** in advance for offerings. Make advance reservations for any table-service restaurant you plan to visit. Minimize wait times by eating when or soon after the restaurant opens. You can always call and cancel if you change your mind. If there are special dietary requests, such as gluten-free foods, have this noted on your reservation. See chapter 6 starting on page 311.

Upon Your Arrival

Keep your regular routine. If your traveler who has ASD is normally up at 7:00 am, then that's when you should get up (you may want to adjust this to reflect your home time zone). If they are used to eating at specific times, do your best to keep that schedule.

Consider whether a **Guest Assistance Card** (see pages 10-11) can provide necessary accommodations for your special needs traveler.

Use FASTPASS at the parks—we can't stress this enough. It will significantly reduce the time you wait in line! One important note, however—some with ASD will not understand why they got in line to get a FASTPASS and then left without riding. Have one member of your group get all the FASTPASSes.

At **character meet and greets**, show the attending cast member your Guest Assistance Card. On occasion and at their discretion, they will provide some special accommodation.

If you are early risers, **Extra Magic Hour** (see page 109) saves you time in lines and also offers a cooler time of day to tour the parks.

Physical issues? You'll do a lot of walking. If your traveler with ASD tires easily, **rent a wheelchair or stroller**, depending on their age.

Each theme park has a **First Aid Station**—if you need a quiet place, see if they have a room you can use. See page 196 for more information.

There are **companion restrooms** located throughout each theme park. Look for these especially if you need a place to change diapers or are especially sensitive to sounds. Most, but not all, have changing tables at counter height and no longer than four feet. For locations, see chapter 5.

Ask the cast member outside each attraction about noise levels, flashing lights, and **potential problems**. Also ask for seating recommendations. If you want to be near an exit, be the first to go down the row in the theaters.

Reader Tip: "Many autism spectrum children are sensory-seeking, not just defensive. I've traveled with two very different autism spectrum kids and, for both, Big Thunder Mountain Railroad was their favorite. Your child's limitations should guide you."—contributed by Alissa Tschetter-Siedschlaw

Take breaks back at your hotel—don't hesitate to leave while everyone is still going strong. The key is not to let things go too long. Time at the pool or resting in the room works wonders for everyone!

Disney resorts can provide **child bed rails** at no additional cost.

[U] Autism Spectrum Disorders (continued)

Having dinner in the parks or resort? **Eat early** (around 4:00 pm) so you don't have long waits.

Know where the gardens and **quiet places** in the parks are (see chapter 5). Most people either don't know where they are or avoid them. For you, these can be a great respite. We note the quiet spots at the resorts in chapter 4.

Consider **character meals** for Disney character interaction instead of the "meets" in the theme parks. At the parks, you can encounter crowds and long waits, especially for the more popular characters. At a character meal, the characters visit each table, without lines or jostling. Once the characters come to your table, their attention can be directed toward you. However, if your traveler is sensitive to loud noises, avoid the really noisy character meals like 1900 Park Fare (Grand Floridian) and Chef Mickey's (Contemporary).

Reader Tip: "I would like to suggest you try Pal Mickey (a speaking, plush Mickey toy available at Walt Disney World) for any child with autism. My son normally "self-stims" (e.g., hand flapping) when he is overstimulated or excited. I was amazed when I noticed that, after getting Pal Mickey, he was no longer stimming. We bought a bottle strap and used it to hang Mickey around his neck. He was so busy trying to feel Mickey wiggle and listening for him to talk that he was no longer stimming. I was so excited! Just having his own Mickey to hold seemed to give him some needed security."—contributed by peer reviewer Carrie Bass

What Are Autism Spectrum Disorders (ASD)?

Autism Spectrum Disorders, also known as Pervasive Developmental Disorders (PDDs), cause impairments in thinking, feeling, language, and the ability to relate socially. They encompass a wide range of symptoms from mild to severe and include diagnoses such as autism or Asperger Syndrome. Unlike people with noticeable physical problems, a person who has ASD may not initially appear any different than one who does not have ASD.

Behaviors that are common to someone who has ASD can include repetitive movements (such as rocking), abnormal responses to sounds and touch, difficulty initiating or maintaining a conversation, tantrums, and laughing or crying for no apparent reason. These behaviors in a public setting can cause occasional awkwardness, yet most families with a member who has ASD have successful and magical trips to Walt Disney World.

Bright Idea: If you are concerned about others who may make comments on your traveler's behavior, considering printing out small cards that explain autism and your child's condition. Then just hand out a card when necessary. You can get preprinted cards at http://www.autism-society.org.

Chronic Fatigue Syndrome/ Fibromyalgia

Chronic fatigue, fibromyalgia, and other similar conditions, like rheumatoid arthritis, all have one common symptom—a severe feeling of being tired that has been going on for months. Additional symptoms may include muscle aches, joint pain, and tender body points. But even if you experience these symptoms, a trip to Walt Disney World can still be fun and fulfilling if you remember several important things.

Your Icon:

C

CHRONIC

(C=Chronic) Look for this symbol in the book for more details on your special need

You probably already know the steps you need to take to deal with your symptoms: Eat well-balanced meals, get plenty of rest, and pace yourself physically, emotionally, and intellectually. This will be especially important to remember when touring Disney's theme parks, as there are so many things to look at and long distances to travel. Don't even try to do it all. You won't be able to and you'll just be miserable!

Planning Ahead

As you plan your vacation, consider going during the **cooler months** with lower attendance, like January and early February or early December. Heat just makes fatigue that much worse.

If you fly to Florida, try to book either **nonstop flights** or flights with sufficient layover so you don't have to rush from gate to gate. You can also request wheelchair assistance in traveling from the airport check-in area to the gate and return. Most airlines will offer preboarding for those needing assistance or extra time. Take advantage of this so you don't have to stand for long periods or struggle to get through the crowded aisles. If you are going to have carry-on luggage, make sure it's on wheels. Ask for assistance getting it in the overhead bin when you board the plane.

If you drive, be sure to factor in **lots of stops** so you can walk around and reduce stiffness in your legs.

When you make a hotel reservation, request a **room near the elevator** as well as one that is handicap accessible, if necessary.

Be sure to **bring all medications**, doctors' names and numbers, and a summary of your medical history in case of delays or layovers.

Planning · Your Special Need · Getting There · Staying in Style · Touring · Feasting · Resources · Index

[C] Chronic Fatigue Syndrome/Fibromyalgia (continued)

Consider whether a **Guest Assistance Card** (see pages 10-11) can provide necessary accommodations for you or your special traveler.

There is a lot of walking at Walt Disney World, both at the theme parks and at the Disney resorts. **Renting an ECV/wheelchair** can save energy for the attractions. You may also want to consider renting an ECV from a local firm so that you have the wheels with you at the resorts, in the parking lots, etc. Disney buses are able to accommodate wheelchairs and ECVs. See pages 201-203 for info on renting wheelchairs and ECVs.

Factor in **midday breaks** at your resort. For convenience, we recommend staying at a Disney resort.

Remember that each theme park has a **First Aid Station** where you can cool off and lie down for a while if you feel overly fatigued. See page 196 for First Aid Station information.

PassPorter Picks

✔ Use **FASTPASS** whenever possible to avoid long waits in line. We note the attractions with FASTPASS in chapter 5.

✔ Take advantage of **Extra Magic Hour**, when one park opens early to Disney resort guests. Crowds are lower, so lines are usually shorter.

✔ Visit popular attractions during **parade times** to avoid long queues.

✔ Make **advance dining reservations**, especially for popular places, to avoid long waits. Dining at off-peak times decreases wait times also.

PassPorter Pans

✔ Unless you have a wheelchair or ECV, avoid attractions with **limited or no seating**, like the 360-degree CircleVision films, which require you to stand for the duration. Review the Attraction Seating Types on page 197.

✔ Avoid long days; **conserve your energy**—staying up for an E-Ride Night might not be a good idea if you have an early morning planned.

✔ Avoid riding with someone on rides whose momentum may cause them to slide to one side of the car or another, like Big Thunder Mountain Railroad. Instead, consider **riding solo**, so no one squeezes up against you.

✔ Rides that are jarring can **cause excess pain** and could start a flare-up. Check out the ride or have someone ride it first to check movement.

Diet

Your Icon:

D

(D=Diet)
Look for this symbol in the book for more details on your special need

Just because you're on vacation, it doesn't mean you have to change the way you eat. Whether your special dietary needs are lifestyle choices (like low-fat, low-carb, vegetarian, or vegan), health-related (low sodium, no sugar added/diabetic, allergies to fish, nuts, eggs, dairy products, wheat gluten), or religious (kosher/halal), all Walt Disney World table-service restaurants that accept advance reservations (see chapter 6 for details) can **meet your needs**, with many chefs treating your need as an opportunity to delight and amaze you.

Planning Ahead

If you or someone in your party has special dietary needs, make advance reservation arrangements by calling **407-WDW-DINE** (407-939-3463) before you leave for your trip. When you do, alert the cast member to your special needs, and they will make a note on the file.

The more time you give the Disney chefs to prepare, the better. Disney restaurants request **72 hours advance notice**, so that they can plan your special requirements. If you forget, though, don't despair! Often, if you discuss your issues with your server, you will still be able to dine without breaking your regimen. Servers will usually bring a chef out from the kitchen to talk with you personally—and they seem to welcome the challenge of preparing a special order.

Reader Tip: The executive chefs from each of the parks can e-mail you a list of items from food carts/fast food stations around the parks that meet your special dietary need, if such a list is available. (We got extensive lists from each park for gluten-free hot dogs, pizza, ice cream, etc.)—contributed by peer reviewer Leanne Phelps

For **dinner shows** like the Hoop Dee Doo Revue or the Spirit of Aloha Dinner, 24-hour notice is required. Call 407-WDW-DINE as soon as you reach the Orlando area to confirm that your special request is noted on your reservation.

If you are staying **off Disney property**, you can still make special requests of Disney restaurants. Just call the main Walt Disney World switchboard (407-824-2222) and ask to be connected to the specific restaurant.

[D] Diet (continued)

Upon Your Arrival

Once you arrive in Orlando, if you are staying at a Disney resort hotel, **speak to a cast member** at the resort's Lobby Concierge desk and let them know again what your specific needs are, and they will call the restaurant for you. The more specific and individual your needs are, the more lead time the restaurant will require. Even with advance notice, however, sometimes the message doesn't get to the right chef. Be sure to talk with your server at the restaurant, who should clue in the chef.

If you have other specific concerns, you can also call the **executive chefs** or Food and Beverage managers directly at the telephone numbers listed below. If no one is available when you call, leave a message and a telephone number so they can get back to you.

Magic Kingdom: 407-824-5967
Epcot: 407-560-7483
Disney-MGM Studios: 407-560-1347
Disney's Animal Kingdom: 407-938-2203

Bright Idea: Even if you've gotten a listing of ingredients or menus from Disney from previous visits, be sure to check prior to each trip—menus, ingredients, and offerings change often.

Kosher meals can be provided with 24 hours advance notice at most table-service restaurants. A credit card is required to guarantee the order, but will not be charged unless the reservation is cancelled within 24 hours or if the party is a no-show. Kosher items are *not* available at these restaurants: the Grand Floridian's Garden View Afternoon Tea, Teppanyaki Dining Room, House of Blues, Planet Hollywood, Fulton's Crab House, Portobello Yacht Club, and Rainforest Café. The table-service restaurants at the Swan and Dolphin (Gulliver's Grill, Palio, Shula's Steakhouse, Todd English's bluezoo, and Fresh Mediterranean Market) do not normally have kosher meals available, but call 72 hours in advance to inquire whether it's possible to order kosher meals.Kosher meals are available without advance notice at these counter-service locations in the resorts and theme parks: Cosmic Ray's Starlight Café at the Magic Kingdom, the food courts at Disney's All-Star Resorts and Pop Century, Sassagoula Food Factory & Floatworks at Port Orleans French Quarter, Riverside Mill Food Court at Port Orleans Riverside, Liberty Inn at Epcot, Pizzafari at Disney's Animal Kingdom, and the ABC Commissary at Disney-MGM Studios.

Reader Tip: The only kosher restaurant in the Greater Orlando area is Amira's Kosher Deli in Altamonte Springs (407-831-0999).—contributed by peer reviewer Robert Feder

If you're not planning on eating every meal out, you can **pick up groceries** with items that conform to your diet in a number of places. For example, Gooding's carries Hebrew National brand kosher hot dogs. Lactose-intolerant folks can find lactose-free milk (Lactaid) in some resort convenience stores, but not much else that addresses their specific needs. Your best bet for purchasing special items is to visit a nearby grocery store, such as Gooding's in the Crossroads Shopping Center.

Bright Idea: If you have specific food allergies or dietary concerns, you may bring your own small snack items into the parks.

Other pointers for those with special dietary needs, contributed by peer reviewer Leanne Phelps, who has several family members with severe food allergies:

✔ **Don't be afraid of buffets**, wondering what ingredients are involved and what cross-contamination might have occurred. Chefs at buffet restaurants are usually just as willing to make special meals as those at table-service restaurants. When you're seated, ask to speak to a chef. Sometimes a chef will point out items from the buffet that you can eat without worry, but usually he or she will ask what types of foods you are interested in and bring you specially prepared food. While you may have to be a little patient, it will be worth the wait.

✔ **Plan for a little extra time**. Even when the restaurants have been notified ahead of time of your dietary need (and especially when they aren't), special meals often take longer to prepare.

✔ **Ask the chef for suggestions**. If you have a special dietary need, you can always ask if a certain menu item could be prepared to meet your needs. However, if you don't have a particular desire, you can ask a chef for ideas. Just mention what ingredients you must avoid.

✔ If you plan to eat quite a few meals at your **Disney resort's food court**, consider calling in advance to see what special accommodations can be made for you. Unlike most food courts in malls and airports, Disney resort hotel food courts can be very accommodating for special diets. Don't hesitate to ask if a Mickey waffle can be made gluten-free or a if dessert can be made sugar-free—many times the answer is yes. If you encounter a cast member that doesn't understand your request, ask to speak to the food court manager on duty.

✔ Some travelers require their food to be **extremely fresh** to avoid bacteria that grows on food that sits for any length of time. If this applies to you, be sure to tell your server. If you would like something from a fast food cart or stand, be very specific about this request, and you can usually watch them prepare your burger or other item on the spot.

[D] Diet (continued)

Passporter Picks

✔ If you follow a vegetarian/vegan diet, check out the guidebook "**Vegetarian Walt Disney World and Greater Orlando**" by Than Saffel and Susan Shumaker (Globe Pequot Press). It's a great resource and provides a good overview of many of the restaurants in the Orlando area. You can get it at bookstores or order it direct from the publisher at http://www.globepequot.com.

© Deb Wills

✔ Even when you don't give advance notice, **servers and chefs** try hard to be accommodating and can be remarkably well-informed. If you have any questions or concerns about the ingredients or preparation of a regular menu item or the availablility of a substitution, don't hesitate to ask your server.

Disney chef Tjetjep ("TJ") at Boma

✔ Some Disney restaurants are **more accommodating** than others when it comes to special requests. We've found Boma (Disney's Animal Kingdom Lodge) and Kona Café (Polynesian Resort) to be especially agreeable to requests for vegetarian/vegan dishes. Many of the restaurants in the deluxe resorts have come up with amazing sugar-free desserts on short notice, too.

PassPorter Pans

✔ If you're **allergic to seafood**, avoid the following restaurants, which primarily feature seafood on their menus: Flying Fish Café (BoardWalk); Fulton's Crab House (Pleasure Island); Tempura Kiku (Japan in Epcot); Coral Reef (Future World in Epcot); Yorkshire County Fish Shop (United Kingdom in Epcot); Restaurant Akershus (Norway in Epcot); Kimono's (Walt Disney World Swan); and Todd English's bluezoo (Walt Disney World Dolphin). While seafood alternatives are often available, cross-contamination is a potential concern.

✔ If you have a **peanut allergy**, avoid the Asian restaurants on property, which tend to use peanut oil in their cooking: Tempura Kiku, Teppanyaki, Yakitori House, Nine Dragons, Lotus Blossom Café (all in Epcot's World Showcase), Tomorrowland Terrace Noodle Station, and Kimono's.

Be sure to read chapter 6 on dining, which contains a wealth information on special diets.

[F] Fears (continued)

Bright Idea: Almost every attraction and all thrill rides have an "out" before you get on the actual attraction. This allows you to see the pre-show and get a feel for the special Disney theming without actually experiencing the ride itself. Don't hesitate to tell the cast member you do not wish to ride. Some great pre-shows include the Tower of Terror (which could also be scary and dark with thunder) and Rock 'n' Roller Coaster. It's easy enough to see these pre-shows, then exit.

Remember that sometimes things others find thrilling may **terrify you** or your fearful child. For example, when Deb Koma's son was little, he noticed the glowing eyes of the tiger in the tunnel of the Jungle Cruise ride—that was enough to scare him on this very gentle, funny ride. And Deb Koma's very brave 5-year-old niece was scared of the lightning scene in The Many Adventures of Winnie-the-Pooh. She refuses to ride that very child-friendly ride again, even three years later! Know yourself or your child.

Whatever you do, don't make the mistake of riding the Magic Kingdom's Snow White's Scary Adventures with youngsters early in your trip. They will think that it is a fun princess ride and it is not—it's dark and quite scary. Some young children are frightened and they will then **associate any ride** that's dark or in a building with their scary experience and refuse to go on another. Trust us on this one!

Sometimes, the roles reverse and the **child is the brave one** for the adult. Deb Wills has "fond" memories of riding the Twilight Zone Tower of Terror with the 7-year-old daughter of a dear friend. She held Deb's hand the entire time to soothe her.

Concerned with crowds? Definitely travel in the off-season. Enter theaters first or last so you are not in the midst of several hundred people. Being last is generally easier, as you don't have to fight the crowds trying to get the "best seat" and you can exit after almost everyone has left.

Claustrophobic? There are certain areas/rides that you should avoid—like the sound booths at Sounds Dangerous and Conservation Station, and the Tower of Terror and Mission: SPACE in Epcot. We note these areas in our individual descriptions in chapter 5.

The 3-D presentations in each theme park have special tactile effects that range from a **spray of water** to the sensation of something running over your feet. In addition, special 3-D glasses are provided to wear during the show. If the 3-D effects bother you or a companion, don't wear (or remove) the special glasses. Hold children on your lap to avoid some tactile effects.

Down Syndrome, Fragile X, and Other Cognitive Disabilities

As we have said throughout this chapter, no matter what your ability or disability, Disney offers something for everyone. The traveler with Down Syndrome, Fragile X, or other cognitive disabilities is no different.

Because these conditions manifest themselves in so many ways, with such a wide variety of symptoms, we attempt to provide you with general information and tips that help you with your trip. Just remember, even if you aren't able to do or see everything you want to, the magic touches everyone. And a smile on the face of your special traveler will be worth all the planning for your trip to Disney.

Your Icon:

Intellectual

I

(I=Intellectual) Look for this symbol in the book for more details on your special need

Planning Ahead

Travelers with cognitive disabilities often have **other issues** to take into consideration, including communication and social skills concerns, as well as personal hygiene issues. We recommend that you read the sections on asthma and allergies, autism spectrum disorders, heart health, mobility, and special diets—they may be applicable to your situation. In addition, other sections of this chapter may also apply—you might want to take the time to browse through the entire chapter.

In all likelihood, a special needs traveler with cognitive disabilities will need closer supervision and guidance while away from home. While one person may have slight difficulty thinking and communicating, another may face major challenges with basic self-care and even physical issues. You really will need to **know the abilities and limitations of everyone** traveling with you ... even yourself!

We've said many times throughout this book, but it bears repeating: If at all possible, **travel in the off-season**, as there will be cooler temperatures and lower crowds!

Be sure to **do your research** prior to the trip. Have a good idea of attractions that will and won't be good matches for the special needs traveler.

Bright Idea: As said elsewhere in this chapter, taking anyone out of his or her normal routine and environment can be unsettling. This is especially true for special needs travelers. Be aware that old issues may resurface. To help combat this, before you leave home, practice or role-play various situations that may occur.—contributed by peer reviewer Robert Feder

[I] Down Syndrome, Fragile X, and Cognitive Disabilities (continued)

Perhaps the most important area to take care of is **personal identification**. In the event members of your group get separated, be sure they not only have a waterproof ID on them, but information as to where you are staying and how you can be contacted. If you have a digital camera, take a photo each morning before you go out; it will be easier to remember clothing and appearance. Have a plan in place in case you are separated so you can spring into action and not panic should the situation arise. We offer more details on personal identification on page 92.

There are **many wide open spaces** around Walt Disney World, with lots of people coming and going—lots of characters, colors, and sounds to offer major distractions. Be on alert especially during times when it's easiest to become separated from your group: during parades, when large theater attractions let out, and near character meet and greets.

If **fatigue and muscle weakness** are a concern, request a room near the elevator or close to the parking lot or bus stop when you make a hotel reservation.

Bring all **medications, doctors' names and numbers, and a summary** of your medical history in case of delays or layovers.

Consider whether a **Guest Assistance Card** (see pages 10–11) can provide necessary accommodations for your special traveler.

Upon Your Arrival

Touring Walt Disney World can involve long days of walking and waiting in lines. **Don't try to do it all**. You simply can't, and trying to do everything will only lead to frustration. Consider mobility issues—if a stroller or wheelchair will help your special needs traveler enjoy more of the day, don't hesitate to rent one (see page 201–203).

If you rely on **Disney transportation**, keep in mind that it can take a long time to get from point A to point B. Plan accordingly. Don't wait until someone has a meltdown or gets overtired and the whole group gets cranky. If one person needs to head back to the room, do it! You'll be glad you did!

Fears

Fears evoke unpleasant feelings. Fear of the dark, spiders, heights, crowds, mice, flying, water, coasters; whatever it is, if it makes you feel uneasy, it might even trigger an anxiety attack. A Walt Disney World vacation is supposed to be magical and relaxing—the last thing you want is to be "surprised" by something that makes you feel uncomfortable or anxious.

Although Walt Disney World is as friendly a place as you can imagine, the special effects or nature of certain attractions may present conditions or objects that make you fearful. Understandably, you want to avoid these sit[...] Knowledge is your best tool! Research the places you'll visit an[...] you'll experience so that there are no scary surprises. Here are so[...] for doing just that:

Planning Ahead

Some attractions come right out and tell you they might scare you[...] are **warning signs** outside the entrance, so heed them! We m[...] anything that you might want to know about in our individual att[...] descriptions in chapter 5.

Important Note: Never coerce anyone (adult or child) to go on an attr[...] If there is one sure vacation mood-killer, that's it. You can always use th[...] Switch option (see page 194), or consider shopping or slurping on a [...] bar while the rest of the group sees the attraction.

When in doubt, **ask a cast member about the attraction**. He or sh[...] answer your questions about what you'll find inside the turnstile[...] could also ask those who are exiting the ride for their opinions.

Traveling with others? Have someone you trust **experience the attra[...] without you and then report back. You may find it is something you[...] to try, or it will confirm that you don't. Remember, once you're on [...] vehicle, you are there for the duration. You can't stop the ride m[...] because you want to get off.

Not all coasters are the same in intensity or effects. While Rock 'n' Roller Coaster and its three loops in the dark might scare you (it does Deb Wills), Big Thunder Mountain Railroad is more family-friendly and might fit the bill for you just fine!

While each of the nighttime shows has lots of fireworks (and bangs), you can still enjoy the show with a lower volume if you **use earplugs** (see page 25) or **watch** from an alternate location. For instance, the Magic Kingdom fireworks can be viewed from any of the Magic Kingdom monorail resort beaches or from a rented pontoon boat. The higher Epcot fireworks can be seen from several of the Epcot resorts, again with lower volume.

Sometimes you can see the attraction itself **without getting on it** to help in your decision whether to ride or not. The big drop on Splash Mountain is clearly visible from the bridge in Frontierland. Continue past the entrance for plenty of viewing areas for Big Thunder Mountain Railroad. Primeval Whirl at Disney's Animal Kingdom is outside, too.

The Disney theme park experience includes fantastic entertainment. Some is improvisational and the cast engages the audience. In other attractions, **audience participation** is possible. For the introverted or shy, we have noted these in the specific attractions/pavilions in chapter 5.

A cast member with an insect in a glass case

At Disney's Animal Kingdom, cast members sometimes carry around glass containers with small animals, insects, spiders, or snakes. This is especially true during the first hour or so the park is open in the Oasis and Discovery Island areas. Cast members with the containers do not approach you; they wait for you to come to them. There are also exhibits in Disney's Animal Kingdom with live small animals. We have so noted in the specific attractions in chapter 5.

Guests who **don't want to get wet** should stay away from Splash Mountain at the Magic Kingdom and Kali River Rapids at Disney's Animal Kingdom, and be aware that some rides either spray/mist water or have a water component that might get you damp (like Voyage of the Little Mermaid and Honey, I Shrunk the Audience). These are noted in chapter 5.

Fear of water? Avoid the Friendship boats, ferry boats, and other boat transportation. Attractions with water include Pirates of the Caribbean, "it's a small world," El Rio del Tiempo, Maelstrom, The Living Seas, Living With the Land, Splash Mountain, and Kali River Rapids.

Service animals are discussed on page 12.

[F] Fears (continued)

Upon Your Arrival

If the attraction you are leery about takes place in a theater or if you are "crowd-phobic," try to **sit near an exit**.

Bear in mind that this is Florida, and **bugs and small lizards** are virtually everywhere outside. In May and September, tiny "love bugs" (so called because there often two or more mating as they fly) are everywhere—they don't bite or sting, but they can bother the bug-wary.

Certain **restaurants can also present situations** that conjure up particular fears. We note them in our individual restaurant descriptions in chapter 6, but here are a few specific tips:

✔ Be aware of places like the Rainforest Café and Sci-Fi Dine-In Theater, which have scary sound and visual effects. If you have a fear of fire, use caution when going to the Spirit of Aloha dinner or the open cooking grill at 'Ohana, both at the Polynesian Resort. There are other restaurants that have showcase open fires—we note them in chapter 6.

✔ Guests who are shy might avoid Prime Time, Whispering Canyon, or 'Ohana, where your server might engage you in some tomfoolery!

✔ If you have fear of bugs and lizards, you might want to avoid Pizzafari, which has depictions of these creatures throughout the seating areas. There are also a lot of bugs in "It's Tough To Be A Bug." For the squeamish, note that there's a skeleton in Restaurantosaurus.

✔ If you have claustrophobia, stay away from small and crowded places like the Plaza Restaurant (the Magic Kingdom) and Beaches & Cream (Yacht and Beach Club).

✔ If you're afraid of heights, don't sit near the window at the California Grill (Contemporary) or ride the monorail.

✔ If you have a problem with the dark, you might want to avoid very dark restaurants like San Angel Inn (Epcot), Sci-Fi Dine-In Theater (Disney-MGM Studios), and Rainforest Café (Disney's Animal Kingdom and Downtown Disney).

Obvious fear triggers at both Blizzard Beach and Typhoon Lagoon water parks are the **very fast, very high slides and raft rides**. We note other fear factors in our individual descriptions of the water park attractions starting on page 281.

Planning

Your Special Need

Getting There

Staying in Style

Touring

Feasting

Resources

Index

DisneyQuest, located in Downtown Disney, has potential scare factors, as does Cirque du Soleil. Much of the action in DisneyQuest's games takes place in **darkened settings**, particularly experiences like Pirates of the Caribbean: Battle for Buccaneer Gold and Buzz Lightyear's Astroblasters. La Nouba, Cirque du Soleil's presentation at Downtown Disney West Side, also takes place in a darkened theater. Many of the acts performed during this show are breath-taking, and many involve performers suspended or climbing to great heights. Be aware that Epcot's IllumiNations evening show has huge fireballs in the opening sequence—you can even feel the heat from many viewing areas.

At Pleasure Island, avoid Adventurers Club's main areas (stay upstairs) and Comedy Warehouse **if you're shy** and don't enjoy audience participation.

At the resorts, there are also some potentially scary situations, which we note in chapter 4. Remember to request a room on the lower level when booking if you have **a fear of heights**.

At Fort Wilderness, there are lots of bugs, lizards, raccoons, and peacocks **walking around**. Both Fort Wilderness and Port Orleans are known to have the occasional gator, but Disney does take steps to control them.

Fear of Giant Mice?

Your favorite Disney characters will come to life as you venture around the theme parks. But while some children (and possibly some adults) eagerly embrace these walk-around characters, others are just as likely to run screaming in the opposite direction. A little work before you encounter any characters may help you avoid the fear and intimidation your child will feel when they realize those little figures of Goofy and Baloo on the television screen are really six feet tall in person.

✔ Talk to your child about the possibility of meeting the characters **before you stand in line** at a character meet-and-greet location. Discuss whether they want to approach the characters or if they'd prefer to enjoy them from afar.

✔ Remind your child that the characters would not hurt them and that **you will be right beside them**.

✔ **If you think it will help**, tell your child that the character is really just a normal person in a costume, pretending to be someone else. (Do this out of earshot of others—you don't want to spoil the magic for anyone!)

✔ For some children, even these reassurances aren't enough—their imaginations are just too good. (Just ask Deb Koma how her son was!) **Tell your child that it will be okay** if they choose to not meet with any characters up close, and mean it! Yes, it's disappointing, but maybe by your next trip, your little one will be ready to meet and greet everyone from sweet Cinderella to cruel old Cruella de Vil.

Foreign Language

It's a Small World, at least that's what the beloved Walt Disney World Fantasyland attraction tells us. And, whether your native language is French, German, Spanish, Japanese, or Portuguese, Disney works to make it even smaller by offering international visitors a number of special aids.

Planning Ahead

The special treatment begins as you start to plan your vacation—**Disney translates its Web site** into a number of languages geared toward a variety of cultures:

For French-speaking visitors:
http://www.disney.ca/vacations/disneyworld/francais

For Spanish-speaking visitors:
http://www.disneylatino.com/disneyvacaciones/waltdisneyworld

For Portuguese-speaking visitors:
http://www.disney.com.br/DisneyViagens/waltdisneyworld/index.html

For Japanese-speaking visitors:
http://www.disney.co.jp/usparks/wdw/index.html

For English-speaking visitors from the United Kingdom:
http://www.disney.co.uk/usa-resorts/waltdisneyworld

For English-speaking visitors from Canada:
http://www.disney.ca/vacations/disneyworld

Once you reach your resort, cast members are ready to provide you with information **in your native tongue**.

Bright Idea: The Walt Disney World Swan and Dolphin, located within walking distance of Epcot, also have a Web site that can be viewed in English, French, Spanish, Portuguese, German, Italian, and Japanese. It not only features the amenities of these two hotels, but a lot of information on the attractions at Walt Disney World and the Orlando area. You can access their Web site at http://www.swandolphin.com.

Your Icon:

Ö

Look for this symbol in the book for more details on your special need

© Debra Martin Koma

International guidemaps

Upon Your Arrival

Begin a visit to each theme park, water park, or Downtown Disney with a stop at **Guest Relations**. Indicated on the theme park guide maps by a blue "i" symbol, Guest Relations is open during regular park hours and can supply international visitors with a wide range of information. Some cast members are fluent in a variety of languages and will be able to help international guests purchase tickets and make advance reservations dining or other arrangements.

Bright Idea: Look closely at the oval name badges worn by every cast member in the parks and at the resorts. If a cast member is fluent in a language other than English, the name badge will sport a flag of the corresponding nation.

Guest Relations also has **guide maps of the parks** in a number of different languages: Spanish, French, Portuguese, German, and Japanese.

Cast name badge with language flags

International guests can also take advantage of **"Ears to the World" Personal Translator Units**. These are portable devices that provide synchronized, translated narration of the scripts of certain attractions into French, German, Portuguese, Japanese, or Spanish. The units resemble lightweight portable cassette players that can be carried around your neck with headphones. The headsets are available at no extra charge (although there is a $100 refundable deposit) at Guest Relations in the theme parks. Attractions with this feature include The Circle of Life, Ellen's Energy Adventure, and The American Adventure (Epcot); Hall of Presidents (the Magic Kingdom); and Walt Disney: One Man's Dream (Disney-MGM Studios). We indicate support for this feature in our individual attraction descriptions in chapter 5.

If you'd like personalized attention, guided tours offered in various languages can be arranged through Guest Relations. If you want to be a bit more independent, there are **tape-recorded walking tours** available in a variety of languages in the Magic Kingdom and Epcot—the equipment may be rented from the theme park's Guest Relations office for a small fee with $100 refundable deposit.

For another type of tour, Spanish-speaking guests can buy a Spanish-speaking **Pal Mickey**, a 10-inch plush Mickey Mouse that talks. (He's also available in English.) Using wireless technology, Pal Mickey points out interesting trivia, reminds you of parade times, and offers tips on where to watch fireworks, among other things. Pal Mickey is available for $65 from most resort gift shops and at locations throughout the theme parks.

[Ö] Foreign Language (continued)

Menus at most resort and theme park restaurants, both table-service and counter-service eateries, are **available in pictorial format**, and sometimes in French, German, Portuguese, Japanese, or Spanish.

Language assistance is available by calling 407-824-2222, which connects guests with a Walt Disney World operator and a phone interpreter (for Spanish, French, Portuguese, Japanese, German, Italian, and additional languages, subject to availability). In addition, all public telephones throughout the Walt Disney World Resort have instructions posted in French, German, Portuguese, Japanese, and Spanish.

Phone cards for international calls are available from vending machines at locations indicated by a yellow star on Disney's park guide maps. Most Disney resort lobbies also have these vending machines.

Foreign currency exchange is available for up to $100 per person at Guest Relations in theme parks and at Lobby Concierge at Disney resorts. The American Express office outside of Epcot offers currency exchange for higher denominations. There is also a foreign currency exchange available at the SunTrust bank on Buena Vista Drive across from Downtown Disney and in Gooding's at the Crossroads shopping center near Hotel Plaza Boulevard.

International Symbols (shown on next page) are used in park maps and on theme park and resort signage.

Disney's International Program

Did you know that Disney invites young people from all over the world to participate in its International Program? Participants can work in a variety of positions throughout the theme parks and resorts as a Cultural Representative, sharing the culture and customs of their countries. Or they can join the International College Program as a student between college semesters. Those in the program live with other participants, making this a multicultural experience for them, too. Look for participants in the International Program in the shops and restaurants located throughout the country pavilions in Epcot's World Showcase. There you can find many natives from the various countries who are more than happy to say a few words in their native tongues or talk about their homelands. Kids can also get in on the fun by visiting the Kidcot Stations around World Showcase—these are staffed by cast members from other countries, who will share some thoughts on their countries and will autograph and stamp the Epcot Passports that are available for purchase in Epcot shops. You can also often find Cultural Representatives during Epcot's Food and Wine Festival in the fall—we've passed the time with natives of countries as diverse as Australia and South Africa who were on hand to discuss aspects of their lands' cultures as they relate to the production of food and wine.

Here is a **measurement conversion factor chart**:

Multiply...	by	to get...	Multiply...	by	to get...
inches	2.54	centimeters	centimeters	0.3937	inches
feet	0.3048	meters	meters	3.281	feet
miles	1.609	kilometers	kilometers	0.6214	miles
ounces	28.35	grams	grams	0.0352	ounces
pounds	0.4536	kilograms	kilograms	2.2046	pounds
gallons	3.785	liters	liters	0.2642	gallons

More conversions are available at http://www.onlineconversion.com.

And a **temperature chart**:

Farenheit	= Celsius	Celsius	= Farenheit
0°F	–17.8°C	–10°C	14°F
32°F	0°C	0°C	32°F
40°F	4.4°C	10°C	50°F
50°F	10°C	20°C	68°F
60°F	15.5°C	25°C	77°F
70°F	21.1°C	30°C	86°F
80°F	26.7°C	35°C	95°F
90°F	32.2°C	40°C	104°F

If you want to check the **most recent currency exchange rates**, visit http://finance.yahoo.com/currency.

Here is a chart with the **international symbols** you'll encounter in Disney guidemaps and on signage:

	restrooms		stroller/wheelchair rental		must be ambulatory
	companion restroom		parade viewing for disabled guests		may remain in chair
	Guest Relations		First Aid Station		must transfer from wheelchair (ECV)
	ATM location	HC	handheld captioning		must transfer to standard wheelchair
	payphone	CC	closed (video) captioning		must transfer to chair, then to vehicle
	TTY payphone	RC	reflective captioning		height requirement
	Baby Center		assistive listening		health warning

Hearing

If you've experienced some hearing loss or impairment, you might think that your enjoyment of Walt Disney World and its attractions may be diminished by all the sounds you'll be missing. And yet, Disney has gone to great lengths to make sure that isn't the case by offering a variety of ways to enhance your vacation.

Your Icon:

H

(H=Hearing)
Look for this symbol in the book for more details on your special need

Planning Ahead

Disney's **special services for guests with disabilities** can be reached by calling 407-939-7807 (voice) or 407-827-5141 (TTY), a special text typewriter telephone line (there's another at 407-939-7670). The cast members that answer these lines can assist you in arranging much of your vacation.

Important Note: Traveling with a service animal that helps with your hearing impairment? See page 12.

Special provisions for hearing impaired visitors run the gamut, from the basic to the sophisticated. At the most basic level, cast members at most locations have access to paper and pens/pencils for communicating. If you would like a sign language interpreter, request it at least two weeks in advance.

If you're taking a **Disney Cruise**, submit a Medical Clearance form at least six weeks prior to sailing to let them know that sign language interpreters will be needed for the shows (they send one to the muster drill as well). Request a Room Communication kit for your stateroom (includes the same things that you get when at the resort—see page 48).

Bright Idea: Bring a waterproof container to store your hearing aid and batteries in, especially when you're aboard a water ride or swimming. If you use a hearing aid, be sure to bring extra batteries with you. Our research around the theme parks and resorts found no place that sells them!

Important Note: A buildup of wax in the ears can make flying extremely painful. Use ear plugs or EarPlanes (http://www.earplanes.com), chew gum, or drink water during take-off and descent to alleviate the pressure, or seek a physician's care.

Upon Your Arrival

Guest Assistance Packets with **dialogue, narrations, flashlights, and pen and paper** are available from cast members near the performance areas for most shows and attractions. Be sure to ask when you first see a cast member at the attraction (they sometimes have to get the packets).

© Debra Martin Koma

TTY phone

Pay phones are equipped with amplified handsets throughout Walt Disney World. There are also TTY pay phones at Guest Relations and a few other locations throughout the parks.

Assistive listening devices, for those with mild to moderate hearing loss, are lightweight, wireless devices that amplify sounds. The devices receive infrared signals from overhead transmitters at various locations. The receivers include a set of lightweight headphones with volume control and are available at Guest Relations. There's a $25 deposit, refundable if you return the device the same day.

Reflective captioning, in which captions are projected via an LED display onto an acrylic panel positioned in front of you, is used at a number of shows performed in theater settings. Ask a cast member at the entrance of the attraction, as the device takes a few minutes to set up properly. It works like this: You are given a device that resembles a flexible microphone stand with a rectangular piece of Plexiglas attached. The Plexiglas must be positioned so that it reflects the captioning from the back wall. It also must be situated so that you can view the stage and see the words at the base of the stage. Ask to be escorted into the theater before the doors "officially" open so you have time to set up the device. We note the attractions at which reflective captioning is available in chapter 5.

Handheld captioning units are another type of portable wireless device that provide synchronized narration of the scripts of certain attractions. The units resemble lightweight portable cassette players that can be

Handheld captioning unit

carried around your neck (although they do feel heavy after a while). The device is available at no charge (although there is a $100 refundable deposit) at Guest Relations in the theme parks. We note the attractions at which handheld captioning is available in our individual descriptions in chapter 5. While the synchronization is not perfect, it provides a great way to know what is being said in the moving attractions.

[H] Hearing (continued)

Video captioning or closed captioning is used on monitors in many attractions for pre-shows. Some of these monitors, indicated on the guide maps with a "CC" symbol, are "caption ready." You can get remote control activators at guest relations for a $25 refundable deposit. Based on the experience of those we spoke with, this device is the least useful of all.

Performances of **some live shows are "signed"** in ASL (American Sign Language) on a rotating basis:

✔ Disney-MGM Studios shows: Sundays/Wednesdays
✔ Magic Kingdom shows: Mondays/Thursdays
✔ Epcot shows: Tuesdays/Fridays
✔ Disney's Animal Kingdom shows: Saturday

The schedules for the signed performances vary from week to week, so it's best to **check with Guest Relations** for up-to-date information.

You can **request free sign language interpretation** for certain other live entertainment, like Epcot's holiday storytellers, at least two weeks in advance by calling 407-824-4321 or 407-827-5141 (TTY).

Bright Idea: Some cast members are trained in sign language—they'll be identified by a special symbol on their name tags.

A cast name tag indicating a sign language ability

Staying at a Disney resort hotel might help lessen any concerns you have about your vacation because of the amenities offered that specifically address concerns of those with hearing impairments. Not only does each Disney resort have rooms with closed captioned television, but there are also **"Room Communication Kits"** available, which include:

✔ Door knock and phone alerts
✔ Bed shaker alarm
✔ Text typewriter (TTY)
✔ Strobe light fire alarm
✔ Phone amplifier

The Guest Relations location at the Main Entrance of both Blizzard Beach and Typhoon Lagoon is the prime source of water park information for guests with a hearing impairment. Guest Relations at both water parks have a **text typewriter (TTY)**. There are also telephones with amplified handsets at various locations, as marked on the water park guide maps.

Bright Idea: Cirque du Soleil's La Nouba (see page 293) is a great show for people who are deaf because there is so little speaking.

Heart Health

If you're recovering from a heart attack or heart surgery, or if you've been diagnosed with high blood pressure, angina, or other heart-related medical conditions, you might think a Walt Disney World vacation is not for you. With some care and planning, your vacation to Walt Disney World can be among your favorite memories.

Your Icon:

Look for this symbol in the book for more details on your special need

Planning Ahead

The first thing to do is **consult your physician**, and get an official medical opinion on how much or how little you should endeavor to undertake.

If you will be flying, be sure to review our general tips for folks traveling with special needs in chapter 3 starting on page 91. In addition, ask your doctor if any testing is needed to ensure that your condition is stable. Recent studies on the effects of air travel on heart disease have found that **in general, the risks are minimal**. There are, however, some people who should not fly, including those who have had a heart attack (myocardial infarction) or a coronary artery stent within the past two weeks; those who have had coronary bypass surgery within the past three weeks (or longer if there were pulmonary complications); those with unstable angina, poorly controlled congestive heart failure, or uncontrolled arrhythmias.

Bright Idea: There appears to be no evidence air travel interferes with pacemakers or implantable defibrillators, but check with your airline to verify that their security screening devices will not harm you. To expedite the security screening process, it's a good idea to carry a Pacemaker Identification Card, available from your physician. Also ask the screener to inspect you via a "pat-down" rather than making you walk through the metal detector or be searched with a handwand. For more tips on going through airport security, visit the Web site of the Transportation Security Administration (TSA): http://www.tsa.gov/public/interapp/editorial/editorial_1376.xml.

As you develop your vacation schedule, plan **low-key days** with frequent breaks. We note quiet spots for breaks in the theme parks in chapter 5.

If necessary, rent an **ECV and/or other equipment** for delivery to your resort—see pages 201–203.

[♥] Heart Health (continued)

Upon Your Arrival

Before your day begins, **check the weather** so that you can plan to be in the cool indoors when the temperature is at its highest. In fact, it's probably best to avoid venturing out in the heat of the day—perhaps sitting in the shade by the pool or meandering in and out of the air-conditioned shops at Downtown Disney would be a better way to spend that time.

The key thing to touring the theme parks is to **pace yourself**. Distances on the park map can be deceptive—things often are farther away than they appear to be, which leads to a lot more walking than you might expect. It's not unusual for us to cover 8, 9, even 10 miles in a day (we can scarcely believe our pedometers). With that in mind, plan your day at a pace that you are comfortable with, not even attempting to cover everything in one day. Perhaps you could even consider renting a wheelchair/ECV to help you conserve your energy. (See "Mobility" on pages 62–66.)

Most of the major thrill rides in the parks carry **health warnings** (see photo for an example)—our advice is to heed them. The coasters, especially attractions like Rock 'N' Roller Coaster or Space Mountain, can really shake a person up, while other attractions, like Mission:SPACE and Stitch's Great Escape, provide thrills that can make even the most-conditioned athlete's heart race!

While enjoying the water parks, avoid the big water slides, which carry their own health warnings. Just getting to the top of a slide like Humunga Kowabunga can be a huge effort. There are **First Aid Stations** at each water park that can provide a cool place to rest as well as basic first aid.

Test Track health warning and height restriction sign

If you're watching your diet, the Disney table-service restaurants (and some counter-service spots, too) **offer heart-healthy entrees**, indicated with a special symbol on the menu. If you have additional dietary concerns, such as requiring a low-sodium diet, read "Diets" on pages 31–34.

If you're in the Walt Disney World area and have further health needs, a list of some of the **nearby medical providers** can be found in the Medical Treatment section of this chapter on pages 58–61.

Taking one of the backstage tours? If you **wear a pacemaker**, be sure to let your guide know before you start out. There may be an area or two backstage you'll want to avoid.

PassPorter Picks

✔ The Disney-MGM Studios is a compact theme park, easy to navigate, and many of its attractions are either indoors or in shaded areas.

✔ Consider staying at one of the smaller Disney resorts, such as Port Orleans French Quarter, which does not require long walks to get around its buildings. As an alternative, consider staying at one of the deluxe resorts, which are more self-contained, with ample elevators/escalators and additional amenities. Request a room location close to the lobby, bus stops, elevators, and/or food service areas and explain that it is for a medical condition.

✔ Dine at some of the restaurants known for their heart-healthy menus, such as California Grill at the Contemporary Resort, or Fresh Mediterranean Market at the Walt Disney World Dolphin Resort.

✔ Try the quiet pool at your resort, which is usually less noisy and crowded than the main themed pool.

PassPorter Pans

✔ Avoid the attractions marked with health warnings—they are designated as problematic for a reason!

✔ Blizzard Beach has very little shade and most of the slides there are "big thrills." This is probably not a good choice if you have heart health concerns—try Typhoon Lagoon instead.

✔ Disney's Animal Kingdom has few indoor/air-conditioned attractions. Visit early in the day, especially in warmer weather.

🔊 Automated External Defibrillators (AED)

You may have seen signs recently in airports and many other public places marking the spot of an **Automated External Defibrillator**. What is it? An AED is a small device that's easy to use and can aid in the treatment of cardiac arrest. Disney has recently installed AEDs throughout its resort area, both onstage and backstage, and has trained many cast members in their use. As of this writing, AEDs can be found with lifeguards in the pool areas, with mobile security units, and with the nurses at First Aid Stations. In addition, Reedy Creek Emergency Services paramedics can reach the theme parks and Downtown Disney within minutes—they, too, are equipped with AEDs.

Planning

Your Special Need

Getting There

Staying in Style

Touring

Feasting

Resources

Index

Planning

Your Special Need

Getting There

Staying in Style

Touring

Feasting

Resources

Index

Infants

Yes, Walt Disney World is for kids, but is it really for the littlest of little ones? Isn't it a hassle to bring newborns to the World? Sure, some folks will give you strange looks when you tell them that you're taking your infant to Walt Disney World. Baby won't remember the trip and it just means a lot of work for you, they'll argue.

While it might not be easy for Mom and Dad to juggle a baby, especially if they're also watching a toddler or preschooler, there are times when it's just not practical (or desirable) to leave the baby behind. Maybe you want your other children to see Walt Disney World. Perhaps you want to see Mickey Mouse yourself. Or, more importantly, you feel it's best to keep your baby with your family for bonding and/or breastfeeding.

Babies

Your Icon:

B

(B=Babies)
Look for this symbol in the book for more details on your special need

No matter the reason, never fear—just as Disney caters to children of all ages, it makes special accommodations for its youngest visitors.

Planning Ahead

Carefully consider the **time of year** to bring your infant. Ideally, you won't want to visit in the heat and crowds of the summer months. A better time to travel with baby would be in the fall when the crowds have dissipated and things have cooled off a bit or in early December or the January–February timeframes when both crowds and temperatures are lower (this is our personal favorite time of year to visit).

If you're flying, seriously consider **purchasing a seat** for your infant. While you can lap carry infants under age two on domestic flights (international flight policies may differ—check with your airline), a lap is not a safe place for your baby. Most infant car seats are FAA-approved (look for a sticker on the car seat) and fit in airline seats using the buckle to secure the seat in place (no need to use the base on infant seats). Most economy seats are 17 in. wide, so you'll want to be sure your seat is 17 in. or less. Note that a car seat may not fit in a bulkhead row if the arm rests do not go up. Also note that booster seats and safety vests are often not allowed on planes. Inquire with the airline on discounted seats for infants when making your reservation. Visit http://www.flyingwithkids.com for details.

Bright Idea: Infants' ears may be more sensitive to the pressure changes during take-off and landing, so offer a bottle or pacifier during these times to encourage baby to swallow.

Having a car at your disposal (whether a rental or your own) gives you some flexibility. You can head back to the room whenever you want, or you can run out for additional diapers or formula when you need them. If you have a car, be sure to have a car seat for baby's safety. (Florida law requires that all children up to age 3 be restrained in a child safety seat. The penalty for not complying is $60 and 3 points against your driver's license!) If you're renting a car, that means you need to either bring your own car seat or reserve one from the rental agency.

Staying on Disney property gets you to and from the parks faster, without the hassle of dealing with parking lot trams and car traffic. You might consider a resort on the monorail line so that getting to and from the Magic Kingdom is easy, particularly if you need to make a midday break. Or consider staying at a resort with a kitchenette or full kitchen so that you can have easy access to a microwave and refrigerator.

Renting a **stroller** at Disney saves you the hassle of transporting it from home. But remember, if you rent, you'll only have a stroller at the parks—you won't have one with you for those long walks to the bus or parking lots or around your resort or airport. We recommend bringing your own stroller—best bet is an easily collapsible umbrella-type. If you bring your own, be sure that the height is appropriate for the person doing most of the pushing, otherwise you may be dealing with a sore back at the end of a long day. Another alternative for a small infant is a baby carrier, such as a sling or backpack, for hands-free touring. Just remember that on a very hot day, holding baby so close to your body for long periods of time could overheat both of you! See page 201-203 for info on renting the various stroller types available at the Disney theme parks, including prices.

Caring for an infant while on vacation can add an extra dimension to your experience. The worry and strain of making sure baby's needs are met can wear on parents, especially if they have other little ones in tow. Consider what amenities you can **bring from home** that might make life on vacation easier—a beloved toy, a white-noise machine to help baby sleep, or even an extra pair of hands! That's right—maybe there's a grandparent or aunt or trusted friend who wouldn't mind tagging along to offer extra help and support—maybe they could even watch the infant (and other children) while the new Mom and Dad have a quiet night out alone.

Bright Idea: Not sure how many diapers or how much formula to bring along? Keep a log of baby's diaper and formula usage in the week before your trip to see how much is typically used. Divide by 7 to get the daily amount, and then multiply by the number of days in your trip. Add 10% to the total to be on the safe side. Now you've got just what you need! If luggage space for all those diapers is an issue, consider using a private town car service that includes a stop at a local grocery store. Or pack a cardboard box of your supplies—when you're done, either toss the box or use it to pack all your souvenirs.

[B] Infants (continued)

Upon Your Arrival

While you may not want to let your infant slow you down, it's probably better if you do. Take things at a **slower pace** than other vacationers, and allow yourself and baby frequent breaks from the hustle and bustle. A midday return to the hotel room for naps all around is a good idea.

If your infant is too small (under 6 months) to slather with **sunscreen**, remember to keep them covered with lightweight, loose clothing that covers their limbs to protect them from the Florida sun. Also make sure your baby stays hydrated—the intense heat and humidity can affect even the littlest park-goers.

Bright Idea: Buy a little battery-powered fan that clips on the handle of the stroller, or maybe even get a small mister to help keep baby cool.

When you're ready for a break, all the restrooms, including men's rooms, have **changing tables** for infants and small children.

Even better than changing tables are **Baby Care Centers**. Each theme park features a bright and clean Baby Care Center located near the First Aid Station. In the Magic Kingdom, the Baby Care Center is behind the Crystal Palace restaurant; in Disney's Animal Kingdom, it's near Creature Comforts on Discovery Island; in Epcot, it's near the Odyssey (on your way to the Mexico pavilion in World Showcase); and at the Studios, it's near the main Guest Relations area at the entrance. In each center, there are private nursing rooms with rocking chairs and low lighting; feeding rooms with highchairs, bibs, and plastic spoons; baby changing tables; restrooms; and a bright child's playroom with kid-sized table and chairs and a television playing videos. There are also the following items available for purchase:

✔ Carnation Good Start Supreme Infant Formula, liquid and powder (the Baby Care Centers are sponsored by Carnation)
✔ baby food and junior food
✔ juice and Pedialyte
✔ baby bottles and nipples
✔ pacifiers
✔ disposable diapers (Huggies)
✔ diaper ointment
✔ baby powder
✔ children's acetaminophen (Tylenol)
✔ moist towelettes (wipes)
✔ sipper cups
✔ teethers

© MediaMarx, Inc.

Highchairs at Magic Kingdom's Baby Care Center

Although your baby may only be a few months old, there are still plenty of **rides and attractions** sure to entertain them. Cinderella's Golden Carrousel, for instance, is bright with happy music—babies seem to enjoy the gentle spinning and up-and-down of the horses, as long as you hold them tight. We note these "infant-friendly" attractions in chapter 5.

For those rides that baby can't go on, though, Disney offers a "**Rider Switch**" option (also known as "child swap") at most rides that makes life a little easier. It works like this: One adult remains with the non-rider in a holding area (usually near the attraction's exit), while the rest of the party rides the attraction. When the riders exit, a cast member will direct the adult who hasn't ridden directly onto the ride, so that he/she can experience the attraction without additional wait time.

If you're **breastfeeding**, don't stop while you're at Walt Disney World—it's not only acceptable according to Disney officials, but it's also permissible by Florida law (a mother can breastfeed her baby in any public or private spot where she is allowed—see http://www.lalecheleague.org/Law/Bills14.html). If you wish to nurse discreetly, there are plenty of dim attractions during which you can nurse your infant. At the Magic Kingdom, try Hall of Presidents, Carousel of Progress, Tomorrowland Transit Authority, and Country Bear Jamboree. In Epcot, try the American Adventure, Impressions de France, Living Seas (movie portion), Spaceship Earth, and Ellen's Energy Adventure. At Disney-MGM Studios, try Voyage of the Little Mermaid and Sounds Dangerous. There are also plenty of other quiet nooks for resting or breastfeeding throughout the parks. We make note of them in chapter 5. You may find it helpful to bring a sling and/or nursing bib for virtually "invisible" nursing wherever you may be. And, of course, the Baby Care Centers make cool, quiet places for nursing.

Nursing in a sling at Disney-MGM Studios

Bright Idea: If your baby is an early riser, consider getting an early start on your day. Take advantage of Extra Magic Hour (see page 109) if you can.

The counter-service/food court area at most Disney resort hotels has a **microwave**, but be very careful about using it to heat formula or baby food—the microwave can develop hot spots in the food and burn your baby. Instead of a microwave, try a cup of hot water to warm bottles and jars instead. Complimentary refrigerators ideal for storing formula or baby food are available at Disney moderate, deluxe, and Disney Vacation Club resorts or for $10/day at the value resorts.

Bright Idea: If you room has a coffeemaker, heat water in it, then place your bottle or baby food jar in the warm water for a while. As always, check the temperature before giving it to baby.

[B] Infants (continued)

All Disney resorts and most other hotels provide "pack 'n' play" type **playpens/cribs** for infants at no extra charge—be sure to request one if you need it when you make your reservations. The pack 'n' plays are usually very clean and in excellent condition, but if you get one that is not up to your standards, call housekeeping for a replacement. The cribs usually come with a fitted sheet, as well as an extra regular bed sheet to use as a mattress pad.

The "general store" areas of the Disney resorts have many **baby basics** for sale, including diapers and baby wipes. Of course, you're paying for the convenience. If you have access to a car, it's more economical to drive to Gooding's at the Crossroads Shopping Center near Downtown Disney or one of the other retail shops in the Orlando/Kissimmee area.

There's a **children's play area** in each of the Disney resorts' main theme pools, perfect for your little one to splash in. If you're thinking of dipping your infant in any of the resort pools, remember they must be wearing snug-fitting plastic pants over their diapers or special swimming diapers. If you forget to bring them from home, they'll be available for purchase from the pool shop or the resort stores.

Disney does have **child care centers** at many of its deluxe resorts, but children under 4 aren't allowed, so parents of infants have to consider other options if they'd like some time sans baby. The most convenient choice is to have a friend or family member along for the trip watch the child, but if that's not possible, there are a few in-room babysitting services available. Kids Nite Out is sanctioned by Disney, and its sitters are fully bonded and insured and come prepared to play. Rates vary depending on the age and number of children. Contact Kids Nite Out at 407-828-0920. There are several other reputable services in the area—one that has been highly recommended to us is Fairy Godmothers (407-277-3724). Babysitters from these firms may also be able to care for children with special needs. Call for specifics. See chapter 7 for more details on child care options.

Should your baby become ill (perish the thought!) while you're on vacation, there are a number of **health care centers** nearby (see page 60).

Disney eateries, both counter and table service, provide **highchairs** for infants (strollers are not always allowed in the restaurants). In addition, your server will be happy to heat a bottle or warm baby food in the kitchen—just be sure to test its temperature after heating.

Your infant may be too young to **sample anything from your plate**, but just in case, you should know that children under the age of 3 may share from an adult's plate at no charge. If you choose to order a child's meal from the menu you will be charged.

The **First Aid Stations at the water parks** offer a quiet spot to cool down for a bit, as well as provide minor first aid care if needed. Remember, though, that Blizzard Beach does not have much shade and is more known as a "thrill" water park. A slightly more sedate experience may be had at Typhoon Lagoon. As mentioned above, if your infant will be playing in any of the water areas, they must be wearing snug-fitting plastic pants over their diapers or special swimming diapers. If you forget to bring them from home, they'll be available for purchase from the pool shop or the resort stores.

You can also bring your infant on a **Disney cruise**, provided she/he is at least 12 weeks old. Request a crib for your stateroom—the Disney Cruise Line will provide a Pack 'n' Play-type porta-crib with a crib sheet, but you'll need to bring your own bedding—we recommend extra-warm jammies rather than blankets for your child's safety. Infant-size lifejackets are also provided—request one from your stateroom host or hostess or at Guest Services upon boarding. Although babysitting is not available in guest staterooms, the cruise ships do have Flounder's Reef Nursery, an infant and toddler group babysitting area that is open every evening and certain times during each day. Reservations for this babysitting are taken on cruise embarkation day from 1:30 pm to 3:30 pm. Space is limited and is available on a first-come, first-served basis. The fee is $6 per hour per child, with a two-hour minimum. This service is only available for children ages 12 weeks to 3 years, and is not available to children who require one-on-one care or babysitter-assisted medical attention. Children who are not toilet-trained cannot play in the cruise ships' pools, but they can splash in the fountain play area near Mickey's Pool, which is designed exclusively for little ones wearing swim diapers. Speaking of diapers, some infant sundries, like diapers and formula, are available onboard, but it's wise to bring most of what you'll need (baby food, pacifiers, bottles, etc.) from home. If your infant is old enough to sit up in a highchair, let Disney know that you'd like a highchair at your table during dinner, and they will note it on your reservation. If your infant is too young for a highchair, you can bring your infant car seat (the type with a handle) into the dining room and set it on a chair (if stable) or beside your chair while you eat.

Four-month-old Alexander snoozes while his parents eat in Parrot Cay

Ongoing Medical Treatment

Just because you're under a doctor's ongoing care doesn't mean you should stay chained to your home—you deserve a Walt Disney World vacation as much, if not more, than anyone! But let's face it—leaving behind your familiar physicians and caregivers can be a scary prospect. With adequate planning and preparation, you'll find that the Orlando area can provide you with the quality care you need, while allowing you the freedom to visit the Mouse.

treatment

Your Icon:

T

(T=Treatment)

Look for this symbol in the book for more details on your special need

What do we mean by "Ongoing Medical Treatment"? It's a pretty broad phrase, and to be honest, many of the special needs outlined in this chapter could be classified as requiring ongoing medical treatment. In this section, we're specifically thinking of those **guests who require special medical treatment** such as periodic dialysis or those who are oxygen-dependent. We're also thinking of those who may be fed via a gastric or naso-gastric tube, or other conditions that require ongoing care such as cystic fibrosis, spina bifida, or cerebral palsy. We also take into account those whose conditions require continuing medication or monitoring, such as diabetes, sleep apnea, epilepsy, and mental health disorders, such as bipolar disorder, Tourette Syndrome, or depression (see page 13).

Planning Ahead

Obviously, a key factor in making your trip successful is talking with your **health care provider** and working with them to coordinate the services you need in Orlando. Review our general information about traveling with special needs in chapter 3 starting on page 91.

When **making Disney resort reservations**, request a room that is easily accessible, close to the main facilities and a bus stop if necessary. If it's important to you, be sure to request a nonsmoking room. Also remember to request a refrigerator if you have medication that needs to be kept cold. Disney provides complimentary refrigerators in all moderate, deluxe, and Disney Vacation Club resorts, but there's a $10/night charge at the value resorts. If the refrigerator is required for a medical reason, Disney normally waives the $10/night fee.

Important Note: If you are insulin-dependent or require syringe injections, request a disposal box to safely discard used needles and other sharp objects. Boxes are provided free (and discreetly) by Housekeeping at all Disney resorts.

Traveling with a **service animal**? See page 12 for details.

Consider resorts that have a **kitchen or kitchenette** to allow you the freedom to prepare meals and snacks.

While planning your day at a Disney **water park**, keep in mind that Blizzard Beach has very little shade and is also deemed a more "thrill"-oriented water park. Typhoon Lagoon is a slightly more manageable park. Also, there are First Aid Stations at the water parks if you need some minor first aid care or a place to cool off.

The full-size kitchen at Old Key West's one- and two-bedroom villas

Guests with **epilepsy** and/or seizures may rest assured that Disney cast members will be responsive in the event of a seizure. Tips on traveling with epilepsy are at http://allearsnet.com/pl/epi.htm.

If you're cruising and **need dialysis**, discuss your needs with the Disney cruise reservationist at the time of booking.

If you're **cruising and require oxygen**, you must complete the Medical Clearance form and let the Disney Cruise Line know the name, address, and phone number of the oxygen supplier.

For some **additional background information** about traveling while requiring special medical treatment, we've compiled a list of organizations and facilities that might be helpful in chapter 7, starting on page 374.

Upon Your Arrival

When touring the theme parks, many of our recommendations for individuals traveling with **heart health or physical therapy** concerns apply to those traveling with medical treatment needs:

✔ Use FASTPASS whenever possible to avoid long waits in line. Consider whether a Guest Assistance Card (see pages 10-11) can provide necessary accommodations for your special traveler.

✔ Observe attraction health warnings and take breaks during the day.

✔ Remember to stop by the First Aid Stations in the theme parks if you need the aid of a nurse or if you have medication that needs to be refrigerated while you're touring the park.

✔ Consider using a wheelchair or ECV if you would like to conserve your energy and/or stamina.

These suggestions all are **dependent** on your individual health issues, your stamina, and the frequency of the treatment you require.

Planning

Your Special Need

Getting There

Staying in Style

Touring

Feasting

Resources

Index

Is There a Doctor in the House?

What do you do if you get sick while you're visiting the Most Magical Place on Earth? If your illness does not require immediate care, there are a couple things you can do:

✔ If you're in the parks, visit the First Aid Station (see page 196).
✔ If you're at your resort, call the Lobby Concierge. They'll give you information on the options open to you.

There are three locations of Florida Hospital Centra Care close to Disney property—complimentary transportation is available, and most insurance plans are accepted. Here are the locations:

✔ Lake Buena Vista Centra Care (near Crossroads Shopping Center and Hotel Plaza Blvd.), 12500 South Apopka-Vineland Road, 407-934-2273. Open weekdays 8:00am–midnight, weekends 8:00 am–8:00 pm.
✔ Formosa Gardens Centra Care (near the junction of World Drive and Highway 192), 7848 West 192, 407-397-7032. Open weekdays 8:00 am–8:00 pm, weekends 8:00 am–5:00 pm.
✔ Kissimmee Centra Care (near Medieval Times and Bass Road), 4320 W. Vine Street, 407-390-1888. Open weekdays 8:00 am–8:00 pm.

If you'd prefer to consult with a doctor before you head to a clinic or hospital, you can call Centra Care In-Room Services at 407-238-2000 for a free telephone screening.

Other options recommended by Disney:

✔ Doctors on Call Service (DOCS), 407-399-3627
✔ EastCoast Medical, 407-648-5252—a 24 hour-a-day call center staffed by registered nurses and medical ancillary staff.

But what if you need help *now*? You may think to call 911, but if you're using a cell phone that relays to your home area code, that might not be the most expedient way to get help. Those who have had to deal with this type of situation recommend contacting the nearest Disney cast member first. If you're in the theme or water parks, they'll know the fastest way to contact an emergency rescue team right away. If you're in a resort, call the front desk, who will contact emergency services for you.

If you're out and about when an emergency arises, or if you have a car at your disposal, you *may* want to go to a hospital emergency room. The closest hospital to Walt Disney World is the Florida Hospital Emergency Department at Celebration Health (407-303-4000). This facility accepts all medical plans for emergency care. To get there, take either Epcot Center Drive or Osceola Parkway east to I-4, I-4 west to exit 64A, then right on Parkway Boulevard, then right on Celebration Place. Watch for "Emergency Room" signs. Driving south on World Drive to the Celebration exit is much farther and takes quite a bit longer. Taking Sherberth Road from Animal Kingdom/AK Lodge to 192 and then east is slower than taking Osceola Pkwy and I-4. (See chapter 7 for more details.)

That said, it's not always advisable to drive yourself—time saved in the short run must be balanced against the lack of medical staff and livesaving equipment during the drive. Think twice before you "swoop and scoop."

Dental emergency? Call the Celebration Dental Group at 407-566-2222.

Traveling With a Terminally Ill Person

This is probably the hardest section of the book for us to write. Sharing the Magic of Disney during a trip with a terminally ill family member or friend must be one of the **most bittersweet experiences**, one that neither of the authors has done.

Based on our other experience, however, we would recommend that if you are traveling with a person who is terminally ill, you should review our chapter on general travel tips for folks with special needs, and sections in this chapter on Diet, Heart Health, Motion Sickness, Mobility, and Medical Treatment. If the person with a terminal illness is a child, you may want to contact the **Make-A-Wish Foundation** (http://www.wish.org), **Give Kids the World** (http://www.gktw.org), **or Dream Factory** (http://www.dreamfactoryinc.org).

We'd like to **share some thoughts** from an experienced reader who has made this type of trip:

"When touring the parks with someone with a terminal illness, remember that what might be gentle rides for even young children may be physically overwhelming to someone made delicate from their illness.

In Adventureland, Pirates of the Caribbean might be too rough because of the waterfall drop, and the Swiss Family Treehouse involves a lot of walking with no quick exit.

In Fantasyland, both the Many Adventures of ~~Winnie the Pooh~~ and ~~Snow White's Scary Adventures~~ involve sudden turns and bumps. ~~Peter Pan's~~ Flight is gentle, but the side-to-side rocking may be difficult for someone with motion sickness. ~~The Mad Tea Party~~ spin might be gentle enough if no one spins the car, but the tunnels would be horrible for someone with motion sickness. Tomorrowland Transit Authority is gentle, but the speed might be unsettling.

There are still many attractions that would pose little problem.

In Adventureland, the Jungle Cruise and the Enchanted Tiki Room (even "under new management") are gentle enough.

I wouldn't recommend any of the Frontierland rides, but the shows would be fine, and Tom Sawyer Island would be a great place to relax. All of the Liberty Square attractions should be fine.

In Fantasyland, 'it's a small world' is the safest ride. In Tomorrowland, the Carousel of Progress is safe but isn't always open.

There are no hidden surprises in Epcot. Avoid Mission:SPACE, Test Track, Cranium Command, Body Wars, Soarin', and Maelstrom; everything else should be fine.

The only really gentle ride-through attraction in the other two parks is the Great Movie Ride, but there are many shows, walk-through attractions, and other touring opportunities to make visits to them worthwhile."

—contributed by anonymous

Planning

Your Special Need

Getting There

Staying in Style

Touring

Feasting

Resources

Index

Mobility

Walt Disney World is a **huge complex** encompassing 47 square miles. When we say there is a lot of ground to cover here, we mean it! You may get along just fine at home, but at Disney, you'll be walking and standing much more than you may be accustomed to. For travelers with mobility issues, Disney has taken your needs into consideration.

Your Icon:

(M=Mobility)
Look for this symbol in the book for more details on your special need

This section is for you, whether you are a person who uses a wheelchair, cane, or walker on a permanent or temporary basis (accident or surgery/illness recovery); someone who can't stand for long; someone for whom extra walking far exceeds your normal routine; or someone who is unsteady.

Planning Ahead

When you're making your reservations, remember to let any representative you deal with and/or your travel agent know of any special requirements you have. If you need a fully accessible resort hotel room or stateroom, be sure to **book early**, as there are a limited number available. If you need a room close to an elevator for medical reasons, have that noted on your reservation, too. Are you bringing a service animal? This needs to be explained when booking also. Let the Disney representative know you have special needs and have them make notes on your reservation form. See chapter 4 starting on page 107 for details on making reservations

A week or so before your trip, **confirm all arrangements** you've made to make sure everything is ready.

You can **bring your own wheelchair** to Walt Disney World, rent one from local vendors, or rent one at a theme park. Your Disney resort may also have wheelchairs available on a limited, no-charge basis for use on the resort's grounds. For more information on renting and getting around via wheels at Walt Disney World, see "Wheels!" on pages 201-203.

If you are flying and bringing your wheelchair (especially motorized ones), be sure to check with airlines **before you purchase your ticket**. Each has slightly different requirements and restrictions. Don't purchase a ticket first only to find out your needs can't be accommodated.

Traveling with a **service animal**? See page 12.

Most airlines allow **preboarding for passengers needing extra time**, so you'll be able to get settled in before the rest of the passengers start boarding. When you reach the gate on departure day, be sure to inquire with your airline exactly how this works.

Getting **back and forth from the airport** also requires preplanning, depending on your needs.

Once you arrive in Orlando, there are several transportation options for **reaching your resort**. If you need an accessible mode of transportation, you have some different options:

1. Use Disney's Magical Express (see page 98) which can accommodate wheelchairs with advance notice—indicate your need at the time you book your Magical Express request.
2. Make reservations with Mears for an accessible shuttle—call 407-423-5566 or visit http://www.mearstransportation.com.
3. While expensive, Mears also rents accessible vans.

Remember to **bring your handicap parking permit/tag for parking** your vehicle. Those with this tag receive complimentary valet parking at Walt Disney World where available. If you rent a wheelchair from a local vendor, remember that you need to bring your handicapped parking permit/tag from home, along with the permit registration and appropriate ID. If you park in the regular parking lot at the parks, you will not be able to get the wheelchair on the tram.

If you or someone in your group **drives to Walt Disney World**, you'll be able to pack anything special you need with you. If you have an accessible vehicle, this will make your experience a little easier, since you are familiar with that mode of transportation.

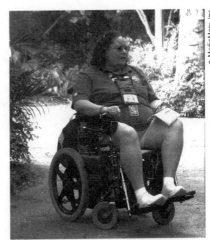

If you are **able to transfer from your wheelchair** into a car and your budget allows, we suggest town car transportation from the airport. They are basically the same price as a taxi and you travel in greater comfort with less wait.

Don't let **pride** get in your way. If you exhaust yourself early trying to walk around, nobody will have a magical time.

Peer reviewer Joanne Ernest at Disney's Animal Kingdom

Planning | Your Special Need | Getting There | Staying in Style | Touring | Feasting | Resources | Index

[M] Mobility (continued)

Upon Your Arrival

Once on Disney property, you'll find that most **Disney transportation is accessible** for wheelchair/ECV users. See "Wheels!" on pages 201–203.

Wheelchair and Electric Convenience Vehicle (ECV) rentals are available at each of the four major theme parks on a **first-come-first-served basis**. These wheelchairs may not be transferred from park to park. ECV rentals are limited to those 18 years of age and older, and you will be required to sign a waiver. The cost is $30 plus a $10 deposit. If you plan to visit more than one park on the same day, you need only pay the rental fee once. When you leave a park, you will need to turn in your ECV/wheelchair, but retain your deposit ticket—you can use it to claim an ECV/wheelchair at each park you visit that day. Keep in mind there is no guarantee an ECV/wheelchair will be available for you. If one is, you will be able to receive a replacement chair at the second park at no additional charge. You will turn in your ECV and deposit slip at the end of your day and receive $10 back. The cost to rent a standard wheelchair is $7 per day, with a $2 refundable deposit.

As you experience the Walt Disney World resort from the oldest sections (like the Magic Kingdom and Polynesian resort) to the newest areas (such as Disney's Animal Kingdom and Pop Century) you'll see a gradual **change for the better** in regards to accessibility from minimal to very comfortable.

Each attraction at Walt Disney World has a **symbol** in the guidemap (and the Disney Guidebook for Guests With Disabilities) indicating how you may experience that particular ride. We detail this information in chapter 5.

The various **options** for experiencing the Disney attractions include:
✔ Stay in your wheelchair.
✔ Transfer from your wheelchair to the ride vehicle. This usually involves several steps and some may be up or down.
✔ Transfer from your ECV to a wheelchair.
✔ Transfer from your ECV to a wheelchair to get through the queue, and then transfer out of the chair to the ride vehicle.

Keep in mind that cast members are not allowed to physically assist anyone in and out of rides.

If you are planning to walk around the park but cannot stand for long periods of time or do not have the stamina to wait in long attraction queues, seriously consider renting a wheelchair or ECV. Consider whether a **Guest Assistance Card** (see pages 10–11) can provide necessary accommodations for your special traveler.

Some attractions have **auxiliary entrances** for those with disabilities. These are intended to offer those in wheelchairs or with service animals a more convenient entrance to the attraction. Auxiliary entrances are not intended to bypass waiting lines. Guests with disabilities and a maximum of five members of their party may enter through these entrances. The rest of the party must use the main entrance.

A few attractions have an actual ride vehicle **on display** outside the main entrance so you can see exactly what you'll be boarding. We mention specifics in the descriptions of those attractions in chapter 5. Space Mountain seating can be especially tricky as it is a small space with a T-bar that fits closely on your lap.

Most cast members stationed at the entrance to attractions are on the lookout for guests in wheelchairs/ECVs and will **explain the procedures** for that ride to you. If you spot them first, approach them and explain what your abilities are as far as transferring, walking, or controlling body motion. Based on the information you provide, the cast member will give you instructions. Follow them and you're all set.

Once you get inside an attraction, you may be asked again for the same information by a different cast member. Although it may be annoying, remember that **your safety** is their chief concern and they want to give you the appropriate instructions. If something doesn't sound right to you, though, or you are not clear on the instructions, be sure to ask, ask, and ask!

If you travel with a **service animal**, be sure to check with the cast member at each attraction before entering (read about service animals on page 12). We note attraction information for service animals in chapter 5.

If you will be **leaving your wheelchair/ECV**, ask where the ride will unload and where your chair will be at that point. Sometimes you will load and unload in the exact same location. Other times, the chair will be moved to the unload area.

Each of the theme parks has some **companion-assisted** restrooms. We've noted where they are for you in chapter 5. Most resorts do not have companion restrooms, however, although all have accessible restrooms.

For the most part, you should be able to go through the full-service Disney restaurants in your ECV/wheelchair. However, **counter-service** spots often have narrow queues formed by railings. These spots often are more crowded, which means there's much less room to maneuver in. You may want a member of your party to assist with transporting your food, or ask a cast member for assistance. On the plus side, though, some eateries have low counters that are easily accessible. We have marked the ones we've discovered in our individual descriptions in chapter 6.

Planning

Your Special Need

Getting There

Staying in Style

Touring

Feasting

Resources

Index

Planning

Your Special Need

Getting There

Staying in Style

Touring

Feasting

Resources

Index

[M] Mobility (continued)

Merchandise locations are also accessible, but again can be very difficult to navigate when crowded, especially at the end of the day. We suggest doing your shopping **early in the day**. By all means take advantage of merchandise delivery back to your Disney hotel (see page 110) so that you don't have to carry your purchases around.

A few of the resorts have **"zero-entry"** swimming pools and pool wheelchairs, which allow easier access into the pool. Cast members are not allowed to assist you, but the gradual entrance area makes it much easier to get into the water. See page 106 for more information.

It's only logical that the newer resorts have more accessible features. Not only does Saratoga Springs have a zero-entry pool, it also has a **"transfer tier"** located at one of its small slides, and it has an accessible hot tub. Many of the older hotel swimming pools are equipped with the transfer tiers, but these are most useful to those who have some upper body strength and can lift themselves out of their chairs.

Both Blizzard Beach and Typhoon Lagoon water parks are wheelchair/ECV accessible to a degree. A number of the rides **require stair walking** to get to the entrance. See chapter 5 for details.

The shops and eateries at Downtown Disney and the BoardWalk are all accessible, yet some are **so crowded with merchandise** they make navigating via wheelchair/ECV nearly impossible. We note which places are least chair/ECV-friendly in our individual descriptions in chapter 5.

Important Note: When you are getting on (or off) an attraction with mobility issues, you should not rush! Rushing can lead to accidents. The cast member will wait for you.—contributed by peer reviewer Joanne Ernest

Disney Cruise Line offers accessible staterooms, with ramped bathroom thresholds, open bed frames, added phones in the bathroom/nightstand, bathroom and shower handrails, fold-down shower seats, hand-held shower heads, lowered towel and closet bars, and emergency call buttons. Note that there are only four stateroom categories that are handicapped accessible: category 3 (one-bedroom suite with veranda), category 5 (deluxe balcony), category 8 (deluxe oceanview), and category 11 (standard inside).

One final word. While Walt Disney World is ADA-compliant and the resort is as accessible as possible, there are some areas that are a bit **tricky to navigate**. We have tried to note those throughout this book as appropriate.

Motion Sensitivity

Motion sickness or vertigo occurs when your brain receives conflicting information about your body's position. It may make you lightheaded, dizzy, or unsteady. For some, the room may spin or you feel nausea. For instance, your inner ear detects that the vehicle you're in is moving, but your eyes are stationary—it creates a feeling that your spatial orientation, balance, or equilibrium is off and you can feel "carsick" or "seasick." These are usually temporary conditions and **can often be avoided with proper planning**. (There are some conditions that cause motion sickness that are medical in origin, such as inner ear infections or Meniere's Disease, and they require medical treatment.) Whatever your symptoms, all you know is you want to avoid feeling that way, especially when you are at Walt Disney World!

Your Icon: Queasy

Q

(Q=Queasy)
Look for this symbol in the book for more details on your special need

Sometimes you can **control your environment**. For example, don't go on the Mad Tea Party's spinning teacups. Other times, the environment may be out of your control and you have to find ways to deal with the symptoms (such as when you're on a cruise ship). Here are some tips and advice to follow.

Planning Ahead

Prior to your trip, **talk to your physician** about taking a motion sickness remedy. Some are over-the-counter (OTC), some require a prescription, and some are holistic. Whichever method you choose, try it out a few weeks before you leave home so you'll know exactly how it makes you feel in case there are any side effects.

Co-author Deb Wills recently developed motion sensitivity and has had great success with the over-the-counter medicine called Bonine (generic name: meclizine). In fact, she starts taking it **several days before** she is scheduled to get on the cruise ship. Some folks report Bonine and Dramamine help them on theme park attractions, too!

Reader Tip: "I had good luck with Sea Bands, the bands that apply pressure to certain points on your wrists. No negative side effects. They're reusable and over-the-counter. It seems to help me with what I'd call very slight, occasional motion sickness, especially after the 360-degree films."—contributed by Kitty Smith

Bright Idea: In an airplane, request a window seat and try to be seated over the wings to minimize motion sickness.

[Q] Motion Sensitivity (continued)

Be aware of your triggers and try to avoid those types of attractions. Disney has **warning signs** outside of attractions that may affect those with motion sensitivity, and we have noted them in chapter 5. Heed the warnings!

If you've had problems in the past with **big-screen movies**, decide whether entering a Disney attraction featuring a movie is a good idea. A number of them are 360 degrees or extra large, extra wide screens, which can cause greater problems.

Some rides **go in circles** and their potential for causing motion sickness is high, from Astro Orbiter, Dumbo, and the Mad Tea Party in the Magic Kingdom to TriceraTop Spin and Primeval Whirl in Disney's Animal Kingdom. You can see all of these rides without having to stand in line—decide for yourself if their spinning would affect you.

The following is a list of attractions that **may cause motion sickness**:

✔ Magic Kingdom: Dumbo, Magic Carpets of Aladdin, Mad Tea Party, Cinderella's Golden Carrousel, AstroOrbiter, Walt Disney's Carousel of Progress (theater slowly moves in circular motion), Big Thunder Mountain Railroad, Space Mountain, Barnstormer, Buzz Lightyear's Space Ranger Spin (you control the spinning), Timekeeper (CircleVision 360 movie).

✔ Epcot: Mission:SPACE, Body Wars, Test Track, Soarin', the CircleVision 360 movies: O Canada and Reflections of China. Also, the Garden Grill restaurant slowly revolves.

✔ Disney's Animal Kingdom: Kali River Rapids (rough water raft ride), Primeval Whirl, Dinosaur, TriceraTop Spin, Kilimanjaro Safari.

✔ Disney-MGM Studios: Star Tours (motion simulator), Twilight Zone Tower of Terror (sudden drops), Rock 'n' Roller Coaster.

There are also some rides where you might **unexpectedly** have a problem, such as the Haunted Mansion and Spaceship Earth. Both of these rides have cars that rotate and travel backwards. Also avoid sitting in the backward seat of Magic Kingdom's Tomorrowland Transit Authority if that causes motion sickness for you. Disney buses have sideways seats in addition to forward-facing ones.

If you exit an attraction and aren't feeling quite right, **don't hesitate** to ask a cast member for assistance. They will lead you to a bench to sit and wait a few minutes. Remember, you can always go to the First Aid Station to rest.

Bright Idea: If you feel queasy after an attraction, try small sips of a carbonated drink or nibble crackers to settle your stomach. Another tip is to sniff rubbing alcohol—you can bring small packets of alcohol wipes with you from home. And remember, don't eat right before going on spinning or thrill rides that you think might cause motion sickness, such as Mission:SPACE, Rock 'n' Roller Coaster, or Primeval Whirl.

Feeling a bit **seasick** on your Disney cruise? Go on deck and look out at the horizon. Also, the Infirmary is stocked with anti-motion-sickness over-the-counter medications.

PassPorter Picks

✔ While your group is riding rides that might bother you, browse the shops or **scout out a good place to eat**. If you can bear to watch, take photos of your family/friends riding.

✔ The movies at Body Wars and Star Tours can be experienced **without** the motion simulator running during non-busy times. Inquire with a cast member at the attraction.

✔ On the monorail, bus, or boats, try to **avoid reading**, sit close to the front seat, look out into the distance, and always face forward.

PassPorter Pans

✔ If you frequently get seasick, you might want to **avoid boat transportation** (ferry, launches, Friendships) around the resorts.

✔ The following attractions include **boats that travel along water**. Most are gentle rides, but if you are ultra-sensitive, avoid:

© Deb Wills

- Magic Kingdom: "it's a small world," Jungle Cruise, Liberty Belle Riverboat, Pirates of the Caribbean, Splash Mountain, and the Raft to Tom Sawyer's Island.

- Epcot: Living with the Land, El Rio del Tiempo, and Maelstrom.

- Disney's Animal Kingdom: Kali River Rapids.

Water warning sign at Kali River Rapids

Physical Therapy/Rehabilitation

You are recovering from surgery or an accident, working to maintain your strength or mobility, or just trying to mend what "ails" you. A portion of your healing involves physical therapy—can you stick to your regimen while on vacation? Yes, you may be able to continue (with your health care provider's approval) your rehabilitation during a vacation to Walt Disney World.

Your Icon:

P

(P=Physical)

Look for this symbol in the book for more details on your special need

Planning Ahead

Consult with your medical team before leaving home to determine what you can do. Likewise, be sure to find out what you should avoid!

Remember to pack anything you may need for your **exercises** (like exercise bands or workout clothes).

Remember, too, to bring an adequate supply of any medications you may be taking. Also bring along a **copy of your prescriptions**, just in case you need to get a refill!

Upon Your Arrival

You'll have access to ice machines at the resorts, but if you need heat, you'll want to **pack your own heating pad** or try the Thermacare heat packs available at drug stores. Don't forget zipper-close bags if you need to ice down.

All of the Disney resort hotels have swimming pools. Some even have a **"quiet" pool** where you can do your exercises (or laps) without disruption. Some of the pools have zero entryways to allow for easy transition into the pool. Early morning is usually the best time. While the water parks have lots of activities, they won't be a place for you to do any exercises.

Depending on the exercise(s), you may be able to do them right in your hotel room. If you need more space, there are **fitness clubs** at a number of resort hotels. If you're over 14 and staying at a resort with a fitness club, you can use the facility at no additional charge. (Children 14–17 must be accompanied by parent or guardian.) Most fitness centers have Cybex machines, treadmills, stairmasters, bicycles, and free weights (see next page for a listing of fitness center locations).

Disney Vacation Club (DVC) members may use the fitness club at any DVC resort as long as they are staying at Walt Disney World. A $12 fee will be charged if the DVC member uses a fitness center at a non-DVC resort and they are not staying there.

If you are not staying at a Disney resort with a health club but are staying on Disney property, **you may use a fitness club for $12 per day**.

If you belong to a health club at home, check before you leave to see if there are any **reciprocal privileges** at clubs in the Orlando area.

There are also a number of spas on Disney property where you can receive a **massage** or have access to a sauna, steamroom, or whirlpool (see next page for locations). The purchase of a spa treatment includes use of the adjacent fitness center for the day of treatment.

Perhaps **renting** a wheelchair or an ECV for touring the parks is the way to go (see Mobility on pages 62–66).

If you want to do some concentrated walking or jogging for cardiac rehab, use one of the **walking/jogging/biking trails** at most Disney resorts. Stop by the Front Desk of the Disney resort and ask for a "jogger's map." These will give you a path to follow with approximate mileage. There is a wonderful wooded trail from the Fort Wilderness Campgrounds to the Wilderness Lodge and a riverside trail from Port Orleans French Quarter to Riverside. A large loop can be made to include Epcot, the Epcot resorts and Disney-MGM Studios. The three All Star Resorts are all back to back so you can walk from one to the next to the next and back. Caribbean Beach, Coronado Springs, and Port Orleans Riverside are all large enough to provide their own walking areas. Be aware there are no paths to walk at Disney's Animal Kingdom Lodge.

If you need to contact local doctors/visiting nurses/hospitals during your stay, see **Medical Treatment** on pages 58–61.

[P] Physical Therapy/Rehabilitation (continued)

First Aid Stations are available in the theme parks and water parks—see page 196 for details.

Disney Cruise Line has the Vista Spa, an adult-only section of the ship housing the fitness center, aerobics studio, spa treatment rooms, and more. The fitness center is free for your use during the cruise, as is the aerobics studio when classes are not in session (classes may be offered free of charge—check with the spa for details upon your arrival). The fitness center has free weights, Cybex weight machines, treadmills, stair-steppers, ab-rollers, and stationary bikes. The fitness center is usually empty—only on at-sea days does it become busy.

Here is a current listing of **Fitness Centers and Spas** offered at Disney Resorts:

✔ Disney's Animal Kingdom Lodge—Zahanati Fitness Center and Spa

✔ Disney's BoardWalk—Muscles & Bustles Health Club

✔ Disney's Contemporary Resort—Olympiad Fitness Center

✔ Disney's Coronado Springs Resort—La Vida Fitness Center

✔ Disney's Grand Floridian Resort & Spa—Disney's Grand Floridian Spa & Health Club

✔ Disney's Old Key West Resort—R.E.S.T. Exercise Room

✔ Disney's Saratoga Springs Resort & Spa—Disney's Saratoga Springs Resort & Spa Fitness Center

✔ Disney's Wilderness Lodge and The Villas at Disney's Wilderness Lodge—Sturdy Branches Health Club

✔ Disney's Yacht & Beach Club Resorts and Disney's Beach Club Villas—Ship Shape Health Club

✔ Walt Disney World Dolphin Resort

Pregnancy and Fertility

It's wonderful—you're expecting your own "little souvenir" just like the cute little girl mentions on those Walt Disney World television commercials. But is it really wise to walk all those miles, standing in long lines in the Florida heat?

Obviously, every expectant woman is different, and it's best to consult with your doctor as to whether you should attempt a trip to Walt Disney World. But once you get the medical go-ahead, here are some things to consider.

expectation

Your Icon:

E

(E=Expectant)
Look for this symbol in the book for more details on your special need

Planning Ahead

Just because you're going on vacation, don't think you can ignore all the **normal rules and advice** that pregnant women should follow. You'll need comfy shoes that provide lots of support; loose, lightweight clothing; and plenty of sunscreen.

You'll also want to be sure to **stay hydrated**. Pregnant women are supposed to drink more water than usual anyway, and the Florida heat can be unrelenting at times. Because you're drinking more often, you'll need to find the restrooms more often—be sure you have a guide map with you so you can locate the nearest one when you're traveling in the parks or Downtown Disney.

Remember that park distances on the guide maps can be deceiving. You'll be doing a lot of walking around, so plan on taking it slow, and be sure to **take frequent rests**. If you can, you may want to even plan a midday break by returning to your hotel for a dip in the pool, or take an afternoon nap in the air-conditioned room.

While you're walking around, remember to be extra careful. The joints of pregnant women tend to become unstable (it's a hormone thing!) and you may lose your footing or your balance more easily. Pay close attention to places with **uneven surfaces**, like the play areas floored with spongy material, and the pathways at Disney's Animal Kingdom. Pay even closer attention when getting in and out of vehicles, especially those you have to step down into or up out of, like some of the boat rides.

Planning · Your Special Need · Getting There · Staying in Style · Touring · Feasting · Resources · Index

[E] Pregnancy and Fertility (continued)

Be sure to eat enough—**don't skip meals** just because you're on the go. It's easy to get caught up in having a good time and neglect to eat lunch.

Also be sure to continue to eat nutritiously. Sure, those yummy cinnamon rolls they sell at the BoardWalk Bakery are awesome, but are they really that good for you? You're on vacation, but you and baby-to-be still need the right nutrients. A better idea is to **pack nutritious snacks** so you don't get overly hungry and eat the wrong things.

Along with eating enough and eating right, remember that you may be experiencing **food cravings** or aversions. When Deb Koma was pregnant, she says she couldn't even look at a hamburger without feeling queasy. Be sure to plan your mealtimes around places that serve food you can actually eat.

If there are any **"creature comforts"** that you can bring along with you, try to squeeze them in your suitcase. Maybe it's your comfy robe and plain crackers to combat morning sickness or the white-noise machine that lulls you to sleep every night.

Upon Your Arrival

When touring the theme parks, Disney has **health warnings** on many of its thrill rides and strongly advises that pregnant women not ride these. We suggest you follow this advice, regardless of what stage you are at in your pregnancy.

But don't fret, there's **plenty to do** that doesn't require you getting shaken up or turned upside-down. Disney-MGM Studios, for instance, has many live entertainment shows that are either indoors or in the shade. And don't forget, while others in your group are riding thrill rides like Mission:SPACE or Dinosaur!, there are plenty of shops for you to browse through.

There are health warnings on many of the water slides at Blizzard Beach and Typhoon Lagoon water parks, and we suggest you heed them. A better bet is to **plant yourself in a raft** and float around the gentle "lazy rivers," like Castaway Creek at Typhoon Lagoon. So remember to pack a maternity bathing suit if you plan on pool time.

Back at your resort, don't hesitate to **call Housekeeping** if there's something that could make your stay in the room more comfortable. For example, you can get extra pillows if you need them for additional support for your pregnant tummy. Keep in mind that many of Disney's value and moderate resorts are spread out, with long walks between services and facilities. You may instead want to consider staying at a more self-contained resort, such as the Contemporary Resort tower or the Wilderness Lodge.

Also, remember that pregnant women must avoid raising their **internal body temperature** too much—check with your doctor before sitting in one of Disney's "spas" (or any hot tubs) or traveling during the hottest months in the summer.

PassPorter Picks

✔ Take advantage of all the quality **live shows** and entertainment around the theme parks. Most of the shows are either indoors or in the shade with plenty of time to sit.

PassPorter Pans

✔ **Avoid the big thrills**, just for this trip. When you return with the fruit of your labor (pun intended), then you can have a family member or friend hold baby while you spin and coast to your heart's content!

Fertility

Have you been trying to get pregnant? Maybe this trip to Disney is just what you need to relax a little before conceiving. First and foremost, it's important to follow all the rules for pregnant women as you may not realize you're already pregnant (as editor Jennifer Marx discovered on her Disney vacation). Avoid hot tubs like the plague—this applies to women (bad for the egg and embryo) and men (bad for the sperm). If you're on medication, bring enough for the trip plus a little extra (and don't forget a copy of your prescriptions just in case). Don't discount the value of relaxation as a fertility booster either—many women have gotten pregnant on vacations (it's not just a myth). And speaking of making babies, don't forget those little things you may need for "smooth" operations. (We have seen personal lubricants for sale on property, but they aren't generally the fertility-friendly types.) If you're having long-term issues conceiving as Jennifer did, be mentally prepared for the masses of children and babies you will encounter at Walt Disney World. If it becomes overwhelming and positive thinking isn't helping, take a night off for Pleasure Island where kids are few and far between—just skip or go light on the adult beverages.

Planning

Your Special Need

Getting There

Staying in Style

Touring

Feasting

Resources

Index

Religion

PG·236 chuRch (handwritten)

With millions of visitors from all over the world pouring into the Orlando area, houses of worship of every denomination are plentiful. No matter your religious preference, you should be able to find appropriate services in the Walt Disney World area.

Certain religious services were held regularly on Disney property at one time, but that practice was discontinued in 2002. Exceptions are on Easter and Christmas Day— sometimes a few Catholic and Protestant services are held at the Contemporary Resort's Fantasia Ballroom.

WoRship (handwritten)

Your Icon:

W

(W=Worship)
Look for this symbol in the book for more details on your special need

Bright Idea: If you observe a special diet as part of your religion (e.g., kosher) be sure to read our section on Diets on pages 31–34.

Planning Ahead

Below is a selection of area religious services. For additional information, churches, or services, consult a current **local telephone directory** when you arrive in the Orlando area.

Most of these services can be reached **via taxi** if you do not have the use of your own transportation. Call Mears taxicab service at 407-422-2222.

Bright Idea: As an alternative, consider calling a town car service. It often is even cheaper than a taxi for a local run to a house of worship!

Roman Catholic Services:
Mary, Queen of the Universe Shrine, 8300 Vineland Avenue
Phone: 407-239-6600; Web:
Mass schedule: Sunday: 7:30 am, 9:30 am, 11:30 am, and 6:00 pm
Saturday: 6:00 pm
A priest hears confession daily.

The **shrine** is located 2.5 miles northeast of Lake Buena Vista on the I-4 frontage road. Traveling south on SR 535 from Hotel Plaza Boulevard/ Crossroads, drive to the second traffic signal, turn left (Vineland Avenue) and continue approximately one mile.

Bright Idea: If you're taking a taxi to the church, it may be difficult to get one for the return trip. Try walking over to the shopping center next door and getting a cab from there.

Protestant Services:

Celebration Presbyterian Church, 635 Celebration Avenue
Phone: 407-566-1633; Web: http://www.commpres.org/connect.html
Directions: To get to **Celebration Presbyterian Church**, take I-4 West
to exit 64A which will take you to 192 (heading toward Kissimmee). Travel
two traffic lights down, make a right turn onto Celebration Avenue. Follow
Celebration Avenue into town and the church is located one-quarter mile
down the road on the right-hand side.

First Baptist Church of Kissimmee, 1700 North John Young Parkway
Phone: 407-847-3138; Web: http://www.fbckiss.org
Directions: To get to the **First Baptist Church of Kissimmee**, go east on
highway 192 (West Irlo Bronson Memorial Highway) toward Kissimmee.
Turn left onto North John Young Parkway. After one block, turn left into
the First Baptist Church.

Islamic Services:

Islamic Center of Orlando, 11543 Ruby Lake Road
Phone: 407-238-2700
Directions: To get to the **Islamic Center of Orlando**, take I-4 East to
Lake Buena Vista exit. Turn left onto SR 535; continue on 535, and the
mosque will be on the right-hand side of the road (approximately two
miles from I-4 exit).

Masjid Al-Rahman Mosque
http://www.iscf.org//About_ISCF_Masajid.asp?masajid=1

Islamic Society of Central Florida
http://www.iscf.org

There is also a designated **meditation/prayer room** open from 11:00 am
to 9:00 pm daily located inside the Morocco pavilion museum in Epcot's
World Showcase. Small rugs are available for guest use.

Jewish Services:

Celebration Jewish Congregation (Reconstructionist), 607 Celebration Ave.
Phone: 407-596-5397; Web: http://www.jrf.org/cjc/index.htm
Directions: To get to **Celebration Jewish Congregation**, take I-4 West to
exit 64A, which will take you to 192 (heading toward Kissimmee). At the
second traffic light, make a right turn onto Celebration Avenue. Follow
Celebration Avenue into town.

For a **full list** of Orlando's houses of worship, visit:
http://www.orlandowelcome.com/pray/pray.htm.

Seniors

Your Icon:

S

(S=Seniors)
Look for this
symbol in the
book for more
details on your
special need

Congratulations! You've reached senior status and you still want to go to Walt Disney World! We hope we never think we're too old to experience the magic.

We realize that many seniors are fit and healthy and have more energy than we do! But maybe you'd like to take your time and stop to smell the roses. Or maybe you or a senior you're traveling with is among those who have some special needs. If so, you might have to adapt your plans to meet the demands an **older and wiser body** makes on you. Also, be aware that a vacation with the kids and grandkids can be far more active than you're used to. Even if your health is good, you may encounter unexpected limitations. If you do, don't fight them—every family vacation deserves a happy ending. You'll find pertinent advice throughout this book. And if you experience any unexpected discomfort, the nearest Disney cast member will know how to get you the help you need.

So what really differentiates a mature traveler from a younger vacationer? Obviously, it's hard to make generalizations, but for the purposes of this section, we're assuming that if you're a mature traveler, you're looking for a **different kind of Walt Disney World experience**—maybe one that's more low-key or less hectic than the average Disney-goer's. Even if you're visiting the theme parks with your grandchildren, you still need time that is just for you.

Planning Ahead

If you have specific health concerns, **consult** with your regular physician before undertaking a trip to Walt Disney World. Our tips and suggestions are in no way a substitute for medical advice. And if you do have some special considerations, there are other sections in this chapter that might be of interest to you: Diet, Heart Health, Ongoing Medical Treatment, Mobility, Hearing, and Vision.

So what types of things should you focus on when you're visiting Walt Disney World? First of all, **take everything at your own pace**. Don't get up early to be the first one in the theme parks, unless you *want* to be there at rope drop. Schedule leisurely meals at off-peak hours; you'll avoid long waits and noisy crowds. Make sure you allow yourself plenty of breaks. Possibly head to the resort in the middle of the day for a dip in the pool, or just some quiet time in the cool of your room.

Also, there's no reason to keep the whole group together for every activity. **A mix of family togetherness and alone time is key** to everyone enjoying themselves. Seniors may want to spend fewer hours in the park, rejoining the family at a designated time and place. Grandparents can be their kids' heroes by taking the grandchildren back to the room for a midday rest or by babysitting while others spend a late night at the parks. But remember you deserve a break, too, so make sure your kids return the favor!

While all of the Disney theme parks have something to offer the mature traveler, you may find **some activities are more appealing than others**. Epcot in particular is filled with cultural and educational experiences that might be more entertaining to you than the rides in the Magic Kingdom's Fantasyland. Disney's Animal Kingdom, with its myriad live animals and related exhibits scattered throughout the park, is equally interesting.

When booking your room, consider any special health needs you might have and follow our suggestions in the appropriate sections in this chapter. If you need a **larger room**, for example, or if you prefer to be away from the noise of the pools, be sure to request it when making reservations.

Also, choose a resort that reflects the type of vacation you're looking for. If you're staying at a Disney resort looking for **peace and quiet**, that does not mean one of the value All-Stars or Pop Century, which are frequently filled with high school cheerleading and sports groups. Instead, if the budget allows, consider treating yourself to a stay at one of the deluxe resorts, which offer convenience in transportation and location, as well as some enriching experiences. Disney's Animal Kingdom Lodge, for example, has its own game preserve right on the grounds—you can book a room with a savanna view, with giraffes, wildebeest, and other wild animals greeting your morning. And if your budget stretches even further, why not really spoil yourself and stay in a concierge room at one of the deluxe resorts? Amenities there include a special lounge with all-day snacks and beverages.

All of the Disney resort hotels have swimming pools, and most have at least one **"quiet" pool** where you are more likely to enjoy the water without lots of noise. Early morning is usually the best time for a quiet dip. Some of the pools have zero entryways to allow for easy transition into the pool, too. (See sidebar on page 106.)

If you'd prefer a **laid-back lounge for a cocktail** before or after your meal, we've enjoyed Martha's Vineyard (Beach Club), the Belle Vue Room (BoardWalk), and Mizner's (Grand Floridian)—these spots usually seem far removed from the "madding crowd."

Planning

Your Special Need

Getting There

Staying in Style

Touring

Feasting

Resources

Index

[S] Seniors (continued)

Upon Your Arrival

Remember that distances around the theme parks **are greater** than you might expect. Consider renting a wheelchair or ECV to help you conserve energy if the heat and activity catch up with you.

Remember to rest frequently, and **hydrate often**! The Florida sun and humidity sap everyone's strength, especially folks who are spending 8–10 hours pounding the hot pavement. (See chapter 5 for quiet spots.)

Don't skip meals! It's easy to forget yourself in the midst of too much fun, but touring the parks on an empty stomach is not a good idea.

Use **FASTPASS** whenever possible; it really is the best way to shorten your time waiting in line. (See page 206 for more details on FASTPASS.)

Take note of where the **First Aid Stations** are located in each park (see page 196). Even if you don't need any of their services, it's a nice, quiet place to cool down if you're feeling overheated or overwhelmed.

If you're looking for peace and quiet, **avoid the children's play areas**, which are loud and filled with high-spirited kids running around and blowing off steam. These include Tom Sawyer Island, Toon Park, and Donald's Boat (the Magic Kingdom); Honey, I Shrunk the Kids Movie Set Adventure (Disney-MGM Studios); and the Boneyard (Disney's Animal Kingdom).

On the other hand, certain parts of Tom Sawyer Island can be a **respite** from the hubbub of the Magic Kingdom—if you can manage the uneven, unpaved pathways, head over there and find a spot on a quiet bench, or sip a cool drink while reading at Aunt Polly's Dockside Inn, with the hustle and bustle of Frontierland in the distance.

Take special care in Disney's Animal Kingdom, where the pathways are often **narrow and uneven**.

If you're curious about how things work, Disney offers a number of **behind-the-scenes tours**, ranging from a few hours to all day. Generally, tour attendees have to be at least 16—you'll definitely be old enough!

If you find that your appetite or your budget isn't as hearty as it used to be, you might not want to dine at the all-you-can-eat meals at Walt Disney World as you won't get your money's worth. A good alternative is to try eating your **main meal at lunchtime**, when portions are slightly smaller and prices are slightly less. Some resorts even offer discounts to Florida residents, annual passholders, and Disney Vacation Club members at lunchtime. Yet another option is to order only appetizers instead of full entrees.

Character meals tend to be on the loud and boisterous side, often with additional noisy entertainment for kids. If you want a **sedate meal**, don't dine with the characters. The loudest offenders include 1900 Park Fare (Grand Floridian), Breakfastosaurus (Disney's Animal Kingdom), and Chef Mickey's (Contemporary).

For **quiet fine dining**, try the table-service restaurants at the deluxe resorts. Among our favorites for a relaxing meal with fantastic food: Artist Point at the Wilderness Lodge, California Grill at the Contemporary, Jiko at Animal Kingdom Lodge, and Flying Fish Café on the BoardWalk. And there's Victoria & Albert's at the Grand Floridian for special occasions!

Co-author Deb Koma (right) takes tea with her mother and sister at the Garden View Lounge

While Blizzard Beach has a reputation for being a big thrill water park, **Typhoon Lagoon** might be more desirable for the mature traveler. Its Castaway Creek lazy river raft ride is a pleasant way to while away a few hours. If you're interested, you can swim with the fishes, or sharks, to boot, in the Shark Reef snorkeling pool. Of course, if the grandkids insist that nothing but Blizzard Beach will do, it, too, has a lazy river ride that you can bob along in while the young'uns tackle the fast body slides like Summit Plummet.

Strolling around both **Downtown Disney** and the BoardWalk is a nice respite from the hustle and bustle of running from ride to ride. There's lots to do in these two areas that get you away from the frenetic pace of the theme parks. Best of all, you can stop in either place for a yummy ice cream cone or cool drink while you sit in shade next to the water and people-watch. The amazing Cirque du Soleil's show La Nouba, at the West Side, is a treat for the eyes that you can only experience in Orlando.

If the idea of rowdy entertainment turns you off, though, be aware that at night Downtown Disney's Pleasure Island becomes one night club after another, with lots of loud, pounding music playing in the streets, where they also serve alcohol. Over at the **BoardWalk**, the entertainment isn't quite so loud, except Jellyrolls with its dueling pianos. It can draw big crowds that get into the spirit of singing along a little too much at times. Likewise, the smoke-filled ESPN Club bar can be a bit loud with overflow crowds.

As a mature traveler, some of your favorite activities may actually be **outside of the theme parks!** Be sure to research your trip as much as possible in advance, so that you know about the many golf courses (not to mention miniature golf), scattered around the resort. In addition, many of the resorts offer swimming, tennis, a variety of other court sports, water craft and bicycle rentals, jogging trails, fitness centers, and spas. If fishing is your game, there are a number of catch-and-release programs available.

Size

Walt Disney World visitors come from countries all over the world, speak a multitude of languages ... and come in **all shapes and sizes**. It's clear that one size does not fit all. No one wants to plan an expensive vacation, then worry that they won't fit in the various rides and attractions. Fear not! Walt Disney World has taken your needs into consideration. In fact, folks often comment how "at large" friendly most of Walt Disney World really is.

Your Icon:

L

(L=Large or Little)

Look for this symbol in the book for more details on your special need

As you experience the Walt Disney World resort from the oldest sections (like the Magic Kingdom park and the Polynesian resort) to the newest areas (Disney's Animal Kingdom and Pop Century resort), you'll notice how accessibility for people of size has **improved** over the years.

Planning Ahead

For people of size, we suggest getting a room with a king size bed. Not only will you be more comfortable, but there will be **one less obstacle** (the other bed) to maneuver around in your room. You will pay a bit more for a King room category, but the comfort will outweigh the cost.

While all of the value resort room sizes are about the same (260 sq. ft./ 24 sq. m.), the **moderates vary**. Caribbean Beach offers the most space at 340 sq ft. (31.6 sq. m.), compared to 314 sq. ft. (29 sq. m.) at moderates such as Port Orleans Riverside, French Quarter, and Coronado Springs.

The Wilderness Lodge and Disney's Animal Kingdom Lodge have the **smallest rooms** of all the Deluxe resorts at 340 sq. ft. (31.6 sq. m.) and 344 sq. ft. (32 sq. m.), respectively. The Contemporary garden wings have the largest regular rooms at 436 sq. ft. (40.5 sq. m.). The following deluxe resorts offer a deluxe room category that has more space: Disney's Animal Kingdom Lodge, BoardWalk, and Yacht and Beach Club. And, of course, there are the villas of the Disney Vacation Club (DVC) resorts. The DVC studios begin at 356 sq. ft./33 sq. m. (376 sq. ft./35 sq. m. at Old Key West) and offer other amenities such as a small refrigerator, microwave, and coffeemaker. Refer to chapter 4 for resort room categories.

Know the **height requirements and ride restrictions** before you get to Walt Disney World to avoid disappointments and surprises. (You'll find this information in the Guidebooks for Guests with Disabilities and online at AllEarsNet.com, http://allearsnet.com/tp/rr.htm.)

Disney Cruise Line offers some of the largest staterooms available on cruise ships. Even non-suite staterooms measure as large as 304 sq. ft. Disney Cruise Line also offers accessible staterooms and suites, with ramped bathroom thresholds, open bed frames, added phones in the bathroom/nightstand, bathroom and shower handrails, fold-down shower seats, hand-held shower heads, lowered towel and closet bars, and emergency call buttons.

Looking for Walt Disney World Logo clothing? Before you go, check online at http://www.disneydirect.com or at local stores like Walmart. At Walt Disney World sizes 3X, 4X, and 5X are sold at the **World of Disney** in the Downtown Disney Marketplace.

For **photographs** of Disney ride vehicles and theater seating to identify size issues, visit: http://allearsnet.com/tp/gal_ride.htm.

For **guest reports**, visit: http://allearsnet.com/tp/ridsiz.htm.

Upon Your Arrival

The two biggest areas of **concern** we hear from people of size are:

1. Will I fit through the turnstiles?
2. Will I fit in the ride vehicle or theater seat?

Folks of size do not ever have to go through a **turnstile**. The entrance to each park has a gate for wheelchairs and strollers right next to the turnstile. Just motion to the cast member you will enter that way or ask if you're unsure. The same is true for the entrances of each attraction—most have a gate that swings open. Just ask the cast member. Be on alert at the Magic Kingdom. Those turnstiles and gates are among the smallest in all of Walt Disney World and can be particularly challenging! We note where to watch out in each attraction section in chapter 5.

Some attractions have an actual ride vehicle **on display** outside the main entrance so you can see exactly what you'll be boarding (ask at Test Track). We'll mention specifics in the descriptions of those attractions. Space Mountain seating can be especially tricky.

Several attractions in each of the theme parks and water parks have **minimum height requirements** and are so noted in chapter 5.

Sit-down restaurants usually have **chairs without arms**. If you don't see one, ask. Better yet, request one from the hostess/host when you check in. Be sure to ask for a booth or table (whichever you prefer) when you check in, too.

Planning

Your Special Need

Getting There

Staying in Style

Touring

Feasting

Resources

Index

[L] Size (continued)

The one theme park dining area where you might encounter a problem is at the **Sci-Fi Dine-In Theater**, where much of the seating is in mock vintage convertibles. A picnic table in the back fits most folks.

Bright Idea: Does the ride vehicle have a seat belt? Be sure and pull it all the way out before you sit down. Seatbelt extenders are available on some attractions. Ask a cast member when you enter the ride.

The restrooms all have handicapped stalls, of course, and these provide more room to move around. Likewise, there are some Companion Restrooms at the parks and these offer a bit more **room to maneuver** as well (see chapter 5 for listings).

If you encounter a problem, do not hesitate to ask a **cast member**. They should be able to get what you need or direct you accordingly.

References to the **various seating types** found in attraction ride vehicles and theaters may be confusing. See page 197 for details and photos.

Important Note: Persons small in stature may have difficulty reaching the overhead hand holds on Disney buses when there is only standing room. Look for the seat-level bars to hold on to.

PassPorter Picks

✔ Many restaurants have chairs without arms. Ask for one at check-in.

✔ Test Track and Rock 'n' Roller Coaster have much more leg room in the front row; Space Mountain has more room in the back seat.

PassPorter Pans

✔ If you're a tall person, look out for rides that we have designated as having "small spaces" in chapter 5.

✔ Don't take the Segway tour in Epcot if you're more than 250 lb. (113 kg.). Likewise, you have to be at least 5 feet (152 cm.) tall to drive a Sea Raycer boat and can weigh no more than 320 lb. (145 kg.).

✔ The Magic Kingdom has really narrow turnstiles.

✔ In those Disney Cruise Line staterooms that have pull-down berths, the weight limit is 220 lb. (100 kg.). Some excursions (such as parasailing) have weight limitations also.

✔ Horseback riding at Fort Wilderness has a 250-lb. (113-kg.) limit.

Vision

Visitors to Walt Disney World who have partial or complete vision loss can enjoy just about any experience the resort has to offer, but their experiences will be slightly different. If you have some degree of vision loss, or if you are traveling with someone who does, you'll be relieved to note that Walt Disney World offers a number of services to help maximize your vacation.

Vision

Your Icon:

V

(V=Vision)
Look for this symbol in the book for more details on your special need

Planning Ahead

Before you head to Orlando, it's a good idea to learn more about the Walt Disney World resort. Some Disney guidebooks are available on **audiotape** through the Library of Congress's National Library Service for the Blind and Physically Handicapped (NLS) at http://www.loc.gov/nls. Contact your local library or bookstores for availability. There are also several services that translate magazine articles into Braille. You might be able to find some travel articles on Orlando through them. Try http://blindreaders.info or the National Federation of the Blind at http://www.nfb.org.

As we go to press, we hope to offer this **guidebook in Braille** and/or audio format. Check http://www.passporter.com/wdw/specialneeds or call toll-free 877-929-3273 for status.

Also, if you require special glasses, it's a good idea to bring an extra pair with you if you have them, or a **copy of your prescription**, in case you need to get an emergency pair.

Remember **sunglasses**, too, if your eyes are sensitive to the light—the summer sun can be very bright and intense!

Be sure to request an **easily accessible** room when you book your reservation, whether you're staying at a Disney resort or off Disney property. A room that's on the main floor is a good idea. Otherwise, a room that's close to the hotel facilities, such as the food court or elevators, is a good choice.

Disney **restaurant menus** are not available in Braille or audio formats. If you have text-to-voice computer software, you can preview the menus at http://www.allearsnet.com/menu/menus.htm.

Planning

Your Special Need

Getting There

Staying in Style

Touring

Feasting

Resources

Index

[V] Vision (continued)

Upon Your Arrival

Even though a person with vision loss can tour the theme parks independently, it's probably better to have a **companion** along, especially during busy peak seasons. A companion can help avoid congested traffic areas and provide direction more easily, while also offering verbal descriptions of the sights and attractions. Besides, Walt Disney World is an experience that's enhanced when you share it with a friend.

Bright Idea: When leading a visually impaired person through busy walkways, yield the right-of-way to strollers. Also, agree on what to do if you become separated. It is usually best for the visually impaired person to stop where they are and wait for their companion to come back to them.

Among the **aids** that Walt Disney World offers:

✔ **Braille guidebooks** are available at Guest Relations for a $25 refundable deposit (if you return the book the same day). It's a good idea to study the guide for a while before touring a park.

✔ Audiotape guides with **portable tape players** are also available at Guest Relations for a $25 refundable deposit. There are two versions of the audio cassettes: an audio guide (with an overview of the services available to those with vision impairments, as well as an idea of the layout of the theme park) and an audio tour (which describes a specific route, giving distances between attractions and important stopping points along the way). These audio guides are not as useful as the Braille guide, as they are sequential and don't allow you to wander or explore at your own discretion.

✔ Braille and **large print park guide maps** are located in each park. In Disney's Animal Kingdom and Disney-MGM Studios, the Braille map stand is located outside of Guest Relations. The Magic Kingdom has Braille maps inside City Hall and adjacent to the Main Street Tip Board. See chapter 5 for locations of the Braille maps in each park.

There are several **3-D movies that require special glasses** to see the 3-D effects. They are: It's Tough to be a Bug in Disney's Animal Kingdom; Mickey's PhilharMagic in the Magic Kingdom; Honey, I Shrunk the Audience in Epcot; and Muppet Vision 3-D in the Disney-MGM Studios. These 3-D glasses are wide enough to fit right over your own glasses, but people with vision loss or impairment may not be able to fully perceive the special effects.

There are hands-on displays in some areas that can provide additional sensory input for those with vision loss. In Disney's Animal Kingdom, there are areas along the Pangani Forest Exploration Trail and at Conservation Station that feature "manipulatives," such as animal skulls and bones, for **tactile exploration**. Often the children's areas during some of Epcot's special events (Food & Wine Festival and Flower & Garden Festival) have additional hands-on experiences that are worth investigating.

A "manipulative" at Disney's Animal Kingdom

Braille signage is available in Disney **elevators** and marks resort rooms to make it easier to locate your destination.

There are no Braille menus available at the Walt Disney World restaurants. If you have some or complete vision loss, a **cast member or companion** can read the menu offerings to you.

There are no special provisions at the **water parks**, but you should be able to experience most attractions if you have a companion to assist you.

There is **Braille signage** on the restrooms located at Guest Relations and in Once Upon a Toy at Downtown Disney, but there are no Braille maps available. Some shops in both Downtown Disney and the BoardWalk may be tricky to negotiate—they are very crowded with merchandise and displays. We have noted other special considerations in our individual descriptions of these areas in chapter 5.

If you use a **service animal**, you'll find that you're able to take it with you around most of Walt Disney World, as long as it's on a leash or a harness. See our information on traveling with a service animal on page 12.

See our information on traveling with a service animal on page 12.

[V] Vision (continued)

PassPorter Picks

✔ Attractions with a **large amount of dialogue**, such as Spaceship Earth or Hall of Presidents, are easier to follow.

✔ People with vision loss can experience **dark thrill rides**, such as Rock 'n' Roller Coaster or Space Mountain, in much the same manner as those without vision impairment.

✔ Consider purchasing **Pal Mickey**, a 10-inch plush Mickey Mouse that talks. Using wireless technology, Pal Mickey points out your location, reminds you of parade times, and offers tips on many other things. Pal Mickey is $65 at most resort gift shops and at locations throughout the theme parks. (There's also a Spanish-speaking Pal Mickey!)

✔ Try to catch some of the **live musical acts** in the parks, like Voices of Liberty in Epcot or Main Street Philharmonic in the Magic Kingdom.

✔ The props, called **manipulatives**, found in certain areas of Disney's Animal Kingdom can give insight through a tactile experience. Animal Kingdom Lodge has similar displays. Often these exhibits are billed for kids, but they can also be useful to those with vision impairments.

PassPorter Pans

✔ For some, the **fireworks shows and parades** are not easily appreciated. Others enjoy the music, sound, and the "impact" of explosions and drums, which can be thrilling.

Reader Story: "It is important to remember that while a visually impaired person cannot enjoy Walt Disney World in the same way as a sighted person, they enjoy it in a different way. What to concentrate on depends on the individual. I have gone multiple times with my husband (who is totally blind) and a friend (who has very limited vision—he can see light and some color). They have different interests. My husband enjoys technology, so his favorite park is Epcot, because of Innoventions and the attractions in Future World. He enjoys listening to the different people at the attractions. My husband also enjoys the thrill rides. His favorite attraction is The Tower of Terror in the Disney-MGM Studios. All of the roller coasters and simulators are the things he wants to do the most. My friend's favorite park is also Epcot, but for a very different reason. He enjoys the food, smells, and shopping in World Showcase, and loves talking to the people from other countries, asking about their country of origin. Since he is also a music lover, we try to catch some of the entertainment, such as Epcot Vybe or Off Kilter. He also enjoys going to the different resorts to check out the atmosphere. It is at the resorts where one can take the most time and give good descriptions of what is around."

—contributed by Lori Kloman Williamson

Your Special Needs Tips and Stories

My husband Sam doesn't like to draw attention to his profound deafness. Before our first Walt Disney World trip in 2001, I researched the options available to us: interpreters, portable hearing aids, or reflective captioning screens. None of these, in his opinion, warranted the bother of asking for them. The whole week, I couldn't convince him to try out the reflective captioning screens available at most of the theater-type shows/attractions. It was a fight every time our hearing daughter wanted to see a show. The cast members tried to help, but that just turned him off even more. Finally, on our 2003 trip with my parents, we convinced him to try the reflective captioning "just once" at the Hall of Presidents. He was hooked! He couldn't believe how much better the presentation was with the reflective captions. Since then, he doesn't complain when we want to see a show; he heads right to the head of the line and asks out loud for the closed caption. (Sam depends on American Sign Language as his main communication, so he doesn't usually talk aloud to strangers, but he likes the RC that much!) We are eagerly waiting to try out the handheld captioning devices now offered on our next trip in 2005.

—contributed by anonymous

Traveling with fibromyalgia can be tough. The mind is willing, the body gives out. Having made four Disney trips with this illness, I have learned a lot. First thing is pace yourself! I am one who wants to see it all *now*! But when I push myself, my body gives out on me—fast. Last year, we had seven wonderful nights at Walt Disney World, and I decided to take it slower, come back to the room for **afternoon rests**, and take in everything at a leisurely pace. The old body held up longer than usual, and I experienced only one really bad day. I came back to the room, put on my swimsuit and spent some time in the **hot tub** to relax my aching body. On our last day, I had trouble walking, but all in all, I had a wonderful time. Without slowing down, I don't think I could have made it past two days. Take time to enjoy the sights and you will be able to enjoy the World!

—contributed by peer reviewer Deb Kendall

While trying to conceive, I made countless trips to Disney, as well as four trips while pregnant. During those trips when my fertility was paramount, I essentially behaved as though I were pregnant—no alcohol, no hot tubs, good diet, daily vitamin, no thrill rides. Not only did this mindset help when faced with hoardes of happy kids with their parents, but on the Disney trip I discovered I actually was pregnant, I was really thankful I'd been taking care of myself all along.

—contributed by editor Jennifer Marx

As a larger guy—6'6", 375 pounds—I find that hotels, bathrooms, and public transportation all present their own obstacles. You have to deal with all of those things, and more, at theme parks. On my most recent trip to Walt Disney World, I decided to really pay attention to how everything works for those of us who are of more-than-average proportions. I'm happy to report that Disney, while perhaps not necessarily perfectly suited to larger visitors, is certainly a Big-Friendly place to be.

—contributed by peer reviewer Joshua Olive

Planning

Your Special Need

Getting There

Staying in Style

Touring

Feasting

Resources

Index

Planning

Your Special Need

Getting There

Staying in Style

Touring

Feasting

Resources

Index

Your Special Needs Tips and Stories
(continued)

I am the mother of a young boy with high-functioning autism.
We have had two wonderful spring vacations at Walt Disney World (he was 3 and 4 years old) even though we are on a budget and it is just us two (I'm a single mother). The nice thing about it being just the two of us is that we can go at a much slower pace than other families. We must have looked at the train display at Epcot for an hour! And we went back to Minnie Mouse's Toontown kitchen as much as he wanted. My son is verbal but picture cards and schedules help him understand what is going on. I went online and found images for just about everything ... our hotel room, the Disney bus, restaurants, and rides (both the outside view of the ride and picture of the ride car itself). Usually the image size is just right for a picture card, which I printed, laminated, and put on a vinyl folder with velcro.

—contributed by anonymous

I have traveled with my mobility-challenged mother on all of my Walt Disney World adventures. She is not yet in a wheelchair. Neither of us are strong enough to load and unload a rental ECV from a car trunk. On our second trip to the World in 2000, we took her handicapped pass and parked in the handicapped parking, but this was generally way too far for my mother to walk to the gate. A parking cast member told us in the future to head toward the normal parking and request a spot at the beginning of any row. She said we should have the handicapped pass visible when we request this. On our last four trips, we have done this and have had only one cast member tells us to go to the regular handicapped lot. We then asked the next cast member and he put us at the beginning of a row. It is much better for my mother, who can now ride the tram up to the gate or Transportation and Ticket Center. Using this method, my mother's legs swell up less and she doesn't have to have as many down days during her vacation.

—contributed by Penny de Geer

This year we attended Mickey's Very Merry Christmas Party with my son, who has an Autism Spectrum Disorder (ASD). We had been waiting in line at the Timekeeper building to get our picture made for the complimentary photograph. When we began to go through the door, my son began to scream "no," and tried to run away. He is scared of buildings with high ceilings, and as we had never been in that building, we were unprepared. Immediately, the cast member at the doorway turned to me and simply said "Autism?" She told him that he did not have to go in there, that they had a special way for him. She led us around the room to where the photographers were. I am amazed and thrilled with how well-prepared the cast members are to deal with the unique needs of individuals with ASD. Way to go, Disney!

—contributed by peer reviewer Carrie Bass

Getting There (and Back!)

You've decided that you are going to visit the Mouse, and now it's time to make your travel plans.

Just what is the best way to travel to Walt Disney World? Well, so much of that depends on you and your special needs. There are obviously pros and cons to each method of travel, which we address a bit in this chapter. We also tell you other special things you need to know to make the journey with ease and confidence.

In addition to our suggestions and tips, you'll also find special phone numbers and Web site addresses to assist you in planning your trip.

No matter which mode of transportation you choose, all special needs travelers should keep the following items on their person or in their carry-on luggage to avoid losing them:

✔ Be sure to bring enough (including extra) of any prescription medications you need, in their original bottles, as well as a copy of the prescription(s), in case you need to get refills. Make a separate list of these medications, including the dosages. If the prescription is with a pharmacy chain, getting a refill at a local branch should not be hard.

✔ Keep a summary of your medical history with you at all times, including the names and phone numbers for your doctor(s). Include a copy of your electrocardiogram if you have heart health concerns. Bring a letter from your doctor(s) describing your health condition and any special relevant information. A doctor's letter stating your condition and requested accommodations while touring the parks will be helpful if you plan to request a Guest Assistance Card (see pages 10-11).

✔ Bring lists of contacts and phone numbers in case of emergency.

✔ Carry identification for each person that includes their name, emergency information, and where you are staying in Florida. We've found the Who's Shoes ID to be great for youngsters and for those travelers unable to verbalize or remember their information—for more details, see http://www.whosshoesid.com.

Planning

Your Special Need

Getting There

Staying in Style

Touring

Feasting

Resources

Index

Personal Identification

We recommend everyone traveling keep personal ID on them at all times. This may be something as simple as a driver's license or state-issued ID cards. For kids, you may want to have them carry a laminated card or attach ID to their clothing, depending on their age. Here are more specific ways to keep ID on yourself and your travelers:

Cruisers—Beginning 12/31/2005, all U.S. citizens must have a passport to reenter the U.S. from the Caribbean. (Prior to this, a driver's license and birth certificate were accepted.)

International Travelers—Carry your passport on you at all times, in the event of a problem or emergency. You may want to consider keeping it in a special passport case tucked inside your shirt, and/or use the PassHolder Pouch (see page 401), which fits most passports.

Medical Needs—Medical alert bracelets (or necklaces) are paramount if you have a special medical issue. You can generally find generic bracelets indicating common special needs such as diabetes, in most drugstores. We recommend you get your ID tag personalized with your contact information, too. You can order these from http://www.medicalert.org.

Other Travelers—There are a variety of products that allow you to wear your identification. You can get bracelets, shoe tags and stickers, and zipper pulls. You can find some of these at http://www.whossshoesid.com.

For **companies** offering ID products, visit http://childrenwithdiabetes.com/d_06_700.htm.

Looking for an inexpensive, low-tech way to record personal information? Here's a **simple ID card** tailored to a vacation—feel free to copy it as many times as needed. Then just fill it out, laminate it, and stick it in a wallet, purse, pocket, backpack, or PassHolder Pouch. Consider including a recent photo on the back side, too!

> Name: _KuDu Boo_____ Age: _28___
> Medical Conditions/Medications:
> _____aye glass far near sight_____
> Address: _____
> Phone: _561-506-9466_ Cell Phone: _561-506-9466_
> Hotel: _____ Phone: _____
> Hotel Room Registered Under Name: _____
> I am traveling with: _____ Cell Phone: _561-506-9466_
> _____ Cell Phone: _561-506-9466_
> Emergency Contact: _561-506-9466_ Phone: _561-506-9466_

Reader Tip: "I make up ID cards for both of my boys to carry in their waist packs. These cards are about credit card size and include their name, my name, the resort name, resort number, length of stay, home phone, and emergency contact. I also include info about their medication and dosage. I also have a doctor's note (with contact information) indicating that they are under his care for ADHD. I put this inside a plastic sleeve—the kind sold for trading cards or the kind that you get to hold your insurance card in. This keeps the ID from getting ripped or wet. I decorate the cards with Disney stickers, of course!"—contributed by peer reviewer Michelle Steiner

A Special Time to Go

A special vacation starts with carefully choosing the best time to go. As we've said, some times are much better than others to visit Walt Disney World. Specifically, the "off-season" is less crowded and more temperate. We know that everyone has different needs, however, so to help you decide, we charted the **fluctuating factors** for each month below. Most Disney veterans agree that the best time to visit is November–February, being careful to avoid the holidays, when parks fill to capacity. Three-day weekends are also to be avoided whenever possible. The latter half of August and September are uncrowded but very hot. For temperature and rainfall data, visit http://www.passporter.com/wdw/bestoftimes.htm.

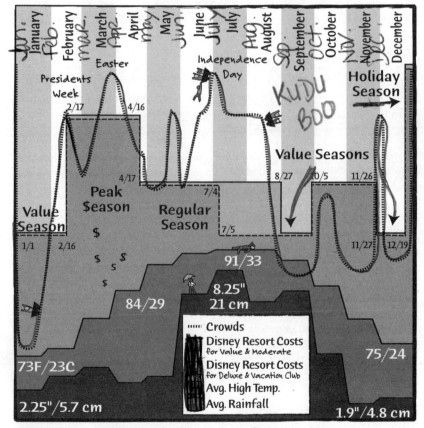

2005 Disney resort cost seasons are as follows:

Value Season is Jan. 1– Feb. 16 (all), Jul. 5–Oct. 4 (deluxe and DVC), Aug. 28–Oct. 4 (value and moderate), Nov. 27–Dec. 19 (all); **Regular Season** is Apr. 17–Jul. 4 (deluxe and DVC), Apr. 17–Aug. 27 (value and moderate), Oct. 5–Nov. 26 (all); **Peak Season** is Feb. 17–Apr. 16 (all); **Pre-Holiday Season** is Nov. 18–Dec. 19 (Ft. Wilderness campsites only); and **Holiday Season** is Dec. 20–31 (all).

Getting There

Depending on where you live and the size of your group, transportation can be a major item in the vacation budget. The two most popular travel options are **personal vehicle and plane**. Bus and train are options, too. There are pluses and minuses to every option; only you can decide what works best for you and your specific situation.

By Personal Vehicle

Many travelers choose to drive themselves to Disney for a variety of reasons, not the least of which is **economy**. In addition, having your own vehicle puts you on your schedule and your schedule alone. You don't have to run through airports or figure out train schedules. For large families, driving can be much less expensive than flying, but a long drive can also seriously reduce your magical time at Disney.

Find out how far away you are from Walt Disney World by using a **AAA TripTik** (http://www.aaa.com, membership required) or by visiting Mapquest.com (http://www.mapquest.com). Select "driving directions," which will also give you estimated travel times.

Reader Tip: "Do an Internet research for restaurants or markets that can accommodate your needs in the cities where you will stop for meals or for the night."—contributed by peer reviewer Leanne Phelps

Taking your own vehicle provides a **number of benefits** for the special needs traveler:

✔ You travel on your **own schedule**, avoiding rushes and potential long waits at airports and train stations.
✔ You're in **familiar surroundings**, which is especially attractive to those with autism spectrum disorders and other developmental disabilities.
✔ Your **own vehicle** is probably more comfortable than standard airline/train seats if you're a person of size.
✔ You can **make stops whenever needed** for stretching, restrooms, and food.
✔ You **won't be dependent** on Disney transportation once you arrive.
✔ It's **easier to pack meals** and snacks.
✔ It's easier to **bring your own wheelchair/stroller** and other special needs items.
✔ If you bring a **service animal**, it is often cheaper to drive. Also, you don't have to worry about anyone bothering the animal or vice versa.

There are some **drawbacks** to driving, however, including:
✔ A very long drive can **take precious time** away from touring.
✔ **More planning is required** to determine routes, tolls, and/or overnight lodging.
✔ If you have to do the driving yourself, it can be **very exhausting**.

By Plane

Most travelers find that flying is not only the **fastest way** to get to Orlando, but it can sometimes also be the least expensive method. Just like with all components of your trip, know the travelers in your party, be sure to research policies, and contact the airlines with any special requests. Once you've made your plans, be sure to confirm and reconfirm them!

When trying for **low airfares**, make sure you research all area airports—a slightly longer drive to an alternate airport might save you lots of money on airfare, especially for large families. Also, start checking prices early on so you know when a good deal pops up and can take advantage quickly! Finally, don't forget to be flexible about what time of day and the day of the week you fly to save even more.

Each commercial carrier has its own specific information regarding traveling with special needs. Check its Web site or call the airline, and be sure to read the information carefully before making final plans. The **Transportation Security Administration (TSA)** also has details for persons with disabilities and medical conditions online at http://www.tsa.gov/public. You'll also find guidelines here for restrictions on carry-on luggage.

General flying **guidelines**:
- ✔ Consider wearing **compression stockings** to limit the risk of blood clots.
- ✔ Periodically stand up and **move around** the plane if possible.
- ✔ Flying can be very dehydrating so **limit your intake** of alcohol and caffeinated drinks, which can actually dehydrate you. Bring a bottle of water and drink plenty of it.
- ✔ Arrange for **wheelchair transportation** to take you to and from your gate if you have mobility or fatigue concerns.
- ✔ Make advance **arrangements for oxygen** if you think you will need it. Since some airlines do not provide oxygen, you may need to ask your doctor to provide a prescription and fill out an airline medical form at least three business days before your departure. Note that many airlines do not allow passengers to bring their own oxygen aboard—be sure to verify this before you book.
- ✔ If you meet the criteria, consider requesting **an exit row**, which offers more legroom.
- ✔ Bring your own **meal/snacks**. Foods meeting your dietary needs may be hard to find in transit. If there'll be an in-flight meal, inquire in advance about special dietary requests.
- ✔ If flying with a **service dog**, request a bulkhead seat so the dog has room to lie down.
- ✔ Occasionally, an airline may ask for a **letter from a doctor** verifying that the special needs traveler is fit to fly. Consider bringing one "just in case."

🔔 Special Seats for Special People

Check with your airline about seats for those with special accessibility needs. People of size may request seat belt extenders if necessary (some airlines will not allow you to use an extender if you are seated in an exit row). While you are allowed to lap carry infants up to 24 months, seriously consider getting them their own seat and bringing an FAA-approved car seat—it's far safer. (Tip: Consider the Sit 'n' Stroll seat/stroller combo at http://www.sitnstroll.com).

Getting Around the Orlando Airport

Orlando International Airport is a large, sprawling hub and one of the better (and cleaner) airports. When you arrive, your plane docks at one of four **satellite terminals**. From there, follow the signs to the automated shuttle train that takes you to the main terminal—there you'll find baggage claim and ground transportation. Once you reach the main terminal (Level 3), follow the signs down to baggage claim (Level 2). Shuttles, taxis, town cars, rental cars, and buses are found down on Level 1 (take the elevators opposite the baggage carousels). Each shuttle and bus company has its own ticket booth, so keep your eyes open. If you get lost, look for signs or an information desk that can get you back on track. For more details on the Orlando International Airport, call 407-825-2001 or visit http://www.orlandoairports.net. Page travelers at 407-825-2000.

Note: Each satellite terminal has a companion restroom.

⚠ Disabled Air Traveler Hotline

Did you know there's a **toll-free hotline for disabled air travelers** operated by the Department of Transportation? The hotline serves two main purposes: education and assistance in resolving disability-related air travel problems. Hotline operators are well-versed in relevant laws and regulations (Air Carrier Access Act and the regulation 14 CFR Part 382) and can provide callers with general information about the rights of air travelers with disabilities. The hotline operators also respond to requests for printed consumer information about air travel rights of the disabled and can also assist in resolving real-time or upcoming issues with air carriers by contacting the carrier and attempting to resolve the issue. Hotline Duty Officers have, for example, contacted air carriers and convinced them to accept service animals and electric wheelchairs onboard flights or to stow folding wheelchairs in the cabin. Air travelers who want information about the rights of persons with disabilities in air travel or who experience disability-related air travel service problems may call the hotline from 7:00 am to 11:00 pm Eastern time, seven days a week, at 800-778-4838 (voice) or 800-455-9880 (TTY).

By Bus and Train

You may not have considered **traveling by bus** to Walt Disney World, but several commercial bus lines, such as Greyhound, do offer accommodations for special needs travelers with adequate advance notice (usually at least 48 hours). Visit Greyhound's Web site for details on their services at http://www.greyhound.com or call 1-800-231-2222.

Traveling by train may be practical for some travelers, especially for those able to take advantage of Amtrak's Auto Train, which allows you to bring your own car without having to drive it all the way to Florida. The Auto Train may be a little more expensive than even flying, but the convenience of having your own vehicle might be worth the expense. The Auto Train leaves from Lorton, VA (just outside of Washington, DC) and arrives in Sanford, FL (about a one-hour drive from Orlando). You board the Auto Train in the late afternoon, eat your meals on board, sleep on board overnight, and arrive the next morning (it's a 16-hour trip) ready to head to Disney. Amtrak offers a variety of accommodations for travelers with special needs—they even have a section on their Web site for special needs travelers with specific guidelines relating to wheelchairs, service animals, oxygen equipment, etc. Some discounts may be available. For more information on the Auto Train or traveling by train in general, visit http://www.amtrak.com or call 800-872-7245.

Commercial Travel Pros and Cons

As in all types of travel, there are positive and not-so-positive features. When considering commercial travel, here are a few of the benefits to consider:

- ✔ Typically takes **less** travel time.
- ✔ You don't have to **drive** yourself.
- ✔ Can be more **economical** for individuals or small groups.
- ✔ If flying and staying at a Disney resort, you may have access to Disney's new **Magical Express ground transportation** (see the next page).

Before booking this type of travel, here are the **drawbacks** to consider:

- ✔ You may **not be able to walk around** to stretch.
- ✔ There are **baggage limitations**.
- ✔ Seating may be unfamiliar and **uncomfortable**.
- ✔ When **confined to a small space** for a long time, the possibility of meltdown increases for some.
- ✔ You may encounter **longer waits** for security, luggage, check-in, etc.
- ✔ Your personal wheelchair may have to be **disassembled** to be stored in the cargo hold.
- ✔ Your stroller may be **inaccessible** during the trip.

Planning

Your Special Need

Getting There

Staying in Style

Touring

Feasting

Resources

Index

Are We There Yet?

OK, now you've arrived in Orlando ... so how do you actually get to Walt Disney World? If you arrived at the airport, bus, or train station, you'll need transportation to Disney. You can take advantage of Disney's newest program, Magical Express, rent a car, take a shuttle or taxi, or hire a town car.

Disney's Magical Express

Beginning May 5, 2005, Disney's Magical Express began offering free transportation between Orlando International Airport and Walt Disney World. If you're a guest of a Disney hotel, you can sign up for this service in advance. You check your bags when you depart from your home airport, then, upon arrival at the Orlando airport, skip baggage claim and proceed directly to a Disney motorcoach (similar to those used by the Disney Cruise Line). Your luggage "magically" appears at your resort when you check in! This service is *free* (during the Happiest Celebration on Earth, which runs through December 2006) for guests staying at Disney hotels who register at least 10 days in advance either through their travel agent, online at http://www.disneyworld.com, or by calling Disney Reservations at 407-934-7639. Magical Express can accommodate wheelchairs and ECVs, but there are a limited number of spaces. Make sure to mention that you have a wheelchair or ECV when making your reservations. The only disadvantage to this service is that you may have to travel to several other Disney resorts to drop off others before reaching your destination.

Bright Idea: Disney's Magical Express is also available for your return trip to the airport. In addition, if you're flying with a participating airline, you can also use the Resort Airline Check-In Service, which allows you to check your luggage and receive your boarding passes at your resort. As of May 2005, participating airlines are American, Continental, Delta (including Song), and United (including Ted).

© Nikki Shenk

Disney's Magical Express motorcoach

Car Rentals

If you're flying and plan to rent a car once you get to Orlando, we suggest you rent from one of the agencies located right at the airport on Level 1: Alamo, Avis, Budget, Dollar, National, and L&M. (Other companies require taking a shuttle from the airport to an off-site location, which can be a major hassle both ways.) When you reserve your car, be sure to make any special requests, such as a child car seat or hand-control-equipped vehicle. You can check out the individual car rental companies' policies on accommodating special needs by visiting their Web sites or by calling their main telephone number directly.

Reader Tip: "If you rent a car, I would suggest that you consider the gas option offered by most companies. This means you can return your car with an empty tank and not worry about stopping to fill up on the way back to the airport."–contributed by peer reviewer Robert Feder

Shuttles and Taxis

Shuttle stands are located at the Orlando International Airport (Level 1), but all other pickup points require advance notice. The major shuttle operator is Mears (800-759-5219). While taxis are available, we don't recommend them for travel due to cost. Large parties may be able to ride in a taxi mini-van economically, however.

Town Cars

A number of companies offer taxi, shuttle, or town car service to Disney. Of the three options, we suggest the **town car** (if your budget allows) for the following reasons:

✔ The driver **meets you in the baggage claim area**, assists with your luggage, and drives you directly to your Disney resort without stopping at other resorts.

✔ Some services even offer a **free stop at a local grocery store** so you can pick up a few necessities and special food items you probably won't find in the Disney shops.

✔ The town car vehicles are usually late model, very clean, and **very comfortable**.

✔ There is **little wait time**, since the town car drivers are usually waiting to greet you.

✔ You can leave the **driving to someone else**, and don't have to worry about getting lost or dealing with traffic.

✔ Depending on the number of people in your group, the town car may actually be **less expensive** per person than shuttle service.

✔ Your party is the only one in the town car—you **don't have to share the ride** with strangers.

Town car services we've used include (in alphabetical order):

✔ Happy Limo (888-394-4277, http://www.happylimo.com)

✔ Quicksilver (888-468-6939, http://www.quicksilver-tour.com)

✔ YourRide (866-240-RIDE, http://www.yourride.net)

Important Note: If you have allergies or asthma, remember to request a smoke-free car that is also free of heavily scented air fresheners.

Packing List

Begin thinking about what you need to pack once you have your transportation decided. Commercial vehicles have restrictions on the size and number of luggage pieces. If you drive yourself, your only limit is the available space in your vehicle. Here is a helpful packing list to guide you—items in bold may be handy to carry around in your day bag.

The Essentials

☑ Casual clothing you can layer—the dress code nearly everywhere at Disney is casual, even at dinner. One "nice" outfit is usually enough.

___ Shorts/skirts   ___ Pants/jeans   ___ Shirts   ___ Sweaters
___ Underwear   ___ Socks   ___ Pajamas   ___ _____

☑ Jacket and/or sweatshirt (light ones for the warmer months)

___ **Jackets**   ___ Sweatshirts   ___ Sweaters   ___ Vests

☑ Comfortable, well-broken-in shoes ... plus a second pair, just in case!

___ Walking shoes   ___ Sandals   ✓ Sneakers   ___ _____

☑ Swim gear (bring one-piece suits for water slides)

___ Suits/trunks   ___ Cover-ups/towels   ___ Water shoes   ___ Goggles

☑ Sun protection (the Florida sun can be brutal)

___ **Sunblock**   ___ **Lip balm**   ___ **Sunburn relief**   ___ **Sunglasses**
___ **Hats w/brims**   ___ **Caps**   ___ **Visors**

☑ Rain gear (compact and light so you don't mind carrying it)

___ Raincoat   ___ **Poncho**   ___ **Umbrella**   ___ **Dry socks**

☑ Comfortable bags with padded straps to carry items during the day

___ **Backpacks**   ___ **Waist packs**   ___ Shoulder bags   ___ **Camera bag**

☑ Toiletries (in a bag or bathroom kit to keep them organized)

___ **Brush/comb**   ___ Toothbrush   ___ Toothpaste   ___ Dental floss
___ Favorite soap, shampoo, and conditioner   ___ Deodorant   ___ **Baby wipes**
___ **Aspirin/acetaminophen/ibuprofen**   ___ **Band aids**   ___ **First aid kit**
___ **Prescriptions** (in original containers)   ___ Vitamins   ___ Fem. hygiene
___ Hair dryer/iron   ___ **Anti-blister tape**   ___ Makeup   ___ Hairspray
___ Razors   ___ Shaving cream   ___ Cotton buds   ___ Lotion
___ Nail clippers   ___ Spare eyeglasses   ___ Lens solution   ___ **Bug repellent**
___ Mending kit   ___ Small scissors   ___ Safety pins   ___ **Insect sting kit**

☑ Camera/camcorder and more film/tape than you think you need

✓ **Camera**   ___ **Cameoorder**   ✓ **Film/tapes**   ___ **Storage cards**
✓ **Batteries**   ✓ **Chargers**   ___ **Camera case**   ___ _____

☑ Money in various forms and various places

___ **Charge cards**   ___ **Traveler's checks**   ✓ **Bank cards**   ___ **Cash**

☑ Personal identification, passes, and membership cards

✓ **Driver's licenses**   ✓ **Other photo ID**   ___ **Passports**   ✓ Birth certificate
___ **AAA card**   ___ **Discount cards**   ___ Air miles card   ___ _____
___ **Tickets/passes**   ✓ **Insurance cards**   ___ **Calling cards**   ___ _____

Tip: Label everything with your name, phone, and hotel to help reunite you with your stuff if lost. Every bag should have this info on a luggage tag as well as on a slip of paper inside it. Use our Luggage Tag Maker at http://www.passporter.com/wdw/luggagelog.htm.

For Your Carry-On

- ☑ Your **PassPorter**, **tickets**, **maps**, **guides**, and a **pen** or **pencil**! ✎ Remember to pack any sharp or potentially dangerous items in your checked luggage, not your carry-on.
- ☐ **Camera** and/or **camcorder**, along with **film**, **tapes**, and **batteries**
- ☑ Any **prescriptions**, important toiletries, **sunblock**, **sunglasses**, **hats**, **bug repellent**
- ☑ Change of clothes appropriate to your destination's weather
- ☑ **Snacks**, ☙ **water bottle**, **juice boxes**, gum, favorite books, **toys**, **games**, blankets

For Young Travelers

- ☑ Snacks and juice boxes
- ☑ Books, toys, games, and a night light
- ☑ Stroller, carrier, and accessories 🛒
- ☑ **Diapers, formula, other baby needs**
- ☐ EarPlanes (http://www.earplanes.com)

For Heat-Sensitive Travelers

- ☐ **Personal fans/water misters** 💨
- ☑ **Water bottles** (frozen, if possible)
- ☑ **Washcloth** to cool off face and neck
- ☑ **Hats** with wide brims
- ☑ **Sunshades** (for baby strollers)

For Special Needs Travelers (see page 91 for a list of items to keep in your carry-on)

- ☑ **Earplugs**
- ☐ **Handheld games** and game magazines
- ☑ Personal music player with headphones
- ☑ **Favorite toy or game**
- ☑ Special diet snacks or food items
- ☑ **Chewable anti-nausea tablets**
- ☐ Disposable thermometers
- ☐ Handicapped tag from home vehicle
- ☐ Heating pad
- ☐ Ben Gay or Icy Hot (sore muscles)

- ☐ Special pillows, white noise machine
- ☐ **Adequate doses of any medications**
- ☐ **Prescriptions in case of refills**
- ☐ **EpiPen**, if you have severe allergies
- ☐ Extra hearing aid batteries
- ☐ Doctor's letter for Guest Assistance Card
- ☐ **Medical history/doctor contact info**
- ☐ Plastic gloves
- ☐ Measuring spoon
- ☐ Special adaptable items

Everyone Should Consider

- ☑ Big beach towels (for pools and water parks)
- ☑ **Penlight** or flashlight (for reading/writing in dark places and to alleviate kids' fears)
- ☑ **Water bottles**, water bottle strap, and personal **fan/water misters**
- ☑ **Snacks** for any time of the day (plus gum, if you chew it)
- ☑ Plastic cutlery for snacks or leftovers ✐
- ☑ **Quarters** and **pennies** (and a way to hold them) for the coin presses and/or laundry
- ☑ Plastic storage bags that seal (large and small), plus trash bags
- ☑ Address book, stamps, and envelopes ✉
- ☑ Laundry detergent/tablets, bleach, dryer sheets, stain removal wipes, and a laundry tote
- ☑ Hand sanitizer or antibacterial wipes, disinfectant wipes
- ☐ Collapsible bag or suitcase inside another suitcase to hold souvenirs on your return

Your Personal Packing List

☑ _____   ☑ _____
☑ _____   ☑ _____
☑ _____   ☑ _____
☑ _____   ☑ _____
☑ _____   ☑ _____
☑ _____   ☑ _____
☑ _____   ☑ _____
☑ _____   ☑ _____

Planning | Your Special Need | Getting There | Staying in Style | Touring | Feasting | Resources | Index

Your Traveling Tips and Stories

I suggest going to a local running shoe store for shoes. I went about a month ahead of time so I could break them in. I looked up a great local running store. The clerk actually observed my walking style, and then suggested the best three shoe styles for me. She suggested that even though I was primarily planning on walking in them, running shoes would be the best option, because they offer the most cushioning (over walking shoes or cross-trainers). They are the best sneakers I have ever bought. They didn't require any breaking in at all! The funny thing is, the woman who was ahead of me in line was also buying shoes for a trip to Disney World!

—contributed by Lorraine Ivester

For those of you who have to bring injections on airlines, you must have a prescription to show baggage checkers. Also, check with your pharmacist or doctor to make sure that the x-ray machines your meds must pass through won't affect the meds. I have an injection that must be refrigerated. I carry it on with me and mention it to the baggage checkers before I put it through. When I get to the Disney resort, the front desk will put it in a refrigerator for me if my room isn't ready. Walt Disney World supplies a complimentary refrigerator rental if you have a medical necessity for it. It's always been a dorm-sized refrigerator, but I've heard there are also small ones (shoebox sized) they sometimes give to guests for meds.

—contributed by Eileen Lloyd

I am in a power wheelchair and use a ventilator 24/7. When traveling, we have to take lots of medical supplies. Our last two trips, we boxed up many of the medical supplies I'd be needing while there. We had them sent to the hotel that we'd be staying at, and upon arrival, they had our box in our room for us. This made our traveling to Disney much easier, since we had fewer things to bring with us on the airplane. We plan on doing this when we go again.

—contributed by anonymous

One advantage to driving yourself to Walt Disney World is something that may be a personal idiosyncrasy of mine: driving allows you to come down a bit more gently from the high of being there. Flying gets you home so fast that you are jolted from the experience, rather than allowing yourself to unwind out of it. At least that's the case with me. I like flying, because I get there that much faster, but I'd prefer to drive home, reminiscing the whole way ... and, possibly, singing Disney songs far too loudly.

—contributed by peer reviewer Joshua Olive

Bring on the plane everything you need to last 24–48 hours. Through various trips, we've been stuck overnight at a connecting airport, redirected to land 100 miles from our destination, and left without luggage for a day! It was very easy to buy a toothbrush but not very easy to replace needed medications and supplies. The well-packed carry-on bag was a lifesaver!

—contributed by peer reviewer Susan Heck

Staying and Cruising in Style

Walt Disney World offers 24 themed resort hotels—one is sure to fit your budget and taste. Why would you want to stay at a Disney hotel? There are numerous advantages, but the biggest is that you will be immersed in the magic for your entire vacation! In fact, most Disney hotels offer so many amenities and have so much to do that even if you never set foot in a theme park, you'll still feel you "got away from it all."

There is something for everyone: the budget-minded value resorts with eye-popping, larger-than-life icons; the modestly priced moderate resorts with larger rooms and increased amenities; the posh deluxe resorts with impeccable appointments, multiple dining options, and closer access to the parks; and the Disney Vacation Club (DVC) Resorts, which feature accommodations ranging from a studio with a kitchenette to a grand villa with three full bedrooms, several bathrooms, a full kitchen, and living and dining rooms.

In addition, when you stay at a Walt Disney World Resort, you have access to special perks, such as:

✔ Disney's Magical Express Service (complimentary through December 2006)—Disney resort guests (excluding the Walt Disney World Swan and Dolphin and the Hotel Plaza hotels) can arrange for free shuttle service from Orlando International Airport to check in at their hotel, while their luggage goes straight from the plane to the room. The service will take you back to the airport when your vacation is over, too.
✔ Extra Magic Hour—Visit a designated theme park one hour earlier or several hours later than the general public each day of the week.
✔ Complimentary package delivery from Disney locations to your hotel.
✔ Free Disney transportation to/from the Disney theme parks.
✔ Free parking at the Disney theme parks.
✔ Chargeback privileges that allow you to charge purchases around Walt Disney World directly to your room.
✔ Special Disney character wake-up calls.

Special Lodging for Special Guests

Because Walt Disney World is a family vacation destination, you expect its hotels to be prepared to accommodate all sorts of families' needs. You'll be pleasantly surprised to learn that they are also able to meet most of the requirements of travelers with a **wide variety of special needs**, too.

Disney resort rooms have **standard accommodations** much like you'd find in any hotel: two double or queen beds, a television, a telephone, a small table with two chairs, a small wall safe, a bathroom with shower/tub, and vanity area. We note in the resort descriptions when Disney resort rooms offer other than these standard accommodations.

In addition, all Walt Disney World resort hotels have at least some rooms with the following **special equipment and facilities** for those with particular requirements. These rooms are available by special request (see pages 107–108). In general, the newer resorts (Pop Century, Coronado Springs, Disney's Animal Kingdom Lodge, and Saratoga Springs), or those most recently refurbished, have more and better special accommodations. The following special equipment or facilities are available:

© Deb Wills

In the **bathrooms**:
- ✔ Wider bathroom doors
- ✔ Bathroom handrails
- ✔ Roll-in showers
- ✔ Shower benches
- ✔ Hand-held shower head
- ✔ Accessible vanities
- ✔ Portable commodes
- ✔ Raised toilet seat with grab bar

In the **guest rooms**:
- ✔ Bed boards and bed rails
- ✔ Adjustable beds, lower beds, and rubber bed pads
- ✔ Open-frame beds
- ✔ Low-level peepholes in doors
- ✔ Refrigerators (charge may apply at value resorts)
- ✔ Closed captioned televisions
- ✔ Both upper and lower door locks on balcony doors
- ✔ Pack 'n' Play-style portable cribs (request when booking and also at check-in)
- ✔ Room Communication Kits with door knock and phone alerts, bed shaker alarm, Text Typewriter (TTY), strobe light fire alarm, and phone amplifier

A roll-in shower with bench, hand-held shower head, and rail at BoardWalk Villas

Some (not all) **accessible rooms** may have the following:
- ✔ Electrical switches 48" (1.2 meters) above the floor (including thermostat)
- ✔ Touch switch lamp
- ✔ Vanity open below sink (roll under)
- ✔ Lower countertops/cabinets
- ✔ Countertop microwave (in Disney Vacation Club resorts)
- ✔ Low threshold at balcony

Bright Idea: Consider Disney's newest resort, Saratoga Springs Spa and Resort—it was built with many special needs accommodations "standard." All accessible rooms in this resort are equipped for those with hearing impairments.

Also available on request at some **deluxe resorts**:

✔ Rollaway beds
✔ Down pillows
✔ Heating pads
✔ International electrical adapter
✔ Strollers
✔ Highchairs
✔ Electrical outlet covers

Reader Tip: "I'm hard of hearing and one of my biggest concerns—no matter where I'm staying—is hearing any alarms during the middle of the night (pretty much nothing wakes me up). So be sure to notify the cast member during check-in if you are hard of hearing so they can note it on your room assignment."—contributed by anonymous

Other special accommodations found throughout the **Disney resorts**:

✔ As mentioned in chapter 5, Disney transportation to and from the resorts is, for the most part, accessible for all vacationers. There are both buses with wheelchair lifts and buses that "kneel" (i.e., they lower to enable easy entry). Ferries, Friendships, cruisers, and monorails also have room and special locations for wheelchairs/ECVs and strollers.

✔ Braille signage (not at all resorts) to identify rooms, shops, restrooms, etc., and on elevator controls.

✔ Standard wheelchairs are available free at each resort on a very limited basis. A deposit is required, but the wheelchair may be used for the duration of your stay.

✔ Many resorts have at least one low counter at check-in for someone who's shorter or using a wheelchair/ECV. These are generally found at one of the far ends of the check-in counter.

✔ In the lobby or main building of all resorts, foreign-speaking visitors will find an international phone calling card machine with instructions in Spanish, Portuguese, German, French, and Japanese.

✔ While there are no companion restrooms in any of the Disney resort hotel lobbies that we could find, the Polynesian has one on the second floor across from 'Ohana restaurant, and there are others located in the pool areas of several resorts. We note their locations in the appropriate hotel description on the following pages.

✔ Accessible parking is available at each resort—be sure to have a valid handicapped parking permit or hang tag. If you are staying at a resort with valet parking, it is complimentary with the handicapped parking permit.

✔ Luggage assistance varies depending on your resort category. Although the value resorts offer luggage assistance, it can take up to 60 minutes for luggage to be delivered to your room. (It can also take that long for luggage pickup when you're departing.) The deluxe resorts offer immediate full-service bell services at check-in.

✔ If you have special dietary needs and plan to eat at your resort's restaurant(s), be sure to call the resort prior to your arrival.

✔ Sharps containers can be requested from Housekeeping.

Bright Idea: Once you arrive, visit the restaurant/food court and ask to speak to a chef—try to do this during off-peak hours if possible. Tell them exactly what your needs are, and be sure to mention any cross-contamination issues, too. Remember, the chefs are most accommodating to your requests when given at least 72 hours' notice. Ask the chef to point out any prepackaged food that would be okay, too!

Special Lodging for Special Guests (continued)

The **resort chefs** we spoke with were very helpful, offering suggestions and asking lots of questions. If you are unsure of anything when dining, ask for an ingredient list or speak with a chef. (We were pleasantly surprised to see the Food and Fun Court at the Contemporary prominently posted the ingredients for many of its baked goods.) See chapter 6 for more details on resort dining with special needs.

Here are more **important things you should know** about staying at the Disney resort hotels with special needs:

✔ Disney supplies soap and shampoo in its resorts; however, there are no brands or ingredients listed. If you use specific soap and shampoo at home due to allergies or sensitivity, be sure to bring them with you.

✔ For those with allergies and/or asthma, Disney's housekeeping service will provide special room cleanings and will also use special, less harsh, cleaning agents (see chapter 2 section on Allergies).

✔ While many of the deluxe resorts have childcare facilities on-site, these are only open to potty-trained children age 4–12. These "kids' clubs" do not babysit special needs children who require one-on-one attention. Speak to the child care club cast members in advance, and explain the special needs to determine whether your child can be accommodated. In-room babysitting is available from outside sources. See page 363.

✔ With the exception of Disney's Animal Kingdom Lodge, you'll find at least one path or walkway available for joggers, power walkers, and those wanting to stroll. If you have physical therapy or other exercises to do while at Disney, all deluxe and Disney Vacation Club resorts, as well as Coronado Springs, offer fitness facilities (see side bar page 72). Use of the facility is free to guests staying at that resort, or you can purchase a day pass for $12.

✔ All Disney hotels have swimming pools. A few have zero-entry access areas (see below). Water wheelchairs are available at most resorts with zero-entry access pools—request one from the lifeguard.

> **What's So Special About a "Zero-Entry" Pool?**
> Some resorts have primary theme pools with a "zero-entry" shoreline. This is a gradual slope into the pool, just like a real beach. It's ideal for those who are unable to step down into a traditional pool - instead, they can just wade into the water. Most pools with zero-entry also have a water wheelchair available, which can wheel right into the pool—ask a lifeguard about availability. The resorts that currently have zero-entry pools are: Disney's Animal Kingdom Lodge, Grand Floridian Resort and Spa, Polynesian Resort, and Saratoga Springs.

Bright Idea: When you check in, ask if there is any "resort activity" information or schedule available. Also check with the lifeguards for daily pool activities.

✔ Automatic External Defibrillators (AEDs) are located in all pool areas and numerous other locations around the resorts—check the resort map for specific locations.

✔ All Disney resort hotels have at least one small playground, as well as an arcade.

✔ Bicycle and boat rentals are available at many resorts. Some offer a "family length-of-stay package," which can offer a good value.

✔ Most of the moderate and deluxe resorts offer hot tubs (called "spas").

✔ In-room doctor/dental care is available if necessary (see page 60 in chapter 2).

Making Special Reservations

Once you have an idea of where you want to stay at Disney, it's time to **make reservations**. You don't need to use a travel agent, but if you have a great travel agent, by all means consult him or her. Here's the lowdown on making reservations when you have special requests:

If you have **common special requests** (i.e., nonsmoking room, close to bus stop, etc.), make your reservations for all Walt Disney World resort hotels at 407-WDW-MAGIC (407-939-6244) or 800-828-0228 (Walt Disney Travel Company). When you make your reservations, explain your special needs and request they be noted on your reservation form. Be sure to state if your request is due to medical reasons so that you are guaranteed it is honored. Disney representatives can offer assistance in English, Spanish, Japanese, French, Portuguese, and German. If you have Internet access, you can research rooms and make reservations at http://www.disneyworld.com (click on "Resorts"). If you prefer, you can also make reservations via mail by writing to Walt Disney World at Box 10100, Lake Buena Vista, FL 32830.

If, however, your **special requests are unusual** and/or involve more than an accessible or a nonsmoking room, ask to speak with Walt Disney World Resort Special Reservations or call directly at 407-939-7807 and press "1" (voice) or 407-939-7670 (TTY). This department works with you to determine what accommodations are available in the hotel(s) you are interested in and then books your reservation. They also note on your reservation what accommodations you need. They will preassign a room and block it for you. If you have a travel agent, make sure they know to talk to the Special Reservations folks when making your arrangements.

Remember to **mention all of your special requests** when making your Disney resort hotel reservations. Here are some request ideas:

✔ Unable to walk long distances or have other mobility concerns? Request a room near a bus stop or near central services.

✔ Have a traveler with an aversion to loud noises? Request a quiet room away from pool/elevator and common areas.

✔ Have a wheelchair or are you a person of size? Request a room with a king bed, which is generally more spacious. (King rooms may carry an additional charge.)

✔ Fear of heights? Request a lower floor.

✔ Traveling with an infant? Request a crib or bed rails. Some resorts have highchairs available, too.

✔ Traveling with someone with medications that need to be kept cold? Request a refrigerator, if not standard in your room.

✔ Does someone in your party have a visual impairment? Request a first floor room that is near the bus stop and/or food court.

✔ Are you a little person or short of stature? Request a stepstool for the room.

Planning

Your Special Need

Getting There

Staying in Style

Touring

Feasting

Resources

Index

Making Special Reservations (continued)

If you have a **particular location or room in mind** (we make suggestions later on), be sure to tell the reservations agent. It's best to make your request as general as possible. You'll have better luck requesting a "ground floor room near a bus stop" rather than simply "room 109." If Disney doesn't know why you want room 109, they can't choose a suitable substitute. Disney will not guarantee a particular room or view, but if your request is "in the system," they will try their best to accommodate you. If you have more than one request, make them in order of priority.

Four to five days prior to arriving at your hotel, call and speak to the front desk and ask for the room assignment cast member. Go over with them what accommodations you requested and **confirm their availability**. If you have specific needs, ask if the room can be blocked for you, so that it isn't given away. The earlier in the day you arrive, the better your chances of being accommodated. We've created an easy, fill-in-the-blanks form for you to use when making phone calls (or when checking in) at: http://www.passporter.com/wdw/resortrequest.htm.

In the rare instance that after all your prearrival work, you arrive and there is no room to accommodate your needs, pull out whatever correspondence you have about the room and **request to be placed in a comparable room** on Disney property that can accommodate your needs.

Checking In

Check-in time at most Disney resorts is either 3:00 pm or 4:00 pm—we specify in the individual resort descriptions. This is a good time to restate your special requests and see if the appropriate room is blocked for you. The problem is, everyone wants to check in at the same time, which makes check-in especially difficult if you have small children or travelers who are unable to wait in long lines for various reasons. Here are some strategies for making check-in a bit easier:

Check in as soon as you arrive, even if it's well before "official" check-in time. Sometimes you may be pleasantly surprised that a room is available. Even if one is not, however, you may still let them know you're on property and then can leave your baggage with Bell Services while you wait wherever you choose—get a meal, visit a theme park, sightsee around the resort, even go swimming. If you check in before your room is ready, some resorts will give you a phone number to call, along with your inactivated room keys. Once the room is ready, they will give you the room number—you don't need to check in again.

If you do encounter a line when you check in, though, there is always a small area with child-size seating and a TV playing Disney videos nearby—a kids' waiting area. Most are in plain view, so while you wait in the queue, you can keep your eyes on the little ones. If you are unable to stand in the line for a long time, check with Bell Services and inquire about the availability of a wheelchair.

Once at the front desk, be sure to go over any special requests you made in advance. This is the best time to correct any problems.

Resort Key

Room Locations—Room locations, such as a building or room number, can be requested, but are not guaranteed. However, if you note your preferences when you make your reservation and again when you check in, there is a chance you will get the room you want. Resort maps and suggestions are given for each resort in this chapter. If you don't like the particular room you've been assigned, do as you would with any hotel and politely ask for another.

Room Occupancy—All resorts have rooms that hold at least four guests, plus one child under three in a Pack 'n' Play crib. There is an extra charge for more than two adults in a single room. Some Port Orleans Riverside (Alligator Bayou) rooms accommodate up to five guests (they have an optional trundle bed). Many of the deluxe resorts and the Fort Wilderness Cabins can sleep five or more in a room. The two-bedroom villas in the Disney Vacation Club resorts can accommodate up to eight.

Amenities—All rooms have the basics: television with remote control, phone, drawers, clothing rod with hangers, small table, chairs, and simple toiletries. Additional amenities differ at each resort and are detailed later. If your room doesn't have a coffeemaker, alarm clock, or iron/ironing board, request it from housekeeping.

Check-Out Time—Check-out time is 11:00 am. If you need to check out a bit later, ask the front desk early that morning. If the resort isn't busy, they may grant your request at no extra cost. You can also leave your bags with Bell Services to go play in the parks. Another option is to use Magical Express or the resort airline check-in process (see page 98).

Childcare—Child care "clubs" are available in some of the deluxe resorts (refer to the chart on page 112), but they only take potty-trained children ages 4–12. Speak to the childcare club cast member in advance to determine whether accommodations for your child are possible. In-room sitting from non-Disney vendors is available. See page 371.

Concierge—All of the deluxe resorts offer concierge services, which give you extra perks like a continental breakfast, afternoon snacks, and planning services. Tell the valet when you arrive at the resort that you are staying on the concierge level and you may be able to bypass the regular check-in line. Concierge services are associated with certain rooms (often on the higher floors) and come at a higher rate.

Data Services (Internet)—All phones have data ports. Look for a local access number before you arrive (Celebration is a local call, Kissimmee is not). Each local call you make is 75 cents. You must include the area code (407) in all local calls. The front desk will also receive your faxes for a fee. Most resorts now have high-speed Internet access for $9.95 for a continuous 24-hour period; some even have public areas with wireless internet (Wi-Fi).

Disabled Access—All Disney resorts offer accommodations and access for differently abled guests. For details and reservations, call Walt Disney World Resort Special Reservations at 407-939-7807 (voice) or 407-939-7670 (TTY). Be sure to ask that "Special Needs" be noted on your reservation.

Extra Magic Hour—A special program for Disney resort guests in which a park opens one hour earlier or stays open several hours later than usual each day. With the lower crowds during these early/late hours, your wait times are minimal—you can often see and do more in that time than you can throughout the rest of the day. We strongly suggest you take advantage of this feature. The schedule changes from week to week—call 407-939-4636 or check http://www.disneyworld.com for the schedule during your visit.

Resort Key (continued)

Food—Every resort has some type of dining option—food courts, cafés, fine dining, and/or room service. All resort eateries are described in detail in chapter 6. If you are looking for snack food or groceries, each resort has a general store with a small selection of foodstuffs and drinks. No gum is sold on property. If you have special dietary needs and plan to eat at your resort, it's best to stop by and speak to the chef early in your visit.

Housekeeping Services—Every Disney resort has daily housekeeping services. Request extra towels, toiletries, rubber sheets, extra linens, pillows, and blankets, as well as hairdryers, irons, and ironing boards from Housekeeping. Disney can also provide special room cleanings for those with allergies or chemical sensitivities. Request these special services when you make your reservations and again at check-in. Note: Disney Vacation Club (DVC) resorts provide less frequent housekeeping services to DVC members or their guests using DVC points.

Ice and Soda—All resorts have ice machines nearby. Most, but not all, have soda machines. If soda is important, pick some up before you arrive. Another option is to purchase a refillable souvenir mug (offered at most resorts) for free refills of soda, coffee, tea, and cocoa at your resort—see "Refillable Mugs" on the next page.

Information—Check the Walt Disney World information channels on your in-room TV (closed caption channels available). These channels are available at every resort and offer a nice introduction for newcomers, plus a peek at what's new for veterans. You can also dial "0" from your Disney resort telephone to ask specific questions (TTY phones are available upon request—see "telephones" on next page).

Laundry—Every resort has either coin-operated machines in a laundry room near the pool (expect to pay eight quarters/load) or a washer and dryer in your room. One- and two-bedroom and grand villas have stacked washers/dryers in the room that come with a small box of powdered laundry soap. Old Key West and The Villas at Wilderness Lodge offer complimentary self-service laundry facilities (no coins needed). Laundry bags and forms are available in your resort room for same-day laundering (but it's very expensive). Store your dirty laundry in the laundry bags.

Lobby Concierge—Formerly known as Guest Services. Each resort has a Lobby Concierge desk where you can purchase park passes, make dining arrangements, and find answers to just about any question. You can also connect to Lobby Concierge (and other Disney services) through a button on your in-room phone. At some resorts, Lobby Concierge is combined with the Front Desk staff.

Merchandise Delivery—Resort guests can have park and Downtown Disney purchases delivered free to their resort, usually by the next afternoon. Inquire before your purchase is rung up. Your package is delivered to your resort's gift shop for pickup, not your room.

Money—Cash, Disney Dollars, traveler's checks, The Disney Credit Card, MasterCard, Visa, American Express, Discover, Diner's Club, and JCB are accepted, as well as personal checks with proper ID. ATMs are located near the front desk. Make your room deposit over the phone or fax with the above credit cards or by mail with a credit card or check.

Parking—Secured, free, gated parking lots are available at all resorts; the deluxe resorts also offer valet ($7/day, free to those with a handicapped parking permit or tag). The Swan and Dolphin charge to park in their self-serve lot ($7) as well as for valet parking ($10/day or $14/overnight). Shades of Green charges $3 a day for regular parking. Show your resort ID or confirmation at the security gate—parking is reserved for resort guests and those using a resort's restaurants or recreation.

Pets—Pets are not allowed in the parks or resorts (except for a few campsites at Fort Wilderness—see page 140) unless they are service animals. Disney kennels will board pets for $6 per day, and resort guests may board their pets overnight for $9 per night. Although the kennels are designed primarily for dogs and cats, they can also accommodate birds, ferrets, small rodents, rabbits, and nonvenomous snakes. Owners must walk their pets three times a day. Epcot's kennel offers a dog-walking service for $2.50/walk.

Pools—Every Disney resort has at least one swimming pool, and most pools have some type of disabled access. Some pools have a platform or "transfer tier" for wheelchair users to lift themselves onto and slide into the water. Others have "zero-entry" entrances for wading into the water (see photo on page 142). Hours of operation vary, but usually the "theme" pools close in the evenings while the "quiet" pools stay open all night. Only guests staying at a resort can use its pool, though some resorts share pools and Disney Vacation Club members using their points have access to all but the Stormalong Bay pool complex at the Yacht & Beach Club and Uzima Springs Pool at Disney's Animal Kingdom Lodge (unless they are staying there, of course).

Recreation—Every resort has something to do, with many offering a wide variety of outdoor activities. You can visit another resort to use its recreational facilities (with the exception of swimming pools). Hours are seasonal—check upon arrival.

Refillable Mugs—Most resorts sell thermal mugs that can be refilled free or for a small fee at your resort for the duration of your stay. Mugs are about $12 and can generally be refilled at a resort's food court or snack shop. Beverages usually available include coffee, sodas, ice tea, and hot chocolate. Milk and juice are occasionally offered as refill options.

Refrigerators—All Disney moderate and deluxe resort rooms are equipped with (or will be soon) a small refrigerator, free of additional charge. In the value resorts (All-Stars and Pop Century) a refrigerator can be requested for $10/day (free if required to store medication). There are no refrigerators at the Swan and Dolphin, although they do have mini-bars.

Room Service—The deluxe resorts and some of the moderate resorts offer room service. Some resorts offer a pizza delivery service after 4:00 pm daily.

Security—Security at Disney has always been good, and since 9/11, security has visibly heightened. A gatehouse guards entry into every resort, and virtually everyone who drives through the resorts' gates is questioned. Show your photo identification and resort identification, or explain that you are checking in, dining, or using the recreational facilities at the resort if you arrive by car. All resort rooms have electronic locks that open with your resort ID for added security. In addition, you can store small valuables in your in-room safe (all Disney resorts have safes) or with the front desk.

Spa (hot tub)—There's at least one hot tub at every Disney resort, with the exception of the All-Stars, Fort Wilderness, Polynesian, and Pop Century. Traditional spa facilities (massages and manicures) are available at some resorts (see page 306).

Telephones—Pay phones equipped with a Text Typewriter (TTY) for those with hearing impairments are available in each resort lobby. Resort rooms with special communication kits are equipped with TTY phones also. All rooms have a phone and details on how to use it. Local, toll-free, and credit card calls are 75 cents each, while long-distance calls are the cost of the call plus a 50% surcharge. Use calling cards or a cell phone instead. Incoming calls are free.

Transportation—Every resort provides free, accessible transit to and from the parks via bus, boat, monorail, and/or pedestrian path. We list each resort's options and in-transit times in this chapter.

Wheelchairs—Wheelchairs can be borrowed from every resort (inquire at Bell Services). A deposit is required and availability is limited. (See Wheels! on pages 201–203.)

Resort Comparisons

It's clear that Disney has tried to address many of your special needs in the amenities and facilities that it provides in its rooms. So **how do you choose** which resort is the best one for you? There are lots of things to consider, obviously. For example, a traveler with allergies or asthma may not want to stay at the Animal Kingdom Lodge, with its wildlife on the resort grounds, or at a resort known for its dense wooded areas—e.g., Port Orleans Riverside or Fort Wilderness, with all the Spanish moss and trees.

In the **hotel descriptions** on the following pages, we've tried to present the information that is most relevant to visitors with special needs to help you in making your resort decision. In general, we provide a resort description (layout, ambience, theme), check-in experience, guest room types, dining options, amenities (pool, arcade, fitness facility, or other activities), quiet spots, and transportation options. At the end of each resort description, you'll find our overall rating, along with any specific special need considerations.

We've also provided the following **overview** of the various resorts' amenities, so that you can make your own quick comparison:

Kitchen facilities are present only in the villas/cabins of the indicated resorts.

	All-Star Resorts	Animal King. Lodge	Beach Club/Villas	BoardWalk Inn/Villas	Caribbean Beach	Contemporary	Coronado Springs	Dolphin	Fort Wilderness	Grand Floridian	Old Key West	Polynesian	Pop Century	Port Orleans	Saratoga Springs	Shades of Green	Swan	Wild. Lodge/Villas	Yacht Club
Resort Category (D=Deluxe, C=Disney Vacation Club, M=Moderate, V=Value)																			
Category	V	D	D/C	D/C	M	D	M	D	–	D	C	D	V	M	C	D	D	D/C	D
Total Rooms	5760	1293	785	910	2112	1041	1967	1509	1195	900	761	853	2880	3056	184	586	758	864	634
Occupancy	4	4-5	4-8	4-12	4	5	4	5	4-10	5	4-12	5	4	4-5	4-12	5	5	4-8	5
Kitchen Facilities*			✓	✓						✓					✓			✓	
Hi-Speed Internet			✓	✓		✓	✓	✓		✓					✓		✓	✓	✓
Monorail						✓				✓		✓							
Restaurants/Cafes	–	2	3	7	1	3	1	3	2	5	1	2	–	1	1	4	3	3	3
Character Meals		✓				✓			✓	✓		✓					✓		
Quick Service	3	1			1	1	1	1		1		1	1	2				1	
Room Service		✓	✓	✓	✓	✓	✓	✓		✓		✓			✓	✓	✓	✓	✓
Pools	6	1	3	3	7	2	4	2	2	2	4	2	6	7	3	2	2	2	3
Kid Pool	3	1	1	1	1	1	1	1	1	1	1	1	2	2	1	1	1	1	1
Health Club		✓	✓	✓		✓	✓	✓		✓	✓				✓	✓	✓	✓	✓
Child Care Club			✓	✓						✓		✓						✓	✓

Planning

Your Special Need

Getting There

Staying in Style

Touring

Feasting

Resources

Index

Disney's All-Star Resorts

The All-Star Movies, Music, and Sports resorts are economical, functional, and quite large. The first value resorts at Disney, they each have 1,920 rooms in themed, three-story, T-shaped buildings with elevators. These connected resorts all display **larger-than-life icons** to match the theming of the area, like the 35 ft. (10.6 m.) Buzz Lightyear in All-Star Movies, a three-story guitar in All-Star Music, and a 38 ft. (11.5 m.) surfboard in All-Star Sports.

Check-In
The main building of each resort (Cinema Hall, Melody Hall, and Grandstand Hall) houses the front desk/check-in, food court, bus depot, arcade, pool bar, and general store. A short-term check-in parking area is available nearby. Due to the size of these resorts, these central areas are often very noisy, with guests coming and going in all directions. **Check-in time is 4:00 pm**. There is often a long wait to check in to the All-Stars resorts due to the sheer number of rooms they have. To avoid the waits, we suggest you check in as soon as you arrive at Walt Disney World—sort of a "pre-check-in." It's a good time to drop off your luggage, too. Then you can leave to shop or play at the theme parks—check in "for real" later, when the crowds have subsided. See our sidebar on page 108 for other check-in strategies.

Important Note: The front desks here don't have low counters for guests in wheelchairs.

When your room is ready, you will have to walk to it—unless you have a car or your own wheels with you. There is **no internal transportation** system at the All-Stars, and the rooms here are very spread out. You can talk to Luggage Services about the availability of a wheelchair, if needed.

Guest Rooms
The 5,760 rooms at the three resorts are small (about 260 sq. ft./24 sq. m.) and fairly standard—they have either two double beds or one king, a TV, and a table with two chairs. Refrigerators are available for $10/night. Room decor varies with the resort's particular theme—Movies features characters from Disney films; Music's motif is, well, musical; and Sports has baseballs, basketballs, footballs, etc.

Guest rooms face a pool, courtyard, or parking lot, with the occasional wooded view. **A $12 premium is added to the "preferred" buildings closest to the Main Hall** (reserved at the time of booking). Preferred buildings are Fantasia (All-Star Movies), Calypso (All-Star Music), and Surf's Up (All-Star Sports). Those farther away are generally quieter, but you'll also be walking/wheeling a distance to and from the bus stops and all other central services. Of the three All-Star resorts, the layout of Music is the simplest to navigate.

Despite being among the **smallest rooms at Walt Disney World**, the All-Star rooms can fit an ECV or wheelchair comfortably if you only have two people. If you have four, no matter if they are very small children, things will be tight with the wheelchair/ECV. If you want more room to move around, request a king room—just keep in mind that these tend to be the barrier-free rooms, and they may only have a shower, no tub.

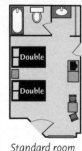

Double

Double

All rooms exit to the outside (no inner corridors), so you are exposed to the elements when you're going to main services or bus stops.

Standard room layout

Disney's All-Star Resorts
(continued)

Guest Rooms (continued)

For a **quieter stay**, request rooms facing away from the pool areas on the top (third) floor. Each building has an elevator, as well as partially covered outdoor stairs.

For **convenience** to food, bus stops, and the main pool, request these buildings: All-Star Movies—101 Dalmatians, Fantasia, or Toy Story; All-Star Sports—Surf's Up; and All-Star Music—Calypso.

© MediaMarx, Inc.

A standard room at All-Star Music Resort

Important Note: Be aware that at various times throughout the year, large and sometimes boisterous youth groups may be staying at these resorts (think cheerleaders, dance competitions, and Pop Warner football). Inquire about this when you check in.

Dining

Other than limited snacks at the general store, the only places to purchase food at the All-Star Resorts are the **food courts**. Each have several stations offering a variety of selections and a refrigerated section with prepackaged items like sandwiches, salads, fruit, etc. Some kosher foods are always available at the food courts without advance notice. There is also limited pizza delivery in the evenings. One microwave is available for guest use in each food court area.

Amenities

Each All-Star Resort has **two pools: a large themed pool and a smaller pool** that usually is less crowded. There are no water wheelchairs or zero-entry access points for the All-Star pools; however, each has a transfer tier for wheelchair users to lift themselves onto and slide into the water. The bathhouse at the All-Star Sports Home Run pool has a roll-in shower with bench and handrails.

Each All-Star Resort has a **small playground area**, good for letting off some steam. There is also a game arcade located in the main building of each resort, as well as a variety store selling souvenirs and sundries.

There are **no spa or fitness center facilities** at the All-Star Resorts, so if you require a gym for physical therapy or an exercise routine, you'll have to visit another resort on-site (see page 72). You may use any of those facilities for $12 per day, based on availability. The purchase of a spa treatment at any Disney health club includes use of the adjacent fitness center for the day of treatment.

Disney's All-Star Resorts
(continued)

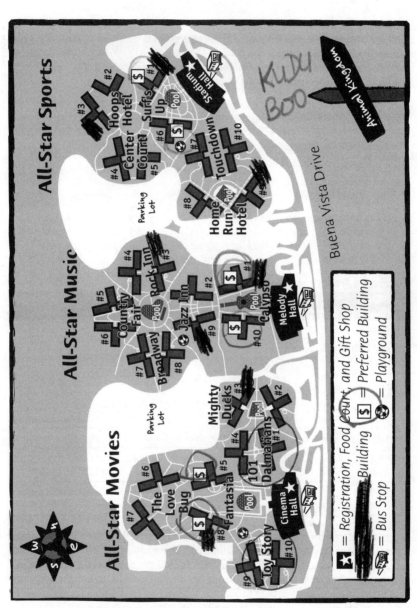

2005 standard room rates begin at $77 in value season, $99 in regular season, $109 in peak season, and $119 in holiday season (seasons are indicated on page 93). Preferred rooms (see preferred buildings marked on map above) run $12 more per room.

Disney's All-Star Resorts
(continued)

Quiet Spots

As big as these resorts are, there are **a few quiet spots** to be found. At All-Star Movies, look for the hammocks behind the palm trees near Fantasia. All-Star Music has picnic tables in the Country Fair courtyard and a small garden with benches in Broadway. All-Star Sports has a large covered pavilion in the back. You'll also find at least one small landscaped area with benches at each resort.

To get away from the loud hustle and bustle of the food court, there are tables and chairs outside that may be quieter. Keep in mind, though, that these are subject to weather conditions and also tend to be smoking areas. You can always bring your food back to the room.

Transportation

Disney transportation to the parks from these resorts is via **buses**. For other destinations, transfer at a nearby theme park (daytime) or at Downtown Disney (evening).

Waits for buses to and from the All-Stars can be long, especially at park opening and closing times. The queues wind around and can get very crowded—in fact, it is not uncommon to have standing room only on the buses. Sometimes a single bus will service all three of the All-Star resorts. All-Star Sports is the first stop in both directions in this case.

Estimated Transportation Times

Magic Kingdom	Epcot	Disney-MGM Studios	Disney's Animal Kingdom	Downtown Disney
direct bus ~20 min.	direct bus ~10 min.	direct bus ~10 min.	direct bus ~10 min.	direct bus ~15 min.

Approximate time you will spend in transit from resort to destination during normal operation.

Our Special Needs Ratings

The All-Star Resorts are great for the budget, but not for amenities. They **rank low to medium**, primarily due to their layout.

[A][U][S]	Can be very busy and noisy in the pools and central areas.
[C][♥][T] [M][P][E]	Unless you are in a preferred building, have a car, or use a wheelchair, we do not recommend the All-Star Resorts due to their sprawling design.
[D][W]	Food court chefs can accommodate with minimum 72 hours' notice. Kosher foods are available on a regular basis at the food courts here.
[F]	Larger-than-life icons could scare some.
[S]	For a more relaxing experience, consider staying at a moderate, deluxe, or Disney Vacation Club resort.
[L]	Be sure to request a king bed.

Disney's All-Star Movies/Music/Sports Resorts

1901/1801/1701 W. Buena Vista Dr., Lake Buena Vista, FL 32830
Phone: 407-939-7000/407-939-6000/407-939-5000
Fax: 407-939-7111/407-939-7222/407-939-7333

Disney's Animal Kingdom Lodge

The **most unique resort on Disney property**, Disney's Animal Kingdom Lodge surrounds you with the sights, sounds, cuisine, and even the animals of Africa. In fact, this deluxe resort was designed to resemble an African "kraal" village and has its own 33-acre savanna, which is home to more than 200 mammals and birds.

Check-In

The self-parking area is a fair distance from the Lodge entrance—there are a few steps or a ramp to reach the main entrance. To avoid this, consider valet parking ($7/night or complimentary with a handicapped parking tag).

Check-in is at 3:00 pm. Bell Services will assist in taking your luggage to your room. Rooms located at the end of a long hallway, or "trail," can be a significant distance from the front desk or elevator—ask at Bell Services if a wheelchair is available if you need one.

Guest Rooms

This deluxe resort offers **two sizes of rooms**, all decorated in African-style prints. The standard rooms (floors 1–4) are 344 sq. ft. (32 sq. m.) and come with either two queen beds, one king bed plus a daybed, or one queen bed with bunk beds. The deluxe rooms (floors 5 and 6) are 381 sq. ft. (35 sq. m.) and have an additional daybed or fold-out chair single bed. All rooms also have a ceiling fan, table and chairs, TV and armoire, and double sinks in the bath area. In addition, they are equipped with a hairdryer, coffeemaker with coffee packets, wall safe, iron, and ironing board. Newspaper delivery, room service, and voice mail are also available. Concierge service offers additional amenities, as well as a lounge and unique animal-viewing safaris (for an additional fee).

Accessible rooms offer a king bed, roll-in shower, tub, and accessible seat for toilet. You can also request a "Room Communication Kit" with visual smoke alarm, bed boards and rails, egg crate mattress pad, bottle warmer, humidifier, rubber bath mat, and "sharps" container for used needles.

Standard room layout

The entire resort is one structure, so **all rooms exit into a hallway**, not to the outdoors. As we noted earlier, though, hallways can be very long—if you have a problem walking/wheeling any distance, remember to request a room close to the lobby.

All rooms have a balcony—the minimum size is four feet long. If animal watching is the main reason you want to stay at the Lodge, be sure to reserve a savanna view. Rooms that face the animal savanna have special restrictions—no smoking and no throwing or dropping things off the balcony (for the protection and safety of the animals). There are security cameras that monitor balcony activity.

Planning

Your Special Need

Getting There

Staying in Style

Touring

Feasting

Resources

Index

Disney's Animal Kingdom Lodge
(continued)

Dining

Disney's Animal Kingdom Lodge's two table-service restaurants, **Boma and Jiko**, are very **vegetarian/vegan friendly**. Even so, as we note in chapter 2, it's important to call 72 hours ahead of time to alert the chefs to your special needs. But if you forget to call in advance, we've found that the chefs at Boma in particular are happy to walk you around the buffet, pointing out what you can and can't eat after you explain what foods you need to avoid. Note that quick service dining at **Mara** or room service are your only lunch options at this resort. See chapter 6 for our in-depth descriptions of dining options.

Amenities

This is a beautiful hotel with many amenities, but there are three major drawbacks: the resort is **isolated**, there are no walking/jogging trails, and the rooms are dark and poorly lit. Those with vision impairments may have problems seeing, especially in the bathroom vanity area.

Most services are within the main resort, but you have to go outdoors to reach the pool; Mara, the quick-service restaurant; Pumbaa's Fun and Games arcade; and the Zahanati Fitness Center. Disney's Animal Kingdom Lodge also has several public savanna viewing areas, located inside as well as outside.

There is one large pool, Uzima Springs, which has **zero-entry access**, as well as a water wheelchair available. There's a play area located nearby. There is no quiet pool here.

If you want to **maintain an exercise routine**, the resort has the Zahanati Fitness Center with exercise equipment, steam room, sauna, and massage therapies (for an extra fee).

Zawadi Marketplace is the **retail shop** celebrating the romantic and adventuresome spirit of Africa through the stories and cultures represented in its merchandise. Limited sundries and food are available here. See below for a list of common items of interest to travelers with special needs, as well as approximate prices.

Typical Grocery/Sundry Items

Found in Deluxe/Disney Vacation Club resort shops (prices as of May 2005)

Item	Price	Item	Price
Off insect repellent (6 oz.)	$7.25	Electrical adapter	$8.50
Imodium (6 caplets)	$5.25	Speedo earplugs	$3.25
Cortaid	$3.25	Fruit	$0.99
Pepcid AC (6 tablets)	$5.00	Muffins (no fat-free available)	$2.99
Advil (20 liquid-filled caplets)	$6.75	Bread	$2.89
Benadryl (24 tablets)	$8.00	Peanut butter	$2.85
Tylenol (24 extra strength)	$6.00	Sugar-free gummy candy (4 oz.)	$2.75
Bayer aspirin	$3.30	Pop-Tarts	$3.25
Dramamine	$2.75	Coffee (Folgers brick)	$4.50
Diapers	$8.50	Fat-free milk (quart)	$1.75
Swimming diaper	$1.60	Good Start Formula (powder)	$13.35
Adult diapers (Serenity Pads, 14)	$11.50	Baby food (jar)	$0.95+

Disney's Animal Kingdom Lodge
(continued)

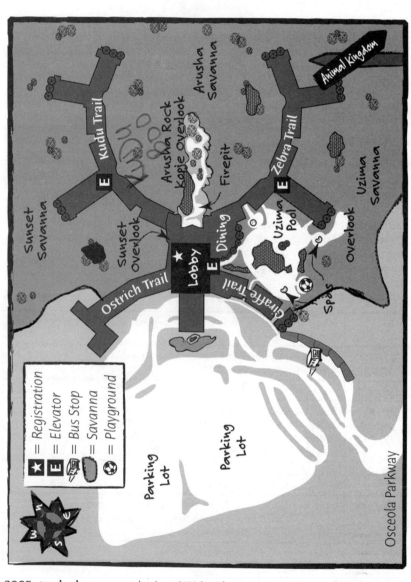

2005 standard room rates begin at $199 in value season, $239 in regular season, $289 in peak season, and $324 in holiday season (seasons are indicated on page 93). Pool view rooms are about $26–$30 higher. Savanna view rooms are $81–$96 higher than standard rooms. Deluxe rooms (available in both water/pool and savanna view) are $86–$186 higher than standard rooms. Concierge rates begin at $435 in value season, $490 in regular season, $555 in peak season, and $620 in holiday season. Suites are also available starting at $640 for a one-bedroom in value season.

Planning
Your Special Need
Getting There
Staying in Style
Touring
Feasting
Resources
Index

Disney's Animal Kingdom Lodge
(continued)

Transportation

All Disney **transportation from this resort is via bus**. As you exit the main lobby, the bus station is down to the left. From here, you can get to the theme parks, water parks, and Downtown Disney. The buses that service the Lodge do not stop at other resorts. If you want to travel to other resorts, travel from Disney's Animal Kingdom or another theme park (day) or from Downtown Disney (evening) and transfer to the appropriate bus.

Estimated Transportation Times

Magic Kingdom	Epcot	Disney-MGM Studios	Disney's Animal Kingdom	Downtown Disney
direct bus ~20 min.	direct bus ~15 min.	direct bus ~10 min.	direct bus ~5 min.	direct bus ~15 min.

Approximate time you will spend in transit from resort to destination during normal operation.

Our Special Needs Ratings

Disney's Animal Kingdom Lodge is one of our favorite places at Disney to relax and get away from it all! It's great for those wanting a quiet, laid-back atmosphere. Author Deb Wills could sit on the balcony all morning watching the animals (in fact, she has done just that!). We rate the lodge **medium-high** with lots of amenities but some drawbacks, as noted.

[G]	The savannas are kept very clean, but depending on allergies/asthma, the animals could be an issue.
[C][♥][T] [M][P][E]	Request a room near the lobby if you need shorter walking/wheeling distances.
[D]	Very accommodating for special dietary requests with 72 hours' notice.
[F]	There are two gas firepits at Disney's Animal Kingdom Lodge, one just off the main lobby and one outside in the Arusha Rock area. Also, the animals are not very close and are behind barriers, but those with a fear of wild creatures may be uncomfortable in this setting.
[Ö]	Many of the cast members at this resort are from Africa and are more than willing to share the language and culture of their native countries.
[L]	For more room, request a king bed or book a deluxe category room. Some rooms have bunk beds—if this would be a problem for you, remember to ask for a room without.
[V]	Rooms tend to be dark with low lighting.

Disney's Animal Kingdom Lodge Resort

2901 Osceola Parkway, Bay Lake, FL 32830
Phone: 407-938-3000 Fax: 407-938-7102

Disney's BoardWalk Inn & Villas Resort

The BoardWalk Inn and its adjacent Disney Vacation Club sibling, the BoardWalk Villas, share a **premium location on Crescent Lake** between Epcot and Disney-MGM Studios. With a seashore theme designed to conjure up the feel of the old-time Atlantic City Boardwalk, these resorts have furnishings in pastel blues, greens, and yellows. The boardwalk that they sit on features fantastic water views, as well as a variety of entertainment and dining options.

Check-In

Ample parking is available at this resort, but the self-parking area is a few minutes' walk/ wheel uphill to the lobby. There's also valet parking ($7/day, or complimentary if you're a DVC member staying using points or if you have a handicapped tag). Check-in for both sides of the resort (**3:00 pm at the Inn; 4:00 pm at the Villas**) is done in the common lobby. On the far left of the check-in counter, there's a lower counter to provide easier access for those in a wheelchair.

Bell Services assists in **delivering your luggage to your room**. Because this is a deluxe resort, all rooms exit into a hallway, not to the outdoors (except for Garden Suites; see below).

Guest Rooms

BoardWalk Inn, located on the right as you stand at the entrance with the parking lot/bus stop behind you, has 378 rooms with water, garden, or standard views. Each room is about 435 sq. ft. (40.4 sq. m.) and has one king or two queen beds, plus a 5-foot daybed or queen sleeper sofa. There are 191 nonsmoking rooms. The BoardWalk Inn also has several suites, including 14 separate romantic Garden Suites (about 1,000 sq. ft./93 sq. m.) that resemble two-story cottages, complete with white picket fence. Suites have a separate living room, sleeper sofa, and a wet bar on the first floor, while the open second floor has a king-size bed, a separate shower, and a large whirlpool tub. Garden Suites have an outside entrance.

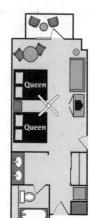

Standard room layout (Inn)

BoardWalk Villas, on the left, feature 532 studios and one-, two-, and three-bedroom suites that range from 359 to 2,142 sq. ft. (33.4 to 199 sq. m.) Because all Villas rooms feature kitchen facilities, these accommodations are ideal for travelers with special dietary needs. Other amenities include a private balcony or patio, hair dryer, iron, ironing board, and vacuum cleaner. All except studios also have a washer, dryer, and DVD player. All rooms also have double sinks, a marble vanity, a table and chairs, sofa, armoire, TV, ceiling fan, toiletries, turndown service (on request), voice mail, and, for most rooms, newspaper delivery. 292 of the rooms are designated nonsmoking.

If you want to **avoid noise**, especially that of the BoardWalk entertainment venues, request a room overlooking the beautifully landscaped courtyards, away from the promenade and the pools.

Planning
Your Special Need
Getting There
Staying in Style
Touring
Feasting
Resources
Index

Disney's BoardWalk Inn & Villas Resort
(continued)

Dining

The BoardWalk is unique, in that most of its dining and entertainment options are **located along the promenade** outside the resort. There are a number of table-service restaurants and quick snack spots, but Spoodles in particular is known for its healthier, lighter Mediterranean menu. Flying Fish is, as the name indicates, primarily a seafood restaurant—it's a great choice for diners who want to eat light and healthy, but those with fish or shellfish allergies might want to avoid it. Room service is also available, and there's a great selection of food items in the Screen Door General Store on the promenade. (Dundy's Sundries, just off the main lobby, has a much more limited selection of items.) See page 118 for a list of typical items available that are of particular interest to special needs travelers. For in-depth descriptions of all the BoardWalk's dining options, see pages 348-349.

Amenities

Trying to maintain an **exercise routine** while on vacation? The BoardWalk has Muscles and Bustles Fitness Center with exercise equipment, steam room, sauna, and massage therapies (for an extra fee). There are also bikes for rent at the resort's recreation center, Community Hall, and surrey bikes on the BoardWalk. In addition, there are two lighted tennis courts. The almost one-mile walkway around Crescent Lake and the path to Disney-MGM Studios are both excellent for walking, jogging, or wheeling.

The main pool, **Luna Park**, has a decidedly carnival feel—in fact, the 200-ft. slide is known as Keister Coaster. Swimmers exit the slide through the mouth of a large clown head—if you have a fear of clowns (we hear some folks do!), you might want to avoid this. Try the two other heated pools or one of the three hot tubs (one near each pool). There's also a wading pool for infants at Luna Park—remember diaper-age children must wear snug-fitting plastic pants or special swimming diapers when in the water. All BoardWalk pools have transfer tiers. Automated External Defibrillators (AEDs) are located at each of the pools and at numerous locations throughout the resort.

The **arcade**, Side Show Games, is located near the health club, and there are also carnival-type games on the BoardWalk itself most nights. If you're looking for a place for your kids to cavort, there's also a playground located adjacent to Luna Park.

Quiet Spots

If you need a quiet retreat, the **Belle Vue Room**, off by itself down the hall from the lobby on the Inn side of the resort, is a good bet during the day, when the bar isn't open. There are overstuffed chairs and sofas to relax in. There are also backgammon, chess, and checkers tables (ask a cast member for game pieces). When the bar is open, it may get crowded with noisy groups. There are several quiet sitting areas scattered throughout the resort's buildings, and the gardens near the Garden Suites have benches perfect for resting and soaking in the sun. If you're over on the Villas side of the resort, some floors have over-sized seating areas in the middle of the hallway that are usually quiet during the day.

Accessible bathroom in the Villas

© Deb Wills

Planning | Your Special Need | Getting There | Staying in Style | Touring | Feasting | Resources | Index

Disney's BoardWalk Inn & Villas Resort
(continued)

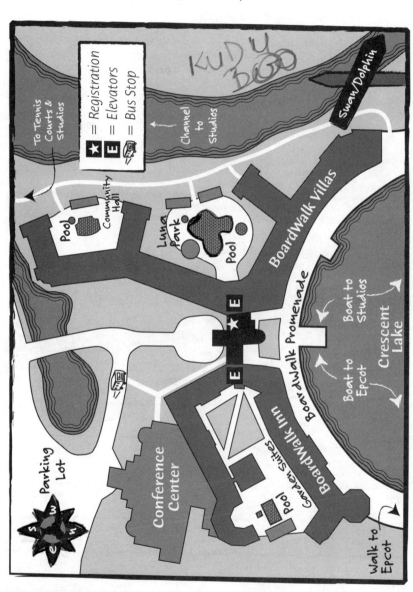

2005 standard room rates at BoardWalk Inn begin at $294 in value season, $334 in regular season, $404 in peak season, and $459 in holiday season (seasons are indicated on page 93). Water view rooms add $76-$96 more. Studio villas at BoardWalk Villas begin at $294 in value season, $334 in regular season, $404 in peak season, and $459 in holiday season. One-bedroom villas are $106-$131 more, two-bedroom villas are $266-$581 more, and three-bedroom grand villas are $1,066-$1,511 more.

Disney's BoardWalk Inn & Villas Resort
(continued)

Transportation

Transportation **options include buses**, which you board in the front of the resort (to the Magic Kingdom, Disney's Animal Kingdom, Downtown Disney, and the water parks) and boats, which depart from the marina (to Epcot and Disney-MGM Studios). You can also walk/wheel to Disney-MGM Studios, Epcot, Yacht & Beach Club, and the Swan & Dolphin. If you want to travel to other resorts, travel to a theme park (day) or to Downtown Disney (evening) and transfer to the appropriate bus.

Bright Idea: The buses and boats that service the BoardWalk also make stops at the other Epcot area resorts (Yacht and Beach Club, Swan and Dolphin) on their way to Epcot and the Studios. It is frequently quicker to walk to your destination if you are able to do so.

Estimated Transportation Times

Magic Kingdom	Epcot	Disney-MGM Studios	Disney's Animal Kingdom	Downtown Disney
direct bus ~20 min.	walk (wheel)/boat ~15/~5 min.	walk (wheel)/boat ~15/~20 min.	direct bus ~10 min.	direct bus ~15 min.

Approximate time you will spend in transit from resort to destination during normal operation.

Our Special Needs Ratings:

The BoardWalk Inn and Villas **rank high** on the special needs convenience scale, although they are not for those on a tight budget. The proximity to two theme parks, numerous dining and transportation options, and other amenities, make the BoardWalk area an attractive choice for vacationers who have a variety of special needs.

[A][U][S]	The pool area and rooms that front the promenade can be noisy, especially in the evenings.
[G] [D]	In-room kitchen facilities at the BoardWalk Villas are ideal for vacationers traveling with special dietary needs.
[R]	On the promenade, you'll find the Big River Grille and Brewing Works, a brewpub; Jellyroll's, a nightclub; and the ESPN Club—any of these might be a temptation for a person recovering from an alcohol addiction.
[B]	The Villas, with in-room kitchen facilities, are also ideal for vacationers traveling with an infant.
[C][♥][T] [M][P][E]	Request a room near the elevator or lobby if you need shorter walking/ wheeling distances.
[D]	Very accommodating for special dietary requests with 72 hours' notice.
[F]	The clown pool can be scary to some.
[V]	Rooms are bright and cheerful, with plenty of light.

Disney's BoardWalk Inn & Villas Resort

2 101 Epcot Resorts Blvd., Bay Lake, FL 32830
Phone: 407-939-6200 Fax: 407-939-5150

Disney's Caribbean Beach Resort

Take a trip to the tropics, mon, and enjoy the lush landscaping and colorful surroundings at the Caribbean Beach moderate resort. The islands, as each grouping of buildings is called, are named after actual islands in the Caribbean (Aruba, Jamaica, Trinidad, etc.) and encircle a 45-acre lake with white sandy beaches.

Check-In

The **Customs House**, front desk, and luggage service are located just inside the entrance to the resort. This is where you will be dropped off (or park) for check-in. Check-in time is 3:00 pm.

Luggage service is available. When your room is ready, check with Bell Services at the Custom House. Someone will take you and your luggage to your building (a wheelchair-accessible van is sometimes available) if you don't have your own car.

Guest Rooms

This resort has 2,112 rooms and is **so spread out** that it has its own internal bus system, which makes a full circle of the resort every 20–30 minutes. Due to the size of the resort, not all rooms are within easy walking/wheeling distance of the Old Port Royale Town Center, where the food court, restaurant, themed pool, and other guest services are housed, or even to the closest bus stop. We recommend renting a car or ECV if you have any mobility or waiting time concerns.

The rooms are located in two-story buildings and are the **largest of all the moderate resorts**—340 sq. ft (31.5 sq. m.). There are no elevators to take you upstairs (it's 17 steps to the second floor), so if a ground floor room is necessary for medical/mobility reasons or you have small children or a stroller, be sure to state that when you make your reservation—or consider another resort! Standard views are parking lot or courtyard, or you can request a water (pool or bay) view. We recommend the courtyard view, as it's difficult to enjoy the premium view—most folks don't want to keep the curtains open to see the view due to privacy concerns or fears.

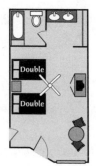

Standard room layout

Rooms have **one king bed or two doubles**, as well as a small table with two chairs, a TV in an armoire, and a ceiling fan. There are no balconies or patios, but there are coffeemakers, refrigerators, and limited room service available. You can also request a rollaway bed ($15) and an international electrical adapter from housekeeping.

A **$10 premium** is added to the rate of buildings closest to Old Port Royale (must be reserved at the time of booking). These "preferred" islands are Martinique and Trinidad North. Those further away will require quite a walk/wheel to and from the food areas. For more "secluded" islands, request Aruba, Jamaica, or Trinidad South.

All rooms exit to the outside (there are no inner corridors) so you will be exposed to the elements when you go to the main services, and passers-by may peer in through your windows. If you are not in one of the preferred islands, you will have a distance to travel to get to Old Port Royale. Your options are to use a car or the internal bus transportation.

126   Chapter 4: Staying in Style   Topic: Caribbean Beach Resort

Planning

Your Special Need

Getting There

Staying in Style

Touring

Feasting

Resources

Index

Disney's Caribbean Beach Resort
(continued)

Dining

Market Street Food Court offers a variety of stations with a central cash register area. Offerings include pizza/pasta, a hamburger shop, grab-and-go market, and Bridgetown Broiler. Some kosher items are available here without advance notice. **Shutters**, the full-service restaurant, is open for dinner only with American cuisine inspired by the flavors of the Caribbean. (See chapter 6.) There is also limited room service available in the evenings—just pizza and sandwiches.

Important Note: Chairs here are sturdy and wooden with no arms. For a less congested area during breakfast and lunch hours, seating is available in the Shutters restaurant area.

Amenities

Old Port Royale Town Center, which houses the gift shop, Market Street Food Court, Spanish fort-themed pool, Banana Cabana pool bar, and Shutters, a full-service restaurant, is located about one mile from the Customs House.

In addition to the main themed pool, **each island has its own "quiet" pool**. While there are no zero-entry pools here, some pools have a transfer tier for wheelchair users to lift themselves onto and slide into the water.

Most of the **"island" pools have ramps** to enter the pool deck area, but Martinique has steps around the pool area. Look behind the pool near the laundry building to find the only ramp. At the other villages, if you find steps leading to the pool area on one side, be sure to check around the "islands." For instance, at Trinidad South, there are steps on the lake side, but flat entrances on the other sides. If you have a car or don't mind hopping on a bus, try another village if one pool is crowded.

Caribbean Beach offers **numerous activities**. You can rent boats and bicycles, jog/walk around the bay, check out the video games in Goombay Games Arcade, swim in the pools, enjoy three playgrounds, or walk to Parrot Cay, a lush hideaway with tropical birds in the middle of Barefoot Bay.

There are **no spa or fitness center facilities** at Caribbean Beach, so those who require a gym for physical therapy or exercise routine will have to visit another Disney resort. You may use any of the Disney facilities for $12 per day, based on availability. The purchase of a spa treatment includes use of the adjacent fitness center for the day of treatment.

Reader Tip: You can actually see Epcot's higher fireworks from the beach between Martinique and Trinidad North. Just look across the water toward Aruba.—contributed by peer reviewer Sue Mickelson

Quiet Spots

Quiet spots can be found throughout the resort. There are a number of small, lush areas with a bench here and there to **enjoy the quiet of the resort**. The beach walk around Barefoot Bay also has places to sit, rock in a hammock, or just enjoy the quiet. It's especially beautiful and peaceful at sunrise.

Disney's Caribbean Beach Resort

(continued)

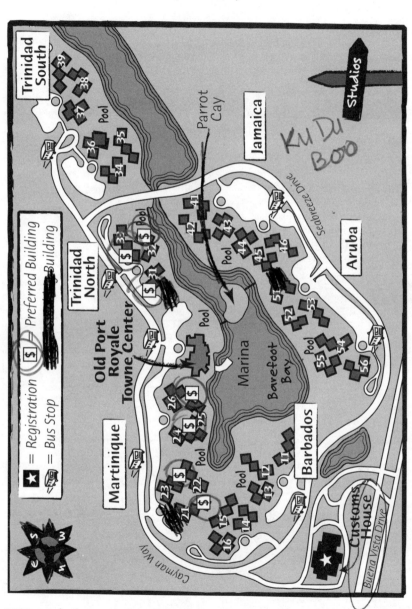

2005 standard room rates begin at $134 in value season, $149 in regular season, $169 in peak season, and $184 in holiday season (seasons are indicated on page 93). A water view, king bed, or preferred room adds $15 more to the above rates. Preferred rooms are in Martinique and Trinidad North, as noted in the map above.

Disney's Caribbean Beach Resort
(continued)

Transportation

All Disney **transportation here is via dedicated bus** (buses don't stop at other resorts en route). There are seven bus stops, one for each island and one at Old Port Royale.

Estimated Transportation Times

Magic Kingdom	Epcot	Disney-MGM Studios	Disney's Animal Kingdom	Downtown Disney
direct bus ~20 min.	direct bus ~15 min.	direct bus ~12 min.	direct bus ~20 min.	direct bus ~25 min.

Approximate time you will spend in transit from resort to destination during normal operation.

Our Special Needs Ratings:

Caribbean Beach Resort is a quiet, well-landscaped resort with a beautiful lake where one can relax and enjoy a slower pace. The large, sprawling layout of the resort and separation of the check-in/luggage facility from the Old Port Royale make it more important for those with special needs to have a car or stay in a preferred location.

Our Special Needs Convenience Scale

[C][♥][T][M][P][S]	Request a preferred building or have a car with you.
[D][W]	A selection of kosher menu items is available at the food court without prior notice.
[P]	Lots of places to walk/wheel and swim. Also has bicycle and boat rentals.
[S]	Active seniors or those with a car will enjoy the quiet, laid-back atmosphere of this resort.
[F]	There are lots of birds around this resort.
[L]	Rooms are largest of the moderate resort category. Remember to request a king-size bed ($15 extra).

Disney's Caribbean Beach Resort

900 Cayman Way, Lake Buena Vista, FL 32830
Phone: 407-934-3400 Fax: 407-934-3288

© MediaMarx, Inc.

Accessible toilet at Caribbean Beach Resort

Disney's Contemporary Resort

One of the two original Walt Disney World hotels, the deluxe Contemporary Resort offers wonderful views of the Seven Seas Lagoon, the Magic Kingdom, and Bay Lake. This is a full-service resort, complete with restaurants, pools, convention center, salon, fitness club, and much more. What's more, it's on the monorail loop that serves the Magic Kingdom.

Check-In
Check-in time is 3:00 pm. As you enter the lobby, you will find the check-in counter on your left (there are no low counters, however). There are some comfy chairs across the way, if you need to wait for others in line.

The resort's 1,041 guest **rooms are spread out** among the large A-frame section (the Tower) and two three-story wings (called Garden Wings). For tower guests, elevators take you to your floor. Those in the wings walk/wheel to their rooms. Bell Services will bring your luggage to your room within 15 to 20 minutes of your request. If you choose to take advantage of the ample self-parking, you can drop your luggage off first, park, and then check in (note that the self-parking area is closer to the Wings than to the Tower). Valet parking is available ($7 or complimentary with a handicapped tag). If you are staying in the Garden Wings, ask the valet to keep your car nearby while you check in so you can drive over.

Guest Rooms
Rooms are spacious (about 436 sq. ft./40.5 sq. m.) and have either two queen beds or one king, as well as a daybed. The decor is very, well, contemporary, with bright colors and geometric patterns. Other furnishings include a table with chairs, an armoire with a TV, coffeemaker, hair dryer, a generous-sized bathroom with two sinks, and a massage shower head. Newspaper delivery and turndown service are both available. Rollaway bed ($15) may be added to king-bed rooms. You may also request an international electrical adapter.

Garden Wing rooms have **standard or garden/water views**; Tower rooms have views of Bay Lake or Seven Seas Lagoon. Tower rooms have balconies, while the Garden Wings offer first-floor patios (very few rooms in the Wings have balconies).

The Contemporary offers **two levels of concierge**—full service on the 14th floor and "concierge light" on the 12th. If this is something you desire, we highly recommend the full-service 14th floor!

Most rooms have two queen beds and a daybed, although there are also king-bed rooms.

If mobility is a concern, reserve a room in the Tower near an elevator, not in one of the Garden Wings. You'll pay a premium to stay in the Tower, but you'll also have most services available inside the main building. If you stay in the Garden Wings, you will be walking/traveling outside, sometimes in uncovered areas, to get to Disney transportation and resort services.

The **North Garden Wing** is closest to the food court, monorail, pathway to the Magic Kingdom, and bus stop. (The North Wing is 100 percent nonsmoking, by the way.) The South Garden Wing is closest to the pool and the convention center. Only the second floor in the South Wing is nonsmoking.

Standard room layout

Disney's Contemporary Resort
(continued)

Dining

The California Grill, on the Contemporary's 15th floor, is **one of the best restaurants** in Walt Disney World, known not only for great food and wine, but for its exceptional view of the Magic Kingdom. Several vegetarian options are always featured on the menu, but for more specific dietary requests, call 72 hours in advance. Chef Mickey's is a very popular character meal, serving breakfast and dinner. The restaurant is large and open, with characters all around and music that the characters dance to—it is a loud, busy place. The Concourse Steakhouse serves three meals a day and is adjacent to Chef Mickey's. The Food and Fun Center fast food area, which is open 24 hours, does not offer any kosher meals; however, they may be available from room service. Room service is available 24 hours a day. See chapter 6 for our specific ratings of the Contemporary's eateries.

Amenities

On the **first floor of the Tower** are the main lobby, check-in, Bell Services, Common Grounds (coffee bar with limited hours), and the Food and Fun Center (fast food and arcade). Some areas in the lobby and throughout this resort also have wireless internet (Wi-Fi) access available.

The **fourth-floor concourse** is where you'll find the monorail station (with service to the Magic Kingdom, Polynesian, Grand Floridian, and Transportation and Ticket Center), gift shops, Chef Mickey's character buffet, the Outer Rim lounge, and the Concourse Steakhouse.

There are **lots of things to do at the Contemporary**—jogging paths, volleyball, shuffleboard and tennis courts, and boat rentals are available. And for the more energetic, there's Sammy Duvall Water Sports Centre (http://www.duvallwatersports.com), which offers a variety of water experiences, including parasailing and skiing.

The **Olympiad Fitness Center** is free to resort guests staying at the Contemporary.

Two adjacent pools serve the resort. There's **no zero-entry pool**; however, there is a water slide and small fountain area for kids. Two hot tub/spas near the pools can help soothe those aching muscles after a day in the parks. The Sand Bar is located by the pool and is open with seasonal hours.

Go out to the beach and **watch the Magic Kingdom's fireworks**, or head to the fourth-floor concourse, which offers inside views. From Bay Lake-view rooms and the beach, you can watch the nightly Electric Water Pageant.

A **pin trading station** is located on the fourth floor across from the gift shops. Friday nights, the Contemporary hosts pin trading meets with special activities for children.

There is a **wheelchair "restroom,"** rather than just a stall, in the lobby restroom. The lobby's women's restroom also has a "Child Protection Seat" in one of the stalls to allow you to strap an infant securely in place while you're using the facilities.

Note that the Contemporary is undergoing a major guest room renovation that will last through 2006.

Disney's Contemporary Resort
(continued)

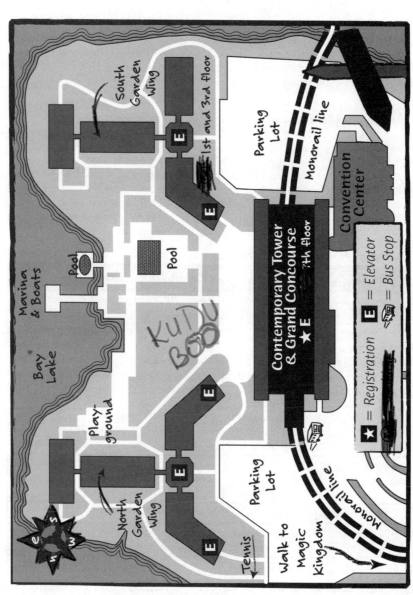

2005 standard room rates begin at $244 in value season, $274 in regular season, $319 in peak season, and $359 in holiday season (seasons are indicated on page 93). Garden Wing rooms are $46 more. Tower rooms are $101–$131 more than standard rooms. Concierge tower rooms start at $405 (add $90 for 14th floor rooms). Suites are also available starting at $800 for one-bedroom and $1,550 for two-bedrooms.

Planning

Your Special Need

Getting There

Staying in Style

Touring

Feasting

Resources

Index

Disney's Contemporary Resort
(continued)

Quiet Spots

There are areas around the grounds by the Garden Wings that offer **quiet places to walk/ wheel** and look out on the waterways. During the day, if there are no conventions, the second floor has a variety of comfy chairs and sofas and is generally unpopulated. In the evening, the second floor area near the elevator is the check-in for the California Grill.

Transportation

There are a **number of transportation options available** at the Contemporary. Disney transportation is via bus or boat, or you can take the monorail, which has an accessible station on the fourth floor. The Magic Kingdom is just a 10-minute walk away. Also on the monorail line are the Polynesian and Grand Floridian Resort and Spa. From the bus stop, located to the right as you exit the front of the resort, you can go to the other theme parks, water parks, and Downtown Disney. (Buses sometimes make stops at other resorts en route.) The boat will take you to Fort Wilderness or the Wilderness Lodge (a rare luxury to have any resort-to-resort transportation). Note that water levels and the type of boat in operation will determine whether it is wheelchair-accessible.

Estimated Transportation Times

Magic Kingdom	Epcot	Disney-MGM Studios	Disney's Animal Kingdom	Downtown Disney
monorail/walk ~20/~10 min.	monorail x 2 ~15 min.	direct bus ~20 min.	direct bus ~20 min.	direct bus ~35 min.

Approximate time you will spend in transit from resort to destination during normal operation.

Our Special Needs Ratings

The Contemporary **ranks very high** on our special needs convenience scale—it has a terrific location close to the Magic Kingdom and is on the monorail line. Convenience comes with a price, though—this is a deluxe-priced resort. The resort's varied transportation options (monorail, boat, bus, walking) and numerous other amenities make it an excellent choice for vacationers who have a variety of special needs.

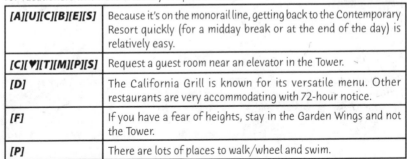

[A][U][C][B][E][S]	Because it's on the monorail line, getting back to the Contemporary Resort quickly (for a midday break or at the end of the day) is relatively easy.
[C][♥][T][M][P][S]	Request a guest room near an elevator in the Tower.
[D]	The California Grill is known for its versatile menu. Other restaurants are very accommodating with 72-hour notice.
[F]	If you have a fear of heights, stay in the Garden Wings and not the Tower.
[P]	There are lots of places to walk/wheel and swim.

Disney's Contemporary Resort
4600 North World Drive, Bay Lake, FL 32830
Phone: 407-824-1000 Fax: 407-824-3539

Disney's Coronado Springs Resort

Coronado Springs, located between Disney's Animal Kingdom and Disney-MGM Studios, is classified a "moderately priced" resort. Yet, because of its convention facilities, it **offers many amenities** normally found only in the deluxe hotels. The architecture and decor reflect the regions of Mexico and the American Southwest.

Check-In

Check-in time is 3:00 pm and takes place in El Centro, the main building, with a spacious lobby and high ceilings. There's one low counter on the far right for wheelchair/ECV accessibility.

The resort is fairly spread out, so getting to your room from El Centro can be as much as a **half-mile trip**. If you need assistance, ask when you check in, and a cast member will give you a lift to your room on a golf cart. Another option for getting around the resort is to hop on a bus at El Centro and ride around the resort to the stop nearest your building. If you require a wheelchair, there is a limited number available for your use at the resort. There's no charge, but a refundable deposit (usually $250) is required.

Guest Rooms

A **sprawling resort** of 1,921 rooms, Coronado Springs has three themed areas of accommodations situated around a 15-acre lake known as Lago Dorado. The main building, El Centro, houses registration and the shops and restaurants. It is located on the south side of the lake. Moving clockwise around the lake, the building areas are the three- and four-story Casitas, which represent the urban areas of the Southwest and Mexico; the rustic Ranchos, themed to reflect rural areas of the Southwest; and the two-story Cabanas, characterized by their sandy shorelines along the beach of the lake. All multistory buildings have elevators. Accessible rooms are located on the first floor of the Casitas 3 building, as well as on the first floor of buildings in the Ranchos and Cabanas.

Rooms are about 314 sq. ft. (29.17 sq. m.) with **two double beds (or one king)**, a television in an armoire with three drawers, table with two chairs, single sink vanity, and bathroom. Other amenities in the room include a four-cup coffeemaker with regular and decaf coffee packets, small refrigerators, a wall-mounted hair dryer, an iron and ironing board, high-speed Internet access, and a small wall safe. Newspaper delivery is available for $1.50/day. A number of junior, one-bedroom, and executive suites are also available.

A number of rooms **connect to the room next door**. Request this type of room if you're traveling with a companion. For nonsmokers, there are 1181 nonsmoking rooms. Smoking-optional rooms are located in Casitas 1, floors 3 and 4, and Cabanas 9A.

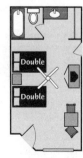

Standard
room layout

Disney's Coronado Springs Resort
(continued)

Buildings in **Cabanas 9B or Casitas 1 or 3 are nearest El Centro** and its bus stop—in fact, the pathway to rooms in the Casitas is fully covered. (To get to other buildings, you'll need to travel outdoors, unprotected from the elements.) Casitas 4, Ranchos 6A or 7B, or Cabanas 8A are near the other bus stops. The Ranchos are closest to the main pool but the farthest from El Centro and its services. We recommend buildings 6B and 8A for the view and proximity to the quiet pool or Cabanas 9B for convenience to El Centro.

© Debra Martin Koma

Roll-in Shower at Coronado Springs

Important Note: This resort frequently hosts large conventions. Inquire about this when you check in so that you can attempt to avoid the large groups.

Dining
Coronado Springs' dining options include the table-service Maya Grill and the nontraditional food court Pepper Market (see page 351). Both of these restaurants will accommodate special requests with 72-hour notice (see "Making Special Requests," chapter 6). Pepper Market in particular **prepares many items to order** using fresh ingredients—it's easy to speak to the chef on the spot to discuss special dietary requirements. For those who would like a light meal or snack, La Tienda, next to Pepper Market, carries fresh fruit, drinks, sandwiches, salads, and wraps. Other spots to grab a quick bite: Siesta's pool bar and Francisco's lounge. Because Coronado Springs caters to a convention crowd, it also offers limited room service in the mornings and evenings.

Amenities
Unlike the other Disney moderate resorts, Coronado Springs has its **own fitness center**. La Vida Health Club has exercise equipment, a whirlpool, and massage treatments. For those who want to stick to their exercise routine on vacation, there's a nature trail and a pathway encircling the lagoon. There are also boats and bikes for rent at La Marina, and there is a volleyball court.

The Dig Site main theme pool is a **10,800 sq. ft. (1,003 sq. m.) miniature water park**. It's built around a stepped Mayan pyramid and features a 123-foot (37.5-meter) water slide, hot tub that holds up to 22 people, and separate children's pool with water jets. There's also a heated quiet pool in each of the three themed accommodation areas. All the pools have a transfer tier for those who are able to lift themselves onto it and then slide into the water. Automated External Defibrillators (AEDs) are located at each of the pools and at numerous locations throughout the resort.

Kids will love the **play area** located at the Dig Site, too, with its swings, slides, and a jungle gym to crawl around on. Nearby is the Iguana Arcade (a second arcade, called the Jumping Bean Arcade, is located at El Centro).

Disney's Coronado Springs Resort
(continued)

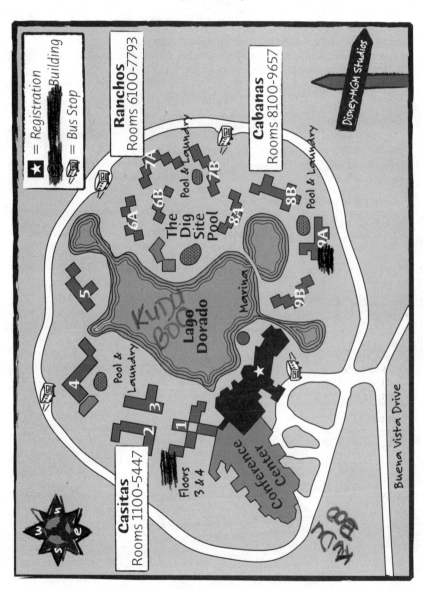

2005 standard room rates begin at $134 in value season, $149 in regular season, $169 in peak season, and $184 in holiday season (seasons are indicated on page 93). Water view and king-bed rooms are $15 more. Junior suites are $290–$455 more than standard rooms. One-bedroom suites are $580–$775. Two-bedroom suites are $860–$1,140.

Disney's Coronado Springs Resort
(continued)

Quiet Spots

If you're looking for a quiet spot to hang out, you've come to the right resort. There are **hammocks located all around Lago Dorado**—they make the perfect place to "chill out." Also, all around the Casitas section are courtyards with beautiful fountains that make nice spots to relax and refresh. The secluded Nature Trail, located behind the Dig Site, is a nice spot for a leisurely exploration, too.

Transportation

All Disney **transportation from this resort is via bus**. There are four bus stops scattered around the resort—the main stop is located down the walkway to your left as you exit El Centro. (Buses often make a stop at Blizzard Beach en route.) A sidewalk connects the resort to Blizzard Beach, and it's a short drive to Disney-MGM Studios or Disney's Animal Kingdom.

Estimated Transportation Times

Magic Kingdom	Epcot	Disney-MGM Studios	Disney's Animal Kingdom	Downtown Disney
direct bus ~15 min.	direct bus ~15 min.	direct bus ~15 min.	direct bus ~10 min.	direct bus ~25 min.

Approximate time you will spend in transit from resort to destination during normal operation.

Our Special Needs Ratings

Coronado Springs **ranks medium-high** on our special needs convenience scale. Even though it's a moderate resort, it has many deluxe amenities—the fitness center, room service—that make it an attractive choice for vacationers who have a variety of special needs. In addition, we've found the cast members here to be extremely helpful and willing to accommodate special requests.

[C][♥][T] [M][P][S]	Resort is spread out; request room close to El Centro or bus stop.
[G]	There's a wide variety of flowering shrubs and plants all around the grounds—allergy/asthma sufferers beware.
[P]	There's a health club facility on-site, as well as a nice pathway encircling the lake.
[L]	Request a guest room with a king bed.

Disney's Coronado Springs Resort

1000 W. Buena Vista Drive, Bay Lake, FL 32830
Phone: 407-939-1000 Fax: 407-939-1001

Disney's Fort Wilderness Resort & Campground

More than just an ordinary campground, Disney's Fort Wilderness offers a number of **different types of accommodations**, as well as a wide assortment of things to do. Nestled among tall, dark pine and cypress trees dripping with Spanish moss, the 700-acre campground is in a secluded spot on Bay Lake, just minutes from the Magic Kingdom theme park.

Check-In

Check in at Fort Wilderness (**1:00 pm for campsites; 3:00 pm for Cabins**) is handled pretty much as it is at any Disney resort. The lobby of the registration building has a stone fireplace and rough-hewn rocking chairs, with wood paneling and other homey touches. Once you've checked in, you can drive directly to your campsite if you have your own car. Otherwise, a cast member will take you and your luggage in a minivan to your cabin.

Guest Rooms

All types of camping are available—tent, pop-up, trailer, and motor home (RV)—throughout the 788 campsites. In addition, there are 407 Wilderness Cabins, for folks who enjoy the rustic setting but aren't interested in truly "roughing it." Located on small loop roads connecting to larger thoroughfares, each campsite or Wilderness Cabin is relatively secluded by trees and shrubs and has its **own paved driveway, charcoal grill, picnic table**, and, in the case of campsites, 110V/220V electrical service.

The **Wilderness Cabins**, located on loops 2100–2800, are modified mobile homes with exteriors made to look like genuine log cabins. Measuring approximately 12' x 42' (504 sq. ft./46.8 sq. m.), these air-conditioned cabins are fully equipped for that "home-away-from home" feeling. They can accommodate up to six guests plus a child under 3 in a crib. Each cabin has a bedroom with double bed and bunk bed, full bathroom, and full kitchen, and living room with an in-wall full Murphy bed. They are furnished with loveseat, television, and two kid-sized chairs and a table. Three kitchen chairs are around a rustic kitchen table along with an upholstered bench that seats three more. Amenities include a porta-crib and sheet, broom and dustpan, sponge mop, iron, ironing board, vacuum cleaner, extra pillows and blanket, wall-mounted hair dryer, voice mail, and daily housekeeping. No tents are permitted outside a Wilderness Cabin.

Some Wilderness Cabins have **wheelchair accommodations**, with these features:
- ✔ Wheelchair-accessible door and hallway
- ✔ Large deck and ramped entry
- ✔ Roll-in shower
- ✔ Lower sink/kitchen counter top

The cabins are, however, **extremely dark**. The décor, in shades of dark browns, burnt oranges, and forest greens with dark wood paneling, is made to seem even darker by the cabins' poor lighting. Because you're nestled amongst trees, the rooms are dark even when there is full sunshine outside. In addition, the lightbulbs are low wattage. Those with vision impairments may find it difficult to see in these cabins. (Deb Koma found it hard to see even without vision impairments!)

Cabin layout

Planning · **Your Special Need** · **Getting There** · **Staying in Style** · **Touring** · **Feasting** · **Resources** · **Index**

Disney's Fort Wilderness Resort & Campground
(continued)

Campsites

There are **three types of campsites**: partial hookups that supply water (in the 1500 and 2000 loops); full hookups with sewer and water (in loops 600, 800–1300, and 1600–1900); and preferred sites (in the 100–500, 700, and 1400 loops) with cable TV, sewer, and water. Preferred sites are closest to the marina and Settlement Depot. Each site accommodates up to ten people and one car; pets are welcome at certain sites. All sites are within walking distance of clean, air-conditioned "Comfort Stations" that have restrooms, private showers, telephones, ice machines (extra fee), and laundry facilities.

Bright Idea: If you use a wheelchair, consider staying near loops 100, 300, 500, 900, and 1400 loops because the Comfort Stations near these are wheelchair-accessible.

If you're staying without a car, **request to be close to a bus stop**—if your campsite or cabin is at the far end of the loop, getting to the bus stop can be quite a haul. To reduce transit time to the parks, request a site in loops 100–800—these are within walking/wheeling distance of Settlement Depot and the marina. The most popular campsites are on loop 400. If you want a full hookup campsite, we highly recommend loop 800.

Getting around the resort can be difficult, since motor traffic is limited to entering/exiting the park. To get anywhere within Fort Wilderness, you must either walk/wheel or use the internal bus system. Three bus routes—Yellow, Orange, and Purple—serve locations within the resort, and all stop at Settlement Depot and Outpost Depot. A quicker way to get around is to rent an **electric golf cart**. Because they are difficult to get, we suggest you reserve one (up to a year in advance) from Fort Wilderness' Bike Barn at 407-824-2742. Rates are $43+tax per 24-hour period.

Dining

You may **cook many of your meals**, ideal if you have dietary concerns. Bring your own groceries, buy them at Gooding's at Crossroads near Downtown Disney, or buy them from one of the two Trading Posts (a more expensive option) on the campground.

If you choose to **eat out** at Fort Wilderness, there aren't many options for you—there's Trail's End Restaurant (see page 351), which serves food buffet-style, or there's the Chuck Wagon and Crockett's Tavern, which serve snacks. For a special night out, there's the Hoop-Dee-Doo Musical Revue dinner show or Mickey's Backyard BBQ (see page 362). Special diets can be accommodated at these dinner shows with at least 24-hour notice.

Amenities

If you need to maintain an **exercise routine** while on vacation, there are a number of choices. Fort Wilderness has no fitness center, but there are many trails perfect for hiking, wheeling, or jogging. There are also two lighted tennis courts, plus places for volleyball, tetherball, basketball, and horseshoes. The marina rents boats or surrey bikes, while the Bike Barn rents canoes or standard bikes. In addition, there are horseback rides at the livery for about $32/person. Note that riders must be at least 9 yars old and 48 inches tall and can weigh no more than 250 pounds. The campground also has two heated pools, a wading pool, and a beach for sunbathers. Automated External Defibrillators (AEDs) are located at each of the pools and at numerous locations throughout the resort. None of the Fort Wilderness pools appear to have transfer tiers.

For the younger set, there are **several playgrounds** around the resort, plus two game arcades: one at the Settlement Trading Post, the other at the Meadows Trading Post.

Disney's Fort Wilderness Resort & Campground
(continued)

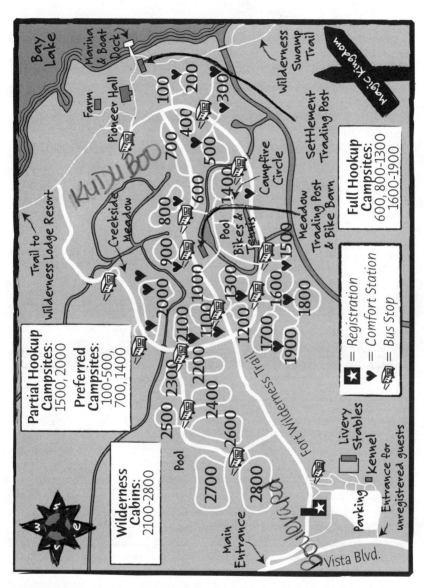

2005 standard campsite rates (partial hookup with electricity and water) begin at $38 in value season, $54 in regular season, $62 in peak season, $72 in holiday season, and $42 in pre-holiday season (seasons are indicated on page 93). Sewer hookup sites add $5–$12 more. Sites with sewer and cable add $12–$17 more to the standard rate. Wilderness Cabins are $234 in value season, $274 in regular season, $309 in peak season, and $339 in holiday season.

Disney's Fort Wilderness Resort & Campground
(continued)

More Amenities

Seniors might enjoy camping at Fort Wilderness due to its low-key pace and the many activities. Try a bass fishing excursion or a quiet canoe trip. The Electrical Water Pageant, a light and music barge parade on Bay Lake, can be seen from the beach at 9:45 pm.

Those who have **fears of animals** should note there are many small creatures, such as squirrels, rabbits, raccoons, armadillos, and peacocks, around the grounds. Pets are also allowed in loops 300, 700, 800, and 1600–1900. The loops are quite dark at night.

Transportation

Since Disney transportation to and from Fort Wilderness requires a transfer from an internal bus to some type of external transport, **a car comes in handy** at this resort to save wait and transit times, not to mention frustration and aggravation. Boats go to the Magic Kingdom, Wilderness Lodge, and the Contemporary. Bus transportation is a little more complicated. Buses for Disney-MGM Studios pick up and drop off at Settlement Depot. Buses for Epcot and Disney's Animal Kingdom/Blizzard Beach pick up/drop off at Outpost Depot. If you need to travel by bus to the Magic Kingdom during park operating hours, you must take the Orange bus from the Settlement Depot, which will take you to the Wilderness Lodge, and then transfer to a Magic Kingdom bus. To return from the Magic Kingdom during park hours, take the Wilderness Lodge bus, then transfer to the Orange bus to get back to Fort Wilderness. If you need to travel to or from the Magic Kingdom after park hours, transfer at the Transportation and Ticket Center. There's a path connecting Fort Wilderness to the Wilderness Lodge, if you're up for the journey. For other resorts, transfer at Magic Kingdom or Downtown Disney.

Estimated Transportation Times

Magic Kingdom	Epcot	Disney-MGM Studios	Disney's Animal Kingdom	Downtown Disney
boat ~15 min.	direct bus ~25 min.	direct bus ~30 min.	direct bus ~30 min.	direct bus ~35 min.

Approximate time you will spend in transit from resort to destination during normal operation.

Our Special Needs Ratings

Fort Wilderness Resort & Campground **ranks low to medium** on our special needs scale, depending on your individual requirements.

[A][U][C][B][♥] [T][M][P][E][S] [L]	The fact that campsites and cabins are so far from guest services, and the difficult internal transportation system are drawbacks for those with mobility concerns, as well as those traveling with children who have difficulty waiting for long periods. If relying on Disney transportation to get around, request a campsite/cabin close to a bus stop.
[G][D]	The ability to prepare your own meals, either at your campsite or in your Wilderness Cabin, is ideal for vacationers with special dietary needs. But the thick tree cover, along with lots of Spanish moss and numerous woodland creatures, may spark asthma/allergy issues.
[A][U]	Fort Wilderness provides ample opportunity for running off steam and for getting away from the hubbub of the theme parks.

Disney's Fort Wilderness Resort & Campground
4510 N. Fort Wilderness Trail, Bay Lake, FL 3283, Phone: 407-824-2900 Fax: 407-824-3508

Disney's Grand Floridian Resort & Spa

A stately **turn-of-the century Victorian hotel**, the gleaming white Grand Floridian sits on Seven Seas Lagoon between the Polynesian and the Magic Kingdom. This is Walt Disney World's most deluxe hotel.

Check-In

Ample parking is available at this resort, but the **self-parking area is across the street**. It's a few minutes' walk/wheel (no incline) to the lobby—you can't park close to your room. There is valet parking, though ($7/day or complimentary with a handicapped tag).

Check-in (3:00 pm) takes place in the Grand Lobby, with its soaring ceiling and exquisite one-ton chandeliers. Unfortunately, there's no low counter for wheelchair accessibility at the registration windows, nor is there a companion restroom available in the lobby area. There are, however, a number of comfy sofas and chairs perfect for waiting while another member of your party checks in.

Once you've checked in, **Bell Services takes you and your luggage to your guest room**, whether you're staying in the Grand Lobby building itself or in one of the outer lodges.

Guest Rooms

There are nearly **900 guest rooms spread out among five lodge buildings** and the Grand Lobby. Rooms are about 400 sq. ft. (37.2 sq. m.) and have marble-topped double sinks and balconies or patios. Most guest rooms, decorated in one of four themes (floral, cameo, swans, or Alice in Wonderland), offer two queen-size beds and a daybed, accommodating five people. The lodge buildings also house the slightly smaller "dormer" rooms, plus suites. Amenities include signature toiletries, turndown service, mini-bar, refrigerator, wall safe, hair dryer, newspaper delivery, 24-hour room service, high-speed Internet access, and luxurious bathrobes.

In addition to the standard room amenities, you can also **request these special items**:

Standard room layout

✔ Bed boards/Bed rails
✔ Down pillows
✔ Heating pads
✔ Cribs
✔ Smoke detectors (for guests with hearing disabilities)
✔ Microwave (limited number available)
✔ Room Communication Kit (for those with hearing impairments)

Conch Key and Boca Chica lodges are all **nonsmoking**, while Big Pine Key has nonsmoking rooms on floors 1, 2, and 3. Smoking optional rooms are: Sago Cay 4th and 5th floors; Sugar Loaf (concierge) 14; and Big Pine Key floors 4 and 5.

Four extra-special types of rooms are available. The lodge tower rooms have a separate sitting area, an extra TV and phone, and five windows. Concierge rooms offer personalized services, continental breakfast, evening refreshments, and a private elevator. Of the concierge rooms, special turret rooms have wet bars and windows all around, while honeymoon suites feature whirlpool tubs.

Disney's Grand Floridian Resort & Spa
(continued)

Guest Rooms (continued)

The **dormer rooms** on the top floors of the lodge buildings may be a bit smaller (they only sleep 4 rather than 5), but they have vaulted ceilings and a secluded balcony. The best views of Cinderella Castle are found in the lagoon view rooms in Sago Cay and Conch Key lodges, but these buildings are quite a distance from the main building. If proximity to the restaurants and guest services is important, request a room in the Grand Lobby or in Sugar Loaf Key. (These rooms are pricier, though, as they are all suites or concierge level.) Note that the latter sees a lot of traffic, however, and can be noisy. Big Pine Key is near to the beach, and its lagoon view rooms offer picturesque views.

Dining

In keeping with the upscale atmosphere of this resort, there are a number of fine dining table-service restaurants, described on pages 352–353, which are happy to accommodate special requests with 72-hour advance notice. Notable among the Grand Floridian's restaurants are Narcoossee's, which has an **extensive vegetarian menu**—just ask!—and Victoria & Albert's, Disney's finest restaurant. In addition, there's a 24-hour food stop, Gasparilla's Grill.

You can also arrange for **private dining** here—eat on your balcony, on the beach, or even on a boat in the lagoon. Make arrangements in advance with room service.

If you need **basic groceries and sundries**, there's Sandy Cove on the first floor of the main building (see our sidebar on page 118).

Amenities

If you need to **maintain a fitness routine** while on vacation, there's the Grand Floridian Spa & Health Club, a fully equipped fitness center (with massage and spa treatments, too). There are also two clay tennis courts (for a fee) and a one-mile jogging path to the Polynesian. Finally, you can rent a variety of boats at the marina.

The **playground** is near the Mouseketeer Clubhouse; the arcade is at Gasparilla's Grill.

The main theme pool at the Grand Floridian features a **"zero-entry" shoreline**. This is a gradual slope into the pool, just like a real beach—ideal for those who are unable to step down into a traditional pool. There is also a water wheelchair available, which can wheel right into the pool—just ask a lifeguard for assistance. Besides the main pool, there is also a heated "quiet pool," which has a transfer tier, for wheelchair users able to lift themselves out of the chair and then slide down into the pool. There's a hot tub located near each pool and a white sand beach for sunbathing (no swimming allowed). Automated External Defibrillators (AEDs) are located at each of the pools, and at numerous locations throughout the resort.

Grand Floridian's main pool with a zero-entry shoreline

Disney's Grand Floridian Resort & Spa
(continued)

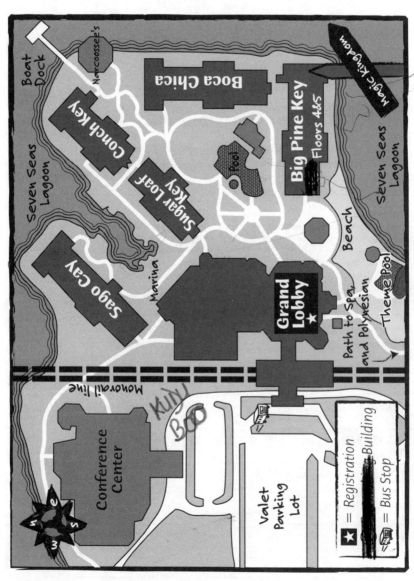

2005 standard room rates begin at $349 in value season, $394 in regular season, $459 in peak season, and $534 in holiday season (seasons are indicated on page 93). Lagoon view rooms are $61–$86 more. Lodge Tower rooms are $81–$116 more than standard rooms. Concierge rooms begin at $460 in value season, $535 in regular season, $620 in peak season, and $685 in holiday season. Suites are available from $915 to $2,535.

Planning • Your Special Need • Getting There • **Staying in Style** • Touring • Feasting • Resources • Index

Planning

Your Special Need

Getting There

Staying in Style

Touring

Feasting

Resources

Index

Disney's Grand Floridian Resort & Spa
(continued)

Quiet Spots
If you're looking for a little privacy, try some of the **benches on the second floor** of the main building. There are also quiet spots along the beach.

Another good spot is the **balcony next to the stairs** on the second floor of the main building—it is very secluded and has a table and chairs.

Transportation is varied and fairly easy at the Grand Floridian. A monorail (accessible station on the second floor) goes to the Magic Kingdom as well as the Contemporary, Polynesian, and the Transportation and Ticket Center, where you can transfer to the Epcot monorail. Boats also take you to the Magic Kingdom and the Polynesian, though they only accommodate folded wheelchairs (no ECVs). For other parks, use the buses in front of the resort. For other resorts, monorail to the Magic Kingdom (daytime) or bus to Downtown Disney (evening) and transfer to a resort bus.

Estimated Transportation Times

Magic Kingdom	Epcot	Disney-MGM Studios	Disney's Animal Kingdom	Downtown Disney
monorail/boat ~3/~10 min.	monorail x 2 ~12+10 min.	direct bus ~10 min.	direct bus ~15 min.	direct bus ~20 min.

Approximate time you will spend in transit from resort to destination during normal operation.

Our Special Needs Ratings
Grand Floridian Resort & Spa **ranks high** on our special needs convenience scale, but staying here is expensive. The resort has a terrific location on the water, is close to the Magic Kingdom, is on the monorail line, and has numerous other amenities that make it an excellent choice for vacationers who have a variety of special needs.

Our Special Needs Convenience Scale

[A][U][C] [B][E][S]	Because it's on the monorail line, getting back to the Grand Floridian quickly (for a midday break or at the end of the day) is relatively easy.
[C][♥][T][M] [P][E][S]	Request a room near an elevator in the main building.
[D]	Narcoossee's has a surprisingly extensive vegetarian menu—be sure to ask. Other restaurants are very accommodating with 72-hour notice. Note that kosher items are *not* available at the Garden View Lounge Afternoon Tea.
[P]	Beautiful health club on site with lots of places to walk/wheel and swim.
[V]	Rooms are bright and spacious, but buildings are spread out.

Disney's Grand Floridian Resort & Spa
4401 Floridian Way, Bay Lake, FL 32830
Phone: 407-824-3000 Fax: 407-824-3186

Disney's Old Key West Resort

The first Disney Vacation Club (DVC) property, Old Key West, stretches across an area situated between Downtown Disney and Epcot. Built to represent a **relaxed Key West vacation spot**, the resort is a favorite with DVC members but is also popular among non-DVC members.

Check-In
Check-in time is **4:00 pm**. Bell Services will assist in taking your luggage to your room if you need help. All buildings except 64 have parking right out front. If you don't have a car, ask a cast member to transport you via one of the resort's golf carts.

Guest Rooms
The accommodations here are the **largest of the DVC resorts** located at Walt Disney World. It's laid-back and low-key and reminds you of being at a seaside resort. The studios have kitchenettes, while all other villas have full-sized kitchens and "family room" areas. Full-sized washers, dryers, and DVD players are at all villas except the studios. There are laundry facilities near each of the pools.

Its **49 buildings** include studios (376 sq. ft./35 sq. m.) and one-bedroom (1086 sq. ft./101 sq. m.), two-bedroom (1392 sq. ft./129 sq. m.) and three-bedroom (2265 sq. ft./210 sq. m.) villas. Each cluster of buildings shares a parking lot. Views include a golf course, water, and wooded areas, making for a peaceful place of respite.

Because all Old Key West villas feature kitchen facilities, these accommodations are **ideal for travelers with special dietary needs or an infant**. Other amenities include a private balcony or porch, hair dryer, iron, ironing board, and vacuum cleaner. All rooms also have double sinks, a marble vanity, a table and chairs, sofa, armoire, TV, ceiling fan, toiletries, housekeeping, voice mail, and wall safes.

Accessible rooms are available, but only the three newest buildings (62, 63, and 64) have elevators. Many buildings have three floors, so be sure to request a first-floor unit if necessary. If you are looking for a nonsmoking unit, remember to mention it when making your reservation. The "smoking optional" buildings are 12, 19, and 41. Also remember to request a one- or two-bedroom unit in buildings 30 and above if having the second entrance to the bathroom is important.

You can also **request special items**, such as bed boards and rails, highchairs, shower seat for disabled, smoke detector and telephone for hearing impaired, toilet seat for wheelchairs, and extra portable cribs.

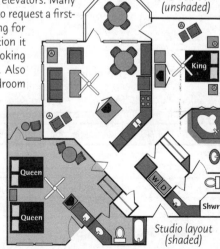

One-bedroom (unshaded)

King

Queen

Queen

W/D

Shwr

Studio layout (shaded)

Entire layout represents a two-bedroom villa

Planning
Your Special Need
Getting There
Staying in Style
Touring
Feasting
Resources
Index

Disney's Old Key West Resort
(continued)

Dining
Dining choices include **Olivia's Cafe**, which serves three meals a day. Many Orlando locals frequent this restaurant, and we feel it's one of the "best-kept secrets" around Disney. Booths and chairs (with and without arms) are part of the seating plan. For quick service, "Goods to Go" is located near the main pool, serving burgers and snacks. The Gurgling Suitcase is adjacent and has drinks and appetizers (but very little sitting room). The Turtle Pond Pool has the Turtle Shack snack bar, which is open seasonally. See page 354 for a more in-depth look at Old Key West's dining choices.

Amenities
If you need to **maintain an exercise routine** while on vacation, there's the R.E.S.T. Beach Recreation Dept., which features traditional exercise equipment, including Nautilus and treadmills. Massage is available by appointment only. Joggers/walkers/wheelers will have a great time exploring the resort as they exercise or even walk/wheel/jog to Saratoga Springs and Downtown Disney. Finally, there are boat and bike rentals.

Playgrounds are located near each of the swimming pools. The Conch Flats Community Hall offers games and organized activities for kids (ask for a schedule). Two arcades, Electric Eel Arcade and the Flying Fisherman, will satisfy the video game players.

The **Conch Flats General Store** is small but offers a fairly nice selection of logo goods, souvenirs, watches, and food items and toiletries, as well as packaged liquor (see page 118).

Transportation
Buses stop at the **resort's five bus stops** to take you to all four Disney theme parks, water parks, and Downtown Disney. In addition, a ferry connects Old Key West to Saratoga Springs and Downtown Disney Marketplace. The ferry is wheelchair-accessible. Go down to the pool area and you'll find the ramp to the dock.

Estimated Transportation Times

Magic Kingdom	Epcot	Disney-MGM Studios	Disney's Animal Kingdom	Downtown Disney
direct bus ~25 min.	direct bus ~10 min.	direct bus ~10 min.	direct bus ~15 min.	bus/boat ~5/~15 min.

Approximate time you will spend in transit from resort to destination during normal operation.

Our Special Needs Ratings
Old Key West is a very relaxing resort with all the comforts of home, including flexibility for dining. Although Old Key West has limited transportation options, we **rate it medium to high**.

[C][♥][T][M][P][S]	Request a room near an elevator and close to a bus stop.
[P]	Old Key West has a health club on site and lots of places to walk/wheel and swim, plus many other activities.
[V]	Rooms are bright and spacious, but buildings are spread out.
[S]	Seniors may enjoy the quiet, relaxing atmosphere here.

Disney's Old Key West Resort
1510 North Cove Road, Lake Buena Vista, FL 32830
Phone: 407-827-1198 Fax: 407-827-7710

Disney's Old Key West Resort
(continued)

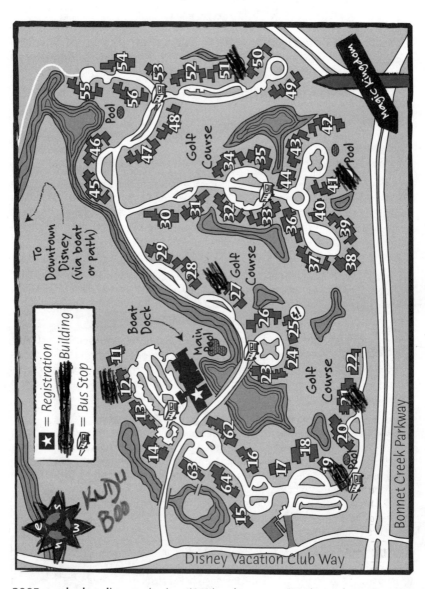

2005 standard studio rates begin at $259 in value season, $289 in regular season, $339 in peak season, and $379 in holiday season (seasons are indicated on page 93). One-bedroom villas are $350–$525. Two-bedroom villas are $490–$805. Three-bedroom grand villas are $1,070–$1,505.

Disney's Polynesian Resort

When Walt Disney World opened in 1971, there were only two Disney resorts: the Contemporary and the Polynesian (known as Disney's Polynesian Village Resort at the time). With its **coveted location** on the monorail and the Seven Seas Lagoon facing Cinderella Castle, the Polynesian Resort brings to life a near-perfect tropical paradise.

Check-In

Check-in time is **3:00 pm** in the gorgeous atrium lobby of the Great Ceremonial House. As at many deluxe resorts, the self-parking area is a few minutes' walk/wheel from the main lobby. Consider valet parking ($7/day; free with handicapped tag) instead.

Even though the atmosphere is decidedly tropical, with a splashing waterfall nearly hidden amidst the lush foliage in the center, the echoes make the lobby a **somewhat noisy place**. In addition to the registration desk, located on your right as you enter the lobby, there's an Island Guide desk, immediately on your left when you enter. The guides here can not only answer your questions about the resort but are experts on the cultures of South Pacific island people. Their service is just an extra touch that helps to enhance your visit to this resort.

Once you've checked in and the cast member drapes a colorful, artificial flower lei around your neck, Bell Services will **assist you with your luggage**. Some of the buildings are a few minutes away—Bell Services can transport you via golf cart.

Guest Rooms

There are 853 guest rooms distributed among **11 longhouses representing "islands"** in the South Pacific. The longhouses are two or three stories high; the first-floor rooms have patios, and many of the upper-floor rooms have balconies. The room furnishings include bamboo bed frames with woven rattan mat canopies, a bamboo daybed, bamboo nightstand … you get the idea.

The **standard guest rooms**, which are 409 sq. ft. (38 sq. m.), all include the standard furnishings and two queen-sized beds, a nightstand with telephone, table with two chairs, armoire with television, in-room safe, iron and ironing board, refrigerator, coffeemaker with coffee packets, and hair dryer in the bathroom. Each room can accommodate five, because it features a daybed. The bathrooms are fairly spacious, with one or two sinks of green marble outside the green marbled shower/tub area and the toilet tucked modestly in a nook behind the sinks. Suites and concierge-level rooms housed in the Tonga and Hawaii longhouses offer personal service and great views.

Amenities for all resort rooms include toiletries, 24-hour room service, housekeeping, turndown service (on request), and voice mail. All first-floor rooms have patios, and all third-floor rooms have balconies. Most second-floor rooms have no balconies, with the exception of Tahiti, Rapa Nui, Tokelau, and Tonga, which were built later.

Exceptional water views looking out at the Castle can be found in Hawaii (concierge building). The first-floor rooms in Tahiti facing away from the water have secluded patios, as do those in Rapa Nui and Rarotonga.

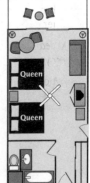

Standard room layout

Disney's Polynesian Resort
(continued)

Guest Rooms (continued)

If you opt for a **standard view**, we recommend Aotearoa for an up-close view of the monorail. For added privacy, request a room on the top floor. It tends to be noisy in the pool areas (near Samoa, Niue, Hawaii, Rarotonga, and Tokelau). Request a room in Tonga (which houses all the resort's suites) or Rarotonga if you want to be close to the Great Ceremonial House and its guest services.

Most of the **wheelchair-accessible rooms** are in Rapa Nui, and all of the rooms with a roll-in shower are here. This building is next door to the Transportation and Ticket Center, making it a fair distance from the Great Ceremonial House services. There are balconies on all of the floors. With one exception, all buildings have their own elevators.

Important Note: Niue, the smallest building at the Polynesian, is located next to the Great Ceremonial House and is just a few steps from either of the pools, but there is no elevator in the building. To gain access here, you have to enter the Rarotonga building, take the elevator to the second floor, and enter Niue using the connecting walkway.

Dining

Of the dining choices at the Polynesian (detailed on page 354), the **Kona Café** is well-known as a restaurant eager to please those with special dietary needs, particularly vegetarian and vegan diets. 'Ohana is the family style, all-you-can-eat breakfast and dinner restaurant across the way on the second floor, while the 24-hour Captain Cook's Snack Company is on the first. As a special treat, the Polynesian is home to an outdoor, luau-style dinner show, the Spirit of Aloha (see pages 365–366). Special diets can be accommodated at this dinner show with at least 24-hour notice.

Trader Jack's and Samoa Snacks can be found on the second floor of the Great Ceremonial House, if you need **basic groceries** and sundry items. See page 118 for typical items.

Amenities

For those who want to **keep up with their exercise routine**, the Polynesian does not have its own health club. Guests at the Polynesian may use the nearby Grand Floridian Spa & Health Club free of charge, however. Walkers, wheelers, and joggers can take advantage of the Walk Around the World that partially encircles the lagoon and a 1.5-mile path that winds through the resort (ask at Lobby Concierge for a map). Boaters can rent Sea Raycers and other watercraft at the marina. There are also surrey bikes for rent.

Bright Idea: There's a Sea Raycer out of the water—this comes in handy to help you determine whether you will fit and allows to you practice entering and exiting the vehicle.

In addition to a heated quiet pool is the Nanea Volcano theme pool, which features a large pool "fed" by a spring, a water slide, warm water areas, underwater music, and a **zero-entry section** (pool wheelchair available—ask a lifeguard). There's also a kids' water play area—remember that children in diapers must wear snug-fitting plastic pants or special swim diapers when in the water. There is no hot tub here, but there is a beach for sunbathing (no swimming allowed). Automated External Defibrillators (AEDs) are located at each of the pools and at numerous locations throughout the resort. Note that the pool does not have a transfer tier, but the zero-entry access should make up for that.

Planning

Your Special Need

Getting There

Staying in Style

Touring

Feasting

Resources

Index

Disney's Polynesian Resort

(continued)

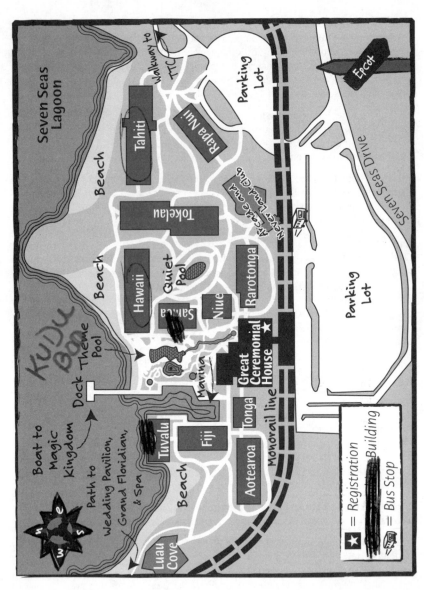

2005 standard room rates begin at $304 in value season, $354 in regular season, $419 in peak season, and $484 in holiday season (seasons are indicated on page 93). A lagoon-view room adds $96–$101. Concierge garden rooms are $410–$595, and concierge lagoon-view rooms are $510–$720. One-bedroom suites are $510–$1,000, two-bedroom suites are $1,232–$1,845, and the King Kamehameha Suite is $1,850–$2,550.

Disney's Polynesian Resort
(continued)

More Amenities
There's a **playground** near the main pool and a game arcade, Moana Mickey's, by the Never Land Kids' Club.

You can find **other shops** in the Great Ceremonial House—apparel and Wyland Galleries on the first floor and souvenirs and sundries on the second.

The **Electrical Water Pageant** passes by the Polynesian around 9:00 pm. If you can't see the lagoon from your room, watch it from the beach or at the end of the dock near the marina.

Quiet Spots
The beach in front of Hawaii and Tahiti has **bench swings and hammocks**.

Transportation
Options abound at the Polynesian. The **monorail** (accessible station on the second floor) can whisk you to the Magic Kingdom, Grand Floridian, and Contemporary, as well as the Transportation and Ticket Center (TTC) in a matter of a few minutes. The small launches to the Magic Kingdom and Grand Floridian are *not* wheelchair/ECV accessible—they have steps in and out and can carry a folded wheelchair, but ECVs cannot be boarded at all. To reach Epcot, take a short walk/wheel to TTC and board the monorail. To reach other parks and Downtown Disney, take a bus. If you're feeling ambitious, you can walk/wheel to the Grand Floridian. To reach resorts that aren't on the monorail, take a monorail to the Magic Kingdom and transfer to a resort bus (daytime), or bus to Downtown Disney and transfer to a resort bus (evening).

Estimated Transportation Times

Magic Kingdom	Epcot	Disney-MGM Studios	Disney's Animal Kingdom	Downtown Disney
monorail/boat ~10/~5 min.	monorail x 2 ~10+10 min.	direct bus ~15 min.	direct bus ~15 min.	direct bus ~25 min.

Approximate time you will spend in transit from resort to destination during normal operation.

Our Special Needs Ratings
The Polynesian Resort **ranks high** on our special needs scale. It has a terrific location on the water, is close to the Magic Kingdom, is on the monorail, and has many other amenities that make it an excellent choice.

Our Special Needs Convenience Scale

[G]	The variety of lush vegetation may cause asthma or allergy issues.
[A][U][C][B] [E][S]	Because it's on the monorail, getting back to the Polynesian quickly (for a midday break or at the end of the day) is relatively easy.
[C][♥][T][M] [P][E][S]	Request a room near an elevator—remember that Niue does not have its own elevator.
[D]	Restaurants are very accommodating with 72-hour notice. Kona Cafe is particularly vegetarian/vegan friendly.
[P]	There's no health club but lots of places to walk/wheel and swim.
[V]	Rooms are a little on the dark side.

Disney's Polynesian Resort
1600 Seven Seas Drive, Bay Lake, FL 32830, Phone: 407-824-2000 Fax: 407-824-3174

Disney's Pop Century Resort

The **newest of the value resorts**, Pop Century is colorful and sports larger-than-life icons similar to the All-Star Resorts. Pop Century is a much larger resort, though, and once completed (currently only the Classic Years' 2,880 rooms are open), there will be more than 5,700 rooms. As of this writing, there is no opening date for Phase II.

Check-In

Check-in time is **4:00 pm** in Classic Hall, which houses the front desk/check-in, food court, lounge, bus depot, arcade, and general store. The "Everything Pop" area contains the food court, lounge, and general store—these are all open and share the same space, making it quite noisy and busy! The central areas are often very noisy with guests coming and going in all directions. A short-term check-in parking area is available nearby.

As we noted about the All-Star Resorts, you can **expect medium to long lines at check-in** here. To avoid the waits, we suggest you check in as soon as you arrive at Walt Disney World—sort of a "pre-check-in." It's a good time to drop off your luggage, too. Then you can leave to shop or play at the theme parks—check in "for real" later when the crowds have subsided. See page 108 for check-in strategies.

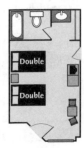

Bright Idea: There is a low check-in counter at either end of the long front desk area to make registration easier for folks in wheelchairs/ECVs.

As in other Disney resorts, there is **special kids' waiting area**, but at Pop Century, this space is just off the lobby, and you are unable to see it from the check-in line.

Pop Century's kid's waiting area

© MediaMarx, Inc.

Guest Rooms

The four-story buildings of this resort are **very spread out**. A $10 premium is added to the '60s buildings, which are the closest to the main shopping/eating area, Everything Pop!, and must be reserved at the time of booking. Those farther away are generally quieter but also require quite a walk/wheel to and from the bus stops and food areas. Room views include the pool, parking lot, or woods. For quieter rooms, request rooms facing away from the pool/parking areas.

Despite being among the **smallest rooms** at Walt Disney World (260 sq. ft./24 sq. m.), they are quite comfortable and are furnished with two double beds or one king, TV with armoire, small table with two chairs, and a chest. An ECV or wheelchair will fit comfortably if you only have two people—otherwise, it may be difficult to get a wheelchair in the room and close the door. If you have four, no matter if they are very small children, things will be tight with the wheelchair/ECV. If you want more room to move around, request a king room.

All **rooms exit to the outside** (no inner corridors), so you will be exposed to the elements when walking to bus stops or services.

Standard room layout

Disney's Pop Century Resort
(continued)

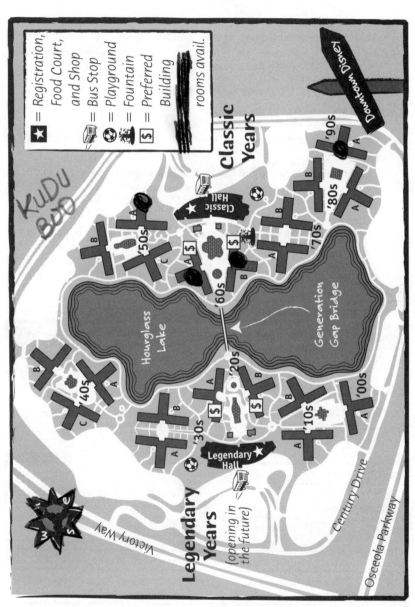

2005 standard room rates begin at $77 in value season, $99 in regular season, $109 in peak season, and $119 in holiday season (seasons are indicated on page 93). Preferred rooms (see preferred buildings marked on map above) run $12 more per room.

Planning

Your Special Need

Getting There

Staying in Style

Touring

Feasting

Resources

Index

Disney's Pop Century Resort
(continued)

Other than limited snacks at the general store, the only place that food is available is at the **Everything Pop! food court**. You enter an area with several stations offering a variety of selections. There is also a refrigerated section with already packaged items like sandwiches, salads, fruit, etc. Refills for refillable mugs may include lemonade and apple juice. One positive note is that some kosher foods are always available at the food courts without advance notice. See chapter 6 for more dining details.

Amenities
Pop Century has **three themed pools**, a small playground area for letting off some steam, and an arcade. The laundry room has a front loading/accessible washing machine.

Quiet Spots
To get away from the **loud hustle and bustle** of the Food Court, there are tables and chairs outside that may be quieter. Keep in mind, these are then subject to weather conditions and also tend to be smoking areas. You can always bring your food back to the room.

Transportation
All Disney **transportation from this resort is via bus**. (There is currently only one bus stop.) Waits for buses to and from Pop Century can be long, especially at park opening and closing. The queues wind around and can get very crowded—in fact, it is not uncommon to have standing room only on the buses. There is a designated area next to the queue for wheelchair guests to wait, making pre-boarding easier.

Estimated Transportation Times

Magic Kingdom	Epcot	Disney-MGM Studios	Disney's Animal Kingdom	Downtown Disney
direct bus ~25 min.	direct bus ~20 min.	direct bus ~15 min.	direct bus ~15 min.	direct bus ~20 min.

Approximate time you will spend in transit from resort to destination during normal operation.

Our Special Needs Ratings
Pop Century is great for the budget, but not for amenities. It's **low** on the special needs convenience scale, primarily due to the layout. However, we do recommend Pop Century as your value resort of choice.

[A][U][S]	This resort can be very busy and noisy in the pools and central areas.
[C][♥][T] **[M][P][E]**	Unless you are in a preferred building location, have a car, or use a wheelchair, we do not recommend Pop Century due to its spread-out design.
[D][W]	Food Court chefs can accommodate with minimum 72 hours' notice. Note that some kosher items are generally available without advance notice.
[F]	The larger-than-life icons could scare some.
[S]	For a more relaxing vacation, stay at a moderate, deluxe, or Disney Vacation Club resort.
[L]	Be sure to request a king bed.

Disney's Pop Century Resort
1050 Century Drive, Lake Buena Vista, FL 32830
Phone: 407-938-4000 Fax: 407-938-4039

Disney's Port Orleans Resort

Located along the banks of the Sassagoula River, north of Downtown Disney, Port Orleans is actually an **amalgamation of two resorts**: the former Dixie Landings (now known as Port Orleans Riverside) and Port Orleans (now known as Port Orleans French Quarter). Several faces of the Old South are represented at Port Orleans. The French Quarter evokes the feeling of historic New Orleans as it prepares for Mardi Gras; Riverside houses the rustic, moss-covered buildings of Alligator Bayou and the serene, stately mansions of Magnolia Bend.

Check-In

Port Orleans has two front desks, one in each district. Be sure to check with Disney before arrival to find out which district's front desk you should use. Check-in time is **3:00 pm**.

The Mint is your first stop in the **French Quarter**, a large building with wrought ironwork details and a soaring glass atrium that safeguards the district's front desk, guest services, and shop. A step outside reveals narrow cobblestone lanes, complete with "gas" lamps, wrought iron benches, and grand magnolia trees.

A leisurely ten-minute walk or wheel along the Sassagoula takes you to **Riverside**. Banjo music and southern hospitality greet you as you enter Riverside's Sassagoula Steamboat Company, a replica of an old riverboat depot. The depot is the crossroads of this quaint settlement, housing the district's front desk and services. Venture out along meandering paths and wooden bridges to antebellum mansions in one direction or the bayou in the other.

Once you check in, you can drive yourself to your building and park fairly close to your room. Alternatively, **Bell Services will take your luggage** and you to your room.

Guest Rooms

The **French Quarter has six large buildings** with 1,008 rooms. Most buildings have their own gardens in front, charmingly fenced with wrought iron. Riverside itself has two distinct sections—the Southern plantations of Magnolia Bend have 1,024 rooms, as do the more rustic buildings in Alligator Bayou.

Important Note: Large and often boisterous youth groups (cheerleading competitions, Pop Warner football) frequently stay in the Riverside section of this resort. If you're looking for peace and quiet, inquire about this when you check in so that you can attempt to avoid the large groups.

All rooms are 314 sq. ft. (29.2 sq. m.) and have a similar layout, varying only in decor and theme. In the French Quarter, you find **faux French Provincial** furniture, gilt-edged mirrors, and Venetian blinds. Riverside's Magnolia Bend rooms are appointed with cherry furniture and brocade settees.

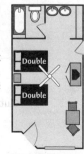

Standard room layout

Planning   Your Special Need   Getting There   Staying in Style   Touring   Feasting   Resources   Index

Disney's Port Orleans Resort
(continued)

Guest Rooms (continued)

Rooms in **Riverside's Alligator Bayou** sport beds made of hewn "logs" and patchwork quilts. All rooms accommodate up to four and come with either two extra-long double beds or one king bed (king bed rooms are located on building corners). Alligator Bayou's 963 rooms house up to five guests at no additional charge by offering a trundle bed (see photo at right), which slides out from under the double bed and fits a child or small adult. Rooms include a TV, armoire, table and chairs, ceiling fan, and a separate vanity area with double pedestal sinks. Every room has a window (corner rooms have two), but none have private balconies. Other room amenities include toiletries (soap

A Port Orleans Riverside trundle bed

and shampoo only), housekeeping, coffeemaker and coffee packets, limited room service, in-room safe (most rooms), voice mail, refrigerator, and hair dryer.

Note that Alligator Bayou buildings **do not have elevators**. If you have mobility concerns, request a ground floor room in one of these buildings.

Port Orleans is **exceptionally large and sprawling**, and room location can really make a difference in your resort experience. Request the style that suits you best—when you make your reservation, you can specify whether you want a room in Riverside or the French Quarter.

Most rooms in the French Quarter are **within easy distance** of Lobby Concierge, the gift shop, and the food court. If being close to the center of things is important, request Buildings 2–5. The best views are of the Sassagoula River, as the opposite river bank is pristine—consider upgrading to a water view room (specifically request a river view). The buildings in French Quarter do have elevators.

The grand "mansions" of **Magnolia Bend** in Riverside conjure a Gone With the Wind feel. The Magnolia Terrace building is a good pick for proximity to recreation and dining. (Only the Oak Manor building is smoking-optional here.) The buildings in Alligator Bayou are smaller (only two stories) and have lush landscaping. Building 14 is near the main building, Ol' Man Island, a quiet pool, and a bus stop—it has no bad views, as it is nestled between buildings and the river. Buildings 15 and 18 are also good choices—note that 18 is smoking-optional. For a quieter room, request the second or third floor. Magnolia Bend buildings have elevators.

Bright Idea: If you'd like a brighter room, request one on a corner—it will have two windows.

Because Port Orleans is so spread out, getting around can take some walking. You may want to **hop a bus to get around** the resort.

Disney's Port Orleans Resort
(continued)

Dining

Port Orleans' only table-service restaurant is **Boatwright's Dining Hall**. This restaurant in the Riverside district offers breakfast and dinner—see page 355 for details. Two large food courts—Sassagoula Floatworks and Food Factory in the French Quarter and the Riverside Mill at Riverside—offer breakfast, lunch, and dinner. A selection of kosher foods is generally available at the food courts without advance notice, but 72 hours' notice is required for more specialized requests. Limited room service (mostly pizza and sandwiches) is offered after 4:00 pm.

If you want to keep some snacks or some **simple groceries** in the room, Jackson Square Gifts & Desires (French Quarter) and Fulton's (Riverside) stock sundries and the basics. See our sidebar on page 118.

Amenities

If you're **keeping to an exercise routine** while on vacation, there is no fitness center at Port Orleans, but there is still plenty to do. In Riverside, you can rent bikes, including surrey bikes, from the Dixie Levee marina, and there are two walking/jogging/biking/wheeling routes mapped out around the two resorts. Ask for a map at Lobby Concierge. The Dixie Levee marina also rents pedal boats and other watercraft.

The **French Quarter's Doubloon Lagoon** is a medium-sized theme pool with a huge dragon water slide (you slide right down its tongue). A Mardi Gras band of crocodiles shoots water at unsuspecting swimmers. The French Quarter also has a wading pool and a hot tub nearby. In Riverside, Ol' Man Island in the middle of the district offers a "swimmin' hole", complete with a water slide, a waterfall cascading from a broken sluice, and a fun geyser. A hot tub and kids' wading area are also available here. There's a transfer tier at both theme pools for wheelchair users able to lift and lower themselves into the water. Riverside also has five quieter, heated pools throughout Magnolia Bend and Alligator Bayou.

Wheelchair transfer tier at Doubloon Lagoon

© Debra Martin Koma

The **two spas (hot tubs)** near the theme pools are great after a long day at the parks. The spa in the French Quarter is a bit secluded (look near the laundry) but large enough for several people to soak comfortably. Automated External Defibrillators (AEDs) are located near all the pools and are scattered throughout the resorts.

There's a **playground** near each of the two theme pools. An old-fashioned fishin' hole on Ol' Man Island in Riverside lets you hang a cane pole over a pond stocked with catfish, perch, bass, and bluegill (catch and release only). For more adventure, you can book a fishing excursion down the Sassagoula. Enjoy an evening carriage ride through the two sister resorts. Carriages depart from in front of Boatwright's in Riverside between 6:00 pm and 9:00 pm. (Cost is $30 for a 30-minute ride for up to four adults or two adults and two to three children.)

Disney's Port Orleans Resort

(continued)

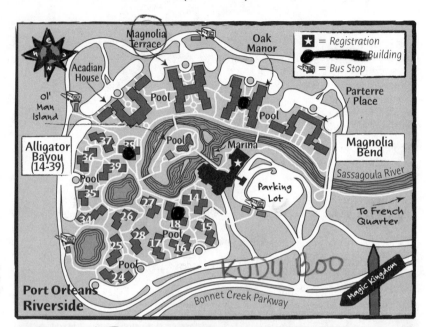

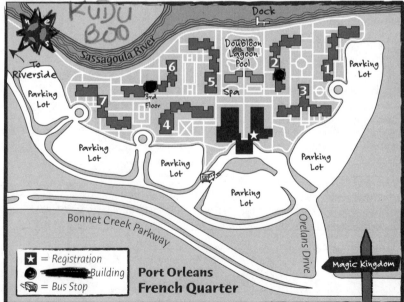

2005 standard room rates begin at $134 in value season, $149 in regular season, $169 in peak season, and $184 in holiday season (seasons are indicated on page 93). Water view and king bed rooms are $15 more.

Disney's Port Orleans Resort
(continued)

Quiet Spots

The resort's grounds are beautifully landscaped with **small parks and gardens**, plus plenty of benches for sitting and soaking in the atmosphere.

Transportation

Disney transportation to the theme parks, water parks, and Downtown Disney is via **bus**. Buses usually stop first at French Quarter's one bus stop, then go to the four stops in Riverside. To get to other resorts and destinations, take a bus to Epcot (when open) or to Downtown Disney (evening) and transfer to the appropriate bus. An accessible boat also picks up from Riverside and the French Quarter and goes to and from Downtown Disney Marketplace until 10:00 pm. Boats run about every 20 minutes (weather permitting) and are relaxing but leisurely.

Estimated Transportation Times

Magic Kingdom	Epcot	Disney-MGM Studios	Disney's Animal Kingdom	Downtown Disney
direct bus ~10 min.	direct bus ~10 min.	direct bus ~15 min.	direct bus ~15 min.	direct bus/boat ~15/~20 min.

Approximate time you will spend in transit from resort to destination during normal operation.

Our Special Needs Rating

Port Orleans Riverside **rates medium** on our special needs convenience scale, but French Quarter is **medium-high**, due to its compact size and charming atmosphere.

[A][U][S]	It can be very busy and noisy in the pools and food court areas.
[C][♥][T][M] [P][E][S] (Riverside Only)	If mobility issues are a concern and you do not have a car or a wheelchair, request a building close to services—this resort covers a lot of ground. Also, Alligator Bayou buildings do not have elevators—consider requesting a room on the ground floor.
[D][W]	Food court chefs are happy to accommodate with minimum 72 hours' notice. In addition, food courts at both Riverside and French Quarter usually have kosher items available.
[G]	There are many, many trees covered with Spanish moss around the Riverside area—allergy/asthma sufferers beware.
[F]	Alligators have been spotted in the Sassagoula River here.
[M]	The playground at Riverside is all sand, making it difficult for those with mobility issues.
[S]	Seniors will enjoy the French Quarter district.
[S][V]	Low lighting in Alligator Bayou rooms may not be good for those with vision impairments.

Disney's Port Orleans Resort

2201 Orleans Dr. and 1251 Dixie Dr., Lake Buena Vista, FL 32830
Phone: 407-934-5000 (French Quarter) or 407-934-6000 (Riverside)
Fax: 407-934-5353 (French Quarter) or 407-934-5777 (Riverside)

Disney's Saratoga Springs Resort and Spa

This is **Disney's newest resort**, located on the site of the former Disney Institute, adjacent to the Lake Buena Vista Golf Course and across Village Lake from Downtown Disney. The 65-acre Saratoga Springs Resort and Spa will eventually have 828 units, making it the largest Disney Vacation Club property to date. As of now, however, only 184 units are open as part of Phase I. Phases II and III are set to be completed in 2005 and will add an additional 368 units, while Phase IV won't be ready until 2007.

Modeled on **Saratoga Springs, New York**, the historic vacation escape famous for its healthful spa waters and thrilling horse races, this resort features Victorian-styled buildings peppered with thematic details such as a horse weather vane and a "stable" gate.

Check-In
The resort's check-in area (**check-in time is 4:00 pm**) is found in the Carriage House, an airy and bright space. Once you've checked in, you can drive over to your cluster of buildings. There's ample parking next to each building, although you can't park right in front of your room as you can at Old Key West Resort. Alternatively, Bell Services assists you with your luggage and takes you to your room. Another option is to board the bus that stops in front of the Carriage House and take it to the bus stop closest to your building. There are currently just two stops in operation.

Guest Rooms
Each of the sections of Saratoga Springs ties in to one aspect of the "Health, History, Horses" motif. The only section open currently is **Congress Park**, named for the real city's central greenspace, a favorite of both athletes and artists. (The Springs and The Paddock will open in the future.) This cluster of four Victorian-style buildings borders on the lake looking out to Downtown Disney and is the area of Saratoga Springs closest to that shopping and eating district. Rooms are decorated in soft shades of seafoam green, sand, cream, and pale yellow with dark wood furnishings and accents with a decidedly equine motif.

The Saratoga Springs Villas, with their **kitchen facilities**, are ideal for cooking meals for yourself. Studio villas (355 sq. ft./33 sq. m.) host up to four guests with one queen bed, a sofa bed, double sink, microwave, toaster, coffeemaker, and a small refrigerator. The one-bedroom (714 sq. ft./66.3 sq. m.) and two-bedroom (1,075 sq. ft./100 sq. m.) villas host up to four or eight guests each and offer master suites with king beds and whirlpool tubs, DVD players, sofa beds, full kitchens, and washers/dryers. The two-story Grand Villas (2,113 sq. ft./196 sq. m.) sleep up to 12 and feature three bedrooms, four bathrooms, a full kitchen, and dining room.

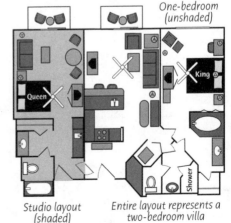

One-bedroom (unshaded)

Studio layout (shaded)

Entire layout represents a two-bedroom villa

Disney's Saratoga Springs Resort & Spa
(continued)

Guest Rooms (continued)

Since only Congress Park is open at press time, your **room choices are limited**. One consideration is that the fireworks from Pleasure Island across the lake go off at midnight each night. If the fireworks are a concern at all, request a room away from the lakeside and close to the quiet pool. Ask to be close to the footbridge, which leads to the Carriage House if mobility is a concern. There are no "preferred" or premium-priced guest rooms. Rooms in the Springs (second phase) will be closest to the Carriage House and theme pool areas, with views of Saratoga Lake or gardens/parking. The Paddock (third phase) is most spread out and distant from other facilities.

Dining

The kitchen facilities in the Villas are perfect for those with **special dietary needs**, allowing you to prepare at least some of your meals for yourself. Dining out at Saratoga Springs is limited to The Artists' Palette, a modified food court designed to resemble an artist's workspace. Open all day, it features a variety of prepackaged items, as well as some made-to-order offerings, such as pizzas, salads, and sandwiches. The Artists' Palette also stocks some basic groceries and sundries. See the sidebar on page 118 for an idea of typical items and prices.

Amenities

For those who wish to maintain an exercise routine while on vacation, the Saratoga Springs Spa has a **fully equipped fitness center** (as well as a full range of spa treatments for an extra fee, of course). There are also a jogging path, two clay tennis courts, basketball, shuffleboard, and bicycles for rent at Horsing Around Rentals. Additionally, right next door is the Lake Buena Vista Golf Course.

The High Spring Rock pool features a **"zero-entry" shoreline**. This is a gradual slope into the pool, just like a real beach— ideal for those who are unable to step down into a traditional pool. There is also a water wheelchair available, which can wheel right into the pool—just ask a lifeguard for assistance. In addition, there's a special transfer tier at the pool with an accessible platform for wheelchair users able to lift themselves out of the chair. Besides the main pool, there is also a heated "quiet pool" in each of the themed areas, which have transfer tiers. There are two hot tubs located near the main pool— one is equipped with a special wheelchair lift. There are also hot tubs near each quiet pool. Automated External Defibrillators (AEDs) are located at each of the pools and at numerous locations throughout the resort.

Saratoga Springs' zero-entry shoreline

Disney's Saratoga Springs Resort & Spa
(continued)

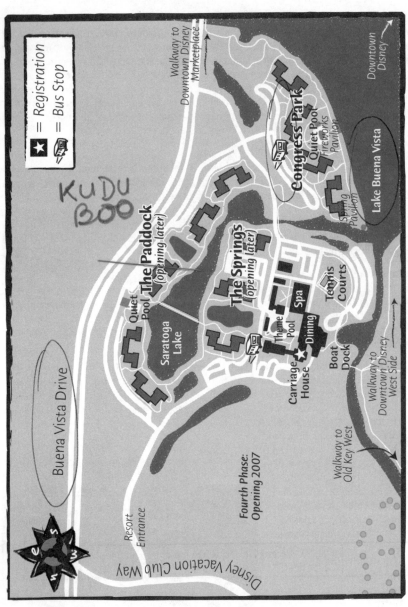

2005 standard studio rates begin at $259 in value season, $289 in regular season, $339 in peak season, and $379 in holiday season (seasons are indicated on page 93). One-bedroom villas are $350–$525. Two-bedroom villas are $490–$805. And three-bedroom Grand Villas are $1,070–$1,505.

Disney's Saratoga Springs Resort & Spa
(continued)

Quiet Spots

In spite of the **construction** that's ongoing, there are a few quiet spots here. There's a barbecue pavilion, a fireworks pavilion, formal gardens, and gazebos/fountains, all perfect for sitting and relaxing or reading in the sunshine. The Turf Club Lounge is another quiet spot, as is the patio located directly outside the Turf Club.

Transportation

Direct buses to the four theme parks, water parks, and Downtown Disney stop at the resort's bus stops (only two as of this writing). These buses also provide internal transportation within the resort. An accessible boat from the dock near the Carriage House goes to the Marketplace at Downtown Disney, stopping at Old Key West en route. Walking/wheeling paths connect the resort with Downtown Disney Marketplace and West Side (West Side pathway crosses the footbridge near the boat dock). There is also a path connecting this resort to Old Key West (see map on previous page).

Estimated Transportation Times

Magic Kingdom	Epcot	Disney-MGM Studios	Disney's Animal Kingdom	Downtown Disney
direct bus ~25 min.	direct bus ~10 min.	direct bus ~15 min.	direct bus ~20 min.	walk/bus/boat ~15/~10/~7

Approximate time you will spend in transit from resort to destination during normal operation.

Our Special Needs Ratings

Saratoga Springs Resort and Spa **ranks medium** on our special needs convenience scale. While the kitchen facilities available in the rooms here make it an excellent choice for vacationers with infants or special dietary needs, we find the resort remote from the theme parks with restricted transportation options and only one eatery. In addition, the current construction is noisy and unsightly. Also, buildings are spread out and most are located far from the main resort services.

[C][♥][T][M] [P][E][S]	If mobility issues are a concern, request to be in a guest room near an elevator.
[D]	Food court chefs are happy to accommodate with a minimum of 72 hours' advance notice.
[♥][P]	This resort has gorgeous spa and fitness facilities. When construction is completed, it will be beautifully landscaped and pleasant to walk/wheel around.
[S]	If you're interested in golf, you're just a few minutes away from a golf course here.

Disney's Saratoga Springs Resort & Spa

1960 Broadway, Lake Buena Vista, FL 32830
Phone: 407-827-1100 Fax: 407-827-1151

Disney's Wilderness Lodge & Villas

The rustic setting, log interior, and enormous lobby of the Wilderness Lodge transports you from the hustle and bustle of the theme parks to a quieter, more **serene location**. Along with its neighboring Disney Vacation Club (DVC) Villas, this is one of those Disney resorts that is so complete an experience, you don't have to enter a theme park during your vacation and yet you'll still feel like you got away from it all. It was designed by the same architect responsible for Disney's Animal Kingdom Lodge.

Check-In

Self-parking at the Lodge is a distance from the lobby entrance, up a short incline. Consider valet parking ($7/day or complimentary with handicapped tag). Check-in for both the Lodge (a deluxe resort) and the DVC Villas is **3:00 pm**. Services, including registration, for both the Lodge and the Villas are shared. Valet parking is free to DVC members staying on points.

The Lodge is the **main building** with left and right wings that surround the courtyard and themed pool area. The Villas are off to the right, connected to the main building by an outdoor covered walkway.

Guest Rooms

The Lodge has 728 guest rooms and suites. Some **open into the main lobby**, but most are along the wings with wooded or pool/water view. Standard view rooms may overlook the roof or parking areas. Regular rooms (about 350 sq. ft./32.5 sq. m.) have two queen beds, though a few have bunk beds in lieu of the second queen. All Lodge rooms have a balcony or patio, small table and chairs, TV, wall safe, refrigerator, coffeemaker and coffee packets, and hair dryer in the bathroom. Double sinks in the bathroom vanity area are standard, as are newspaper delivery and voice mail. Turndown service is available on request.

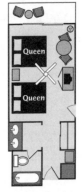

If you think you'd like a little more space, request a king room—these double as the barrier-free rooms and have a large shower but no tub. Concierge service is available also.

Standard Lodge room layout

The Villas have **136 studio, one- and two-bedroom villas**. The studios have a kitchenette, while the one- and two-bedroom villas offer full kitchens, a common area, and a stacked washer and dryer. Access to the main lobby from the Villas is via a long, inclined ramp.

For **quieter rooms**, request the top floor or a woods view. Lower floors facing the courtyard and pool can be a bit noisy.

No rollaway beds are available at the Lodge.

© Deb Wills

The kitchenette of a Wilderness Lodge Studio

Disney's Wilderness Lodge & Villas
(continued)

Dining

Wilderness Lodge hosts one of Disney's finest restaurants, **Artist Point**, which features many game items and cuisine specialties of the Pacific Northwest. They are especially accommodating to special requests with 72-hour notice. The Lodge's counter-service spot, Roaring Fork, can be quite crowded, but in the seating area, there is a microwave for warming foods. Whispering Canyon Cafe, just off the main lobby, has noisy, all-you-can-eat, family-style fun. An a la carte menu is also available. There's a good assortment of grocery items in the Wilderness Lodge Mercantile (see page 118). For a more in-depth look at the resort's dining options, see chapter 6.

Amenities

There are **plenty of activities** at the Wilderness Lodge—and even more if you visit neighboring Fort Wilderness Resort and Campground. Nonaccessible boats connect the two resorts. At the Wilderness Lodge, you can rent boats or bicycles, enjoy the Sturdy Branches health club, play at the Buttons and Bells arcade, swim in Silver Creek or the quiet pool at the Villas (both have transfer tiers), or explore the art and artifacts located throughout the resorts.

Central services are easily located off the **main lobby** and include front desk, Lobby Concierge (guest services), Whispering Canyon Café (serves three meals a day), Artist Point (a full-service dinner featuring the tastes of the Pacific Northwest), Roaring Fork (a fast-food spot), and Territory Lounge, as well as Trout Pass Pool Bar. Whispering Canyon Café is a restaurant that's open to the lobby. It can get quite boisterous at the Canyon when the tomfoolery begins! Pony races for the kids (and sometimes adults) are not uncommon.

Bright Idea: Ask for a kids' activity book at the front desk, and don't forget to look for all the Hidden Mickeys.

The Lodge also offers a **resort tour** some mornings. For a special treat, inquire at check-in about being a Flag Family. Steep stair-climbing is required to participate.

The famous **Fire Rock Geyser** spouts off hourly, and the Electric Water Pageant is visible from the beach every evening.

© Deb Wills

The beach at Wilderness Lodge & Villas Resort

Disney's Wilderness Lodge & Villas
(continued)

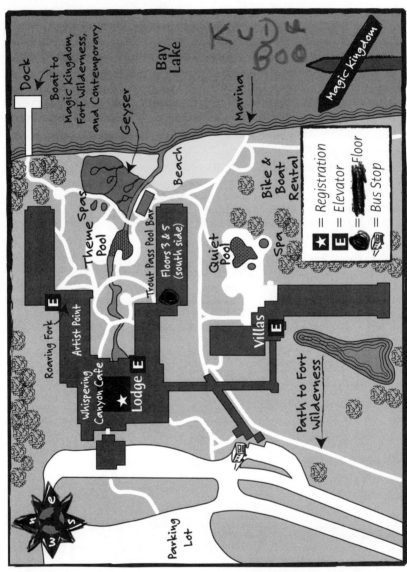

2005 standard room rates begin at $199 in value season, $239 in regular season, $289 in peak season, and $324 in holiday season (seasons are indicated on page 93). Woods-view rooms are $31–$36 more. Courtyard-view rooms are $56–$71 more than standard rooms. Standard concierge rooms are $360–$490. Studio villas are $284 in value season, $324 in regular season, $389 in peak season, and $449 in holiday season. One-bedroom villas are $390–$580. Two-bedroom villas are $555–$1,015.

Disney's Wilderness Lodge & Villas
(continued)

Transportation

Even though the Wilderness Lodge is near the Magic Kingdom, it's **not on the monorail line**, nor can you walk/wheel to the Magic Kingdom or the Transportation and Ticket Center (TTC). Disney-provided transportation is via boat (to the Magic Kingdom) or bus (to all other locations). Feedback on the transportation runs hot and cold, so if waiting is an issue, we suggest renting a car. Nonaccessible boat transportation is available to Fort Wilderness and the Contemporary. Boat transportation to the Magic Kingdom is occasionally not accessible due to water levels. When this occurs, take a bus to TTC.

Estimated Transportation Times

Magic Kingdom	Epcot	Disney-MGM Studios	Disney's Animal Kingdom	Downtown Disney
boat ~8 min.	direct bus ~10 min.	direct bus ~15 min.	direct bus ~15 min.	direct bus ~25 min.

Approximate time you will spend in transit from resort to destination during normal operation.

Our Special Needs Ratings

Wilderness Lodge is a great place to relax and enjoy the theming. Kitchen facilities available in the Villas make it an excellent choice for vacationers with infants or special dietary needs. We rate it **medium-high** on our special needs convenience scale—our only reservation is that even though all services are centrally located, the resort is remote from most Disney locations other than the Magic Kingdom and Fort Wilderness.

[A][U][S]	Main pool area can get very crowded. A smaller, quiet pool is available at the Villas. Roaring Fork—the quick-service spot—can be crowded and noisy.
[C][♥][T] [M][P][E]	Request a room near an elevator if you have mobility concerns.
[D]	Chefs are very accommodating with 72 hours' notice.
[P]	Fitness facility is on premises, as well as plenty of walking/wheeling trails and other activities.
[L]	Be sure to request a king bed—definitely not a bunk bed room, which has even less floor space.
[V]	Rooms may seem dark and poorly lit, partially due to the dark wood furnishings.

Disney's Wilderness Lodge and Villas Resort

901 W. Timberline Drive, Bay Lake, FL 32830
Phone: 407-824-3200 Fax: 407-824-3232

Disney's Yacht & Beach Club & Villas Resorts

The Yacht Club and Beach Club are **sister resorts**, perched on the bank of Crescent Lake, directly across from Disney's BoardWalk. The Beach Club Villas, a Disney Vacation Club (DVC) resort, joined these resorts in 2002. All are within walking/wheeling distance of both Epcot and the Disney-MGM Studios.

Like the BoardWalk across the lake, these resorts were designed to evoke the feel of the **seashore in the early 1900s**. The Yacht Club is the gray clapboard half of the building, with a dilapidated ship on its beach. The Beach Club's side is sky blue, with a white sandy stretch of beach. Adjacent to the Beach Club, in a separate seafoam green structure, are the Beach Club Villas.

Check-In

The Yacht and Beach Club have **separate entrances and separate front desks**. Unfortunately, neither has a low counter for check-in. Beach Club and Beach Club Villas guests check in at the Beach Club's front desk. Check-in time at both resorts is 3:00 pm.

Parking is available, but the lot is a lengthy (though level) walk/wheel from the lobby. Valet parking is available ($7/day or complimentary to DVC members staying at the Villas using points or to those with a handicapped parking permit). Bell Services will assist you with your luggage, but note that some rooms are located quite a long distance from the front desk. Ask if a resort wheelchair is available to save you the steps.

Guest Rooms

Standard rooms (634 at the Yacht Club, 580 at the Beach Club) are 380 sq. ft. (35.3 sq. m.) and are decorated in pastel colors. The Yacht Club has a decidedly more nautical feel to the decor (anchors, compasses, and the like), while the Beach Club and Villas are rather more seaside in tone. Rooms have one king-size or two queen-size beds, a daybed, double sinks, a makeup mirror, a small table and chairs, refrigerator, coffeemaker with coffee packets, and an armoire with a television and a mini-bar. Some slightly smaller rooms have a king-size Murphy bed and an extra sink and counter. Many rooms, but not all, have balconies or patios. Other room amenities include room service, hair dryers, iron and ironing board, newspaper delivery, turndown service (on request), wall safe, toiletries, and voice mail. Both the Yacht Club and the Beach Club offer a concierge service with slightly larger rooms on the fifth floor. In addition, 40 special suites (20 in each resort) range in size from a junior suite to a two-bedroom suite to the ultimate Presidential Suite.

Upon request, the Yacht and Beach Club can provide the following **special items**:

- ✔ Rollaway beds ($15 plus tax per day)
- ✔ Bed boards and rails
- ✔ Cribs
- ✔ International electrical adapter
- ✔ Smoke detectors for hearing impaired
- ✔ Heating pads
- ✔ Down pillows

Standard room layout

Disney's Yacht & Beach Club & Villas
(continued)

Guest Rooms (continued)

The 205 **Beach Club Villas**, with their kitchen facilities, are ideal for those who prefer to cook at least some meals and snacks for themselves. Rooms are studio, one-, and two-bedroom villas. Studios accommodate up to four guests with one queen-size bed, a double-size sofa bed and a kitchenette (with a sink, microwave, and a small refrigerator). The one- and two-bedroom villas accommodate up to four or eight guests respectively, and offer full kitchens, DVD players, king-size beds, and whirlpool tubs in the master bedroom, double-size sleeper sofas in the living room, and washers/dryers. Amenities for all villas include room service, iron and board, hair dryer, newspapers, high-speed Internet access, turndown service (on request), in-room safe, toiletries, and voice mail. The only smoking-optional rooms (just 24 of them!) in the Beach Club Villas are on the fourth floor.

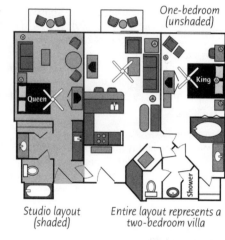

One-bedroom (unshaded)

Studio layout (shaded)

Entire layout represents a two-bedroom villa

Upon request, the Beach Club Villas can provide the following **special items**:

✔ Bed boards and rails
✔ Full-size cribs
✔ Extra portable cribs
✔ Down pillows
✔ Highchairs
✔ Electric mixer
✔ Booster seat
✔ Shower seat and toilet seat for disabled
✔ Smoke detector and telephone for hearing impaired
✔ Electric adapters
✔ Tea bags and decaf coffee

If mobility is a concern, request a room closer to the lobby for **easier access**. Also, there's a bank of elevators near each resort's lobby to serve most rooms. If your room is at the far end of a hall, though, look for a single elevator or stairway. If you're heading to Epcot, the exit near Beach Club's quiet pool is most convenient.

Stormalong Bay, the mini-water park between the Yacht & Beach Clubs, is very popular, and can be **quite noisy**, even into the night. Request a room away from it if noise is a concern.

All rooms on the first floor have patios. Most rooms on the top floor have full balconies, as do some on other floors. Be aware that some balconies are **standing room only**, however. If a full-size balcony is important, request it.

Some rooms have a **king-size Murphy bed**. These are slightly smaller than other rooms. If you desire a slightly larger room, consider the Beach Club's fifth floor concierge level.

Planning | Your Special Need | Getting There | Staying in Style | Touring | Feasting | Resources | Index

Planning

Your Special Need

Getting There

Staying in Style

Touring

Feasting

Resources

Index

Disney's Yacht & Beach Club & Villas
(continued)

Dining

Because the Yacht and Beach Clubs **share restaurants**, there are a number of fine dining options here (see pages 358–359). The Yacht Club Galley and the Crew's Cup Lounge are especially good for those looking for lighter fare. In addition, the Beach Club Villas, with their kitchen facilities, give you the chance to prepare some meals and snacks in the room. The resorts' shops (Fittings and Fairings at the Yacht Club; Beach Club Marketplace at the Beach Club) offer a good selection of grocery and sundry items. (See page 118.) Also, the newly opened Beach Club Marketplace, adjacent to the Emporium, offers made to order and prepackaged sandwiches, salads, and sweet treats. Room service is always available.

Amenities

If you need to **maintain an exercise routine** while on vacation, there's the Ship Shape Health Club, a complete fitness club offering a spa, sauna, and massage therapies. The resorts also have two lighted tennis courts and a sand volleyball court. The Bayside Marina rents watercraft and surrey bikes as well.

Three sandy-bottom swimming pools along with whirlpools, bubbling jets, a water slide in a shipwreck, and two hot tubs (spas) form the three-acre mini-water park known as **Stormalong Bay**. Stormalong Bay is for Yacht and Beach Club and Villas resort guests only (resort ID required). Unfortunately, there is no zero-entry access at Stormalong Bay, but there are several spots where you can wade into shallow pool areas of $2\frac{1}{2}$ to 3 feet of water. There is also a transfer tier for wheelchair users who are able to lift and lower themselves into the water. Lifeguards here suggest that if you're mobility-challenged, but can handle a few steps up, you might be able to go down the slide at the kids' pool. Quiet pools with transfer tiers are located at the far ends of the resorts. The Villas has its own quiet pool, called "Dunes Cove," and a hot tub. Automated External Defibrillators (AEDs) are located at each of the pools and at numerous locations throughout the resort.

Near Stormalong Bay, there's a **playground**, while the game arcade, Lafferty Place, is located adjacent to the pool area.

Quiet Spots

Quiet spots abound around these resorts. Just off the Beach Club Lobby is the The Solarium, near the entrance to the Villas is The Drawing Room, and near the Villas' quiet pool is The Breezeway. Over at the Yacht Club, there are chairs on the first floor, just behind the shop, that are often vacant and usually very quiet. Other chairs in the hallway on the way to the quiet pool offer another quiet area.

Disney's Yacht & Beach Club & Villas
(continued)

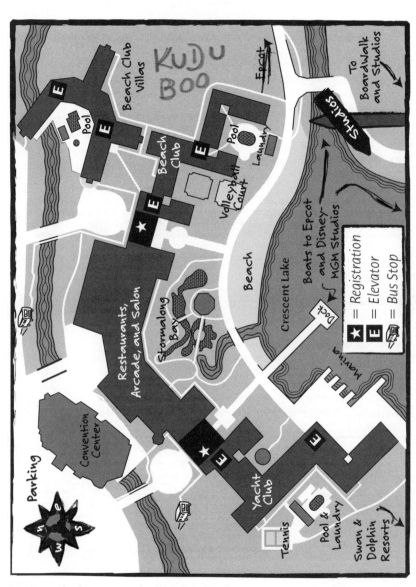

2005 standard room rates begin at $294 in value season, $334 in regular season, $404 in peak season, and $459 in holiday season (seasons are indicated on page 93). Water/pool view rooms are $61–$66 more. Garden-view concierge rooms are $435–$625. Beach Club Villa studios are $294 in value season, $334 in regular season, $404 in peak season, and $459 in holiday season. One-bedroom villas are $400–$590. Two-bedroom villas are $560–$1,040.

Disney's Yacht & Beach Club & Villas
(continued)

Transportation

There are a **number of transportation options available** at the Yacht and Beach Club resorts. Accessible Friendship boats (which also stop at the BoardWalk and the Swan and Dolphin) leave from the marina for Epcot and Disney-MGM Studios. Buses to the Magic Kingdom, Disney's Animal Kingdom, and Downtown Disney leave from the front of the Beach Club and Yacht Club—they also service the other Epcot area resorts. The BoardWalk, Dolphin, and Swan are all within walking and wheeling distance, as is the International Gateway to Epcot. Although the inclines on the bridges to BoardWalk and Swan/Dolphin are a challenge, you can avoid the incline on the path to Epcot via a waterside bypass. You could also walk or wheel to Disney-MGM Studios along the path beside the BoardWalk Villas. Reach other destinations by transferring at a nearby theme park (day) or Downtown Disney (evening).

Estimated Transportation Times

Magic Kingdom	Epcot	Disney-MGM Studios	Disney's Animal Kingdom	Downtown Disney
bus ~20 min.	walk/boat ~10/~10 min.	walk/boat ~20/~15 min.	direct bus ~20 min.	direct bus ~15 min.

Approximate time you will spend in transit from resort to destination during normal operation.

Our Special Needs Ratings

We rate the Yacht Club and Beach Club and Villas **very high** on our special needs convenience scale, even though they are among the more expensive Disney resorts. The kitchen facilities available in the Villas makes them an excellent choice for vacationers with infants or special dietary needs. In addition, the resort is centrally located, convenient to both Epcot and Disney-MGM Studios, as well as the Walt Disney World Swan and Dolphin hotels and the BoardWalk Inn and Villas. Transportation and dining options abound, and among the restaurants located in the vicinity are some of the most accommodating for travelers with special needs.

Our Special Needs Convenience Scale

[A][U][S]	Stormalong Bay pool area can get very noisy and crowded. Smaller quiet pools are available. Beaches and Cream restaurant, located near the pool, can also be quite crowded and noisy.
[C][♥][T][M][P][E]	Request a room near an elevator if you have mobility concerns.
[D]	Chefs are very accommodating with 72-hour notice.
[♥][P]	Excellent fitness facilities available on the premises; in addition, there are great walking paths and numerous other activities.
[L]	Be sure to request a king bed.

Disney's Yacht and Beach Club and Villas Resorts

1700/1800 Epcot Resorts Blvd., Bay Lake, FL 32830
Phone: 407-934-7000/8000 Fax: 407-934-3450/3850

Shades of Green Resort

Shades of Green is a **U.S. Armed Forces Recreation Center** right in the heart of Walt Disney World. It is exclusively for active and retired military personnel, as well as reservists, National Guard, Department of Defense civilians, and U.S. Public Health Service officers. The resort reopened in 2004 after an extensive renovation and expansion.

Guest Rooms
The rooms are **among the largest** at Disney at 450 sq. ft. (42 sq. m.). The 575-plus rooms are all nonsmoking, as are most central areas. Rooms are located in two buildings, one three stories and the other five stories. The building to the left of the lobby is closest to the parking garage, fitness center, and Mangino's restaurant. The building to the right of the lobby surrounds the Millpond Pool. Also nearby is a playground, Evergreen Sports Bar and Grill, hot tub, and business center. There are rooms facing the Millpond Pool itself. If you have mobility concerns, ask to be in a room closest to the lobby. There are ADA-compliant rooms—inquire at booking. Eleven family-style suites that sleeps six or eight are also offered.

Dining
Garden Gallery offers a la carte and buffet breakfast and dinner. The dinner buffet has a different theme each night. Evergreen Sports Bar and Grill serves salads, sandwiches, and burgers, while Mangino's serves dinner Italian-style. Light fare can be obtained at the Eagle's Lounge, which also has a wheelchair ramp for access to the outer lower deck with beautiful woods views. Room service offers breakfast and dinner service. Express Café near the bus area has food to go.

Amenities
For activities, there are **two pools** (Millpond and Magnolia), as well as a kids' pool and hot tub. An arcade is also near Millpond Pool. One 9-hole and two 18-hole golf courses are adjacent to the resort. AAFES General Store sells snacks, sundries, and limited Disney items.

Quiet Spots
The resort has lots of **landscaped paths and walkways**, with benches sprinkled throughout. The expansive lobby area also offers areas to sit and relax, gaze into the fireplace, or sit outside on the deck overlooking the central grounds and, in the distance, the golf course.

Transportation
Shades of Green has its own transportation (separate from Disney's) which is provided via the **bus stop** located outside the lobby in the lower level. Be sure to read the bus schedule you receive at check-in. Buses have ramps for wheelchair access. Parking is $3.

Our Special Need Ratings

[A][U][S]	The pool area can get very crowded and noisy.
[C][♥][T][M] [P][E][S]	If you have mobility concerns, we suggest renting a car and requesting a room near an elevator.
[D]	Chefs are very accommodating with 72-hour notice.
[L]	Be sure to request a king bed.

Shades of Green Resort
P.O. Box 22789, Bay Lake, FL 32830, Phone: 407-824-3400 Fax: 407-824-3460
For more information: 888-593-2242, 407-824-3400, http://www.shadesofgreen.org

Swan and Dolphin Resorts

With its sculptures of swans and heraldic dolphins, the Walt Disney World Swan and Dolphin resorts tower above nearby Epcot. Some find their design striking; others find it surreal. Westin and Sheraton, both of which are divisions of Starwood Hotels, jointly manage this pair of luxury hotels popular with **business and international visitors**.

Check-In
Each of these resorts has its own **separate check-in area**. Both areas are very open with loud echoes, particularly the Swan with its noisy splashing fountain. Check-in time at both resorts is 3:00 pm.

Parking is available for $7/day, but the lot is a **few-minutes' walk from the hotel entrance**. Valet parking is available for $14/day.

Once you've checked in, **Bell Services** will assist you with your luggage, but note that some rooms are located quite a long distance from the front desk. Ask if a resort wheelchair is available to save you the steps.

Guest Rooms
Rooms feature either one king-size bed or two double-size beds, separate vanity and bath areas, two 2-line phones, minibar, hair dryer, iron, and in-room safe. A mandatory "resort fee" adds a coffeemaker, free local phone calls, health club access, newspapers, and high-speed Internet access. In-room movies and Nintendo are extra. Some rooms have balconies, and 195 suites offer a bit more room. Guest rooms at both resorts were **recently renovated** and now sport a modern design (by Michael Graves) and "Heavenly Beds" with pillow-top mattresses and down comforters. The resorts also offer concierge (Royal Beach Club Level) and conference facilities, plus many of the same amenities and benefits found at Disney resort hotels.

Reader Tip: The Dolphin had the nicest handicapped room we've used at Disney. Large and spacious, just steps from the elevator, and with a huge shower/bath area. It was planned for the disabled.—contributed by peer reviewer Pam Passwater

Important Note: These resorts frequently host large conventions.

Dining
Between the two resorts there are quite a number of **dining options**, from the 24-hour Tubbi's (Dolphin), to the full-service Palio's (Swan) and the upscale seafood extravaganza Todd English's bluezoo (Dolphin). In addition, the Swan and Dolphin are just a short walk/wheel from the BoardWalk and the Yacht and Beach Club Resorts and their eateries (see pages 348–349 and 358–359). Notable for its willingness to cater to special diets is Fresh Mediterranean Market, which features a healthful buffet and made-to-order items. Note that kosher items are not generally available at Swan and Dolphin restaurants, even with advance notice. Note, too, that the Swan and Dolphin feature restaurants with a great emphasis on seafood: Kiku (sushi) and Todd English's bluezoo.

Swan and Dolphin Resorts
(continued)

Amenities

If you need to **maintain a fitness routine** while on vacation, both the Swan and Dolphin feature fully equipped fitness centers that include saunas and massage therapies. Several walking/wheeling/jogging routes, ranging from one to four miles, have been mapped out—ask at the fitness center for a map. There are also four lighted tennis courts between the two hotels, as well as basketball and volleyball areas. And if you're not up to a round of real golf at one of Disney's golf courses, the Fantasia Gardens Miniature Golf is just a short walk away.

Each hotel has a **heated quiet pool**, perfect for swimming laps. Located between the two resorts is the three-acre Grotto Pool, which has a waterfall and slide. There's also a kiddie pool for the little ones and four whirlpools. There's also a small playground located at each resort, not too far from the pools.

Each resort has its own **game arcade**—the Dolphin's is slightly larger and is located near Tubbi's 24-hour buffeteria.

Guests receive most of the **same benefits** enjoyed at the Disney-owned resorts, including package delivery, but they cannot charge Disney purchases to their room.

Transportation

Disney **buses** take you to Disney's Animal Kingdom, the Magic Kingdom, the water parks, or Downtown Disney. The bus stop is at the front of either resort (exit the hotel and walk/wheel down the sidewalk to the left). Note, however, that buses stop at other Epcot area resorts (BoardWalk, Yacht Club, and Beach Club) en route. There are accessible Friendships, which also stop at the Epcot area resorts, that run to Disney-MGM Studios and Epcot from the dock located between the two hotels. Walking/wheeling to Epcot or Disney-MGM Studios is also an option from these two very conveniently located hotels.

Our Special Needs Ratings

We rate the Swan and Dolphin resorts **high** on our scale. The convenient location, close to two theme parks, and numerous dining and transportation options make them a very good choice for guests with special needs. Also, many discounts and special rates (for teachers, AAA, Disney Annual Passholders, etc.) are available.

[A][U][S]	The Grotto Pool area can get very crowded and noisy. Smaller quiet pools are available.
[C][♥][T][M][P][E]	Request a room near an elevator if you have mobility concerns.
[D][W]	No kosher items are available at the restaurants here.
[L]	Be sure to request a king bed.

Walt Disney World Swan and Dolphin Resorts

1500 Epcot Resorts Blvd., Bay Lake, FL 32830
Phone: 407-934-3000 (Swan) or 934-4000 (Dolphin)
Fax: 407-934-4499 (Swan) or 407-934-4099 (Dolphin)
For reservations, call 800-828-8850 or 407-934-6244
For more information, visit http://www.swandolphin.com

Disney Vacation Club

The Disney Vacation Club (DVC) is Disney's version of vacation ownership, a sort of **mouse-friendly timeshare**. Unlike traditional timeshares (where you purchase a set place for a set time of year), the DVC works on a point system, providing flexibility regarding accommodations and when you want to travel.

Currently, there are **seven DVC resorts**: Old Key West (see pages 145–147), BoardWalk Villas (see pages 121–124), Villas at the Wilderness Lodge (see pages 164–167), Beach Club Villas (see pages 168–172), Saratoga Springs Resort and Spa (see pages 160–163), Vero Beach (along the Florida coast), and Hilton Head Island (South Carolina). Accommodations offered range from studios to one-, two-, and three-bedroom villas. Housekeeping is limited.

DVC accommodations can be **rented** just like all the other Disney resort hotels or can be reserved by members. For those traveling with special needs, more at-home amenities are offered in DVC resorts, making them a great choice. Studios have a kitchenette and access to laundry machines, while the one-, two-, and three-bedroom villas have full kitchens, washer and dryer, whirlpool tub, and space!

Disney Vacation Club

200 Celebration Place, Celebration, FL 34747-9903
Phone: 800-500-3990 Fax: 407-566-3393
DVC information kiosks are at most Disney parks and resorts.
Sales offices and models are at Disney's Saratoga Springs.
DVC Web site: http://www.disneyvacationclub.com

© MediaMarx, Inc.

The master bedroom of a one-bedroom villa at Saratoga Springs Resort

Other Hotels

Below are a few hotels and motels near Walt Disney World (but not on property) that either our editors and publishers Jennifer and Dave Marx stayed in and recommend or at which our readers report good experiences.

Hotel Name (in alphabetical order)	Starting Rates	Year Built	Year Renovated
Holiday Inn Family Suites	**$114+**	**1999**	**2005**

Jennifer and Dave had the pleasure of staying at this 800-suite resort in July 2002. Besides the resort's close proximity to Walt Disney World (just 3 miles/5 km.), the hotel offers unique and very convenient "Kidsuites" with a living room, kitchenette, master bedroom, and kids' room. The kids get a bunk bed, TV, Nintendo (fee applies), and a small table and chairs. If you don't have kids, you can get a room with a different configuration, such as the SweetHeart Suite (whirlpool tub and 50" TV), the CinemaSuite (60" TV with stereo surround), Residential Suite (full kitchen), or the Two-Bedroom Suite. Guests get a full, hot breakfast buffet from 6:30 am to 11:00 am. Kids eat free when they dine with adults. The resort also has a large pool, water playground, two hot tubs, and a small miniature golf course. There is a free scheduled shuttle bus to Walt Disney World, but we found it more convenient to drive. The resort was being revamped with a Nickelodeon theme in spring 2005. Visit http://www.hifamilysuites.com or call 407-387-5437 or 877-387-5437. Hotel address: 14500 Continental Gateway, Orlando, FL 32821

Radisson Resort Parkway	**$79+**	**1987**	**2001**

Jennifer and Dave enjoyed our recent stay at this 718-room, 6-story deluxe hotel just 1.5 miles (2.5 km) from the gates of Walt Disney World. Guest rooms accommodate up to four guests with either one king-size bed or two double-size beds. Rooms come in either pool or courtyard views and feature modern Italian furniture and marble bathrooms. Amenities include a 25" TV, stocked mini-bar, in-room safe, coffeemaker, iron and ironing board, hair dryer, makeup mirror, voice mail, and data ports. For a fee, you can add WebTV and Nintendo. The resort has two pools, a water slide, a wading pool, and two hot tubs, as well as lighted tennis courts, fitness center, playground, and arcade. Food service includes a full-service restaurant (open for breakfast and dinner), a deli with Pizza Hut items, a sports bar, a pool bar, and room service. Note that kids under 10 eat free when accompanied by a paying adult. There is a free scheduled shuttle bus to attractions. For the best rates, visit http://www.radissonparkway.com/offers/index.asp?adsvc=02PASS or call 407-396-7000 and ask for the "Y-PASS" rate code. 2900 Parkway Boulevard, Kissimmee, FL 34747

Sheraton Safari Resort	**$85+**	**1994**	**1998**

While this isn't equivalent to Disney's Animal Kingdom Lodge, this safari-themed resort is a winner with kids and adults alike. The 489-room, 6-story hotel is located just $1/4$ mile ($1/2$ km.) from the Disney property (you can't walk to it, but it is a short drive or ride on the scheduled shuttle). Guest rooms come in standard (one king-size or two double-size beds), Safari Suites (with kitchenette and separate parlor), and deluxe suites (with full kitchens and large parlors). Standard rooms accommodate up to four guests or five guests with the rental of a rollaway bed. All rooms have a balcony or patio, TV with PlayStation, two phones with voice mail, data ports, high-speed Internet access, hair dryer, makeup mirror, coffeemaker, iron and ironing board, and in-room safe. The resort features a large pool with a 79-ft. water slide, wading pool, hot tub, fitness center, and arcade. One full-service restaurant (Casablanca's) offers breakfast and dinner (kids under 10 eat free with paying adults), along with the Outpost Deli (for lunch and dinner), the ZanZibar Watering Hole, and room service (6:30 am–10:00 pm). Visit http://www.sheratonsafari.com or call 407-239-0444 or 800-423-3297. Hotel address: 12205 Apopka-Vineland Road, Orlando, FL 32836.

Disney Cruise Line

The Disney Cruise Line combines many of your favorite things from the Disney theme parks and transforms them into two magnificent cruising ships for a **unique vacation experience**. The Disney Magic and the Disney Wonder boast outstanding customer service, unique dining and entertainment experiences, Disney characters, and, of course, magic.

Whether you're sailing on the Magic or the Wonder, you'll receive in your stateroom each evening a newsletter, the **Navigator**, packed with information on the next day's activities. This guide provides you with dining hours and locations, special activities, and show descriptions and times. Extra copies of the Navigator are available at Guest Services. Visit: http://www.dcltribute.com/navigators to become familiar with the Navigator and activities before you go. The Magic and the Wonder are almost identical, so all descriptions here apply to both, unless otherwise noted.

Adults without children sometimes hesitate to go on a Disney cruise because they equate Disney with "family," but co-author Deb Wills loves the **adult-only areas** of the ship and Castaway Cay and has never felt inundated with young ones.

Cruise veterans will find the Disney **staterooms larger than most other cruise lines**. Standard in each room category are a television, phone, and in-room safe. Bathrooms contain hair dryer and tub. Almost half of all staterooms offer a verandah where you can sit and enjoy your morning coffee or evening beverage.

Before You Go

You can **book your Disney Cruise vacation** yourself through Disney Cruise Line. Call 888-325-2500. Outside the U.S., call 407-566-6921 (representatives offer assistance in English, Spanish, Japanese, French, Portuguese, and German). For information via TTY, call 407-566-7455. You can also reserve your cruise through http://www.disneycruise.com or contact a travel agent.

Whatever you decide, when you book your cruise, you'll also be **selecting your stateroom**. Before you call, make sure you have a list of any special needs/requirements and preferences to discuss with the reservation agent. This is when you'll note everything from special dietary requests, to accessible staterooms, to the need for a special communications kit.

If you have any special medical needs or require an accessible room, you need to submit a **special medical form**. Request this from your travel agent or Disney directly. The earlier you book your cruise, the better your chances of obtaining an accessible cabin in the category you desire.

You will be asked if you prefer the **early or late dining seating**. Early is at 6:00 pm and late is 8:30 pm. If eating at a specific time is necessary for you, be sure to mention this when you book your reservations. Remember any time zone changes when deciding on early or late seating. It is quite possible that you will be sitting with "strangers" at meal time.

Bright Idea: *If you wish to have your own table (no others seated with you), be sure to request this in advance. Once onboard the ship, check with Guest Services to see if your request was granted. If not, you will have the opportunity to request dining changes at that time.*

Staterooms on the Disney Cruise Line

Inside Staterooms (Categories 10-12)
Inside staterooms are the **least expensive**. There are no windows (don't reserve if you are claustrophobic), which makes the rooms fairly dark. Category 10 rooms are 214 sq. ft. (20 sq. m.) and categories 11 and 12 are 184 sq. ft. (17 sq. m.). Category 12 sleeps only three people. Categories 11 and 12 do not have the split bathroom (separate toilet and bath). Room locations range from deck 2 to deck 7 (most on the lower decks).

Outside Stateroom With Porthole (Categories 8-9)
These are not the small portholes you might associate with a ship—these are large round windows that let in a **good amount of light** (except deck 1's outside staterooms, which have two tiny portholes). No verandahs though. Category 8 rooms have 214 sq. ft. (20 sq. m.) and are on decks 5-7, but most are in the front of the ship (avoid if you have motion sensitivity).

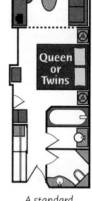

Outside Stateroom with Verandahs (Categories 4-7)
Staterooms are 268-304 sq.ft. (25-28.2 sq. m.). Your verandah is your own **private deck** for watching the sights.

Outside Stateroom Suites With Verandas (Categories 1-3)
These are huge rooms with extra amenities, such as concierge service and expanded room service. All suites are on deck 8 and are pricey!

Bright Idea: To view the location of accessible staterooms, visit the Disney Cruise Line "Deck Plans" page at http://disneycruise.com or check the stateroom chart in P"assPorter's Field Guide to the Disney Cruise Line and its Ports of Call" guidebook.

A standard category 9 stateroom

Reader Tip: "When we booked our cabin, we were told my electric wheelchair would most likely fit in the room and, if not, we could leave it in the hallway. When we checked in, they said it would not fit, but the stateroom host would stow it. The stateroom host told us he had no place for it and would have to leave it by the elevator. Fortunately, we were able to upgrade. With something important like this, call and call again! Even then, be flexible once you board the ship."–contributed by peer reviewer Joanne Ernest

An accessible stateroom (category 11) has a lot of space   An accessible, roll-in shower

Embarking on the Disney Cruise Line

Documentation

Your **cruise documents** will arrive approximately two weeks prior to your cruise. Be sure to fill these out before you leave home. Double-check to make sure you have the proper identification with you. Current photo identification and valid birth certificates are accepted for U.S. residents at the time of writing, but only until 12/31/2005, when passports are required for all persons (adults and children, U.S. resident or otherwise) reentering the United States from the Caribbean.

Packing

Be sure to **pack a day bag** with anything you might need from the time you depart for the cruise terminal until dinner. Depending on where you are coming from and your mode of transportation, it is possible you will not see your luggage from early morning to that evening!

Small personal coolers are allowed for medications, baby food, or dietary needs.

Check-In

Check-in is the time to **reconfirm** that Disney Cruise Line has a record of any special needs requests you made in advance. If you need special assistance boarding, discuss this with the crew member at the terminal when you check in—you may be able to wait off to the side rather than stand in the line. Alas, there are no accessible counters at check-in.

© MediaMarx, Inc.

The terminal and entrance to the gangway (through Mickey's head); seating to the right is used by those who have special boarding needs and those booked in categories 1-3

Safety Drill

Before each ship leaves Port Canaveral, a **mandatory safety drill takes place at 4:00 pm**. In your stateroom closet, you'll find bright orange life jackets. Check the jackets when you arrive in your stateroom. If you need different sizes, contact your stateroom host/hostess right away. An announcement over the stateroom and ship loudspeakers (complete with sounding alarm) will notify you of the drill. You must put on your life jacket and report to your designated location on the ship. Your assembly station is mapped on the back of your stateroom door, and your station location is noted on your life jacket. While most locations are on the outer decks of the ship, some are inside, such as at Animator's Palate. It gets quite crowded and noisy in these inside areas. Once you arrive at your drill assembly station, a crew member will take attendance (be sure to check in when called). You will be required to wait in a group until the "all clear" is sounded. This can be 15–20 minutes. Keep your life jacket on until you return to your stateroom.

If you **require assistance** during the safety drill, stop by Guest Services soon after you board and let them know your situation. People with mobility issues will be assisted (and will be able to use the elevators). A limited number of larger-size life jackets are available upon request. Ask your stateroom host or hostess, or call Guest Services once you board.

Dining on the Disney Cruise Line

Where to Eat

You have a **choice of places** to dine and snack throughout your cruise: buffet, table-service restaurant, snack bars, room service. You are assigned a dining table location and rotation for dinner. Your servers stay with you as you move to different dining rooms each night.

Special dietary requirements are accommodated on the Disney Cruise ships, provided you make your requirements known before you cruise. A notation will be made on your reservation and you may be instructed to meet with the Food and Beverage team the afternoon you board ship (check the Welcome Navigator for time/location). You'll have the chance to explain your needs, and the Food and Beverage team will discuss what they can do for you. This information will be passed to your servers, who wil be with you each evening throughout your cruise (except if/when you dine at the premium restaurant, Palo). Be sure to remind your servers (and the head waiter) of your dietary requests on the first evening.

If you wait until you are onboard to request a special meal, your **choices will be very limited**. Basics such as vegetarian (two choices) or grilled chicken/fish are always available at the table-service restaurants, but obtaining foods without sauces or making other special request, isn't always possible due to the "en masse" kitchen preparation.

Bright Idea: When you're breakfasting at Triton's/Lumiere's/Parrot Cay, Egg Beaters egg substitutes are available upon request. Because these take longer to prepare, be sure to order them as soon as you are seated.

Kosher meals are available at the table-service restaurants only when requested in advance of your cruise. Sugar-free desserts are offered during lunch and dinner in the table-service areas.

Kids' menus are available at table-service restaurants (adults can order from them, too). Basic items usually include hot dogs, macaroni and cheese, pizza, chicken strips, grilled cheese, soda, milk, or juice. Smoothies are $3.50 extra.

Room service is available 24 hours a day, whether you are at sea or in port (except on debarkation morning). Although the menu is very limited, you don't have to leave your cabin to eat. Special dietary items are limited with room service, though. Selections include chef salad, soup, fruit, sandwiches, burgers, mac and cheese, peanut butter and jelly, and pizza.

Deb Wills has cruised while on **Weight Watchers** and, after seven days, remained the same weight as when she set foot onboard. She did splurge a bit at Palo, but she made sure to get some exercise in and was able to maintain her diet.

Co-author Deb Wills (right) and Linda Eckwerth at Palo

Entertainment on the Disney Cruise Line

What to Do

The cruise just wouldn't be Disney's without **characters and first-rate shows**. The entertainment starts during the Sail Away Party (5:00 pm) on decks 9 and 10. The party is very high energy, noisy, and crowded. That said, it's one of our favorite parts of the cruise experience. And there's nothing so thrilling as hearing "When You Wish Upon A Star" from the ship's horn as you pull out of port!

The nighttime **theater shows** are high-quality entertainment, too, and are very popular. Early diners attend the later shows, and late diners the early shows.

People of all ages love the Disney characters. In addition to appearances during the day, **characters are available for photographs** each evening in the atrium just outside Triton's/Lumiere's. Lines tend to be very long at these times, especially when Mickey and Minnie are in their formal attire. It also can get very crowded and noisy during these photo sessions.

The **Vista Spa** is a delightful adults-only area where you can get pampered and keep in shape. You can get spa treatments and salon services, take exercise and nutrition classes, and work out in the fitness center (the perfect place to maintain an exercise routine).

Travel Insurance

While no one likes to think their vacation might get canceled at the last minute, it can happen. If you have **medical issues**, you may be especially vulnerable to needing to cancel a planned trip or for emergency medical evacuation once aboard. In addition, weather concerns (traveling from the north in winter, cruising the Caribbean during hurricane season), can delay your arrival to the port.

Most **travel insurance policies** will offer trip cancellation/interruption, delay protection, emergency medical, and baggage coverage. The Disney Cruise Line offers a policy for as little as $49 per person. However, if you use the Disney Cruise Line policy and do not book your airfare with them, that portion of your trip may not be covered. Also, some preexisting conditions are not covered, so be sure to inquire.

You can also call your insurance agent or visit http://www.insuremytrip.com or http://quotetravelinsurance.com. Don't delay if you want travel insurance, as some insurance policies must be **purchased within a week of paying your deposit** for the cruise.

Reader Tip: "Buy your travel insurance within a few days of making your initial cruise deposit. The travel insurance companies will only cover preexisting conditions if you purchase their coverage within 7 to 21 days (varies from company to company and plan to plan) of making your initial deposit. I've searched and have yet to find a company that will cover preexisting conditions, at any price, if you purchase the plan outside the 7- to 21-day window."—contributed by peer reviewer Amy Warren Stoll

Special Needs on the Disney Cruise Line

Special Requests

When you're making your special requests for the cruise, remember that everything is handled by the Disney Cruise Line reservations staff on land. In other words, these are not the same people who will be traveling with you on the ship. That's why it's so important to **double check that all requests** have been recorded once you receive your final boarding documents. Then, once you are onboard, and before the ship sails, visit Guest Services (deck 3 midship) to verify that all your requests have been noted. The crew members onboard will do everything possible to accommodate you, but they must get the information from Disney Cruise Line reservations first—otherwise, they won't know just what it is that you require and make sure it's around.

Allergies

For many cruisers, traveling south means **different vegetation and flowers**. If you are sensitive to pollen, grasses, etc., be sure to bring your allergy medication with you. Bedcovers in the staterooms are changed after every cruise, along with your bed linens. If you require any special cleaning, discuss this when you make your reservations.

Disney **restricts smoking** to certain areas of the ship and enforces it. No smoking is allowed in the main dining areas or staterooms. Smoking is allowed in the dance club, adults-only lounge, and open areas, such as decks 9 and 10. No smoking is allowed in the Mickey pool area. Guests can smoke on their verandahs, however, and the smoke can travel.

ADD/ADHD/ASD

The **Disney Cruise Line DVD** is a great way to become familiar with the ship and your upcoming voyage—you can request the free DVD by calling 888-325-2500 or visiting online at http://www.disneycruise.com.

All outside railings facing the water have solid bottoms to **discourage climbing**.

Be sure to bring **earplugs for loud areas** (such as the open decks and buffet areas).

All verandah staterooms have a second lock high up on the verandah door that must be unlocked to access the verandah.

Be sure to visit Guest Services once you board if you will need special accommodations during the **mandatory safety drill**.

You might encounter **lines and/or waits** in these spots:
- ✔ At check-in at the terminal. Lines are usually short unless the cruise is "sold out."
- ✔ Waiting to board the ship prior to embarkation time. Folks who arrive at the terminal tend to get in line after they check in. There is no real reason to do this unless you want to make sure you get a reservation at Flounder's Reef or Palo, the adults-only restaurant.
- ✔ During the safety drill. You will be required to wait at your designated location until all staterooms have checked in and the "all clear" is given.
- ✔ On excursions. While Disney excursions are very organized, you often have to gather and wait several times. Also, some excursions may have a fair amount of travel time, so ask before booking.
- ✔ For character photographs. Lines can be long during the evening hours when everyone wants a photo with Donald and Daisy or Mickey and Minnie.
- ✔ At Guest Services, especially during your last 24 hours onboard.
- ✔ At the buffet meals.

Special Needs on the Disney Cruise Line
(continued)

Addiction Recovery

There are **Friends of Bill W. meetings** onboard the Disney Cruise Line. The 7-night cruise has meetings every day except boarding and debarkation day. The 4-night cruise has meetings on day 2 and 3 (again, not on boarding or debarkation day). The 3-night cruise has meetings on the second day (again, not on boarding or debarkation day). Check your daily Navigator for times and locations, or contact Guest Services onboard to obtain meeting information.

Important Note: Remember, alcohol is everywhere onboard and there is always a "drink of the day." Drinking age is 21.

Chronic Fatigue

Try not to let the jam-packed personal Navigator alarm you! While there is plenty to keep you entertained and active during the cruise, you can also choose to **just kick back** and watch the water go by if you desire. You don't even have to leave the ship until you return to port if you choose.

If you have a room in category 7 or above, you can sit and smell the sea air right from your **stateroom's verandah**. Order room service for meals and you're all set. Category 8 allows you to sit at the window and watch the water. Deck 4 offers lounge chairs under shade facing the water—this area is generally quiet. The Tropical Rainforest at the Vista Spa is a great place for quiet and relaxation, complete with soothing heat and steam.

Use caution when selecting excursions. Some of them take the entire day, with much of the time used to get back and forth from the ship.

Fears

If you or someone you are traveling with doesn't like heights, book an inside stateroom and stay away from the edges of the decks. Fear of water? Avoid the outside decks.

Foreign Language

The Directory of Services book found in your stateroom has brief information sections in the back written in **Spanish, French, German, and Japanese**. Dining room menus are also available in those languages. Have your reservation noted and remind your servers the first evening.

Crowded Areas

- ✔ Topsiders/Beach Blanket Buffet Lunch on embarkation day
- ✔ Before and after the evening dinner seatings
- ✔ Before and after a stage show ends
- ✔ Character Meet and Greets
- ✔ Atriums during photography sessions
- ✔ Shutters, where photographs are displayed (especially the last 24 hours)
- ✔ Debarkation at a port—at the initial time you are able to leave the ship
- ✔ Embarkation at a port—as the time to be back onboard nears
- ✔ Kids' and family pools, especially on "at sea" days when it's hot
- ✔ Safety drill assembly stations
- ✔ Elevators, especially midship

Special Needs on the Disney Cruise Line
(continued)

Hearing Impaired

Assistive listening systems are available for the Walt Disney and Buena Vista theaters, WaveBands/Rockin' Bar D, and Studio Sea. A $25 refundable deposit will be charged to your stateroom. Inquire at Guest Services.

Closed captioning is available for stateroom televisions and select onboard video monitors. American Sign Language interpretation is available for live performances on designated cruises. You must make arrangements when you book your cruise.

Communication kits are available for your stateroom and contain door knock and phone alerts, phone amplifer, bed shaker, strobe light smoke detector, and TTY.

Guest Assistance Packets containing show scripts, flashlights, and pen/paper are available at Guest Services. You can sign out these packets and keep them until the night before debarkation, then return them to Guest Services.

Infants/Children

Traveling with young ones? You can **request Pack 'n' Play-type cribs**, bed rails, and highchairs from your stateroom host/hostess. Crib blankets are not provided (nor recommended for young infants).

© MediaMarx, Inc.

Formula for infants (milk-based Isomil and Similac) are sold in the Treasure Ketch (deck 4). You can also purchase diapers, wipes, diaper ointment, pacifiers, and a few other items—baby food is not available for purchase nor is it offered in the restaurants. Keep in mind the ship's stores have limited hours and are closed when in port. It's best to bring your own supplies!

If your child is between 12 weeks and 3 years, or not toilet-trained, you can use **Flounder's Reef Nursery**, the ship's full-service childcare center. (If your child

A Pack 'n' Play-type crib aboard the Disney Cruise Line

is older, see the Oceaneer Club and Lab sidebar on the next page.) Located on deck 5, near the Buena Vista Theatre, Flounder's is equipped with a playroom and toys, Disney movies, baby bouncers, and rocking chairs, as well as a separate sleeping area with cribs

© MediaMarx, Inc.

for infants and mats for toddlers. There is also a small diaper changing room. Babies in Flounder's Reef may be given apple juice and saltine crackers, as appropriate for their age. No other food is given to them.

Flounder's Reef is **$6/per hour** for the first child and $5/hour for additional children, with a two-hour minimum. Flounder's is open daily, usually from 1:00 pm to 4:00 pm and 6:00 pm to midnight. Times can vary depending on port, so be sure to check your Navigator for times.

Flounder's Reef play area

Special Needs on the Disney Cruise Line
(continued)

Oceaneer Club and Lab

The Oceaneer Club (ages 3-4 and 5-7) and the Oceaneer Lab (ages 8-9 and 10-12) are activity centers designed just for kids. Special age-appropriate programs run here throughout the day and evening, and there is no additional fee—it's included in the price of your cruise. Children must be potty-trained; however, exceptions are made for special needs children. If your special needs child is not potty-trained, they will be admitted to the club unless they require one-on-one care or have more demanding needs. You will have a pager and will be called to take care of the child's toileting needs. If there are special medical needs, you must file a medical form when you make your reservation.

On the first afternoon of the cruise, visit the children's area (deck 5 midship) to speak with the counselors and (if desired) sign in your kids. As you're filling out the registration form (it's quite lengthy!), be sure to talk with the counselors to explain any special needs your child has. We've been told some parents do not mention "special needs" for fear their child won't be accepted—rest assured the staff makes every effort to accommodate every child and strives to make sure every child has a special cruise. Be sure to include all special considerations, including allergies, illnesses, limitations, medical conditions, medications, fears, etc. The more information you share, the better the staff can assist your child. You may stay with your child in the club or check on him/her whenever you like. The clubs can be very loud, so be sure to bring earplugs if you or they have a sensitivity to noise.

The club issues pagers to parents so you can be contacted quickly in case a problem arises. Parents are paged when children require bathroom assistance (staff cannot change diapers or help children with the toilet). If your special needs child is in the kids' program while in port, be sure to leave a responsible adult aboard the ship.

Make sure you understand the rules and the schedule for the clubs. For safety reasons, there are times of transition (when the groups are changing locations) when you will not be able to sign your child in or out.

If you are unsure how your child will react in the club, start out slowly. Leave them there for just a short amount of time. Next time, they can stay a little longer. Remember, be flexible!

If at any time your child wants to leave the club, they can let the counselors know, and you will be paged.

There are various age groupings for kids' activities. While the Disney Cruise Line is very strict and will not allow you to move your child up to an older age group, you may be able to move down, depending on your child.

The Disney Cruise Line is unable to provide one-on-one care for any child with special needs, and counselors are not allowed to administer any medications. If your child will be in the club and it's med time, you will have to give the medication yourself.

Special Needs on the Disney Cruise Line
(continued)

Medical Treatment

Disney has a well-equipped **medical facility** on deck 1 staffed by two doctors and three registered nurses from Vanter Cruise Health Services (http://www.vanterventures.com). The center is open daily in the morning and early evening, and a physician and nurse are on call 24 hours a day. The Disney Cruise Line contracts out for the medical care. Any usage fees you incur will be charged to your stateroom and must be paid before you leave the ship. You will be provided a form to file with your insurance company after the cruise. There is a very limited pharmacy onboard for emergencies and unexpected illnesses. All regular medications must be brought with you. In extreme circumstances, Disney will arrange to have a passenger taken back to the nearest port to receive medical care (costs will vary).

If you need to have your **blood pressure checked**, stop by the first aid center during normal working hours.

Bright Idea: We strongly urge you to take out travel insurance when you book your cruise (see page 182). Be sure to inquire about coverage for preexisiting conditions.

A small refrigerator, actually more like a beverage cooler, comes in each stateroom. It's set at approximately 55° F/ 13° C. It is 8" deep x 12" wide x 16.5" high. This is not a suitable storage area for your medications. Request a real refrigerator when making your reservation and confirm just prior to sailing. The onboard medical center has a limited supply of **compact refrigerators for medications**.

Housekeeping will provide a **container for "sharps,"** or used needles—just ask your stateroom host or hostess upon arrival.

Mobility/Accessibility

Sixteen **handicap-accessible, barrier-free staterooms** are available in categories 3, 5, 6, 8, and 11. These rooms are larger than normal and also feature open bed frames, additional phones in the bathroom/nightstand, bathroom and shower handrails, fold-down shower seats, hand-held shower heads, lowered towel and closet bars, and emergency call buttons. Those with mobility concerns who do not use a wheelchair should book a stateroom near an elevator.

© Deb Wills

Peer reviewer Chet McDoniel in an accessible category 8 stateroom

Most **standard wheelchairs do not fit through the regular cabin doors** onboard. Some standard chairs can easily fold, and if so, they can be taken inside the room.

A pool transfer tier can be found at the Quiet Cove pool (multistep, not automatic).

Companion restrooms are located on deck 3 aft by Parrot Cay, deck 4 forward by the Walt Disney Theatre, deck 9 forward by Vista Spa, and deck 10 aft by Palo.

The **Walt Disney Theatre** has places for wheelchairs in the back. If you can transfer from your chair, you can request seating in the front row. Ask the crew member when you arrive at the theatre. They'll take you inside and get you set up before everyone else enters.

Special Needs on the Disney Cruise Line
(continued)

Mobility/Accessibility (continued)

The handicapped viewing area for the **Sail Away Party** is on deck 10 overlooking the pool. It's a great place for everyone to watch the party, but be aware there is <u>no</u> shade! There is also a "participation" area for the party on deck 9 near the gazebo. Check with crew members 30 minutes prior to the activity for exact location.

Elevators are small and often crowded. Avoid the midship elevators in particular.

To **access** Lumiere's/Triton's (deck 3) go through the side entrance—the main entrance has steps. Access to the raised seating at Rockin' Bar D/Wavebands (also deck 3) is via ramp located in the bar area.

Wheelchairs are available on a limited basis from Guest Services. If you will need a wheelchair or ECV while onboard or in ports, bring your own or rent one (call 866-416-7383 or visit http://brevardmedicalequip.com) with delivery and pickup right at the ship.

The **Port of Nassau is semi-wheelchair friendly**. There are some sidewalk cut-outs and some accessible shops. If you book an excursion through Disney Cruise Line, they will not transport your electric wheelchair, but they may be able to provide a manual one for you to use. At this time, there are <u>no</u> excursions that can accommodate powered chairs.

The Disney Cruise Line makes every attempt to **dock directly** at the port's pier, allowing gangplank loading and unloading (accessible for wheelchairs), but there may be times when this is not possible. In those cases, cruise guests are "tendered" from the ship to the shore. Tendering involves transportation via small boats. You must be able to transfer from your wheelchair to the tender boat and out again, and your wheelchair must be folded and transferred to the tender. In certain situations, it will be impossible for guests in wheelchairs to transfer due to safety concerns.

A limited number of **beach wheelchairs** are available at Disney's private island, Castaway Cay. They are located on the left at Shuttle's Cove, the first tram stop. If you plan to spend your day at Serenity Bay (the adult-only beach), beach wheelchairs are available there also. The lifeguards will keep your personal wheelchair at their stations.

Bright Idea: If you plan to get out of your wheelchair at the beach, bring a cover to reflect the heat (and protect against the salt water).

Getting around **Castaway Cay can be a challenge** from a mobility standpoint, as much of the surface area is sand. The only companion restroom on Castaway Cay is in the First Aid building across from the family beach (but quite a distance from the adult beach). Tram service on Castaway Cay is available, but because the space is smaller than normal Disney buses, be aware that some motorized scooters and wheelchairs may not fit. (Right behind the driver, in the first "row" of seats, there is a section of seating that can be pulled up for a wheelchair to fit in. No lifting is involved. A manual ramp is pulled out from the floor in that seating section by the driver.)

The **Disney Cruise Line buses** are chartered through Mears. Each bus can accommodate two electric wheelchairs. If there are more than two in your party, be sure to discuss this when you book the transport. The restroom onboard the buses is wheelchair-accessible.

Special Needs on the Disney Cruise Line
(continued)

Service animals are allowed onboard the Disney Cruise Line (you'll need to file a special medical form—see page 178); however, they may not be allowed off the ship at certain ports. Special paperwork must be filled out once you make a reservation—this includes separate paperwork for the Bahamas. Be sure to check with your travel agent or Disney representative for specifics. Service animals are allowed in all public areas of the ship, except some areas of the Vista Spa. Stop at Guest Services once onboard to find "rest areas" for your service animal. If you book a Category 6 or better stateroom, Disney can provide "turf" for your service animal to use on the verandah. Many of the break areas are not in guest areas and while you may accompany your animal while on break, many cast-member-only areas are a tight squeeze for a wheelchair. See page 12 for more information on bringing service animals.

Motion Sensitivity

Disney Cruise Line ships have two huge stabilizer fins that diminish the worst of the ship's motion. Beyond that, we recommend you consider one of these remedies:

✔ **Purely natural**—Go topside, take deep breaths, get some fresh air, and look at the horizon. The worst thing you can do is stay in your stateroom. Drink lots of water and have some mild food, such as saltine crackers—avoid fatty and salty foods, and eat lightly.

✔ **Herbs**—Ginger is reported to help reduce seasickness. It comes in pill and cookie form—even ginger ale can help. It's best to begin taking this in advance of feeling sick.

✔ **Bonine, or "Dramamine Less Drowsy Formula"**—These are brand names of meclizine, which has far fewer side effects than original formula Dramamine (which we don't recommend for adults). Take it a few hours before departure for maximum effectiveness. Note that Bonine is only for those 12 years or older; use original formula Dramamine for kids ages 2 to 12. The onboard medical facility provides free chewable meclizine tablets (25 mg.) from a dispenser next to its door on deck 1 forward. Guest Services (on deck 3 midship) may also have some meclizine if you can't make it down to deck 1.

✔ **Sea Bands**—These are elastic wrist bands that operate by applying pressure to the Nei Kuan acupressure point on each wrist by means of a plastic stud, thereby preventing seasickness. Some people swear by them; some say that they don't work. Either way, they are inexpensive (unless you buy them on the ship) and have no medical side effects.

✔ **Scopolamine Transdermal Patch**—Available by prescription only. It is the most effective preventative with the least drowsiness, but it also comes with the most side effects, such as dry mouth and dizziness. For more information about scopolamine, speak to your doctor and visit http://www.transdermscop.com.

✔ **Ship Location**—A low deck, midship stateroom is generally considered to be the location on a ship where you'll feel the least movement. If you know you're prone to seasickness, consider requesting a stateroom on decks 1-2, midship. But if once you're onboard, you find yourself feeling seasick, the best thing to do is get out of your stateroom, go to deck 4 midship, and lie down in one of the padded deck chairs.

✔ **Choose Excursions Wisely**—Those prone to motion sickness may want to avoid shore excursions that rely heavily on smaller boats such as ferries and sailboats.

Special Needs on the Disney Cruise Line
(continued)

Pregnancy

Women past their 24th week of pregnancy are **not allowed to sail** on the Disney Cruise Line. Prior to this, cruising is actually very comfortable for pregnant women as there isn't a huge amount of walking and it's easy to graze all day long. Be aware that you should not take any medications for nausea without your doctor's permission (SeaBands are just fine, however). Check with your doctor prior to the cruise as well as the Vista Spa staff for the treatments available while pregnant.

Religion

Those on 7-night cruises can attend an **interdenominational service** in Diversions (deck 3 forward) on Sunday at 9:00 am. Erev Shabbat (Jewish Sabbath Eve) services are held in Diversions Fridays at 5:30 pm. You can attend services in Cape Canaveral on 3- and 4-night cruises on Sunday. Western Caribbean cruises can attend afternoon services on Sunday in Key West. See http://www.marinersguide.com/regions/florida/capecanaveral/churches.shtml.

Chill Out Time

If you're looking for a place to just sit and be for a while, here are some places that we've found onboard:

- ✔ Grab a padded lounge chair on deck 4—you can enjoy the scenic views and stay shaded, too (great for naps).

- ✔ Deck 7 aft has a secluded and usually quiet deck.

- ✔ Enjoy the warmth of the sun on deck 10 (pools are on deck 9).

- ✔ Peace and quiet can be yours for lunch at Lumiere's/Triton's when most of the passengers are out exploring the port of the day.

- ✔ The Fantasia Reading Room (deck 2 midship, Disney Magic only) is a quiet place to read, play cards, or just chill. Kids using the room must be accompanied by an adult.

- ✔ Ask for a Hidden Mickey Challenge from Guest Services and see how many you can find.

- ✔ Take an early morning or late night stroll around deck 10. It's breezy up there, so bring a jacket.

- ✔ Treat yourself at the Vista Spa (see page 182).

- ✔ Serenity Bay on Castaway Cay is an adults-only beach where the only noise you'll hear is the lapping of the waves. Lounge chairs and umbrellas available on a first-come, first-serve basis.

Bright Idea: If you book a Land/Sea package, we definitely recommend doing the theme parks first and the cruise second for maximum relaxation.

Special Needs on the Disney Cruise Line
(continued)

Size

Check your life jacket once you're in your stateroom on the afternoon of embarkation day. If you need a larger size, ask your stateroom host or hostess prior to the safety drill at 4:00 pm.

Ask your head server for chairs without arms in the main dining areas. Folding chairs are available upon request for the back of the theaters.

Most stateroom bathrooms can be uncomfortable as the sink and toilet are very close together. Elevators are small and often crowded—avoid the midship elevators when possible, as they are very narrow.

Reader Tip: "My husband, who is a very large man, found it better to use a restroom outside our stateroom. He could go into the handicapped stall and it gave him lots more room than trying to use the restroom in our inside stateroom, which was a very tight fit."—contributed by peer reviewer Lori Jones

Visual Impairments

Services for those with visual impairments are limited onboard the cruise ships. All elevators do have Braille buttons; however, **Braille menus are not available**. A limited number of children's books in Braille are available for participants in the Oceaneer Club.

Palo, Spa, and Excursion Reservations

Once your cruise is paid in full, you can access your reservation online, and at specific intervals, you can make your reservations for Palo, the spa, and excursions. Concierge Cruisers: reservations can be made up to 105 days before embarkation. Castaway Club Members: 90 days prior to embarkation. All other sailors: 75 days prior to embarkation.

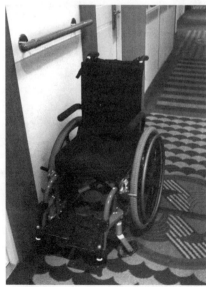

© MediaMarx, Inc.

More Information

Looking for more information? There's an entire PassPorter guidebook dedicated to the Disney Cruise Line and its ports! Visit http://www.passporter.com/dcl/guidebook.htm and see page 403. We also recommend the unofficial Magical Disney Cruise Guide, which is located online at http://allearsnet.com/cruise/cruise.shtml.

Two other web sites that are very informative regarding the Disney Cruise Line are http://www.castawayclub.com and http://www.dcltribute.com.

Visit http://www.disneycruise.com or call 888-214-2500.

A cruiser keeps their personal wheelchair in the hallway to save room in their stateroom

Planning

Your Special Need

Getting There

Staying in Style

Touring

Feasting

Resources

Index

Your Lodging Tips and Stories

We leave a <u>large</u> chunk of time each day for swimming at the resort and "chill-out" time. A child with ADHD tends to get overstimulated very quickly, and Disney is a place that can overstimulate the most timid person! We do plan late evenings, but they are always followed by a morning to sleep in or a low-key day. Any child who is tired and hungry, with or without ADHD, is not going to have a great time at Walt Disney World!

—contributed by Ann Berry

The value resorts are nice because they have exterior hallways. If you need to leave the confines of the room because of a crowded feeling, it's nice to be able to walk outside without having to navigate hallways. The biggest drawback is that the check-in area is tiled and can be noisy, and the food court is extremely noisy with the buzz of all the people, plus music and TVs.

—contributed by Karen Sears

We have been <u>very</u> lucky with both our Autism Spectrum Disorder kids in that they have really loved each of the resorts we've chosen. This last trip, we stayed at the Beach Club and I admit it was very difficult when it came to meals. Both of our kids will only eat certain foods (one of which is chicken strips), and that's usually a sure bet when all else fails. At the Beach Club there was literally nothing they would eat at Cape May or Beaches and Cream. Staying at other resorts, like Port Orleans Riverside, that was never a problem, since we could find a wide variety at their food court. We *loved* the resort and would definitely stay there again. I would just really have to plan meals more carefully.

—contributed by Michelle Suit

My husband (who is blind) and I spend the first evening at our resort walking to specific places, such as the outdoor seating area of the food court. This gives him enough independence to go to there and sit while I get ready in the mornings. It is also important to let a person with visual impairments get used to the room and the layout. Most visually impaired individuals are good with mobility, although some have more difficulty with being disoriented than others.

—contributed by peer reviewer Lori Kloman Williamson

I am in a wheelchair, and I go to Disney every year. I just love this place, because it is what some would say is barrier-free. I always stay at the All-Star Resorts. They are perfect for me; they have roll-in showers and the flip-down bench.

—contributed by Cheryl Giffear

When I filled out the form at the cruise's kid's club, I described my son's disability and his needs. One of the major things about him is that he is socially about three years younger than his chronological age. So, even though he was 11 at the time of the trip, his social skills were more like those of an 8-year-old. After the staff read my form, they discreetly asked me if I wanted him to be considered in the 8- to 9-year-old group vs. the 10- to 12-year-old group. I was pleased that they would consider that, but I told them that I thought he'd do okay with the 10- to 12-year-olds. I explained that he didn't consider himself to be that age and that would have hurt his self-esteem. He wanted to be with the other 11-year-olds, even though he didn't always act like them. I just wanted the staff to be aware that if they saw immature behavior from my son, there was a reason.

—contributed by peer reviewer Michelle S.

Touring
the
Parks

Perhaps you've never considered a trip to the Walt Disney World Resort before—maybe you thought your special needs would be too limiting. We're here to show you how it *can* be done.

Yes, Walt Disney World is a big place, and yes, taking on its theme parks can seem a daunting task. What about the crowds? What about the lines? How can I get around? What if I don't fit in the seat? These are all valid questions and concerns for anyone, but especially for you if you have special health- or lifestyle-related requirements.

We've tried to take the guesswork out of touring the Disney theme parks. We've not only rated each attraction, but we've assessed them for their special needs user-friendliness. We've looked at the size and type of seating, the nature of the attraction, the location of the queues, fear factors, and any special accommodations that the attractions offer. In addition, we've talked to real people who've experienced these rides and shows themselves, to learn firsthand what works and what doesn't. From their shared knowledge, we've also compiled tips and stories that we hope will help enhance your vacation. As part of this process, we conducted a rather elaborate survey, from which we've gleaned our readers' top picks for attractions that accommodate their special needs the best. We've also found attractions that our readers suggest certain special needs travelers avoid. We indicate these Best Choices and Worst Choices in our individual attraction descriptions later in this chapter.

In this chapter, we familiarize you with some Disney buzzwords and discuss some key Disney features that can help make your experience more enjoyable. We also talk about your transportation options and other mobility concerns. Finally, we break down the attractions at the four major theme parks, as well as the water parks and other fun places to visit in the Disney universe.

Touring With Special Needs

The single most important thing to remember before you ever enter a theme park is **preparation**, as emphasized in chapters 1 and 3. This is particularly true for travelers who have special needs. Have a general plan of where you're going and when, how you're going to get there, when and where you're going to eat, and what you're going to do if things don't go as planned.

In practical terms, we strongly recommend you make a **rough schedule** of your days. Include which park(s) you're going to visit and which attractions you're going to experience. Reading this chapter is the first step. We also urge you to make advance reservations if you plan to dine in the World (see chapter 6) and figure out transportation in advance (see pages 198–200).

To help you get started, here are some Disney **buzzwords** that you'll find helpful to understand as you read through this chapter:

Admission Media—Park passes (tickets). See pages 204–205 for pass details and rates.

Attraction—An individual ride, show, or exhibit (see page 218).

Baby Care Center—A special facility found in each major park, near the First Aid Station, where you can nurse, feed, and change a baby. It also has most baby care supplies on hand. See page 196. (Note: All restrooms, even men's rooms, have diaper changing facilities.)

Cast Member—A Disney employee.

Child Swap—A system available at most rides that allows one adult to wait with a non-riding child (or special needs traveler) while the other person rides an attraction (see below).

🔔 Rider Switch (also known as "Child Swap")

When a non-rider needs a companion but the companion also wants a chance to ride, take advantage of Rider Switch. It's available at most of the attractions at Walt Disney World.

Here's how it works: The entire party proceeds through the standard queue area. Part of the group experiences the attraction while a companion waits with the individual or service animal who will not ride (due to age/height restrictions, fears, or special needs, etc.). At the conclusion of the ride, the companions change places, permitting the waiting companion to also experience the attraction without additional wait time. In fairness to everyone, only those individuals who did not ride the first time accompany the second rider.

We've noted attractions where Rider Switch is most useful in our individual attraction descriptions. If you have any questions, ask the first cast member you encounter at the specific attraction.

Planning

Your Special Need

Getting There

Staying in Style

Touring

Feasting

Resources

Index

ECV–Electric Convenience Vehicle. A three- or four-wheeled motorized scooter. These can be rented at the theme parks and elsewhere. (See Wheels! on pages 201-203.)

Extra Magic Hour–Disney resort hotel guests can enter certain parks one hour early or stay up to three hours later on certain days (see page 109).

FASTPASS–Disney's timed-ticket system (see page 206).

First Aid Station–See sidebar on next page.

Guest Relations–The primary information desks located at each park.

Lockers–Available near the entrance of each park and the Ticket and Transportation Center. Cost is $5/day plus $2 refundable deposit. Save your receipt for a new locker at another park on the same day.

© Debra Martin Koma

Queue–A waiting area or line leading to an attraction or character greeting.

A typical queue

Seating Types–Different vehicles and shows have different types of seating (see page 197).

Single Rider Line–Available only at certain attractions. This system allows riders to bypass the regular standby line if they're willing to ride separately from their group. This works well if the rider is traveling with a special needs traveler who does not wish to experience a ride and doesn't need a companion.

Smoking–Prohibited in most park areas. Designated smoking areas are noted on maps.

Strollers and Wheelchairs–Single and double strollers, as well as manual wheelchairs, are available for rent at all parks and many other locations. (See Wheels! on pages 201-203.) For some special needs children, strollers may be used as wheelchairs with a Guest Assistance Card (see page 10).

Rider Switch–See sidebar on previous page.

Restrooms–Available everywhere and indicated on all maps. Companion restrooms are also available (indicated on park maps and in the Guidebooks for Guests With Disabilities).

Noisy Restrooms at Walt Disney World

Some adults and children who are sensitive to loud noises may be fearful of self-flushing toilets found in the theme park restrooms. The "red eye" sensor located behind the toilet on the back wall detects movement and will automatically flush–sometimes while you're still seated! To cope with the auto-flush feature, try one of the following:

✔ Cover the sensor with a sticky post-it note until you are finished.
✔ If you're assisting a child, cover the sensor with your hand.
✔ Wear earplugs or headphones.

Remember to remove any paper you've placed over the sensor when you're through–and don't use regular stickers, which may not be easily removed. Note that there are also several new automatic hand dryers in some restrooms at Disney's Animal Kingdom. These new dryers are super loud, so avoid them if such noises are an issue. Paper towels are still available in all restrooms.

Touring With Special Needs
(continued)

First Aid Stations and Baby Care Centers

First Aid Stations are on hand for you in each of the four theme parks and the two water parks. First Aid Stations are staffed by licensed practical nurses or registered nurses who can assist with most non-emergency needs. (If you have an emergency, contact the nearest cast member or call 911!) They are also able to refrigerate medication or cool-down vests for service animals, and will store small medical equipment that you need to have handy, like nebulizers. The stations also have small private rooms/cubicles with cots if you need to lie down to recover from motion sickness, the heat, etc. Most stations have companion restrooms, as well as a TTY phone nearby. The First Aid Stations are located:

✔ In the Magic Kingdom: To your left as you face the Crystal Palace Restaurant, just off Main Street U.S.A.

✔ In Epcot: In the Odyssey Center, between Future World and World Showcase.

✔ In Disney-MGM Studios: Near Guest Relations on your left, just after you pass through the turnstiles.

✔ In Disney's Animal Kingdom: In Discovery Island just behind the Creature Comforts shop.

✔ In Typhoon Lagoon: Just to the left and slightly behind Leaning Palms.

✔ In Blizzard Beach: The First Aid Station is located near the park entrance in between Lottawatta Lodge and Beach Haus.

Baby Care Centers are located in each of the four theme parks. At the Baby Care Centers, you can change, nurse, or feed your baby; purchase supplies (diapers, baby powder, formula, etc.); pick up lost children; have a quiet snack (you provide the food) with young children; cool down from the heat, etc. Baby Care Centers have a small kitchen where you can heat bottles or food, as well as highchairs, rocking chairs, and a small play/TV area for young children who are waiting for mom. Some stations, like the one in Epcot, have changing tables that can accommodate larger or older children. The Baby Care Centers are located near the First Aid Stations listed above.

The changing room at Magic Kingdom's Baby Care Center

© MediaMarx, Inc.

Attraction Seating Types

To experience an attraction at Walt Disney World, you may have to walk, stand, fasten a seat belt, wear a harness, etc. We describe the basic terms here so you understand them as you read our individual attraction details:

Bench Seat—A seat with no arms that may fit anywhere from two to 20+ people in the row. Bench seats may or may not have backs. Examples are Kilimanjaro Safaris and Country Bear Jamboree (with backs) and Flights of Wonder (without backs).

A bench seat with back at Country Bear Jamboree

The overhead harness at Stitch's Great Escape!

Harness—A padded mechanism that comes down over your shoulders to keep you in place in your vehicle. Examples: Rock 'n' Roller Coaster and Mission:SPACE.

Low/high lap bars—A low bar is one that is pressed into your lap to restrict your movement. A high bar rests (more gently) on your lap or may not even be lowered at all. Examples: Big Thunder Mountain Railroad (low lap bar) and Haunted Mansion (high lap bar).

A low lap bar on Big Thunder Mountain

Seat belt—Lap or lap-and-shoulder belt very similar to car seat belts. Examples: Twilight Zone Tower of Terror, Dinosaur, and Dumbo the Flying Elephant have lap belts; Test Track has lap-and-shoulder belts.

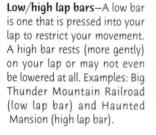

A lap seat belt on Dumbo, which is also an example of a small space

Small space—This term means different things to different folks, but basically, it indicates space is limited in some manner. Examples: Mad Hatter's Tea Party, Dumbo the Flying Elephant, and Astro Orbiter.

Standing—An attraction that requires you to stand for a significant portion of the presentation. Some 360-degree movies that require standing offer "lean rails" for you to rest against. Examples: Reflections of China and O Canada!

Theater seating at Mickey's PhilharMagic

Theater seating—The type of seating you would find in a movie theater. Seat sizes vary in width and leg room. Wheelchair/ECV areas are provided in attractions with theater seating. Examples: Honey I Shrunk the Audience and Mickey's PhilharMagic.

Lean rails for standing at Reflections of China

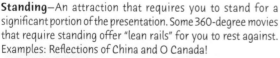

Getting Around the Resort and Parks

We've said it before, but it bears repeating—Walt Disney World is *huge*! The entire resort—theme parks, water parks, hotels, the whole works— encompasses 47 square miles! That's a lot of ground to cover, so be sure you're prepared for some major walking or wheeling before you go.

Bright Idea: Pick up a Disney Transportation Guide at your Disney resort for hints on the quickest way to get to and from most Disney parks.

Just how you get around the World really depends on your individual situation. Those reliant on wheelchairs or ECVs, for example, may find having a **vehicle at your disposal** to be indispensable. Driving yourself from place to place allows you the freedom to come and go on your own schedule—especially important if you're traveling with an infant, or with someone who tires easily. Having your own vehicle (your personal car or a rental) also affords you the ability to venture off Disney property easily—perhaps to buy more formula and diapers or special dietary items, or to attend religious services. Should you decide to rely on Disney's complimentary transportation, however, here's what's available:

Our friend Nancy Tynes, using a Disney bus lift

Bus transportation is available within Walt Disney World (with proper Disney resort hotel ID) every 15 to 30 minutes. Bus destinations are posted on signs as well as on bus marquees (illuminated signs atop each bus). Buses can accommodate a wheelchair/ECV as long as it will fit on a standard bus lift (32" x 48"). Buses can hold up to two non-collapsed wheelchairs/ECVs—if you can fold your wheelchair and sit in a regular seat, more chairs can be accommodated. If you have a longer or wider wheelchair than will fit on the lift, or if you have three or more wheelchairs/ECVs in your party, contact the front desk at your Disney resort for travel options. Bus drivers will assist you in boarding the bus through the rear entrance and ensure that your chair is secured appropriately. There are currently three types of wheelchair/ECV access in use on Disney buses: 1. The oldest buses have stairs that convert to form a lift (see photo). These are a tight fit for most wheelchairs/ECVs, and oversized scooters/ECVs will not fit. The wheelchair/ECV user backs onto the platform and sets the brakes. The front of the ramp folds up so you don't roll off, and then it rises to floor level. If you are in a wheelchair pushed by someone else, they back onto the platform pulling the wheelchair toward them, and they stay on the ramp, too. 2. Some buses have a ramp that slides out of an enclosure in the base of the bus floor. The wheelchair/ECV user backs onto this ramp into the bus. 3. The newest buses have a ramp that flips outward. These ramps are wider and are also found on "kneeling buses," which allow them to go down lower, making the ramp less steep and easier for wheelchair/ECV users to back onto. These buses that "kneel" actually dip down in front, too, making it easier for everyone to climb aboard the stairs. Strollers are permitted on all types of buses, but they should be folded prior to boarding, unless being used as a wheelchair for a special needs child.

Important Note: Disney bus drivers are required to board passengers in wheelchairs/ECVs first. Be sure to wait in the designated queue, or wait in a place where the driver can see.

Monorail transportation (a futuristic, elevated railway with a single track) is available between the Ticket and Transportation Center (TTC), the Magic Kingdom, and Epcot from about 7:00 am until 1.5 hours after each park closes. Service to the resorts is available until 11:00 pm or two hours after the Magic Kingdom closes, whichever is later. The resort monorail services the Contemporary, Polynesian, and Grand Floridian resorts. Monorails are wheelchair/ECV accessible, but there's a small step up from the platform to the train car. A monorail pilot will place a ramp on the platform so you can wheel into the accessible car (which is appropriately marked). Note that the ramps leading to the monorail stations at the Magic Kingdom, Epcot, and TTC are quite steep—it may be difficult to push a manual wheelchair here

Taking a stroller on the monorail

(Epcot's station has an elevator). Strollers are also permitted on the monorail and they do not need to be collapsed. Note that side-by-side double strollers fit best in the wheelchair-accessible cars. Ask a cast member if you need assistance.

Important Note: The ramp for boarding the monorail car may be steep for your ECV/wheelchair. Ask the monorail cast member to be sure the exit doors on the opposite side of the monorail car are closed, in case you require a lot of acceleration to board. You don't want to fall out the other side!

Boat service is available in a number of locations around Walt Disney World. The Magic Kingdom Ferry takes you between the TTC and the Magic Kingdom. Smaller launches connect the Magic Kingdom area resorts (Disney's Fort Wilderness Resort and Campground, Contemporary, Wilderness Lodge, Grand Floridian, and Polynesian) to the Magic Kingdom. Friendships connect Epcot to Yacht & Beach Club, Swan & Dolphin, BoardWalk, and Disney-MGM Studios. The Disney Vacation Club Ferry connects Disney's Old Key West Resort and Saratoga Springs Resort & Spa to Downtown Disney. There is also a ferry that connects Port Orleans Resort to Downtown Disney. All boats can accommodate strollers—sometimes they must be collapsed before boarding. Ask a cast member. Unfortunately, not all boats can handle wheelchairs/ECVs. The large ferries connecting the Magic Kingdom and the TTC are accessible, but the small launches that run between the Magic Kingdom area resorts to the Magic Kingdom may only accommodate folded wheelchairs and require you to take a step or two in and out. The Friendships in the Epcot area are usually accessible with normal water levels, but when water levels are higher or lower than usual, it may not be possible to roll on board. (In these cases, a sign is posted on the dock.) Even when water levels are normal, rough water or wind may make it impossible to roll on board or off.

The Magic Kingdom Ferry

Walking is by far the most common way to get around the parks themselves. There's very little in the way of intra-park transportation. Be sure to bring comfortable, well-broken-in shoes if you're going to be hoofing it.

Getting Around the Resort and Parks
(continued)

Parking at Walt Disney World

Parking lots are huge, and during peak times of the year, they can fill up. The rows are very, very long, and unless you have a handicapped parking permit, you won't have a choice of where to park. Cast members direct cars very systematically to an exact space. Each lot is assigned a name, and all rows are numbered, so be sure to write down your lot and row numbers before leaving the area! Tram service is provided from parking areas to the park.

Bright Idea: Take a photo of the row number with your digital or cell phone camera, or leave yourself a voice mail with the location of your car.

Parking is free if you're staying at a Disney resort or have an Annual Pass; otherwise it's $8/car or $9/camper or RV. Parking is also free if you have a disabled parking permit, so be sure it's visible as you approach the toll-gate for the park. Ask the cast member where disabled parking is located. (If you don't have a disabled permit but are traveling with a wheelchair/ECV, ask the cast member for the best place to park.)

Parking lot trams are used in the four major theme parks but do *not* service the disabled parking area. Even though the designated disabled parking area is the closest parking to the park entrance, it still may be quite a way to the actual turnstiles, not to mention the wheelchair/stroller rental location, so use the passenger drop-off area instead if you're able (follow signs to the drop-off location). If you have an easily folded wheelchair and can climb in unassisted, the tram may be a better option for you than parking in the disabled parking area. Note that cast members *cannot* assist you in boarding, however. A limited number of courtesy wheelchairs (designated by blue flags, backs, and seats) are sometimes available in the disabled parking area, but we've seldom seen them as the day goes on. If you're taking the tram from the parking lot, you'll need to step up into it and sit on hard bench seats. Be sure that small children are seated in the middle of tram benches and that strollers are collapsed. The trams will take you near the entrance of the park (or, in the case of the Magic Kingdom, to the TTC), but you'll still need to walk a bit to get to the turnstiles and stroller/wheelchair rental spot. When departing the theme park, you reverse the procedure, returning to the parking lot via tram again. There is only one tram stop per section, so be sure to listen carefully when your section and row are announced. Note that there's no tram service at Downtown Disney, Blizzard Beach, Typhoon Lagoon, or Wide World of Sports.

© Deb Wills

A Walt Disney World tram

Wheels!

The wheel: Whatever did we do before its invention? Wheels make getting around so much easier, particularly for those of us with small children or mobility issues. Whether you need a stroller, a wheelchair, or an ECV to help you navigate, here's what you need to know about wheels in the Walt Disney World Resort.

First of all, any wheeled vehicle you use to get around Disney has to have **at least three wheels**. Why? Disney's policy is that guest-operated, two-wheeled vehicles, no matter the type, are not permitted on the transportation systems or inside the parks, including Downtown Disney and Disney's Wide World of Sports. This is primarily directed at the use of Segway Human Transport Vehicles (see sidebar below) but also applies to bicycles and scooters. For safety reasons, two-wheeled vehicles are only permitted on established bike paths or other areas that allow the use of recreational bicycles. In most circumstances, maneuverability is difficult, and others may not easily see or avoid these vehicles, creating a potential safety concern.

Various other options exist for those who need to use a **wheelchair or ECV/ scooter**. At the theme parks and Downtown Disney, you can bring your own or rent one on a first-come, first-served basis. In addition, several medical supply companies in the Orlando area rent these types of vehicles—they even will deliver them to your resort, with Disney's full cooperation.

The main advantage to **bringing your own** stroller or wheelchair/ECV is that you can keep it with you. You'll be able to use it both at the parks and the resorts, getting to and from your transportation, plus you'll have it with you at the airport or train station if that's how you're traveling. Note that you may be able to rent a complimentary wheelchair at your resort, for a refundable ($250–$300) deposit. See chapter 4 for more details.

⏻ Segways (Human Transport Vehicles)

Cast members in Epcot and other areas of Walt Disney World began using Segways in 2003 to help them cover large distances quickly. In addition, Epcot now offers a tour, Around the World on a Segway, which allows guests to try the nifty gadgets for a few hours at a cost of about $80. Visitors, however, are **not permitted to bring personal Segway units** into the Walt Disney World Resort. According to Disney, the restriction is based on concern for guest safety. There is also the concern that a Segway operator may have difficulty with Disney's peak season crowds. It should also be noted that Segways have not yet been approved by the Food and Drug Administration as medical devices. So, as of this writing … leave your Segways at home.

Planning
Your Special Need
Getting There
Staying in Style
Touring
Feasting
Resources
Index

Wheels!
(continued)

If you choose to **rent from a Disney theme park**, consider this:

1. Disney only has a limited number of strollers/wheelchairs/ECVs for rent each day, and you're not able to reserve these in advance. If you get to the theme park too late (which could mean mid-morning), you may be out of luck and not get a stroller/wheelchair/ECV.
2. Disney rental ECVs have four wheels and may seem cumbersome and low-powered to people accustomed to riding a more maneuverable three-wheeled scooter.
3. You will only have use of the wheels while you're in the theme park, which means you'll need to walk to the bus/tram stop or to your car and then from the bus stop to your room at the resort or hotel.

If you decide to rent from one of the Disney theme parks, however, here are the current prices at the time of writing:

Single Stroller	$8 per day with $1 Disney Dollar refunded upon return.
Double Stroller	$15 per day with $1 Disney Dollar refunded upon return.
Wheelchair	$8 per day with $1 Disney Dollar refunded upon return .
ECV	$30 per day plus $10 refundable deposit. You must be 18 years old or older to rent ECVs.

If you plan to visit more than one park in a day, **hang on to your receipt**. When you get to the second park, show your receipt and you can get another stroller/wheelchair/ECV, if one is available, at no additional charge. When you turn in your wheels, you can request a transfer wheelchair to get to your car.

You also have the option of renting a stroller, wheelchair or ECV for multiple days—Disney calls it a **"Length of Stay Rental."** You'll pay once for as many days as you want, plus you'll get a small (10%) discount. Then when you return the next day, just show your receipt to the cast member and you'll be shown through the queue with little or no wait. The "Length of Stay" rentals do not guarantee a stroller, wheelchair, or ECV.

Bright Idea: "Express Stroller Rental" is sometimes offered outside the turnstiles at park opening—look for the sandwich board sign and cast member for quick stroller rentals without waiting in the standard line.

You can rent strollers, wheelchairs, and ECVs from the following locations:

© Deb Wills

Magic Kingdom: Rentals are located to your right, inside the entrance turnstiles. Wheelchairs can also be rented at Mickey's Gift Station at the TTC. Replacement strollers and wheelchairs can be obtained at the Tomorrowland Arcade, Tinker Bell's Treasures, and Frontier Trading Post. Replacement strollers are also available to railroad passengers at stations of the Walt Disney World Railroad.

Magic Kingdom strollers

Wheels!
(continued)

Strollers, wheelchairs, and ECVs rental locations (continued from previous page):

Epcot: Wheelchairs can be rented at The Gift Spot, on your right just before the main entrance; wheelchair/ECV and stroller rentals at the shop to the left of Spaceship Earth; and at the International Gateway. Replacements can be obtained at the Glas und Porzellan shop in the Germany Pavilion in the World Showcase.

Disney-MGM Studios: Rentals are located on your right after you pass through the turnstiles just beyond Oscar's. Replacements can be obtained at the Writer's Stop shop at the end of Commissary Lane. Just show your receipt. Replacement strollers can also be obtained at Tatooine Traders.

Disney's Animal Kingdom: Wheelchairs can be rented at The Outpost shop on the left *before* you enter the park. Wheelchair, stroller, and ECV rentals are on your right just after you pass through the turnstiles. Replacement strollers can be obtained at Creature Comforts and Mombasa Marketplace. Complimentary loaner strollers are provided for all at the Conservation Station as you exit the Wildlife Express train.

You can also rent strollers, wheelchairs, and ECVs at **Downtown Disney**. Charges for rentals here vary slightly from the theme parks:

Single Stroller (no double strollers)	$7 per day with a $20 refundable deposit.
Wheelchairs	$7 per day with a $20 refundable deposit.
ECVs	$8 per hour (two-hour minimum), plus $10 key deposit; maximum $30 per day. An imprint is taken of a major credit card; if you fail to return the ECV, your credit card will be charged for its replacement. You must be 18 years or older to rent an ECV.

You can rent strollers, wheelchairs, and ECVs from Guest Relations at the **Marketplace**, located near Once Upon a Toy. You can rent single strollers and wheelchairs (not ECVs) from Guest Relations at Downtown Disney's West Side, located near the bridge that connects the West Side with Pleasure Island.

Renting a stroller/wheelchair/ECV from a **local company** means that you'll have the wheels with you for the duration of your vacation. For about the same cost per day as Disney, these companies will not only rent you the chair/ECV, but will even deliver the wheels to your requested destination. There are many vendors located in the Orlando area (check the local phone book)—here are a few vendors for which we have firsthand knowledge:

For Wheelchairs/ ECVs:	Care Medical: 407-856-2273 or 800-741-2282 Walker Medical: 407-518-6000 or 888-SCOOTER (726-6837) Apria: 407-291-2229 or 800-338-1640 Randy's Mobility: 863-679-1550
For ECVs ONLY:	Scootarama: 877-RENT-ECV (736-8328)
For Strollers:	Family Rentals: 407-909-0042 Medical Travel (Special Needs Strollers): 800-778-7953

Park Passes

On January 2, 2005, Disney revamped its admission options, bringing more flexibility and more confusion. It's safest to budget **$64**/day for ages 10+ (**$51**/kids ages 3-9), the single-day/single-park base price for the major parks in 2005. The new "Magic Your Way" multiday passes emphasize flexibility and savings, so you can do more at a lower price. Here's the deal on passes (prices include tax):

■ Magic Your Way Tickets	*Actual 2005 Rates*

*Magic Your Way tickets are available for 1-10 days. Guests can stick to basic admission or add one or more options at the time of purchase (see explanations below). Magic Your Way replaces single-day passes and all varieties of Park Hopper passes. A Magic Your Way **Base Ticket** ($64-$223) is good for entry to a single major park (Magic Kingdom, Epcot, Disney-MGM Studios, or Disney's Animal Kingdom) for each day of the ticket. Multi-day Base Tickets bring substantial discounts (see chart on the next page), so it pays to buy your admission all at once. Multi-day Base Tickets expire 14 days after the first use, but they do not have to be used on consecutive days. Buy only as much admission as you'll actually need for your visit to Disney. Note that multi-day Base Tickets are imprinted with the guest's name, so they are not transferable. The **Park Hopping** option (add $37) lets you visit more than one major park on the same day, for the length of your ticket. Available with any Base Ticket, this option is costly unless you spend four or more days at the parks, but it's indispensable if you plan to visit all four parks in fewer than four days and it can maximize the enjoyment of any longer stay. The Magic Your Way **Magic Plus** option (add $48) adds a limited number of single-day, single-park admissions for the minor parks (Blizzard Beach, Typhoon Lagoon, Pleasure Island, DisneyQuest, and Wide World of Sports) to any Base Ticket. Each Magic Plus option is worth $10-$36, depending on where you use it. Purchase this feature with 1- to 3-day Base Tickets and you receive two Plus Options, 4- to 5-day Base Tickets receive three options, 6-day Base tickets receive four options, 7- to 10-day Base Tickets receive five options. Regardless of how many Plus options you receive, the cost to add this feature is always the same. As long as you make a minimum of two visits to the more costly minor parks, you'll get your money's worth. The **Premium** option (add $85) is a combination of a Base Ticket, Park Hopping, and Magic Plus options (but at no additional savings). The **No Expiration** option (add $10-$107) is best suited for those who plan to save the unused portion of a multi-day ticket for a future vacation. The 14-day life span of a Base Ticket is generally enough for any one vacation. Prices for the various tickets are listed in the comparison chart on the next page.*

■ Annual Pass	*Actual 2005 Rates*

Unlimited admission to the four major parks for a full year, plus special privileges. An Annual Pass ($421/$358) costs less than two 3-day Magic Your Way Base Tickets with Park Hopping. Annual Passes also kick in great discounts on resorts (based on availability) and other privileges, such as a newsletter and events. There are also annual passes for the water parks ($106/$86), Pleasure Island ($59), DisneyQuest ($84/$67), and water parks plus DisneyQuest ($137/$105). You cannot share an Annual Pass (or any other multiday pass).

■ Premium Annual Pass	*Actual 2005 Rates*

A Premium Annual Pass ($548/$466) offers the same privileges as the regular Annual Pass plus unlimited admission to the minor parks (including DisneyQuest) for $128 more. Five minor park visits cover the added cost. A Premium Annual Pass costs less than two 3-day Premium Magic Your Way tickets with a No Expiration option, and it is good for a full year.

Special Needs Admissions: No special tickets, discounted or otherwise, are available for those with special needs. Kids under 3 are admitted into the parks for free (and get a free ride if the ride allows someone that small). Anyone 10 and over is considered an adult in the eyes of the ticket booth. Passes for kids ages 3-9 cost up to 20% less than adult passes. Also, the option-filled pass you buy for yourself is usually more than your child needs, especially if you use childcare programs.

Old Ticket Media: Prior to "Magic Your Way," Disney issued "Park Hopper" passes. If you have an old Park Hopper with unused days on it, you may use or upgrade it.

Upgrades and Exchanges: Upgrade or apply the unused value of an unexpired park pass to a better pass. Visit Guest Relations (parks) or Guest Services (resorts) for details.

Advance Purchase Discounts: Discounts of between $8 and $12 are possible on tickets of five days or longer duration, if you purchase them in advance at Disney's web site, or include them in the cost of a vacation package. This is significantly less than the value of advance purchase discounts available in the past.

AAA: Members can expect some sort of discount (historically 5%) on some passes. You must purchase tickets directly from AAA to get the discount.

Florida Resident Discounts: It pays to live nearby. Florida Resident Seasonal Passes work like Annual Passes, but with blackout dates in busy seasons. There are some other special deals for Florida residents only.

Disney Vacation Club Discounts: Discounts of about $100 are available on Annual Passes for members of the immediate family residing in the same household. See page 176.

Military Discounts: Discounts of roughly 7%–8% may be available on admission—check with your Exchange shop or MWR (Morale, Welfare, and Recreation) office. Some offices may need to preorder your tickets, so we advise you check with them well in advance. Keep an ear out for special programs for active military personnel—in recent years, Disney offered all active military personnel a free five-day park hopper, with discounted admission for up to five family members or friends. To check on current specials and buy tickets, phone 407-939-4636 or visit Shades of Green (see page 173) upon arrival.

Online Ticket Brokers—These folks sell legitimate, unused tickets at good rates. Try http://www.ticketmania.com (877-822-7299), http://www.floridaorlandotickets.net (888-723-2728), or http://www.mapleleaftickets.com (800-841-2837). Be wary of others hawking tickets, including eBay and timeshares.

Pass Comparison Chart: Options and prices for your number of days in the parks. *(Prices are the actual 2005 costs of adult, non-discounted passes, including tax.)*

Pass Type	Days: 1	2	3	4	5	6	7	8	9	10	11	12	13	14
Base (single day/park)	$64	$127	$182	$197	$206	$209	$212	$215	$218	$223				
Base + No Expiration		$137	$193	$213	$243	$257	$271	$322	$325	$329				
Base + Park Hopping	$101	$164	$219	$234	$243	$246	$249	$252	$256	$260				
Base + Park Hop. + No Exp.		$175	$230	$250	$280	$294	$308	$359	$362	$366				
Base + Magic Plus	$112	$175	$230	$245	$253	$257	$260	$263	$266	$271				
Base + Magic Plus + No Exp.		$185	$241	$261	$291	$305	$318	$370	$373	$377				
Premium	$149	$212	$267	$282	$291	$294	$297	$300	$304	$308				
Premium + No Exp.		$223	$278	$298	$328	$342	$356	$407	$410	$414				
Annual Pass										$421	→			
Premium Annual Pass											$549	→		

For more details and updates, visit http://www.allearsnet.com/pl/ticket.htm.

Touring Advice

In interviewing fellow Disney vacationers, we heard several recurrent themes as to what makes touring Walt Disney World with special needs most enjoyable. We'd like to share some **hard-earned advice** with you in the hopes that it will make your trip easier and more pleasurable.

1. Plan and be prepared! Visit http://www.disneyworld.com (look for the **Guests With Disabilities** link) or write ahead to Disney to obtain copies of the current Guests With Disabilities Guides (there's one for each of the major parks) so that you're familiar with procedures.

2. Know the **abilities and limitations** of everyone in your group, including yourself. Don't push, don't try to experience everything—because you just can't do it. Take midday breaks.

3. Take advantage of **Disney's programs** that help you save time and waiting, such as Extra Magic Hour, FASTPASS, and Rider Switch.

4. Don't be afraid to **ask a cast member for help**. They are there to make your experience the best it can be and are more than willing to offer advice and aid. While they can't physically assist you, they can suggest the best ways for you to experience attractions and can point you in the direction of additional aids, such as special parade viewing areas.

Disney's FASTPASS

Just what is this FASTPASS you've been hearing so much about? For the special needs Disney-goer, it is probably the single most important program that Disney offers in its theme parks. FASTPASS is basically a timed-ticket system that allows you to wait in line "virtually," while you go off shopping or eating or riding something else. It works like this: Insert your park admission pass into a FASTPASS machine located near the attraction. Your FASTPASS pops out, marked with the time later in the day that you can return to ride/experience the show, bypassing the regular, or "standby" line. You can go about your business until your time "window" opens, thereby avoiding long waits in line. You generally can hold only one FASTPASS at a time, but check the FASTPASS itself, which will usually tell you how soon you can obtain another. This feature is especially attractive to those who can't tolerate standing in one place for long periods, such as children with ADHD or those with chronic fatigue. One of the best things about FASTPASS (besides how it eliminates wait times!) is that it's free to all Disney park guests. We've indicated which attractions have FASTPASS throughout this chapter and encourage you to take advantage of it as much as possible. FASTPASS is sometimes not used in the off-season or on slow days, but during busy seasons, FASTPASSes for certain attractions can be gone as early as noon!

Character Meet and Greets

One of the highlights of a visit to Walt Disney World for most kids is **meeting the characters** that they've seen so often on TV and movie screens. But getting to meet the characters isn't always so easy, especially for children with special needs who may not be able to tolerate waiting in long lines for a variety of reasons. As one mom writes: "What to do with a kid who is absolutely nuts over Disney (typical for autism spectrum disorder children), but who also finds the sounds, smells, touches, and inescapable crowds about as appealing as dental surgery?" Here are some tips to minimize wait times for those popular characters:

1. If there is a particular character you want to meet, speak to a cast member at Guest Relations when you enter the park. They have a **special number** to call to determine if, when, and where specific characters will appear.

2. Check the **times guides** for special character greeting times in each theme park. Arrive at the designated spot a few minutes early to get in the front of the queue if possible. If you have several members in your party, perhaps one can wait in line while another walks around with the impatient, tired, or fidgety child.

3. If you're waiting at a **character greeting location**, speak to the cast member handling the character. They may, at their discretion, choose to help you through the queue more quickly. They may also alert the character to your child's special requirements.

4. **Be flexible**. If your child is unable to wait for Pooh or Mickey today, perhaps trying again later or another day will make all the difference. Also, if your child gets to the front of the line and realizes that the *big* Tigger standing in front them is too intimidating, do not force them to embrace the character. Try again later or another day. In fact, some children are satisfied to see their favorite characters from a distance.

5. Visit a **show or parade** that features the character(s) your child wants to see, rather than waiting in a long line.

6. Take your child to a **character meal**. In this setting, a variety of characters come around to your table and spend several minutes, giving you their undivided attention.

Adults, these characters are there for you, too! Don't be shy or embarrassed about having your photo with your lifelong favorite Mr. Smee, Mickey, or Chip and Dale.

···>

Planning

Your Special Need

Getting There

Staying in Style

Touring

Feasting

Resources

Index

Understanding and Using
the Attraction Descriptions and Ratings

If you've used a PassPorter guidebook before, you know that our custom-designed attraction charts include background, tips, restrictions, queue conditions, accessibility details, enhanced ratings, and much more. We use a special attraction chart to organize all this information, allowing you to find what you need for touring the theme parks at a glance.

Description Key

Icons[3]   Ratings[4]

1 **Attraction Name** [D-3[2]]	*FP* 🚹	# # #
Description offering an attraction overview, what to expect with a focus on how the queue, waiting area, and the attraction itself can affect your special needs. We also offer our suggestions for the best seating/viewing/riding, tips, and height/age restrictions. Tips for each special need, when available, follow special needs letter icons (see page 8). We also include Best and Worst Choices as they relate to a particular special need, based on our special needs travelers' survey results.		**Type**[5]
		Scope[5]
		Ages[6]
		Thrill Factor[7]
		Avg. Wait[7]
		Duration[7]

[1] Each chart has an empty **checkbox** in the upper left corner—use it to check off the attractions you want to visit (before you go) or those you visited during your trip.

[2] **Map coordinates** are presented as a letter and a number (i.e., A-5). Match up the coordinates on the park's map for the attraction's location within the park.

[3] Icons indicate when an attraction has FASTPASS (*FP*) or a height/age restriction (🚹).

[4] Our **ratings** are shown on the far right end in the three boxes, on a scale of 1 (poor) to 10 (don't miss!). The first is co-author **Deb Wills'** rating, the second is co-author Deb Koma's rating, and the third is our **Readers'** ratings. We offer our personal ratings to show how opinions vary, even between people like us who like many of the same things. Use our opinions as a point of reference. For example, we both love the details and the little things that make Walt Disney World unique, and we are fondly nostalgic over the oldest attractions. But where Deb Wills dislikes spinning, gets dizzy over inversions, and is sensitive to overly loud noises, Deb Koma enjoys all the coasters and thrill rides and finds herself drawn repeatedly to rides that shake her up and turn her upside-down.

[5] The boxes on the right below the numeric ratings give basic information. The first box is **attraction type**. The second box is always **attraction scope**, which we rate with the guest with special needs in mind as follows:

- E-Ticket   A major crowd-pleaser—don't miss it! (Expect long lines.)
- D-Ticket   Excellent, try not to miss it.
- C-Ticket   A good attraction enjoyed by most.
- B-Ticket   OK, but don't fret if you don't have time for it.
- A-Ticket   A simple diversion, often overlooked.

[6] **Age-appropriate ratings**. For example, we may say "All Ages" when we feel everyone, from infant on up, will get something out of the experience. More common is "Ages 4 & up" or "Ages 8 & up" for attractions we think will be best appreciated by vacationers who are at least 4 or 8. This is *only* our guideline and not a Disney rule.

[7] **Thrill/scare factor**, **average wait**, and **duration** follow the age ratings, though we eliminate these if they don't apply or expand them if deserving. We did our best to format this information so you can understand it without having to check this key, too!

Magic Kingdom

For many the **Magic Kingdom**, which opened on October 1, 1971, is Walt Disney World. With its gleaming Cinderella Castle as a focal point, the theme park is known for both its gentle kid-pleasing rides, like Dumbo the Flying Elephant, and its high-energy thrill attractions, such as Space Mountain.

This dream-made-real is home to **seven themed lands** and scores of attractions that appeal to all ages, covering 107 sprawling acres. With all there is to experience in this wonderland, the thought of trying to navigate this theme park can be daunting, especially for people who must deal with special needs. But armed with a little knowledge and aided by careful planning, a trip to the Magic Kingdom will make you feel like a little kid again.

Guest Relations is located in two spots: on your right before you pass through the turnstiles and on your left as you enter the park, in the City Hall building. This is where you can obtain current guide maps, times guides, and Guidebooks for Guests With Disabilities; obtain a Guest Assistance Card (see pages 10–11); rent hearing or vision devices; obtain the current schedule for Sign Language Interpreted attractions; and ask any special questions you might have. Wheelchair/ECV users enter City Hall via one of the ramps on either side of the building.

Bright Idea: If you're getting to the Magic Kingdom via the Ticket and Transportation Center, you can rent a wheelchair from Mickey's Gift Station there. Wheelchairs are kept out of sight, so just ask—it may be more convenient than renting at the Magic Kingdom itself.

To help you plan your days, you should know that the Magic Kingdom is **laid out like a wheel**, with the hub centered directly in front of Cinderella Castle (see map on pages 212–213). Pathways act as the spokes leading to the following themed areas:

Main Street, U.S.A.—A glimpse of a younger, simpler America. Many of the the shops lining Main Street, U.S.A. are interconnected—you could walk or wheel its length without going outdoors. Folks using wheelchairs/ECVs or strollers, however, may find the shops hard to navigate, as they are cluttered with merchandise displays, not to mention lots of browsing shoppers. Unless you're trying to stay out of the weather, you'll usually find it easier to move down Main Street's sidewalks or the street itself. Beware of the grooves and trolley rails in the street, which can wreak havoc with a stroller or wheelchair/ECV.

More
Magic Kingdom

Adventureland—Home to attractions that tap into the adventurer in all of us, including the famous ground-breaking Audio-Animatronics of Pirates of the Caribbean and the Jungle Cruise. This land has several wide open spaces that are easy to navigate, although its outdoor plaza shops are difficult to get around. If you're in a wheelchair, be aware of the ramp leading to Adventureland from the hub—its incline is misleading, and may require that someone push you or that you enter Adventureland from Frontierland via Liberty Square.

Frontierland—The spirit of the Old West lives on in attractions such as Big Thunder Mountain Railroad and Splash Mountain. The streets of the frontier get very congested, though, particularly around parade times, so you may find it hard to pass through if you're on wheels. One other word of warning—the gulls in this area have gotten particularly aggressive. Beware if you have a fear of birds—or if you just want to keep your french fries safe!

Liberty Square—Colonial times revisted via a trip on an old river boat and a stay with the presidents of our nation. It's fairly easy to move about outdoors, but Liberty Square's shops are a problem with narrow entryways and cramped quarters.

Fantasyland—A child's dream come true, with attractions featuring such popular childhood characters as Peter Pan, Snow White, and Winnie the Pooh. Fantasyland crowds can be extremely difficult to navigate, even if you're on foot. Crowds here are worst on Saturdays and Sundays.

Mickey's Toontown Fair—A kid-sized place that allows youngsters to visit with their favorite Disney characters. Geared to the grade-school set and younger, the streets here are fairly easy to get around, although getting through some of the structures can be difficult if crowds are thick.

Tomorrowland—A look at the future through retro eyes, featuring thrill rides like Space Mountain and the new Stitch's Great Escape. This very popular area is most congested around Buzz Lightyear's Space Ranger Spin entrance and over near Space Mountain.

Wait Times

Each park has a tip board in a central location that tells you approximate wait times for each attraction. A cast member stationed there updates the board frequently, but sometimes the tip board, or even the wait times signs posted at individual attractions (see photo to right) may not be accurate. This happens for a variety of reasons, including minor problems that actually shut the attraction down temporarily. If you want to verify the expected wait time, don't hesitate to ask the cast member at the attraction's entrance.

© Deb Wills

Snow White wait time

Getting to the
Magic Kingdom

The Magic Kingdom attracts locals and tends to be **busiest on Saturday and Sunday**. To avoid crowds as much as possible, we suggest going on a Monday. Tuesday and Wednesday may be good days, too, depending on the Extra Magic Hour schedule (see page 109). The most popular attractions, like Space Mountain, are best if done first thing in the early morning to avoid long lines. Parents of young children are better off doing Fantasyland or Toontown Fair first—they get busier later in the day. Go to big thrill rides during parades. Shop in the afternoon to avoid crowds. And most importantly remember to take breaks throughout the day and drink plenty of water.

By Car—For many special needs travelers, it may be more convenient to travel by car. Take I-4 to Exit 67 (West) or exit 62 (East) and continue about 4 miles to the toll plaza. All-day parking is $8 (free to Disney resort hotel guests and Annual Passholders) and the pass is valid at other Disney parks' lots on the same day. Cast members will direct you to the accessible parking area if you need it.

By Monorail—From the Contemporary, Polynesian, or Grand Floridian resorts, take the monorail directly to the park. Each of these deluxe resorts have elevators that will take you to the monorail platforms. If you're using a wheelchair or ECV, cast members will assist you in boarding. From Epcot, you'll have to take the monorail to the TTC and transfer to the Magic Kingdom express monorail or the ferry boat. There are accessible ramps for boarding each of these transportation methods.

By Boat—From the TTC, a ferry will take you over to the Magic Kingdom. The Polynesian, Grand Floridian, Fort Wilderness, and the Wilderness Lodge & Villas also have launch service to the Magic Kingdom. The launches normally used on the Grand Floridian/Polynesian route and occasionally used on the Ft. Wilderness/Wilderness Lodge route cannot accommodate ECVs, and wheelchairs must be folded. Use available buses or the monorail instead.

By Bus—From all other resorts, buses take you directly to the Magic Kingdom. From the Disney-MGM Studios or Disney's Animal Kingdom, you must take a bus to the TTC, then transfer to monorail or boat. From Downtown Disney, the easiest route is to take a bus to the Polynesian and take the monorail.

By Land—You can walk or wheel from the Contemporary along a path, paved with Walk Around the World bricks.

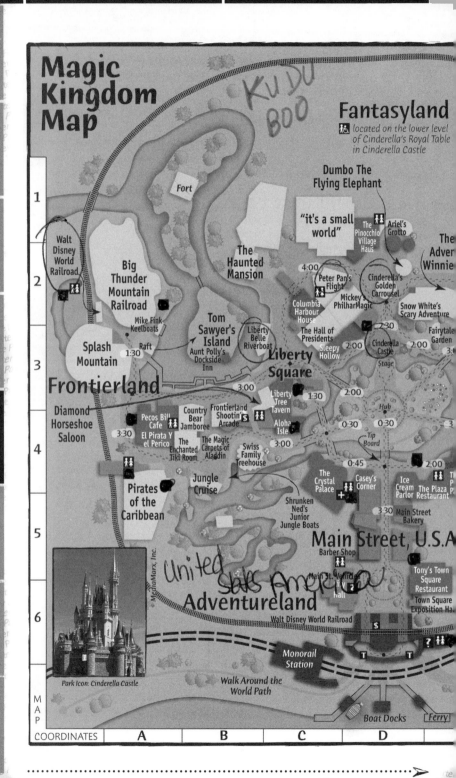

Magic Kingdom Map

Fantasyland

located on the lower level of Cinderella's Royal Table in Cinderella Castle

KUDU BOO

Fort

Dumbo The Flying Elephant

"it's a small world"

The Pinocchio Village Haus

Ariel's Grotto

The Adventures of Winnie

Walt Disney World Railroad

Big Thunder Mountain Railroad

The Haunted Mansion

Peter Pan's Flight

Cinderella's Golden Carrousel

Mickey's PhilharMagic

4:00

Columbia Harbour House

Snow White's Scary Adventure

Mike Fink Keelboats

Tom Sawyer's Island

Liberty Belle Riverboat

The Hall of Presidents

2:30

Fairytale Garden

Splash Mountain

Raft
1:30

Aunt Polly's Dockside Inn

Liberty Square

Sleepy Hollow

2:00

Cinderella Castle
Stage

2:00

Frontierland

3:00

Liberty Tree Tavern

1:30

2:00

Hub

Diamond Horseshoe Saloon

3:30

Pecos Bill Cafe
El Pirata Y el Perico

Country Bear Jamboree

Frontierland Shootin' Arcade

Aloha Isle

0:30

0:30

Tip Board

The Enchanted Tiki Room

The Magic Carpets of Aladdin

Swiss Family Treehouse

3:00

0:45

2:00

Jungle Cruise

Shrunken Ned's Junior Jungle Boats

The Crystal Palace

Casey's Corner

Ice Cream Parlor

The Plaza Restaurant

Pirates of the Caribbean

3:30

Main Street Bakery

Main Street, U.S.A.

Barber Shop

United States America

Adventureland

Main St. Vehicles
Town Hall

Tony's Town Square Restaurant

Town Square Exposition Hall

Walt Disney World Railroad

Monorail Station

Park Icon: Cinderella Castle

Walk Around the World Path

Boat Docks

Ferry

© MediaMarx, Inc.

COORDINATES | A | B | C | D

MAP

Planning · Your Special Need · Getting There · Staying in Style · Touring · Feasting · Resources · Index

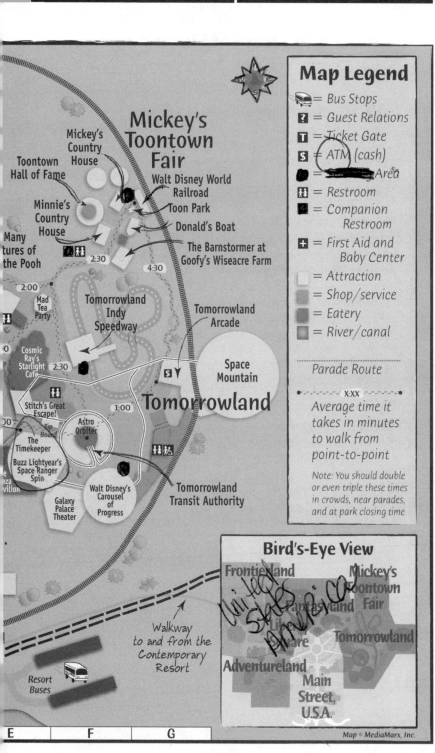

Map Legend

= Bus Stops
? = Guest Relations
T = Ticket Gate
S = ATM (cash)
= ~~Area~~
= Restroom
= Companion Restroom
+ = First Aid and Baby Center
= Attraction
= Shop/service
= Eatery
= River/canal

Parade Route

•—————— X:XX ——————•

Average time it takes in minutes to walk from point-to-point

Note: You should double or even triple these times in crowds, near parades, and at park closing time

Mickey's Toontown Fair

Mickey's Country House
Toontown Hall of Fame
Minnie's Country House
Many ...tures of the Pooh
Walt Disney World Railroad
Toon Park
Donald's Boat
The Barnstormer at Goofy's Wiseacre Farm

2:30
4:30
2:00
Mad Tea Party

Tomorrowland Indy Speedway
Tomorrowland Arcade

Cosmic Ray's Starlight Cafe 2:30

Space Mountain

Stitch's Great Escape!
1:00
Astro Orbiter
Tip Board
The Timekeeper
Buzz Lightyear's Space Ranger Spin
Galaxy Palace Theater
Walt Disney's Carousel of Progress

Tomorrowland

Tomorrowland Transit Authority

Bird's-Eye View

Frontierland
Mickey's Toontown Fair
Fantasyland
Liberty Square
Tomorrowland
Adventureland
Main Street, U.S.A.

Walkway to and from the Contemporary Resort

Resort Buses

E   F   G

Map © MediaMarx, Inc.

Planning
Your Special Need
Getting There
Staying in Style
Touring
Feasting
Resources
Index

Making the Most of Magic Kingdom

After you pass through the Magic Kingdom's turnstiles, the **wheelchair/ECV and stroller rentals** are on your right. There are only limited numbers of wheelchairs and ECVs, and reservations are not taken, so be sure to get there early to rent. (Or consider renting equipment from an off-site vendor—see Wheels! on pages 201-203.)

It would be easy to waste a lot of time zigzagging across the park to experience the various rides and shows. Instead, **plan your day** and move around the park in a way that best conserves not only your time but your energy. We suggest starting in Tomorrowland and working your way around the park counterclockwise—many visitors head to the most popular attractions like Space Mountain, Splash Mountain, and Big Thunder Mountain Railroad, or they tend to start in Adventureland, not realizing that many attractions aren't open in Adventureland until 10:00 am!

The **First Aid Station** is located to the left of the Crystal Palace, just off Main Street, U.S.A. See page 196 for services available there.

The Magic Kingdom's **Baby Care Center** is located adjacent to the First Aid Station. There you'll find changing tables, highchairs for feeding, a kitchen for heating bottles and food, a communal nursing room with about four rocking chairs, and a cast member who can sell you basic baby care items like diapers.

The nursing room has several rocking chairs and subdued lighting

There is **no alcohol sold** anywhere in the Magic Kingdom—not even in the restaurants. This is especially attractive to those recovering from an alcohol addiction.

You'll find a large **Braille map** on a stand located in Main Street U.S.A.'s City Hall (Guest Relations). There's also a Braille map of the park near the tip board on Main Street, U.S.A., near the hub.

Entertainment at the Magic Kingdom

The daily 3:00 pm parade is, at the time of writing, the 20-minute **Share a Dream Come True parade**, featuring giant snowglobes with favorite Disney characters. There's also an evening parade on certain nights, the dazzling lights of **SpectroMagic** (co-author Deb Koma's favorite!). There are several special viewing areas for those in wheelchairs/ECVs: Town Square in Main Street, U.S.A.; on the Tomorrowland side of the Partners statue near Cinderella Castle; and across from the Liberty Tree Tavern in Liberty Square. Speak to a cast member to gain access to these areas. These areas fill up quickly, so arrive early to get a spot. During peak periods, access may be limited to the special needs traveler plus one member of their party. If you're traveling without a wheelchair and want to use these areas, you will need a Guest Assistance Card (see pages 10–11). If you don't like to be close to others, these viewing areas may not be a good choice. Wheelchairs are usually parked within inches of each other.

The afternoon parade has **American Sign Language (ASL)** interpretation at the Liberty Square viewing area on certain dates. Speak to Guest Relations for the schedule. You'll need to be in the area next to the Liberty Bell about 20 minutes before the parade starts.

The Magic Kingdom has **live entertainment** performed along its streets throughout the day. Check your Times Guide for exact times and locations, or visit http://pages.prodigy.net/stevesoares. One such performance, the Sword in the Stone, is performed in Fantasyland adjacent to Cinderella's Golden Carrousel. This show is performed in ASL on certain dates (check with Guest Relations). There's nowhere to sit, but if you arrive about 5 minutes before the scheduled show time, wait in the left section of the audience.

The 12-minute **Wishes fireworks show** takes place in front of the castle on most nights. Although you can view the fireworks from around the Magic Kingdom, the best viewing spot is directly in front of the castle, standing in the middle of Main Street, U.S.A. between Casey's Corner and the Ice Cream Parlor.

Seniors and former military personnel should note that veterans may participate in the daily **Flag Retreat** in Town Square around 5:00 pm daily. Ask early in the day about participating at Guest Relations.

Schedules for **sign language shows** are made a week at a time. Ask at Guest Relations for the current schedule.

Finding Your Place at the Magic Kingdom

SPECIAL PLACES

Attractions With Hearing Devices Chart

Assistive Listening	Hall of Presidents, Mickey's PhilharMagic, Galaxy Palace Theater, Timekeeper, Stitch's Great Escape!, Jungle Cruise, Enchanted Tiki Room, Country Bear Jamboree, Carousel of Progress, Judge's Tent (in Toontown), and Castle Forecourt Stage
Handheld Captioning	Haunted Mansion, "it's a small world," Peter Pan, Snow White's Scary Adventures, The Many Adventures of Winnie the Pooh, Walt Disney World Railroad, Tomorrowland Transit Authority, Carousel of Progress, Buzz Lightyear, Pirates of the Caribbean, Jungle Cruise, and Enchanted Tiki Room
Reflective Captioning	Hall of Presidents, Mickey's PhilharMagic, Timekeeper, and Country Bear Jamboree
Closed Captioning	Judge's Tent (in Toontown), Space Mountain pre-show, Carousel of Progress intro, Timekeeper pre-show, and Stitch's Great Escape pre-show
ASL Interpretation	Jungle Cruise, Liberty Belle Riverboat, Castle Forecourt Stage show, and Fairytale Garden (storytime)
Ears to the World (Translation Devices)	Walt Disney World Railroad, Enchanted Tiki Room, Jungle Cruise, Hall of Presidents, Haunted Mansion, Tomorrowland Transit Authority

Quiet areas for a break or time-out:

- The Fairy Tale Garden, to the right and behind the castle, has several shows of Storytime with Belle, but in between performances, it's a quiet, shaded spot.
- Down by the old Swan Boat dock (along the rose garden path near the castle) is quiet and secluded, and the way to get there is solitary and peaceful.
- The Tomorrowland Terrace Noodle Station counter-service restaurant (leading up to Tomorrowland) is actually very quiet during off-peak hours—stop there before the lunch rush or mid-afternoon for a shady break.
- Town Square Exposition Center theater is good. There are also quieter areas on either side of the theater, some with tables and benches.
- Indoor restaurant seating areas between Pecos Bill's and El Pirata y El Perico are often quiet.
- The pathway between Mickey's Toontown Fair and Tomorrowland along the railroad tracks is a relaxing area.
- Outside the park, follow the "Walk Around the World" path west past the monorail station to benches, lawns, and a sandy beach (no swimming).
- A cool, but not necessarily quiet, spot is just to the left of the Tomorrowland Light & Power Co. (the video game arcade next to Space Mountain). There are benches there and the doors to the arcade are usually open—on a hot day, the cool air-conditioned air just pours over you. This is a wonderful spot if you can stand the background noise of the arcade and the nearby Speedway.

Finding Your Place at the Magic Kingdom

Companion restroom locations in the Magic Kingdom:
- At the First Aid Station near Crystal Palace in Main Street, U.S.A.
- In the lower level of Cinderella's Royal Table restaurant in the castle
- Near Splash Mountain in Frontierland
- In Mickey's Toontown Fair
- To the right of Space Mountain in Tomorrowland
- At the Transportation and Ticket Center's East Gate

Attraction Seating Chart
See page 197 for explanations of each type of seating listed below.

Astro Orbiter	small space
Barnstormer at Goofy's Farm	high bar
Big Thunder Mountain Railroad	bench seat and low bar
Buzz Lightyear's Space Ranger Spin	bench and high bar
Carousel of Progress	theater
Cinderella's Golden Carrousel	straddle horse or bench
Country Bear Jamboree	padded bench with backs
Dumbo The Flying Elephant	small space
Enchanted Tiki Room	bench
Fairytale Garden	bench or standing
Galaxy Palace Theater	bench (no backs)
Hall of Presidents	theater
Haunted Mansion	high bar
"it's a small world"	bench
Jungle Cruise	bench
Liberty Belle Riverboat	standing or bench
Mad Tea Party	small space
Magic Carpets of Aladdin	small space
Many Adventures of Winnie the Pooh	high bar
Mickey's PhilharMagic	theater
Peter Pan	high bar
Pirates of the Caribbean	bench (with backs)
Snow White's Scary Adventures	bench
Space Mountain	straddle bench/small space
Splash Mountain	bench and high bar
Stitch's Great Escape!	harness
Timekeeper	standing
Tomorrowland Indy Speedway	small space/lap belt
Tomorrowland Transit Authority	bench (with backs)
Town Square Exposition Hall	theater
Walt Disney World Railroad	bench (with backs)

SPECIAL PLACES

Planning

Your Special Need

Getting There

Staying in Style

Touring

Feasting

Resources

Index

Charting the Attractions
at Main Street, U.S.A.

	Deb Wills' Rating	Deb Koma's Rating	Readers' Rating

☐ Main Street Vehicles [D-5] — 2 | 2 | 5

A one-way ride between Town Square and Cinderella Castle (either direction) in vintage vehicles. Horseless carriages, trolleys pulled by Belgian horses, and even a fire engine. These vehicles are fun to ride in if you're willing to wait in the slow, long lines. **[A][U][C]** There are often long waits for the vehicles, standing in unshaded areas. **[G]** Avoid the horse-drawn vehicles if allergic to horses. **[F]** The horses are quite large—those with a fear of animals might want to avoid. **[M]** Guests must transfer from ECV/wheelchair to ride (the trolley can take a folded wheelchair). All vehicles require at least two steps up. **[Q]** You must sit sideways on the omnibus, fire engine, and two jitneys. **[L]** The omnibus has narrow doors and stairway.

Vehicles
A-Ticket
All ages
Gentle ride
Long waits

☐ Town Square Exposition Hall [D-6] — 3 | 4 | 5

Don't pass by this museum dedicated to cameras—it's also the Camera Center! Walk inside to see early Mickey Mouse cartoons playing, and check out the interactive kiosks, photo cutouts, and character greetings! **[M]** May remain in wheelchair/ECV. Use ramp to your right as you face the building.

Exhibit
A-Ticket
Ages 3 & up
Simple fun

☐ Walt Disney World Railroad—Main Street Station [D-6] — 5 | 5 | 7

Circle the Magic Kingdom on a steam train, with stops at Main Street, U.S.A., Frontierland, and Mickey's Toontown Fair. You'll catch glimpses of all but Liberty Square and Fantasyland along the 1.5-mile journey. Ride the full route, or disembark at any stop. Attraction is closed during the fireworks. **[C][S][L][V]** Use the railroad to travel around the park without wasting energy. **[M]** ECV/wheelchair users take the ramp next to the station, then go to the front of the train near the engine. Do <u>not</u> use the exit ramps from inside the train station. The engineer will assist in loading you into the first car—there is a bench seat for your chairless companions. **[B]** Fold personal strollers before passing through the turnstiles. Replacement rental strollers may be available at other stops (hold on to your nametag!) but are not guaranteed. **[Ö]** Ears to the World can be used here. **[H]** Certain segments have handheld captioning. **[F]** There are two short, dark tunnels between the Main Street and Frontierland stations.

Train Ride
B-Ticket
All ages
A bit loud
Gentle ride
Short waits
20-min. ride (roundtrip)

⊡ What Is and Isn't an Attraction?

We define an "attraction" as an individual ride, show, or exhibit. These are the destinations at the park and almost invariably come with a queue. We cover virtually all the attractions that Disney lists in its own guidemaps, plus a few that aren't listed that we think are deserving of the "attraction" title (such as Ariel's Grotto). Like Disney, we don't consider things like talking trash cans (yes, they exist!) to be attractions, as they rarely have a queue. We also don't consider parades or fireworks to be attractions, either—we cover these under the Entertainment sections in the park introduction pages. Character greeting areas are less straightforward—if Disney considers one to be an attraction or we feel it offers more than simple character greetings, we include a description of it. For a list of character greeting locations, refer to the guide map upon your arrival and see page 207 for more tips.

Charting the Attractions at Adventureland

	Deb Wills' Rating	Deb Koma's Rating	Readers' Rating

"The Enchanted Tiki Room–Under New Management" [B-4]

	6	6	6

This Disney fixture (formerly known as Tropical Serenade) has enchanted visitors for years. Infused with new life a few years ago with the addition of Iago and Zazu, it's a showcase for Audio-Animatronics. You wait in a shaded outdoor queue (standing only) and are entertained by a short pre-show. **[A][U]** Enter row first to be closest to exit. **[U][B][F]** There are periods of darkness, thunder, lightning, and some scary-looking tiki gods chant loudly. **[G][U]** There is often an unpleasant odor in this room. **[M]** Wheelchair users must enter pre-show area at a designated gate to the right of the turnstiles at the direction of a cast member. You'll be shown to the special seating area. **[Ö]** Ears to the World available. **[H]** Handheld captioning and assistive listening are available.

Show
D-Ticket
Ages 4 & up
Dark, loud at times
Short waits
2-min. intro 9-min. show

Jungle Cruise [B-4]   **FP**

	8	8	7

A silly sail along the "Rivers of the World" in a craft reminiscent of The African Queen. Even though you cruise by Audio-Animatronics animals and restless natives, the only real danger is that you'll split your side from the skipper's corny jokes. You may get slightly damp. The shaded outdoor queue snakes for what seems like an eternity some days, with no place to sit while you wait. Boat has cushioned bench-type seats. **[A][U]** Must stay in vehicle for entire ride. **[A][U][F]** There are periods of darkness as you ride through a tunnel; there are also realistic-looking Audio-Animatronics snakes and other animals. **[A][U][F][I]** Be aware there is a loud, sudden gunshot noise that may startle some. **[A][U][C][♥][T][I][M][P][E][S]** Use FASTPASS to minimize wait times. **[Ö]** Ears to the World available. **[H]** Assistive listening is available. Sign language interpreted performances on designated days; check with Guest Relations for schedule. Arrive at least 10 minutes in advance; enter to the LEFT section through the wheelchair entrance. **[M]** Wheelchair/ECV users must use the ramped pathway to the right of the Swiss Family Treehouse exit to access the attraction's area. Enter the attraction through the designated queue to the left of the FASTPASS machines. If able, you must transfer from your chair to the boat; otherwise you will have to wait for an accessible boat. **[Q]** This is a real, though gentle, boat ride, so those with extreme motion sickness may want to avoid. **[C][M][S][L][V]** You must step down to get into the boat–since the boat is floating, this can be tricky.

Boat Ride
D-Ticket
Ages 3 & up
Dark, fake snakes and wild animals
FASTPASS or long waits
10-min. ride

The Magic Carpets of Aladdin [B-4]

	5	5	5

Ever wanted to fly on a magic carpet? This is your chance! You control the height and front-to-back rocking motion on this ride that's very similar to Dumbo the Flying Elephant. Watch out for the spitting camels. Outdoor queue is partially shaded–waiting for your turn to fly can get quite hot. Carpets have two rows of bench seats. **[U][F][Q]** Although you control it, your carpet can soar high, and spins around at a fairly good speed. **[M]** Wheelchair/ECV users enter using the regular queue. If able, you must transfer from your chair to the carpet, otherwise you will have to wait for an accessible vehicle. ECV riders who cannot transfer to the vehicle must transfer to a standard wheelchair. One carpet accommodates a single wheelchair. **[L]** Each row of the carpet can accommodate two average-sized adults; people of size may require their own seat. **[H][T][M][V]** Service animals are NOT permitted.

Ride
D-Ticket
Ages 3 & up
Flies high
Long waits
1½-min. ride

⟶

Side tabs: Planning · Your Special Need · Getting There · Staying in Style · Touring · Feasting · Resources · Index

Charting the Attractions
at Adventureland
(continued)

	Deb Wills' Rating	Deb Koma's Rating	Readers' Rating

Pirates of the Caribbean [A-4]

10 **10** **9**

Boat Ride
E-Ticket
Ages 6 & up
Dark, slight drop, scary to young kids
Medium waits
10-min. ride

Yo Ho! A Pirate's Life for me! The inspiration for the recent blockbuster movie, this slow, dark ride takes you through a subterranean world of buccaneer Audio-Animatronics and their booty. Lines can be slow, but most of the wait is in the cool indoors. One medium drop; you may get splashed. **[L]** The turnstiles to this attraction are <u>very</u> narrow—just 15" wide. Ask a cast member to let you in via the wheelchair entrance if necessary. Inclined moving walkway at exit. **[A][U]** Must stay in vehicle for entire ride. Many Guest Assistance Card holders report difficulty using it at this attraction. **[U][F][I]** Queue can be very crowded and create claustrophobic feelings during busy seasons. This boat ride is completely in darkened surroundings. There are some depictions of mild violence and loud noises, such as cannon shots. **[H]** Handheld captioning is available. **[I]** A Reader Worst Choice (see page 193).**[M]** Wheelchair guests enter using the regular queue. You must transfer from your wheelchair to the boat; folding wheelchairs will be stowed on the boat. ECV guests and those in non-folding wheelchairs must transfer to a wheelchair provided at the ride. Manual wheelchair users may find the steep ramps difficult. An elevator is available to take you back up to the main floor at the end of the ride. **[M][S][V]** Parts of queue very dimly lit, with uneven floor. **[L]** The turnstiles are narrow, but the boats have bench seats with backs and ample room for all body types. **[H][T][M][V]** Break area for service animals nearby; ask a cast member.

© Deb Wills

The 15" wide turnstiles here are a tight squeeze

Shrunken Ned's Junior Jungle Boats [B-4]

2 **3** **3**

Arcade
A-Ticket
Ages 6 & up

Got a couple of bucks? Then you might want to pass a few minutes steering these remote-controlled miniature Jungle Cruise boats around the little lagoon. Two minutes for one dollar. **[M]** Wheelchair/ECV accessible. **[A]** Outdoor fun, may be good place to let off some steam.

Swiss Family Treehouse [B-4]

4 **6** **4**

Walk-Thru
B-Ticket
Ages 4 & up
Lots of stairs
Allow 15-30 min. to walk through

If you've seen the classic Disney movie "Swiss Family Robinson," then you'll really appreciate the details of this representation of the shipwrecked family's treehouse home. **[A][G][U][C][B][♥][T][I][M][P][E][S][L][V]** This attraction involves <u>lots</u> of stairs (137 steps, to be exact) and is <u>not</u> wheelchair/ECV or stroller accessible. **[B]** Leave strollers in the designated area to the left of the treehouse entrance, or cast members will move them. **[F]** Once at the top of the treehouse, you have a terrific view of Adventureland below, but those with a fear of heights might find it unsettling. **[I][M]** Reader Worst Choice (see page 193).

Charting the Attractions at Frontierland

	Deb Wills' Rating	Deb Koma's Rating	Readers' Rating

☐ Big Thunder Mountain Railroad [A-2] 🄵🄿 🕴

Ratings: 10 10 9

This high-speed (35 mph) coaster is a runaway mine train with lots of twists and turns, sudden stops, and sharp drops. The outdoor queue is partially shaded, but the waits here can be quite long, with only a few rocks or fences here and there to lean against. Seats are bench-style with a low bar. **[A][U][I][S]** This is a big thrill ride, so it could cause overstimulation. **[A][U][C][♥][T][I][M][P][E][S]** Use FASTPASS to minimize wait times. **[C][♥][T][Q][P][E][S]** You can really get shaken up on this rough roller coaster, so those with motion sickness, heart- or back-related issues, as well as pregnant women, should avoid. **[H][T][M][V]** Service animals are NOT permitted. **[B]** Use Rider Switch. **[F]** There are some dark moments along the way as the train passes through tunnels. Anyone with a fear of heights or falling should also avoid this ride. **[M]** Wheelchair/ECV users, use FASTPASS. If FASTPASS is unavailable, enter through the exit on the right and speak with a cast member. You must transfer out of your wheelchair/ECV to ride. Keep in mind that if an emergency evacuation is necessary, you'll have to deal with stairs or else wait until someone can help you. **[B][L]** You must be at least 40 in./102 cm. to ride. **[L]** People of size may need their own row; lap bar may be uncomfortable.

Coaster
E-Ticket
Ages 6 & up
Rough, fast ride with lots of twists and turns
FASTPASS or long waits
5-min. ride

☐ Country Bear Jamboree [B-4]

Ratings: 8 5 5

Audio-Animatronics bears perform country-western music in this hokey show, accented by jokes and dancing. Some wait time outside. **[A][I][U]** Theater has padded bench seats. Show can be loud; may overstimulate. **[A][I][L][U]** The turnstiles to this attraction are <u>very</u> narrow. Ask a cast member to let you in via the wheelchair entrance if necessary. **[B]** Leave stroller in the designated area to the left of the entrance, or cast members will move it. Dark theater for discreet nursing. **[F]** Show takes place in a darkened theater. Also, talking animals may scare some. **[H]** Assistive listening and reflective captioning available. **[M]** Wheelchair/ECV users, enter through door on the left side of the building. You may remain in your chair during the show.

Show
C-Ticket
Ages 2 & up
Loud
Medium waits
15-min. show

☐ Frontierland Shootin' Arcade [B-4]

Ratings: 2 5 3

OK, pardner—set your rifle sights on these targets from the Old West! You get 25 shots for 50 cents. **[A][U][I]** Can be loud; may overstimulate. **[M]** Wheelchair accessible rifles located on the left side of the counter, up the ramp.

Arcade
A-Ticket
Ages 9 & up

☐ Frontierland Station–Walt Disney World Railroad [A-3]

Ratings: 5 5 7

Ride the full route, or disembark at any stop. Attraction is closed during the fireworks. **[U][♥][C][M][S][L][V]** Use the railroad to travel around the park. **[B]** Fold personal strollers before climbing the entry stairs. Replacement rental strollers may be available at other stops (hold on to your nametag!) but are not guaranteed. **[Ö]** Ears to the World available. **[H]** Certain segments have handheld captioning. **[M][S][L]** If you have difficulty climbing stairs, you can be admitted via the wheelchair ramp; see a cast member for assistance. Wheelchair/ECV users should also see a cast member for admission via the wheelchair ramp, which is fairly steep. **[F]** There are two short, dark tunnels between the Main Street and Frontierland stations.

Train Ride
B-Ticket
All ages
A bit loud
Gentle ride
Short waits
20-min. ride (roundtrip)

Sidebar tabs: Planning · Your Special Need · Getting There · Staying in Style · Feasting · Resources · Index

Charting the Attractions at Frontierland
(continued)

	Deb Wills' Rating	Deb Koma's Rating	Readers' Rating

■ Splash Mountain [A-3] FP 🧍 🍴

	10	9	9

Everybody has a Laughing Place, and this log flume with Br'er Rabbit, Br'er Fox, and other characters from the Uncle Remus stories might be yours! First 10 minutes of the ride are calm, taking you through an Audio-Animatronics wonderland. But watch out for the five-story drop near the end–it's a doozy! There's a play area near the exit called the Laughin' Place for youngsters too small or fearful to ride. Queue is outdoors, mostly uncovered until you get quite close to the ride. There's a good chance you'll get wet on this ride–in fact, the seats are often wet from previous riders. Bring a towel, poncho, or something to sit on if this bothers you. **[A][U][I]** This is a big thrill ride, so it could cause overstimulation. **[A][U][C][♥][T][I][M][P][E][S]** Use FASTPASS to minimize wait times. **[A][U]** Must stay in vehicle for entire ride. **[H][T][M][V]** Service animals are <u>not</u> permitted. Break area for service animals behind parade gates; ask a cast member. **[♥][T][Q][E][S]** Because of the steep drop and other dips and turns, those with motion sickness, heart- or back-related issues, as well as pregnant women, should avoid this ride. **[B]** Use Rider Switch. **[B][L]** You must be at least 40 in./102 cm. to ride. **[M][S][V]** Parts of queue very dimly lit, with uneven floor. **[L]** The logs have smallish bench type seats, which may be uncomfortable for people of size, including taller people. **[F]** There are some dark moments along the way and, of course, the big drop–anyone with a fear of heights or falling should avoid this ride. **[M]** Wheelchair/ECV users should use FASTPASS. If FASTPASS is unavailable, speak with a cast member. Otherwise, enter through the regular queue. There are stairs at the point where the queue enters the building, so wheelchair/ECV users, as well as those with crutches or canes, will be diverted around this area. (Others who need to avoid stairs will need a Guest Assistance Card.) You then must transfer out of the chair to the boat, then step down into the boat (and step up to get out at the end of the ride). Keep in mind that if an emergency evacuation is necessary on this ride, you might have to deal with stairs or else wait until someone can help you.

Boat Ride With Thrills
E-Ticket
Ages 9 & up
Sharp drop!
FASTPASS or long waits
12-min. ride

■ Tom Sawyer Island [A-3]

	5	6	5

There are caves, tunnels, and an old fort with air guns on this little island themed to Mark Twain's popular Tom and Huck novels. You have to take a raft to reach the island. Closes at dusk. **[A][U]** This is a good place to run around and blow off steam. **[G][U]** There is often a musty or unpleasant odor in the tunnels. **[C][♥][T][E][V]** The island trails and tunnels involve lots of walking and some climbing, although there are places to stop and rest along the way. **[F]** The tunnels and caves here are <u>very</u> dark and close–if you have claustrophobia, you won't want to try them. There are also a few rickety bridges that might bring on a fear or two. **[S]** Seniors may want to avoid the island simply because there are so many youngsters running wild and there is a lot of walking involved. **[B][M][P]** You must be ambulatory to get around the island easily–there are stairs, bridges, and narrow tunnels not made for strollers or wheelchairs. In addition, the rafts transporting guests to the island cannot take ECVs. Instead, wheelchair users may wait at the island's dock, maybe play a game of checkers, or wheel over to Aunt Polly's Dockside Inn for a drink or snack, if it's open. **[L]** Some of the tunnels are very narrow–larger body types might not be able to squeeze through comfortably.

Playground
C-Ticket
All ages
Some dark tunnels and caves
Short waits for raft
Allow at least an hour

Charting the Attractions at Liberty Square

	Deb Wills' Rating	Deb Koma's Rating	Readers' Rating

■ Diamond Horseshoe [B-3]

	4	4	5

Love those Toy Story 2 characters? Then stop in to this converted, air-conditioned saloon to see Woody, Jessie, Bullseye, and friends up close and personal. *[M]* Wheelchair/ECV users enter using the ramp to right of the entrance. *[A][U][C][♥][T][M][P][E][S]* The waits are fairly short; limited seating.

Character Meet
A-Ticket
All ages

■ The Hall of Presidents [C-3]

	7	7	6

Audio-Animatronics at their best—all of this country's presidents take the stage and are represented, down to the most minute detail, following a patriotic 180-degree film of our history. Shows every half-hour. Theater holds 700. *[A]* Reader Worst Choice (see page 193). *[A][U]* Enter row first to be closest to exit. *[B]* Dark theater for discreet nursing. *[F]* Show takes place in a darkened theater. *[Ö]* Ears to the World can be used here. *[H]* Assistive listening and reflective captioning are available. *[M]* If using a wheelchair/ECV, enter the lobby through the right side of the turnstiles and ask to be directed to the special seating area. *[L]* Theater-style seats may be tight squeeze for larger body types.

Show
C-Ticket
Ages 10 & up
Dark theater
Short waits
23-min. show

■ The Haunted Mansion [B-2] *FP*

	10	10	9

Travel on a slow-moving track through the other-worldly home of 999 Grim Grinning Ghosts. There's no gore, but plenty of things that go "boo!" Outdoor queue is mostly uncovered, but lines move steadily. Some standing once indoors for the pre-show. Be aware that at times your "Doom Buggy" ride vehicle travels backward. *[A][U][C][F][♥][T][I][S]* Ask cast member to bypass pre-show to avoid claustrophobic feelings or standing for a long time. Doom Buggy vehicle wraps around you and can create a very closed-in feeling. After the pre-show, boarding area is very dimly lit and lines merge so that you are very close to, even touching, others. *[A][U][I][V]* You must board and exit using a moving walkway. *[A][U][B][F][♥][T][I][S]* The entire ride is <u>very</u> dark, and although the scares are meant to be mild, some sensitive souls may find them too intense. *[A][U][C][♥][T][I][M][P][E][S]* Use FASTPASS to minimize wait times. *[A][U]* Must stay in vehicle for entire ride. *[Ö]* Ears to the World available. *[H]* Handheld captioning is available. *[B]* Leave stroller in the designated area to the right of the entrance. Use Rider Switch. *[M]* Wheelchair/ECV users should use FASTPASS; otherwise, speak to a cast member for boarding instructions. The moving walkway can be slowed or stopped to make boarding/getting off easier. *[L]* Vehicles may be a tight squeeze for larger body types—consider riding alone in a vehicle.

Track Ride
E-Ticket
Ages 6 & up
Very dark, some scares
FASTPASS or med. waits
3-min. intro
7-min. ride

■ Liberty Belle Riverboat [B-3]

	5	5	5

This steam-powered sternwheeler features a narration by "Mark Twain," as you travel around Tom Sawyer Island. Sometimes characters ride along with you. Cruises depart on the half-hour. You wait on a shaded dock, with benches nearby. Beware of standing downwind, as you may feel the warm steam from the smokestacks. *[C][♥][T][P][E][S][L]* There's limited seating on the boat, so be prepared to stand. *[H]* Sign language interpreted on designated days; check with Guest Relations. Arrive at least 10 minutes in advance. Interpreter will be on first level. *[M]* If using a wheelchair/ECV, enter through the exit ramps on either the left or right side of the landing. Speak with a cast member before boarding. Note there are stairs between decks. *[Q]* This is a real boat ride, even though it's gentle.

Boat Ride
C-Ticket
All ages
Gentle rides
Med. waits
20-min. ride

Planning | **Your Special Need** | **Getting There** | **Staying in Style** | **Touring** | **Feasting** | **Resources** | **Index**

Charting the Attractions at Fantasyland

Deb Wills' Rating · Deb Koma's Rating · Readers' Rating

▪ Ariel's Grotto [D-1]

3	3	3

If the Little Mermaid is your favorite character, this is the place to meet her! Spend some one-on-one time and have your photo taken with Ariel here. The ceiling inside the "cave" area drips water. **[A][U][C][♥][T][M][P][E][S]** The wait to see Ariel can be quite lengthy. Outdoor queue has very limited shade, some umbrellas; there is a comfortable height low wall around a portion of the queue where you can lean or sit. Once inside the "cave," it is air-conditioned. **[M]** If using a wheelchair/ECV, use the regular queue. A recent renovation enables wheelchair/ECV guests to pull up next to Ariel for photographs.

Character Meet
A-Ticket
All ages
Long waits

▪ Cinderellabration [D-2]

6	5	5

On the Castle Forecourt Stage several times a day, Cinderella celebrates the art of giving, with a character meet and greet opportunity following the festivities. A recent renovation removed the walls and raised planters in the Hub, creating a clearer view of the stage. **[C]** Unless you're lucky enough to find a bench to sit on, you'll have to stand for the duration of this show. **[F]** Some Disney villains appear onstage—might be scary to young children. The show concludes with daytime fireworks whose sudden loud sounds could be startling. **[H]** Handheld captioning and assistive listening are available. Sign language interpreted performances on designated days; check with Guest Relations for schedule. Arrive at least 15 minutes before the show and stand in the <u>right</u> section of the audience. There is no seating. **[M]** Special Wheelchair/ECV viewing area available—ask a cast member.

Live Show
C-Ticket
All ages
Few scares
15-min. show

▪ Cinderella's Golden Carrousel [D-2]

5	5	6

Ride this beautiful merry-go-round that dates back to the early 1900s redone with scenes from Cinderella and music from Disney movies. The queue area is mostly shaded, and the line moves fairly quickly. **[A][U][I]** The noise level on this merry-go-round is high—it could cause overstimulation. **[A][U]** Must stay in vehicle for entire ride. **[B][F]** The height of the carousel horses might be a bit scary to some. **[B]** Leave stroller in the designated area, or cast members will move it. **[M]** Wheelchair/ECV guests enter at the exit to the right of the main entrance; a cast member will direct you on how to board. Tip: Send a quicker member of your party ahead to claim your horse/seat. Note you may get on and off at different spots. You must transfer out of your chair and sit on either a horse (they all move up and down) or in the one stationary chariot. The chariot, which is wooden with padded seats, is located in the middle of the horses, not on the outside row. You must be able to step into it; could be awkward. It has two rows with room for two adults in each row. **[Q]** Those who are very motion sensitive might want to avoid this ride. **[H][T][M][V]** Check with a cast member before bringing a service animal on this attraction. **[S][L]** Height of horses may make getting on or off difficult.

Ride
B-Ticket
Ages 2 & up
High horses can be scary
Short waits
2-min. ride

© MediaMarx

Cinderella's Golden Carrousel is a kid favorite

Charting the Attractions
at Fantasyland
(continued)

Planning

Your Special Need

Getting There

Staying in Style

Touring

Feasting

Resources

Index

	Deb Wills' Rating	Deb Koma's Rating	Readers' Rating

Dumbo The Flying Elephant [D-2] — 5 5 5

A classic carnival ride featuring the famous Disney elephant flying in circles over Fantasyland. The queue is mostly in the shade, but the waits here can be long, with no place to sit. **[U][F][Q]** Although you control it, your elephant can soar high, and spins around at a fairly good speed. Those who are afraid of heights or who are very motion sensitive might want to avoid this ride. **[B]** Leave stroller in the designated area away from the entrance, or cast members will move it. **[M]** Wheelchair/ECV users enter at the marked gate next to the regular entrance. You must transfer from your chair to the elephant. **[L]** Elephants can comfortably accommodate one large person and one child; people of size may require their own seat. **[H][T][M][V]** Service animals are <u>not</u> permitted.

Ride
D-Ticket
All ages
Spins high in the air
Long waits
2-min. flight

Fairytale Garden [E-3] — 7 6 5

Belle of Beauty and the Beast fame stops by to reenact her story with the aid of audience members. There's even a chance for character meet and greet afterward. Bench seats without backs. **[A][U]** Show can get very crowded, with people standing or sitting very close to one another. **[H]** Sign language interpreted performances on designated days. Arrive at least 20 minutes before the show and sit or stand in the <u>left</u> section of the audience. **[M]** Wheelchair/ECV accessible.

Live Show
B-Ticket
All ages
No scares
15-min. story

"it's a small world" [C-2] — 8 7 6

This ride first debuted at the World's Fair in 1964 and has been charming visitors ever since with its dolls from around the world, not to mention its unforgettable song: "It's a world of laughter, a world of tears …" Most of the queue is in the shade. **[A][U]** Must stay in vehicle for entire ride. With so much music and movement, ride can be overstimulating. **[B]** Leave stroller in the designated area to the left of the attraction, or cast members will move it. Reader Best Choice (see page 193). **[H]** Handheld captioning is available. **[M]** ECV users must transfer to a wheelchair to negotiate the queue. There are boats that can accommodate wheelchairs, though. Talk with a cast member at the attraction.

Boat Ride
C-Ticket
All ages
That song!
Short to med. waits
11-min. cruise

Mad Tea Party [E-2] — 4 6 6

Spin like crazy in giant teacups in this ride themed to Alice in Wonderland's Mad Tea Party. Turning the metal wheel in the center makes you spin faster. Mostly shaded queue area. Seating in teacups is very cramped, even for normal-sized adults. **[A][U]** The noise level in this ride is high—it could cause overstimulation. **[B]** Leave stroller in the designated area, or cast members will move it. **[M]** Wheelchair/ECV guests enter at the exit to the right of the operator's control booth. Tip: Send a quicker member of your party ahead to claim your teacup. Note you may get on and off at different spots. You must transfer out of your chair to ride. Those who have trouble maintaining an upright position on their own should not ride, since the spinning creates a great centrifugal force. **[Q]** This is the ultimate spinning ride. Those who get dizzy easily should definitely avoid it! Reader Worst Choice (see page 193). **[L]** The center wheel may make teacups a tight squeeze for people of size. **[H][T][M][V]** Service animals are <u>not</u> permitted on this attraction.

Ride
C-Ticket
Ages 4 & up
Spinning!
Short waits
2-min. spin

Charting the Attractions at Fantasyland
(continued)

| | Deb Wills' Rating | Deb Koma's Rating | Readers' Rating |

☐ The Many Adventures of Winnie the Pooh [E-2] *FP* | 6 | 6 | 7 |

Take a tour through the Hundred Acre Wood in a bouncing hunnypot as you pass by Pooh, Tigger, Piglet, and friends in scenes from several of their well-known stories. A preschooler pleaser! Luckily, the long lines here are mostly in shaded areas, but there's no place to sit while you're passing the time. **[A][U][C][♥][T][I] [M][P][E][S]** Use FASTPASS to minimize wait times. **[A][U]** Must stay in vehicle for entire ride. **[H]** Handheld captioning is available. **[F]** Most of the ride is in darkened surroundings; there's even a simulated rainstorm that can be scary to young children. **[B]** Leave stroller in the designated area, or cast members will move it. **[M]** ECV users must transfer to a wheelchair to negotiate the queue. There are some wheelchair-accessible hunnypots, but you may have to wait for one. **[L]** Each row of the hunnypot vehicles seats two average adults comfortably. People of size might prefer own seat; lap bar might be uncomfortable. **[H][T][M][V]** Check with a cast member before bringing a service animal on this ride.

Track Ride
D-Ticket
All ages
Some dark spots could be scary
FASTPASS or long waits
3-min. ride

☐ Mickey's PhilharMagic [D-2] *FP* | 9 | 8 | 9 |

The newest 3-D movie with other sensory effects is named after Mickey but is really Donald Duck's show. Scenes take you through popular animated classics, like Aladdin and The Lion King, all set to the corresponding music. Most of the queue area outdoors is shaded; indoors the waiting is cool and comfortable. **[A][U][I]** Show is very loud—could cause overstimulation. **[A][U]** Enter row first to be closest to exit. Gusts of air are blown into your face several times; also, there is the simulated scent of apple pie. Water is also sprayed on you several times. To prevent this, search for the sprayer on the seat back in front of you before the show starts, then cover it with your hand. **[A][U][C][♥][T][I][M][P][E][S]** Use FASTPASS. **[A][U][F][I][Q][S][V]** You must wear special 3-D glasses; they fit over regular glasses. Those with vision impairments may not fully appreciate the effects. **[G]** Artificial scents blown in face. **[U]** Reader Worst Choice (see page 193). **[C][H][I][M][L][V]** Reader Best Choice (see page 193). **[B]** Leave stroller in the designated area, or cast members will move it. **[F]** Most of the show is in darkened surroundings; some special 3-D effects are intense and loud. **[H]** Reflective captioning; assistive listening. **[M]** Wheelchair/ECV accessible. Once inside, head toward the right for accessible seating. Notify a cast member for help. **[L]** Theater-style seats may be tight squeeze for people of size.

Show
E-Ticket
Ages 5 & up
Dark, loud; some effects may be scary
FASTPASS or med. waits
10-min. show

☐ Peter Pan's Flight [C-2] *FP* | 8 | 7 | 8 |

Off to Neverland in a pirate ship, you'll soar over scenes from the movie Peter Pan—London, Mermaid Lagoon, and don't forget the evil Captain Hook. The long lines here are mostly in the shade. **[A][U][C][♥][T][I][M][P][E][S]** Use FASTPASS to minimize wait times. **[B]** Leave stroller in the designated area, or cast members will move it. **[F]** Most of the ride is in darkened surroundings; there's evil Captain Hook and the crocodile in many scenes, possibly scary to young children. Also, your ride vehicle is suspended from the top and sides—those with a fear of heights might be uncomfortable. **[M]** Wheelchair/ECV users should use FASTPASS; otherwise speak with the cast member at the entrance for direction. You must be able to step on the moving walkway and into the moving vehicle to ride—the walkway will not be stopped. There may be an area that is more accessible, however, if you speak with a cast member. **[H]** Handheld captioning is available. **[L]** Each "ship" holds two average-size adults comfortably. People of size might prefer own vehicle; lap bar. **[H][T][M][V]** Service animals are <u>not</u> permitted.

Track Ride
D-Ticket
Ages 3 & up
Dark, heights, could be scary
FASTPASS or long waits
4-min. ride

Charting the Attractions at Fantasyland (continued) and Mickey's Toontown Fair

Deb Wills' Rating
Deb Koma's Rating
Readers' Rating

Snow White's Scary Adventures [D-2] — 5 6 5

Traveling in a three-rowed mining car, you go through the highlights of Disney's classic "Snow White and the Seven Dwarfs," complete with the scariest Wicked Witch ever. **[A][U][I]** The noise level in this ride is high—it could cause overstimulation. **[B]** Leave stroller in the designated area away from the entrance, or cast members will move it. **[F]** Most of the ride is in darkened surroundings; some of the effects are intense and loud, especially the Wicked Witch, who repeatedly pops out at you. **[H]** Handheld captioning is available. **[T][Q]** This ride makes many sudden turns and jerks. If you have back and/or neck problems, you might want to avoid this ride. **[M]** Wheelchair/ECV users enter at the marked gate at the far right of the attraction. You must transfer out of your chair to ride. **[L]** People of size might prefer to ride in their own row. The back seat of the car is better for adult sizes. **[H][T][M][V]** Check with a cast member before bringing a service animal on this attraction.

Track Ride
C-Ticket
Ages 5 & up
Dark, scary for small children
Short waits
3-min. ride

The Barnstormer at Goofy's Wiseacre Farm [F-2] — 6 8 6

Short, but kid-friendly coaster that swoops through Goofy's barn. The long, winding outdoor queue is partially shaded, with many diversions (such as the cornfields) along the way. Each plane has bench seats with a high bar. **[A][U][C][♥][T][Q][P][E][S]** Even though it's billed as a "kiddie coaster," you can really get shaken up on this ride, so those with motion sickness, heart- or back-related issues, as well as pregnant women, should avoid it. **[B]** Leave stroller in the designated area, or cast members will move it. Use Rider Switch. **[M]** ECV users must transfer to a wheelchair to negotiate the queue. You must then transfer from your chair to ride. Talk with a cast member at the entrance for directions on boarding. **[L]** You must be at least 35 in./89 cm. to ride. The vehicles don't have much leg room, and may be too small for some taller/larger adults. Avoid seats with "roofs," which may make entry and exit awkward. **[H][T][M][V]** Service animals are _not_ permitted.

Coaster
D-Ticket
Ages 4 & up (35" and up)
Fast turns
Med. waits
1-min. flight

Donald's Boat [G-1] — 3 3 4

Interactive water play area. Allow 20-30 minutes. See our sidebar on page 252 for water play areas. **[A][U]** Great play area for blowing off some steam. **[A][U][F]** You may get wet or squirted. **[M]** Wheelchair/ECV accessible, but spongy flooring is difficult to move around on. Upper level access by stairs only.

Playground
A-Ticket
All ages

Mickey's Country House and Judge's Tent [F-1] — 5 5 6

See Mickey's home with whimsical details, including his sports equipment and gardening tools. After meandering through his house, meet the Big Cheese himself. The lines to meet Mickey are long, but they are mostly in the cool indoors of his tent. **[A][U]** Visit during parade times or later in the day to avoid long waits. **[H]** Handheld captioning and assistive listening are available in the Judge's Tent character greeting area. In addition, the Judge's Tent monitors have closed captioning. **[M]** Wheelchair/ECV accessible. Go through the regular queue, through the house, and into the Judge's Tent.

Walk-Thru
B-Ticket
All ages
Long waits
Allow 20 min. to 1 hour

Planning
Your Special Need
Getting There
Staying in Style
Touring
Feasting
Resources
Index

Charting the Attractions at Mickey's Toontown Fair
(continued)

	Deb Wills' Rating	Deb Koma's Rating	Readers' Rating

◼ Minnie's Country House [F-1]

	5 5 6
Miss Minnie's home is full of hands-on activities, including a microwave that pops popcorn and a refrigerator that blasts cool air. Minnie's not usually here, but still, this house is worth a look. Allow 20 minutes to 1 hour. **[M]** Wheelchair/ ECV accessible. Go through the regular queue, through the house. **[H][M][V]** Break area for service animals nearby; ask Cast Member.	**Walk-Thru**
	B-Ticket
	All ages
	No scares
	Short waits

◼ Toon Park [F-1]   🛝

	4 4 6
Kids' play area. **[A][U]** Great play area for blowing off some steam. **[L]** You must be <u>under</u> 40 in./89 cm. to play. **[M]** Wheelchair/ECV accessible, but spongy flooring is difficult to move around on.	**Playground**
	A-Ticket
	Ages 1–4

◼ Toontown Hall of Fame [F-1]

	4 3 6
Meet Minnie Mouse and other favorite Disney characters here. Don't miss the new Princess Room, dedicated to the likes of Snow White, Aurora, Belle, and others. Most of the lines here are long, but at least they are in the cool indoors. Visit when Toontown opens at 10:00 am to see the characters sing and dance before dropping the rope. **[A][U][C]** Waits to meet the characters can be quite long. **[M]** Wheelchair/ECV accessible. Go through the regular queue.	**Character Meet**
	A-Ticket
	All ages
	Long waits

◼ Walt Disney World Railroad–Toontown Station [G-1]

	5 5 7
Hop out here to see Toontown or walk over to Fantasyland and Tomorrowland. Or stay on board for the Main Street U.S.A. station—a great shortcut to the exit. Closed during fireworks. **[U][C][M][S][L][V]** Use the railroad to travel around the park. **[B]** Personal strollers must be folded before boarding. Replacement rental strollers may be available at other stops (hold on to your nametag!), but are not guaranteed. **[F]** Two short, dark tunnels between the Main Street and Frontierland stations. **[Ö]** Ears to the World available. **[H]** Certain segments have handheld captioning. **[M]** Wheelchair/ECV users enter on far right of station.	**Rail Ride**
	B-Ticket
	All ages
	A bit loud
	Gentle ride
	Short waits
	20-min. ride

ⓘ Turnstiles

Traditional turnstiles (with the rotating arms that you have to push forward to enter) are located at the entrance of all the theme parks to count daily visitors. Magic Kingdom's turnstiles are the narrowest—probably because it was the first park built and standards were different at the time. You'll find the same type of turnstiles at the entrance of most Magic Kingdom attractions. (At the other parks, you only encounter an occasional old-fashioned turnstile at the individual attractions— the other parks use photo cells embedded in the attractions' entryways to count visitors.) People of size, as well as those with mobility issues, strollers, and service animals, do <u>not</u> have to enter through a turnstile. There are alternate entrances at all attractions—ask a nearby cast member for help. Tip: If you're helping someone through the turnstile, be aware of where the arms are going to strike him or her to avoid a painful experience.

© Debra Martin Koma

A old-style turnstile

Charting the Attractions at Tomorrowland

Deb Wills' Rating
Deb Koma's Rating
Readers' Rating

■ Astro Orbiter [F-4] — 3 · 7 · 3

	Ride

Like Dumbo, this ride spins you 'round and 'round in rocket ships that you can control. The differences are the space-age theme, the faster speed of spinning, and the fact that you must ride an elevator to reach the vehicles. The long queues for the elevator here are outdoors but shaded—if you must wait for this ride, try first thing in the morning or in the evening when it's cooler. **[A][U][Q]** *Although you control it, your vehicle can soar high and spins around at a fairly good speed. Those who are very motion sensitive might want to avoid this spinning ride.* **[F]** *To reach this ride, you must take a very small elevator up—it holds about 10 adults in a VERY cramped space. In addition, there's a slight odor that many find offensive in this elevator. The ride itself is very high and has a commanding view of Tomorrowland. Those with a fear of heights might want to avoid it.* **[A][U][C][♥][T][I][M][S]** *Queues for this attraction can be quite long as you wait to board the small elevator up to the ride itself and stretch into mostly unshaded areas.* **[M]** *Wheelchair/ECV users enter through the regular entrance. The cast member will direct you past the turnstiles onto the elevator. You must transfer from your chair to the vehicle.* **[L]** *Vehicles can comfortably accommodate two average-sized adults sitting one in front of the other; people of size may require their own vehicle.* **[H][T][M][V]** *Service animals are* not *permitted.*

Ride
C-Ticket
Ages 5 & up
Flies high!
Long waits
1½-min. flight

■ Buzz Lightyear's Space Ranger Spin [F-4] — *FP* — 9 · 10 · 8

	Ride

Shoot at electronic targets in this ride that's like a giant arcade game featuring characters from Disney's Toy Story. Your vehicle spins at your command, and your laser "ion cannon" is homed in on the evil Emperor Zurg for a chance to save the universe! While much of the queue is indoors, during busy times, the lines can stretch outside into unshaded areas. **[A][U]** *Must stay in vehicle for entire ride. Reader Best Choice (see page 193).* **[A][U][I]** *The noise level in this ride is high, almost like being* inside *a giant arcade game—it could cause overstimulation.* **[A][U][I][V]** *You must board and exit using a moving walkway.* **[A][U][C][♥][T][I][M][P][E][S]** *Use FASTPASS to minimize wait times.* **[H]** *Handheld captioning available.* **[M]** *Wheelchair/ECV guests should use FASTPASS; otherwise go through the standby queue. ECV users must transfer to a wheelchair to negotiate the queue. Ask a cast member for a wheelchair accessible vehicle. Note that some wheelchairs might be a tight fit. If this is the case, you can switch to a standard wheelchair if available. The moving walkway can be slowed or stopped. Ask a cast member for assistance.* **[Q]** *Although you control the spinning of the vehicle, you do need to rotate from side to side to aim at targets—motion sensitive folks may find the spinning disorienting.* **[I]** *Swirling red lights in tunnel and flashing white lights (where they're taking your photo) near end of ride.* **[L]** *Vehicles can comfortably accommodate two average-sized adults; people of size may require their own vehicle. Sitting in the middle of the seat may be more comfortable, but makes aiming/shooting awkward.* **[H][T][M][V]** *Service animals should not ride.*

Ride
D-Ticket
Ages 4 & up
Mild "space flight" effects
FASTPASS or med. waits
4-min. flight

Planning
Your Special Need
Getting There
Staying in Style
Touring
Feasting
Resources
Index

Charting the Attractions
at Tomorrowland
(continued)

| | Deb Wills' Rating | Deb Koma's Rating | Readers' Rating |

■ Walt Disney's Carousel of Progress (seasonal) [F-4]

10 10 6

This attraction, which is (sadly) seasonal, debuted at the World's Fair in 1964–65. It tracks the path of modern technology from the turn of the century to the present day, with Audio-Animatronics that tell the tale. Theater turns with the passing of each scene, although the stage remains stationary. Limited operating hours. The outdoor queue is partially shaded, but waits are not usually very long. **[A][U]** Enter row first to be closest to exit. **[B]** Dark theater for discreet nursing. **[H]** Assistive listening and handheld captioning are available. The pre-show portion of Carousel of Progress is close-captioned. **[M]** Wheelchair/ECV users enter through the regular entrance, where the cast member will direct you to the seating area. **[L]** Theater-style seats may be tight squeeze for larger body types. **[H][T][M][V]** Break area for service animals nearby; ask a cast member for details.

Show
C-Ticket
Ages 6 & up
No scares
Short waits
22-min. show

■ Galaxy Palace Theater (seasonal) [F-5]

2 2 4

Partially covered outdoor theater is home to a variety of live shows throughout the year. Bench seats are hard and backless. **[M]** Wheelchair/ECV users may remain in chairs. Ask a cast member to be directed to special viewing area.

Live Show
B-Ticket
All ages

■ Stitch's Great Escape! [E-4] FP 🚹

3 3 5

This attraction, which debuted in November 2004, features Stitch the alien before the events in the movie "Lilo & Stitch" occur. The attraction contains some of the most sophisticated Audio-Animatronics technology ever developed and features characters straight out of Lilo & Stitch, including the Galactic Federation's Grand Councilwoman and Captain Gantu, with voices supplied by the movie's original actors. Covered queue area, but during busy times, queue can extend into main, unshaded pathway. Standing pre-show. Theater-style seating, but an overhead harness rests on your shoulders during the show. **[A][U][C][♥][T][I][M][P][E][S]** Use FASTPASS to minimize wait times. **[A][U]** Enter row first to be closest to exit. **[G]** Simulated chili dog smell is quite strong. **[V]** Check with a cast member before bringing a service animal on this attraction. **[A][U][F]** Most of the show takes place in darkness, with loud sudden noises and tactile effects. Cries and screams from others in audience can also

Show
E-Ticket
Ages 7 & up
Could be scary for young kids
FASTPASS or long waits
6-min. intro 12-min. show

be unsettling. Note that you are restrained by harness—could create feelings of being trapped. **[B]** Use Rider Switch. **[Ö]** Ears to the World can be used here. **[H]** Assistive listening and handheld captioning are available at this attraction. The pre-show portion of this attraction is closed captioned. **[M]** If in a wheelchair/ECV, ask a cast member to be seated in an accessible area, where you can remain in your chair and still use the harness so that you experience the special effects. **[L]** Theater-style seats may be a tight squeeze for larger body types. Seats are hard, molded plastic and are only 20" wide. **[B][L]** Height restriction of 40 in./102 cm.

© Deb Wills

Theater-style seats with overhead harnesses

Charting the Attractions
at Tomorrowland
(continued)

Deb Wills' Rating / Deb Koma's Rating / Readers' Rating

☐ Space Mountain [G-3]   FP 👤   7 8 9

This high-speed coaster is entirely in the dark with lots of twists and turns and sharp drops. The outdoor portion of the queue often stretches out into exposed sunshine, while the indoor queue is very dark. Watch your step! **[A][U][C][♥] [T][I][Q][P][E][S]** You can really get shaken up on this rough roller coaster, so those with motion sickness, heart- or back-related issues, as well as pregnant women, should avoid this ride. **[A][U][C][♥][T][I][M][P][E][S]** Use FASTPASS to minimize wait times. **[B][♥][L]** Reader Worst Choice (see page 193). **[F]** This coaster is completely in the dark. Anyone with a fear of heights or falling should also avoid this ride. **[H]** The video pre-show portion is close-captioned. **[M]** Wheelchair/ECV users should use FASTPASS. If FASTPASS is unavailable, speak with a cast member at the entrance. The standby line is not accessible, so if you do not have a FASTPASS, the cast member will issue you a written one. ECV users must transfer to a wheelchair to negotiate the queue. You must then transfer out of your chair to ride. You need to be able to step down into the vehicle to ride, and there is a steep, moving walkway at the exit. Keep in mind that if an emergency evacuation is necessary on this ride, you'll have to deal with a catwalk and ladders or else wait until someone can help you. If you want to stay in your wheelchair, you can see the pre-show and post-show sections and avoid the ride altogether. Manual wheelchairs users may find the steep ramps difficult. Be sure to lock brakes on wheelchairs/ECVs on the moving walkway. **[B]** You must be at least 44 in./112 cm. to ride. Use Rider Switch. **[I]** Some flashing lights and jerky movements may trigger seizures. **[L]** Riders straddle t-bar, and the space is small. Entry/exit may be awkward. People of size might find lap bar uncomfortable. **[H][T][M][V]** Service animals are <u>not</u> allowed.

Coaster
E-Ticket
Ages 8 & up
Twists and turns all in the dark
FASTPASS or long waits
2½-min.

☐ The Timekeeper (seasonal) [E-4]   9 8 6

Audio-Animatronics robots, Timekeeper and 9-Eye, take you on a journey through the major highlights of history. This 360-degree CircleVision film is only seasonal, alas, but well worth a visit. Waiting area is indoors. **[A][U]** Enter row first to be closest to exit. **[C][♥][T][M][P][S]** You must stand for the entire presentation—there are no seats, only "lean rails" to lean against. **[F]** Very loud at times, with sudden outbursts and even sparks. **[H]** Assistive listening and reflective captioning are available. The pre-show portion is close-captioned. **[M]** If in a wheelchair/ECV, a cast member will direct you to the front row, where you'll be able to see while seated. **[Q]** Note that CircleVision films can be disorienting and create motion sickness. **[V]** This is a 360-degree CircleVision film—those with vision impairments may not fully appreciate the special effects.

Show
C-Ticket
Ages 4 & up
Dark, some scary scenes
Med. waits
4-min. intro
16-min. show

☐ Tomorrowland Arcade [G-3]   2 3 3

Located at the exit of Space Mountain, this noisy arcade is a great place to wait while other members of your group are riding the coaster. Most games are 50 cents to $1.00 per play. **[A][U]** The noise level in this arcade is high—could cause overstimulation. **[M]** While the arcade itself is wheelchair/ECV accessible, only some games are.

Arcade
B-Ticket
Ages 6 & up

Side tab labels: Planning, Your Special Need, Getting There, Staying in Style, Touring, Feasting, Resources, Index

Charting the Attractions at Tomorrowland
(continued)

| | Deb Wills' Rating | Deb Koma's Rating | Readers' Rating |

☐ Tomorrowland Indy Speedway [F-3]

🧍 .   **5** **5** **4**

What kid doesn't want a chance to drive before they're 16? This ride gives them that chance. The top speed is only 7 mph and the gas-powered cars are on a track, but that doesn't matter—this is one popular attraction. **[A][U][♥][T][Q][P][E][S]** Another car may bump you from behind on this ride, so those with motion sickness, heart- or back-related issues, as well as pregnant women, should avoid this ride. **[A][U]** Can be extremely noisy. Must stay in vehicle for entire ride. **[G]** Exhaust fumes from cars can be irritating. **[M]** Wheelchair/ECV users go through regular queue to the access gate, where a cast member will direct you. You must be able to transfer out of your chair into the vehicle, and you must be able to depress the gas pedal and steer if driving. **[L]** You must be at least 52 in./132 cm. to drive the car. The cars may be too small for people of size. **[V]** You must steer a car on a track for this ride—those with vision impairments may not be able to judge distances between cars. **[H][T][M][V]**: Service animals should not ride.

Ride
C-Ticket
Ages 4 & up
Some bumps and sudden stops
Long waits
4-min. drive

☐ Tomorrowland Transit Authority [F-4]

6 **6** **6**

Get a grand tour of Tomorrowland on this elevated people-mover that takes you through Space Mountain and several other Tomorrowland attractions. No waiting usually, but you must take a moving conveyor belt that travels up a steep incline before boarding. **[A][U]** Must stay in vehicle for entire ride. **[A][U][I][V]** You must board and exit using a moving walkway. **[B]** Dark stretches for discreet nursing. **[F]** Long stretches of this ride pass through complete darkness. Offers sneak peek into Space Mountain, for those who think they may be too afraid to ride. **[Ö]** Ears to the World available. **[H]** Handheld captioning is available. **[M]** You must be ambulatory to ride—there's a sharply inclined moving walkway to enter, then there's a moving platform. You must then board your vehicle, which is moving at the same speed. **[Q]** If traveling backwards bothers you, be sure to choose a forward-facing seat. **[L]** Vehicle has two rows facing each other. People of size may require their own row.

Ride
B-Ticket
All ages
Dark in spots
Very short waits, if any
12-min. grand tour

© Deb Wills

A Tomorrowland Transit Authority vehicle

Epcot

At three times the size of the Magic Kingdom, Epcot is huge! It is divided into two worlds: Future World encompasses the front section of the park, while the 11 pavilions in World Showcase circle a manmade lagoon. If you have any energy or mobility concerns, we highly recommend touring Epcot in a wheelchair/ECV (especially in the hotter months).

Future World has been **slowly evolving** from the original collection of rides it opened with in 1982, to more high-tech, innovative attractions like Soarin', Turtle Talk with Crush, and Mission: SPACE. The good news is there is much more to Epcot than simply the attractions. Live entertainment is the norm rather than the exception. In addition, six museum-quality galleries offer glimpses of art and artifacts. Generally speaking (if you bypass Mission: SPACE and Test Track), Epcot is the most laid-back of all the parks—it lends itself to "take it one step at a time" touring no matter what the ages or special needs of any of its guests.

There are three **Guest Relations** locations at Epcot. You'll find one on the far right, before you pass through the park turnstiles. The main Guest Relations location is located to the left and rear of Spaceship Earth. The third is outside the turnstiles at the International Gateway. Guest Relations is where you can obtain current Guidebook for Guests With Disabilities, obtain a Guest Assistance Card (see pages 10–11), rent hearing or vision devices, obtain the current schedule for Sign Language Interpreted attractions, and ask any special questions you might have.

After you pass through the **Epcot front entrance turnstiles**, the wheelchair/ECV and stroller rentals are on your left. There are only limited numbers of wheelchairs and ECVs, and reservations are not taken, so be sure to get there early. (Or consider renting equipment from an off-site vendor—see page 203). If you enter through the International Gateway, go left after the turnstiles to rent your wheels. There are very few rentals available at this location.

The pathways in Epcot are wide and **easy to navigate**. Unlike some of the other parks, Epcot's layout is very straightforward with little confusion as to what direction you need to travel. The pavilions are mostly friendly to travelers who use wheelchairs/ECVs, those with mobility issues, health issues, youngsters, and seniors; however, during crowded times (park closing, holidays) stores and outdoor pathways become congested, making movement difficult.

AMBIENCE

PARK LAYOUT AND NAVIGATION

Planning

Your Special Need

Getting There

Staying in Style

Touring

Feasting

Resources

Index

Getting to Epcot

Epcot's **Future World is more crowded when the park opens** because World Showcase does not open until 11:00 am. If there are long lines, either obtain a FASTPASS or circle back later in the day, once the crowds have found their way into World Showcase. The exceptions to this rule are Test Track and Mission:SPACE, which are so popular that they have long lines all the time. Parts of Future World closes at 7:00 pm, so crowds are more concentrated in World Showcase. The variety of ethnic restaurants available also makes World Showcase popular in the evenings.

Epcot is unique in that there are **two separate entrances**, making it the only park to which you can travel via all modes of transportation: car, bus, boat, walking/wheeling, or the monorail. The front entrance has the Disney resort bus stops, car parking lot, taxi and charter bus zones, and the monorail. At World Showcase's International Gateway, you can arrive by land or boat. If you enter through World Showcase before 11:00 am, you will need to walk or wheel into Future World (past Canada and the United Kingdom).

By Car—Special needs travelers may find it more convenient to travel via car. Take I-4 to exit 67 (westbound) or exit 62 (eastbound) and continue to the Epcot toll plaza.

By Monorail—From the Magic Kingdom, Contemporary, Polynesian, or Grand Floridian, take the monorail directly to the Transportation and Ticket Center and then transfer to the Epcot monorail. If you're using a wheelchair or ECV, cast members will assist you in boarding. Note that the entrance and exit ramps to the monorail platform are steep. There is a bypass elevator; ask a cast member for access.

By Boat—The Friendship boats make a huge loop from Epcot to the BoardWalk, Yacht and Beach Club, Swan and Dolphin, and Disney-MGM Studios. The boat is a gentle ride, giving you a chance to sit and get out of the weather, but it does take some time, depending on where you board. Friendship boats are wheelchair/ECV accessible. Strollers can be pushed on without folding; enter at the rear of the boat. Ask a cast member if you need a small ramp for access.

By Bus—From all other resorts, buses take you directly to Epcot. Some of the bus stations are a long walk/wheel from the front gate.

By Land—From the BoardWalk Inn & Villas, Yacht and Beach Club/Villas, Swan, Dolphin, and the Disney-MGM Studios, Epcot is within walking/wheeling distance. Follow the pathways toward the International Gateway, which emerges between France and the United Kingdom.

Making the Most of Epcot

TIPS

If members of your party don't mind getting split up, take advantage of the **single rider line** found at Mission:SPACE and Test Track. These lines are often faster than FASTPASS and definitely faster than the standby line. Test Track cars sit three across, while Mission: SPACE pods hold four. If there are vacant spaces, cast members will fill them with individuals from the single rider line. The drawback is you will be separated from your group.

Kidcot Fun Stops (suggested ages 6–10) are located at each World Showcase Pavilion and Test Track's gift shop. In World Showcase, international cast members will talk with children about their native lands, engage them in a craft, stamp their World Showcase Passports (kids of all ages) if they have one, and sign a personal message in the language of the country. Kid's Guides with facts and pictures of Epcot are available at Guest Relations or the turnstiles and can be stamped and signed, too.

Seniors will love Epcot, so allow extra time. Consider a guided tour like Gardens of the World or Hidden Treasures (see page 305).

Theaters are large, so once a show ends, there is a lot of **congestion** as folks exit the immediate area and decide where to go next.

SPECIAL CONSIDERATIONS

Friendship boats provide transportation across World Showcase—docks are located in front of Morocco and in front of Italy (see map on next page). There are often long waits for the boats, and unless you need a rest or particularly enjoy the boats, you'll get to your destination more quickly by walking/wheeling.

The **First Aid Station** (with companion restroom) is located at the junction of Future World and World Showcase, in the Odyssey Center, near Mexico. The Baby Care Center is right next door. See sidebar on page 196 for services available there.

Braille maps are located outside the Electric Umbrella in Future World and on the International Gateway Path in World Showcase, as well as at Guest Relations in Future World.

Alcohol is sold throughout Epcot, both inside and outside buildings and restaurants; this is especially true during the International Food and Wine Festival in the autumn.

Planning

Your Special Need

Getting There

Staying in Style

Touring

Feasting

Resources

Index

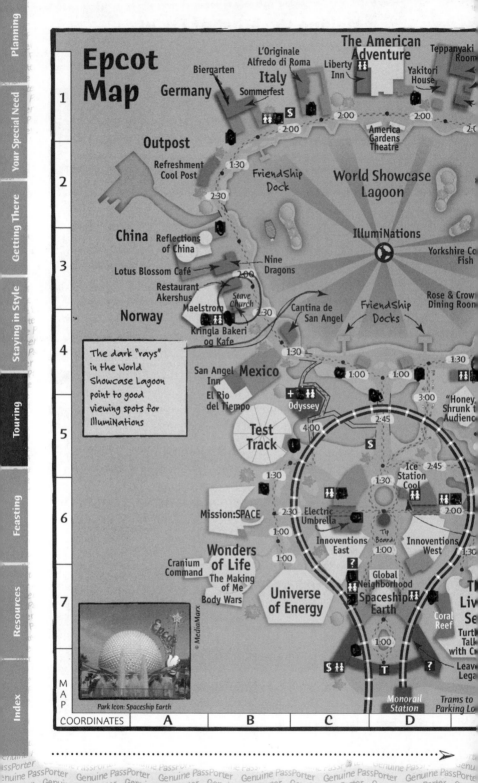

Epcot Map

Germany
Biergarten
L'Originale Alfredo di Roma
Italy
Sommerfest
The American Adventure
Liberty Inn
Teppanyaki Room
Yakitori House

Outpost
Refreshment Cool Post
Friendship Dock
America Gardens Theatre
World Showcase Lagoon

China
Reflections of China
Lotus Blossom Café
Nine Dragons
IllumiNations
Yorkshire Co Fish

Restaurant Akershus
Stave Church
Cantina de San Angel
Friendship Docks
Rose & Crow Dining Room

Norway
Maelstrom
Kringla Bakeri og Kafe

The dark "rays" in the World Showcase Lagoon point to good viewing spots for IllumiNations

San Angel Inn
Mexico
El Rio del Tiempo
Odyssey
"Honey, Shrunk t Audience

Test Track

Ice Station Cool

Mission:SPACE
Electric Umbrella
Innoventions East
Tip Board
Innoventions West

Wonders of Life
Cranium Command
The Making of Me
Body Wars
Universe of Energy
Global Neighborhood
Spaceship Earth
T Liv Se
Coral Reef
Turt Talk with C
Leave Lega

Park Icon: Spaceship Earth
© MediaMarx

Monorail Station
Trams to Parking Lo

COORDINATES | A | B | C | D

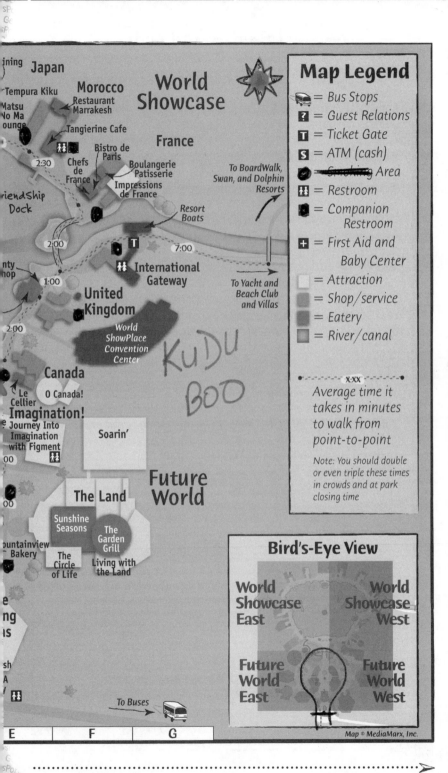

Map Legend

- = Bus Stops
- **?** = Guest Relations
- **T** = Ticket Gate
- **$** = ATM (cash)
- = ~~Smoking~~ Area
- = Restroom
- = Companion Restroom
- **+** = First Aid and Baby Center
- = Attraction
- = Shop/service
- = Eatery
- = River/canal

•·······X:XX·······•

Average time it takes in minutes to walk from point-to-point

Note: You should double or even triple these times in crowds and at park closing time

World Showcase

Japan
Tempura Kiku
Matsu No Ma Lounge
Morocco
Restaurant Marrakesh
Tangierine Cafe
France
Bistro de Paris
Chefs de France
Boulangerie Patisserie
Impressions de France

Friendship Dock

2:30
2:00
1:00
7:00

To BoardWalk, Swan, and Dolphin Resorts

Resort Boats

International Gateway

To Yacht and Beach Club and Villas

nty hop

United Kingdom

2:00

World ShowPlace Convention Center

KuDu BOO

Canada
Le Cellier
O Canada!

Future World

Imagination!
Journey Into Imagination with Figment

Soarin'

The Land
Sunshine Seasons
The Garden Grill
ountainview Bakery
The Circle of Life
Living with the Land

Bird's-Eye View

World Showcase East   World Showcase West

Future World East   Future World West

To Buses

Map © MediaMarx, Inc.

E   F   G

Planning | Your Special Needs | Getting There | Staying in Style | Touring | Feasting | Resources | Index

Entertainment at Epcot

ENTERTAINMENT

Live entertainment can be found throughout the park. You can spend your entire day watching each of the live performers. Enjoy musical acts, improvisation, alien contortionists, and incredible a cappella singing! (Check times guide for details.) As your trip gets closer, check out the unofficial Walt Disney World Entertainment web site for times: http://pages.prodigy.net/stevesoares/index.htm.

Disney characters are found all around Epcot. They travel several times a day (check times guide) in a character bus and make stops at the Future World/World Showcase junction and several countries. A plethora of characters come off the bus and form impromptu lines for autographs and photos. This is a great way to meet a variety of characters, some seldom out and about. If you look around, you can generally find someone all by themselves, just waiting for you. Characters are also known to frequent the pavilion most representative of their origins; Beauty and the Beast in France; Aladdin, Jasmine, and Genie in Morocco; and so on. See page 207 for more details.

Schedules for **sign language interpreted shows** are made a week at a time. Times may vary. The best thing to do is check at Guest Relations, and they can print out the latest one for you.

Attractions With Hearing Devices Chart

Assistive Listening Device	Ellen's Energy Adventure, Innoventions (certain sections), Circle of Life, Living Seas (movie), The Making of Me, Honey I Shrunk the Audience, Test Track, America Gardens Theatre, Impressions de France, Maelstrom, O Canada, American Adventure, and Cranium Command
Handheld Captioning	Ellen's Energy Adventure, Journey Into Imagination With Figment, Living With the Land, Spaceship Earth, Test Track, El Rio del Tiempo, and Maelstrom
Reflective Captioning	Circle of Life, Living Seas (certain areas, not Crush), The Making of Me, Honey I Shrunk the Audience, Impressions de France, Maelstrom (film), O Canada, American Adventure, and Cranium Command
Closed Captioning	Living Seas (certain areas), Body Wars, Honey I Shrunk the Audience, Mission:SPACE, Test Track (Briefing Room), and Soarin' (pre-show)
ASL	Turtle Talk With Crush and World Showcase Players
Ears to the World (Show Translators)	Spaceship Earth, Innoventions, Ellen's Energy Adventure, Cranium Command, Mission:SPACE, Test Track (Briefing Room), Circle of Life, Honey I Shrunk the Audience, Journey Into Imagination, Reflections of China, American Adventure, and O Canada

Finding Your Place at Epcot

Those wishing or needing a **quiet area** for breaks, time-outs, or baby nursing should consider:

- The right side of Living Seas near the entrance to Coral Reef restaurant.
- Turning right into World Showcase, just past the store, is an alcove with benches and some shade.
- During the day and early evening, the IllumiNations viewing areas by the United Kingdom and France are generally unoccupied.
- On the right side of Morocco is a quiet area with shade and benches.
- Short but lush vegetation trail to the right of the Mexico pavilion.
- In the Canada pavilion, the benches on second level are in a quiet area.
- In the United Kingdom, the garden in the back (when there are no shows).
- Ellen's Energy Adventure has a line of benches (some shaded)
- The far left side of Test Track near the entrance to the Cast Access area. You can still hear the noise of Test Track, but it's generally not populated here.

Companion restrooms are located in the following areas:

- Near Spaceship Earth (on both sides)
- Future World East opposite Test Track
- Future World West opposite The Land
- Refreshment Port (right side)
- First Aid Station (near Odyssey Pavilion)
- Norway (near Viking ship), Germany (right side), and Morocco (right side)

Attraction Seating Chart

American Adventure	theater
Body Wars	theater with seat belt
Circle of Life	theater
Cranium Command	bench without back
El Rio del Tiempo	bench with back (boat)
Ellen's Energy Adventure	bench with back
Honey I Shrunk the Audience	theater
Impressions de France	theater
Journey Into Your Imagination	moving, bench with back, high bar
Living Seas	"The Seas" movie: bench with back; Turtle Talk: bench without back, some floor seating
Living with the Land	bench with back (boat)
Maelstrom	bench seat (boat); bench with back (theater)
Making of Me	bench without back
Mission:SPACE	harness, low bar
O Canada	standing with lean rails
Reflections of China	standing with lean rails
Spaceship Earth	moving, bench with back, small space
Soarin'	seat belt
Test Track	automobile seating with shoulder/lap belts

SPECIAL PLACES

Planning

Your Special Need

Getting There

Staying in Style

Touring

Feasting

Resources

Index

Charting the Attractions at Future World (East)

	Deb Wills' Rating	Deb Koma's Rating	Readers' Rating

☐ Spaceship Earth [D-7]

9 8 8

Epcot's shimmering geosphere icon stands 180 feet tall and features the history of communications from caveman to the future as told by 65 Audio-Animatronics. A moving, inclined walkway takes you to the loading area, where you step onto a moving platform to board the vehicle of this continuously loading ride. The walkway can be further slowed or stopped if necessary—ask cast member before entering queue area. Your "time machine" has two rows of hard plastic seats; side door opens for entrance/exit. Gentle ride, but last half is backward and downhill. Speaker is located on headrest. Companion restrooms are nearby. **[A][U][F][T][I][Q][V]** Fluorescent lighting similar to strobes in "tunnel" area may trigger seizures in those prone. **[A][U][F]** Ride vehicles may unexpectedly pause briefly; periods of darkness, narrow and enclosed spaces. **[A][U]** Must stay in vehicle entire ride. **[G][F]** Smell of wood burning in Rome scene. **[U][B][♥][Q][L]** Reader Best Choice (see page 193). **[B]** Dark ride for discreet nursing. **[Ö]** Ears to the World available. **[H]** Handheld captioning available—provides about 80% of narration. **[M]** Main queue is not accessible for wheelchairs/ECVs—entrances on both sides. Transfer from wheelchair to vehicle. Check with cast member for loading procedures. If an emergency evacuation is necessary, you'll have to deal with stairs or else wait until someone can help you. **[F][Q]** Vehicle gently rotates and then travels backward downhill during last part of ride. **[A][Q][P][E][V]** Slow-moving load/unload platform. **[H][T][M][V]** Check with cast member before entering with service animals. The smell of burning wood might upset some service animals. **[L]** Each row can fit one large adult and one small child; a large adult may need to sit in their own row.

Track Ride
E-Ticket
Ages 5 & up
Dark, steep incline, some backward travel; gentle
Short waits except at park opening
15-min. ride

☐ Innoventions East [C-6]

5 5 6

"The Road to Tomorrow"—Disney partners with hi-tech vendors who exhibit cutting edge technologies via demonstrations, hands-on activities, and video games. This is a walk-/wheel-around exhibit area with very few benches. It can be very loud and crowded. Take the House of Innoventions tour, see the Segway demonstration, UL Testing Lab demos and hands-on, Fantastic Plastic Works (make your own take home plastic robot), and visit the Disney Interactive Zone to send a 10-second video/audio email! Check with cast member at each exhibit for special accommodations. **[A][U][F][I][S]** Very noisy with lots of stimulus. **[Ö]** Ears to the World available for Intro to Innoventions. **[H]** Assistive listening and video captioning available at some exhibits. Sign language interpreted performances at House of Innoventions on designated days; check with Guest Relations for schedule. Arrive at least 20 minutes in advance; meet interpreter at entrance. **[H][T][M][V]** Check with cast member before entering with service animals.

Playground
B-Ticket
All ages
Very noisy
Short waits
Allow 30–60 min. to explore

Charting the Attractions
at Future World (East)
(continued)

| | Deb Wills' Rating | Deb Koma's Rating | Readers' Rating |

☐ Universe of Energy (Ellen's Energy Adventure) [B-7] — **7 7 7**

Comedian Ellen DeGeneres dreams of winning "Jeopardy!" but the Energy category stumps her. Bill Nye the Science Guy saves the day. Standing pre-show (sets the story) in cool, dark room with handful of benches. Travel in slow-moving, 97-passenger hard plastic vehicles (long bench seats with backs) past primeval dinosaurs, view widescreen dramatic film. Shows start every 17 minutes. Indoor queue with uncovered outdoor queue overflow. **[A][U][B][F][♥]** Dinosaur area is dark, loud, and may be scary. **[A][U]** Must stay in vehicle entire ride. Show is very long! **[C][♥][T][E][S]** Sit in air-conditioning to rest and enjoy. Enter last row so you don't have to move all the way down the bench to enter and exit. **[C][♥][M]** Reader Best Choice (see page 193). **[B]** Dark ride for discreet nursing. **[Ö]** Ears to the World available. **[H]** Assistive listening and handheld captioning available. **[H][T][M][V]** Break area for service animals nearby; ask a cast member. **[M]** Must transfer from ECV to standard wheelchair at entrance. May remain in wheelchair for show, but some wider-/longer-than-average wheelchairs may be a tight fit. After pre-show, move right into loading area and wait for cast member assistance.

Sidebar: Film/Ride · D-Ticket · Ages 4 & up · Dark, loud, dinosaurs · Med. waits · 8-min. intro · 37-min. ride

☐ Wonders of Life (seasonal) [B-7] — **5 5 7**

Health and fitness area that includes a thrill ride, shows, and hands-on exhibits. Open seasonally. **[M]** Restrooms have large accessible handicapped stalls.

Sidebar: Pavilion · C-Ticket

☐ Fitness Fairgrounds (seasonal) [B-7] — **3 3 5**

Hands-on health and fitness exhibits and demos. Inside Wonders of Life.

Sidebar: Playground

☐ Body Wars (seasonal) [B-7] 🚶‍♀ — **4 6 6**

Motion simulator inside Wonders of Life transports you through the human body with sharp movements and herky-jerky motion! Intense special effects. **[A][U]** Must stay in vehicle for entire ride. Back rows give roughest ride. Cast member can provide a 4-point harness for those who have a hard time holding on with just the seat belt. **[A][U][C][F][♥][T][I][M][Q][P][E][S][V]** Rough/fast ride with sudden movements. Must be in good health, free from heart, back or neck problems. Expectant mothers should not ride. Ask cast member to view film without motion simulator running—at the cast member's discretion, you may be asked to return later for experience without motion. **[B]** Use Rider Switch. **[F]** Loud noises, claustrophobia factor medium. Simulates graphic travel through the bloodstream—squeamish folks should avoid. **[H]** Assistive listening and video captioning available in pre-show. **[H][T][M][V]** Service animals not allowed. **[♥][L]** Reader Worst Choice (see page 193). **[M]** Transfer from wheelchair to vehicle. Position wheelchair in front of theatre for easy transfer to seat; cast member will remove the wheelchair for actual ride. **[L]** Minimum height 40 in./102 cm. Seat with retractable belt may be a tight fit for persons of size; armrest may also be uncomfortable. **[T]** Brief period of strobe light.

Sidebar: Thrill Ride · D-Ticket · Ages 6 & up · Very rough · Med. waits · 1-2 min. pre-show · 5-min. ride

Charting the Attractions at Future World (East)
(continued)

Deb Wills' Rating | _Deb Koma's Rating_ | _Readers' Rating_

▢ Cranium Command (seasonal) [A-7]

9 **10** **8**

See what it's like to be inside an adolescent boy's brain! Cute, funny show especially enjoyed by pre-teens and parents. Star-studded cast including George Wendt from "Cheers", Dana Carvey, Jon Lovitz, and Charles Grodin. Animated pre-show is standing on a floor with a 10-15° slope—stand in back for best view of screen. Sit on bench seats with backs in theater. Located inside the Wonder of Life. **[U][B][F]** Very loud noises. **[C][♥][T][E][S]** Sit in air-conditioning to rest and enjoy. **[Ö]** Translation with Ears to the World device **[H]** Assistive listening and reflective captioning available (ask a cast member at entrance). **[M]** Wheelchair/ECV users use regular queue and ask cast member to be directed to special seating area.	**Show**
	D-Ticket
	Ages 3 & up
	Loud noises
	Short waits
	5-min. intro
	12-min. show

▢ The Making Of Me (seasonal) [B-7]

5 **5** **5**

Martin Short takes you on a sensitive and touching journey about childbirth and family. No sex, just family love, marriage, and romance. Parental discretion advised. Located inside the Wonders of Life. **[H]** Assistive listening and reflective captioning (request from cast member at entrance). **[M]** Enter to the left of the main entrance and request assistance to the special seating area.	**Film**
	C-Ticket
	Ages 8 & up
	15-min. film

▢ Mission:SPACE [B-6] _FP_ 🧍

4 **9** **8**

The International Space Training Center will prepare you for a mission to Mars! Long, winding queue weaves inside and outside. Four-person ride vehicles are attached to a centrifuge that simulates liftoff and space flight. Very enclosed space with individual harness. Must be in good health; free from high blood pressure, heart, back, or neck problems and motion sickness. Very intense—you may become queasy and dizzy like co-author Deb Wills or love it like co-author Deb Koma! Heed the warnings. Post-show area (wheelchair accessible) has games and hands-on fun for all ages. Play area for small kids (huge tubes to climb on). **[A][U][C][♥][T][M][P][E][S][L]** Use FASTPASS to minimize wait times, or try the single rider line. **[A][U][C][F][♥][T][I][M][Q][P][E][S][V]** If uncomfortable with enclosed dark spaces, simulators, spinning, or loud sounds, you should not ride. **[A][U]** Must stay in vehicle entire ride. **[C][M][Q][L]** Reader Worst Choice (see page 193). **[B]** Use Rider Switch. **[Ö]** Ears to the World available in pre-show. Mission:SPACE video kiosk available in English, Spanish, Japanese, German, Portugese, and French. **[F]** You should not ride if you're claustrophobic. **[H]** Closed-captioning for pre-show. **[H][T][M][V]** Service animals not allowed. **[M]** Transfer from wheelchair to training capsule. **[B][L]** Height requirement is 44 in./112cm. Vehicle is very small. Seat room is ample, but the "rocket" closes down, similar to a car trunk. Persons large through the stomach note the "rocket" may not be able to lock—if it's not locked, you won't go on your mission. **[C][♥][T][Q][S][E]** Should not ride.	**Thrill Ride**
	E-Ticket
	Ages 8 & up
	Disorienting
	FASTPASS or long waits
	7½-min. pre-show
	5-min. ride

Side tabs: Planning / Your Special Need / Getting There / Staying in Style / Touring / Feasting / Resources / Index

Charting the Attractions
at Future World (East)
(continued)

	Deb Wills' Rating	Deb Koma's Rating	Readers' Rating
Test Track [B-5] FP 🏃	8	9	9

Experience General Motors' car testing procedures. Travel up to 65 mph in open-air vehicles (with two rows of three). Queue area is very loud and slow-moving; there's lots of loud banging and collision simulations. Standing pre-show takes place in a small room. Shoulder/lap belts on ends, lap belts only in middle seat. Fast, banked sharp curves, sudden stops, bumps, abrupt temperature changes. Must be in good health and free from high blood pressure; heart, back, or neck problems; and motion sickness. Companion restroom nearby. Exit into GM Showroom. You can bypass the ride by entering through the gift shop and auto showcase area. There's an optional six-minute virtual reality film called Dreamchaser, which is not worth a long wait. Just outside is the Cool Wash Coca Cola misting station (operating during warmer months) as well as a butterfly garden (a great place to take a breather). **[A][U][C][♥][T][M][P][E][S][L]** Use FASTPASS to minimize wait times or ask for the Single Rider Line. **[A][R][U][C][F][♥][T][I][M][Q][P][E][S][V]** Rough/fast ride with various lighting and environmental changes. **[A][R][G][U][F][♥][T][I][M][S][V]** Mechanical arm shoots mist towards vehicle in corrosive testing room. **[A][U]** Must stay in vehicle entire ride. **[Ö]** Ears to the World available for Briefing Room. **[F]** Unless there are three in your party, you will be seated with strangers. **[C][♥][M][L]** Reader Worst Choice (see page 193). **[H]** Assistive listening, closed-captioning, and handheld captioning available for Briefing Room. **[H][T][M][V]** Service animals not allowed. **[M]** Accessible FASTPASS machine on far right. Check with cast member for directions. Transfer from wheelchair to vehicle. **[M][L]** Note that there is a stationary vehicle in a private area if you want to practice boarding and exit. Ask a cast member. **[♥][E]** Guests with these conditions should not ride. **[Q]** Use caution if prone to motion sickness. **[C][M][S]** If you cannot step down into the car, ask to be loaded at the seat belt stop where it might be easier, with a shorter step. You can also transfer from wheelchair to vehicle easier at this stop. A grab bar is available upon request—it can be secured in the car for someone who needs to pull themselves out of the wheelchair and into the car. **[Q]** Seats in post-show Dreamchaser move with film. Ask cast member about using a seat that does not move. **[B]** Use Rider Switch. **[B][L]** Height restriction 40 in/102 cm. Larger people may not be completely comfortable in this ride, as it has bucket seats. Middle seats are the least comfortable, back row has very little leg room, front row has leg room to spare. If no one is in the middle seat, a larger person might be OK in one of the outside seats, but if it's a full car, a larger person literally might not fit. The seat belts are very ample, but it might help to lift your bottom off the seat to get the seat belt closed. Otherwise ask a cast member for assistance.	**Thrill Ride** E-Ticket Ages 7 & up Fast, jerky, bumpy FASTPASS/ single rider line, or very long waits 3-min. intro 5-min. ride

🎄 Holidays Around the World

Each year from Thanksgiving to New Year's, Epcot celebrates Holidays around the World. The entire park is decorated in red and white poinsettias, garland, fir trees, lights—and there's even special entertainment! Each World Showcase country has a holiday storyteller who performs a cute and informative short skit (standing only for most performances) on the customs of various lands and cultures, after which you can ask questions.

Charting the Attractions at Future World (West)

Deb Wills' Rating
Deb Koma's Rating
Readers' Rating

Innoventions West [D-6] — 5 5 6

Part two of Epcot's high-tech trade exhibit. Demonstrations (Where's the Fire), hands-on activities, and games. Send an email to your family and friends. This is a walk-around exhibit area with very few benches. It can be very loud and crowded in some areas. **[A][U][F][I][S]** Some areas very noisy with lots of stimulus. **[Ö]** Ears to the World available for Innoventions introductions. Send a postcard in one of six languages: kiosk available in English, Spanish, Japanese, German, Portuguese, and French. **[H][T][M][V]** Check with cast member before taking service animals. **[H]** Assistive listening and closed captioning available at some exhibits.

Playground
B-Ticket
Ages 6 & up
Noisy
Short waits
Allow 30–60 min. to explore

Ice Station Cool [D-6] (closed until December 2005) — 4 5 7

Cool down and quench your thirst! Pass through the "igloo" into a unique tasting room sponsored by Coca Cola. Taste international flavors of sodas and check out Coca Cola merchandise. Before tasting room, you must go through the "ice station" with chilly air and sometimes even snow. Heavy plastic strips form the entrance/exit to this area—awkward to move and hard to navigate, especially in a wheelchair. Bypass unless you need to cool down or want the free soda. **[A][U]** Noisy and small area, abrupt temperature change. **[A][U][T][M][P][E][S][V]** Floor is cold, sometimes wet/sticky. **[G][D][E]** No list of ingredients and no sugar-free beverages. **[C]** Not worth the energy except to cool down. **[B]** Cold and damp. **[F]** Refreshus Maximus (man) is frozen in ice on the left before you get to tasting room; may be spooky for youngsters. **[M]** Accessible soda stations, but description signs too far away. Exit ramp located to left of the stairs behind cash register.

Walk-Thru
A-Ticket
Ages 2 & up
Noisy, cold, sticky floor
Unlimited

The Living Seas [E-7] — 7 7 6

The world's largest saltwater aquarium, now with "Finding Nemo" theming throughout. View sharks, rays, manatees, and don't miss Turtle Talk with Crush! Low lights and soft music in standing pre-show area with 360-degree screen. You have two choices: (1) Go to the doors on right for 7-minute movie "The Seas" in a theater with bench seats with backs. The movie has loud noises during earth formation sequence. After movie, exit to Hydrolators, simulated elevators that go to Sea Base Alpha. Hydrolators hold 25–30 people in a confined area. You may feel cramped. Ask cast member to show you the elevator bypass. (2) Go through doors on left to bypass the movie and go straight to Hydrolators. Sea Base Alpha requires lots of walking and standing (except for Crush) with few places to sit. **[B]** Dark theater for discreet nursing **[B][H]** Reader Best Choice (see page 193). **[F]** Claustrophobia alert—ask to bypass Hydrolators. Sharks and other sea life in exhibits. **[H]** Assistive listening and reflective captioning in theater (ask cast member at entrance). Video captioning available in some areas of Sea Base Alpha. Sign language interpretation on designated dates; check with Guest Relations for schedule. Arrive at least 10 minutes in advance; enter through regular queue; see cast member for directions. **[H][T][M][V]** Use caution if traveling with service animal. Marine life is in full view (floor to ceiling windows). If your service animal is sensitive to other animals, you might need to correct it continually. **[M]** Ramped entry queue is winding and can be difficult to navigate in larger ECVs (including Disney rentals) or wheelchairs (sharp turns). You will be encouraged to transfer from ECV to wheelchair, but you don't have to. Restroom stalls too small for door to close with some wheelchairs.

Pavilion
D-Ticket
All ages
Unique aquarium
Short waits
7-min. movie Allow about one hour for exhibits

Charting the Attractions
at Future World (West)
(continued)

	Deb Wills' Rating	Deb Koma's Rating	Readers' Rating

☐ The Land [E-6] | 8 | 8 | 7 |

Explore agriculture and our environment. Brand new Soarin' attraction, gentle boat ride, movie, newly renovated food court, and sit-down character meals. Elevator inside to the left of Garden Grill restaurant. **[B]** Strollers must be parked outside. **[M]** Wheelchair entrance on right. Restrooms are very difficult for someone using wheelchair; small tight spaces and small stalls.

Pavilion
E-Ticket

☐ The Circle of Life [F-6] | 8 | 6 | 6 |

The Lion King's Timon and Pumbaa host this environmental film with a message for us all. Spectacular photography. Music can get loud. Standing indoor queue area with limited bench seating. Theater seating inside. **[A][U]** Enter row first to be closest to exit. **[C][F][♥][T][M][P][S][V]** Steep steps up/down theater. **[B]** Dark theater for discreet nursing. **[Ö]** Ears to the World. **[H]** Reflective captioning available (ask cast member at entrance). Assistive listening for movie. **[M][P]** Cast member will direct you to seating area. Wheelchair/ECV area is in back of theatre–open area without seats. Others in party will be encouraged to sit in row ahead. One person may remain with wheelchair but must stand. **[L]** Theatre seats may be too narrow for some body types.

Film
D-Ticket
Ages 3 & up
Short waits
12-min.
film

☐ Living With the Land [F-6]   🅵🅿 | 7 | 6 | 7 |

A gentle boat ride through Epcot's agriculture farm. Learn about hydroponics and aquaculture. **[A][U][C][♥][T][M][P][E][S][L]** Use FASTPASS to minimize wait times. **[A][U]** Must stay in boat entire ride. **[F]** When crowded, queue design could trigger claustrophobic feelings; dark in areas (especially beginning), simulated thunderstorm. **[H]** Hand-held captioning includes about 75 percent of narration but doesn't always coincide well. Sign language interpreted performances on designated days; check with Guest Relations for schedule. Arrive at least 10 minutes in advance; enter through the wheelchair entrance to the right of the standard queue. **[M][P]** Follow signs to wheelchair entrance to right of ride entrance. Must transfer from ECV to standard wheelchair. All boats have ramp for wheelchairs (one wheelchair per boat). **[Q]** Gentle ride, but use caution if VERY sensitive to motion.

Boat Ride
D-Ticket
Ages 4 & up
Dark
FASTPASS or
long waits
13-min. ride

☐ Soarin' [F-6] (New for 2005)   🅵🅿 🕴 | 10 | 10 | 10 |

Soarin' takes you on a simulated, hang-glider flight over the grandeur of California, the Golden State. You are lifted 40 feet inside a giant projection screen dome (think IMAX). Sights, smells, gentle motion, and even wind make you feel aloft. Sit side by side on one of the three rows (10 seats per row). Bench seats, legs dangle, seat belts. Entrance queue and the exit path are long! The paths go up and down. **[A][U][C][♥][T][M][P][E][S][L]** Use FASTPASS to minimize wait times. **[A][U]** Must stay in seat entire ride. **[A][U][F][♥][T][M][Q][P][S][V]** The seats will rise up and simulate flight (think of hang gliding). **[G]** Scents of pine, orange, and the seashore. **[B]** Use Rider Switch. **[F]** Heights, flying, feet dangle. **[Q]** Could produce motion sickness. **[H][T][M][V]** Service animals are not allowed. **[M]** Must be able to transfer to ride vehicle, at press time; no option to remain in wheelchair/ECV and view from floor. **[C][♥][T][Q][S][E]** Should not ride. **[B][L]** Height restriction 40 in./102 cm.

Simulator
E-Ticket
Ages 7 & up
Simulated
heights
FASTPASS or
long waits
Very long
waits
5-min. ride

Charting the Attractions at Future World (West)
(continued)

	Deb Wills' Rating	Deb Koma's Rating	Readers' Rating

☐ Honey, I Shrunk the Audience [E-5]   FP | 9 | 8 | 8 |

Dr. Wayne Szalinski (Rick Moranis) demonstrates his newest invention, receives the Inventor of the Year award, and, well, someone gets shrunk again! Standing pre-show on slanted floor to view 12 flat-screen monitors (some monitors in second row have subtitles). Theater seating with slight padding. Loud noises, intense special effects (some tactile), theater vibrates. May be too intense for children and some adults. Video monitor on left side of 3D screen to view without 3D glasses. **[A]** Reader Best Choice (see page 193). **[A][U][C][♥][T][M][P][E][S][L]** Use FASTPASS to minimize wait times. **[A][U][B][F][♥][T][I][Q][S]** Effects include wind, water, movement, loud noises, other tactile effects. **[A][U]** Enter row first to be closest to exit. **[F]** When cast member finishes the intro in the theater, smoke comes out of the podium. Film features lions, snakes, mice, and other scary moments. **[A][U][F][I][Q][S][V]** Wear special 3-D viewing glasses—they fit over regular glasses. **[Ö]** Ears to the World available **[♥][T][M][Q][P][E][S][L]** Pre-show area has a 10- to 15-degree slope. Stand in back of pre-show area to lean against partial wall (just in front of wheelchair area). **[H]** Reader Best Choice. **[H][T][M][V]** Check with cast member before entering with service animals. Break area for service animals nearby; ask cast member. **[H]** Reflective captioning available—see cast member at entrance. Assistive listening and video captioning available. **[M]** Wheelchair entrance on left. Transfer to seat to experience all special effects. Only one person can accompany wheelchair to special seating area. **[Q]** Theater vibrates when "shrunk." Mild motion sensitivity may occur when Adam "picks up" the theater.	3-D Film E-Ticket Ages 8 & up Very loud, dark, snakes, mice FASTPASS or med. waits 5-min. intro 13-min. film

☐ Journey Into Your Imagination With Figment [E-5] | 7 | 7 | 3 |

Figment, the lovable purple dragon, returns to stimulate your imagination with sight, sound, smell, and musical fun! This is a gently moving ride in four-person, hard plastic vehicles, but special effects may be intense. Vehicles stop periodically. After ride, exit into Image Works. Located inside the Imagination pavilion. **[A][U][C][B][F][♥][T][I][Q][S][V]** Vehicle vibrates in sound lab; loud noises, flashes of light, darkness. Smell lab has mild skunk scent, air blows in your face. **[A][U]** Must stay in vehicle entire ride. **[C][♥][T][I][M][Q][P][E][S][L][V]** Vehicle boarding area flat; cars do stop for loading. **[B]** Dark ride for discreet nursing. **[Ö]** Ears to the World available. **[H]** Handheld captioning available. **[H][T][M][V]** Break area for service animals nearby—ask cast member. **[M]** Wheelchairs enter on left. Wheelchair accessible vehicle available. Some longer or wider than average wheelchairs may be a tight fit. If able, transfer to an available manual wheelchair. **[L]** Each row can fit one large adult and one small child, or a large adult will need to sit in their own row; back row slightly wider than front.	Track Ride C-Ticket Ages 5 & up Portions are dark with loud noises and flashes Med. waits 6-min. ride

☐ ImageWorks: Kodak "What If" Labs [E-5] | 4 | 6 | 7 |

Hands-on sound and image exhibits, digital photo, and unique photographic gift items. Located inside the Imagination pavilion. **[A][U][C][B][F][♥][T][I][S]** Very noisy. **[A][U]** Lots of activities are good for burning off some excess energy. **[M]** If crowded, it can be hard to maneuver around.	Playground B-Ticket All ages Allow 20 min.

Charting the Attractions
at World Showcase
(listed in clockwise order)

	Deb Wills' Rating	Deb Koma's Rating	Readers' Rating

☐ Mexico [B-4] — 7 8 8

Travel south of the border and enjoy unique exhibits, a Mexican shopping plaza, San Angel Inn restaurant, and a twilight setting with a volcano in the distance. Restrooms inside pavilion. Entertainment in courtyard standing only. *[F][S][V]* Very low lighting in marketplace and restaurant. *[Ö]* Many cast members working here are from Mexico and are fluent in Spanish. *[H][T][M][V]* Break area for service animals nearby; ask cast member. *[M]* Access pavilion via ramp on right of main entrance. Hard to maneuver wheelchair in shopping areas, especially when crowded.

Pavilion
D-Ticket
All ages
Low light

☐ El Rio del Tiempo [B-4] — 5 7 5

A gentle boat ride takes you from Mexico's past to the present with a combination of Audio-Animatronics (the Mexican version of "it's a small world" with the dancing dolls), music and film clips. You must step down into boat. A few boats have wheelchair ramps. Some mist in beginning of ride. Very dark in spots. Fiber-optic fireworks in ceiling near end. *[A][U]* Must stay in boat entire ride. *[B][F]* Skeleton-costumed band; simulated fireworks display. *[B]* Dark ride for discreet nursing. *[H]* Handheld captioning available. *[M]* Proceed through exit so cast member can assist with boarding. Must transfer from ECV to standard wheelchair. *[Q]* Boat ride is gentle, but still rocks a little.

Boat Ride
C-Ticket
All ages
Dark, but tame
Short waits
7-minute cruise

☐ Norway [B-3] — 5 6 7

A visit to Scandinavia includes a Viking ship play area, Maelstrom boat ride, eateries, live entertainment, shops, and trolls. Shops are difficult to maneuver as they go from large to small spaces. A replica of a Gol Stave Church from Oslo is open to explore. The Stave Church has two entrances, one with stairs, the other with level access. Wheelchairs/ECVs fit through the church door, but the door is heavy. A wheelchair-bound guest traveling alone will have trouble opening this door by themselves. Entertainment is in the courtyard, but it is standing only. A companion restroom is to the right of the Viking ship. *[C]* The Stave church is quiet and cool, though there is no place to sit. *[F]* A very large troll statue is in the shop. *[Ö]* Many cast members here are from Norway and speak Norwegian. *[M][L]* Small hallways make the Stave Church difficult to walk through.

Pavilion
C-Ticket
All ages
Allow 30 min.

© MediaMarx, Inc.

Norway

Planning · Your Special Need · Getting There · Staying in Style · Feasting · Resources · Index

Charting the Attractions at World Showcase
(continued)

	Deb Wills' Rating	Deb Koma's Rating	Readers' Rating

☐ Maelstrom [B-3] `FP` — 8 8 7

Travel to a Norwegian fishing village via a mythical forest with trolls, storms, and polar bears. There's a short, steep drop; short backward ride; and Vikings. Boat seats have backs but no padding. One ride sequence has boat going toward a pulsating, spinning light, similar to a strobe light. If boats back up waiting to unload, they bump each other and you get jostled. Exit the boat into a small theater for brief movie about Norway—seats have slat backs and padded seats. To bypass theater, walk right through. **[A][U][C][B][F][♥][I][S]** Movie is very loud. **[A][U][C][♥][T][M][P][E][S][L]** Use FASTPASS to minimize wait times. **[A][U][B][F][♥]** Special effects may be scary. Large trolls/polar bears, lightning, and darkness. **[A][U]** Must stay in boat entire ride. **[B]** Use Rider Switch. **[F][Q][V]** Boat turns and travels backward briefly. **[H]** Handheld captioning available for ride. Assistive listening and reflective captioning available for movie—ask cast member at entrance. **[H][T][M][V]** Check with cast member before bringing service animals onboard. **[M][S][V]** Two steps to load/unload boat. Rails separating boarding area limit space available to assist person boarding/exiting the boat. **[M]** Reader Worst Choice (see page 193). FASTPASS area hard to access. Wheelchair is brought from loading to unloading zone. If an emergency evacuation is necessary, you need to be able to handle stairs, or else wait for help. Theater not very wheelchair-friendly; ends of rows recessed for wheelchairs. Back row does not allow access for wheelchair. Go to the far side of the theater (near exit) and reposition your wheelchair. **[Q]** Boat ride can be rough at times. You may experience slight problems with movie—sit in back of theater, not sides or front.

Boat Ride
D-Ticket
Ages 5 & up
Small drops, backwards, dark
FASTPASS or med. waits
15-min. ride

☐ China [B-3] — 6 7 6

Majestic architecture, exhibits, gardens, shopping, live entertainment, and eateries transport you to China. Land of Many Faces gallery offers unique exhibits. Entertainment in courtyard—standing or sitting on the ground only. **[Ö]** Most cast members in this pavilion are natives of China and speak Chinese. **[H]** Pay phone with TTY in plaza. **[M]** Wheelchair/ECV accessible.

Pavilion
C-Ticket
All ages
Allow 20 min.

☐ Reflections of China [A-3] — 6 6 7

The 360-degree CircleVision movie allows you to see China's people, cities, and cultures. Waiting area indoors with benches (see photo below). Live entertainment in pre-show area by Chinese musicians—check times guide. Theater is standing only, no seating—just lean rails. **[A][U]** Enter row first to be closest to exit. **[C][♥][T][M][Q][P][S][L][V]** Lean rails available. **[Ö]** Ears to the World available. **[H]** Reflective captioning—see cast member. Assistive listening available. **[Q]** You may experience motion sickness—if 360-degree movies make you a little dizzy, stand near the back of the room or don't go. **[M]** Position in rear of theatre.

360° Film
D-Ticket
Ages 6 & up
Could cause dizziness
Short waits
13-min. show

© Debra Martin Koma

Benches in the pre-show area

Charting the Attractions at World Showcase
(continued)

Deb Wills' Rating | Deb Koma's Rating | Readers' Rating

☐ Germany [B-1] — 3 | 5 | 7

Fantasy, folklore, and the sounds of Oktoberfest. Live entertainment in restaurant, seating based on availability for non-dining guests. Watch the outdoor clock tower on the hour. Don't miss the model train village. Companion restroom on the right side of the pavilion. ***[R]*** *Wine tastings sold.* ***[Ö]*** *Most cast members in this pavilion are natives of Germany and speak German.*

Pavilion | B-Ticket | All ages

☐ Italy [C-1] — 3 | 6 | 6

Shops, architecture, and restaurant, represent the beauty of Italy, Venice in particular. Entertainment in courtyard, limited patio furniture seating, standing or sitting on the ground only. ***[R]*** *Wine tastings sold.* ***[F]*** *Improv group selects participants from the audience.* ***[Ö]*** *Most cast members in this pavilion are natives of Italy and speak Italian.*

Pavilion | C-Ticket | All ages

☐ The American Adventure [D-1] — 7 | 8 | 7

The American Adventure is the large building directly across the lagoon as you enter from Future World. Enjoy an Audio-Animatronics show, outdoor amphitheater, fast food eatery, and small gift shop. Spirit of America Fife and Drum Corps may play outside. Live entertainment pre-show by a cappella group Voices of Liberty in the lobby of the pavilion with limited benches, standing, or sitting on the floor. You can listen to the singers without seeing show. American Heritage Gallery located to the right of the building lobby. ***[H]*** *Pay phone with TTY in Liberty Inn.* ***[H][T][M][V]*** *Break area for service animals is nearby—ask cast member.* ***[M]*** *Gift shop has little room to maneuver.*

Pavilion | D-Ticket | All ages

☐ The American Adventure Show [D-1] — 9 | 7 | 7

American history buffs will love this multimedia show with Mark Twain and Ben Franklin as your guides! Two escalators and a set of stairs lead to main theater; for elevator (on right as you enter Rotunda), see cast member. Theatre seating. Located inside The American Adventure. ***[A][U]*** *Enter row first to be closest to exit.* ***[C][♥][T][M][E][S]*** *Theater is cool with comfortable seating.* ***[B]*** *Dark theater for discreet nursing.* ***[F]*** *Mild violence (not graphic) from war scenes, dark at times. Bright camera flash in Civil War photography scene, thunder and lightning in Chief Joseph scene.* ***[Ö]*** *Ears to the World available.* ***[H]*** *Reader Best Choice (see page 193). Reflective captioning available—see cast member at entrance. Assistive listening also available.* ***[M]*** *Wheelchair area in back of theater, maximum 12 wheelchairs per show. Wheelchairs will be brought upstairs in elevator to listen to pre-show singers from above. While waiting to enter theater, you will be in a roped-off area with other wheelchair/ECV guests. Floor is sloped 10–15 degrees. May be difficult to hold wheelchair, so set brakes. When you enter theater, wheelchair seating immediately on left. Don't go past this area, as rest of floor is sloped. Cast will assist getting you settled in theater prior to crowds arriving.* ***[Q]*** *May experience motion sensitivity during scene with Frederick Douglass.* ***[L]*** *Theater seats may be too narrow for some body types.*

Show | E-Ticket | Ages 5 & up | Dark at times | Med. Waits | 15 min. pre-show with singers | 3- min. show

Planning | Your Special Need | Getting There | Staying in Style | Touring | Feasting | Resources | Index

Charting the Attractions
at World Showcase
(continued)

	Deb Wills' Rating	Deb Koma's Rating	Readers' Rating

America Gardens Theatre (seasonal) [D-1] — 7 | 7 | 6

Home to a wide variety of special entertainment, from '60s bands to the Candlelight Processional, and more. Check times guide for shows. Front area may be reserved for those with special dining packages. Open-air bench seating; very little shade, sun/heat may be intense. Located at The American Adventure pavilion. **[B]** Quiet spot for discreet nursing on days when no performances are being held. **[H]** Assistive listening available. **[M]** See cast member for wheelchair area.

Show	
D-Ticket	
All ages	
Waits vary	
Usually 25 min.	

Japan [D-1] — 8 | 7 | 7

The bright Torii gate welcomes you. Beautiful area—hill gardens with water, rustic bridges, flowers, and koi pond. The Bijutsu-kan-Gallery hosts traveling exhibits. Mitsukoshi Department store and several eateries. Entertainment in courtyard; traditional drums are very loud—standing or sitting on the ground only. Tip: Between Japan and Morocco are areas with benches and shade. **[R]** Sake wine tastings sold. **[C][♥][T][M][E][S][L][V]** Small elevator near shop entrance brings you to restaurants. Very limited maneuvering room, crowded waiting area. **[F]** Elevator can trigger claustrophobia. **[Ö]** Most cast members in this pavilion are natives of Japan and speak Japanese.

Pavilion	
C-Ticket	
All ages	
Short waits	
Allow 20 min.	

Morocco [E-1] — 6 | 8 | 7

Architecture, shops, entertainment, and foods of this North African country are showcased here. Gallery of Arts displays science, music, and technology. Entertainment lagoon side on stage, few benches (no backs). Free 15-minute tours offered daily; inquire in shop. Companion restroom on far right side of pavilion. **[Ö]** Most cast members in this pavilion are natives of Morocco and speak Arabic. **[H]** Pay phone with TTY available. **[M]** Shops, alleys, and café, hard to negotiate in wheelchair. **[W]** There is a designated meditation/prayer room (Islamic) open daily from 11:00 am to 9:00 pm located inside the museum; small rugs are available for use.

Pavilion	
C-Ticket	
All ages	
Short waits	
Allow about 20 min. to explore	

France [F-2] — 7 | 7 | 7

Journey back to the France of 1870-1910 through Impressions de France movie, restaurants, and shops. Live entertainment in courtyard—very limited bench seating. **[R]** Wine tastings sold. **[G]** Designer fragrances and perfumes in several shops. **[C][F][♥][T][M][P][E][S][L][V]** Second-floor gallery in Plume et Pallette shop only accessible by stairs. **[Ö]** Most cast members in this pavilion are natives of France and speak French.

Pavilion	
D-Ticket	
All ages	

Impressions de France [F-2] — 7 | 7 | 7

Palais du Cinema is home to a French travelogue set to classical music. Beautiful views of Normandy, Loire Valley, Paris, etc. Theater seating. Music can be loud. Located in France pavilion. **[A][U]** Enter row first to be closest to exit. **[C][♥][T][M][E][S]** Waiting area has no seating but is in cool indoors. Theater is cool with comfortable seating. **[B]** Dark theater for discreet nursing. **[H]** Reflective captioning available—see cast member at entrance. Assistive listening also available. **[M]** Enter left side of hallway; cast member will assist you. **[L]** Theater seats may be too tight for some body types.

Film	
D-Ticket	
Ages 5 & up	
Dark theater	
Short waits	
18-min. film	

Charting the Attractions
at World Showcase
(continued)

Deb Wills' Rating | Deb Koma's Rating | Readers' Rating

☐ United Kingdom [E-3] | 7 | 9 | 7

The British Isles represented by music, improvisational performers, shops, gardens, pub, eateries, and architecture. Entertainment in courtyard—limited benches, standing, or sitting on the ground. Hedge maze in back for kids. Tip: Tables and umbrellas located to the right of Yorkshire Fish and Chips (unless reserved). **[R]** Pub featured prominently. **[G]** Designer fragrances and perfumes in Queen's Table Shop adjacent to Tea Caddy. **[F]** Improv troupe selects folks from the audience. **[H]** Sign language interpreted performances of World Showcase Players on designated days; check with Guest Relations for schedule.	**Pavilion** C-Ticket All ages

☐ Canada [E-4] | 7 | 7 | 7

Many international influences on our neighbor to the north are showcased with a Native Indian village, French chateau, and beautiful English gardens. Live entertainment, shops, movie, and eateries. Entertainment in courtyard with bench seating or standing—music can be very loud. **[M]** Wheelchair ramp in front of pavilion. **[Ö]** Some cast members in this pavilion speak French.	**Pavilion** C-Ticket All ages

☐ O Canada! [E-4] | 7 | 7 | 6

360-degree CircleVision movie with breathtaking views of the Canadian countryside, including British Columbia, Calgary Stampede, and the Changing of the Guard. Waiting area is small but inside and cool. Theater is standing with lean rails, no seating! You may experience motion sickness—if 360-degree movies make you a little dizzy, stand near the back of the room or avoid. **[A][U]** Enter row first to be closest to exit. **[[F]** You might feel claustrophobic in waiting area. **[Ö]** Ears to the World available. **[H]** Reflective captioning—see cast member at entrance. Assistive listening also available. **[M]** Position wheelchair/ECV in rear of theater. To gain access to movie, wheelchairs must enter through Victoria Gardens past Le Cellier restaurant over a wooden walkway through a canyon. Although level, this area is extremely narrow. When a wheelchair is on this walkway, there will not be room for any opposing foot traffic. **[Q]** Motion sensitivity possible.	**360° Film** C-Ticket Ages 5 & up Dark, a little dizzying 18-min. film

🛈 Epcot's Festivals

Epcot is home to **two major festivals**, one in the spring and one in the fall, in addition to being the showcase for December holiday decorations. Every spring, Epcot hosts the International Flower & Garden Festival, while each fall brings the International Food & Wine Festival. Both offer unique displays, exhibits, and seminars (most free with admission). During the Flower & Garden Festival, Disney boasts thousands of blooms throughout the park. If you have allergies (including to molds), or asthma or are sensitive to smells, use caution touring Epcot during the festival. The Flower and Garden Festival usually has a kids' play area where they can let off a little steam. Crowds tend to be higher during the festivals, especially on weekends. During the Food and Wine Festival, World Showcase is *very* crowded, especially on weekends. Alcohol is sold at almost every food kiosk, and there are many seminars offering free wine and beer tastings. Check with individual booths for ingredient listings which may or may not be available.

IllumiNations: Reflections of Earth

IllumiNations: Reflections of Earth is the multimedia nighttime show that concludes each day at Epcot. Fireworks, lasers, lights, torches, water fountains, and music mesmerize you for 15 minutes. Very limited seating; standing or sitting on the ground is the norm. Fire, explosions, and, depending on wind (check direction), smoke. Viewing areas for wheelchairs/ECVs include in front of each Showcase Plaza shop, in front of Canada and Italy. These spots tend to fill quickly, so arrive early. After the show, there are huge crowds exiting the park; sit on a bench and enjoy the music while waiting for the park to empty. Noise can be a major distraction for service animals here—some may shy away from it.

Fountain/Water Play Areas

What kid doesn't like to play in a water fountain? Your little ones can delight in a number of fountains and water play areas around the World. Two magical water fountains are located in Epcot—one in Future World East on the way to Mission: SPACE and another on the pathway connecting Future World to World Showcase. The base of these areas is made from a soft, spongy material, and the water spurts up at odd angles unpredictably. There's another such fountain at Downtown Disney in the Marketplace. These are great places for little ones to cool off and let off some steam, especially in the summer. Just be sure they take off their shoes and socks first—remember to bring a change of clothes and towel for them, and a plastic bag to put the damp stuff in. (Or maybe they can wear a bathing suit underneath their regular clothes.) They *will* get wet—and love it!

Other locations for fun water play (note that during periods of cooler weather or drought the fountains may be turned off):

✔ Magic Kingdom: Donald's Boat in Mickey's Toontown Fair, Tiki God Statues in Adventureland

✔ Epcot: Cool Wash mister near Test Track; Jumping Fountains near Imagination Pavilion (see photo)

✔ Disney-MGM Studios: Honey I Shrunk the Kids playground; Coca-Cola bottle mister near the Backlot Tour

✔ Animal Kingdom: The Boneyard

© Deb Wills

Epcot's Jumping Fountains water play area

Disney-MGM Studios

Walt Disney first had the idea for a park based on the movies more than 40 years ago, but it wasn't until May 1989 that the Walt Disney Company unveiled the **Disney-MGM Studios**. Here, guests of Walt Disney World can witness the inner workings of movie and television production facilities.

Through its exciting attractions, Broadway-caliber shows, first-rate entertainment, and hands-on participation, the Disney-MGM Studios not only entertain but educate. The Studios have nearly doubled in size in the last ten years and continue to expand, but it still remains a fairly compact theme park, easily experienced in a day.

Disney-MGM Studios isn't as easy to navigate as other parks due to its free-form layout (see map on pages 256–257). There are two Guest Relations locations at this theme park. The first is located to your left before you pass through the turnstiles. The second is to your left after you enter the park. This is where you can obtain current guide maps for disabilities, obtain a Guest Assistance Card (see pages 10–11), rent hearing or vision devices, obtain the current schedule for Sign Language Interpreted attractions, and ask any special questions you might have. Here are the five areas of Disney-MGM Studios:

Hollywood Boulevard—The main street of this 1930s town, the street is fairly easy to negotiate, but its shops, which are interconnected like those in the Magic Kingdom, are very congested.

Echo Lake—Attractions and eateries circle this quiet lake, which features the towering Dinosaur Gertie. Although accessible, there are several areas with steps—be sure to check out where the ramps are.

Sunset Boulevard—The very popular street that's home to the park's two biggest thrill rides, Rock 'n' Roller Coaster featuring Aerosmith and the Twilight Zone Tower of Terror, and the nighttime Fantasmic! amphitheater show. Be prepared to fight the crowds. The open-air food court here, Sunset Ranch, features more healthy options than most places, but its setup is very crowded and difficult to get around in.

Streets of America—Recently renovated to include facades of the streets of San Francisco, with Chicago skylines to come, the Streets of America is home to a huge amphitheater for the Lights! Motors! Action! Extreme Stunt Show.

Mickey Avenue—A variety of soundstages and the Animation Courtyard make up this area, which is fairly easy to get around.

Planning

Your Special Need

Getting There

Staying in Style

Touring

Feasting

Resources

Index

AMBIENCE

PARK LAYOUT AND NAVIGATION

Getting to Disney-MGM Studios

BEST TIMES TO GO

Disney-MGM Studios can be **enjoyed in one day**, although it is best to visit the most popular attractions earlier to avoid long lines. Arrive before the scheduled opening time for the best advantage. The most popular attractions—Rock 'n' Roller Coaster and the Twilight Zone Tower of Terror—generate very long lines. Make a beeline for these rides first thing, unless you've just eaten breakfast!

Several of the shows have **limited seating capacity** (such as Voyage of the Little Mermaid) and can require a lengthy wait if busy.

Wherever possible, get a **FASTPASS**. Check the entertainment schedule in the park's times guide for show times.

Take the **length of the show times** into account when planning your route, and keep in mind that viewing several shows can take a considerable amount of time.

Many attractions and restaurants empty immediately before and during a **parade**, affording shorter lines or the chance to get a table without advance reservations.

GETTING THERE

By Car—For many special needs travelers, it may be most convenient to travel by car. Take I-4 to exit 67 (west) or exit 62 (east) and continue on to Disney-MGM Studios. All-day parking is $8 (free to Disney resort guests and Annual Passholders), and the pass is valid at other Disney parks' lots on the same day.

By Boat—From Epcot's International Gateway, BoardWalk, Yacht & Beach Club, and Swan and Dolphin, take a "Friendship." These boats are fully accessible for wheelchairs/ECVs and strollers.

By Bus—Take a direct bus from all resorts (other than those mentioned above), Epcot's main entrance, and Disney's Animal Kingdom. From the Magic Kingdom, catch a bus at the Transportation and Ticket Center. From Downtown Disney, Typhoon Lagoon, or Blizzard Beach, take a bus or a boat to a resort and transfer to a Disney-MGM Studios bus.

By Land—You can walk or wheel from the BoardWalk, Swan & Dolphin, and Yacht & Beach Club, and even Epcot's International Gateway. Follow the paths marked along the canal beside the BoardWalk Villas.

Making the Most of Disney-MGM Studios

The **First Aid Station** is located near Guest Relations on the left, just after you pass through the turnstiles. The Baby Care Center is right next door. See sidebar on page 196 for services available there.

We think **seniors will enjoy this park**, which is filled with nostalgia for an era gone by. Caricatures of old-time actors line the walls of the Hollywood Brown Derby restaurant, and movie memorabilia adorns Sid Cahuenga's shop near the entrance of the park. There's even an attraction that pays tribute to Walt Disney—One Man's Dream—whom many of today's seniors must certainly recall.

There are quite a few **live shows** in the Studios, most either in air-conditioning or in the shade. Take advantage of them!

Character greeting spots abound in the Studios, but the lines can be long. Check your daily times guide for exact times and locations, then plan to be there several minutes early to avoid long waits in line.

Many shows at Disney-MGM Studios (such as Indiana Jones Epic Stunt Spectacular, Backlot Tour, and Who Wants To Be A Millionaire—Play It!) feature **audience participation**. Even one of the restaurants, the '50s Prime Time Café, is known for its interaction with the clientele. If you're the shy, retiring sort, you may want to avoid these, or at least take steps to avoid being called on.

The Disney-MGM Studios has several uniquely Disney themed **dining experiences**, but they are not without special needs concerns. The Sci-Fi Dine-In Theater, for example, has a very dark setting and projects snippets of old science fiction movies on a drive-in style screen. The '50s Prime Time Café involves lots of interaction with the servers, which may not be for the shy and introverted. Be sure to investigate the atmosphere of the restaurant before dining.

A large **Braille map** mounted on a stand is located just outside Guest Relations on your left, after you enter the park.

TIPS

SPECIAL CONSIDERATIONS

Planning · Your Special Need · Getting There · Staying in Style · Touring · Feasting · Resources · Index

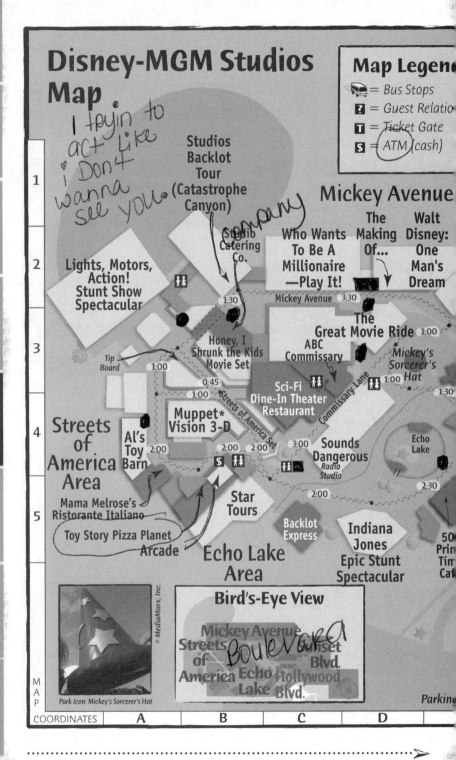

Planning
Your Special Need
Getting There
Staying in Style
Touring
Feasting
Resources
Index

Disney-MGM Studios Map

Map Legend

🚌 = Bus Stops
❓ = Guest Relations
🎫 = Ticket Gate
💲 = ATM (cash)

i tryin to act like i Don't wanna see you

Studios Backlot Tour (Catastrophe Canyon)

company

Studio Catering Co.

Mickey Avenue

The Making Of...

Who Wants To Be A Millionaire —Play It!

Walt Disney: One Man's Dream

Lights, Motors, Action! Stunt Show Spectacular

1:30

Mickey Avenue 3:30

Honey, I Shrunk the Kids Movie Set

The Great Movie Ride 1:00

ABC Commissary

Mickey's Sorcerer's Hat

1:00

1:30

Tip Board 1:00

0:45

1:00

Streets of America Set

Sci-Fi Dine-In Theater Restaurant

Commissary Lane

Streets of America Area

Muppet* Vision 3-D

Al's Toy Barn 2:00

2:00 2:00

3:00 Sounds Dangerous Radio Studio

Echo Lake

2:30

Mama Melrose's Ristorante Italiano

Star Tours

Backlot Express

Indiana Jones Epic Stunt Spectacular

50's Prime Time Café

Toy Story Pizza Planet Arcade

Echo Lake Area

2:00

© MediaMarx, Inc.

Park Icon: Mickey's Sorcerer's Hat

Bird's-Eye View

Mickey Avenue

Streets of America

Boulevard

Sunset Blvd.

Echo Lake

Hollywood Blvd.

Parking

COORDINATES	A	B	C	D

M A P

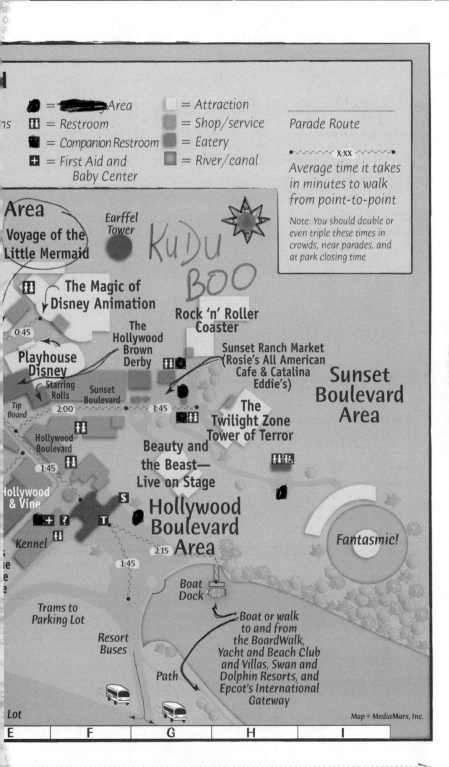

● = ____Area   ☐ = Attraction

🚹 = Restroom   ☐ = Shop/service   *Parade Route*

■ = Companion Restroom   ☐ = Eatery

➕ = First Aid and Baby Center   ☐ = River/canal

●·····XX····● *Average time it takes in minutes to walk from point-to-point*

Note: You should double or even triple these times in crowds, near parades, and at park closing time

Area
Voyage of the Little Mermaid

Earffel Tower

KUDU BOO

🚹 **The Magic of Disney Animation**

Rock 'n' Roller Coaster

0:45

Playhouse Disney

The Hollywood Brown Derby

Sunset Ranch Market (Rosie's All American Cafe & Catalina Eddie's)

Sunset Boulevard Area

Starring Rolls

Sunset Boulevard

Tip Board   2:00   1:45

🚹

The Twilight Zone Tower of Terror

Hollywood Boulevard   1:45   🚹

Beauty and the Beast— Live on Stage

🚹

Hollywood & Vine

➕ ❓ $ T

Hollywood Boulevard Area   2:15

Fantasmic!

Kennel   🚹

1:45

Boat Dock

Trams to Parking Lot

Resort Buses

Boat or walk to and from the BoardWalk, Yacht and Beach Club and Villas, Swan and Dolphin Resorts, and Epcot's International Gateway

Path

Lot

Map © MediaMarx, Inc.

E   F   G   H   I

Planning · Your Special Need · Getting There · Staying in Style · Touring · Feasting · Resources · Index

Entertainment at Disney-MGM Studios

ENTERTAINMENT

The afternoon parade here is **Stars and Motor Cars** and features a variety of themed vehicles bearing a multitude of Disney characters. There are two special viewing spots for those in wheelchairs/ECVs located at the end of Hollywood Boulevard—one in front of the giant Sorcerer's Hat icon, the other in front of the Keystone Clothiers shop. Speak to a cast member for access. An ASL translation is done in front of the ABC TV Theater, across from Echo Lake/Min & Bill's Dockside Diner. Arrive at least 15 minutes early and stand in the designated viewing area on the steps in front of the building. See a cast member for assistance.

The nighttime fireworks and laser display is known as **Fantasmic!** Held in an amphitheater toward the end of Sunset Boulevard, Fantasmic! is extremely popular. Obtaining a seat often means getting there more than an hour before the scheduled show time. If there are two shows, try to attend the later one—it will be much less crowded. (Or consider using the Fantasmic! Dinner Package—see page 337). Other special considerations at Fantasmic!: If you're attending Fantasmic! in a wheelchair/ECV, you enter through the regular queue. Talk to a cast member for direction to the special wheelchair seating area. Cast members will direct those in wheelchairs/ECVs to the back row, but if you wish to sit in the front row, just ask. There is limited accessible seating there. There is a companion-assisted restroom available in the amphitheater. There is a TTY phone located at these restrooms, also. Assistive listening and reflective captioning are both available during Fantasmic! Talk to a cast member for more information about the use of these devices here. Those seated in the front rows of this show often get wet—sit back further if this is a potential problem. Those who are sensitive to loud, sudden noises, minor explosions, and special smoke and light effects may wish to avoid Fantasmic! as it includes all of these things. The Fantasmic! amphitheater can hold nearly 10,000 when it's filled to standing-room-only capacity—be aware that crowds at the show's conclusion can be crushing as they try to exit. Strollers must be parked in a designated area.

Attractions With Hearing Devices Chart

Assistive Listening	Beauty and the Beast, Fantasmic!, Indiana Jones Epic Stunt Spectacular, Muppet*Vision 3D, Playhouse Disney, Sci-Fi Dine-In Theater Restaurant, Sounds Dangerous, The Great Movie Ride (pre-show only), The Magic of Disney Animation, Voyage of the Little Mermaid, Who Wants To Be A Millionaire, One Man's Dream (theater only), Lights, Motors, Action! Extreme Stunt Show
Handheld Captioning	Backlot Tour, The Great Movie Ride, Playhouse Disney, and One Man's Dream
Reflective Captioning	Fantasmic!, Muppet*Vision 3D, The Magic of Disney Animation (theater), Little Mermaid, and One Man's Dream Theater
Closed Captioning	Backlot Tour (queue ramp and prop warehouse only), Muppet*Vision 3D (pre-show only), Playhouse Disney (queue only), Star Tours (boarding area only), The American Film Institute Showcase, and Tower of Terror (pre-show only)
ASL Interpretation	Stars and Motor Cars Parade, Beauty and the Beast, Indiana Jones, and Who Wants To Be A Millionaire.
Ears to the World	Sounds Dangerous, Muppet*Vision 3D, One Man's Dream, Backlot Tour pre-show, and Tower of Terror pre-show

Finding Your Place at Disney-MGM Studios

Those wishing or needing a **quiet area** for breaks, time-outs, or baby nursing should consider:
- Behind Sid Cauenga's One-of-a-Kind shop near the entrance
- The Writer's Stop, around the corner from Sci-Fi Dine-In Theater
- The little corridor leading to Radio Disney studio, next to Sounds Dangerous

There are a number of **companion restrooms** available at the Disney-MGM Studios:
- Near the Twilight Zone Tower of Terror
- Across from the Star Tours ride
- To the right of Lights, Motors, Action! amphitheater
- Inside Lights, Motors, Action! amphitheater
- In Fantasmic's amphitheater
- Near Rock 'n' Roller Coaster
- Right side of Millionaire building on Mickey Avenue

Attraction Seating Chart

Backlot Tour	standing/bench
Beauty and the Beast	bench (no backs)
The Great Movie Ride	bench
Honey I Shrunk the Kids	playground
Indiana Jones Epic Stunt Spectacular	bench (no backs)
Lights, Motors, Action! Extreme Stunt Show	bench (no backs)
The Magic of Disney Animation	theater/stool
Muppet*Vision 3D	theater
One Man's Dream	walking/wheeling and theater
Playhouse Disney Live!	floor seating
Rock 'n' Roller Coaster	harness
Sounds Dangerous	theater
Star Tours	theater with seat belt
Tower of Terror	seat belt
Voyage of the Little Mermaid	theater
Who Wants to Be a Millionaire? Play It!	theater

SPECIAL PLACES

Sidebar tabs: Planning · Your Special Needs · Getting There · Staying in Style · Touring · Feasting · Resources · Index

Charting the Attractions in the Echo Lake Area

	Deb Wills' Rating	Deb Koma's Rating	Readers' Rating

▮ Indiana Jones Epic Stunt Spectacular [D-5] 🅵🅿 | 8 | 8 | 8

Get a behind-the-scenes look at how the amazing stunts from the Indiana Jones movies were done. Adults may be chosen to participate in the show. Outside queue is unshaded. Seating in the amphitheater is on hard metal bleacher-like backless benches. **[A][U][I]** The noise level in this show is high—could cause overstimulation. **[A][U]** Enter row first to be closest to exit. **[A][U][C][♥][T][I][M][P][E][S]** Use FASTPASS to minimize waits. **[F]** After sunset, the amphitheater is very dark for some portions of the show. Also, there are lots of sudden, loud noises, explosions, fire, and some staged fight scenes. **[H]** Assistive listening available. Sign language interpreted performances on designated days; check with Guest Relations for schedule. Arrive at least 20 minutes before the show and proceed to the main entrance. Sit in the <u>center</u> section of the audience, to the right of the tech booth. **[M]** Wheelchair/ECV users should use FASTPASS; speak to the cast member at the entrance to be directed to special seating area. **[L]** The bench seats here have no backs.	**Live Show** E-Ticket Ages 4 & up Loud, fire, violence FASTPASS or med. waits 30-min. show

▮ Sounds Dangerous [C-4] | 4 | 6 | 6

Comedian Drew Carey takes you through a humorous program showcasing state-of-the-art sound effects. This queue is mostly shaded, with television monitors providing pre-show entertainment. **[A][U][F]** Much of this show takes place in complete darkness. You must wear earphones to experience the special audio effects. Those sensitive to loud noises may wish to avoid. **[A][U]** Enter row first to be closest to exit. **[B]** Dark theater for discreet nursing. **[Ö]** Ears to the World available. **[H]** Handheld captioning and assistive listening available. **[M]** Wheelchair/ECV users use regular queue; speak to the cast member at the entrance to be directed to special seating area. **[L]** Theater-style seats are very small—may be tight for people of size; ask cast member about seats with armrests that can be raised. (They should be located near the rear of the theater on the left side as you face the screen.)	**Film** C-Ticket Ages 7 & up Takes place in darkness, very loud noises Short waits 12-min. film

▮ Star Tours [B-5] | 🅵🅿 🏃 | 9 | 10 | 8

Inspired by the Star Wars movies, this popular attraction combines a flight simulator with action-packed video for a rough ride. The indoor queue weaves all around—during very busy times, there is even a line outside (mostly shaded). The giant AT-AT machine above you just before the entrance sprays mist during hot weather. A companion restroom is opposite the entrance. A TTY phone is at these restrooms. **[A][U][I]** The noise level in this ride is high—could cause overstimulation. **[A][U] [C][♥][T][I][M][P][E][S]** Use FASTPASS to minimize wait times. **[F]** Dark/violent at times. **[C][♥][T][Q][P][E][S]** You can really get shaken up on this simulator, so avoid it if you have motion sickness, heart- or back-related issues, or if you're pregnant. Roughest ride is in the back row! **[F][♥][T][I][M][E][S]** During non-peak times, cast members may run the movie without running the simulator. Be sure to ask! **[H]** Video at boarding area is close captioned. **[I][T]** Strobe-like lights flash throughout attraction. **[M]** Wheelchair/ECV users should use FASTPASS; otherwise speak to the cast member at entrance. ECV users must transfer to wheelchair to negotiate queue. You must transfer out of chair to simulator seat. Manual wheelchair users may find the steep ramps difficult. **[B]** Use Rider Switch. **[B][L]** Height restriction: 40 in./102 cm. Seats (with retractable belts) may be tight for people of size; armrest may be uncomfortable. **[T][I][M]** Cast members can provide a 5-point harness for those who require more than just a seat belt. **[H][T][M][V]** Service animals are not permitted. Break area for service animals nearby; ask cast member.	**Thrill Ride** E-Ticket Ages 8 & up Rough, rocky, may cause motion sickness FASTPASS or long waits 3-min. intro 5-min. flight

Charting the Attractions in the Streets of America Area

Deb Wills' Rating
Deb Koma's Rating
Readers' Rating

Planning
Your Special Need
Getting There
Staying in Style
Touring
Feasting
Resources
Index

☐ Honey, I Shrunk the Kids Movie Set Adventure [B-3]   5 5 6

Kids' play area themed to the popular movie series. Listen for the ant sounds and the sniffing dog's nose! **[A]** Reader Best Choice (see page 193). **[F]** Some tunnels are very closed-in spaces and completely dark. Also, giant ants and bugs are depicted—if you have a fear of insects, you may wish to avoid. There is a possibility of getting sprinkled with water from the dripping Super Soaker. **[I]** Reader Worst Choice (see page 193). **[M]** Not recommended for ECV users. Wheelchair users go through regular queue to the access gate. **[C][♥][T][M][E][S][L][V]** Flooring is uneven, and the spongy surface may be difficult to negotiate. Lots of small spaces between slides and other equipment. **[B]** Leave stroller in the designated area away from the entrance to the playground, or cast members will move it.

Playground
B-Ticket
All ages
Giant bugs, dripping water
Short waits
Allow 30 min.

☐ Muppet*Vision 3-D [B-4]   9 8 9

Kermit, Miss Piggy, and other Muppet friends take you through a demonstration of 3-D technology with added sensory effects. Indoor waiting area is dimly lit—there's really nowhere to sit while you're waiting, but you are entertained by the Muppets in a pre-show video on overhead monitors. Floor in pre-show slopes downward sharply. **[A][U][I]** The noise level in this show is high—it could cause overstimulation. Sensory effects like spraying water and air blowing in your face may be disconcerting. Also, real bubbles float gently down from ceiling. **[A][U]** Enter row first to be closest to exit. **[A][U][F][I][Q][S][V]** You must wear special 3-D glasses; fit over regular glasses. Those with vision impairments may not fully appreciate the effects. **[F]** Avoid this show if you're sensitive to loud noises. **[Ö]** Ears to the World can be used here. **[H]** Handheld and reflective captioning and assistive listening available here. Film portion of pre-show is also closed captioned. **[M]** Wheelchair/ECV users enter through the standby queue to the access gate at the turnstiles. The cast member in the waiting area will direct you to the seating area. **[L]** Theater-style seats may be tight squeeze for people of size. **[V]** Reader Worst Choice (see page 193).

3-D Film
E-Ticket
Ages 4 & up
Loud, some violence
Med. waits
10-min. intro 18-min. film

☐ Get Involved ... or Not!

Disney-MGM Studios is well-known for its band of actors who roam the park's streets looking to involve visitors in their improvisational comedy acts. Known as Streetmosphere, these performers take on personalities ranging from old-time movie stars to ordinary plumbers and workers. They're lots of fun, if you're into that kind of thing, but if you're on the fearful/introverted side, you might want to avoid them. Here are a few other places or groups that often try to enlist the audience's participation—you decide if you want to become part of the act!

In Epcot: World Showcase Players; Turtle Talk With Crush
In the Magic Kingdom: Storytime with Belle and Sword in the Stone Ceremony
In Disney's Animal Kingdom: Flights of Wonder and DeVine
In Disney-MGM Studios: Indiana Jones; Backlot Tour; '50s Prime Time Cafe; Lights, Motors, Action! Extreme Stunt Show; Who Wants To Be A Millionaire—Play It!
Outside the Theme Parks: Whispering Canyon Cafe; 'Ohana; Spirit of Aloha; Hoop Dee Doo Musical Revue; Comedy Warehouse; and Adventurers Club

Charting the Attractions in the Streets of America Area
(continued)

	Deb Wills' Rating	Deb Koma's Rating	Readers' Rating

■ Streets of America Movie Set [B-4]

3 **4** **6**

Newly revamped facades of buildings along popular city streets (New York, San Francisco) provide an interesting movie set backdrop. Other details, like city noise sound effects, add to the atmosphere. Currently under construction with additional new facades to debut sometime in 2005. *[M]* Wheelchair/ECV accessible. *[H][T][M][V]* Service animal break area is located backstage to the left of the Courthouse here—speak to a cast member for assistance.

Walk-thru
A-Ticket
All ages
No scares
Take as long as you want!

■ Toy Story Pizza Planet Arcade [B-5]

3 **3** **6**

Designed to resemble the pizza place in Disney's original "Toy Story," this arcade is adjacent to a counter service restaurant. Typical video game arcade, with most games requiring two to four tokens (which cost 25 cents each). *[A][U][I]* The noise level in the arcade is high—it could cause overstimulation. *[M]* Wheelchair/ECV accessible.

Arcade
A-Ticket
Ages 5 & up
No scares
Few waits

■ Lights, Motors, Action! Extreme Stunt Show [A-2] (New for 2005)

8 **8** **—**

Fresh from Disneyland Paris, prepare to be wowed by an epic display of the stuntperson's art. Cars, motorcycles, and jet skis roar across the set while a giant video screen shows how the special effects action is turned into movie magic. A 5,000-seat amphitheater is ready to pack in the audiences. Seating in the amphitheater is on hard metal, bleacher-like backless benches. There is a companion

Show
E-Ticket
Ages 3 & up
Loud!
30-min. show

© MediaMarx, Inc.

The original Lights, Moteurs, Action! show at Disneyland Paris

restroom located in this theater. *[A][U][I]* The noise level in this show is high—could cause overstimulation. *[A][U]* Enter row first to be closest to exit. *[A][U][C][♥][T][I][M][P][E][S]* Use FASTPASS to minimize wait times. *[F]* There are lots of sudden, loud noises, explosions, and fire. *[H]* Assistive listening available. *[M]* Wheelchair/ECV users should use FASTPASS; speak to the cast member at the entrance to be directed to the elevator (to your left after you pass through the main entrance). The accessible section is about halfway up the theater. *[L]* The bench seats here have no backs.

Charting the Attractions in the Mickey Avenue Area

	Deb Wills' Rating	Deb Koma's Rating	Readers' Rating

The Magic of Disney Animation [F-2]　　5　5　8

Tour what used to be Disney's Florida animation studio. This revamped attraction now features a short film in a small theater with an animator and Mushu, from Disney's "Mulan," explaining the animation process. There's a hands-on program at the end of the tour, during which an animator talks you through the process of drawing your own Disney character, which you can keep as a souvenir. Seating for latter portion is at artist desk on stool—spectators can sit on benches. Outdoor queue is mostly shaded. **[H]** Reflective captioning and assistive listening available. Film portions are also closed captioned. Some portions are sign language interpreted on designated days; check with Guest Relations for schedule. Arrive at least 5 minutes in advance; meet interpreter at entrance. **[M]** Wheelchair/ECV users enter through the regular queue. Ask the cast member to be directed to an accessible seat during the drawing section. **[H][T][M][V]** Break area for service animals nearby; ask cast member.

- Film/Walk-Thru/Hands-On
- D-Ticket
- Ages 4 & up
- No scares
- Med. waits
- Allow 45 min.

Walt Disney: One Man's Dream [D-2]　　9　9　8

Trace Walt Disney's path in this exhibit of hundreds of artifacts from his youth and early days in the business and throughout his career. After perusing the displays, view the film, which features Walt himself talking about his amazing journey. **[A][U]** Enter row of theater first to be closest to exit. **[B]** Dark theater for discreet nursing. **[Ö]** Ears to the World available. **[H]** Handheld and reflective captioning and assistive listening available. **[M]** Wheelchair/ECV users enter through the regular queue. **[L]** Theater-style seats may be tight squeeze for people of size. **[H][M][V]** Break area for service animals nearby; ask cast member.

- Walk-Thru
- D-Ticket
- Ages 10 & up
- Short waits
- Allow 30 min. for exhibit
- 20-min. movie

Playhouse Disney—Live on Stage! [E-3]　　7　7　8

Perfect for preschoolers, this show spotlights characters from the Disney Channel's popular daytime programs: Bear in the Big Blue House, JoJo and Goliath, Stanley, and Pooh and friends. Outdoor queue is mostly in the sun. **[A][U]** Sit at far ends of sections for easy exit if necessary. Separate unmarked entrance for those with Guest Assistance Card—ask a cast member. Note that real bubbles float gently down from ceiling. **[B]** Music and dancing—Baby should love this! Reader Best Choice (see page 193). **[H]** Handheld captioning and assistive listening available. Film portions are also closed captioned. **[M]** Wheelchair/ECV users enter through the regular queue. Ask a cast member for directions to special seating area. **[S][L]** You must sit on the carpeted floor for this show—there is only limited bench seating at the rear of the theater.

- Live Show
- C-Ticket
- All ages
- No scares
- Med. waits
- 20-min. show

Fantasmic! Dinner Package

The Fantasmic! Dinner Package includes a fixed-price dinner at one of the participating Disney-MGM Studios restaurants (Hollywood Brown Derby, Mama Melrose Ristorante Italiano, or Hollywood & Vine) and reserved seating in the Fantasmic! amphitheater (usually on the far right side of the theatre) at no additional charge. This means that instead of waiting in line for 60–90 minutes outside the theater, you can walk right up to the theater 30–45 minutes before show time and still have a good seat. (Note that these seats are still first-come, first-served.) Ask about the package when you call to make your reservations.

Charting the Attractions
in the Mickey Avenue Area
(continued)

Deb Wills' Rating — Deb Koma's Rating — Readers' Rating

Studios Backlot Tour [B-2] | 8 | 8 | 7 |

See how sea battles are filmed, tour Disney's backlot, and brave Catastrophe Canyon, a special effects tour de force. Audience members can be chosen to participate in the first part of the tour. Outdoor queue is shaded, which is good, since waits can be quite long. You're entertained by a video on overhead monitors while you wait. The first portion of the tour is all standing with nowhere to sit, and you may get splashed. Tram tour portion also includes the danger of getting wet—those seated on the left (as you face front) get wettest. You can use the restroom after the standing portion of the tour. **[A] [U]** Queue may be overstimulating during long waits, as the loud movie clips repeat and many people are crowded into a very small area. **[A][U][F][I]** Parts of the tour have sudden, very loud effects. The Catastrophe Canyon portion is not only loud, with explosions, but also with rushing water and fire. **[F][Q]** Tram shakes and trembles during Catastrophe Canyon portion. **[Ö]** Ears to the World available at pre-show. **[H]** Film portions are closed captioned. Sign language interpreted performances on designated days; check with Guest Relations. Sea battle and tram tour interpreted. Meet interpreter at entrance. **[M]** Wheelchair/ECV users enter through the regular queue; stay to the right. The access gate will be to your right. You may stay in your wheelchair/ECV and ride in an accessible vehicle, or fold wheelchair and stow on the tram ride.

Show/Ride
D-Ticket
Ages 6 & up
Explosions, fires
Long waits
40-min. tour

Voyage of the Little Mermaid [E-2]   *FP* | 9 | 7 | 8 |

A mingling of live action, puppetry, and film make this show a must-see for any Ariel fan. The popular Disney animated film is reenacted with fun results! You may feel like you sit close to the front of theater. Most of this queue is outdoors, but in the shade. **[A][U][I]** Parts of this show have very loud special effects. Also, there are flashing light effects used here. **[A][U][C][♥][T][I][M][P][E][S]** Use FASTPASS to minimize wait times. **[A][U]** Enter row first to be closest to exit. **[F]** Parts of this show are in the dark. Also, Ursula the Sea Witch can be very menacing. **[H]** Reflective captioning and assistive listening available. **[M]** Wheelchair/ECV users should use FASTPASS; otherwise speak to the cast member at the entrance for direction. **[L]** Theater-style seats may be tight squeeze for people of size.

Live Show
E-Ticket
Ages 3 & up
Dark, strobe effects
FASTPASS or long waits
17-min. show

Who Wants To Be A Millionaire—Play It! [D-2] | 9 | 10 | 9 |

This is your chance to sit in the Hot Seat and win a Disney Cruise Line cruise! The set is an exact replica of the famous TV show with real hosts encouraging you to go all the way. The outdoor queue is not covered, but waits usually aren't too long, unless you just missed a show starting time. Ask a cast member if you want to sit in the very front row (the Fastest Finger seats). A companion restroom is located next door. There is a TTY phone located at these restrooms, also. **[A][U][C][♥] [T][I][M][P][E][S]** Use FASTPASS to minimize wait times. **[A][U]** Enter row first to be closest to exit. **[H]** Assistive listening available here. Sign language interpreted performances on designated days; check with Guest Relations. Arrive at least 15 minutes before the show and proceed to the main entrance. Sit in the low section of the audience between seats 592-600 or 557-563. **[M]** Wheelchair/ECV users should use FASTPASS; otherwise speak to a cast member. Wheelchair seating on left as you enter. Limited number of seats have handheld game pads; ask cast member. **[L]** Very close seats, 14" wide, no arms, molded plastic—may be tight squeeze for people of size. Also, the control panel is located at a low angle; might be awkward to reach. Roomy Hot Seat has arms and is one step up. **[H][T][M][V]** Service animal break area is located at the backstage gate here—speak to a cast member.

Live Show
E-Ticket
Ages 7 & up
Exciting!
Medium waits
30-min. show

Planning — Your Special Need — Getting There — Staying in Style — Touring — Feasting — Resources — Index

Charting the Attractions in the Sunset Boulevard Area

	Deb Wills' Rating	Deb Koma's Rating	Readers' Rating

Beauty and the Beast—Live On Stage [G-4]

	7	6	8

A reenactment of Disney's animated film about a girl who finds love with an enchanted prince, featuring dazzling costumes, music, and sets. **[A][U][I]** There are some sudden loud noises in this show. **[A][U]** Enter row first to be closest to exit. **[H]** Handheld captioning and assistive listening are available. Sign language interpreted performances on designated days; check with Guest Relations for schedule. Arrive at least 20 minutes before the show and sit in the <u>right</u> section of the audience. **[M]** Wheelchair/ECV users enter using the ramp on the left; seating is in rows in the front and the back—we suggest the front row, although the stage is slightly elevated and you will have to look up a bit. **[H][T][M][V]** Break area for service animals nearby; ask a cast member. **[I]** Reader Best Choice (see page 193).

Live Show
E-Ticket
Ages 5 & up
Loud sound effects
Med. waits
10-min. intro 25-min. show

The Great Movie Ride [D-3]

	8	7	8

Take a trip through movie history on this tram tour that combines film with amazing Animatronics and some live-action surprises. Queue snakes around indoors, while you watch movie clips projected on huge screens. During busy times, queue may overflow to the unshaded outdoors. **[A][U][I]** The noise and excitement levels during this ride can be high at times. Alien scene may be too intense for some. **[A][U]** Must stay in vehicle for entire ride. Queue area can also be overstimulating during long waits, as the loud movie clips repeat multiple times, and many people are crowded into a very small area. **[U][C][♥][M][L][V]** Reader Best Choice (see page 193). **[C][♥][T][M][E][S]** If there are long waits in the queue area, there's nowhere to sit—only rails to lean against. **[F]** Certain scenes during this ride are in very dark surroundings. There's also an extraterrestrial alien scene, a realistic wicked witch, representations of snakes and other animals, and some staged violence. **[H]** Handheld captioning is available at this attraction. Assistive listening is available for the pre-show portion only. **[H][T][M][V]** Certain elements may be distracting to service animals—check with cast member before bringing onboard. **[M]** If in a wheelchair/ECV, see a cast member when you enter the queue with the large movie screen. You'll be directed to an alternate entrance. There is a wheelchair-accessible car at the rear of the train.

Film/Ride
D-Ticket
Ages 4 & up
Some dark scenes, aliens, loud noises
Long waits
3-min. intro 18-min. ride

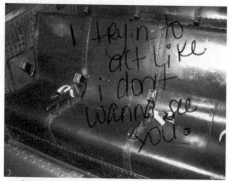

© Debra Martin Koma

Seating on the Twilight Zone Tower of Terror (see next page)

Planning

Your Special Need

Getting There

Staying in Style

Touring

Feasting

Resources

Index

Charting the Attractions in the Sunset Boulevard Area
(continued)

Deb Wills' Rating
Deb Koma's Rating
Readers' Rating

■ Rock 'n' Roller Coaster Starring Aerosmith [G-3] *FP* ♿

| 9 | 10 | 9 |

This high-speed coaster goes from 0 to 60 mph (96.5 kph) in 2.8 seconds! There are lots of twists and turns, inversions, and sharp drops—all completely in the dark. Music is fed, very loudly, through speakers in headrest. The shaded outdoor queue winds around—once inside, you must stand during a brief pre-show video featuring Steven Tyler and his Aerosmith cohorts. A companion restroom is located in the plaza. **[A][U][I]** The noise and excitement levels in this ride are very high—it could cause overstimulation. **[A][U][C][♥][T][I][M][P][E][S]** Use FASTPASS to minimize wait times. **[♥][T][Q][P][E][S]** There are several inversions during this ride—you can really get shaken up, so avoid it if you have motion sickness; heart-, neck- or back-related issues; or if you're pregnant. **[F]** The ride is completely in the dark. Anyone with a fear of heights or falling should also avoid this ride. **[M]** Wheelchair/ECV users should use FASTPASS; otherwise enter through the standby queue. ECV users must transfer to a wheelchair—speak with a cast member to obtain one. You must transfer out of your wheelchair to ride, but you have only 30 seconds to accomplish this. If you'd like to practice boarding beforehand, you can use a stationary vehicle kept in a private area. If you anticipate difficulty boarding, ask the cast member about a special boarding car, which may be available. Keep in mind that if an emergency evacuation is necessary on this ride, you'll have to deal with stairs and narrow walkways or else wait until someone can help you. **[B]** Use Rider Switch. **[B][L]** You must be at least 48 in./122 cm. to ride. Front seats of the "limos" seem to be roomier, as do odd-numbered rows. Adjustable u-bar restraint seems to accommodate most body types. **[H][T][M][V]** Service animals are not allowed. **[M][Q][L]** Reader Worst Choice (see page 193).

Coaster
E-Ticket
Ages 8 & up
Very dark, very loud, very fast!
FASTPASS or long waits
2-min. pre-show 1.5-min. ride

■ The Twilight Zone Tower of Terror [H-4] *FP* ♿

| 10 | 10 | 9 |

A haunted hotel houses a "malfunctioning" elevator that drops you again and again, unpredictably. The outdoor queue is partially shaded, but progresses up a hill through a tangle of unkempt trees. A companion restroom is located opposite the entrance. There is a TTY phone located at these restrooms, also. **[A][U][C][♥][T][Q][P][E][S]** There are intense special effects, including some lightning. There are also a number of sharp, sudden drops, so avoid if you have motion sickness; heart-, neck-, or back-related issues; or if you're pregnant. **[A][U][C][♥][T][I][M][P][E][S]** Use FASTPASS to minimize wait times. **[Ö]** Ears to the World available during the pre-show. **[H]** Film portions of pre-show are closed captioned. **[F]** The ride is almost completely in the dark, except for a moment when the doors open, allowing you to look out onto the theme park below. Anyone with a fear of heights or falling should avoid this ride. **[M]** Wheelchair/ECV users should use FASTPASS; otherwise speak to a cast member at the attraction entrance. ECV users must transfer to a wheelchair—speak with a cast member to obtain one. You must transfer out of your wheelchair to ride. **[B]** Use Rider Switch. **[B][L]** You must be at least 40 in./102 cm. to ride. Seats have retractable belts. While the belts are long enough, the space allotted on the bench may be a tight squeeze for people of size. To give yourself a little more room, do NOT sit near a wall—request an aisle seat. Be aware that as you lift out of your seat during the ride, you may land on hardware uncomfortably. **[H][M][V]** Service animals are not permitted.

Thrill Ride
E-Ticket
Ages 8 & up
Dark, sudden drops, very scary
FASTPASS or long waits
10-min. intro 5-min. ride

Disney's Animal Kingdom

Disney's Animal Kingdom, which opened in 1998, is the newest and largest of the Walt Disney World theme parks. It was initially called a "New Species of Theme Park," and it is just that! Part zoo, part theme park—lush landscaping, detailed architecture, animals, birds, shows, and rides all make up Disney's Animal Kingdom.

Just through the turnstiles, the Oasis provides a peaceful transition from daily life to the beauty of the park. As you emerge from the Oasis, before you stands the 145-foot-tall (44 meters) **Tree of Life**, a magnificent icon. The branches span 160 feet (49 meters). Twenty artists carved more than 300 animals into the 50-foot-wide (15 meter) trunk, branches, and roots. You'll spot different animals depending on your location.

Guest Relations is located to your left both outside and inside the park turnstiles (see park map on pages 270–271). Visit here to obtain the Guide Book for Guests With Disabilities, a Guest Assistance Card (see pages 10–11), hearing or vision rental devices, the schedule for Sign Language Interpreted attractions, and ask any questions.

Oasis/Discovery Island—A lush tropical area with paths to transition you from parking lot to park. Once you arrive in Discovery Island, you'll set your eyes on the Tree of Life. You'll find animal- and bird-viewing areas, with shaded areas and benches for sitting. Headliner attraction: It's Tough to Be a Bug!

Africa/Rafiki's Planet Watch—Swahili architecture shapes Harambe village, complete with eateries, marketplace, and a safari unlike any you've experienced outside of Africa! Board a train to visit Rafiki's conservation exhibits.

Asia—The mythical Kingdom of Anandapur surrounds you with the crumbling ruins of an ancient village, hand-painted walls, temples, Mt. Everest, and even a maharajah's palace.

DinoLand, U.S.A.—A tribute to dinosaurs real and imagined! Kids play in a dig site, enjoy Chester and Hester's tacky and wacky fossil fun games and rides, and the headline attraction, Dinosaur!

Camp Minnie-Mickey—Reminiscent of the Adirondacks, this especially kid-friendly area includes Festival of the Lion King, Pocahontas and her Forest Friends, and Character Greeting Trails.

AMBIENCE

PARK LAYOUT AND NAVIGATION

Planning

Your Special Need

Getting There

Staying in Style

Touring

Feasting

Resources

Index

Getting to Disney's Animal Kingdom

Planning | Your Special Need | Getting There | Staying in Style | Touring | Feasting | Resources | Index

BEST TIMES TO GO

Disney's Animal Kingdom can be enjoyed in one day, although it is best to **visit the most popular attractions earlier** to avoid long lines. Arrive before the scheduled opening time for the best advantage.

Co-author Deb Wills particularly enjoys Disney's Animal Kingdom on **Extra Magic Hour mornings**. Not only are the animals generally awake and moving around, but there is a peaceful quiet to the park. Especially during off-peak times, get a breakfast goodie and coffee from Kusafiri Bakery and then find a quiet animal viewing location in the Discovery Island Trails.

Wherever possible, **get a FASTPASS**. Check the entertainment schedule in the park's times guide for show times. Take the length of the show times into account when planning your route, and keep in mind that viewing several shows takes a lot of time. Many attractions and restaurants are empty immediately before and during the parade, affording shorter lines.

The most popular attraction—**Kilimanjaro Safaris**—generates very long lines, especially first thing in the day. Get a FASTPASS for Kilimanjaro Safaris and visit the nearby Pangani Forest Exploration Trail while you wait.

Remember that once a show ends, there will be **lots of congestion** as folks exit the immediate area and decide where to go next.

GETTING THERE

By Car—For many special needs travelers, it may be most convenient to travel by car. Take I-4 to exit 65 (east or west) and follow signs to Disney's Animal Kingdom parking. All-day parking is $8 (free to Disney resort guests and Annual Passholders), and the pass is valid at other Disney parks' lots on the same day.

© MediaMarx, Inc.

Parking lot and tram loading zone at Disney's Animal Kingdom

By Bus—Take a direct bus from all resorts, Epcot's main entrance, Transportation & Ticket Center, and Disney-MGM Studios. From Downtown Disney, Typhoon Lagoon, or Blizzard Beach, take a bus or a boat to a resort and transfer to a Disney's Animal Kingdom bus.

Making the Most of Disney's Animal Kingdom

The park has its share of **small and large hills and uneven paths**. To simulate the "real" outdoors, pebbles, rocks, animal tracks, sidewalk cracks, and roots were formed in the pathways throughout the park. ECV riding is fine, but those pushing a wheelchair or unsteady on their feet may have difficulty.

Disney's Animal Kingdom is the **hottest of all the parks**, especially in the summer. Most shows and rides are outside. Be sure to wear protective clothing and sunscreen, and stay hydrated!

For animal protection and conservation, **no straws or drink lids** are available. Should you require a straw for drinking, you must bring your own, or you can purchase a souvenir cup with a built-in straw ($7).

A large **Braille map**, mounted on a stand, is located near the Disney Outfitters store, adjacent to Safari Coffee, across the bridge from the Oasis and near the Tip Board.

Access to most of the attractions is via **regular queue**, however some of the queues have tight corners, making wheelchair and especially ECV maneuvering tricky. The prime example of this is the Dinosaur attraction.

Need your **medicine refrigerated**? Take it to the First Aid Station, and they'll take care of that for you. The First Aid Station also has a companion-assisted restroom. There is a TTY phone located here, also. The **First Aid Station** and Baby Care Center are located behind the Creature Comforts shop in Discovery Island (see page 196).

Throughout the theme park, you will find hands-on items called **manipulatives**. Those with vision impairments can instead feel the size and shape of animal heads, bones, etc. Three areas that have these manipulatives are the Pangani Forest Exploration Trail, Maharajah Jungle Trek, and Rafiki's Planet Watch—these can sometimes be found at the kid's activity stations, too!

Service animals are allowed, but the closeness of animals throughout the park could cause problems for some. Be aware!

Reader Tip: "The parrots in The Oasis take exception to my dog. They become very loud. This could cause a problem for many service animals and disturb nearby humans, too!"—contributed by Donna Jagodzinski

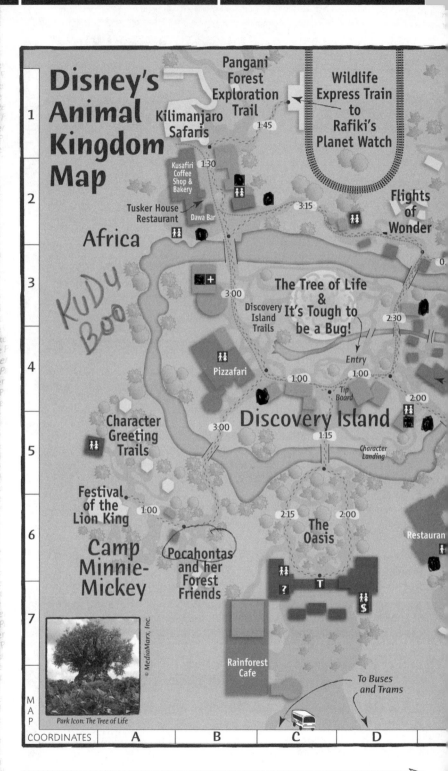

Disney's Animal Kingdom Map

1

Pangani Forest Exploration Trail

Kilimanjaro Safaris

1:45

Wildlife Express Train to Rafiki's Planet Watch

2

1:30

Kusafiri Coffee Shop & Bakery

Tusker House Restaurant — Dawa Bar

3:15

Flights of Wonder

Africa

3

KUDU Boo

3:00

The Tree of Life & It's Tough to be a Bug!

Discovery Island Trails

2:30

0.

4

Pizzafari

Entry

1:00

1:00

Tip Board

2:00

Discovery Island

5

Character Greeting Trails

3:00

1:15

Character Landing

6

Festival of the Lion King

1:00

Camp Minnie-Mickey

Pocahontas and her Forest Friends

2:15

2:00

The Oasis

Restauran

7

© MediaMarx, Inc.

?

T

$

MAP

Park Icon: The Tree of Life

Rainforest Cafe

To Buses and Trams

COORDINATES | A | B | C | D

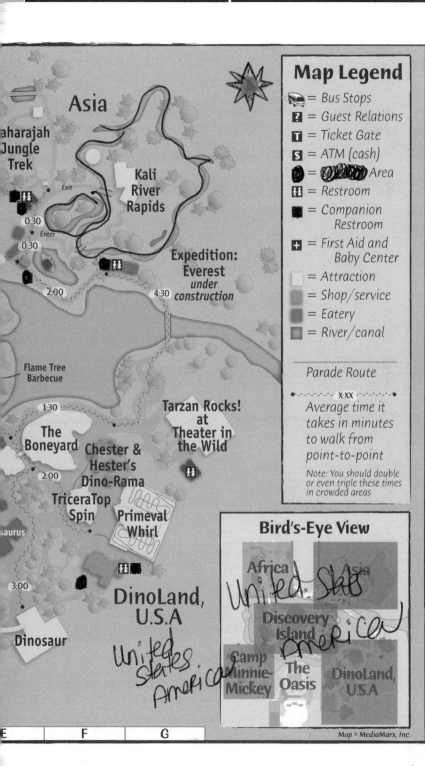

Map © MediaMarx, Inc.

Entertainment at Disney's Animal Kingdom

ENTERTAINMENT

Live entertainment includes a talking palm tree (Wes Palm), a wandering vine (DeVine), and occasional musical acts.

Schedules for **sign-interpreted shows** are made a week at a time. Check at Guest Relations for the most recent schedule.

Festival of the Lion King is the most popular live show and one you shouldn't miss! Check the times guide and try to make the first or last show of the day.

The afternoon **Mickey's Jammin' Jungle Parade** is a bright, festive treat for the eyes, as giant-sized whimsical puppets meander through the park. There are special viewing areas for those in wheelchairs/ECVs:

- Near the Dawa Bar in Harambe, Africa
- Across from Beastly Bazaar on Discovery Island

Kid's Discovery Clubs offer brief (and sometimes hands-on) learning experiences. A kid's guide map is sometimes available, too.

Attractions With Hearing Devices Chart

Assistive Listening	Kilimanjaro Safaris, Rafiki's Planet Watch, Wildlife Express Train, Pocahontas and Her Forest Friends, Festival of the Lion King, Flights of Wonder, Tarzan Rocks!, It's Tough to Be a Bug, and Dinosaur (pre-show)

© Deb Wills

An assistive listening device

Handheld Captioning	Festival of the Lion King, Pocahontas and Her Forest Friends, and Tarzan Rocks!
Reflective Captioning	It's Tough to Be a Bug
Guest-Activated Captioning	Kilimanjaro Safaris (queue), Pangani Forest Exploration (Gorilla Falls Overlook), Rafiki's Planet Watch, Dinosaur (pre-show)
ASL Interpretation	Mickey's Jammin' Jungle Parade, Festival of the Lion King, Pocahontas and Her Forest Friends, Tarzan Rocks, Flights of Wonder, and Rafiki's Planet Watch
Ears to the World	It's Tough to Be a Bug and Kilimanjaro Safaris

Finding Your Place at Disney's Animal Kingdom

You can't get there from here! Unlike the other parks, Animal Kingdom offers **no real orderly sense of direction** once you are inside. Discovery Island is the closest thing to a "hub" and paths from all the lands lead back here. Africa, Asia, and DinoLand U.S.A. are connected by a path. To reach Camp Minnie-Mickey, you have to return to Discovery Island, and Rafiki's Planet Watch via a train from Africa. Be sure to have a guide map with you! Signage provides attraction names and directions, so look for it.

Those looking for a **quiet area** for breaks, time-outs, or baby nursing/napping should consider:
- Inner parts of the Discovery Island trails are rarely populated and offer benches
- Upcountry Landing, when not used for character greets
- Path from Africa to Asia, via back side of Tree of Life—near Flights of Wonder are tables and chairs facing the water, quiet viewing area
- Far right part of the Character Greeting Trails, near the restrooms
- Area behind Drinkwallah
- Immediately to the right of Drinkwalla (entrance to Asia)—look for the pagoda

Companion restrooms available at Disney's Animal Kingdom:
- Opposite Flame Tree Barbecue, just before DinoLand, U.S.A. entrance on right
- Rafiki's Planet Watch
- In the Mombasa Marketplace in Harambe, Africa
- Near Chester and Hester's Dinosaur Treasures in DinoLand, U.S.A.
- Near Maharajah Jungle Trek, on left just before entrance
- Inside Maharajah Jungle Trek, to the right as you exit the Bat House
- First Aid Station on Discovery Island near Creature Comforts shop

Attraction Seating Chart

Dinosaur	narrow seat with bars at hips, seat belt
Expedition Everest	Unknown at time of writing
Festival of the Lion King	bench seats (no backs)
Flights of Wonder	bench seats (no backs)
It's Tough to be a Bug	bench seats (with backs)
Kali River Rapids	narrow seats with seat belts
Kilimanjaro Safari	bench seats (with backs)
Pocahontas and her Forest Friends	bench seats (no back)
Primeval Whirl	small area, low bar, bench seats (with backs)
Tarzan Rocks!	bench seats (with backs)
Triceratop Spin	small space
Wildlife Express to Rafiki's	bench seats (with backs)

SPECIAL PLACES

Planning

Your Special Need

Getting There

Staying in Style

Touring

Feasting

Resources

Index

Charting the Attractions at The Oasis and Camp Minnie-Mickey

Deb Wills' Rating
Deb Koma's Rating
Readers' Rating

The Oasis [C-6]

	8	8	7

Walk-Thru
B-Ticket
All ages
Allow 20 min.

Lush tropical vegetation allows you to decompress as you enter this new species of theme park! Winding paths with viewing areas—give the birds and animals a chance to appear. Have your camera ready. **[G]** Heavy vegetation, grasses, molds, pollen, and animals are present. **[F][V]** One spot along one of the paths has a small "cave" to pass through, but it can be bypassed. **[M][P][E][S]** Watch for roots and ruts in the paths; they have been artificially placed to appear lifelike. **[V]** The heavy vegetation makes the natural lighting dim in spots, especially some of the viewing areas.

Camp Minnie-Mickey Character Greeting Trails [A-5]

	6	7	6

Pavilion
B-Ticket
All ages
Med. waits

Visit Disney characters among the trees in an Adirondacks-like setting. Each trail is marked with characters appearing; each character has their own queue. Have your camera ready. Note: They don holiday apparel in December! **[A]** Waits can be long at times; go while Festival of the Lion King is being performed. **[F]** Large characters may be scary to some.

Festival of the Lion King [A-6]

	9	9	9

Live Show
E-Ticket
Ages 2 & up
Long waits
30-min. show

This Broadway-class show in the round based on The Lion King is not to be missed with its beautiful music, singing, dancing, acrobats, stilt walkers, and floats. The theater is enclosed and offers bench seating (no backs) and air conditioning. Outdoor queue is uncovered with little shade. See the first or last show of the day for shortest waits. Audience members in the front rows (typically children) may be briefly included in the "show." Must climb stairs or sit in first row (reserved for wheelchair travelers and guests). Entertainers will interact with those in the front rows, and some audience participation occurs. **[A][U]** Lots of action from all directions especially front rows. **[A][C][B][H][♥][M][Q][L][V]** Reader Best Choice (see page 193). **[U]** Reader Worst Choice. **[C][♥][T][M][E][S][L]** No backs on seats. **[F]** One act involves fire twirling. **[H]** Assistive listening and handheld captioning available. Sign language interpreted performances on designated days; check with Guest Relations for schedule. Arrive at least 20 minutes in advance; see cast member. **[M]** Wheelchair seating areas in front; see cast member when arriving. Arrive at least 30 minutes prior to show time, and cast member will seat you first before allowing everyone else in. **[H][T][M][V]** Persons with service animals should check with cast members

Pocahontas and Her Forest Friends [B-6]

	5	7	4

Live Show
C-Ticket
Ages 3 & up
Live animals, snakes, and birds
13-min. show

Live forest animals (like ducks, raccoon, skunk, and snake) take the stage with Pocahontas in this show geared toward kids. Wait in an outdoor queue with limited tree shade. Outdoor theater has sheer netting over most bench seats without backs. First four rows are darker colored and for kids only. Certain performances are animal training sessions (check guide map for times). **[F]** Small animals, snake and birds on stage. **[Ö]** Pre-show instructions given in English followed by Spanish. **[H]** Assistive listening and handheld captioning available. Sign language interpreted performances on designated days; check with Guest Relations for schedule. Arrive 10 minutes in advance and sit on right side of theatre when offered. **[M]** Ask for wheelchair/ECV seating in the front of the theater for kids.

Charting the Attractions at Discovery Island

	Deb Wills' Rating	Deb Koma's Rating	Readers' Rating

☐ It's Tough to Be a Bug! [D-4]   *FP*

	8	8	9

3-D Show
E-Ticket
Ages 6 & up
Dark, smells, spiders, "stings"
FASTPASS or med. waits
8-min. show

In the dark caverns at the base of the Tree of Life is a special 3-D attraction. Hosted by Flik the ant from It's a Bugs Life, the show also includes the evil Hopper. Special effects may be too intense for some and include: things dropping from ceiling, dry ice "smoke," stink bug smells, tactile effects, and spraying water. Effects may be less intense in the back. Queue winds through Tree of Life roots (with carvings). Once through turnstiles, queue area is inside and air-conditioned. Theater with bench seating (with backs) is dark and has a high ceiling. The show gets very loud! Please use caution, especially with children. This can be a VERY scary attraction! Heed the warning signs. If unsure, don't go in! **[A][U]** Enter row first to be closest to exit. Reader Best Choice (see page 193). **[A][U][D][B][F][♥][T][P][E][S]** Show takes place in very dark theater and includes spiders, things falling from ceiling, smells, insects, tactile effects in seats, and a menacing villain. **[A][U][C][♥][T][M][P][E][S][L]** Use FASTPASS to avoid waiting in line. **[G]** Dry ice smoke. **[B]** Use Rider Switch. **[U]** Reader Worst Choice. **[F]** 3-D effects (remove 3-D glasses to alleviate fear), insects, loud buzzing sounds, "stings," darkness, and claustrophobia in pre-show area. **[Ö]** Ears to the World translation. **[H]** Assistive listening with rental device. Reflective captioning available; ask cast member at entrance. **[H][T][M][V]** Check with cast member regarding service animals—they are allowed, but make sure your animal can tolerate the noise level and sudden appearance of characters and props. **[M]** Wheelchair/ECV accessible through main queue. When exiting, use exit ramp on left. Wheelchair seating in back or front at the ends of the rows. Front row is easier to transfer to seat. Let cast member know your preference at the entrance. **[V]** Darkened theater. You must wear 3-D glasses, which fit over other glasses, to experience special effects.

☐ The Tree of Life and Discovery Island Trails [C-3]

	8	8	8

Walk-Thru
A-Ticket
All ages
Allow 30 min.

Lush gardens with animal viewing areas surround the Tree of Life and its 325 carvings. This area is often overlooked, especially first thing in the morning. Have camera ready. **[A][U][B]** Semi-secluded areas for quiet time. **[G]** Lots of greenery and animals—those with allergies should be aware. **[C][♥][T][P][E][S]** Look for shaded benches on out of the way paths. **[M]** Wheelchair/ECV accessible on regular pathway.

© MediaMarx, Inc.

A rental wheelchair in front of The Tree of Life

Planning
Your Special Need
Getting There
Staying in Style
Touring
Feasting
Resources
Index

Charting the Attractions at Africa

Deb Wills' Rating | Deb Koma's Rating | Readers' Rating

■ Kilimanjaro Safaris [B-1] *FP* 🏃‍♂️   10 | 10 | 9

Enjoy the beauty of the 100-acre animal reserve aboard modified open-air covered trucks with hard plastic bench seating with minimal padding. Driver will point out wildlife, and there is a story line about poaching. No stopping for photo ops, so have camera ready or just enjoy the view. Children should sit on the inside portions of the bench. Very bumpy, jerky, rough ride on rugged terrain. Each ride is a different experience. Outdoor queue is very long but covered with a few ceiling fans. Loading area ramps downward. There is a small, netted area to place items in, but it's awkward to get things in and out. *[A][U]* Must stay in vehicle for entire ride. *[A][U][C][♥][I][E][S][L]* Use FASTPASS to minimize wait times. *[A][U][M][L]* Reader Best Choice (see page 193). *[G]* Heavy vegetation, grasses, molds, pollen, and animals are present. *[B]* Strollers must be left in designated area, partway into the queue. From stroller park to beginning of loading area is about 40 feet (12 meters). *[F]* When crowded, queue design could trigger claustrophobic feelings. *[Ö]* Ears to the World available. *[H]* Assistive listening and video captioning (queue area) are available. May not be able to hear driver identifying animals or the themed commentary on poaching. *[H][T][M][V]* Check with cast member regarding service animal on vehicle; may be allowed as long as they stay in a "lay down" position. Break area for service animals nearby; ask cast member. *[C][B][♥][T][Q][P][E][S]* Very rough ride with bumps and jolts. *[M]* Follow signs to designated loading area (you will unload at the same place to retrieve your wheelchair). Must transfer from ECV to either vehicle seating or standard wheelchair.

Ride	
E-Ticket	
Ages 3 & up	
Bumpy, live birds and animals, "close escapes"	
FASTPASS or long waits	
19-min. vehicle ride	

■ Pangani Forest Exploration Trail [B-1]   8 | 8 | 7

Gorillas, meerkats, hippos, and birds all make their home along the self-paced walking trail that's just under half a mile long. Between the heavy vegetation and some covered viewing areas, there is some shade. Still, it can get quite hot in here during summer months. Be sure to listen and ask questions of the animal guides. Some hands-on exhibits in the Naturalist's hut. Some areas can become very congested (underwater hippo area, first gorilla area). Binoculars (heavy) available from cast member in aviary. *[A][U][C][♥][I][E][S][L]* Lots of walking. *[G]* Heavy vegetation, grasses, molds, pollen, and animals are present. *[C][B][M][S][V]* Doors in/out of Research Center are awkward and heavy (no automatic opening). *[F]* Research Center has hands-on and small exhibits with spider, snakes, and lizards. Some birds in aviary may be on the ground or low on branches. *[A][U][C][F][♥][T][I][M][Q][P][E][S][L][V]* As you leave the enclosed gorilla area, you will cross a wobbly, wooden bridge. A second, smaller wobbly bridge follows the bachelor gorilla group area. *[Ö][H]* Video with closed captioning in Research Center. Go left as you enter, instead of straight to the glass viewing. *[H][T][M][V]* Check with cast member at entrance before bringing service animals. Some service animals not allowed in aviary and must use bypass. *[M]* Wheelchair/ECV accessible along main path. *[V]* Manipulatives available for exploring at several points along trail—compare human and gorilla skulls.

Walk-Thru	
D-Ticket	
All ages	
Spiders in enclosed cases	
Short waits	
Allow at least 30 minutes	

Charting the Attractions at Rafiki's Planet Watch

Deb Wills' Rating
Deb Koma's Rating
Readers' Rating

Wildlife Express Train to Rafiki's Planet Watch [C-1] `3` `3` `5`

The only way to reach Rafiki's Planet Watch is via this slow-moving train where all seats face outward/sideways. There are two rows of seats and room for one wheelchair per car (you'll need to back in). There is a long walk once you exit the train until you get to Rafiki's Planet Watch. If there is a long wait for the train going out, expect at least that much wait returning. Narration and animal buildings as you travel to Rafiki's Planet Watch. Covered queue with ceiling fans; however, line can extend outside. **[A][U]** Must stay in vehicle for entire ride. **[B]** Stroller (unless collapsible) must remain at train station and you must carry child; use a courtesy stroller at destination. **[H]** Assistive listening with rental device. **[M]** Mainstream queue, some turns are tight, especially 180-degree ones. At turnstile, go left for wheelchair entrance and then straight ahead, wait for cast member. You may stay in your wheelchair/ECV.

- **Train Ride**
- A-Ticket
- All ages
- Glimpses of backstage
- Short waits
- 15-min. ride (each way)

Rafiki's Planet Watch [off map] `S` `5` `5`

Conservation and animal care themed exhibits and activities. Outdoor Affection Section allows hands-on interaction with small domestic animals. Animal Cam shows animal care area; huge colorful mural full of Hidden Mickeys! Most exhibits indoors, includes hands-on, tasting animal food, characters, and Song of Rainforest sound booths (narrated by Grandmother Willow). Might see animal surgeries. **[A][U][F]** Sounds of Rainforest booths have extremely low lighting and require headset. Sounds include birds, animals, mosquitoes, and thunderstorms. **[G]** Hands-on animal area inside and outside. **[G][D][E][W]** Selected animal foods available for tasting. **[H]** Assistive listening. Video captioning in interactive area of Conservation Station. Sign language interpreted performances on designated days; check with Guest Relations for schedule. Arrive at least 5 minutes in advance to see animal presentation at the indoor stage. Rainforest booths feature all sounds through earphones. **[H][M][V]** Service animals not allowed in Affection Section; break area for service animals nearby—ask cast member. **[M]** Wheelchair can enter Rainforest booths, but will have to back out.

- **Exhibit**
- C-Ticket
- All ages
- Backstage, educational fun
- Live animals
- Short waits
- Allow at least 90 minutes for a good exploration

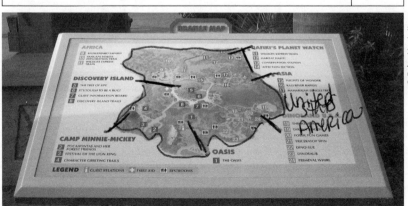

The Braille Map of Disney's Animal Kingdom, located on Discovery Island

© Debra Martin Koma

Planning | Your Special Need | Getting There | Staying in Style | Touring | Feasting | Resources | Index

Charting the Attractions at Asia

Also see Expedition Everest on next page.

Deb Wills' Rating · Deb Koma's Rating · Readers' Rating

Flights of Wonder [D-2] — 6 7 7

The outdoor Caravan Stage is home to more than 20 species of free flying birds including macaws, cranes, hawks, and owls. The whimsical show also has a conservation theme, so it's educational as well as fun. Bench seating with no backs. Bleachers on left/right side offer elevated viewing. Mostly shaded theater. For an up-close look, head to the stage area when the show is over! Great photo ops too. Outdoor queue is uncovered. No food or beverage allowed in theater. Adults with video/still cameras may be chosen during the show to come on stage and photograph. **[A][U][C][♥][I][E][S][L]** No queue area per se—just wait outside theater for opening. **[B]** Leave strollers at theater entrance. **[F]** Audience participation. **[F][V]** Birds fly low over the audience. **[H]** Assistive listening. Sign language interpreted performances on designated days; check with Guest Relations for schedule. Arrive at least 15 minutes in advance; sit in the <u>left</u> section of the audience. **[M]** Wheelchair/ECV accessible through regular queue—special seating on far left in front and also in back.

Live Show	
C-Ticket	
Ages 3 & up	
Live birds overhead	
Med. waits	
25-min. show	

Kali River Rapids [F-2] 🅵🅿 🧍 — 6 9 8

Water raft ride through a jungle jeopardized by illegal logging. There may be flames, but there are also geysers and you will get wet! Wear a poncho to reduce getting soaked. Small storage area in the raft's center to keep items dry, but it really doesn't (bring trash bag or large resealable bag). Must wear shoes to get on ride, but then you can remove them and place in bag to keep dry. High speed in places with a drop. A portion of the ride goes through a simulated burning forest, you will feel the heat and smell fire. Outdoor covered queue is incredibly themed, with intricate details—don't rush through. Once past the turnstiles, the loading area is a large rotating disc that moves at same speed as rafts. Step down into raft and seatbelt yourself in. Rafts seat 12, in six separate seats for two. Special effects may be too intense for some. **[A][U]** Must stay in vehicle for entire ride. **[A][U][C][♥][I][E][S][L]** Use FASTPASS. **[G]** Flower scents in the beginning and fire and smoke in parts. **[B]** Use Rider Switch. **[B][M][L]** Reader Worst Choice (see page 193). **[F]** You will get wet! **[H]** Assistive listening in queue. Take extra precaution to ensure hearing aids are removed and kept in dry place. **[H][T][M][V]** Service animals not allowed. **[M]** Transfer from ECV/wheelchair to raft. Separate loading area for wheelchairs. The raft will be docked, and there is plenty of time to load. Raft is flagged so you are returned to same location at end. **[C][♥][T][Q][P][E][S]** Should not ride. **[B][L]** Minimum height 38 in./97 cm. **[L]** Two persons of size will not fit comfortably on one seat, but a person of size will be comfortable sharing the seat with a child or petite person.

Raft Ride	
E-Ticket	
Ages 7 & up	
Med. drop, flames, geysers, and you will get wet!	
FASTPASS or long waits	
5-min. cruise	

Maharajah Jungle Trek [E-1] — 9 8 7

Lush path with beautiful Asian/Indian architecture and tigers, bats, birds, tapirs, and komodo dragon. There is no glass between you and the bats; however, there is a barrier that prohibits the bats from entering the viewing area. Multiple viewing areas for tigers. Be sure to listen and ask questions of the animal guides. Parts of the open-air trail are covered; some areas can become very congested (tiger areas) and you may have to wait. **[A][U][C][♥][I][E][S][L]** Lots of walking. **[G]** Heavy vegetation, grasses, molds, pollen, and animals are present. **[F]** Bypass bat house if you wish. **[H][T][M][V]** Service animals may be allowed; check with cast member at entrance. Some service animals not allowed in aviary and must use bypass. Break area for service animals nearby; ask cast member. **[V]** Manipulatives available.

Walk-Thru	
D-Ticket	
All ages	
Bats!	
Short waits	
Allow at least 30 minutes	

Charting the Attractions
at Asia (continued) & DinoLand U.S.A.

	Deb Wills' Rating	Deb Koma's Rating	Readers' Rating

☐ Expedition Everest [G-3] (Opens 2006)   – – –

A high-speed train ride with coaster-like thrills, some backward movement. Come face-to-face with Yeti (abominable snowman)! Two seats in each row, and each seat has an individual low bar. **[A][U][C][♥][I][E][S][L]** Use FASTPASS to minimize wait times. **[A][R][U][C][F][♥][T][I][M][Q][P][E][S][V]** Rough/fast ride. **[F]** Portions of ride in dark. **[A][U]** Must stay in vehicle entire ride. **[B]** Use Rider Switch. **[H][T][M][V]** Service animals not allowed. **[M]** Transfer from wheelchair to vehicle. **[♥][Q][E]** Guests with these conditions should not ride.	Coaster
	E-Ticket
	Ages 8 & up
	Long waits

DinoLand, U.S.A.

☐ The Boneyard [F-5]   5 5 6

Kids can let off steam by climbing and sliding in the Boneyard. Flooring is spongy mat-like material. There are some places to sit. Bring a towel and dry clothes. There is virtually no shade except for the mammoth dig site, which is covered with a couple of large fans. Good photo ops. Some bridges are made of net and very wobbly. Take ramp or stairs across walkway to Mammoth Dig Site. Sift through sand to find bones. This is an outdoor but covered area. Shovels/pails provided for kids, wheelchair ramp into sand. **[A][U][F]** Lots of kids in a confined area. **[G]** Sand pit could cause problems. **[C][T][I][M][P][E][S][L][V]** Spongy floor makes walking/wheelchair travel difficult. Not recommended for those in an ECV. **[C][B][♥][T][E][S][L]** Very hot in here during summer months, so be sure to bring water with you. **[F]** Small "cave" with a low ceiling behind T. Rex.	Playground
	B-Ticket
	Ages 1 & up
	Allow 20 min.

☐ Dinosaur [E-7]   FP 🧍   7 7 8

Travel back 65 million years to the Cretaceous period in search of an Iguanadon. Save him before the meteor shower gets everyone! Outside queue covered with ceiling fans, inside winds around with tight corners. Standing pre-show. Ride in 12-person vehicles; each rider has seat belt. Very dark, turbulent, rough ride with loud noises and flashes of lights (especially at beginning and end). Big dinosaurs jump out at you. Sharp turns, sudden stops, herky-jerky motion—think of a bucking bronco ride! Intense special effects. Must be in good health, free from heart, back, or neck problems and motion sickness. **[A][U]** Must stay in vehicle for entire ride. **[A][U][C][♥][I][E][S][L]** Use FASTPASS to minimize wait times **[A][U][C][F][♥][T][I][M][Q][P][E][S][V]** Loud/rough/fast ride with various lighting changes and sudden movements. **[U][C][B][♥][M][Q][L]** Reader Worst Choice (see page 193). **[C][B][♥][T][Q][E]** Guests with these conditions should not ride. **[C]**[L[**[M][S][L]** There are 16 steps down to the loading bay and 16 back up after the ride, or use bypass elevator (see cast member). When you exit the pre-show briefing room, pass through a hallway into the loading bay. As you enter, look to your left for the elevator. Transfer from wheelchair to vehicle. **[B]** Use Rider Switch. **[F]** Queue has insect/reptile photos. When crowded, inside queue design could trigger claustrophobic feelings; darkness, loud noises, dinosaurs jump out at you but don't touch you. **[H]** Assistive listening and video captioning (TV monitors to far right in "Briefing Room") available in pre-show. **[H][T][M][V]** Service animals not allowed. **[L]** Seats are narrow due to seatbelt hardware, can hurt when jostled. If you are large-breasted, this attraction may actually be painful at times. Minimum height 40 in./102 cm.	Thrill Ride
	E-Ticket
	Ages 7 & up
	Dark, scary, very loud, dinosaurs
	FASTPASS or med. waits
	3.5-min. ride

Charting the Attractions at DinoLand, U.S.A.
(continued)

	Deb Wills' Rating	Deb Koma's Rating	Readers' Rating

☐ Tarzan Rocks! [G-4] (attraction will close in early 2006) — 8 7 7

High energy, very loud, rock concert with singers, dancers, acrobats, and musicians, featuring songs and characters based on the animated film. Tarzan, Jane, and Terk join in the fun. Rollerbladers skate through the theater. Not a place to relax, but you will get re-energized! Outdoor queue is standing with no shade. Theater is open-air but covered. Bench seats with backs. Must climb up and down stairs to reach seats. Both queue and theatre can get very hot—bring water. Some seats adjacent to stage with no barriers; must not touch stage or performers. Cast members sometimes walk through selling beverages before show begins. [B] Park strollers outside theater. [B][F][♥][E][S] Very loud rock and roll concert. Consider sitting further back from the speakers. [H] Assistive listening and handheld captioning available. Sign language interpreted performances on designated days; check with Guest Relations for schedule. Arrive at least 20 minutes in advance; sit in the right section and see cast member. [T] Flashing and strobe lights part of show. [M] Three accessible seating levels at this theater; front row, middle row (where the rollerbladers skate through), and the back row. You can request any of the rows; however, the front row and the middle row get filled the quickest.	**Live Show**
	E-Ticket
	Ages 4 & up
	Very loud
	Med. waits (check times)
	28-min. show

☐ Primeval Whirl [G-6] — FP 🚶 — 5 10 8

Herky-jerky coaster whose cars spin, make sudden turns, and short, sudden drops. "Time machines" are designed to seat four, with two sections for two people and a low bar for safety. Must be in good health, free from heart, back, or neck problems, and motion sickness. Small person seated next to large person will get jostled. [A][U] Must stay in vehicle for entire ride. [A][U][C][♥][I][E][S][L] Use FASTPASS. [A][U][C][F][♥][T][I][M][Q][P][E][S][V] Rough spinning ride with sudden movements. [B] Use Rider Switch. [H][T][M][V] Service animals not allowed. [B][♥][Q][E] Guests with these conditions should not ride. [♥][Q][L] Reader Worst Choice (see page 193). [M] Wheelchair/ECV users must transfer to ride vehicle. If unable to brace yourself with legs and arms, you may not be able to stay seated. [B][L] Minimum height 48 in./122 cm. [L] Persons of size can comfortably sit in one of the double seats. If you have a smaller person with you, you may be able to share the seat. Use caution with lap bar being too snug and	**Coaster**
	D-Ticket
	Ages 7 & up
	Fast, drops
	FASTPASS
	2.5-min. ride

☐ TriceraTop Spin [F-6] — 5 3 7

Dumbo-like ride that circles a hub as four-person cars shaped like dinosaurs go up and down. [A][U] Must stay in vehicle for entire ride [F] Heights, spinning [H][T][M][V] Service animals not allowed. [M] Accessible car available. You are required to transfer from ECV to standard wheelchair. Some longer or wider than average wheelchairs may be tight fit—if so, transfer to available manual wheelchair. [Q] Ride goes in circle and up and down. [L] Each row can fit one large adult and one small child, or a large adult will need to sit in their own row.	**Ride**
	C-Ticket
	Ages 2 & up
	1.5-min. ride

☐ Dinorama Fossil Fun Games [F-6] — 2 5 7

Cheesy carnival games of skill or chance. Cost is $2 a game, which include: Raptor Race, Meteor Strike, and Fossil Fueler, occasional walk-around Dinosaur. [A][U] Very loud area with lots of stimulation. [M] Wheelchair/ECV accessible—see a cast member for where to sit for each game.	**Arcade**
	A-Ticket
	Ages 2 & up
	1.5-min. ride

Touring the Water Parks

On a sultry summer day, or even a warmish winter one, Disney's two water parks sure are inviting. Choose from either Typhoon Lagoon, which opened in June 1989 with its back story of a tropical storm gone wild, or Blizzard Beach, which debuted in April 1995 with the theme of a freak snowstorm taking over a resort in Florida. While they may not have as many amenities for the special needs visitor as the theme parks or resort hotels, they do make a number of provisions that will make your visit easier.

Guest Relations, located in front of the entrance to each water park, will provide you with a park guide map (available also in Spanish, French, Portuguese, German, and Japanese), as well as information on services for guests with disabilities. Also at Guest Services, you'll find a text typewriter (TTY).

You can **borrow a standard wheelchair** from Guest Services, although they have a limited number available. Just leave a driver's license or other valid ID as a deposit.

Ticket booths have one lower accessible counter. Lines can be very long at opening time, so either buy in advance or use the Ticket Vending Machines located near the booths.

Most water park attractions require you to **transfer from your wheelchair** either by yourself or with the assistance of a member of your party. Water park cast members are not permitted to physically assist guests.

Water wheelchairs may be available for use in the shallow water areas. Ask a lifeguard. Note that all wheelchairs are only permitted in water up to the axle on the main wheels.

Most **food and merchandise** locations at the water parks are accessible, although some eateries have very narrow queues that are difficult to negotiate. If you have someone with you, have them order and carry your food, or ask a cast member for assistance.

If you have **special dietary concerns**, contact the water park's food and beverage manager before your visit.

The **First Aid Stations** at the water parks are not as large as at the theme parks and only have very basic supplies; however, each does have a companion restroom and the ability to refrigerate medications or cool-down vests for service animals.

Drinking fountains are wheelchair accessible, but you may also request cups from the nearest restaurant or refreshment stand.

Cast members have access to **paper and pencils/pens** if they are necessary to communicate with guests.

Phones with amplified handsets are available in each park; see guide map for location.

Be sure to **remove hearing aids** and keep them in a dry place, such as a plastic bag.

Smoking is permitted in designated areas only. Consult a map if you wish to avoid them.

Note that **wait times** increase as the day wears on. Also, the water parks will refuse additional visitors if they reach capacity. This can happen as early as 10:00 am during the weekends or peak seasons. Consider going early in the day.

Planning | Your Special Need | Getting There | Staying in Style | Touring | Feasting | Resources | Index

Touring the Water Parks (continued)

If you have a **prosthesis**, you must follow a number of special requirements. Cover any exposed metal, sharp edges, or nonskid material before going on any water slide. Coverings, which must be smooth cloth and strong enough to keep the prosthesis from protruding, must be preapproved by water park management. Pick up a specific prosthesis information sheet at Guest Services, but in general, the guidelines are:

✔ If your prosthesis is below the knee, you may ride all the attractions with or without the prosthesis.

✔ If your prosthesis is above the knee and non-bending, you may ride everything with the prosthesis (except where noted for individual attractions). Note that some slides require you to cross your legs at the ankles.

✔ If your prosthesis is above the knee and bends, you may not ride Typhoon Lagoon's Humunga Kowabunga or Blizzard Beach's Summit Plummet.

✔ If your prosthesis is hip level, you may not ride Humunga Kowabunga or Summit Plummet.

✔ If your prosthesis is an upper limb or arm, you can ride all the attractions with or without the prosthesis.

Service animals are welcome at the water parks as long as they remain harnessed/leashed at all times. Follow the same entrances as those using wheelchairs. Animals are not permitted to ride any of the water attractions or enter the water anywhere at the park. Someone must be with the animal at all times. There are designated break areas for service animals as follows (ask a cast member for assistance):

At Typhoon Lagoon	At Blizzard Beach
backstage gate at Shark Reef	backstage gate at main entrance
backstage gate at Ketchakidde Creek	backstage gate near Runoff Rapids
backstage gate at main dressing rooms	

Although there is some shade around the parks, be sure to apply **sunscreen** frequently, and wear a hat, sunglasses, and long sleeves for extra protection from the sun.

The water is **heated** in all attractions, except Typhoon Lagoon's Shark Reef.

The **pavement** can get very hot—wear flip-flops or surf shoes for extra protection. If the pavement in an area is very wet, be on the lookout for low-level squirting water jets.

Lockers and towels can be rented at Typhoon Lagoon's Hi 'N Dry Towels or Blizzard Beach's Snowless Joe's. It's $5 for a small locker and $7 for a larger size with a $2 refund when you return your key. Towels are $1. Lifejackets are free with a refundable deposit and ID. Note that fanny packs are not allowed on rides. Tip: Bring your own towels (from home or your hotel) to save the towel rental fee.

Tips for Wheelchair Users at Water Parks

✔ Since prolonged exposure to water can remove oil/grease from wheel bearings, avoid getting your wheelchair axle wet.

✔ Sand can cause a lot of damage, so stay on the paved pathways.

✔ Use care as you wheel around—if one of your wheels goes off the sidewalk, you can tip over!

✔ You'll be sitting in the sun for a long period, so remember to use lots of sunscreen, or cover up.

Typhoon Lagoon Water Park

Typhoon Lagoon spreads out across 56 lush acres located near Downtown Disney. Note that there are no elevators here and many water slides require walking up and down stairs.

Disney's back story of this water park claims that a **terrible storm** blew through the once-calm resort of Placid Palms, leaving wild waters in its wake, not to mention the shrimp boat Miss Tilly impaled on a mountaintop called Mount Mayday. There are plenty of thrills to be found here, and we think that Typhoon Lagoon is slightly friendlier to visitors with special needs than Blizzard Beach.

The focal point of Typhoon Lagoon is its **2.5-acre wave pool**, which sits below Mount Mayday. Circling the park's perimeter is a slow-moving "lazy river" known as Castaway Creek, perfect for tubing. Cascading down the mountain are an assortment of body slides and raft rides. We describe these attractions beginning on page 285.

By Car—Take exit 67 off I-4, take the first exit and turn right on Buena Vista Dr.—the park is on the right. From Downtown Disney, turn right to Buena Vista Dr.—the park is on the left. Free parking. Parking for park-goers with disabilities is directly across from the entrance plaza. A valid disability parking permit is required.
By Bus—All Disney resorts have direct buses to Typhoon Lagoon. From the Magic Kingdom, Epcot, Disney-MGM Studios, and Disney's Animal Kingdom, take a bus or monorail to a nearby resort and transfer to a Typhoon Lagoon bus (which may also be the Downtown Disney bus). Allow about 30–60 minutes if you travel by bus. Buses deposit park-goers at stops to the left of the Guest Services plaza.

Guest Relations is to the left at the entrance to Typhoon Lagoon.

The small **First Aid Station** (see page 196) is just to the left and slightly behind Leaning Palms (as you're facing it). There's also a companion restroom.

Lost children are entertained at a special desk near Singapore Sal's shop.

International phone card vending machines are located near the restrooms behind Singapore Sal's.

Planning
Your Special Need
Getting There
Staying in Style
Touring
Feasting
Resources
Index
AMBIENCE
LAYOUT
GETTING THERE AND AROUND

Making the Most of Typhoon Lagoon

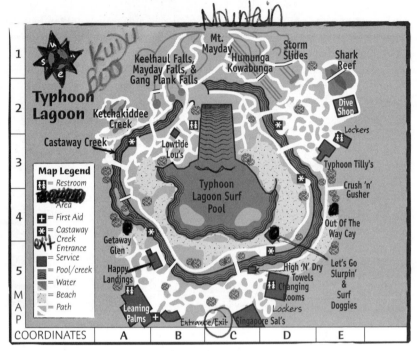

DINING

Leaning Palms is the **main counter-service eatery** at Typhoon Lagoon. It features sandwiches, wraps, burgers and salads. If you have special dietary concerns, contact the Food & Beverage manager at least 24 hours before your visit to the water park (see chapter 6 for our guidelines on requesting special meals.) Other eateries at the water park include Happy Landings for ice cream (sugar-free available), the seasonal Lowtide Lou's and Typhoon Tilly's for more sandwich-type items, Surf Doggies for hot dogs and turkey legs, and Let's Go Slurpin' for snacks and alcoholic beverages (non-alcoholic beer available). Menus for the water parks' eateries are both in pictorial format and are translated into Spanish, Portuguese, French, German, and Japanese. There are also three picnic areas with shade and tables—you could bring your own food and beverage in to the park (especially if you have special dietary needs), although no coolers, alcoholic beverages or glass containers are permitted.

Charting the Attractions
at Typhoon Lagoon

☐ Typhoon Lagoon Surf Pool [C-4]   10 10 9

One of the world's largest inland wave pools! There is a two-hour cycle of waves: 90 minutes of high surf waves that come every 90 seconds, followed by 30 minutes of gently bobbing waves. There is a small chalkboard at the edge of the beach near the front of the park on which the day's wave schedule is posted. The surrounding white sand beach offers plenty of places to relax in the sun—shady areas are harder to find. Surf waves are very turbulent and strenuous. Bathers can lose their footing, bump into one another, and scrape body parts on the pool bottom. Water depth changes rapidly. **[F]** *The six-foot high waves can be intimidating.* **[C][♥][T][M][P][S][L][V]** *The shoreline of the pool is just like a real beach, very gradually sloping downward. Just wade into the water—no step down required.* **[M]** *Water wheelchairs may be available—ask a lifeguard or at the High 'N' Dry Towel and Locker Rentals. Regular wheelchairs can enter from the pathway and zero-depth entry points located at Blustery Bay below the Clock Tower and at Whitecap Cove near Surf Doggies and the Coffee Wagon. Wheelchairs are only permitted into the wave pool up to the axle on the main wheels of the wheelchair. ECVs are NOT permitted in the water—transfer to a regular wheelchair.* **[B]** *Children wearing diapers must either wear snug-fitting plastic pants or swim diapers.*

Pool
E-Ticket
All ages

☐ Castaway Creek [Entry points: A-3, A-2, D-2, D-3, D-5]   9 10 8

Take a tube for a relaxing, 2,100-foot trip around the park. Adult supervision is required. There are several entrance/exit points, so it may be confusing. Entrances are marked with distinctive symbols—be sure everyone knows what to symbol to look for. **[C][♥][T][M][P][S][L][V]** *There is one accessible entrance with a platform, or "transfer tier," located at Seahorse Landing #5 (across from Let's Go Slurpin'), but you must be able to lower yourself into the water or a tube, or have a friend or family member assist you.* **[B]** *Children wearing diapers must either wear snug-fitting plastic pants or swim diapers.* **[L]** *People of size may be uncomfortable in the tubes.*

Lazy River
D-Ticket
Ages 3 & up

© Debra Martin Koma

Transfer tier at Castaway Creek

☐ Crush 'n' Gusher [E-3] (new for 2005)   🔼   – – –

Crush 'n' Gusher is a new water coaster that sends you both up and down along a series of flumes and spillways through a rusted-out tropical fruit facility. You can choose from three different routes, Banana Blaster, Coconut Crusher, and Pineapple Plunger, each ranging between 410 and 420 feet in length. Guests ride in two-person rafts. **[A][U][C][F][♥][T][P][S]** *Fast drop! May be too intense for some adults and children.* **[C][M][P][S][T][♥]** *Follow the sign for wheelchair/ECV access—it leads to an elevator, which takes you to the top of the slides. A cast member will return your wheelchair/ECV to the pool area below to await you after you slide down.* **[B]** *Use Rider Switch.* **[E]** *Pregnant women are not permitted to ride.* **[B][L]** *48 in./122 cm. height restriction.*

Raft slide
E-Ticket
Big drop!
Ages 9 & up

··➤

Charting the Attractions
at Typhoon Lagoon
(continued)

	Deb Wills' Rating	Deb Koma's Rating	Readers' Rating

☐ Ketchakiddee Creek [A-2]   👤

5	6	7

Fun geared to 2- to 5-year-olds, with slides, geysers, and fountains. *[B]* Children wearing diapers must either wear snug-fitting plastic pants or swim diapers. *[B][L]* Height restriction: 48 in./122 cm. tall or under.

Playground
B-Ticket
Ages 2-5

☐ Bay Slides [A-2]   👤

5	5	7

Gentle water slide just for the little ones, ends in its own special corner of the surf pool. *[B]* Children wearing diapers must either wear snug-fitting plastic pants or swim diapers. *[B][L]* Height restriction: 60 in./152 cm. tall or under.

Jr. slide
C-Ticket
Ages 2-5

☐ Keelhaul Falls [B-1]

5	6	7

Take a one-person tube through caves and waterfalls. *[A][U][C][F][♥][T][P][S]* May be too intense for some adults and children. *[♥][T][S][L]* To ride, you must be free of head, neck, back, and heart problems. Also, you must carry your own raft. This ride is for strong swimmers. *[A][U][C][♥][T][P][S][L][V][M]* You must climb many steps to reach the top of this slide. It is NOT wheelchair/ECV accessible. Also, during busy seasons, waits (all standing, little to no shade) can be quite long. *[B]* Use Rider Switch. *[F]* This ride takes you through darkened areas and moves at a white-water pace. *[Q]* May experience motion problems as tube can rotate as you go through turns. *[E]* Pregnant women are not permitted to ride. *[B][L]* Children under age 4 must take a smaller tube.

Tube slide
C-Ticket
Ages 7 & up

☐ Mayday Falls [B-1]

6	6	7

Another one-person tube ride, this takes you past rocky falls at a slightly slower pace than Keelhaul Falls. *[♥][T][S][L]* To ride, you must be free of head, neck, back, and heart problems. Also, this ride is for strong swimmers. *[A][U][C][♥][T][P][S][L][V][M]* You must climb many steps to reach the top of this slide and you must carry your own raft. It is not wheelchair/ECV accessible. Also, during busy seasons, waits (all standing, little to no shade) can be quite long. *[B]* Use Rider Switch. *[F]* This ride takes you through darkened areas and moves quickly. *[Q]* May experience motion problems as tube can rotate as you go through turns. *[E]* Pregnant women are not permitted to ride.

Tube slide
C-Ticket
Ages 7 & up

☐ Gang Plank Falls [B-1]

5	9	6

Families can ride together on this quick white-water rafting adventure. *[C][♥][T][P][S][L][V][M]* You must climb many steps to reach the top of this slide, and a member of your group must carry your own raft. It is not wheelchair/ECV accessible. If you can manage all the steps, however, there is a spot where you may be loaded into the raft with your group to experience this ride. Ask a cast member for direction. *[F]* There are several spots where water is sprayed at you or dumped on you. *[Q]* May experience motion problems as tube can rotate as you go through turns. *[E]* Pregnant women are not permitted to ride.

Raft slide
C-Ticket
Ages 4 & up

Charting the Attractions
at Typhoon Lagoon
(continued)

	Deb Wills' Rating	Deb Koma's Rating	Readers' Rating

Humunga Kowabunga [C-1] 　　🧍 | 1 | 6 | 7 |

The highest body slide (actually three of them) at this park, it only takes 10 seconds to shoot to the bottom. You must go down feet first, with your ankles crossed—remember to cross your arms over your chest. **[A][U][C][F][♥][T][P][S]** Fast (30 mph) drop! May be too intense for some adults and children. **[A][U][C][♥][T][P][S][L][V][M]** You must climb many steps to reach the top of this slide. It is not wheelchair/ECV accessible. Also, during peak seasons, waits (all standing, little to no shade) can be quite long. **[B]** Use Rider Switch. **[E]** Pregnant women are not permitted to ride. **[B][L]** 48 in./122 cm. height restriction.

Body slide
E-Ticket
Ages 9 & up
Very fast, steep drop

Storm Slides [D-1] | 4 | 5 | 7 |

Three different body slides (Rudder Buster, Stern Burner, and Jib Jammer) take you through caves and tunnels at a fast pace. **[A][U][C][F][♥][T][P][S]** May be too intense for some adults and children. **[A][U][C][♥][T][P][S][L][V][M]** You must climb many steps to reach the top of this slide. It is NOT wheelchair/ECV accessible. Also, during busy seasons, waits (all standing, little to no shade) can be quite long. **[B]** Use Rider Switch. **[E]** Pregnant women are not permitted to ride.

Body slides
E-Ticket
Ages 8 & up

Shark Reef [E-1] | 9 | 10 | 8 |

Snorkel among the colorful tropical fish and live (but safe) sharks (hammerheads) and rays, too. There's also the chance for a longer scuba-assisted snorkeling experience for a fee. **[C][♥][T][P][S][L]** Those with heart problems should not attempt to snorkel, nor should those prone to seizures. This attraction is for experienced swimmers, although life jackets are provided. If you are not a strong swimmer, you may still snorkel and float across the pool. **[L]** Children under 10 must be accompanied by an adult. **[M]** Underwater viewing area is wheelchair accessible via path that goes under the shipwreck. Wheelchair users may snorkel if they are able to get into the water on their own, or have a companion to assist them. **[F]** Viewing area under shipwreck is dark and very closed in, with eerie underwater sounds piped in. **[Ö]** Foreign language instructions are printed and hanging from posts at the platform before entering the reef.

Pool
E-Ticket
Ages 6 & up
Cold, salty water

© Debra Martin Koma

Shallow areas like this at Typhoon Lagoon are ideal for a water wheelchair

Blizzard Beach Water Park

Blizzard Beach brings the chills and thrills of a Colorado winter to the warm Florida sun. Ski jumps, toboggan rides, and slalom runs zip you past snow that never melts in Disney's most action-oriented water park. There are no elevators here, and many water slides require walking up and down stairs.

AMBIENCE

According to legend, a freak winter storm developed over the western end of Walt Disney World Resort and covered the area with a thick blanket of powdery white snow. Soon plans were underway for **Florida's first ski resort**. Ski lifts were put up, toboggan runs were laid down and an entire resort area blossomed around the mountain of snow. Yet another sudden temperature change returned temps to their normal Florida levels, and the powdery snow quickly turned into slippery slush. The ski resort became known as Disney's Blizzard Beach, the most slushy, slippery, exhilarating water park anywhere!

GETTING THERE

By Car—From westbound or eastbound I-4, take exit 65 (west on Osceola Parkway), exiting at Buena Vista Drive. Free parking.

By Bus—All resorts and Disney's Animal Kingdom have direct buses to Blizzard Beach. From Disney-MGM Studios, take the Coronado Springs bus. From Epcot, take the Disney's Animal Kingdom Lodge bus. From the Magic Kingdom and Downtown Disney, take a bus or monorail to a Disney resort and board a bus to Blizzard Beach. We recommend you take Disney transportation when you can, because the parking lot can fill up on busy days.

The **First Aid Station** is near the park entrance in between Lottawatta Lodge and Beach Haus. There are companion restrooms here and also behind the locker area. Lost person area located between Lottawatta Lodge and First Aid. See page 196.

Charting the Attractions at Blizzard Beach

	Deb Wills' Rating	Deb Koma's Rating	Readers' Rating

☐ Summit Plummet [D-2]

| | | 1 | 6 | 9 |

The world's highest body slide, which drops 120 feet (36.5 meters) at 60 mph (96.5 kph)! Go feet first, cross your arms, and it's over in 8 seconds. Very steep drop! Must climb stairs to access entrance. [A][U][C][♥][T][P][S][L] Long wait times during peak seasons [A][U][C][F][♥][T][P][S] May be too intense for some adults and children. [C][♥][T][P][E][S] Guests with these conditions should not ride. [B] Use Rider Switch. [F] Fast, straight, steep, long drop! [M] Not accessible by wheelchair/ECV. [B][L] 48 in./122 cm. height restriction.

Body Slide / E-Ticket / Ages 9 & up

☐ Slush Gusher [D-2]

| | | 1 | 6 | 8 |

90-foot (27-meter) high double-humped slide. Wear one-piece suits! Go feet first, lay down, cross arms. [A][U][C][♥][T][P][S][L] Long wait times in peak seasons [A][U][C][F][♥][T][P][S] May be too intense for some adults and kids. [C][♥][T][P][E][S] Guests with these conditions should not ride. [B] Use Rider Switch. [F] Fast, straight, steep, long drop! [B][L] 48 in./122 cm. height restriction.

Body Slide / D-Ticket / Ages 8 & up

☐ Downhill Double Dipper [C-2]

| | | 2 | 5 | 8 |

Side-by-side tube racing slides enclosed for part of the run. The slides are set up as a race and run straight down the hill. Travel up to 25 mph (40 kph). [F] Enclosed area midway [C][♥][T][P][E][S][M] Must climb stairs to access slide entrance. [B] Use Rider Switch. [M] Not accessible by wheelchair/ECV. [Q] Dipper humps may bother those with motion sensitivity. [B][L] 48 in./122 cm. height restriction.

Tube Slide / D-Ticket / Ages 8 & up

☐ Snow Stormers [C-2]

| | | 7 | 6 | 8 |

Switchback slalom-style slides. Mat pickup at top of Mt. Gushmore. Family-friendly. [C][♥][T][P][E][S] Must climb stairs to access slide entrance. [M] Wheelchairs/ECVs may access from an auxiliary gate at the top of the attraction. Must transfer from wheelchair to foam mat for experience.

Mat Slide / C-Ticket / Ages 6 & up

☐ Toboggan Racers [D-2]

| | | 3 | 5 | 7 |

Eight-lane toboggan. Mat pickup at top of Mt. Gushmore. [C][♥][T][P][E][S] Must climb stairs to access slide; small step to get in and out. Ages 6 & up.

Mat Slide / D-Ticket

☐ Teamboat Springs [E-2]

| | | 5 | 8 | 9 |

World's longest family raft ride for up to 6 persons; 1,400 feet (366 meters) along twisting ride. Family-friendly fun. [A][U][C][♥][T][P][S][L] Popular ride, long wait times during peak seasons. [F] May be combined with other groups to fill raft. [M] Access via Mt. Gushmore Chairlift (see next page). Water wheelchair can return in separate raft. [Q] May experience motion problems. [L] Only one plus-size person per raft.

Raft Slide / D-Ticket / Ages 4 & up

☐ Runoff Rapids [D-2]

| | | 5 | 6 | 7 |

Three different open and enclosed inner tube runs. Two can share tube on open runs. Tube pickup at bottom of Mt. Gushmore. Family-friendly fun. Ages 6 & up.

Tube Slide / C-Ticket

Sidebar tabs: Planning · Your Special Need · Getting There · Staying in Style · Touring · Feasting · Resources · Index

Charting the Attractions
at Blizzard Beach
(continued)

	Deb Wills' Rating	Deb Koma's Rating	Readers' Rating

☐ Cross Country Creek [Entry points: B-4, A-4, B-2, C-1, E-3, D-4] | **9** | **9** | **7** |

Float around in tube along continuous flowing creek, encircling park. Tubes at each of the seven entrances. Waterfalls, snow-making machine, and shooting water along the way. Family-friendly fun. Children under 10 should be accompanied by adult. Weak swimmers should use personal floatation device or swimmer's aid. Current is strong at times. Water depth is 2 feet 6 inches (76 cm). **[A][U]** Multiple entrances and exits, may be confusing to find way back. **[M]** Wheelchair/ECV accessible at the following landings: Manatee Landing next to the Warming Hut; Ice Gator Landing across from Avalunch; and Polar Bear Landing between the two main bridges. If you don't get out of the exit where your wheelchair/ECV is parked, you may have to go all the way around again, as water current pushes you in one direction. **[L]** People of size may be uncomfortable in tube.	**Lazy River** D-Ticket Ages 2 & up 20 min.

☐ Melt Away Bay [D-4] | **7** | **7** | **7** |

One-acre (4,046 sq. m.) wave pool at the base of Mt. Gushmore. Constant bobbing gentle waves. **[A][U]** Put your beach chair in the water and be up close to watch your child. **[M]** ECV users must transfer to a standard wheelchair to enter. Wheelchair users can enter from the pathway and zero-depth entry points across from the Warming Hut and from the ramp from the Boardwalk near the Iced Cappuccino wagon. Standard wheelchairs only permitted in the pool as far as the axle on the main wheels.	**Pool** C-Ticket All ages

☐ Ski Patrol Training Camp [D-3] | **7** | **6** | **7** |

Pre-teen fun with floating icebergs, tube slalom, and slides. Ages 6–12.	**Playground**

☐ Tike's Peak [D-5] | **6** | **6** | **7** |

Miniature version of Blizzard Beach for those age 0–6 and their folks. **[B]** Children in diapers must wear snug-fitting plastic pants or special swim diapers. **[L]** Must be 48 in./122 cm. or shorter. **[M]** Wheelchairs can enter Tike's Peak wading pool via zero-depth entry points surrounding the area.	**Playground** C-Ticket

☐ Mt. Gushmore Chair Lift [D-5] | **2** | **3** | **7** |

Wooden bench-seat gondolas take you up to Mt. Gushmore's family of rides. **[B]** Use Rider Switch—no infants or lap seating allowed. **[F]** Heights, no lap bar, feet dangle, travel upward. **[♥][T][M][P][E]** Those with back or neck problems and expectant mothers should not ride. **[M]** Persons traveling in wheelchairs and one companion may access Mt. Gushmore via the lift. Enter to the right of the main queue, remainder of party proceed through standard queue. Guest must transfer from ECV or electric wheelchair to water wheelchair (obtain it from cast member if available). Use chairlift to travel to observation deck or to access Teamboat Springs. **[L]** Weight limit of vehicle is 375 lbs./170 kg.	**Lift to Rides** C-Ticket Ages 3 & up

© Deb Wills

Chairlift in front of Summit Plummet

Downtown Disney

Looking for a delightful break from the theme parks? **Downtown Disney** reigns as a shopping, dining, and entertainment mecca. With the world's largest Disney Store, a unique non-circus circus, and restaurants ranging, quite literally, from soup to nuts, you're sure to find something fun to do.

More than a pedestrian mall, Downtown Disney has **three unique districts**: The Marketplace, which is mostly shops and eateries; Pleasure Island, Disney's nightlife capital; and the newest section, the West Side, with trendy shops and unique restaurants and entertainment venues. Downtown Disney offers the special needs traveler the chance to get away from the hectic pace of the parks. Here you can stop and grab a cappuccino, sit by the water, and people watch. Or, if you'd prefer, you can truly "shop 'til you drop."

By Car—From I-4, take exit 67, then take the first exit and turn right on Buena Vista Dr. Parking is free. The disabled parking spots are located right in front. Tip: The Downtown Disney Marketplace and Pleasure Island parking lots are often packed, especially on the weekends. Try the huge West Side parking lot and stroll/wheel over to the other end of Downtown Disney at your leisure.

By Bus—Buses are available from every Disney resort. From the Magic Kingdom, Epcot, Disney-MGM Studios, or Disney's Animal Kingdom, bus or monorail to a nearby resort and transfer.

By Boat—Resort guests at Port Orleans, Old Key West, and Saratoga Springs can take a boat to the Marketplace.

By Land—Guests at Saratoga Springs Resort, Old Key West, and Hotel Plaza Resorts may find it quicker to walk or wheel.

Admission to Downtown Disney is free, although there is admission charged to enter the clubs on Pleasure Island (see page 301–304).

Most areas in Downtown Disney are **wheelchair/ECV accessible**, and you can rent both wheelchairs and ECVs at Guest Relations at Downtown Disney Marketplace. Wheelchairs can be rented for $7/day with a $20 refundable deposit; ECVs for $30/day with a credit card imprint. (When you return the ECV, the imprint is returned to you; otherwise, you will be charged $500!) You can also rent wheelchairs at the Guest Relations office on the West Side for the same charge. Wheelchairs cannot be rented on Pleasure Island.

AMBIENCE

GETTING THERE

Planning

Your Special Need

Getting There

Staying in Style

Touring

Feasting

Resources

Index

Making the Most of Downtown Disney

TIPS

Strollers cannot be rented on Pleasure Island, but can be rented from either Guest Relations location mentioned on the previous page (single strollers only, no doubles!). Cost is the same as for wheelchairs: $7/day with a $20 refundable deposit.

To get from Pleasure Island to the West Side, avoid the steep stairs by using the **pathway** along the parking lot (near Planet Hollywood) or the elevator at the West End Stage (near the restrooms).

There's a **ramp** that leads along Rainforest Café in the Marketplace, down to Cap'n Jack's. There's another ramp leading up from the marina there that goes along the waterfront and leads up from the Dock Stage, making the area completely wheelchair/ECV accessible.

Companion-assisted restrooms are located behind Once Upon a Toy. There is also a companion restroom located in the Once Upon A Toy shop. Other restrooms scattered around Downtown Disney have at least one accessible stall.

© Debra Martin Koma

Companion restrooms are roomy

Text Typewriter TTY Phones are located on Pleasure Island near Motion, on the West Side near the AMC Movie Theatre, and near the restrooms outside of Cirque du Soleil. And a multilingual information kiosk can be found at the West Side.

For **international visitors**, a prepaid international phone card vending machine is located near the Marketplace's Guest Relations office.

Kids love to frolic in the **water play fountain** (see page 252) near the Marketplace bus stop entrance and Once Upon a Toy.

Although most of the **restaurants** located at Downtown Disney are owned and operated by outside interests (Cap'n Jack's being the notable exception), most will still strive to accommodate special diets if they have adequate notice. Follow our procedures for making special dietary requests in Chapter 2. We assess each of the eateries in Downtown Disney in Chapter 6.

For **more information** and answers to questions, call Downtown Disney Guest Relations at 407-828-3058.

Making the Most of
Downtown Disney

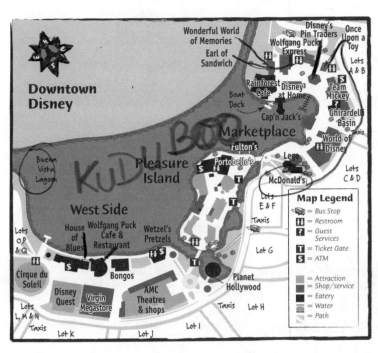

Downtown Disney

Wonderful World
of Memories
Earl of
Sandwich

Disney's
Pin Traders
Wolfgang Puck
Express

Once
Upon a
Toy

Lots
A & B

Rainforest Disney
Cafe at Home

Boat
Dock

Team
Mickey

Cap'n Jack's

Ghirardelli
Basin

Marketplace

World of
Disney

Fulton's

Buena
Vista
Lagoon

Pleasure
Island

Portobello's

Lego

Lots
C & D

McDonald's

West Side

Taxis

Lots
E & F

Lot G

Lots
O,P
& Q

House
of
Blues

Wolfgang Puck
Cafe &
Restaurant

Wetzel's
Pretzels

Cirque du
Soleil

Bongos

Disney
Quest

Virgin
Megastore

AMC
Theatres
& shops

Planet
Hollywood

Lots
L, M & N

Taxis

Lot K

Lot J

Lot I

Taxis

Lot H

Map Legend

= Bus Stop
= Restroom
= Guest
  Services
T = Ticket Gate
S = ATM

= Attraction
= Shop/service
= Eatery
= Water
= Path

The new-age circus company **Cirque du Soleil** has a show on the West Side called La Nouba (from the French "to live it up"). It is a remarkable performance featuring acrobats, clowns, jugglers, dancers, aerialists, and original music (and not one animal!). While the bright lights and costumes and loud music may be overstimulating to some, it is still a fantastic 90 minutes worth experiencing if you can! Note that there are some strobe light effects at the beginning of the performance. The huge theater is accessible for wheelchairs and ECVs, as is the boutique located on the lower level. Remember to request wheelchair seating when purchasing your tickets. Shows are at 6:00 pm and 9:00 pm, Tues.-Sat. Tickets are $63-$91/adults and $42-$63/kids ages 3-11. Not recommended for very young children. Call 407-939-7600 or visit the box office on the West Side.

The **theaters** at the AMC 24 Theatres Complex sport stadium seating, most with retractable armrests. Theaters offer wheelchair seating. Some shows offer reflective or closed captioning, assistive listening, or descriptive listening devices (which describe the action/scenes in a movie for people with vision impairment). Visit: http://moviewatcher.com/theatres/theatre_information.jsp?unit=572.

SHOPPING

Shopping at Downtown Disney

Most **shops** in the Marketplace open at 9:30 am, while West Side shops open at 10:30 am. Closing is at 11:00 pm, with seasonal variations.

Just as at the theme parks, your Downtown Disney **purchases** can be delivered to your Disney resort. In fact, at Once Upon a Toy, there are touch-screens near the cashier's desk that allow you to arrange for this service yourself.

While all of the shops in the Marketplace are accessible in theory, many are so **crammed with merchandise** that they are difficult to get around in. In addition, they all have heavy manual doors—no electric doors—making entry and exit awkward for someone in a wheelchair/ECV or struggling with a stroller. Some shops are also worth singling out for aspects that matter to special needs travelers:

Basin, which features bath and facial products, has many of its soaps and fragrances out in the open—if you are sensitive to strong scents, you may want to avoid this shop.

Once Upon a Toy, which opened in the last few years, is very accessible, as mentioned previously. Not only does it have a companion restroom, all restrooms feature handrails, and there is Braille signage.

Lego Imagination Center has an extensive play area outside, perfect for letting off some steam.

Ronald's Fun House (a.k.a. McDonald's) also has a whimsical play area for kids.

World of Disney (the world's largest Disney Store, is huge—it's easy to get lost or disoriented when wandering around in here.

Goofy's Candy Company features some sugar-free choices.

West Side shopping is also mostly accessible. Some shops to note in this section for special needs considerations:

Disney's Candy Cauldron features some sugar-free items.

Hoypoloi is so crowded with merchandise that a wheelchair or ECV user would find it nearly impossible to maneuver.

Sosa Family Cigars often has the odor of cigar smoke emanating from its doors—those sensitive to smoke should avoid it.

Starabilias (collectibles) specifically requests that no strollers be brought into the store. Wheelchairs/ECVs are welcome, of course, but users might find it hard to navigate in narrow aisles.

DisneyQuest

DisneyQuest is an indoor "theme park" housed in a big, blue, five-story building at Downtown Disney West Side. It features ride simulators, high-tech games, and hands-on activities for young and old alike. Attractions run the gamut from simple video arcade games to a build-your-own coaster simulator. Here's general information about DisneyQuest for the visitor with special needs:

Hours vary by season. Peak season: 11:30 am–11:00 pm, Sundays–Thursdays, and 11:30 am–midnight on Fridays and Saturdays.

As with Disney's theme park admission, you pay a single all-day price and enjoy **unlimited use** of all rides, games, and activities (excluding games that award prizes—a 20-credit card costs $5). Adults pay $36.21 for a full day, and kids ages 3-9 pay $29.82. Children under 10 must be accompanied by an adult, but you can leave the older kids here while you shop elsewhere. Annual passes are available—see page 204. DisneyQuest admission is included in the Magic Your Way with Plus Pack Option and Premium Annual Passes, but it is not an option on the old Park Hopper Plus passes. Discount admissions may be available after 10:00 pm. Note that DisneyQuest will turn guests away once they have reached maximum capacity.

Best times to visit are during the mornings and afternoons and on the weekends. It gets pretty busy in the evenings, after other parks are closed. Crowds are *huge* on foul-weather days.

No strollers are allowed in the DisneyQuest building. Stroller parking is located right outside the main entrance, but most of the experiences here are for older children. This might be one time when it's better to leave Baby at home with a sitter.

Smoking is prohibited throughout the DisneyQuest building.

The main **Information Desk** is located on the first floor, to the left. This is also a Lost & Found. Coat check is on the opposite end of the first floor. There is a TTY phone located on the first floor along with the standard phone bank.

Restrooms are all wheelchair/ECV accessible, with at least one accessible stall, but there are no companion-assisted restrooms. Restrooms are located on the first, fourth, and fifth floors.

Planning

Your Special Need

Getting There

Staying in Style

Touring

Feasting

Resources

Index

INFORMATION

Making the Most of DisneyQuest

There is a **height measuring station** located on the first floor entrance—it's Genie from the movie Aladdin. Measure your group members before you start out, to avoid disappointment later.

Important Note: To purchase any of the Create Zone items (excluding Sticker Shot!), you must do so at the Guest Gallery within 10 minutes after making your creation.

Your adventure begins when you **board the "Cybrolator"** (elevator)—you're treated to a short film featuring the Genie from Aladdin, who briefs you on the experiences to come. When you reach the Ventureport on the third floor, you'll find you can enter four zones: Explore Zone, Score Zone, Create Zone, and Replay Zone. Each zone groups the attractions (described below) by theme. Each zone spans at least two floors, with various stairs, elevators, and pathways linking them. This makes for a bewildering maze—study the map to orient yourself before you get started.

First-time visitors should **spend time exploring** the entire place before splitting up. While you're at it, choose a meeting place and time. The Wonderland Café is a good choice with places to sit, and the Ventureport on the third floor is highly visible.

Allow at least 4-5 hours to tour, more if you love arcades. Be sure to wear a wristwatch—it's easy to lose track of time! It's faster to use the stairs to go up or down one level, if you can. On the other hand, the elevators are less disorienting than the curving staircases.

Relatively quiet cool-down spots include VenturePort on level 3 and Wonderland Cafe and its Internet alcoves on level 4.

The Cheesecake Factory operates two accessible counter-service eateries in DisneyQuest. FoodQuest is located on the top floor (see page 344) and offers a variety of pizzas, burgers, sandwiches, and wraps, including some vegetarian options (pasta with marinara sauce, salads, chips and salsa), plus a few tempting desserts. On the fourth floor below, the Wonderland Café (see page 345) features more in the line of snacks and desserts, as well as fancy coffee concoctions. As a diversion, you can also jump online and surf the Internet on limited-use computer terminals located in some of the booths.

Questions? Call 407-828-4600 or visit http://www.disneyquest.com. There's also a DisneyQuest kiosk in Downtown Disney Marketplace.

Charting the Attractions at DisneyQuest

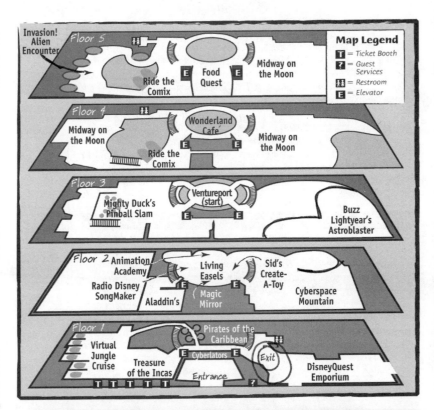

Aladdin's Magic Carpet Ride [Floor 2, Explore Zone]

	6	8	6

Don virtual reality goggles for a wild ride on Aladdin's magic carpet. Swoop through Agrabah and the Cave of Wonder to search for jewels and free the Genie. Seating is similar to sitting astride a motorcycle. **[Q]** There's a real chance of motion sickness here, due to all the swooping and flying you do on your "carpet". **[A][U][I]** The noise level is high—could cause overstimulation. Also there are lots of bright, flashing lights. **[A][U][C][♥][T][I][P][E][S][L]** Often has long waits with few places to sit. **[F][V]** The area is very dark. **[H]** Closed captioning available. **[M]** Wheelchair/ECV users may remain in chair, since the low seats can be adjusted. **[V]** You must wear special goggles to experience the effects of this ride.

Virtual
D-Ticket
Ages 6 & up
Dizziness
4-min. ride

Animation Academy [Floor 2, Create Zone]

	6	6	6

Take your seat at a computer workstation as an instructor draws out your artistry. Hands-on lessons in drawing and/or animating characters. Several 20-minute lessons are offered. After the class, you can buy your creation. **[A][U][C][♥][T][I][P][E][S][L]** Often has long waits with few places to sit and wait. **[M]** Wheelchair/ECV users may remain in chair. **[V]** May have difficulty viewing the computer screen images.

Hands-On
D-Ticket
Ages 6 & up
20 min.

Charting the Attractions at DisneyQuest
(continued)

	Deb Wills' Rating	Deb Koma's Rating	Readers' Rating

☐ Buzz Lightyear's Astroblasters [Floor 3, Replay Zone] 🧍

5 9 7

Ride fully enclosed two-person bumper cars mounted with "cannons" that shoot large rubber balls. The driver pilots to scoop up ammo, and the gunner fires on other cars to make them spin out of control. You can ride solo, but it really is better with a companion. **[Q]** Motion sickness possible—bumper cars spin when hit by rubber balls. **[A][U][I]** The noise level is high—could cause overstimulation. Lots of flashing lights, too. **[♥][T][M][P][E][S]** Because the bumper cars collide frequently, you should be in good health and free from high blood pressure, heart, back, or neck problems. Expectant mothers should not ride. **[M]** Wheelchair/ECV users must transfer out to experience. **[F][S][V]** The area is very dark. **[F]** The cars have doors that close them in—can create a very claustrophobic feeling. **[S][L]** Enclosed cars may be difficult to get in and out of quickly. **[L]** 51 in./130 cm. height restriction.

Bumper Cars
D-Ticket
Ages 9 & up
Very bumpy

☐ CyberSpace Mountain [Floor 2, Create Zone] 🧍

2 8 9

Design and ride your own coaster! Start by choosing a theme and designing the coaster tracks on a computer screen. Then get strapped into a two-person flight simulator (seats are very small!) to experience your coaster, or choose from a ready-made coaster program. Be prepared to be shaken, rattled, and rolled on a ride more dizzying than the real thing. Note: Anyone can create a coaster, but you must meet the height restriction to board the simulator. **[Q]** The simulator rotates a full 360 degrees, creating a sensation that you are inverting like a real coaster. Motion sickness potential is high. **[A][U][I]** The noise level is very high—could cause overstimulation. **[A][U][C][♥][T][I][P][E][S][L]** Often has long waits with few places to sit. **[♥][T][M][P][E][S]** You should be in good health and free from high blood pressure, and heart, back, or neck problems. Expectant mothers should not ride. **[M]** You must be ambulatory to experience. There is a wheelchair lift to bring you to the ride simulators, but you must climb up and then down a couple of steps to get into the simulators themselves. **[F][V]** The area is very dark. In addition, the simulators are very closed in. If you have a fear of small spaces, you may not be comfortable, but there is a "panic button" that you can press at any time to stop the ride immediately. **[L]** 51 in./130 cm. height restriction. People of size may have trouble fitting comfortably in the simulator seats.

Simulator
E-Ticket
Ages 9 & up
Upside-down during inversions

☐ Invasion! An ExtraTERRORestrial Alien Encounter [Floor 5, Score Zone]

2 5 5

Dash across the galaxy to rescue Earth colonists from an invading horde in this simulator ride that borrows characters and fun from the former Magic Kingdom attraction. One teammate pilots the rescue vehicle, while three other teammates keep the bad guys at bay. Great pre-show film. **[Q]** Motion sickness warning. **[A][U][I]** The noise level is high—could cause overstimulation. **[A][U][C][♥][T][I][P][E][S][L]** Often has long waits with few places to sit. **[F][V]** The area is very dark. **[H]** Closed captioning available. **[M]** Wheelchair/ECV users must transfer out to the "cockpit" to experience. **[S][L]** Enclosed cockpit may be difficult to get in and out of quickly.

Simulator
E-Ticket
Ages 7 & up
Violent theme

Charting the Attractions
at DisneyQuest
(continued)

	Deb Wills' Rating	Deb Koma's Rating	Readers' Rating

☐ **Living Easels** [Floor 2, Create Zone] — 5 5 4

Use a touch-sensitive screen to draw animated landscapes. You can buy printouts of your finished product at the Guest Gallery. **[A][U][C][♥][T][I][P][E][S][L]** *Often has long waits with few places to sit and wait.* **[M]** *Wheelchair/ECV users may remain in chairs.* **[V]** *May have difficulty viewing images on the screen.*

Hands-On / B-Ticket / Ages 3 & up

☐ **Magic Mirror** [Floor 2, Create Zone] — 4 5 5

Turn a photo of yourself into a wacky portrait. You can buy your creation at the Guest Gallery. **[A][U][C][♥][T][I][P][E][S][L]** *Often has long waits with few places to sit and wait.* **[M]** *Wheelchair/ECV users may remain in their chairs.*

Hands-On / B-Ticket / Ages 4 & up

☐ **Midway on the Moon** [Floors 4 & 5, Replay Zone] — 7 8 5

Disney-themed versions of arcade games like Ursula's Whirlpool and traditional games like Skeeball. Purchase "points" to play ($5 for 20 credits) then redeem for prizes. **[M]** *Wheelchair/ECV users may remain in their chairs.*

Arcade / A-Ticket / Ages 5 & up

☐ **Classic Games** [Floors 3 & 5, Replay Zone] — 7 8 5

Walk down Arcade Memory Lane, with games that were popular in years gone by, like Defender, Pac Man, and Donkey Kong. No additional charge. **[M]** *Wheelchair/ECV users must be able to stand to access these older games.*

Arcade / A-Ticket / Ages 5 & up

☐ **Sports Arena Arcade** [Floor 4, Replay Zone] — 6 6 5

Sports-themed arcade games. No additional charge. **[M]** *Wheelchair/ECV users must be able to stand to access many of these games. Ages 5 & up.*

Arcade / A-Ticket

☐ **The Underground Arcade** [Floor 3, Replay Zone] — 5 7 5

Popular video arcade games. No additional charge. **[M]** *Wheelchair/ECV users must be able to stand to access many of these games. Ages 5 & up.*

Arcade / A-Ticket

☐ **Mighty Ducks Pinball Slam** [Floor 3, Score Zone] 🏃 — 5 8 7

Imagine you're inside an old-style pinball machine and you have the idea behind this game. You stand on a platform with handles and use body motion/weight to move a "puck" around the huge screen projected in front of you. You must also "body check" opponents on this simulator. **[A][U][C][♥][T][I][P][E][S][L]** *There are very few places to sit and wait.* **[A][U][I][S][♥][T][M][P][E][S]** *Strenuous! You need to be able to rock your body back and forth and around to maneuver your "puck" on the screen. You may experience some sudden, sharp movements. For these reasons, you should be in good health and free from high blood pressure, heart, back, or neck problems. Expectant mothers should not ride. There is one stationary platform if you don't want to rock, but want to watch the play up close. If there are no children waiting, you may be able to use it. Ask a cast member.* **[M]** *Wheelchair/ECV users may remain in their chair.* **[Q]** *Moving platform and wide-screen video may be disorienting.* **[B][L]** *48 in./122 cm. height restriction. Those under 48" should talk with a cast member—there is one stationary platform with a joystick for little ones who don't weigh enough to move the puck, yet still want to pretend they are playing.*

Simulator / D-Ticket / Ages 9 & up

············· ▶

Sidebar tabs: Planning | Your Special Need | Getting There | Staying in Style | Touring | Feasting | Resources | Index

Charting the Attractions
at DisneyQuest
(continued)

Deb Wills' Rating · Deb Koma's Rating · Readers' Rating

■ Pirates of the Caribbean: Battle for Buccaneer Gold [Floor 1] 🧍‍♂️

5 · **10** · **9**

You and up to four shipmates enter this 3-D simulated sea battle in quest of pirate gold. Fire virtual cannonballs against your foes and feel the deck shudder when hit. **[A][U][C][♥][T][I][P][E][S][L]** Lines can be very long, and there are very few places to sit. **[A][U][I][S][V]** You must wear special goggles to experience the 3-D effects. **[♥][T][M][P][E][C][S]** You need to move from cannon to cannon, pulling a cord to fire on the enemy ships. As your "ship" is hit, you feel the impact. The deck rocks like a real ship. Thus, you should be in good health and free from high blood pressure, heart, back, or neck problems. Expectant mothers should not ride. **[F]** The attraction takes place in a darkened, enclosed booth. During the experience, buccaneer skeletons fly out at you. There are also many perilous situations—being shot at, boat sinking, etc. **[M]** ECV users must transfer into a standard wheelchair. The movement effects will be turned off for those in a wheelchair. **[Q]** Realistic film and moving deck create sensation of being on the water—motion sickness potential is high. **[B][L]** 35 in./89 cm. height restriction. **[S][V]** The booth is very dark, and as the motion simulator rocks back and forth, footing becomes unsteady.

Simulator
E-Ticket
Ages 7 & up

Violent theme

■ Radio Disney SongMaker [Floor 2, Create Zone]

5 · **5** · **4**

Create your own hit song in a soundbooth. Combine styles and lyrics for laughs. You can buy a CD of it. **[A][U][C][♥][T][I][P][E][S][L]** Often has long waits with few places to sit. **[M]** Wheelchair/ECV users may remain in their chairs.

Hands-On
D-Ticket
Ages 4 & up

■ Ride the Comix [Floors 4 and 5, Score Zone]

2 · **7** · **5**

Swing your laser sword to battle comic strip villains in this 3-D virtual reality game. **[A][U][I]** The noise level is high—could cause overstimulation. Lots of flashing lights/lasers, too. **[A][U][C][♥][T][I][P][E][S][L]** Often has long waits with few places to sit and wait. **[♥][T][M][P][E][C][S]** Strenuous! You battle with a heavy "sword." **[F]** Lots of scary monsters "attack" you. **[M]** Wheelchair/ECV users must be able to sit on a stool. **[Q]** High potential for motion sickness. **[S][V][C][T][P]** You must wear heavy virtual reality headgear to see the 3-D effect.

Virtual
D-Ticket
Ages 8 & up
May feel dizzy
4 min.

■ Sid's Create-A-Toy [Floor 2, Create Zone]

3 · **4** · **5**

Create a demented toy from spare toy parts—on a computer screen. You can buy a real version of your creation. **[M]** Wheelchair/ECV users may remain in chairs.

Hands-On
B-Ticket

■ Virtual Jungle Cruise [Floor 1]

5 · **9** · **6**

Board a raft, grab a paddle, and take a whitewater river cruise back in time on this motion simulator ride. Dr. Wayne Szalinski guides you and your teammates on this riotous journey over waterfalls and into the age of the dinosaurs. **[A][U][I]** You occasionally get spritzed with water. **[♥][C][P][T][M][P][E][S]** You need to paddle as if on a raft—can be quite difficult. For this reason, you should be in good health and free from high blood pressure, heart, back, or neck problems. Expectant mothers should not ride. **[F]** Lots of dinosaurs spring out at you. There are also many perilous situations—going over waterfalls, into fire, etc. **[M]** Wheelchair/ECV users must transfer out and board the raft to experience this. The raft on the far left is accessible. **[Q]** Realistic film of whitewater rafting creates sensation of being on the water—motion sickness potential is high.

Simulator
E-Ticket
Ages 6 & up

Paddling

Pleasure Island

If you're looking for nightlife, **Pleasure Island** is the place. You can celebrate New Year's Eve every midnight, dance until 2:00 am, or go for the gags at a comedy club. Located smack-dab in the middle of Downtown Disney, Pleasure Island is an entertainment extravaganza.

Pleasure Island also has its share of small shops: Changing Attitudes (clothing), DTV (Disney fashions), Reel Finds (movie memorabilia), SuperStar Studios (star in a video/record a song), and Zen Zone (massage beds). (Pleasure Island eatery details are on page 343.)

The West End Stage is the focus of the nightly New Year's Eve show at midnight. A live band performs much of the evening, and at midnight, there are fireworks overhead. Farther down the street, the Hub Video Stage occasionally hosts performances by smaller bands. The small Waterfront Stage is used on special occasions. We describe the nightclubs themselves starting on page 303.

By Bus—Frequent buses are available from Disney resorts. From a park, bus or monorail to a nearby resort and transfer to a Downtown Disney bus. Get off at the second Downtown Disney stop.
By Car—Follow signs to Downtown Disney. Parking is free. If you intend to drink, please designate a driver. Designated drivers: As you pass through the turnstiles, let the cast member know that you're not imbibing, and you will get two free soft drink coupons.
By Boat—From Port Orleans, Old Key West, and Saratoga Springs, take a boat to the Marketplace and walk or wheel.

Most Pleasure Island **clubs are open** from about 7:00 pm to 2:00 am most nights to guests 18 years and older (younger kids can come with a parent or legal guardian). You'll need a valid driver's license or state ID (with photo). They really do "proof" you at the door, and if you're over 21, you'll get a special wristband that allows you to imbibe. You must be over 21 to enter BET SoundStage Club and Mannequins Dance Palace (some nights)! If you bring kids, be prepared for some good-natured ribbing from performers.

Time flies here, so **arrive early** in the evening to make the most of your visit. The clubs start hopping as soon as they open at 7:00-9:00 pm.

Mondays and Thursdays are **Cast Member Nights** and tend to be crowded. To escape the crowds and noise, consider the Comedy Warehouse during the busiest times of the evening—usually between 10:00 pm and midnight.

Planning

Your Special Need

Getting There

INFORMATION

Staying in Style

Touring

Feasting

Resources

Index

Making the Most of
at Pleasure Island

Don't miss the nightly **New Year's Eve show** at the West End Stage, beginning at 11:45 pm. Note that stairs and restrooms near the West End are closed before and during the New Year's Eve fireworks show. A good spot to watch the nightly New Year's Eve show is from the access ramp in front of Adventurers Club. The area immediately in front of the West End Stage is reserved for wheelchair viewing.

Pleasure Island's streets are now **admission-free** at all times. Stroll through—some clubs may be open for a free "sample" and the live stage is rocking for all. Admission is checked at club entrances, and tickets can be bought at some shops as well as the ticket booths.

Pleasure Island **Multi-Club ticket** good for all clubs on the island for one evening: $22.32/person (adult or child). Pleasure Island Single-Club Ticket, good for only one club/evening (not including Comedy Warehouse or Adventurers Club): $10.60. Ask about discounts.

Alcoholic beverages are even served on the streets of Pleasure Island. Adults 21 and older get wristbands to show they can drink. All Pleasure Island clubs are **nonsmoking**.

If you find the excitement too much, or just want to go somewhere romantic with that special someone, head for the "**hidden patio**." Go down the stairs beside the Adventurers Club, or go down the stairs beside the West End Stage (or take the elevator) and turn right before the bridge for ramp access.

A **TTY phone** is located with standard phones near the Motion club.

All areas are **wheelchair accessible**. All clubs have elevators. There's a long, steep incline rising from the Hub Stage to the West End Stage.

Elevators and stairs at West End entrance may be closed from 11:30 pm to midnight for fireworks—you must detour to the entrance by Mannequins (see map).

Wheelchairs cannot be rented on Pleasure Island. You can rent both wheelchairs and ECVs elsewhere in Downtown Disney, however. Guest Relations at Marketplace rents both ECVs and wheelchairs; West Side rents only wheelchairs (see page 203 for details). Strollers cannot be rented on Pleasure Island, either, but can be rented from either Guest Relations location mentioned above (single strollers only, no doubles!).

Charting the Attractions at Pleasure Island

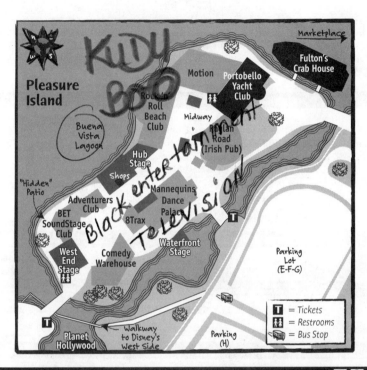

Planning
Your Special Need
Getting There
Staying in Style
Touring
Feasting
Resources
Index

8Trax

	9 8 6
Disco in all its Saturday Night Fever glory! The sound is classic '70s (Thursday is '80s night the floor is packed and illuminated, and dancers are enthusiastic! **[A][U][C][♥][T][I][P][E][S][L]** Lines for this popular nightspot can be VERY long, and there are very few places to sit and wait. **[M]** Wheelchair/ECV accessible. **[S][V]** The club is very dark, and the floor is uneven.	**Dance**
	C-Ticket

Adventurers Club

	10 10 8
In all ways, this is the most "Disney" of the clubs on Pleasure Island (and our absolute favorite). Come with a sense of adventure and be ready to join in. You can be inducted into the fictitious club, learn the secret greeting, and sing the club song! Be prepared for the unexpected, the quirky, and the hilarious. In true Disney fashion, the décor matches the theme here perfectly. The walls are covered with trophies, mementos (some even talk!), and photos amassed by the club members! You may be greeted by the club's stoic butler, the matronly Club President, or even a French maid. Different shows are held throughout the night in the Mask Room, Treasure Room, and Library. Though the Adventurers Club can seem a little confusing at first, just wait a while—something's sure to happen wherever you are, when you least expect it. **[F]** If you're shy, be aware that cast members do involve the audience in the improvisation here. **[M]** Wheelchair/ECV users may remain in their chair. Elevator is located immediately to the left after entering club. When club is crowded, it is difficult to maneuver from room to room.	**Comedy**
	E-Ticket
	Shows run continuously from 8:00 pm to 1:00 am
	Audience participation

Charting the Attractions
at Pleasure Island
(continued)

Deb Wills' Rating
Deb Koma's Rating
Readers' Rating

BET SoundStage Club

| | 5 | 5 | 4 |

Contemporary music and dancing for guests 21 and over. The club is one of the smaller ones, but the intimate atmosphere can be enjoyable. **[M]** Wheelchair/ECV accessible. **[S][V]** The club is very dark, and the floor is uneven.

Dance
C-Ticket

Comedy Warehouse

| | 9 | 9 | 9 |

Houses the Who, What, and Wherehouse Players, a comedy improvisation troupe that delivers hilarious skits, standup acts, sketches, and adult humor "Disney-style." **[A][U][C][♥][T][I][P][E][S][L]** Lines for this popular nightspot can be VERY long if you've just missed a show, and there are very few places to sit and wait. **[F]** If you're shy, be aware that cast members do involve the audience in the improvisation here. **[M]** Wheelchair/ECV users may remain in their chair. Accessible entrance is located on the left side as you're facing the Warehouse, down a long ramp. Ask a cast member for directions.

Comedy
D-Ticket
Rib-tickling

Mannequins Dance Palace

| | 3 | 7 | 6 |

Voted the #1 dance club in the Southeast, this is the place for the hottest dance mix and the biggest sound and lighting system. Bouncers in tuxes proof you and let in a few people at a time. Very, very loud. **[A][U][C][♥][T][I][P][E][S][L]** Lines for this popular nightspot can be VERY long, and there are very few places to sit and wait. **[M]** Wheelchair/ECV accessible. **[S][V]** The club is very dark, and the floor is uneven.

Dance
E-Ticket
Must be 21+

Motion

| | 4 | 6 | 7 |

A big dance floor and clean, open layout are all that distinguish this large club. Top 40 and alternative dance. **[M]** Wheelchair/ECV users may remain in their chair.

Dance
C-Ticket

Rock 'n' Roll Beach Club

| | 7 | 7 | 6 |

Offers fans of classic and modern rock a crowded dance floor, live "cover" bands, and a DJ. You can also play pinball and munch out on nachos. **[M]** Wheelchair/ECV users may remain in their chair.

Dance
D-Ticket

Irish Pub Coming to Pleasure Island

Raglan Road, an authentic Irish pub and restaurant, is scheduled to open in summer 2005 in the space formerly occupied by the Pleasure Island Jazz Company. The pub will offer traditional and contemporary Irish music, storytelling, and dance. It will be owned and operated by Great Irish Pubs Florida, Inc., which is responsible for "Nine Fine Irishmen" at the New York-New York Hotel & Casino in Las Vegas. The menu for the new restaurant is expected to be a blend of traditional Irish fare with modern twists. Pleasure Island club admission will not be required for entry into the pub.

Other Things to Do

Behind the Scenes Tours—Curious about how the magic is made at Walt Disney World? Want to learn more about your favorite park? Then perhaps you want to take one of the special tours offered at Walt Disney World. For a price, you can spend hours learning about the art and architecture of World Showcase in Epcot, take a full day tour of the theme parks and backstage areas, or learn about the Magic Kingdom. Most tours have age requirements (usually 16 and up)—be sure to inquire before booking at 407-WDW-TOUR. **[G][D]** Some tours include a meal (such as the Keys to the Kingdom and Backstage Magic). If you have special dietary needs, make sure you mention this when booking the tour, or at least several days before you arrive. **[B]** Strollers provided for small children on the Behind the Seeds Tour. **[M]** Most tours are accessible by wheelchair/ECV. ECV users must transfer to standard wheelchair for Behind the Seeds Tour. Be sure to mention that you will have a wheelchair when booking. **[C][♥][T][M][P][E][S][L][V]** Most tours require a great amount of walking outdoors. Tour participants should be in good health and free from heart, head, neck, and back ailments, or consider using an ECV. **[H]** The Wild by Design Tour in Disney's Animal Kingdom is presented with special amplifying headsets. **[H][T][M][V]** When making tour reservation, be sure to notify cast member if you will have a service animal so that they can make proper arrangements. **[E]** Pregnant women may not participate in the Segway around the World tour or the Dolphins in Depth experience. **[L]** Most tours have no size

© Deb Wills

Co-Author Deb Wills dons a wetsuit during the Epcot Seas Aqua Tour

requirements, but the Segway around the World tour does have a 250 lb./113 kg. limit. **[V]** Special one-on-one guided tours for those with vision impairments can be arranged through Disney's VIP Tours at 407-560-4033. Other tours can accommodate those with vision impairments—just be sure to mention your requirements when booking.

BoardWalk—Pleasure Island doesn't have a monopoly on nightclubs in Walt Disney World—the BoardWalk resort has its own entertainment complex with clubs, restaurants, and entertainment. Jellyrolls is a dueling piano bar that serves drinks and free popcorn ($7 cover, 21 and up, smoking allowed). Atlantic Dance Hall serves specialty drinks while open-request DJ music lures you onto the floor (no cover, 21 and up, open Tuesday–Saturday). ESPN Club (see page 348) is a popular sports bar. Midway games and street performers add to the fun. For details and directions to the BoardWalk resort, see pages 121-124. **[R]** Several nightclubs here encourage the sale of alcoholic beverages. **[U]** Arcade and carnival-type games here are fun and good for blowing off steam. **[M]** Wheelchair/ECV users may remain in their chair, but some shops and restaurants have narrow entrances and are difficult to navigate. **[M][S][V]** The BoardWalk boards may be uneven in spots.

Planning

Your Special Need

Getting There

Staying in Style

Touring

Feasting

Resources

Index

Other Things to Do
(continued)

Golf—The Walt Disney World Resort boasts 99 holes of golf on five championship courses and one nine-hole course, and it consistently lands on a variety of prestigious "top golf resort" lists. All courses are open to the public and feature full-service facilities, including driving ranges, pro shops, cafes, and lessons. If you're staying at a Disney resort hotel, you'll get free transportation to the links for your scheduled tee times. For more details and to reserve tee times, call 407-WDW-GOLF. We also recommend Marc Schwartz's Unofficial WDW Golf Site at http://www.wdwgolf.com. **[C][♥][T][I][M][P][S][L]** Courses are accessible for wheelchair/ECV users. If you can use a regular golf cart, Disney will give you a "limited mobility" flag that can be put on the cart to identify to other players that you may require more time than usual. If you cannot use a regular cart, there is <u>one</u> special golf cart available that enables you to rotate the seat to hit the ball without having to leave the cart. The golf bag is specially positioned for access to the clubs as well. The cart also has hand controls and a limited mobility flag. It is kept at the Lake Buena Vista golf course, but with at least a half-day notice it can be moved to the other courses as required. Request this cart when you're arranging your tee time, then reconfirm a few days ahead of time by calling the golf event manager at the Lake Buena Vista course. For more information on rules for golfers with disabilities, visit http://www.usga.org/playing/rules/golfers_with_disabilities.html. **[S]** Seniors may enjoy a round of golf instead of another day at the parks!

Fort Wilderness—The campgrounds here offer a respite from the hubbub of the theme parks and get you back to nature with canoeing, boating, fishing excursions, biking, tennis, horseback trail rides, horse-drawn carriage rides, and hayride. The petting farm is free (pony rides cost $3), and so is a visit to the blacksmith shop. There's a nightly campfire program (with character visits and free movies). Trail ride at the resort's Tri-Circle D Livery is a good entry-level horseback riding experience for riders age 9 and up and costs $32. Phone 407-824-2832 for reservations. For more information on Fort Wilderness, see pages 137–140. **[A][U]** Lots of open spaces for running around and blowing off steam. **[G]** Animals, tree pollens abound. Allergy sufferers beware. **[C][B][♥][T][M][P][E][S][L]** Distances between points of interest can be great. **[F]** Lots of animals on the grounds—roaming peacocks, lizards, raccoons, armadillos. **[M]** Wheelchair/ECV users may remain in their chair around the campgrounds. **[L]** Children (ages 2–8) must weigh no more than 80 lbs. (36 kg.) for pony rides. Riders on the horses must weigh no more than 250 lbs. (113 kg.).

Health Clubs & Spas—Many of the deluxe resorts have health clubs with exercise equipment—some even offer massage treatments, steam rooms, and saunas. If you're looking to relax, we recommend the new Saratoga Springs Spa or the Grand Floridian Spa and Health Club. These world-class, full-service centers offer many beauty and wellness treatments, nutrition and fitness counseling, and lots of pampering. If you're hoping to keep up an exercise regimen, visit one of the health clubs located at the deluxe resorts. If you're a guest of that resort, your membership at the club is free. If you're staying elsewhere, you can still work out—you'll just be charged a fee. See our descriptions of the individual resorts starting on page 113 for more details on the health clubs and spas. **[M]** Wheelchair/ECV accessible. **[H][T][M][V]** Service animals may be permitted in some locations—ask in advance. **[♥][P]** Health clubs are great for keeping up exercise routines.

Other Things to Do
(continued)

Tennis—There are seven sets of courts are available around Walt Disney World. Try the Racquet Club at the Contemporary Resort, with six state-of-the-art hydrogrid courts. Call 407-939-7529. *[M]* Most tennis courts are wheelchair/ECV accessible. Ask for details about the individual resort's tennis court when making reservations.

Waterways, Boating, Fishing—If you love the water, you'll surely find something to do on it here. You can rent boats at nearly every deluxe and moderate resort and Downtown Disney. Probably the most popular rentals craft are little, two-person speed boats called Sea Raycers. They're available at most marinas around Disney for $23 per half-hour. Fishing excursions and cane pole rentals are also available in most of those same locations. In 2004, Disney announced an enhanced

© Debra Martin Koma

A Sea Raycer personal watercraft

bass fishing program, in association with BASS, the leading bass fishing organization. You can reserve two-hour, guided, catch-and-release bass fishing expeditions at many Disney marinas. All equipment is provided (even a digital camera to document your catch). Fishing licenses are not needed thanks to the state-licensed guide on board, and participants get a free subscription to Bassmaster Magazine. Excursions accommodate up to five guests and cost $195–$215. Kids 6–12 can go on special one-hour excursions for $30. Phone 407-WDW-BASS for reservations. *[L]* Sea Raycers have a weight limit of 320 lbs./145 kg. *[M][L]* At most rental locations, there's a docked SeaRaycer that you can practice getting into/out of. *[M][S][L]* You must step down into the watercraft. Likewise, getting out may be difficult. *[M]* The pontoon boats can accommodate some wheelchairs. If the chair fits through the gate of the boat railing, you can wheel a manual wheelchair for boarding, then leave it on the boat. The wheelchair user must sit in a boat seat for the ride.

Walt Disney World Speedway—Disney has its own speedway—a one-mile, tri-oval track for auto racing. The race track is home to the Richard Petty Driving Experience, in which participants get to drive or ride at speeds up to 145 mph (233 kph)! You don't really have to be a fan to get a thrill out of this experience. You must be at least 16 for the ride-along program—otherwise there are no health restrictions, but check first with your doctor if you have any concerns. You need to be at least 18 and have a valid driver's license to participate in the driving programs. Riders are subject to strong g-forces. Required to wear special coveralls and helmet in a high-temperature environment. Five-point lap and shoulder harness in vehicle. For Richard Petty Experience details, call 407-939-0130. *[L][M][S]* You need to be able to enter the race car through a window 15″ (38 cm.) high by 30″ (76 cm.) wide, which is 36″ (91 cm.) from the ground. The car doors do not open. *[L]* Usually people who are less than 6′ 8″ (203 cm.) and 280 lbs. (127 kg.) can participate. However, these numbers can vary up or down according to an individual's flexibility and weight distribution.

Other Things to Do
(continued)

Disney's Wide World of Sports Complex—Disney's state-of-the-art athletic center features a 9,500-seat baseball stadium, a 30,000-square-foot fieldhouse, a track and field complex, volleyball, tennis, baseball, softball, football, and more. Because this is a fairly new complex, it is completely accessible, with Braille signage marking restrooms and floor numbers. In 2005, Disney will add another 20 acres of baseball, softball, and multi-sport fields under the sponsorship of Amerada Hess. Admission is $10.75/adults or $8/kids 3–9, tax included. You can enjoy the Multi-Sport Experience covering sports such as football, baseball, and basketball. The 200-acre center is also home to amateur and professional sports, including Atlanta Braves Spring Training and the Tampa Bay Buccaneers training camp. Call 407-828-FANS (407-828-3267), or visit http://www.disneyworldsports.com for more information. *[M]* Wheelchairs are available at the complex's turnstiles (no ECVs). There is no charge, but you must leave some valid form of ID as a "deposit." There is a companion restroom located near the First Aid Center in the baseball stadium, just under the archway for Sections 113–114. Also, there are special wheelchair/ECV seating areas located in the following sections of the stadium: 109 and 111-114 on the lower level; 208, 210, 212, 214, 216, 218, 220 on the upper level. Note that it's a long way up a steep ramp from the parking area to the turnstile and wheelchair rental location. During popular activities like Braves Spring Training games, most parking is in unpaved grassy fields. Guest drop-off area is near the entrance. *[H]* Assistive listening devices can be rented from D-Sport, just past the ticket booths, and may be used at several locations in Disney's Wide World of Sports, including the Baseball Stadium and the Field House. *[V]* Braille signage throughout stadium.

Miniature Golf—Yes, you can even play miniature golf at two themed locations at Disney. Tee times are available for play on the day of; however, you must make these in person. Cost is about $10 for adults and $8 for children, with discounts for Annual Passholders. Hours: 10:00 am to 11:00 pm. Disney's miniature golf courses are as follows:

Fantasia Gardens is located near the Walt Disney World Swan and offers two 18-hole courses. One course is whimsically based on the scenes, characters, and music of Disney's classic animated film, "Fantasia." The other is a "grass" course for the "pro" mini-golfer with wildly undulating par-three and par-four holes from 40–75 feet (12–23 meters) long. There's a companion restroom here, as well as a video game arcade. *[M]* The courses are very accessible by wheelchair, no steps involved. A sidewalk follows the perimeter of the course for those wanting surer footing or wheeling, and there are plenty of benches for sitting and resting. The more challenging course, Fantasia Fairways, may also be more difficult for those with mobility concerns due to its steeper slopes. *[V]* We asked about special "beeping balls" for those with vision impairments, but they are not available.

Winter Summerland is adjacent to Blizzard Beach water park and also offers two courses—one celebrates holidays in the tropics, the other snow! There's medium shade throughout the courses from very tall pine trees. There is no companion restroom here. The background music here gets you in the holiday spirit. *[M]* The courses are very accessible by wheelchair, no steps involved. A sidewalk follows the perimeter of the course for those wanting surer footing or wheeling. *[V]* No special "beeping balls" for those with vision impairments are available here either.

Your Touring Tips and Stories

My boyfriend has multiple sclerosis and is reaching a point where a wheelchair is necessary for any stroll over 50 feet. Disney was the first place we went where he used a wheelchair, and the folks there are so terrific. Every bus was accessible (I'm given to understand that is not always the case, but every bus we saw or rode had the blue and white sign), every employee was kind and helpful, and everywhere we went was much easier than we had feared. Top marks to the folks at Disney for making a life-changing illness a little easier to bear.

–Contributed by anonymous

We have been to Walt Disney World many times over the years, both before our daughter with special needs was born and after. One of the issues our daughter struggles with is endurance. When we know we are going to be in the park late for a show, fireworks, etc., we always rent a stroller late in the day. At the end of the night when everyone is tired (parents included), we can put our daughter in the stroller and not have to carry her through the crowds toward the exit. With our daughter being 6 years old now, she can still fit in the stroller and is more than a handful to have to try and carry.

–Contributed by John Marrinson

I have a child on the autism spectrum and one of the most important things when touring Disney is to use a "tot strap." Even though my child is 10, this strap connecting her to me lets her walk without fear of getting separated from me. It is just too crowded at the parks to take a chance. Also, I buy glowsticks/glow bracelets from home and put them on her in the evenings. When it becomes very dark at night, I can see her easily.

–Contributed by Kalli Mulchi

A few years ago we traveled with my dad, who needed oxygen and was in a wheelchair at the time. When we arrived at the Disney parks, we went directly to Guest Relations and explained our situation. All the parks let us store our extra tanks at their First Aid Stations so that we could change them out at the parks without leaving. Everyone, and I mean *everyone* at the parks was always very willing to help us in any way. We only had to ask.

–Contributed by J. A. Anderson

We had cards with us explaining autism. We handed these cards to people who complained that we were "queue jumping." It worked well most of the time.

– Contributed by an anonymous reader

My daughter was afraid to go on Test Track although she was old enough and tall enough to ride. The cast member pulled her aside and took her to the monitors to see us on the ride in action. She was ready to take a ride after that and loved it. In general, the cast members can make some of the individual attractions a wonderful experience if you have an apprehensive child or adult. I would never have thought I could ask a cast member to show my child how much fun an attraction could be and ease her fear. Prior to this experience I would only ask for general assistance from the cast members.

–contributed by peer reviewer Lydia Economou

Your Touring Tips and Stories
(continued)

Due to arthritis and a variety of medical conditions, my husband can only tour Walt Disney World in a wheelchair. We take his own transport chair, which I push. Disney has to be one of the easiest places in the world to get around in a wheelchair, but there are a couple of odd things to keep in mind. First of all, I would never attempt to travel during a busy time. The bus drivers always load us first, but this is a lot easier and less apt to cause bad feelings among your fellow guests if there is not a huge line waiting to board. Even though the World is relatively flat, there are a couple of spots that nearly did me in—for example, the bridge going over the International Gateway at Epcot is very steep. Finally, time your dining reservations carefully. I made the mistake of trying to get from the front gate of the Magic Kingdom to Cinderella Castle for dinner while the rest of the world lined up for a parade. I now know how salmon must feel trying to swim upstream.
— contributed by Sally Brush

Our son, now 15, has ADHD. Our first trip to Walt Disney World in 2000 was really exhausting for us as we tried to keep up with him and his high level of "energy." Unfortunately, for kids (and adults, I would imagine) who suffer with ADD and ADHD, it is often described as living with a slide show constantly in their head. It is very hard to stay focused on one thing at a time. We figured out that giving Adam the park map to hold on to and focus on was really helpful for those moments when we were not on a particular attraction. It gave him something to look at, hold, and focus on without getting "sensory overload" from all the action taking place around him. He would tell us which attraction, or country in the case of World Showcase, was coming up next and what times the shows were taking place. For him, it was a great way to keep his mind focused and his attention on something helpful and informative. It also gave him a sense of being the "guy in charge," since he was holding the map and had all the answers. Now any time we are at the parks, Adam feels more in control and we never have to deal with that sense of edginess, and that "hyperactive" energy is channeled to something fun and useful!
— contributed by Bradley Smith

This was when I fell in love with Walt Disney World and realized how magical it is: I was traveling with my sister and her family. Her 5-year-old son had two major open heart surgeries, plus several other surgeries. So when we arrived at Star Tours, I was left outside with my nephew and his baby sister. However, he was old enough to know he was missing out on something, so he began to cry when his parents and older brother and sister went inside. There wasn't a crowd, so I explained the situation to the cast member and asked if I could just walk him through so he could see R2D2, C3PO, and the other robots, but not ride the ride. She said yes ... she then told me she had arranged a "test flight" for us. We went up the wheelchair ramp entrance, and when we were at the top, I told the cast members we were there for the "test flight." The three of us were put into a "shuttle" all by ourselves, and they ran the movie of the flight without using the motion. The floor stayed still, and my nephew left with a huge smile on his face! Thanks to Disney's philosophy of making everyone feel welcome, they put smiles on the faces of these kids who have a tough life in the "real" world. It also puts a smile on our (the adults') faces, to leave the stress and worry of everyday life behind for a short time, and partake of some heartwarming "magic."
—contributed by Frances McCarthy

Dining Your Way

Can you believe that the Walt Disney World Resort has more than 300 places to eat? With that many choices, you're sure to find an eatery that meets your special needs, whatever they may be. If anything, there are *too* many choices! So how do you go about deciding which eateries are best for you? That's where we come in. We've been to nearly every restaurant on property at least once and probably several times. We've poured our experience into these pages to help you make the best dining decisions.

This chapter gives you an overview of all your dining options with a variety of special situations in mind so that you can make well-informed decisions. You'll find descriptions of nearly all table-service and counter-service restaurants at both the theme parks and resort hotels, as well as some of the snack shops and carts at the theme parks. Descriptions are organized alphabetically within each park and resort, so you are able to choose the eateries that best meet your needs.

© Elizabeth Shorten

Peer reviewer Elizabeth Shorten gets a special treat

As you make decisions about your meals, be sure to make note of those table-service restaurants for which Advance Reservations (formerly called "Priority Seatings") may be made. These restaurants are the ones that are best able to address your concerns, especially if your special needs are dietary.

Planning

Your Special Need

Getting There

Staying in Style

Touring

Dining

Resources

Index

Deciding on Dining

The first thing to do is **decide how often you want to eat out**. Depending on your situation, you may find it advantageous to bring or buy some food for snacks or meals in your room. Most Disney resorts supply a complimentary refrigerator (it's $10/day additional for value resorts), many include a coffeemaker, and Disney Vacation Club resorts have kitchen facilities, too. You could, of course, eat out for every meal, but if you're traveling with children with ADHD or autism spectrum disorders, for whom long waits are difficult, or with a person who has diabetes or other special dietary needs, it might make sense to have some meals, particularly breakfast, in your room. Light breakfasts are the most practical and the easiest to prepare. It's easy enough to run to the resort's sundries shop and purchase bagels and cream cheese or some cold cereal and milk.

Bright Idea: Bring some favorite snacks/treats from home! Especially remember harder-to-find items like sugar-free candy, low-sodium pretzels or crackers, or dairy-free/gluten-free products. You can also ship snacks from home to arrive at your Disney resort when you do.

What Disney Does for Special Dining Needs

Disney recently revamped all its menus to include what it calls "Balanced Menu Choices and Lifestyle Dining Options." In fact, a special line has been added to all table-service menus: "We are happy to discuss with you and attempt to accommodate any dietary or special needs diets." According to the official statement, all Walt Disney World Resort table-service restaurants that accept Advance Reservations offer "balanced menu choices, and will accommodate lifestyle dining options (such as no-sugar-added, low-fat, low-sodium, low-carb, vegetarian, or vegan)." Counter-service locations also offer balanced menu choices and can accommodate most lifestyle dining options. Menus and guide maps now carry an "Apple Mickey" icon to identify those balanced menu choices. If a special menu request is needed, you should speak with a cast member. Note that dinner shows require 24-hour notice for any special menu request.

Examples of Balanced Menu Choices and Lifestyle Dining Options include: more vegetarian dishes; reduced-fat and reduced-calorie meals and snacks, including no-sugar-added items; and reduced portion options for ice cream, French fries, and popcorn.

Disney has also recently added milk, juice, or a no-sugar beverage (Minute Maid Light Lemonade) as alternatives to soft drinks.

Other special dietary needs: All Walt Disney World Resort table-service restaurants that accept Advance Reservations can accommodate special dietary needs (such as allergies to gluten or wheat, shellfish, soy, lactose or milk, peanuts, tree nuts, fish, or eggs). Special dietary needs can be accommodated if requested at least 72 hours in advance at 407-WDW-DINE (407-939-3463). Also see Kosher Meals on pages 318–319.

Advance Reservations

Nearly every table-service restaurant within Walt Disney World allows you to make Advance Reservations. Prior to May 1, 2005, these were known as "Priority Seatings," but that's about the only difference. Unlike traditional reservations, in which a table would be held for your party at a designated time, Disney's advance reservation system gives you the **first table that becomes available**. The only Disney table-service restaurants that don't accept advance arrangements are some Downtown Disney restaurants, Big River Grille and Brewing Works, and ESPN Club (see detailed listings in this chapter). Additionally, some restaurants DO take traditional reservations, such as Victoria & Albert's, the Swan & Dolphin restaurants (see pages 356–357), and the character meals at Cinderella's Royal Table and Restaurant Akershus (see pages 361–363 for reservation details/policies).

Advance Reservations can be **made before your trip** by calling 407-WDW-DINE (407-939-3463). Call up to 90 days in advance for reservations at most restaurants. (We note any different policies.) We suggest you visit Scott Thomas's handy Priority Seating Calculator at http://pscalculator.net for more Advance Reservation details. Arrangements can also be made the same day in person at Guest Relations, a resort's Lobby Concierge, or by touching *88 on any Disney pay phone or 55 on your Disney resort in-room phone. Be sure to mention if someone in your party uses a wheelchair/ECV.

When you call, you will be asked to **supply the name of the Disney resort** at which you are staying and your date of arrival. If you aren't staying at a Disney resort, no problem—you'll simply need to provide a daytime phone number. Also note that character meals at Cinderella's Royal Table and some special meals require a credit card guarantee—in some cases (Spirit of Aloha Dinner Show, Hoop Dee Doo Musical Revue), your credit card will actually be charged when you make the reservation. You will receive a confirmation number for each successfully arranged reservation. If you are unable to get a reservation, call back about one week before the desired date.

Check in at the restaurant's podium **15 minutes before your seating time**. You may also need to wait anywhere from 5 to 30 minutes for a table to become available, depending upon how busy it is. Some restaurants issue a pager, and most have a comfortable waiting area or bar.

If you later decide not to eat at a particular restaurant, just call Disney again and **cancel your advance reservation**. In the case of the special dinner shows and those meals that require a credit card guarantee, however, be aware that there is a 48-hour cancellation policy.

Planning
Your Special Need
Getting There
Staying in Style
Touring
Dining
Resources
Index

Making Special Dietary Requests

As we mentioned in chapter 2, all Walt Disney World table-service restaurants that accept Advance Reservations (see page 313) try to meet your special needs if you give them adequate notice—at least 72 hours is now required. In fact, even the counter-service eateries and resort food courts are happy to "take requests" with enough fair warning. And, as we found through talking with Disney chefs at various locations, the more warning they have, the better they are able to serve you. The key is to **plan ahead** when you're dealing with a special diet. Here's our step-by-step approach to making special dietary requests:

1. **Choose your restaurants**. A good way to determine your dining spots is to preview the menus. Most of the Disney eatery menus are available online at AllEarsNet.com (http://allearsnet.com/menu/menus.htm). Menus give you an idea of the prices and types of foods available, including many of the ingredients used.

2. Once you've decided on your meals, **make Advance Reservations** for as many eateries as possible. It's best to call (407-939-3463) before you leave for your trip. Tell the cast member you speak to about your specific dietary concerns and s/he will make a notation on your record.

3. For information about dining in the theme park restaurants, you can **call the theme park restaurant management** directly at the telephone numbers listed below. (If no one is available when you call, leave your name and telephone number so they can get back to you!)

   ✔ Magic Kingdom: 407-824-5967
   ✔ Epcot: 407-560-7483
   ✔ Disney-MGM Studios: 407-560-1347
   ✔ Disney's Animal Kingdom: 407-938-2203

4. If you are staying at a Disney resort hotel, **speak to a cast member** at the resort's Lobby Concierge desk upon your arrival to confirm that your specific dining needs have been noted on your dining arrangements. Ask that they call the restaurant for you, so you can speak to a chef. The more specific and individual your needs are, the more lead time the restaurant will require. If you are staying off Disney property, call the main Walt Disney World switchboard (407-824-2222) and ask to be connected to the specific restaurant so that you can confirm they are aware of your special needs.

Important Note: Don't forget to confirm your special dietary requests for any dinner shows you may plan to attend. Events like the Spirit of Aloha dinner require at least 24 hours' notice.

5. If you'll be dining at a resort's food court, visit it or phone during an off-peak time (after the lunch rush, for example) and ask to **talk to a chef**. We've found that most chefs are happy to answer all of your questions about how foods are prepared and which foods are available. Many, if not all, will even ask you specifics so that they can order any special items ahead of time. For example, many places keep a certain number of kosher meals on hand. If you have a large group, though, letting them know in advance allows them to order additional quantities and serve you exactly the foods you want.

6. **Visit theme park counter-service eateries** you want to dine at in the morning to make special requests, like kosher food or sugar-free desserts. Note that counter-service eateries have a book of ingredients used in their offerings—just ask a cast member. Ask to speak to the manager on duty if you have any additional concerns or questions.

7. Even with all these advance plans, however, the message sometimes fails to reach the restaurant or the chef. Be sure to **alert your server at the restaurant** to your special requirements. Most often, the chef will come to your table to discuss what your needs are and then concoct a dish or dishes to your specifications. Also, not all restaurants on Disney property are operated by Disney, so their guidelines on accommodating special dietary needs may be different.

Bright Idea: Disney sometimes changes vendors and recipes, so remember to get updated dietary information before every trip and even while at the restaurant during the visit.

Vegan Snacks

"I'm happy to report that vegan treats abound all over Walt Disney World, if you know where to look. Salty snacks, popcorn, and soft pretzels are available in all four parks. Roasted cashews and cinnamon-glazed almonds and pecans are easy to find. Apple and cherry turnovers from the BoardWalk Bakery are vegan, as are the bear claws found at the Kringla Bakeri og Café in the Norway pavilion. The Main Street Confectionary has a sticky treat called "coconut cashew crisp," very similar in consistency to peanut brittle but minus the peanuts and the butter. There are also a number of prepackaged candies and cookies available in different shops that are vegan—just be sure you read the ingredients. Some of my best finds were cookies in the Norway and Canada pavilions and dark chocolate in the Germany pavilion, as well as some of the prepackaged taffy found in several locations. Obviously, healthier options are available, but if you're looking to satisfy a vegan sweet tooth, don't despair—it's very easy at Walt Disney World!"—contributed by peer reviewer Kitty Smith

Gluten-Free Dining

What does "gluten-free" mean? Gluten is a set of proteins found in wheat flour. (Only wheat is considered to have true gluten, but rye and barley have similar proteins. Oats are also often avoided due to potential cross-contamination during harvesting.) Some folks can't process these proteins properly and need to eliminate them from their diet. If you're one of those individuals, here are the counter-service eateries and snack places, and their foods, we've found around the theme parks that are **safe bets** (and some definite no-no's):

General Food Carts: The turkey legs, strawberry and orange juice bars, frozen lemonade, and Itzakadoozie bars are all gluten-free.

Disney's Animal Kingdom: In Asia, the stir-fry at Chakranadi Chicken Shop is gluten-free. On Discovery Island, Flame Tree Barbecue's ribs, chicken, and salad are all gluten-free. In Africa, there's fresh fruit at Harambe Market and Tusker House's rotisserie chicken, grilled salmon, and salad. The fries at Tusker House may be cross-contaminated. Other gluten-free foods can be found in DinoLand at Restaurantosaurus (salad, french fries, hamburgers) and Petri-Fries (french fries).

In Epcot: The Liberty Inn sometimes has gluten-free pizza available; it contains milk, sunflower seeds, and soy. The meat in the beef burgers, chicken sandwich, and all-beef hot dogs are gluten-free, but the rolls are not. Sometimes gluten-free rolls/bread are available—ask to speak with a manager.

In Magic Kingdom: Cosmic Ray's has rotisserie chicken; El Pirata y el Perico has gluten-free nachos, taco shells, and salsa. Also gluten-free: Scuttle's Landing frozen beverages; ToonTown Farmer's Market and Liberty Square Market for fresh fruit; and Aloha Isle's Dole Whips (vanilla, chocolate, and pineapple). Main Street Ice Cream Parlor has gluten-free ice cream—ask for the manager, as it's kept in the back.

Disney-MGM Studios: Disney chefs do not recommend you order fries from the ABC Commissary—they are in very close proximity to the batter-dipped fish area. The counter-service areas can provide gluten-free pizza or pasta with advance notice.

You can also obtain current info on gluten-free dining by e-mailing Walt Disney World **Guest Communications** through the form on their web site at http://www.disneyworld.com.

Weight Loss Surgery

You should be so proud of yourself! With the help of a surgical procedure—either gastric bypass, lapband surgery, or some other surgical method—you've finally been able to lose a significant amount of weight. But now you're vacationing at Walt Disney World, and guess what? You can't eat as much as you used to—in fact, the surgery you've had physically restricts your stomach capacity and you can only eat very small portions. Will you still be charged full price at the buffets or all-you-can-eat meals? Are there any alternatives to ordering full dinners? Will you be frowned upon for ordering light meals or special items?

While there is as yet **no official Disney policy** on dining for those who have had such weight loss surgery, most travelers we spoke to report having positive experiences at Disney restaurants.

Ask to **speak to a manager** when you arrive at the restaurant, particularly if it's an "all you can eat" meal, and explain your situation—that your surgery physically limits the amount of food you can eat. Bring with you a personalized card or physician's note that states you've had the surgery.

Almost all restaurants at Disney will allow you to **share dishes** (although there may be a minimal plate charge). When eating at a counter-service restaurant, ask the cast member to provide you with a second plate and cut your sandwich or entrée in half so you can easily share it.

Many Disney buffets only charge you the **kid's meal price**, though others (usually those with characters) charge you an "entertainment fee."

Some buffet restaurants, like Fresh at the Walt Disney World Dolphin, offer a continental breakfast (i.e., just fruit and baked goods) and/or a soup and salad bar buffet (again, no hot entrées) at a **reduced price**. This is generally not well-advertised, so ask the host/hostess, your server, or the manager.

If you cannot drink carbonated beverages, **bottled water** is widely available in the parks. Recently, Disney eateries began offering sugar-free, non-carbonated soft drinks such as light lemonade. In addition, the sports drink PowerAde is available at many locations; other sugared drinks, such as lemonade, fruit punch, and iced tea, can also be found.

Other tips:
- ✔ When you make your Advance Reservations, be sure to have your surgery noted as a special dietary request on the reservation.
- ✔ Each park has at least one fresh fruit stand (see page 319).
- ✔ Ask your server if a grilled chicken breast is available, even if it's not on the menu.
- ✔ Consider ordering an appetizer in lieu of an entrée. Combine that with a beverage and a small dessert for a small meal instead of a full-course one.
- ✔ Remember to bring some good snacks with you in the parks!

Kosher Meals

Almost all Walt Disney World Resort table-service restaurants that accept Advance Reservations can accommodate kosher needs if requested at least 72 hours in advance at 407-WDW-DINE. A credit card is required to guarantee the order, but will not be charged the full price of the meal(s) unless the reservation is canceled within 72 hours or the party is a no-show.

Important Note: Kosher meals are not offered at certain restaurants—we note them in the individual restaurant descriptions later in this chapter.

Kosher products offered at Walt Disney World are **Glatt Kosher** and are certified by the OK Kosher Certification Organization (http://www.okkosher.com). Entrées are plated on a three-compartment plastic dish, wrapped in a kosher labeled bag. Entrées include a vegetable and starch accompaniment, dinner rolls, and stainless utensils.

Pricing for kosher meals is as follows as of May 2005, but like everything at Walt Disney World, it is subject to change without notice:

Table-Service Restaurants	Dinner Shows	Buffets and All-You-Care-to-Eat Locations
Breakfast = $9.99 Entrée = $17.99 Kid's Meals = $5.99 Soup = $4.99 Dessert = $5.99	Regular current dinner show prices. You will only receive one meal, not all-you-can-eat, however.	Regular current buffet/all-you-care-to-eat price. You will only receive one meal, not all-you-care-to-eat, however. This includes character and fixed-menu meals.

Vacationers using a **Disney package** (Magic Your Way Plus Dining or any previously booked packages) get the following as part of their kosher meal: one soup, one entrée, and one dessert per guest.

Kosher Meals Available without Advance Notice

Theme Parks:
Disney's Animal Kingdom: Pizzafari
Disney-MGM Studios: ABC Commissary
Epcot: Liberty Inn at American Adventure
Magic Kingdom: Cosmic Ray's Starlight Café in Tomorrowland

Resort Hotels:
All Star Food Courts: World Premiere (Movies), Intermission (Music), and End Zone (Sports).
Caribbean Beach: Old Port Royale Food Court
Pop Century: Everything Pop! Dining
Port Orleans French Quarter: Sassagoula Floatworks and Food Factory
Port Orleans Riverside: Riverside Mill Food Court

As of May 2005, these are the **types of kosher meals available**. All come with kosher flatware pack and items are subject to change at any time.

Breakfast:
✔ Cheese blintzes with hash browns, large twist rolls
✔ Cheese omelet with home fries, large twist rolls

Entrée:
✔ Beef brisket with brown gravy, oven-browned potatoes, mixed vegetables, and large twist rolls
✔ Honey glazed breast of chicken, toasted almond couscous, ratatouille, and large twist rolls
✔ Cheese lasagna, asparagus, and large twist rolls
✔ Baked fillet of salmon, baby carrots and rice medley, and large twist rolls

Kid's Meal:
✔ Kid's hot dog on bun with potato croquettes
✔ Kid's macaroni and cheese
✔ Chicken strips with potato croquettes

Soup:
✔ Matzo ball soup
✔ Garden vegetable soup

Dessert:
✔ Chocolate cake
✔ Apple strudel
✔ Non-dairy cheesecake

Special **Passover** meals, including a Seder plate, are also available for about a week around Passover.

Fresh Fruit Finds

Many counter-service restaurants offer fresh fruit cups, baby carrots, or whole fresh fruit. When buying a "combo meal," **ask if fruit or carrots can be substituted for fries**. The following spots have whole fruit or fruit cups on their regular menus.

Disney's Animal Kingdom: Harambe Fruit Market

Disney-MGM Studios: Anaheim Produce on Hollywood Blvd

Epcot: Refreshment Outpost in World Showcase

Magic Kingdom: Toontown Farmer's Market; Liberty Square Market

All resort food courts/fast food areas

Fresh fruit at Refreshment Outpost in Epcot

© Debra Martin Koma

Dining Basics

Alcoholic Beverages—Most eateries serve alcoholic drinks, with the notable exception of those in the Magic Kingdom. Bars and lounges are located around the "World." Some areas sell alcohol in the walkways, such as Pleasure Island and Epcot. Legal drinking age is 21 and they do check your identification.

Character Dining—Dine with Disney characters! See pages 361–363.

Children's Meals—Nearly every eatery has a children's menu at parent-friendly prices. Perennial kid faves macaroni and cheese and chicken tenders can be found even at the most exotic of restaurants—ask your server. In addition, Disney recently revamped its quick service and food court menus to include one "balanced meal" kids' option with items including turkey wrap pinwheels; salads; veggies and dip; macaroni and cheese with salad; and chicken nuggets with applesauce and fruit. Note that counter-service eatery kids' meals are 10 percent to 28 percent smaller than adult portions.

Bright Idea: Remember if you need a highchair, just ask! They are available at all full-service restaurants and most counter-service spots, too.

Counter Service—This is essentially fast food. The quality varies, and so do the offerings. Most counter-service spots in the Magic Kingdom serve up the traditional burgers, dogs, and fries, while at Disney's Animal Kingdom, you'll find more exotic rotisserie chicken, barbecue, and even grilled salmon!

© MediaMarx, Inc.

Food order/pickup at a counter-service eatery

Dietary Requirements—Low-cholesterol, low-salt, low-fat, and/or vegetarian meals are a regular part of the menu in most restaurants. Look for special Mickey Apple icons on Disney menus for healthy or vegetarian options. With 72-hour advance notice, restaurants can meet kosher and other special dietary needs—see pages 314–315. At least one eatery in each theme park now has kosher items available without advance notice (see page 318)—ask if you don't see the menu posted. We also recommend the travel guidebook, "Vegetarian Walt Disney World and Greater Orlando—Second Edition," by Susan Shumaker and Than Saffel, published by The Globe Pequot Press. The book is available through bookstores and at http://www.globepequot.com. We include Susan and Than's "vegebility" ratings—see page 323 for details on these ratings.

Dinner Shows—Disney offers several dinner shows, combining all-you-care-to-eat meals with live entertainment. Special dietary requests for these shows must be made at least 24 hours in advance. See pages 364–366 for Special Meals.

Dress—Casual clothing is appropriate for all eateries except Victoria & Albert's in the Grand Floridian (see page 353) and Wolfgang Puck's upstairs dining room (see page 345). Several spots have "no tank top" rules. We note these rules, when present, in an eatery's description later in this chapter.

Entertainment—Some restaurants supply entertainment (Restaurant Marrakesh, Biergarten, and Rose and Crown bar area) while others like the Whispering Canyon Cafe and 'Ohana provide activities for kids or server/guest interactions.

Menus—Most menus at counter-service locations are pictorial, so that foreign-speaking guests should have no trouble interpreting them. We have found no Braille menus at any Disney restaurant, presumably because they change so frequently. Many menus can be previewed, though, at Guest Services. Co-author Deb Wills' AllEarsNet.com Web site (http://www.allearsnet.com) also has a nearly complete and very current collection of menus brought back by fellow vacationers.

Money—Cash, Disney Dollars, traveler's checks, the Disney Credit Card, Disney Visa Reward Vouchers, MasterCard, Visa, American Express, JCB, Discover, Diner's Club, and Disney Resort room charge cards are welcomed. Gratuities may be applied automatically to large parties.

Smoking—Florida law now prohibits smoking in all enclosed restaurants and other indoor public spaces. Only outdoor establishments and free-standing bars (no restaurants or hotel lobbies allowed) can allow smoking, but Disney has chosen to ban smoking at most of these, too. Smoking is permitted inside Jellyrolls and at the bar in ESPN Club (both on the BoardWalk).

For Particular Palates

Some children—and some adults as well—aren't the most adventurous eaters. In fact, they'll often only eat certain foods. In our conversations with special needs travelers, we've found that many of these finicky eaters want one of several very simple dishes: peanut butter and jelly sandwich, macaroni and cheese, chicken nuggets, or a grilled cheese sandwich. Here's a sampling of what we found around the theme park counter-service spots—read the individual restaurant descriptions for more details:

Magic Kingdom:
Pecos Bill's: chicken strips
Columbia Harbour House: mac and cheese; chicken strips
Cosmic Ray's Starlight Cafe: chicken nuggets

Epcot:
Electric Umbrella: mac and cheese; chicken nuggets
Liberty Inn: chicken nuggets
Refreshment Port: McDonald's chicken nuggets
Sunshine Seasons: mac and cheese
Tangierine Cafe: pizza; chicken strips

Disney's Animal Kingdom:
Pizzafari: peanut butter and jelly sandwich; chicken strips
Restaurantosaurus: McDonald's chicken nuggets
Tusker House: mac and cheese

Disney-MGM Studios:
ABC Commissary: chicken nuggets
Backlot Express: chicken nuggets; chicken strips

Tips for Diners With Special Needs

✔ Many counter-service eateries have **wheelchair/ECV accessible** cash registers, usually located on the far ends of the counter.

✔ Consider eating **earlier or later than traditional mealtime hours**. You'll be more likely to get a seat and be served quicker (if you haven't made advance reservations), or simply find the restaurant less crowded and noisy.

✔ Most items at counter-service eateries can be ordered **a la carte**. If you don't want fries with that burger "meal," just ask, and you'll usually pay a reduced price.

✔ Resort eateries are frequently **less crowded** than those in the parks, especially during lunch. Consider a visit to a nearby resort restaurant before, during, or after a park visit. The Contemporary, Polynesian, and Grand Floridian resorts are a short monorail ride from the Magic Kingdom, while the Yacht & Beach Club, BoardWalk, and Swan & Dolphin restaurants are near Epcot.

✔ Some full-service eateries have a **separate vegetarian menu**—if you don't see it, ask!

✔ Most full-service restaurants have at least **one sugar-free dessert** on request.

✔ Most counter-service restaurants have an **ingredients list** behind the counter. If the cast member serving you doesn't know about it, ask to speak to a manager.

✔ Fryer oil for french fries, etc., is **100% soybean oil**, but be sure to consider the potential for cross-contamination with other nearby food items, such as batter-dipped or seafood items. McDonald's fries include beef flavoring.

✔ Be sure to inquire about the **oil type** used and what items have been fried in that oil.

✔ If you're traveling alone, cast members will **assist you with your tray** or with reading the menu—just ask!

✔ Special meals sometimes **take longer to prepare**, so allow extra time when dining.

✔ When dealing with buffets and family-style servings, **cross contamination** is always a possibility. Talk with a chef—they may need to prepare a separate plate for you.

✔ Many **familiar chain restaurants** are located nearby, off Disney property. Two helpful books listing these are "Vegetarian Walt Disney World and Greater Orlando—Second Edition" (Globe Pequot) and "Orlando Chow" by Bob Mervine (Intrepid Traveler).

✔ If you require your foods to be **mixed in a blender**, just ask your server. Table-service restaurants can very easily handle this request. It may even be possible at counter-service eateries if you give them enough advance notice—stop by and speak to the manager several hours before you plan to dine.

✔ If for some reason your **intake of food is limited** in some way (e.g., you are fed through a gastric tube, you've had gastric bypass surgery), be sure to speak to the manager, especially at an "all-you-can-eat" meal. Disney does not seem to have a set policy on charging in such cases—you may not be charged at all, or if you're dining at a character meal, you may be charged an entertainment fee. Find out ahead of time what you will be charged.

Reader Tip: "Gluten-free diners don't have to stick with their usual fare. A Disney trip is a good excuse to ask for pasta dishes, pancakes, waffles, and sandwiches. Don't be shy about asking for anything on the menu to see if accommodations are possible."—contributed by peer reviewer Leanne Phelps

Understanding and Using the Eatery Descriptions and Ratings

Our capsule reviews of Disney eateries cover all table-service restaurants, as well as counter-service eateries at the parks, and most food outlets at the resorts. We offer the information you need to know for your specific situation, plus our ratings. We even include most snack carts.

Description Key

Ratings[7]

[1] **Eatery Name** [D-2[2]]	**B/L/D/S**[3]	**$**[4]	[5] [6]	#	#
Description offering an overview of the eatery, including comments on the theming, quality, and menu range. We try to give you an idea of what sort of foods you'll find at a particular eatery, along with our recommendations. We also include information on the availability of lighter fare, children's meals, and alcoholic beverages. Whenever possible, we describe the type of seating (tables, booths, etc.) and whether it is indoor or outdoor.				**Type**[8]	
				Cuisine[8]	
				Noise Factor[8]	
				Seating[8]	
				Avg. Wait[8]	
				Hours[8]	

[1] Each chart has an empty **checkbox** in the upper left corner—use it to check off the eateries that interest you (before you go) or those at which you ate (after your return).

[2] **Map coordinates**—match them up to park maps in chapter 5 for locations.

[3] Meals are indicated by letters: B (breakfast), L (lunch), D (dinner), and S (snack).

[4] **Dollar figures** represent the average cost of a full adult dinner. Table-service meal costs include appetizer, entrée, dessert, soft drink, tax, and tip. Whenever possible, we also provide in parentheses the average cost of a lighter dinner, such as a sandwich, pizza, or entrée salad plus dessert, soft drink, tax, and tip. Average counter-service meal costs include entrée (with fries when appropriate), dessert, soft drink, and tax. Average counter-service snack prices include a snack, soft drink, and tax. Use these only as a guide.

[5] The **orange symbol** indicates an eatery is vegetarian-friendly and has a good "vegebility" rating from the "Vegetarian Walt Disney World and Greater Orlando—Second Edition" guidebook published by The Globe Pequot Press. Please note that these veggie-friendly eateries are the best bets for vegetarians in each location, especially for folks who eat eggs and dairy—but these eateries are not necessarily the best veggie restaurants in the country. For information on vegan meals and to be certain that a menu has not changed since the time of publication, please call Disney to speak directly with a chef at the restaurant in advance of your visit. Remember, too, that all the table-service restaurants can accommodate special dietary requests with at least 72 hours' notice.

[6] Eateries with a reasonable selection of healthy items (low-fat/low-sodium/low-calorie) are indicated with a **tape measure symbol**. These are also friendly to weight watchers!

[7] The two white boxes on the right show **ratings** on a scale of 1 (poor) to 10 (loved it!). The first rating is **Deb Wills'** and the second is Deb Koma's. We offer our personal ratings to show how opinions vary, even between two like-minded people. You can also use our ratings as a point of reference—Deb Wills likes eateries with extensive theming and foods that aren't too exotic or spicy. She also enjoys eating vegetarian meals, but avoids seafood—she has a severe shellfish allergy. Deb Koma's tastes run the gamut, from basic meat and potatoes to seafood to unusual, spicy dishes, but she tries to eat healthily, avoiding heavy sauces and overly rich desserts. Both authors consider it a real treat to relax with glass of wine and a fine meal at the end of a tough day touring the theme parks.

[8] The boxes on the right beneath the numeric ratings give **basic information**: eatery type, cuisine, noise factor, seating, average wait time, and the eatery's hours.

Planning

Your Special Need

Getting There

Staying in Style

Touring

Dining

Resources

Index

Magic Kingdom Eateries

The Magic Kingdom may be magical in many ways, but dining with special needs is not one of them. There are several table-service restaurants in this theme park—all of them catering to a distinctly younger crowd—but most food served here comes from counter-service spots or even less sophisticated "quick-service" snack carts. On the plus side, though, for recovering alcoholics, this park serves no alcohol in any of its establishments.

Aunt Polly's Dockside Inn [B-3] S $5	6 6
Isolated over on Tom Sawyer Island, this little seasonal spot is great for getting away from the mania. Main items: snacks, cold drinks, and Smucker's Uncrustables (defrosted pb&j sandwiches). **[A] [U]** Open-air environment is good spot for letting off steam. Can also be good quiet spot since eatery is often closed, but watch out for birds and the loud passing riverboat. **[M] [Q] [S] [T] [U]** Seating areas can be difficult to navigate. **[M]** The rafts to Tom Sawyer Island are not ECV-accessible.	Counter American Quiet Outdoor seating

Casey's Corner [D-4] L/D/S $10	4 6
Need a quick hot dog and fries? Casey's is the spot for a fast All-American lunch. Most seating is outdoors; indoor seating is at just a few small tables or on wooden bleachers. **[M] [E] [S] [L] [V]** Tables are very close together; seating areas can be difficult to navigate. **[F]** Birds of all types (sparrows, even ibises!) love to come and scrounge a fry or crumbs—if you have a fear of them, avoid the outdoor seating area. **[A] [U]** Indoors features black-and-white Disney cartoons with a sports theme; outside often features an old-time piano player. **[M]** The first register on the left is wheelchair/ECV accessible. **[B]** Just around the corner from this eatery is the Magic Kingdom Baby Care Center.	Counter American Noisy Mostly outdoor seating Short waits 11:00 am-park closing

Cinderella's Royal Table [D-3] B/L/D $50 🎗	4 6
Everyone's a princess or prince inside Cinderella Castle! The character breakfast (adults $21.99/children under 9 $11.99) here is ultra-popular, which means ultra-noisy. Lunch recently became a character meal, too (adults $23.99/children 3-9 $12.99). Dinner's not a character meal and so is a bit quieter. Even still, the princess herself may visit, or at least be "holding court" in the lobby. Main dinner entrées: prime rib, steaks, seafood, and chicken. **[A] [U]** Very noisy at breakfast, but character meals are better meet-and-greet opportunities than in the parks. **[R]** All-you-care-to-eat pre-plated breakfast. **[D]** A number of chicken and seafood entrées for health-conscious diets. Always offers at least one vegetarian selection, like Grilled Portobello Mushrooms and Roasted Asparagus. Important Note: We have found this restaurant to be inflexible at breakfast when it comes to accommodating special requests without advance notice. **[F]** Narrow winding stairs to get to restaurant, or take small elevator. **[M]** Restaurant is on second floor; use elevator or walk up steep stairway. **[F]** Breakfast and lunch feature costumed characters who frequently make the rounds—if anyone has a fear of costumed characters, you may want to avoid. **[S]** Can be quite noisy at breakfast.	Table Service American Medium noise Reservations and credit card deposit essential for breakfast ~8:00 am-10:20 am, noon-3:00 pm, 4:00 pm-park closing

Eatery descriptions and ratings are explained on page 323.

Magic Kingdom Eateries
(continued)

Deb Wills' Rating
Deb Koma's Rating

Columbia Harbour House [C-2] L/D/S $11   7   7

A seafarer's waystation, this is a cozy, nautically themed spot that has some unusual lunch offerings. Main items: Soups, sandwiches, fried chicken strips, and fish. **[M]** The first register on left is wheelchair/ECV accessible. Additional seating upstairs is via an elevator. **[M] [E] [S] [L] [V]** The seating area can be  difficult to negotiate. **[D]** Some vegetarian options are available, like vegetarian chili ($4.99). We recommend the Lighthouse Sandwich—hummus with tomato & broccoli slaw ($6.39). **[Ö]** Pictorial menu available for foreign-language speakers. **[A] [U] [B] [S]** Upstairs seating area is usually much quieter than downstairs. **[A] [U] [D]** Macaroni and cheese is available.

© MediaMarx, Inc.

A Columbia Harbour House meal

Counter
American
Med. noise
More seating upstairs
Short waits
11:00 am–1 hr. before closing

Cosmic Ray's Starlight Café [E-3]   L/D/S $12   7   7

Several different counters serve up a variety of meals in this space-age setting—burgers on one side, soup/salads on another, and chicken on the third. **[D]** Kosher menu items available without advance notice. Chicken and salad items for the health-conscious diner. Veggie burger ($6.19), no-sugar-added brownies ($2.49)! Rotisserie chicken is gluten-free. Veggie burger may not be vegan—ask to see ingredient list. **[D] [G]** Gluten-free rotisserie chicken, fries, hot dogs, and hamburgers available. **[F]** Audio-Animatronics Sonny Eclipse performs in one corner—may be frightening to some. **[Ö]** Pictorial menu for foreign-language speakers. **[H]** Assistive Listening offered for Sonny Eclipse's performance. **[M]** First register on left of Blast-Off Burgers and Starlight Soup-Salad-Sandwich and first register on right of Cosmic Chicken are wheelchair/ECV accessible.

Counter
American
Very noisy
Indoor seating
Avg. waits
10:00 am–closing

Crystal Palace [C-4]   B/L/D $28   8   8

All-day character buffet in a Victorian-era conservatory with hanging plants and stained glass windows. Breakfast is fairly typical bacon/eggs/waffles fare ($17.99 adults; $9.99 children 3-9). Main lunch/dinner items: carved meats, chicken, some fish and pasta items. (Adult lunch $19.99/dinner $22.99; children 3-9 $10.99.) Special kid's buffet with mac and cheese, chicken nuggets. **[A] [U]** Very noisy, but character meals are better meet-and-greet opportunities than in the parks. **[R]** All you can eat buffet. **[D]** Some chicken and fish entrées on the buffet for health-conscious diets. Vegetarian offerings include cheeses, salads, grilled vegetables. **[M]** Entrance ramp located to the left of the main entrance. **[B]** Just around the corner from the Baby Care Center and First Aid. **[F]** All meals here feature Winnie the Pooh and friends, who frequently make the rounds—if little ones have fear of costumed characters, you may want to avoid. **[S]** Can be quite noisy.

Buffet
American
Very noisy
Reservations strongly suggested
Long waits
8:00 am–10:30 am, 11:30 am–3:00 pm, 4:00 pm–park closing

El Pirata Y el Perico [A-4]   L/D/S $10   5   7

This seasonal spot, just a stone's throw from Pirates of the Caribbean, serves up out-of-the-ordinary fast food in a South of the Border atmosphere. Limited menu features tacos, taco salad, and beef empanada. Seating area shared with Pecos Bill's. **[D]** Nachos, taco shells, and salsa are gluten-free. **[Ö]** Pictorial menu for foreign-language speakers. **[V]** Dimly lit.

Counter
Mexican
Med. noise
In/Outdoor

Planning
Your Special Need
Getting There
Staying in Style
Touring
Dining
Resources
Index

Magic Kingdom Eateries
(continued)

Deb Wills' Rating Deb Koma's Rating

■ Liberty Tree Tavern [C-3]　L/D　$33　　8　7

Colonial America is the theme at this warm and cozy tavern. All-you-can-eat character meal at dinnertime (adults $22.99/children 3-9 $10.99); no characters at lunch. Lunch menu features wider selection, including vegetarian and low-fat options. Main dinner items: turkey, roast beef, pork chops. **[A] [U]** Very noisy, but character meals are better meet-and-greet opportunities than in the parks. **[D]** Vegetarian selections include salads and "Amber Waves of Grain," a veggie/grain combo. Note: Readers report that chefs here are particularly sensitive to those with special diets. Macaroni and cheese available. **[M]** Ramp is located to the left of the lobby area. Once inside, speak to a cast member for directions on seating. **[F]** Dinner features costumed characters who frequently make the rounds—if anyone has a fear of costumed characters, you may want to avoid. **[R]** Dinner is an all-you-can-eat meal. **[S]** Can be quite noisy at dinner with lots of small children.

Table
American
Medium noise
Advance reservations suggested
Average waits
11:30 am–3:00 pm 4:00 pm–park closing

■ Main Street Bakery [D-5]　B/L/D/S　$5　　8　8

Just follow your nose to this mecca of all manner of fresh baked goodies—but be aware it's very crowded at park opening as everyone else is doing the same. Also serves up specialty sandwiches and coffees. **[D]** Specialty sandwiches include vegetarian selections such as tomato-mozzarella with basil. No-sugar-added selections available, as well as fresh fruit. **[M]** Queue is difficult to navigate in wheelchair/ECV.

Counter
American
Med. noise
Outdoor
Med. waits
Open all day

■ Pecos Bill Café [A-4]　L/D/S　$13　　7　7

You can't beat this rustic cowboy hangout for standard fast food—it even has an expanded fresh fixings bar, which sets it apart from its counterparts. Lots of seating—try the area in back for fewer crowds/less noise. Main items: burgers, hot dogs, fresh chicken salad. **[D]** A few low-fat options, such as chicken salad and chicken wrap. Salad available without chicken or cheese, making it a good vegan choice. **[F]** Beware of the low-flying birds in Frontierland. They have been known to swoop down and take food off trays! **[Ö]** Pictorial menu for foreign-language speakers. **[M]** Two registers in middle are wheelchair/ECV accessible.

Counter
American
Noisy
In/Outdoor
Med. waits
10:00 am–1 hour before closing

Eatery descriptions and ratings are explained on page 323.

Best Bets in Magic Kingdom for Special Dietary Needs

✔ The table-service restaurants (Liberty Tree Tavern, Crystal Palace, Tony's Town Square and Cinderella's Royal Table), for their ability to take Advance Reservations and advance special requests.
✔ Cosmic Ray's Starlight Café, for its no-advance-notice kosher menu.
✔ Toontown Market, for its variety of fresh fruit.
✔ Pecos Bill Café, for its health-conscious salad and wrap offerings.
✔ Columbia Harbour House, for its vegetarian options, including its vegetarian chili.

Magic Kingdom Eateries
(continued)

	Deb Wills' Rating	Deb Koma's Rating

☐ Pinocchio Village Haus [D-1]   L/D/S $?   — —

At press time, we were awaiting notice of the changeover to a new menu (we hear it will be all Italian fare and include pizza). The Swiss chalet setting of this counter-service eatery is charming. One unique thing—you have a view down into "it's a small world" from here! Seating is available both indoors and outdoors. **[M]** Third register from left is wheelchair/ECV accessible.	**Counter**
	Italian
	Med. noise
	11 am–1 hour before closing

☐ Plaza Restaurant [E-4]   L/D/S $25   6 7

The old-fashioned ice cream parlor feel is captured in this eatery's cozy decor. Main items: classic Reuben sandwiches, club sandwiches, burgers. Note there are no restrooms in this restaurant; you need to exit to go to the restrooms next door. **[D]** A chicken and pear salad and a vegetarian wrap are nods to health-conscious diets. Some no-sugar-added ice cream available. **[M] [E] [S] [L] [V]** Very crowded conditions in this small space make it difficult to navigate.	**Table**
	American
	Reservations suggested
	11 am–1 hour before closing

☐ Tomorrowland Terrace Noodle Station [E-4] L/D/S $10   6 6

This recently renovated terrace eatery is also a shortcut between Main Street and Tomorrowland. Seating is covered, but not enclosed—and not exactly air-conditioned. Revamped menu includes Asian-inspired dishes like chicken, shrimp, or vegetarian noodle bowl, pork steamed bun with Asian slaw, stir fry, fried egg rolls, pot stickers, and mandarin orange and cashew chicken salads, with a ginger-infused creme brulee for dessert. **[G]** Request "no MSG" if sensitive. Note that peanut oil may be used in some cooking here. **[Ö]** Pictorial menu for foreign-language speakers. **[M]** First register on the left is wheelchair/ECV accessible.	**Counter**
	Asian
	Med. noise
	Outdoor, covered
	11:00 am–1 hour before park closing

☐ Tony's Town Square Restaurant [E-6] L/D $45   ☒   7 7

Italian cuisine in a setting straight out of Disney's animated classic "Lady and the Tramp." Limited outdoor seating. Main items: Pasta, veal dishes, strip steak. **[D]** A few chicken and seafood entrées for health-conscious diets. At least one vegetarian selection, like Eggplant and Ricotta Roulade, is also available. **[D] [G]** Some gluten-free pasta available—ask to speak to the chef. **[M]** Ramp located to far right, near Main Street Station tunnel.	**Table**
	Italian
	Reservations suggested
	12–3 pm 5 pm–closing

Selected Magic Kingdom Snack Shops and Carts

Name	Specialties
Main Street Ice Cream Parlor	Ice cream treats; sugar-free/fat-free/dairy-free
Aloha Isle	Dole Whips (gluten-free)
Sunshine Tree Terrace	Citrus Swirl (orange juice/soft-serve)
Frontierland Fries	McDonald's Fries
Liberty Square Market	Fresh fruit
Enchanted Grove	Strawberry Swirl
Sleepy Hollow	Ice cream; funnel cake
Mrs. Potts' Cupboard	Ice cream treats
Scuttle's Landing	Frozen drinks (gluten-free); chips; cookies
Auntie Gravity's	Ice cream treats; smoothies; reduced-fat ice cream
The Lunching Pad	Turkey legs; frozen drinks
Toontown Market	Fresh fruit

Planning
Your Special Need
Getting There
Staying in Style
Touring
Dining
Resources
Index

Epcot Eateries

Epcot offers a **smorgasbord of tastes and cuisines**. We know of few places where you can dine in Mexico, Norway, the United Kingdom, China, and Morocco all on the same day (if you so desire). And when it comes to special dietary needs, you'll find some places incredibly accommodating.

Many Disney guests find Epcot **the place to dine in the evening** with the variety of choices available. The restaurants are extremely popular during the holiday Candlelight Processional season, and long waits are the norm.

Alcohol is served in all table-service and most counter-service restaurants in Epcot, as well as from kiosks located along the walkways and shops in World Showcase. During Epcot's Food and Wine Festival (see 335), alcohol is available at just about every outside booth throughout World Showcase.

Gluten-free breads, as well as special desserts, are available at most full-service restaurants.

Soft pretzels and chocolate chip cookies at Epcot counter-service eateries are processed in a plant that contains **peanuts and tree nuts**, so be careful!

Fresh fruit cups are sold at all counter-service venues. Some counter-service eateries can substitute fruit for fries.

■ **Restaurant Akershus** [B-3]	B/L/D	$34	🎗	6	7

	Preplated
*Home of the Princess Storybook Dining Experience, this replica Norwegian palace hosts royalty all day long. Characters visit your table. The preplated breakfast is basic American fare with scrambled eggs, bacon, sausage, pastries, and hash browns. ($21.99/$11.99) Lunch ($23.99/$12.99) and dinner ($27.99/$12.99) have family-style appetizers and individual entrée selections. Ask for ingredients of desserts! Unless you have to see the Princesses, we don't recommend dining here at breakfast. **[A] [U]** Very noisy, but character meals are better meet-and-greet opportunities than in the parks. Nearby Viking ship for playing and letting off steam.*	Norwegian
	Noisy
	Reservations recommended
	Med. waits
	Call 90 days

| *[G] [D]* Preplated food means little accommodation possible at the last minute. Be sure to request special meals 72 hours in advance! *[F]* Costumed characters make rounds—if anyone has fear of characters, consider avoiding this. *[C][T][M][P][S][L]* There are several rooms of tables and some can be very close together, making maneuvering difficult. | 8:30 am– 10:10 am, 11:40 am– 2:50 pm, 4:20 pm– 8:20 pm |

© Mediamarx, Inc.

Chef Wade at Restaurant Akershus

Epcot Eateries
(continued)

				Deb Wills' Rating	Deb Koma's Rating

☐ L'Originale Alfredo di Roma Ristorante [C-1]   **L/D**   **$52**   ⚓ | 6 | 8 |

This upscale Italian restaurant is designed in rich Florentine style. Alfredo's is based on a famous Roman restaurant of the same name. Fettuccine Alfredo is the restaurant specialty. Other main dishes: Pastas, Ossobucco Maiale (pork shank), veal scalloppine. **[A][U]** Waits are often long and waiting area can get very crowded during dinner. **[A][U][T][I][S]** Can be very noisy—could cause overstimulation. **[D][♥]** Many foods high in fat and with heavy sauces. **[D]** Vegetarian choices limited to salads and pasta. Some pasta is made without eggs—be sure to inquire. **[C][T][M][P][S][L]** Tables are close together. **[Ö]** Most servers here are from Italy and/or speak Italian. **[L]** Some tables have bench seating with backs.	**Table** Italian Very noisy Reservations strongly recommended Call 90 days 12-4:15 pm 4:30-closing

☐ Biergarten [B-1]   **L/D**   **$35** | 6 | 8 |

Oktoberfest is the setting for this buffet restaurant, complete with large wooden tables and live entertainment, including an oompah band and Alpenhorns! Buffet includes sausages, chicken schnitzel, kraut, pasta salads, vegetable salads, and seafood salads. A fish entrée is added at dinner ($20.99 adults/$8.99 children 3-9). Lunch is $15.99/$7.99. **[A][U][F]** May be seated with other parties; request separate table if desired. **[A][U][T][I][S]** Can be very noisy—could cause overstimulation. **[L][M][E]** Tables are very close together making maneuvering difficult. **[R]** All-you-care-to-eat buffet. **[C][L]** Wooden chairs, no arms. **[V]** Low lighting with entertainment. **[Ö]** Most servers here are from Germany and/or speak German. **[H]** Assistive listening devices work for the live performances held here.

Buffet
German
Very noisy
Reservations recommended
Call 90 days
Short waits
Noon-3:45 pm,
4:00-8:30 pm

© Debra Martin Koma

Co-author Deb Koma with peer reviewer
Lydia Economou and their families

☐ Bistro de Paris [F-2]   **D**   **$62** | 7 | 8 |

On the second floor above Chefs de France is the quieter, more elegant, and pricier Bistro de Paris. The restaurant is accessible via a winding staircase or elevator. Offerings include delicacies such as pan-seared foie gras, truffles, grilled lobster, and roasted quail. Desserts are outstanding ($6.50-$8.00). The wine list is excellent, but the cheapest bottle is $42. Ask for a window seat and linger until IllumiNations. No tank tops are allowed. **[A][U][B][S]** Quiet, elegant atmosphere. **[D]** No vegetarian items on regular menu, but ask! **[D][♥]** Many rich, high-fat foods. **[C][F][♥][T][M][P][S][L][V]** Elevator available; ask cast member. **[L]** Some tables have padded bench seating. **[Ö]** Many servers here speak French.	**Table** French Very quiet Reservations strongly recommended Call 30 days 6:00 pm-8:45 pm

☐ Boulangerie Patisserie [F-2]   **L/D/S**   **$11** | 9 | 9 |

Great French pastries and sandwiches; always crowded. Very limited indoor/outdoor seating, some covered. Indoor seating across the way at Galerie les Halles. **[D]** Nothing low-fat or low-cal here! Cheese plate for low-carb diets. **[A][F][U][M][L]** Very small inside area, usually very crowded.	**Counter** French Long waits ~11 am-closing

Planning

Your Special Need

Getting There

Staying in Style

Touring

Dining

Resources

Index

Epcot Eateries
(continued)

Planning | Your Special Need | Getting There | Staying in Style | Touring | Dining | Resources | Index

Deb Wills' Rating / Deb Koma's Rating

☐ Cantina de San Angel [B-4] L/D/S $12 🐶 🦑 6 | 6

Open-air dining with tacos and burritos. Tables have umbrellas and offer some shade. It offers great view of World Showcase Lagoon. No substitutions were allowed on most recent visit. **[R]** Outdoor margarita and beer bar. **[D]** Burritos, nachos, and taco salad can be made vegan or vegetarian upon request. **[U][B][F][I][S]** Beware of the seagulls and other low-flying birds in this immediate area. They have been known to swoop down and take food off trays! **[C][L]** Outdoor seating, wood chairs (no arms) and benches (no backs), neither moves.

| Counter |
| Mexican |
| Med. noise |
| Med. waits |
| Outdoor seating |
| ~11 am-closing |

☐ Les Chefs de France [F-2] L/D $50 🐶 🦑 6 | 7

A little taste of France in America, this restaurant features the creations of its three famous owner-chefs: Paul Bocuse, Gaston Lenotre and Roger Verge. Typical items: Escargot ($9), French onion soup ($5.25), beef au poivre ($28) sautéd sole ($25), and duck with cherries ($25). **[A][U][T][I][S]** Can be very noisy—could cause over stimulation. **[D]** At least one vegetarian option (like vegetarian lasagna, $16) on menu. Lunch offers lighter fare including salads. **[Ö]** Many servers here speak French.

| Table |
| French |
| Very noisy |
| Reservations recommended |
| Noon-3 pm |
| 5 pm-closing |

☐ Coral Reef [D-7] L/D $54 🦑 7 | 8

Incredible tile work and a wonderful view of the Living Seas Aquarium make this a most unique dining experience. Primarily seafood entrées; chicken and beef are also offered. Inquire about fixed-price lunch. **[A][U]** The aquarium will keep kids and adults mesmerized for much of your meal. Ask to be seated on the lower level if you want a close-up look at the fish. If seated further away, kids may be tempted to go up to the glass for a close look, which could disturb other diners. **[G]** Allergy alert: edible playdough for kids is made with peanut butter. This is primarily a seafood restaurant, so those with fish/shellfish allergies may want to avoid. **[D]** A number of fish entrées for health-conscious diets. At least one vegetarian entrée, such as Roasted Squash and other veggies, on menu. **[F]** An occasional shark and rays swim by in the aquarium. **[L]** Wooden chairs no arms. **[V]** Low lighting.

| Table |
| Seafood |
| Noisy |
| Reservations recommended for dinner |
| Call 90 days |
| Med. waits |
| 11:30-3 pm, 4:40-8:00 pm |

☐ Electric Umbrella [C-6] B/L/D/S $11 🐶 🦑 6 | 8

This bustling counter-service spot serves up good food fast. Limited breakfast menu is available. Basic burgers and deli sandwiches, plus a fixin's bar. Quieter seating available upstairs. Indoor/outdoor seating. **[D][♥]** Healthier fare includes chicken salad. **[D]** For vegetarians: veggie burger ($6.19) and black bean soup are available. Turkey wrap for kids. Macaroni and cheese available. **[F]** Beware of birds and squirrels if eating outside. **[M]** Ask cast member to operate elevator for upstairs seating. You will also have to find a cast member to return to the main floor.

| Counter |
| American |
| Med. noise |
| Short waits |
| 9:00 am-7:00 pm |

☐ Fountainview Bakery [D-6] B/S $6 🐶 8 | 7

Baked goods, pastries, sweet treats, as well as specialty coffees. Limited indoor/outdoor (covered) seating. On breezy days, the spray from the Fountain of Nations may get you wet. **[D]** Sugar-free cheesecake offered. **[M]** Stairs in front, ramp access from inside on left. Queue area is small, difficult to maneuver.

| Counter |
| American |
| Noisy |
| Hours vary |

Eatery descriptions and ratings are explained on page 323. ⟶

Epcot Eateries
(continued)

	Deb Wills' Rating	Deb Koma's Rating

The Garden Grill Restaurant [F-6]   L/D $28 | 6 | 6 |

This Land pavilion restaurant recently reopened with a whole new menu and new way of serving lunch (adults $19.99/children 3-9 $10.99) and dinner (adults $21.99/children 3-9 $10.99). Starter, salad, and dessert served family-style, but you choose from among assorted fish, seafood, chicken, and steak entrées. Character dining with semicircular booth seating—each booth looks out. **[A][U]** We recommend this character meal—much better than meet-and-greet opportunities in the parks; much less confusion and noise. **[D]** At least one vegetarian selection, like mushroom and asiago ravioli, offered. **[Q][U]** Restaurant rotates slowly and overlooks part of the Living With the Land boat ride. **[M]** Restaurant has two tiers of seating (a couple steps to get to upper level). **[U]** Sound effects from boat ride below may be bothersome.

Table
American
Med. noise
Reservations not always needed
Call 90 days
Short waits
11:00 am-3:00 pm, 4:30-closing

Kringla Bakeri og Kafé [B-3]   L/D/S $10   ♂ | 8 | 8 |

Pastries and Norwegian sandwiches; limited outdoor seating is covered. **[D]** Chocolate mousse is loaded with cream and chocolate, but sweetened with aspartame. Fruit cup, salads available. All seating is outside. **[M][L]** Very small space inside, usually very crowded. **[A][U]** Viking ship play area next door for children.

Counter
Norwegian
Med. noise
Long waits
~11 am-9 pm

Le Cellier Steakhouse [E-4]   L/D $50   ♂ | 8 | 9 |

This is a very popular steakhouse located in a "stone cellar," featuring red meat and seafood paired with the wines and beers of Canada. The restaurant does not sell mixed drinks, however—only beer and wine. **[D]** Lots of rich sauces on the dishes—tell server if you don't want them. Good menu for low-carb diners. At least one vegetarian entrée (like Grilled Portobello and Sweet Potato Stack, $16) is offered. **[F]** This is a dark restaurant with no windows—possible claustrophobia alert. **[L]** Chairs with no arms. **[V]** Low lighting with no natural sunlight. **[Ö]** Some servers here speak French.

Table
Canadian
Med. noise
Reservations recommended
Long waits
Noon-3 pm 4:00-closing

Liberty Inn [C-1]   L/D/S $12 | 7 | 5 |

Bright and busy fast-food, with lots of seating indoors and out. Main items: hamburgers, hot dogs, and chicken strips. Good fixin's bar. **[D][W]** Kosher meal available without advance notice. **[D]** Vegetarian salad. French fries and hot dogs are gluten-free. Gluten-free bread also available. Grilled chicken sandwich is marinated in canola oil and Italian spices, garlic, salt, and pepper. Gluten-free pizza may be on hand in the freezer. No-sugar-added ice cream and dairy-free ice cream also available. **[Ö]** Pictured menu items. **[L]** Outdoor seating has padded seats without arms.

Counter
American
Med. noise
Short waits
Indoor/outdoor seating
~11 am-closing

Lotus Blossom Café [B-3]   L/D/S $11 | 4 | 7 |

Chinese counter-service eatery with offerings that include stir fry, egg rolls, and a daily special. Limited covered seating is available inside. Ask to see the ingredients list. **[D]** Chicken stock and fish paste is used in many dishes. Vegetable lo mein is made with chicken stock. **[D][G]** Avoid this eatery if you have nut allergies, as peanut oil is used in cooking. **[G]** Request "no MSG" if sensitive.

Counter
Chinese
Med. noise
Med. waits
~11 am-closing

Side tabs: Planning · Your Special Need · Getting There · Staying in Style · Touring · Dining · Resources · Index

Epcot Eateries
(continued)

	Deb Wills' Rating	Deb Koma's Rating

Restaurant Marrakesh [F-1] L/D $44 5 | 8

Traditional Moroccan cuisine and live entertainment, including a belly dancer, in a beautiful Middle Eastern setting. Main items: lamb, chicken, couscous. Great desserts. We have found this restaurant to be inflexible in accommodating special requests, even for a simple grilled chicken meal. **[D]** Vegetable couscous (not vegan). **[F]** Diners can be invited up to dance with belly dancer. **[L]** Wooden chairs without arms. **[W]** There is a designated meditation/prayer room open daily from 11:00 am to 9:00 pm located nearby (inside the museum); small rugs are available for use. **[Ö]** Many servers here speak Arabic.

Table
Middle Eastern
Noisy
Reservations not required
11:30 am–3:45 pm, 4 pm–closing

Matsu No Ma Lounge [E-1] L/D/S $37 8 | 8

Often a quiet respite from the park's hustle and bustle, this lounge offers a variety of hot and cold appetizers, as well as sushi by the piece or on a platter. Great place to people-watch, as it has large windows overlooking World Showcase. **[G]** Avoid if you have nut allergies, since peanut oil used in cooking. **[D]** Chilled tofu, edamame for vegetarians. Kosher foods <u>not</u> offered. **[M]** Located on second floor above Mitsukoshi Department Store, elevator is to the left of store entrance on first level. **[C][T][M][P][S][L]** Space is very small; wheelchair/ECV maneuvering is difficult. **[Ö]** Many servers here speak Japanese.

Lounge
Japanese (Sushi)
Med. noise
Med. waits
~11:00 am–park closing

Nine Dragons [B-3] L/D/S $37 6 | 5

This elegant dining room serves standard Chinese fare. Various regions of China are represented in the food offerings. The food is of average quality. **[D]** Chicken stock and fish paste are used in many dishes. Gluten-free soy sauce available for food preparation and table use upon request. **[D][G]** Avoid this eatery if you have nut allergies, as peanut oil is used in cooking. **[G]** Request "no MSG" if sensitive. **[Ö]** Many servers here speak Chinese. **[L]** Wooden chairs without arms.

Table
Chinese
Med. noise
Reservations suggested
12 pm–4:30 pm, 4:45 pm–9 pm

Rose & Crown Pub and Dining Room [E-3] L/D $37 6 | 6

A bit of Merry Olde England in our midst! Convivial atmosphere featuring Harry Ramsden's famous fish and chips, meat pies, bangers and mash, prime rib with Yorkshire pudding, and ale! Live entertainment includes pub pianist or magician (pub hours: 11:30 am–park closing). Some outdoor seating, perfect for viewing IllumiNations, as long as the wind is blowing in the other direction! **[A][U][T][I][S]** Indoors can be very noisy—could cause over stimulation. **[D]** At least one vegetarian offering is available (such as curried vegetables and tofu for $13). **[M][L]** Indoor seating is close together; difficult to maneuver.

Table
English
Very noisy
Reservations strongly recommended
Noon–4:00 pm, 4:30 pm–close

San Angel Inn [B-4] L/D $35 6 | 6

Your table sits in a dimly lit romantic setting of Mexican twilight, while a volcano steams in the distance. Typical menu items: beef tenderloin with black beans ($23) and roasted pork with chorizo sausage ($18). Advance reservations are strongly recommended. **[D]** Separate menu available for vegetarians—be sure to ask. **[C][L]** Wooden chairs without arms. **[M]** Tight space; hard to maneuver a wheelchair in dining room. Ramp is left of check-in near El Rio del Tiempo. Ask cast member for assistance. **[M][V]** Very low lighting. **[Ö]** Many servers here speak Spanish. **[U]** May be troubled by close seating or sound effects from volcano.

Table
Mexican
Noisy
11:30 am–4:00 pm 4:30–closing

Epcot Eateries
(continued)

				Deb Wills' Rating	Deb Koma's Rating

Sommerfest [B-1]	L/D/S	$12		**5**	6

Very limited quick food menu of bratwurst and frankfurters with sauerkraut. Limited covered seating can be crowded. Noisy eatery. **[R]** Emphasis on German beer and schnapps. **[M]** Very tight area for maneuvering wheelchair/ECV.

Counter
German
11 am–closing

Sunshine Seasons [F-6]	B/L/S	$13		**6**	6

This eatery recently reopened to coincide with the debut of the new Soarin' attraction in the Land pavilion. Sunshine Seasons is a "fast-casual" dining area, combining the convenience of a counter-service spot with unusual menus more typically found at table-service restaurants. Items are prepared in an open kitchen and are available at five stations themed to the seasons of the year: Wood-Fired Grill Shop (fall), with grill and rotisserie items like ancho-rubbed beef with chimichurri sauce and grilled Atlantic Salmon; the Soup and Salad Shop (spring), with fresh herbs and vegetables grown in the Land greenhouse; the Asian Wok Shop (summer), with a Mongolian barbecue and wok station, and menu items including Mongolian vegetable beef stir fry; the Sandwich Shop (winter) with hearty sandwiches like Black Forest ham and salami grinder, turkey muffuletta, all on artisan breads; and the Bakery, with muffins, croissants, bagels, danish, desserts, and coffee. Each station also offers vegetarian and children's options, as well as prepackaged "grab 'n' go" items. **[D]** Vegetarian-friendly, with items like vegetarian noodle bowl with tofu and grilled Cuban veggie sandwich. **[G]** Avoid Asian station if you have nut allergies, as peanut oil may be used in cooking. Request "no MSG" at Asian station if sensitive. **[Ö]** Video menu screens used to identify items.

Counter
Mixed
Noisy
Med. waits

Tangierine Café [E-1]	L/D/S	$14		**8**	8

Chicken, lamb, hummus, and couscous in an open-air café serving traditional Middle Eastern cuisine. Great place for a healthy lunch without feeling stuffed! Desserts are yummy, but not lo-cal at all! Indoor/outdoor seating. **[D]** Vegetarian-friendly. Vegetarian platter ($8) is vegan. **[C][T][M][P][S][L]** Tables and chairs are close together and difficult to maneuver with wheelchair/ECV. **[Ö]** Many servers speak Arabic.

Counter
Middle Eastern
Med. noise
Noon-closing

Eatery descriptions and ratings are explained on page 323.

Best Bets in Epcot for Special Dietary Needs

✔ Sunshine Seasons—The Land
✔ Liberty Inn—American Adventure, for all the special products kept on hand, including kosher meals available with no advance notice and many gluten-free items.
✔ Tangierine Café—Morocco
✔ Teppanyaki—Japan (unless you have a seafood or peanut allergy!)

Important Note: L'Originale Alfredo di Roma Ristorante (Italy), San Angel Inn (Mexico), and Restaurant Marrakesh (Morocco) are operated by third parties (not Disney) and are not always the most flexible and accommodating when it comes to special orders.

Planning · Your Special Need · Getting There · Staying in Style · Touring · Dining · Resources · Index

Epcot Eateries
(continued)

				Deb Wills' Rating	Deb Koma's Rating

Tempura Kiku [E-1] — L/D/S — $40 — 5 | 7

Tucked away between the Teppanyaki Dining Room and the Matsu No Ma lounge, Tempura Kiku serves battered and deep-fried meats, seafood, and veggies. Sushi-bar style seating only. *[G]* Avoid if you have nut allergies, since peanut oil used in cooking. Request "no MSG" if sensitive. *[D]* Chilled tofu, edamame for vegetarians. Kosher meals *not* offered. *[M]* Located on second floor above Mitsukoshi Department Store—the elevator is to the left of store entrance on the first level. *[C][T][M][P][S][L]* Space is very small; wheelchair/ECV maneuvering is difficult. *[Ö]* Many servers here speak Japanese.

Table
Japanese
Med. noisy
Advance reservations recommended
Med. waits
~11 am-closing

Teppanyaki Dining [E-1] — L/D — $42 — 8 | 8

Ever been to a Benihana restaurant? Then you have the general idea behind this restaurant, which serves up seafood, beef, chicken, veggies, and rice, prepared with panache right in front of you on a hot Teppan grill. You are seated around the grill in tables that accommodate up to eight—your table may include other parties. *[G]* Avoid if you have nut allergies, as peanut oil is used in cooking. Request "no MSG" if sensitive. *[D]* Kosher meals *not* offered. Great for low-carb diets. Beware of sugar content in some sauces. If you have seafood or other allergies, notify your server, so your food can be cooked first or separately. *[M]* Located on second floor above Mitsukoshi Department Store—the elevator is to the left of store entrance on the first level. *[C][T][M][P][S][L]* Space is very small; wheelchair maneuvering is difficult. *[L]* Padded seats without arms. *[O]* Many servers here speak Japanese.

Table
Japanese
Noisy
Advance reservations a must
Call 90 days
Long waits
12-3:45 pm,
4:30 pm-
park closing

Yakitori House [D-1] — L/D/S — $13 — 6 | 8

Quick-service eatery offering skewers of grilled chicken, and beef, shrimp tempura, and udon noodles. Indoor/outdoor tables. *[G]* Avoid if you have nut allergies, as peanut oil is used in cooking. Request "no MSG" if sensitive. *[D]* Udon noodles usually made with wheat flour, salt, and water—ask about ingredients. *[M]* Located across the courtyard, with steps in front. Use the ramp through the garden instead. *[V]* Nearby restroom very dark.

Counter
Japanese
Med. noise
Long waits
~11 am-closing

Yorkshire County Fish Shop [E-3] — L/D/S — $10 — 6 | 8

Harry Ramsden's fish and chips are the order of the day, every day! Outdoor patio seating is available to the right rear, overlooking the World Showcase Lagoon. Some tables are shaded with umbrellas. *[D]* Very limited menu of fried fish and hot dogs. *[U][B][F][I][S]* Beware of the seagulls and other low-flying birds in this immediate area—they have been known to swoop down and take food off trays!

Counter
English
Outdoor seating
Med. waits
~11 am-closing

Eatery descriptions and ratings are explained on page 323.

Selected Epcot Snack Shops and Carts

Treat	Found at
Fresh fruit	Outpost (between Germany and China)
Rice cream with strawberry topping	Norway (Kringla Bakeri og Kafé)
Kaki Gori (fruit-flavored shaved ice, vegan)	Japan (along promenade)
McDonald's fries	Refreshment Port (near Canada)

Epcot Food & Wine Festival

Each fall, Epcot is host to the **International Food & Wine Festival**, recently expanded to run six weeks! Small food and beverage booths are set up all along the World Showcase Promenade offering appetizer portions ($2–$6) of a wide variety of cuisines from around the world, including Peru, Greece, South Africa, and Poland, to name but a few. Small glasses of wines, beers, champagnes, ports, and cognac are also available for purchase. Most special dieters will find something of interest here, but be sure and inquire about an ingredients list at the booths! Other than leaving off a sauce/topping or side, no special orders here!

Special food and wine **"hard-ticket" events** (that means you have to buy a separate entry ticket) are plentiful during the Festival, some costing as much as $185 a person. As a rule, no special dietary requests are available—in fact, they don't even make a special menu (or offer a reduced price) at these events for children. We have found an alternative entrée was offered at the Lunch and Learn events we attended (based on what is available in the kitchen). We don't know if we lucked out or if it's part of the regular operations. Check in early and let the host/hostess know of your dietary needs. It is possible that your special requests may be honored (although there's no guarantee). The bottom line is, due to the expense of these events, be wary of going with restricted dietary concerns or picky palates, as you may leave disappointed—not to mention hungry.

The one exception to the above is the very popular **Party for the Senses**, with numerous areas set up with appetizer portions of gourmet foods, wines, and even a beer and scotch table! Low-carb diners should have no problem with the expansive cheese table, fish, poultry, and meat offerings. Food is prepared right in front of you, so you can ask the chef for a sauce or side to be left off, but basically, what is offered is what's available. The chefs who prepare the food are right at the table, so you can easily find out the ingredients of any dish you are curious about. Sadly, these events are not very vegetarian/vegan friendly. The menus are set and no special requests are available.

© Deb Wills

Co-author Deb Koma talks to Mark Newman at Party for the Senses

Disney-MGM Studios Eateries

Where the Magic Kingdom and Disney's Animal Kingdom may be lacking in dining options for the traveler with special needs, Disney-MGM Studios makes up for their shortages. Several table-service restaurants **accommodate special diners with sufficient notice**, and even the counter-service spots offer many good alternatives. One important note—this is the only theme park that does not currently host a character meal at any of its restaurants. A few of the restaurants have very special themes, however—be sure to check them out before you go to be sure that they're up your alley.

☐ **ABC Commissary** [C-3] B/L/D/S $12	4	7
Nicer than any true movie set commissary, this art deco spot features television monitors plugging the latest ABC-TV shows. Plentiful indoor seating; some outdoor seating, too. **[D]** International cuisine features vegetarian as well as low-fat selections. Fries here may not be gluten-free—chance for cross-contamination with deep fryers. **[D] [W]** Kosher meals on regular menu without advance notice. **[Ö]** Pictorial menu for foreign-language speakers. **[M]** First register on left is wheelchair/ECV accessible. **[H]** Television monitors are closed captioned.	**Counter** Multi-Ethnic Indoor Seating Med. noise Med. waits Open all day	

☐ **Backlot Express** [C-5] L/D/S $11	7	7
A great place for standard fast food fare, this place gives you a behind-the-scenes look at a movie set, complete with props. Main items: burgers, hot dogs, sandwiches, chicken strips. Indoor/outdoor seating. **[D]** Vegetarian sandwich offered ($7). Also grilled turkey sandwich ($6.59) for lighter fare. **[Ö]** Pictorial menu for foreign-language speakers. **[M]** Use ramp on far right.	**Counter** American In/Outdoor Noisy 11 am-closing	

☐ **Catalina Eddie's** [G-3] L/D/S $13 ☝ ♿	5	5
Part of the outdoor food court known as the Sunset Ranch Market, Eddie's specializes in pizzas with side salads. Gets very crowded and noisy at peak mealtimes. Short waits. Outdoor seating. **[D]** Garden salad is the only vegetarian selection available.	**Counter** American Med. noise 11 am-closing	

☐ **50s Prime Time Cafe** [E-5] L/D $32 ☝ ♿	8	8
A '50s-style diner with an interactive twist: the servers are all one big, happy family and often chide patrons to eat all their veggies or keep the elbows off the table. Main entrées: meat loaf, fried chicken, pot roast (all $13). Our readers report the chefs here are very accommodating! **[A][U][I][S]** Can be very noisy—could cause overstimulation. Televisions scattered throughout restaurant play old TV clips on a continuous loop. **[D]** A number of low-fat entrées (grilled chicken, tuna, salmon) for health-conscious diets. At least one vegetarian selection available, such as stuffed pepper ($12.49). **[F]** Cast members frequently put diners "on the spot" as part of the role-playing here. Be sure to tell them if you want to be left alone.	**Table** American Noisy Reservations a must Call 90 days Long waits 11 am-4 pm, 4:00 pm-park closing	

Eatery descriptions and ratings are explained on page 323.

Disney-MGM Studios Eateries
(continued)

Deb Wills' Rating   Deb Koma's Rating

Hollywood & Vine [E-5]   D $27   7   7

A '40s-style diner with art deco decor and stainless steel touches this restaurant serves a buffet dinner only ($22.99 adults/$10.99 children 3-9). Ask about the Fantasmic! Dinner Package available here, which offers special seating at Fantasmic! show without the long waits (see below). **[A][U][I][S]** Can be very noisy—could cause overstimulation. **[R]** All-you-can-eat buffet. **[D]** A number of turkey, chicken, and fish entrées are on the buffet for health-conscious diets. Vegetarian selections, like vegetable lo mein and pasta salads, also available.

Buffet
American
Noisy
Reservations recommended
Call 90 days
4 pm-closing

The Hollywood Brown Derby [E-3]   L/D $47   🍴 ☺   9   9

A chic spot of brass and mahogany, the Brown Derby recalls the bygone era of the silver screen. Caricatures of old-time celebrities adorn the walls, while starched linens and white-coated servers take your order. Main entrées: pork tenderloin ($22), seafood, famous Cobb Salad ($13, enough for two!). Ask about the Fantasmic! Dinner Package available here, which offers special seating at Fantasmic! without the long waits (see below). **[D]** A number of chicken and seafood entrées for health-conscious diets. At least one vegetarian selection, like Thai noodle bowl with tofu ($17), is also available.

Table
American
Med. noise
Reservations recommended
Call 90 days
11:30 am-3 pm
3:30 pm-close

ⓘ What is the Fantasmic! Dinner Package?

The Fantasmic! Dinner Package includes dinner at one of the participating Disney-MGM Studios restaurants and reserved seating for Fantasmic! (see page 263). This means that instead of waiting in line for 60–90 minutes outside the theater, you can walk into the theater 30–45 minutes before show time (no waiting in line!) and still have a seat.

There is no additional charge for the package itself. Just call 90 days in advance and book your reservation at one of the participating restaurants. Your credit card will be charged at the time of booking, and there is a 48-hour cancellation policy. As of this writing, only Brown Derby, Mama Melrose, and Hollywood & Vine are participating. Prices (not including admission, tax, gratuity, or alcoholic beverages) for the fixed-price dinners are as follows:

Hollywood Brown Derby—$36.99 adult/$10.99 child (3-9). Your choice of appetizer, soup, or salad; entrée; and dessert from menu.

Mama Melrose—$28.99 adult/$10.99 child (3-9). Your choice of one wood-fired flatbread to share from Mama's rustic on-stage kitchen, as well as family style salad, choice of entrée, and Mama's signature Fantasmic! Tiramisu.

Hollywood & Vine—$22.99 adult/$10.99 child (3-9). All-you-care-to-eat buffet.

Report to your restaurant ten minutes before your Fantasmic! Dinner Package reservation, and you'll receive your special Fantasmic! seating pass at that time. They'll also give you instructions on where and when to enter the amphitheater. Although you do not have a reserved seat with this package, you have access to the reserved section, which is on the far right (the Witch section) of the amphitheater. Seating is on a first-come, first-served basis. The amphitheater is set up so that there really are no *bad* seats, except you will get wet if you sit in the first few rows.

Disney-MGM Studios Eateries
(continued)

	Deb Wills' Rating	Deb Koma's Rating

☐ **Mama Melrose's Ristorante Italiano** [A-4] L/D $38 ($30) 🗑️🍷 | **8** | **8**

*Hollywood Italian—need we say more? Main entrées: wood-fired flatbreads ($12), pasta, chicken parmesan ($16). Ask about the Fantasmic! Dinner Package available here, which offers special seating at Fantasmic! without the long waits (see page 337). **[D]** A number of chicken and seafood entrées for health-conscious diets. At least one vegetarian selection (like Eggplant Napoleon, $15) is also available. **[D] [G]** Gluten-free pasta available; speak to the chef.*	**Table** Italian Reservations suggested Noon–3 pm 3:30 pm–close

☐ **Rosie's All-American Cafe** [G-3] L/D/S $12 🗑️ | **5** | **5**

*Also part of the outdoor food court called Sunset Market Ranch, Rosie's is your basic burger stand. Area gets very crowded and noisy at peak mealtimes. Main items: hamburgers, cheeseburgers, chicken strips, fries. Outdoor seating. **[D]** Vegetarian burger on menu ($5.69). **[M]** First register on right is wheelchair/ECV accessible.*	**Counter** American Med. noise Med. waits 11 am–closing

☐ **Sci-Fi Dine-In Theater Restaurant** [C-4] L/D $36 🗑️ | **5** | **7**

*Designed to resemble a drive-in theater, diners sit in reproductions of vintage cars while watching clips from black and white sci-fi films. A sample car sits outside the restaurant so you can see if you'd prefer table seating. Main items: Pasta, fish, ribs ($16). **[D]** A number of seafood entrées for health-conscious diets. At least one vegetarian selection, like Vegetable Potato Bake ($14), is also available. **[M] [L] [S]** "Car" tables may be awkward; request standard table seating. (Regular table seating is limited; may increase your wait time.) Picnic table in rear should accommodate all. **[A] [U] [I] [F]** Very dark setting, with potentially scary movie scenes on the screen. **[V]** Very dimly lit—may be difficult for those with vision impairments. **[H]** Assistive listening devices can be used here. **[H] [M] [T] [V]** Close tables leave limited room for service animals.*	**Table** American Noisy Reservations strongly recommended Call 90 days Med. waits 11 am–4 pm 4 pm–closing

☐ **Starring Rolls Cafe** [E-3] L/D/S $8 🗑️🍷 | **8** | **8**

*Recently revamped, this former bakery now features specialty sandwiches and salads, mini-desserts, gourmet chocolates, and a fresh-roasted house-blend coffee. Outdoor seating. **[D]** Turkey on focaccia, vegetarian pita (both $7), and smoked salmon on a bagel ($5.79) are among the items for health-conscious diets. **[M]** First register on left is wheelchair/ECV accessible.*	**Counter** American Noisy Med. waits 10 am–closing

Eatery descriptions and ratings are explained on page 323.

🔔 Best Bets in Disney-MGM Studios for Special Dietary Needs

- ✔ The table-service restaurants (Hollywood Brown Derby, Mama Melrose's Ristorante Italiano, 50s Prime Time Café, Sci-Fine Dine-In Theater, and Hollywood & Vine), for their ability to take Advance Reservations and advance special requests.
- ✔ ABC Commissary, for its no-advance-notice kosher menu.
- ✔ Anaheim Produce, for its variety of fresh fruit.
- ✔ Starring Rolls, for its health-conscious salad and sandwich offerings.

(sidebar labels, left margin: Planning · Your Special Need · Getting There · Staying in Style · Touring · Dining · Resources · Index)

Disney-MGM Studios Eateries
(continued)

Deb Wills' Rating / *Deb Koma's Rating*

☐ Studio Catering Co. [C-4] L/D/S $11 — | 7

This spot was closed for a while, but recently reopened to accommodate the crowds anticipated for the nearby new Lights! Motors! Action! Stunt Show. The new menu includes more unusual items, such as flatbread sandwiches (cumin-spiced lamb kefta with baba ghanoush and harissa sauce, tandoori chicken with tomato and cucumber raita, steak "gyro" with roasted red pepper hummus and tomato and onion relish). The kids' menu includes items such as a grilled chicken wrap with lettuce and cream cheese, while desserts include seasonal fruit tarts, lemon curd in a meringue shell, and panna cotta with strawberries. **[D] [G]** Gluten-free items available on request. **[M]** Register on far right is accessible.

Counter · Mixed · Outdoor seating · Med. noise · Average waits · 11:00 am–park closing

☐ Toluca Legs Turkey Co. [G-3] L/D $8 4 | 3

Part of the outdoor Sunset Ranch Market mini food court on Sunset Blvd. As you may have guessed, you can get a turkey leg ($4.69) to munch on. You can also get foot-long hot dogs with chili and/or cheese ($3.69–$4.89). Seating is outdoors at covered picnic benches. Other stands nearby offer burgers, chicken strips, soup, ice cream, McDonald's fries, and fresh fruit.

Counter · American · Noisy · Med. waits · 11 am–closing

☐ Toy Story Pizza Planet [B-5] L/D $11 5 | 6

Pizza and salads in a spot patterned after the kids' eatery in the original Toy Story movie. Seating is available both indoors (wide open upstairs area) and outside. Game arcade adjacent to first-floor seating area. **[A][U][I][S]** Can get very noisy due to arcade. **[D]** Veggie pizza ($5.99) available. **[D][G]** Also has gluten-free pizza available (not on the menu, just ask!). **[Ö]** Pictorial menu for foreign-language speakers. **[M]** First register on right is wheelchair/ECV accessible. Reach second-floor seating via elevator located in arcade area.

Counter · American · Very noisy · Long waits · 11:00 am–1 hour before park closing

☐ Writer's Stop [A-4] B/L/S $8 7 | 6

Coffee bar, featuring fresh-brewed java and iced concoctions, as well as baked goodies and very friendly cast members. **[M]** Wheelchair/ECV accessible, but difficult to negotiate around displays and seating.

Counter · American · Avg. noise

Selected Disney-MGM Studios Snack Shops and Carts

Treat	Found at
Ice cream treats	Dinosaur Gertie's
Stuffed pretzels, drinks	Min & Bill's Dockside Diner
Non-alcoholic beverages	Peevy's Polar Pipeline
Lounge with specialty drinks	Tune-In Lounge
Fresh fruit	Anaheim Produce
Ice cream treats; sugar-free/fat-free/dairy-free	Hollywood Scoops
McDonald's fries	Fairfax Fries
Smoothies, coffees	KRNR The Rock Station

Disney's Animal Kingdom Eateries

Disney's Animal Kingdom has a **limited number of places to eat**. In fact, there is only one full-service restaurant, the Rainforest Café, located at the park entrance.

For the safety of the animals here, **no straws or lids are available** with your beverages, although you can purchase an Animal Topper Sports Bottle for $6.79 (comes with beverage).

Beer is sold at some counter and quick-service spots, and the Dawa Bar and Rainforest Café offer **full bar service**.

Bright Idea: Strawberry juice bars and "Itzakadoozie" ice pops found at many snack carts are all gluten-free.

Flame Tree Barbecue [E-4] L/D/S $13	7	7
The place for BBQ ribs or smoked beef, chicken, and pork. Also serves up sandwiches, salads and fries. Shaded outdoor seating, some areas even semi-secluded and quiet. **[A][U][T][S]** There are some very nice quieter areas with shade—you'll just need to walk a little to find them. Follow the signs for additional seating. **[D]** Ribs, chicken, and salad are gluten-free and dairy-free. Tortilla shells on the salad contain gluten; request without the tortilla shells. **[F]** Birds and small animals may be found in seating areas. **[G][D][♥]** BBQ chicken salad ($7) offered for lighter/veggie fare.	**Counter** American/ Barbecue Quiet Med. waits 10:00 am– 5:00 pm

Pizzafari [B-4] L/D/S $9	7	7
Beautifully painted restaurant with themed rooms serving pizza, deli sandwiches, and salads. Light breakfast fare occasionally offered, must go inside to see. Frozen lemonade available for hot days, but beware of sugar content. **[A][U][T][I][S]** Can be very noisy—could cause overstimulation. Look for less crowded room. **[D]** **[W]** Kosher items available without advance notice. **[D]** Grilled chicken Caesar salad for lighter fare ($6.39). Plain pizza ($5.49) is the only vegetarian option.	**Counter** Italian Very noisy Seating in/outdoors 10 am–5 pm

Selected Disney's Animal Kindom Snack Shops and Carts

Treat	Found at
Fresh cookies	Chip 'n' Dale's Cookie Cabin
Full bar	Dawa Bar
Fresh fruit; juices	Harambe Fruit Market
Baked goods; special coffees	Kusafiri Coffee Shop and Bakery
Ice cream; smoothies	Tamu Tamu Refreshments
Ice cream	Anandapur Ice Cream
Pot stickers; stir fry chicken	Chakranadi Chicken Shop
Gluten-free/dairy-free ice cream	Dino Bite Snacks
Ice cream, drinks	Dino Diner
McDonald's fries	Petrifries

Disney's Animal Kingdom Eateries
(continued)

Deb Wills' Rating
Deb Koma's Rating

Rainforest Cafe [B-7] B/L/D $45 ($32) 6 | 5

Similar to Downtown Disney Rainforest Cafe, this one serves breakfast as well as lunch and dinner. Access this restaurant, the only table-service spot at Disney's Animal Kingdom, from inside or outside of theme park. Very themed dining areas with lots of sounds, lights, and movement, including a thunderstorm and gorilla beating his chest. Huge menu that should satisfy most needs. Food portions large. **[A] [U] [T] [I] [S]** Can be very noisy. **[F]** Some effects might be scary—lightning, loud thunder, animatronic animals. **[D]** Portobello and veggie sandwich ($11.99) for vegetarian diets; other items (such as Hong Kong Stir-fry) may be available sans meat. **[M]** Tables are very close together, maneuvering can be tricky. **[V]** Dimly lit at times.

Table
American
Noisy
Reservations recommended
8:30–10 am, 10:30 am–1.5 hours after park closting

Restaurantosaurus [E-6] B/L/D/S $11 5 | 6

In the morning, this eatery is Donald's Breakfastosaurus—a character buffet with the Duck, Mickey, Goofy, and Pluto ($17.99/adults, $9.99/kids 3–9). Very basic breakfast food; no fancy items here. Make any special dietary requests in advance. Long waits at breakfast. Lunch/dinner is McDonald's burgers, fries, salads, and Happy Meals. **[A] [U][T] [I]** Can be very noisy—could cause overstimulation, but character meals are better meet-and-greet opportunities than in the parks. Small, quieter rooms further away from main serving area. **[R]** Breakfast is all-you-can-eat buffet. **[D]** Veggie burger on menu ($6.19). **[D] [G]** Gluten-free burgers (not buns) available. Salad can be made gluten-free on request. Dairy-free ice cream on request.

Counter
American
Very noisy
Reservations at breakfast
8:00–10:30 am 11:30 am– 3:30 pm

Tusker House Restaurant [B-2] B/L/S $14 8 | 7

Our favorite place to dine at Disney's Animal Kingdom offers rotisserie chicken ($8) and salmon ($8). Very limited breakfast items. Lots of indoor seating; some outside available, too. **[D]** Salads, fish, and turkey wrap for lighter fare. Vegetable sandwich on menu ($7.29). Rotisserie chicken, salmon, and salad are gluten-free. Fries may not be, due to cross-contamination.

Counter
American
9:30–10:30am, 11:00 am– varies

Best Bets in Animal Kingdom for Special Dietary Needs

✔ Dino Bites, for its gluten-free/dairy-free ice cream
✔ Harambe Fruit Market, for its fresh fruit items
✔ Pizzafari, which has Kosher items without advance notice
✔ Rainforest Cafe, for its ability to make advance reservations and advance special requests
✔ Tusker House, a counter-service with an unusual menu (grilled salmon!)

Meal Plus Certificate

Disney's Animal Kingdom offers a unique money-saving program at its restaurants. Called the Meal Plus Certificate, it is good at Restaurantosaurus, Flame Tree Barbecue, Pizzafari, and Tusker House. The certificate is redeemable for the following: a counter-service entrée and beverage; one box of popcorn or ice cream bar; and one bottled drink (soda or water). You can purchase the certificates at counter-service restaurants or at Disney's Animal Kingdom's Guest Relations office. Price: $11.99 for adults (10 & up), $5.99 for children (3–9).

Planning | *Your Special Needs* | *Getting There* | *Staying in Style* | *Touring* | *Dining* | *Resources* | *Index*

Downtown Disney Marketplace Eateries

☐ **Cap'n Jack's Restaurant**	L/D	$49	♋	3	3

A casual nautical restaurant overlooking Lake Buena Vista. Menu includes crab cakes, shrimp, salmon, chicken and ribs. Advance Reservations are not accepted. **[G]** Primarily a seafood restaurant—those with seafood/shellfish allergy may want to avoid. **[D]** Grilled portobello mushroom sandwich ($9) at lunch; no vegetarian entrées on regular dinner menu.

Table
Seafood
Short waits
11:30 am–10:30 pm

☐ **Earl of Sandwich**	B/L/D/S	$10		7	7

Hot sandwiches, salads, wraps and "grab and go" food. Limited breakfast items, kids' selections. Open 8:00 am–11:00 pm. **[D]** Tuna, fruit, and chicken salad. Hot Caprese sandwich ($5) for vegetarians. **[M]** Ordering and pickup queues may be a little difficult for wheelchair/ECV users.

Counter
American
Noisy
8 am–11 pm

☐ **Ghirardelli Soda Fountain & Chocolate Shop**	S	$8	✗	9	10

Straight from San Francisco comes this famous chocolate maker! Best hot fudge sundaes at Disney. Sundaes, shakes, and malts. On cold nights, stop in for a hot chocolate. Limited tables and counter/stools. Indoor/outdoor seating. Friday/Saturday hours: 9:30 am–midnight. **[D]** Sugar and fat-free ice cream available. **[M]** Wheelchair/ECV accessible, but difficult to negotiate around displays and seating.

Counter
American
Noisy
Med. waits
10:30 am–11:00 pm

☐ **Rainforest Cafe**	L/D	$45 ($32)		6	5

Similar to Disney's Animal Kingdom's Rainforest Cafe, with very themed dining areas that have lots of sounds, lights, and movement, including a thunderstorm and gorilla beating his chest. There's even a volcano that periodically erupts! Huge menu should satisfy most needs—food portions here are large. Open until midnight on Fridays and Saturdays. **[A][U][F][T][I][S]** Can be very noisy—could cause overstimulation. Some effects might be scary—dark, flashes of lightning, loud thunder, animatronic animals. **[D]** Hong Kong stir fry and portobello and veggie sandwich for vegetarian diets; other items may be available sans meat. **[D][W]** Kosher items not available here. **[V]** Dimly lit at times—may be difficult for those with vision impairments. **[M]** Dark and crowded seating areas may be difficult to negotiate.

Table
American
Noisy
Call for reservations: 407-827-8500
Very long waits
11:30–4 pm, 5–11 pm

☐ **Ronald's Fun House (McDonald's)**	B/L/D/S	$8		2	4

Your basic McDonald's, just like at home. Open 8:00 am–1:00 am. **[A][U][T][I][S]** Can be very noisy—could cause overstimulation. **[A][U]** Outdoor play area. **[D]** High-calorie, high-fat foods. Go with salads and use lemon for dressing if you're looking for light eating. **[D][G]** McDonald's Web site at http://www.mcdonalds.com/usa/eat/nutrition_info.html has information on gluten-free items, ingredient lists, and allergens . Gluten-free items include burger patty (no bun), fries, apple dippers with caramel, and side salads.

Counter
American
Very noisy
Med. waits
8:00 am–1:00am

☐ **Wolfgang Puck Express**	B/L/D/S	$14	✗	6	6

Fast food for the upscale set. Inside and outside dining. Features pizzas, pastas, soups, and salads. Some sushi and sandwiches prepackaged. Drink homemade lemonade, frozen cafe mocha, wines by the bottle and glass, and beer on tap. Dine outside or take out. **[M]** Queues and indoor/outdoor seating areas are tight for guests using wheelchairs/ECVs.

Counter
American
Noisy
8:30 am–10:00 pm

Downtown Disney Pleasure Island Eateries

Fulton's Crab House L/D $65

Owned and operated by the Levy Corporation, Fulton's is housed in a beautiful, old-style steamboat and serves up a variety of seafood specialties, like Cioppino ($19), fresh fish, crab legs, and lobster dishes. Advance Reservations are accepted and suggested. **[D]** Non-seafood entrées include filet mignon ($33) and a very good double-cut pork chop ($25). **[D]** **[W]** Kosher items are not available here. **[G]** Primarily a seafood restaurant—those with seafood/shellfish allergy may want to avoid this restaurant.

	7 7
Table	
Seafood	
Med. noise	
Avg. waits	
11:30 am–4:00 pm, 5:00 pm–11:00 pm	

© Deb Wills

New Zealand Orange Roughy with Shrimp ($30)

Missing Link Sausage Co. S $10

One of the few places to grab a quick bite on Pleasure Island. Limited menu of sausage, burgers, and hot dogs. **[D]** Portobello mushroom wrap for vegetarians ($5.25). **[D][W]** Kosher items are not available here. **[M]** Wheelchair/ECV accessible, but difficult to negotiate.

	3 3
Counter	
American	
Noisy	
7 pm–1 am	

Portobello Yacht Club L/D $57 ($29)

Upscale Italian in a club atmosphere. Owned and operated by the Levy Corporation, which also runs the neighboring Fulton's Crab House. Main menu items: pasta, veal, seafood. Reservations accepted. **[D]** A number of chicken and fish entrées for health-conscious diets. **[D][W]** Kosher items not available here. **[M]** Wheelchair/ECV accessible, but difficult to negotiate around seating.

	7 7
Table	
Italian	
Med. noise	
Avg. waits	
11:30 am–11 pm	

Raglan Road

An authentic Irish pub and restaurant, scheduled to open in summer 2005 in the space formerly occupied by the Pleasure Island Jazz Company. The pub will offer traditional and contemporary Irish music, storytelling, and dance. It is owned and operated by Great Irish Pubs Florida, Inc. The menu for the new restaurant is expected to be a blend of traditional Irish fare with modern twists. Pleasure Island club admission will not be required for entry into the pub.

	? ?
Table	
Irish	
Other factors not known at time of writing	

Eatery descriptions and ratings are explained on page 323.

Downtown Disney West Side Eateries

Bongos Cuban Cafe — L/D — $33 — 7 7

Latin flavor in the kitchen and in the theming of Gloria Estefan's beautifully decorated restaurant. Salads, sandwiches for lunch; salads, seafood, chicken, and beef for dinner. Additional seating upstairs. Hours: 11:00 am-10:30 pm at restaurant, 10:30 am-11:00 pm at express window. **[A][U][F][L][M]** Tables and chairs very close together. **[D]** Salads for lighter fare. Special vegetarian plate ($14) available. **[H]** Tile floors and walls create lots of echoes; very noisy environment. **[L]** Padded metal chairs with no arms.

Table	
Cuban	
Very noisy	
No advance reservations	
Long waits	

FoodQuest — L/D/S — $12 — 6 6

When hunger pangs hit you at DisneyQuest, run up to this fast food place. (Must have DisneyQuest admission to enter.) Several counters serve up different items—pizza, pasta, sandwiches, salads, hot and cold wraps. Several booths have Internet access. **[D]** Several vegetarian options available, including spinach/artichoke dip with chips ($6.50), pasta with marinara (meatless) sauce ($6.50), pizza. Herbal teas available. **[M]** Lines to get food can wind around and be difficult to negotiate. Located on upper level of DisneyQuest—take the elevator.

Counter	
American	
Noisy	
Med. waits	
11:30 am-10:30 pm	

House of Blues — L/D — $39 ($30) — 5 5

American food with a Cajun flair offering traditional foods plus gumbo, jambalaya, and etouffée. Sunday Gospel Brunch disappointing, food quality and service low. Located near Cirque du Soleil and DisneyQuest, "HOB" looks like a weatherbeaten wharfside dive. Inside is an equally aged interior with comfy booths. Live blues bands keep the joint cookin' (and make conversation difficult). Headliners play at the concert hall next door. A Gospel Brunch is held every Sunday. Open to midnight Tue-Wed., and until 2:00 am Thu.-Sat. **[A][U][T][I][S]** Can be very noisy—could cause overstimulation. **[D]** Few items on the light side. **[D][W]** Kosher items are not available here.

Table	
American	
Very noisy	
Reservations for dinner	
Long waits	
11 am-11 pm (open later on Tue.-Sat.)	

Planet Hollywood — L/D — $40 — 6 5

The big blue world planted outside of Downtown Disney's West Side is the Orlando outlet of this global chain that features movie and TV memorabilia as it serves up sandwiches and burgers, entrée salads, pasta, and more. Portions are generous, but quality is just so-so. **[D][W]** Kosher items are not available here. **[A][U][H][T][I][S]** Can be very loud. **[V]** Dimly lit.

Table	
American	
Very noisy	
Long waits	
11 am-1 am	

Wetzel's Pretzels — S — $4 — 5 5

Gourmet pretzels with dips, hot dogs, and Haagen Dazs Ice Cream. A second kiosk in the Marketplace. Indoor seating. Open 10:30 am-11:00 pm Sun-Thu, 10:30-midnight Fri-Sat (West Side), and 10:30 am-11:30 pm (Marketplace). **[D]** Sorbet, frozen lemonade, and granitas available.

Counter	
American	
Med. noise	

Eatery descriptions and ratings are explained on page 323.

Downtown Disney West Side Eateries
(continued)

			Deb Wills' Rating	Deb Koma's Rating

☐ **Wolfgang Puck Grand Cafe**	L/D	$41 ($32)	7	7

Hearty soups, wood-fired pizzas, salads, pasta, rotiserrie, grill, sushi, and sashimi (that's raw fish to you and me!). Seating is available inside, at the bar, and outside. Seating is crowded. Try for a late lunch instead of dinner. **[A][U][T][I][S]** This restaurant can be very noisy—could cause overstimulation. **[D]** Turkey burger ($11) as well as other lighter options are on menu. Some vegetarian choices, like pumpkin ravioli ($14) and penne with spinach and goat cheese ($14). **[L]** Tables for two are very small.

> **Table**
> American
> Very noisy
> Reservations for dinner
> Very long waits
> 11:30 am–11 pm

☐ **Wolfgang Puck Dining Room**	D	$56	8	8

Puck's Dining Room is upstairs, upscale, and pricey. Noise carries up from the café downstairs. Seafood, duck, lamb, beef, and risotto. Reservations recommended. Open 6:00 pm–10:30 pm. Dress code is "business casual" (no swimwear/tank tops/flip-flops) and is strictly enforced. **[G][D]** Be sure to call in advance for special dietary concerns.

> **Table**
> American
> Long waits

☐ **Wolfgang Puck Express**	L/D	$13	⌀	6	6

Fast food for the upscale set. Inside and outside dining. Features pizzas, pastas, soups, and salads. Some sushi and sandwiches prepackaged. See page 342 for the Marketplace location. Open 11:00 am–11:00 pm. **[M]** Shop and the outdoor seating are tight for wheelchair/ECV users.

> **Counter**
> American
> Med. noise

☐ **Wonderland Cafe**	S	$8	6	6

Located inside DisneyQuest (admission required), this is the spot for a quick pick-me-up or a sweet treat. Lots of gorgeous desserts (the place is run by the Cheesecake Factory, after all) and specialty coffees. Comfy seating in tables and booths. **[D]** Herbal teas available. **[M]** Located on upper floor of DisneyQuest— just take the elevator!

> **Counter**
> American
> Noisy
> 11:00 am–11:45 pm

© Debra Martin Koma

An Internet station at the Wonderland Cafe

Planning
Your Special Need
Getting There
Staying in Style
Touring
Dining
Resources
Index

Resort Dining

There's a number of really good restaurants at the resorts—in fact, resort restaurants are **generally much better** than those found in the theme parks. That said, there are a few things to keep in mind when dining at your Walt Disney World resort:

Some **kosher items** (usually chicken and hot dogs) are available in the food courts of Disney's value and moderate resort hotels. But be sure to give 24 hours' notice if you'll have a group dining, or if you're at a deluxe resort.

All resorts have at least one **microwave** available for warming foods, located in their food court or counter-service area.

In addition to the prepackaged "grab and go" items found in most of the food courts, the resort general stores **sell some food items**. You'll find the most variety at the Disney Vacation Club resorts, since their units have kitchen facilities. Staples such as bread, milk, donuts, and cereal are generally available—remember, though, that you'll pay a premium. We have found the Hess Express gas stations on Disney property to be less expensive than the resort general store on many items. See page 118 in chapter 4 for a table listing generally available food items at the resort shops.

Bring any **specialty items** you don't want to do without, like sugar-free syrup, Splenda or other sugar substitutes, and low-sodium salt. These types of items are sometimes provided, but may not always be available. We did not find low-carb items for sale in any of the resort general stores, for example. Each venue decides what to offer (such as Splenda), so just because you find an item one place doesn't mean you'll find it everywhere.

© MediaMarx, Inc.

Everything Pop is the food court and general shopping area at Pop Century Resort

Resort Eateries
(All-Star Resorts and Disney's Animal Kingdom Lodge)

Deb Wills' Rating
Deb Koma's Rating

All-Star Resorts Eateries

■ End Zone, Intermission, World Premiere B/L/D/S $13	5	5

Food courts offering typical fast food fare. Breakfast items include eggs and bacon, waffle platter ($5.69). Lunch/dinner serve up burgers, hot dogs, sandwiches, pizza. Grab'n'go items, salads, pastas, and hand-dipped ice cream. Indoor seating with limited outdoor seating. **[D][W]** Kosher meals available without advance notice. Inquire about gluten- and dairy-free items. **[Ö]** Video screen menu aids foreign-language speakers.	**Counter** American Very noisy 6 am–12 am

Disney's Animal Kingdom Lodge Resort Eateries

■ Boma–Flavors of Africa B/D $31 ♨ ✄	9	7

A unique dining experience in one of Disney's most unusual resorts. Boma features a wide variety of foods for every taste and a kitchen staff that goes out of its way to be accommodating. Breakfast ($15.99 adults/$8.99 children 3–9) items include standard fare, roasted meats, a few South African favorites and Frunch, a very sweet but tasty juice! At dinner ($24.99/$10.99), don't miss the hearty soups, smoked meats, grilled fish, and desserts. **[A][U][T][I][S]** Can be very noisy—could cause overstimulation. **[R]** All-you-care-to-eat buffet. **[D]** Open kitchen right behind food stations make chefs very accessible for questions and requests. Huge selection of vegetarian and vegan items included in buffet. **[L]** Heavy wooden chairs, most with no arms. **[Ö]** Traditional Japanese breakfast available upon request.	**Buffet** African Very noisy Reservations a must Call 90 days Long waits 7:30 am– 11:00 am, 5:00 pm– 10:00 pm

© Deb Wills

Boma

■ Jiko–The Cooking Place D $54 ♨ ✄	9	10

Africa meets Asia meets California—fusion cooking reigns supreme in this stylish restaurant! Flatbreads, dips, soups, salads, and creative entrées prepared by well-known Disney chef Anette Grecchi Gray, who has a penchant for designing unique menus. Relaxed atmosphere, knowledgeable servers. No tank tops/swimwear—dress is "smart casual." Wait for your table at the Cape Town Lounge and Wine Bar located at the entrance to the restaurant. **[D]** Fish and vegetarian selections standard. Don't miss the tandoori tofu with grains and veggies (spicy) ($17.50). Many menu items are gluten-free. We've found this restaurant to be very accommodating to special diet requests. **[V]** Dimly lit, may be hard to see for those with vision impairments.	**Table** African Med. noise Reservations a must Call 90 days Short waits 5:30 pm– 10:00 pm

■ The Mara B/L/D $13	8	8

The only option open for lunch at Disney's Animal Kingdom Lodge, this counter-service spot offers grilled items, salads, soups, baked goods, and some prepackaged "grab 'n' go" items. TV plays in the corner of the room. **[A][U][I][S]** Can be quite noisy. **[L]** Chairs are armless, but very uncomfortable. There is banquette seating on two walls—tables move, so a larger person can sit more comfortably there. **[Ö]** Video screen menus aid foreign-language speakers.	**Counter** African Very noisy 6:00 am– 11:30 pm

Planning | Your Special Need | Getting There | Staying in Style | Touring | Dining | Resources | Index

Resort Eateries
(BoardWalk Inn & Villas Resort)

Deb Wills' Rating   Deb Koma's Rating

BoardWalk Inn & Villas Resort Eateries

Big River Grille & Brewing Works	L/D	$41 ($37)	🏳️	6	5

Brewpub with ordinary sandwich/salad fare. Typical items: burgers, steaks, ribs ($19.99), chicken Caesar salad ($10.99). Brewery stays open later than restaurant; last call 1:00 am. Indoor/outdoor seating. **[R]** Recovering alcoholics should be aware that this is a brewpub, with beer made on the premises. **[D]** Some chicken and fish entrées (grilled salmon $18.99) geared to health-conscious diets. No specific vegetarian entrée offered. **[M]** Crowded tables make navigating indoors difficult. Consider sitting outside, weather permitting.

Table
American
Noisy
Reservations
407-560-0253
11:30 am–
11:00 pm

BoardWalk Bakery	B/L/S	$10		7	7

Those yummy aromas emanating from the BoardWalk area early in the morning are probably coming from the ovens here! Fresh baked goods, specialty coffees, breakfast burritos, and light lunches. **[D]** Whole fresh fruit is available, as is a mixed fruit bowl ($3.59). Peanut butter and jelly for kids. Fat-free muffins ($2.29) available. **[L]** Armless chairs available. **[M][L]** Space inside shop is small, hard to navigate. **[A][U][F]** Birds love to hang out here and try to grab a crumb or two from you. **[S]** It's peaceful here in the mornings overlooking Crescent Lake.

Counter
Bakery
Limited
outdoor
seating
6:30 am–
11:00 pm

ESPN Club	L/D	$37		4	4

The ultimate sports bar, with more than 100 television screens—even in the restrooms—all showing some type of athletic endeavors. Seating is cramped—there are booths, tables, and high bar stools. Usual bar fare. Typical items: burgers, grilled meat, sandwiches, and salads. **[A][U][T][I][S]** Can be very noisy—could cause overstimulation. **[R]** Recovering alcoholics should be aware that this is largely a sports bar environment. In addition, those recovering from or with a gambling addiction should be aware that more than 100 televisions fill this restaurant, all televising sporting events. **[D]** A few chicken and fish options are concessions to health-conscious diets. A few vegetarian selections are available (veggie burger $7.99, portobello sandwich $8.99) also available. **[G]** Smoking is allowed in the bar area.

Table
American
Very noisy
No
reservations
Med. waits
Indoor seating
11:30 am–1 am
(Open until
2:00 am on
weekends)

Flying Fish Cafe	D	$65	🦞🏳️	9	9

This beautifully appointed restaurant on the BoardWalk serves up some of the freshest, most inventively prepared seafood we've ever had. Menu changes seasonally, but typically includes several non-seafood choices (veal chop $39, steak $38) in addition to its wide variety of fish and shellfish. No tank tops/swimwear—dress is "smart casual." **[G]** Primarily a seafood restaurant—those with seafood/shellfish allergy may want to avoid. **[D]** Fish entrées for health-conscious diets. At least one vegetarian selection, like Fondutta Ravioli ($21), is also available. **[A][U][I][S]** Crowds can be noisy—for a quieter experience, ask to be seated in the back under the "canopy."

Table
Seafood
Very noisy
Reservations
strongly
recommended
Call 90 days
Med. waits
5:30–10 pm

Resort Eateries
(BoardWalk Resort and Caribbean Beach Resort)

BoardWalk Inn & Villas Resort Eateries *(continued)*

			Deb Wills' Rating	Deb Koma's Rating

Seashore Sweets | S | $6 | 7 | 7

Just the place for your candy or ice cream fix, this old-style shop also has a display of memorabilia from the Miss America beauty pageant, traditionally held in Atlantic City (hence the BoardWalk connection). Hard and soft-serve ice cream in cones, waffle cones, or bowls, shakes and floats, as well as coffee, soft drinks, bulk and packaged candy, including mix your own colors M&Ms. **[D]** Sugar-free candy available. **[L]** Armless chairs available. **[M][L]** Space inside shop is small, hard to navigate. **[A][U][F]** Birds love to hang outside here and try to grab a crumb or two from you.

Counter
Ice cream
Limited
Outdoor
Seating
Med. waits
1:00–
11:00 pm

Spoodles | B/D | $47 | 7 | 7

This popular eatery features fresh seafood, grilled meats, flatbreads, and pastas with Italian, Greek, and Spanish flavors. Breakfast features American food as well as frittatas (open-faced omelets). Indoor seating. Outside pizza window open noon–midnight. **[G]** Current breakfast flatbread made with wheat flour. **[D]** A number of low-fat entrées, including fresh fruit plate ($7.99) at lunchtime, for health-conscious diets. Vegetarian selections include gnocchi with mushrooms ($18) and four-cheese flatbread ($7).

Table
Mediterranean
Reservations
suggested
Med. waits
7:30–11 am
5–10 pm

Caribbean Beach Resort

Old Port Royale | B/L/D/S | $14 | 6 | 6

A collection of fast food stations offering pizza, pasta, burgers, rotisserie items and a grab'n'go area. Extensive indoor seating. **[D]** Vegetable platter ($6.99) available at Bridgetown Broiler. Also has mac and cheese for kids. **[D][W]** Kosher selections available without advance notice. **[L]** Chairs without arms available.

Counter
American
6:30 am–
11:00 pm

Shutters | D | $40 | 6 | 6

Caribbean Beach Resort's only table-service restaurant offers American cuisine with Caribbean flavors. This eatery is open only for dinner. It features surprisingly good char-grilled tuna ($18.99). **[D]** The black bean soup is vegetarian ($4.29). Fettuccini can be vegetarian. Marinated tofu entrée. **[C][L]** Heavy wooden armless chairs with backs.

Table
American
Reservations
suggested
5:30 pm–
10:00 pm

© Debra Martin Koma

Shutters

Eatery descriptions and ratings are explained on page 323.

Resort Eateries
(Contemporary Resort)

Deb Wills' Rating

Deb Koma's Rating

Contemporary Resort Eateries

☐ California Grill	D	$59	🐕🎗	10	10

The magnificent view alone would draw you to this top-notch restaurant at Disney. Open kitchen keeps restaurant noise level constantly high. Main items: Sushi, flatbreads, seafood, and meats—well-known for its pork tenderloin ($22.75) and beef filet ($34.50). Menu changes weekly. No tank tops/swimwear—dress is "smart casual." Check-in at this restaurant is on the second floor—you're escorted upstairs via private elevator. Wait for your table in the lounge area at the restaurant's entrance in overstuffed chairs looking out at the Magic Kingdom below. **[D]** Veggie appetizers, pumpkin lasagna ($20) entrée–vegetarian options specifically indicated on the menu. We've found this restaurant to be particularly accommodating to special needs diners. **[L]** Chairs with no arms in dining room. Cocktail chairs with arms in lounge.

Table
American
Noisy
Reservations recommended
Call 90 days
Med. waits
5:30 pm-10:00 pm
(Lounge is 5:30 pm-midnight)

☐ Chef Mickey's	B/D	$33		7	7

Located on the fourth-floor concourse, with the monorail occasionally gliding by overhead, this is a character dining experience with lots of energy, good food, and fun. Standard breakfast ($17.99 adults/$9.99 children 3-9) fare. Dinner ($26.99/$11.99) is also standard American fare: beef, chicken, pasta, seafood. Kids have their own buffet. Make your own sundae bar a splurge! Restaurant is open–ceiling is ten stories overhead. **[A][U][T][I][S]** Can be very noisy–often there's loud music and napkin twirling as the characters make the rounds. Monorail frequently glides overhead. Could cause overstimulation. **[R]** All-you-can-eat buffet. Waiting area is part of Outer Rim cocktail lounge. **[D]** Call in advance for special needs. Ask available chefs for ingredients' details.

Buffet
American
Very noisy
Reservations suggested
Call 90 days
Med.-long waits
7-11:30 am, 5:00-9:30 pm

☐ Concourse Steakhouse	B/L/D	$42		4	6

This is an open restaurant adjacent to Chef Mickey's–sometimes it's hard to tell where one restaurant ends and the other begins. Not only does the noise filter in, but overflow guests do, too. Breakfast has omelets, pancakes, waffles, and a fruit plate. Lunch features pizza, salads, soups, and sandwiches. Dinner offers ribs, steak, shrimp, and salmon. Solid quality at breakfast and lunch, but spotty for dinner. There are much better steaks at Disney than at this eatery! **[A][U][T][I][S]** This restaurant can be very noisy–could cause overstimulation. **[D]** Be sure to call well in advance with any special dietary needs. **[L]** Chairs without arms are available.

Table
Steakhouse
Noisy
Reservations suggested
Call 90 days
7:30-11 am, noon-2:00 pm, 5:30-10 pm

☐ Food & Fun Center	B/L/D/S	$13		5	5

Fast food area adjacent to game arcade. Indoor seating. **[A][U][T][I][S]** Can be very noisy–could cause overstimulation. **[D]** The grab'n'go area offers a veggie sandwich ($5.69) consisting of portobello mushroom, tomato, yellow squash and zucchini, onions, and red pepper on foccacia roll. One interesting note is that there is a section of breads (bagels, muffins, etc.) with a complete listing of ingredients posted. Chef not usually available for special dietary questions/concerns. **[D][W]** No kosher meals are available.

Counter
American
Noisy
Med. waits
Open 24 hours

Eatery descriptions and ratings are explained on page 323.

Resort Eateries
(Coronado Springs and Fort Wilderness Resorts)

Deb Wills' Rating — Deb Koma's Rating

Coronado Springs Resort Eateries

Maya Grill — B/D — $48 — 6 | 6

© MediaMarx, Inc.

Maya Grill

As the name implies, Mayan architecture inspired the décor and design of this restaurant that holds a daily breakfast buffet ($11.99 adults/$6.99 children 3–9). In the evenings, it becomes a fairly typical steakhouse that caters to the large amount of convention trade that Coronado Springs hosts. Usual dinner items include steaks, ribs ($19), and catch-of-the-day. A lunch buffet could be added in the future. **[R]** Breakfast is an all-you-care-to-eat buffet. **[D]** Some lighter fare are available, such as seafood and grilled chicken breast entrées. Vegetarian selections are available upon request, but are not on regular menu. **[V]** Low lighting.

Buffet/Table
American
Med. noise
Reservations suggested
Call 90 days
Short waits
7:00 am–11:00 am, 5:00 pm–10:00 pm

Pepper Market — B/L/D/S — $20($12) — 7 | 7

This is a unique food court with freshly made items. You go from station to station to choose which foods you want—hot entrées are made to order. Stations include: Mexican, stir fry, American, pasta, pizza, bakery, and a kid's station. **[D]** Chicken and fish entrées available for health-conscious diets. Vegetarian selections also available—ask the chef at the particular station. **[G]** Avoid the wok station if you have nut allergies—peanut oil used in cooking.

Counter
Multi-Ethnic
Noisy
Indoor seats
Med. waits
7 am–11 pm

La Tienda — B/L/D/S — $8 — 6 | 6

This little convenience store is located next to Pepper Market—a great place to grab a light snack or sandwich on the run. Take your food back to your room or outside, where you can sit at umbrella tables overlooking Lago Dorado. **[D]** Whole fresh fruit and juices are available. Also offered are prepackaged sandwiches, including turkey and chicken wraps.

Counter
American
Med. noise
Short waits
6 am–12 am

Fort Wilderness Resort & Campground Eatery

Trail's End Restaurant — B/L/D — $21 — 7 | 7

One of the best values on Disney property, this homey restaurant offers standard buffet fare prepared in a no-nonsense manner. It also has a pizza carryout. Breakfast ($10.99/$6.99), lunch ($10.99/$6.99), and dinner ($16.99/$7.99) are all served from a buffet. Typical lunch/dinner items include: carved meats, fish, ribs, and chicken. Pizza is available for take-out next door. **[R]** All-you-care-to-eat buffet. **[D]** A number of chicken and fish entrées are on the buffet for health-conscious diets. Soup and salad bar special ($11.50) for lighter eaters. **[D][W]** Kosher meals and other special requests are available with advance notice. **[L]** Chairs without arms are available.

Buffet
American
Noisy
Indoor seating
Med. waits
7:30–11 am, noon–2:30 pm, 4:30–9:30 pm

See also Hoop-Dee-Doo Revue (page 364) and Mickey's Backyard BBQ (page 362).

Planning — Your Special Need — Getting There — Staying in Style — Touring — Dining — Resources — Index

Resort Eateries
(Grand Floridian Resort)

Deb Wills' Rating
Deb Koma's Rating

Grand Floridian Resort Eateries

Cítricos | D | $57 | | 6 | 8

This elegant restaurant combines the simple and fresh cooking flavors from the south of France with some unusual dishes. Tables are well-spaced. Typical entrées: grilled fish, lamb chops ($29), filet ($33). Closed Mondays and Tuesdays. No tank tops/swimwear—dress is "smart casual." Indoor seating. **[D]** A number of fish entrées for health-conscious diets. At least one vegetarian selection, such as Braised Autumn Vegetables ($21), is also available on the menu.

Table
Floridian
Med. noise
Reservations
suggested
5:30–10 pm

Garden View Lounge | S | $25 | | 8 | 9

Elegant lounge with starched linens and fine china, offers daily English tea for a quiet mid-afternoon break. Special tea (chocolate milk!) for children also available. Also hosts "My Disney Girl's Perfectly Princess Tea Party" (see character dining on page 363). **[D][G]** Gluten-free sandwiches may be available with sufficient advance notice. **[D][W]** Kosher items are not available here. **[S]** Seniors looking for a quiet break will enjoy a relaxing, refined afternoon tea. **[R]** Serves alcoholic beverages in the evening.

Table/Bar
English Tea
Quiet
Indoor seats
Reservations
Med. waits
2–6 pm

Gasparilla's Grill | B/L/D/S | $14 | | 5 | 5

This counter-service spot offers all-day dining, adjacent to a game arcade. Typical offerings include breakfast croissants and french toast sticks for breakfast; pizza, sandwiches, burgers, and hot dogs for lunch and dinner. Indoor/outdoor seating available. (Note that outdoor seating overlooking marina is an even quieter option.) **[D]** Vegetarian entrée ($6.99), tabbouleh wrap ($5.69), and fattoush green salad ($5.79) available. **[D][W]** Kosher foods are available with advance notice. **[A][U][T][I][S]** Can be very noisy due to the arcade nearby—could cause overstimulation. **[C][L]** Wooden chairs with backs are bolted in place.

Counter
American
Med. noise
Med. waits
Open 24
hours

Grand Floridian Cafe | B/L/D | $33 | | 5 | 5

An upscale café, this spot has a surprisingly extensive menu. Breakfast features the usual suspects (pancakes, eggs, sausage), but also corned beef hash and eggs ($10.99), eggs benedict ($10.99), even a traditional Japanese breakfast ($19.99)! Typical lunch/dinner items: sandwiches, fish, steak, and prime rib. **[D]** Chicken and fish entrées for health-conscious diets. At least one vegetarian selection (e.g., Asian Noodle Bowl for $12.99) also available. Offers special Berry Pyramid for fat-free/no-sugar-added diets. Chef is very accommodating to special diets. **[L]** Armless chairs available. **[Ö]** Traditional Japanese breakfast available.

Table
American
Very noisy
Reservations
suggested
Med. waits
7–11 am,
11:45 am–2 pm,
5–9 pm

Eatery descriptions and ratings are explained on page 323.

Resort Eateries
(Grand Floridian Resort)

Deb Wills' Rating   Deb Koma's Rating

Grand Floridian Resort Eateries *(continued)*

☐ **Narcoossee's**	D	$69	🐾 ♿	8	9

Located on the Seven Seas Lagoon, this casual restaurant reflects the relaxed atmosphere of Florida living, featuring seafood and its famous Key Lime crème brulee. Wait for your table in the lounge—you can also order appetizers and/or desserts here. **[D]** Extensive vegetarian menu available. Be sure to ask for it! Offers special Berry Pyramid for fat-free diets. **[C][♥][M][E][S][L]** This restaurant is located a few minutes' walk away from the main building. **[G]** Primarily a seafood restaurant—those with seafood/shellfish allergy may want to avoid.

Table
Seafood
Noisy
Reservations recommended
Indoor seats
Short waits
6–10 pm

☐ **1900 Park Fare**	B/D	$34	♿	8	7

This gorgeous Victorian restaurant features lively character meals, enhanced by the piping of Big Bertha—the gigantic player organ that goes off periodically. Breakfast ($17.99/$10.99) with Mary Poppins, Alice in Wonderland, and the Mad Hatter is fairly typical fare: bacon and eggs, waffles, cereals, and danish. Dinner ($27.99/$12.99) with Cinderella and friends has items that vary widely from the norm: carved meats, paella, mussels, and chicken piccata. This spot also is home to the Wonderland Tea Party for kids—see page 363. **[A][U][T][I]** Can be very noisy—could cause overstimulation. **[R]** All-you-care-to-eat buffet. **[D]** A number of chicken and fish entrées are on the buffet for health-conscious diets. Several vegetarian selections, like vegetable lo mein and roasted vegetables, also available. Kosher meals and other special requests with advance notice. **[F]** Breakfast and dinner feature costumed characters who frequently make the rounds—if anyone has fear of costumed characters, you may want to avoid. **[S]** Can be quite noisy and overrun with small children.

Buffet
American
Very noisy
Advance Reservations strongly recommended
Indoor seating
Short waits
8:00–11:10 am
4:30–8:20 pm

☐ **Victoria & Albert's**	D	$121	🐾 ♿	10	10

Disney's five-star dining experience. Five-course prix fixe menu ($95) changes daily. This is the place for extra-special occasions. Very quiet and romantic, with a harp to serenade you. All your servers are either "Victoria" or "Albert." Dress code requires eveningwear for women, jacket for men. Reservations are required—call 407-824-1089 up to 180 days in advance. **[G][D]** Special dietary requests must be made in advance. Call 24 hours in advance to confirm.

Table
French
Quiet
Short waits
5:45 pm & 9:00 pm

🔔 Eating 24/7!

Most quick-service areas at the resorts close somewhere between 10:00 pm and midnight, but there are a few places that are open 24 hours. All grills close by midnight, though, so only grab 'n' go, prepackaged foods are available throughout the night.

- ✔ Tubbi's Buffeteria—Walt Disney World Dolphin
- ✔ Captain Cook's—Polynesian
- ✔ Food and Fun Center—Contemporary
- ✔ Gasparilla's Grill—Grand Floridian Resort & Spa
- ✔ Hess Station near Magic Kingdom

Resort Eateries
(Old Key West and Polynesian Resorts)

Deb Wills' Rating
Deb Koma's Rating

Old Key West Resort Eateries

Olivia's Cafe	B/L/D	$40		8	7

A diamond in the rough where you'll find locals enjoying a good meal at reasonable prices. Kitchen does best with simpler entrées. Lunch menu offers half salad/sandwich with soup. Indoor seating; outdoor covered seating sometimes available—check with a cast member. Many menu items are available for take-out—order here, pick up at Goods to Go. **[D]** Salads, chicken, and fish offer lighter fare. **[L]** Chairs with arms.

Table
Floridian
7:30–10:30 am,
11:30 am–5 pm,
5–10 pm

Goods to Go	B/L/D/S	$10	5	5

This counter-service spot offers fast food from ordinary (burgers and sandwiches) to the unusual (conch fritters!). Continental breakfast foods are available in the morning. **[D]** A fruit plate ($5.89) is available.

Counter
American
7:30 am–10 pm

Polynesian Resort Eateries

See pages 365–366 for the Spirit of Aloha dinner

Kona Cafe	B/L/D	$42		9	8

This popular, innovative eatery offers American cuisine with Asian influences. Breakfast includes the famous "Tonga Toast," a banana-stuffed version of French toast. Typical lunch and dinner items: Mahi Mahi, filet, pasta, and teriyaki. Indoor seating. **[D]** Many fish and lighter dishes for health-conscious diets. Vegetarian selections, such as vegetable rice bowl ($13.99), are also available. Chefs here are particularly agreeable to accommodating special requests, especially for vegetarian/vegan diners. **[G]** Peanut oil may be used in some cooking, stir fry here—be sure to ask! Request "no MSG" if sensitive. **[L]** Armless chairs available.

Table
Asian-inspried
Med. noise
Reservations suggested
Short waits
7:30–11:30 am,
Noon–3:00 pm,
5–10 pm

'Ohana	B/D	$40	6	7

This popular restaurant features an all-you-care-to-eat meal brought to your table. Breakfast features standard bacon and eggs, Mickey waffle fare ($17.99 adult/$9.99 child). Dinner features: skewered grilled meats and fish. Kids parade around the dining area periodically with servers or characters ($24.99 adult/$10.99 child). **[R]** All-you-care-to-eat buffet. **[G]** Beware of cross-contamination! Talk to your server/manager in advance—meats and fish are taken off the skewer with the same implements and are brought to the table touching each other. Open fire pit can be smoky at times. **[D]** Vegetarian selections are not on the regular menu but are available if you ask. **[F]** Breakfast features costumed characters who frequently make the rounds—if anyone has a fear of costumed characters, you may want to avoid. **[L]** Chairs have low arms, which can be uncomfortable. **[M]** Companion restroom located just outside restaurant entrance. **[S]** Can be quite noisy at breakfast. Dinner, too, can be noisy with the interactive activities featured.

Table
Polynesian
Noisy
Reservations strongly recommended
Indoor seating
Call 90 days
Med. waits
7:30 am–11:00 am,
5:00 am–10:00 pm

Captain Cook's Snack Co.	B/L/D/S	$10	5	5

Open all day, this is the spot to get a bite to eat on the run. Grill closes around 11:00 pm, but a good selection of prepackaged foods (salads, wraps, sandwiches) is always available. Indoor/outdoor seating. **[D][W]** Kosher meals only available with advance notice. Macaroni and cheese for kids.

Counter
American
Noisy
24 hours

Resort Eateries
(Pop Century, Port Orleans, and Saratoga Springs Resorts)

Deb Wills' Rating / Deb Koma's Rating

Pop Century Resort Eatery

Everything Pop!	B/L/D/S	$12	5	5

A food court offering typical fast-food fare. Breakfast platter is eggs, biscuit, potatoes, and bacon ($5.59/adults, $3.59/kids). Lunch and dinner serve up burgers, dogs, sandwiches, and pizza. See photo on page 346. **[D]** Vegetable frittata available at breakfast ($4.99). Grilled vegetable flatbread ($6.99). **[D]** **[W]** Kosher meals available without advance notice. **[Ö]** Video screen menu aids foreign-language speakers.

Counter / American / Noisy / Med. waits / 6:00 am–midnight

Port Orleans Resort Eateries

Boatwright's Dining Hall	B/D	$38	5	7

A southern flavor pervades the atmosphere here—there are hearty breakfasts of sweet potato cakes ($7.29) and banana-stuffed french toast ($7.99), plus Cajun cooking featured at dinner. Typical dinner items: blackened fish, bourbon-glazed chicken ($14.59), ribs ($18.59), and jambalaya ($16.99). **[D]** A number of chicken and fish entrées for health-conscious diets. Some vegetarian selections, such as four cheese ravioli ($14.29) or summer vegetable medley ($13.99), also available. **[D][W]** Kosher meals available without advance notice. Other special requests with advance notice.

Table / American / Med. noise / Indoor seats / Call 90 days / Short waits / 7:30–11:30 am, 5-10 pm

Riverside Mill	B/L/D/S	$13	7	7

Food court with Riverside Market and Deli, Bleu Bayou Burgers and Chicken, Southern Bakery, and pizza. Broiler closes at 10:00 pm. **[D]** A number of lighter entrées for health-conscious diets. Vegetarian sandwich $5.59. Special requests with advance notice. Chefs seem very willing to accommodate special diets. Grilled cheese and mac amd cheese available for kids. **[D][W]** Kosher meals available without advance notice. **[Ö]** Pictorial menu for foreign-language speakers.

Counter / American / Noisy / Indoor seats / Short waits / 6 am–midnight

Sassagoula Floatworks and Food Factory	B/L/D/S	$13	7	7

Typical Disney food court. Dinner served until 10:00 pm (pizza and bakery open to midnight). **[D]** A number of lighter entrées for health-conscious diets. Vegetarian chili $4.99. Chefs seem very willing to accommodate special diets. **[D][W]** Kosher meals available without advance notice. **[Ö]** Pictorial menu for foreign-language speakers.

Counter / American / Noisy / Med. waits / 6 am–midnight

Saratoga Springs Resort Eatery

Artist's Palette	B/L/D/S	$14	6	6

Prepackaged items along with a selection of made-to-order menu items, in an airy setting resembling an artist's workspace. Main items: flatbreads (pizzas), wraps, and salads. **[D]** A number of turkey, chicken, and fish entrées for health-conscious diets. Fruit and cheese plate ($6.29) is available. Macaroni and cheese is available for kids.

Counter / American / Med. noise / Short waits / 7:30 am–11 pm

Planning / Your Special Need / Getting There / Staying in Style / Touring / Dining / Resources / Index

Resort Eateries
(Swan and Dolphin Resorts)

Deb Wills' Rating

Deb Koma's Rating

Swan and Dolphin Resort Eateries

☐ Cabana Bar and Grill (Dolphin)   L/D/S $13   ☙ ☙ | 6 | 8 |

Pool bar for refreshments alfresco. Mostly lighter fare and finger foods. Grill closes at 5:00 pm. **[D]** A number of tuna, chicken, and fish items for health-conscious diets. Fresh fruit plate is also available. Vegetarian wrap ($8.50) and veggie burger ($8.95) on menu, as well as low-carb chicken wrap ($9.75).

| Counter |
| Snacks |
| Noisy |
| 11 am-7 pm |

☐ Dolphin Fountain (Dolphin)   L/D/S $18   ☙ ☙ | 7 | 7 |

Burgers, etc., and homemade ice cream in a spot made to resemble an old-time soda fountain. Sometimes the servers will even break into song and dance! **[D]** **[W]** Kosher items are not available here. **[D]** Veggie burger ($7) on the menu. Special treat: Billy D. Lite ($4.25), a fat-free vanilla yogurt blended with skim milk, strawberry sauce, and a fresh banana.

| Table |
| American |
| Indoor seats |
| Med. noise |
| 11 am-11 pm |

☐ Fresh (Dolphin)   B/L $24   ☙ ☙ | 8 | 7 |

A Mediterranean-style market that features American foods with flavor. Food prepared as you order, in many cases. In addition to regular buffet, you can order a "continental breakfast" buffet for a lower price. It includes the baked goods, but not the hot foods. "The Market Room" across the hall is often used for business breakfasts, but you can sometimes be seated here with a regular a la carte breakfast menu. **[D]** A number of chicken and fish entrées are on the buffet for health-conscious diets. Vegetarian selections, like lentil and tomato soup or roasted red peppers stuffed with goat cheese, are also available. Many items made to order, so ask the chefs if you have questions about the ingredients. Don't miss the fresh-squeezed juices. **[R]** All you can eat buffet, although there is an a la carte menu to order from for lunch. **[D][W]** Kosher items are not available.

| Buffet/Table |
| Mediterranean |
| Med. noise |
| Indoor seats |
| Call 90 days |
| Med. waits |
| 6:30-11 am, |
| 11:30 am-2 pm |

The chefs at Fresh are always on hand to answer questions

© MediaMarx, Inc.

☐ Garden Grove Cafe/Gulliver's Grill (Swan)   B/L/D $49   ☙ | 7 | 7 |

Monday through Friday (8:30 am-11:00 am), this spacious restaurant offers a breakfast buffet (adults $13.95; children 3-9 $8.50) and even a Japanese breakfast ($17.95). On weekends, though, it hosts a character breakfast with Pluto and Goofy ($16.95/$8.50). And characters attend nightly at dinner, which features family-style themed buffets ($24.95/$10.95) as well as an a la carte menu. Weekend breakfast is 8:00 am-11:00 am. **[R]** Breakfast and dinner are all you can eat buffets. **[S]** Can be quite noisy during the character meals and overrun with small children. **[D] [W]** Kosher meals not available. **[D]** No vegetarian selections on regular menu—ask! **[Ö]** Traditional Japanese breakfast available.

| Buffet/Table |
| American |
| Indoor seats |
| Med. waits |
| Noisy |
| 6:30 am- |
| 11:30 am, |
| 11:30-2 pm, |
| 5:30-10 pm |

Eatery descriptions and ratings are explained on page 323.

Resort Eateries
(Swan and Dolphin Resorts)

Deb Wills' Rating
Deb Koma's Rating

Swan and Dolphin Resort Eateries *(continued)*

■ **Kimonos (Swan)** D/S $44 🍸 ♿	5	5
Sushi, oriental appetizers, and cocktails served with a healthy dose of karaoke singalong. **[D]** A number of fish items for health-conscious diets. Some sushi items (like asparagus roll, $4, and ichiban roll, $5) are vegetarian; there are also items like edamame ($5). **[S]** Can be quite noisy with karaoke. **[G]** Those with seafood/shellfish allergies might want to avoid. Request "no MSG" if sensitive.	**Table** Japanese Noisy Med. waits 5:30 pm-1 am	

■ **Palio (Swan)** D $54	8	7
Upscale Italian cuisine, featuring pastas, fish, and other Italian specialties like Osso Buco ($28.95) and Veal Scalloppine ($24.95). **[D]** Chicken and fish entrées for healthy diets. At least one vegetarian selection such as Fettuccine del Palio ($19). **[D][W]** Kosher meals are not available. **[L]** Standard chairs have arms; ask for an armless chair. **[V]** Dimly lit—hard to even see the menu!	**Table** Italian Quiet Med. waits 6-11 pm	

■ **Shula's Steakhouse (Dolphin)** D $75	7	8
Masculine décor in dark woods reveals this expensive restaurant for what it is—a throwback to the old-fashioned, expense-account-type steakhouse. Direct reservations line is 407-934-1609. **[D]** Only a few concessions to lighter fare—a few chicken and fish entrées. No vegetarian selections on the regular menu—ask if they'll accommodate you! **[D][W]** Kosher meals are not available.	**Table** Steakhouse Quiet Short waits 5-11 pm	

■ **Splash Grill & Deli (Swan)** L/D/S $13 🍸 ♿	6	7
Poolside treats at the main pool area connecting the Swan and Dolphin resorts. Mostly lighter fare and finger foods. Grill closes at 5:00 pm. **[D]** A number of tuna, chicken, and fish items for health-conscious diets. Fresh fruit plate is also available. Vegetarian wrap ($8.50) and veggie burger ($8.95) on menu, as well as low-carb chicken wrap ($9.75). **[A][U][H][T][i][S]** Can be very noisy, as it is located near the main pool.	**Counter** Snacks Very noisy Outdoor seats Short waits 11 am-7 pm	

■ **Todd English's bluezoo (Dolphin)** D/S $69 🍸 ♿	5	9
One of the newest additions to Walt Disney World, this celebrity chef brings his unique take on fresh seafood dishes. Very trendy décor. No tank tops—dress is "smart casual." You may also dine at the raw bar or in the cafe—order items by the piece. **[G]** Primarily a seafood restaurant—those with fish/shellfish allergies may want to avoid. **[D]** A variety of plain grilled fish are lighter entrées for health-conscious diets. Vegetarian selections are also available on request. **[D][W]** Kosher meals are not available. **[V]** Very dimly lit—may be difficult for those with vision impairments.	**Table** Seafood Quiet Reservations in main room; none in cafe 5-11 pm	

■ **Tubbi's Buffeteria (Dolphin)** B/L/D/S $10 🍸 ♿	9	9
A combination cafeteria/convenience store, this 24-hour stop in the lower level of the Dolphin has it all—from healthy fruit and juice to sandwiches and pizza to famous Krispy Kreme donuts. **[D][W]** Kosher meals are not available. **[D]** Whole fruit available. Fruit plate ($4.95) and veggie burger ($7) are good vegetarian options. Grilled cheese and peanut butter and jelly sandwiches for kids.	**Counter** American Med. noise Short waits Open 24 hours	

Planning
Your Special Need
Getting There
Staying in Style
Touring
Dining
Resources
Index

Resort Eateries
(Wilderness Lodge and Yacht & Beach Club Resorts)

Deb Wills' Rating / Deb Koma's Rating

Wilderness Lodge Resort Eateries

Artist Point — D — $56 — 7 | 9

Beautifully appointed restaurant with Mission-style seating and flavorful contemporary fare from the Pacific Northwest—it's not uncommon to find game and other uncommon entrées (buffalo, venison, duck) on the menu. Menu changes seasonally. Signature dish is cedar-planked roasted salmon ($28). Don't miss the berry cobbler ($12)—expensive but so worth it! No tank tops/swimwear—dress is "smart casual." Wait for your table in the adjacent Territory Lounge, where appetizers are available. **[D]** Be sure to call in advance for special dietary requests. At least one vegetarian option on the menu (e.g., Roasted Red Kuri Squash, $21). **[M]** Ramp to restaurant located to the left of check-in desk.

Table | Pacific Northwest | Med. noise | Reservations suggested | Call 90 days | Med. waits | 5:30–10 pm

Roaring Fork — B/L/D/S — $10 — 6 | 6

This quick-service dining spot is open all day—it's a great place to get a bite to eat on the run. **[D] [W]** Kosher meals available with 24-hour notice, ask for manager. **[D]** Veggie pizza ($6.59) at lunch. Peanut butter and jelly sandwiches are available.

Counter | Snacks | Noisy | 6 am–midnight

Whispering Canyon Café — B/L/D — $37 — 7 | 8

A hearty BBQ restaurant that bellows occasionally into the cavernous lobby of the Wilderness Lodge. Servers all take on personas from the Wild West, and engage diners in good ol' fun. It's not uncommon for servers to yell across the restaurant. Periodic kid races with stick ponies. All-you-care-to-eat skillets or a la carte. Breakfast skillet $9.69; lunch $13.99; dinner $21.99. **[A][U]** Lincoln Logs available while waiting. **[A][U][T][I][S]** Can be very noisy—could cause overstimulation. **[D]** Call in advance for special dietary requests. Fruit plate ($6.29) available for breakfast. **[F]** Servers will interact with you, so if you don't wish to partake, be sure to let your greeter and server know right from the start.

Table | Barbecue | Very noisy | Reservations suggested | Long waits | 7:30–11 am, noon–3 pm, 5–10 pm

Yacht and Beach Club Resort Eateries

Beaches and Cream — L/D/S — $20 — 9 | 8

Patterned after an old-time soda shop, complete with jukebox, this spot features some of the best burgers on Disney property. It also has some of the greatest ice cream treats to be found anywhere! Seating available via booth, high stools, or tables. Very small indoor area and small outdoor seating that is covered.

Connected to arcade. **[A][U][H][T][I][S]** Very noisy—located near pool, plus there is a jukebox in the restaurant. **[D]** Several light entrées for health-conscious diets. Veggie burger is $6.99. Kosher meals and other special requests may be available with advance notice. **[D][G]** Dairy-free ice cream available on request. **[F]** Ordering the Kitchen Sink will draw lots of attention—if this bothers you, avoid. **[C][T][M][P][S][L]** Small space with tables close together—maneuvering is difficult.

Table | American | Very noisy | Indoor/outdoor seats | No advance reservations | Long waits | 11 am–11 pm

© MediaMarx, Inc.

Stool seating at Beaches and Cream

Resort Eateries
(Yacht and Beach Club Resorts)

Yacht and Beach Club Resort Eateries *(continued)*

			Deb Wills' Rating	Deb Koma's Rating
Beach Club Marketplace	B/L/S	$12	7	7

Located just off the lobby of the Beach Club, this new stop offers prepackaged and made-to-order items, great for a bite on the go. Breakfast croissant, sandwiches, wraps, salads; fresh-made gelato. **[D]** Grilled veggie wrap ($6.19) at lunch. Peanut butter & jelly sandwiches are available.

Counter
American
Med/noise
8 am–11 pm

Cape May Cafe	B/D	$33	6	8

Character breakfast buffet $17.99/$9.99; clambake buffet dinner $24.99/$10.99. **[A][U][T][I][S]** Can be very noisy—could cause overstimulation, especially during character breakfast. **[R]** All-you-can-eat buffet. **[G]** Dinner buffet features lots of seafood—those with shellfish/fish allergies may want to avoid. **[D]** Some vegetarian choices on buffet. Kids' buffet has mac and cheese. **[F]** Breakfast features costumed characters who frequently make the rounds—if anyone has fear of costumed characters, you may want to avoid. **[S]** Can be quite noisy at breakfast.

Buffet
American
Noisy
Reservations
strongly
suggested
7:30–11 am,
5:30–9:30 pm

Hurricane Hanna's Grill	L/S	$10	6	8

This counter-service spot is operated seasonally and offers fairly typical pool bar food, such as burgers, hot dogs, salads, and sandwiches. It's located next to Stormalong Bay. **[D]** Vegetable wrap is $6.59; fruit boat is $3.99. **[R]** This grill offers a good selection of non-alcoholic drinks.

Counter
American
Noisy
Outdoor seats

Crew's Cup	L/S	$15	8	7

This is a cozy bar that shares the kitchen with the next-door Yacht Club Galley, featuring a light lunchtime menu. Beer and ale are available from around the world, and you can order light appetizers until 10:00 pm. **[D]** Some salads are available. **[L]** Seating is in booths or lounge-type chairs.

Table
American
Med. noise
Noon–mid.

Yacht Club Galley	B/L/D	$35	8	7

This casual eatery with a nautical theme serves up great grub for a reasonable price. Breakfast buffet ($13.99/adults and $6.99/kids) or a la carte, sandwiches, and entrées. This eatery is quieter and less hectic than other restaurants. **[D]** A number of lighter entrées for health-conscious diets are available. Portobello Mushroom Grinder ($9) at lunch; Roasted Portobello Mushroom Salad as entrée ($13) at dinner.

Buffet/Table
American
Short waits
7:30 am–11 am,
11:30 am–2 pm,
5:30–9:30 pm

Yachtsman Steakhouse	L/D/S	$68	8	7

One of the better steakhouses on Disney property, this light, airy restaurant has a varied menu that also includes seafood and vegetarian options. **[D]** A few lighter entrées for health-conscious diets. At least one vegetarian selection, e.g., Winter Squash Ravioli ($21), is available. Be aware that the chefs here seem to go heavy on the seasonings! **[F]** To the left of the podium is a meat case with the beef that is to be cooked—If you're squeamish about seeing raw meat, avoid that area.

Table
Steakhouse
Noisy
Reservations
suggested
Med. waits
5:30–9:45 pm

Planning · Your Special Need · Getting There · Staying in Style · Touring · Dining · Resources · Index

Room Service

Most Disney resorts have their **own version of "room service,"** from simple pizza delivery at the value resorts to full dinner entrées at the deluxe resorts. Room service menus are placed in each room (look by the TV, on the table, or in the nightstand), and most phones have a Room Service button on them. Although we have found the room service at the Walt Disney World Swan and Dolphin to be far superior in food quality than at the other Disney resorts, the food at the other resorts is perfectly adequate for those times when you don't want to or can't leave your room. It's not for the budget-conscious, though—room service meals are not only taxed with an automatic 17%–20% gratuity, but there is also a delivery charge, which may be a set fee or a percentage.

Important Note: Special requests may or may not be honored at the time of ordering. The best thing is to ask!

Available Room Service

Disney's Animal Kingdom Lodge (kosher meals available with 24 hours' notice)	6:00 am—midnight
All Star Resorts—limited pizza, subs, beer, salads	4:00 pm—midnight
Boardwalk Inn/Villas	6:00 am—midnight
Caribbean Beach—pizza	4:00 pm—11:30 pm
Contemporary Resort	24 hours a day
Coronado Springs—limited full-day service	7:00 am—11:00 pm
Grand Floridian Resort & Spa	24 hours a day
Pop Century—limited pizza, subs, beer, salads	4:00 pm—midnight
Port Orleans—pizza, beer, wine, sodas	4:00 pm—midnight
Old Key West—pizza, beer, wine, sodas	4:00 pm—midnight
Polynesian Resort	6:30 am—midnight
Shades of Green	7:00 am—11:00 am and 4:00 pm—11:00 pm
Walt Disney World Swan and Dolphin	24 hours a day
Wilderness Lodge	7:00 am—11:00 am and 4:00 pm—midnight
Yacht and Beach Club	24 hours a day

Note that the following resorts offer room service **24 hours/day**: Contemporary, Grand Floridian, Walt Disney World Swan and Dolphin, and Yacht and Beach Club.

No room service/delivery is available at Fort Wilderness Resort & Campground or at Saratoga Springs Spa & Resort.

Character Meals

Disney offers many opportunities to dine with characters, both those in full guise (like Mickey Mouse) and "face characters" in costume (like Cinderella). While they don't actually sit with you throughout your meal, they roam around the restaurant and visit your table for autograph signing and picture-taking. Character meals are generally higher priced than regular meals (usually $17–$35 for adults and $9–$18 for kids ages 3–9), but the chance to meet the characters in an unhurried atmosphere makes it worthwhile, especially for those who can't tolerate waiting in the typically long "meet and greet" lines you find in the theme parks.

Even if meeting the characters isn't on your agenda, character dinners are a **good value** when you consider all the other factors—the cost of these buffets and family-style meals is usually less than comparable full-service meals when you factor all costs. Character meals are extremely popular—make advance arrangements as far in advance as possible (up to 90 days) at 407-939-3463. Remember to bring your camera and an autograph book!

Be aware that there's a **mad rush** for Advance Reservations at Cinderella's Royal Table in the Magic Kingdom. Folks start phoning at 7:00 am Eastern time, exactly 90 days prior to their desired date, and tables are often gone in a matter of minutes. This may be alleviated a bit with the recent addition of a character lunch at the restaurant, but we expect that will be popular as well. If you get a table at Cinderella's, expect to pay a deposit of $10/adult and $5/child by credit card—this deposit is refunded if you cancel 24 hours in advance. If you miss out, don't despair. Try again once you get to Walt Disney World. Cancellations are common, so it never hurts to ask for a table, even as you're walking through Cinderella Castle. If you are set on dining with a princess, try the recently expanded Princess Storybook Dining at Restaurant Akershus —now three meals with the princesses a day—or the character dinner at 1900 Park Fare. Chef Mickey's character meals also tend to sell out quickly.

✔ Some character breakfasts start prior to park opening. All Disney resorts offer special Disney bus transportation to the early character breakfasts. Be sure to allow plenty of travel time. Look for a special entrance designated for breakfast reservations. A cast member with clipboard will check off your name, allowing you to enter the turnstiles.

✔ For the best character experience, dine off-hours. While Mickey may only give you a quick hello during busy mealtimes, you might end up with a close, personal relationship when tables are empty.

✔ Don't forget to make any special dietary requests in advance! These character meals are preplated or buffets and so are not as flexible when it comes to special requests, unless the kitchen has had adequate advance notice.

✔ Don't be shy, grown-ups! Even if you aren't dining with kids, the characters visit your table. If you'd rather sit things out, though, simply indicate this, and they will simply give you a nod or handshake as they pass by.

✔ The "head" characters don't speak, but that doesn't mean you have to keep quiet. Talk to them and they'll pantomime and play along. They are especially good with special guests—we've seen them treat foreign-language speaking visitors like visiting royalty!

✔ Theme park admission is required for character meals in the parks.

Available Character Meals

(alphabetical by park, then by resort)

"Chip and Dale's Harvest Feast" Garden Grill   Epcot (The Land)

Held at The Land and hosted by Mickey and friends. Serves lunch from 11:00 am to 3:00 pm ($19.99 for adults/$10.99 for kids ages 3–9); and dinner from 4:30 pm to 8:00 pm ($24.99 for adults/$10.99 for kids ages 3–9).

"Princess Storybook Dining"   Epcot (Norway)

This family-style character dining located at Restaurant Akershus in the Norway Pavilion at Epcot features Disney Princesses and friends. Expanded spring 2005 to three meals a day. Hours for breakfast ($21.99 for adults/$11.99 for kids ages 3–9) are 8:30 am–10:10 am; lunch ($23.99 for adults/$12.99 for kids ages 3–9) is 11:40 am–2:50 pm; and dinner($27.99 for adults/$12.99 for kids ages 3–9) is 4:20 pm–8:40 pm.

"Donald's Breakfastosaurus"   Disney's Animal Kingdom

Daily at Restaurantosaurus in DinoLand U.S.A., serving a breakfast buffet from 8:00 am to 10:30 am. Character appearances include Donald Duck and friends. $17.99 for adults/$9.99 for kids ages 3–9.

"A Buffet With Character"   Magic Kingdom

All-day character dining at The Crystal Palace featuring Winnie the Pooh, Tigger, and friends. Breakfast is from 8:00 am to 10:30 am, ($17.99 for adults/$9.99 for kids ages 3–9); lunch is from 11:30 am to 3:00 pm ($19.99 for adults/$10.99 for kids ages 3–9), and dinner is from 4:00 pm and varies with park closing ($24.99 for adults/$10.99 for kids ages 3–9).

"A Fairytale Lunch at Cinderella's Royal Table" Magic Kingdom

Noon to 3:00 pm daily at Cinderella's Royal Table. Family-style character lunch, featuring Cinderella and friends. $23.99 for adults/$12.99 for kids ages 3–9). Reservations required.

"Goofy's Liberate Your Appetite Dinner"   Magic Kingdom

Daily beginning at 4:00 pm at the Liberty Tree Tavern, featuring Minnie Mouse, Goofy, Pluto, and friends. $24.99 for adults/$10.99 for kids ages 3–9.

"Once Upon a Time Breakfast"   Magic Kingdom

Daily from 8:00 am to 11:15 am at Cinderella's Royal Table, featuring Cinderella and friends. $23.99 for adults/ $12.99 for kids ages 3–9. Reservations required. Lunch, also featuring Cinderella and friends, is $23.99 for adults/$12.99 for kids ages 3–9.

"Beach Club Buffet"   Beach Club Resort

Breakfast ($17.99 for adults/$9.99 for kids ages 3–9) with Goofy and friends, daily from 7:30 am to 11:00 am at the Cape May Cafe.

"Chef Mickey's Fun Time Buffet"   Contemporary Resort

Mickey and the gang, daily from 7:00 am to 11:30 am for breakfast ($17.99 for adults/$9.99 for kids ages 3–9) and dinner from 5:00 to 9:30 pm ($26.99 for adults/ $11.99 for kids).

"Mickey's Backyard BBQ"   Fort Wilderness Resort

This seasonal show is offered from March to December only. It's a buffet dinner and dance, with entertainment and characters, held Tuesday and Thursday nights only from 6:30 pm to 9:30 pm at the outdoor pavilion. Cost is $39.01 for adults and $25 for kids ages 3–9 (tax and gratuity included).

Available Character Meals
(continued)

"Supercalifragilistic Breakfast" — Grand Floridian Resort & Spa

Held daily from 8:00 am to 11:10 am at 1900 Park Fare with Mary Poppins and friends. $17.99 for adults/$10.99 for kids ages 3–9.

"Cinderella's Gala Feast" — Grand Floridian Resort & Spa

Held at 1900 Park Fare with Cinderella and her Storybook Friends from 4:30 pm to 8:20 pm daily. $27.99 for adults/$12.99 for kids ages 3–9.

"My Disney Girl's Perfectly Princess Tea Party" Grand Floridian Resort & Spa

Held at the Garden View Lounge on Sunday, Monday, Wednesday, Thursday, and Friday from 10:30 am to noon. Tea or juice, fruit, small sandwiches, plus singalong and storytelling with Aurora. Child gets tiara, bracelet, and collectible doll. One adult and one child (ages 3–9) is $200, including gratuity. Extra adult $65; extra child $135. 72-hour cancellation policy.

"Wonderland Tea Party" — Grand Floridian Resort & Spa

Hosted by Alice in Wonderland and friends, held at 1900 Park Fare. For children only. Price $28.17 per child; available Monday through Friday at 1:30 pm.

"Pirate Adventure" — Grand Floridian Resort & Spa

A kids-only experience for children ages 4 to 10, held Monday, Wednesday, Thursday, and Saturday at 9:30–11:30 am. Price is $28.17 per child; lunch includes peanut butter and jelly sandwich, gummy bears, rice krispy treat, and fruit punch drink box. Will accommodate special dietary needs if stated when reserving.

'Ohana Character Breakfast — Polynesian Resort

Served family style at 'Ohana from 7:30 am to 11:00 am daily with Mickey, Goofy, and Chip 'n' Dale. $17.99 for adults/$9.99 for kids ages 3–9.

"Good Morning Character Breakfast" — Walt Disney World Swan

Held at Garden Grove on Saturday and Sunday from 8:00 am to 11:00 am with Goofy and Pluto. $16.95 for adults/$8.50 for kids ages 3–9. Buffet style. Reservations are not accepted for this character meal.

Gulliver's Grill Character Dinner — Walt Disney World Swan

Disney characters nightly from 5:30 pm to 10:00 pm. $24.99 for adults/$10.95 for kids ages 3–9. A la carte service. Reservations accepted. Call 407-934-3000, ext. 1618.

© Debra Martin Koma

Expert peer reviewer Masayo Kano (right) and friends at 'Ohana character breakfast

Planning

Your Special Need

Getting There

Staying in Style

Touring

Dining

Resources

Index

Special Meals

Hoop Dee Doo Musical Revue

The Hoop Dee Doo Musical Revue, Walt Disney World's longest-running dinner show, will have you **doubled over with laughter and groans** and enjoying plain old country-style fare in spite of yourself.

Performed three times nightly in Pioneer Hall, the Hoop Dee Doo is well-known and beloved by many for its **vaudeville-style shtick**—no joke too slapstick, no pun too lame, for the cast of six players. But even if this singing and dancing, hootin' and hollerin' is not usually your cup of tea, we think you'll find yourself enjoying the show, along with an abundance of salad, fried chicken, barbecued ribs, corn, baked beans, and strawberry shortcake.

There's no plot to the show, and it's not sophisticated humor by any stretch—this is just an **old-fashioned, G-rated, good ol' time**. Before you're shown into the hall, you'll have your photo snapped (servers will come around during your meal to give you the chance to purchase). Once the doors open and everyone's seated, you have a chance to start on the salad and rolls with honey-sweetened butter. The performers introduce themselves with a rousing opening number and mingle a bit with the audience. After another musical number, they leave the stage to allow dinner to be served.

The **all-you-care-to-eat dinner** is slammed on your table in old-fashioned pails—the fried chicken is moist, the ribs a bit smoky. Side dishes are served in the same way—slow-cooked baked beans and corn seasoned with onion and green pepper bits. For choosier children, the servers are more than happy to bring a variety of kid-tested fare—macaroni and cheese, hot dogs, and even peanut butter and jelly sandwiches are available upon request.

If the tall Mason jars filled to the brim with icy water aren't enough to slake your thirst, your server will bring you the **beverage of your choice**: lemonade, milk (white and chocolate), soft drinks, iced tea, coffee, beer, or wine (including cabernet, white zinfindel, chardonnay, and sangria) are all included.

As the main course draws to a conclusion, the **entertainment swings into high gear**. The performers return to engage the audience in celebrating birthdays and anniversaries and mingle once again with the crowd, not forgetting those seated at the upstairs tables. Finally, a rousing rendition of Woody Guthrie's "This Land Is Your Land" gets the audience really cheering, twirling their red gingham napkins wildly overhead.

After one more song, dessert is brought out amongst much fanfare and chorus-line-style high leg kicks—even the servers get into the act! Dishes of delectable **strawberry shortcake** smothered with whipped cream are plonked on the table, and as you gobble up this grand finale (with coffee if you want it), the players enact theirs—a tribute to Davy Crockett that includes the participation of several audience members. As the show draws to its end, servers run through and distribute washboards for the final number so that everyone can join in and make as much ruckus as possible.

Maybe this show is **not for everyone**, but for those who don't mind their ribs barbecued, their chicken southern-fried, and their humor corned, the Hoop Dee Doo is a must-do.

Special Diets: The Hoop Dee Doo Revue will accommodate your special dietary requests (vegetarian, diabetic, etc.) if you call at least 24 hours in advance. Make your requests at 407-824-2803. When you call, be prepared to answer questions about what you want as your meal. Unlike other special requests (which will just alert the restaurant to be prepared for you to show up), this show generally wants to offer you suggestions and have you pick your substitutions on the spot. If you are calling for someone else, be sure you know exactly what they would prefer.

Reader Tip: "The only time I really had to make a special request regarding a menu was when I took my son to the Hoop Dee Doo show, because he would never touch fried chicken or ribs. I gave them about 48 hours' notice, and they gladly provided him with exactly what he wanted: grilled cheese, applesauce, broccoli, and apple juice, certainly not their regular fare. They were very accommodating and helpful; just give them enough notice."—contributed by peer reviewer Peter Johnson

Shows are held at 5:00 pm, 7:15 pm, and 9:30 pm. **Ticket prices** include tax and gratuity (as of June 2005): $50.22/adults; $25.43/kids 3–9. Discounts are sometimes available, usually for annual passholders. Call 407-939-3463 for reservations. Your credit card will be charged at the time the reservation is made. There is a 48-hour cancellation policy.

Bright Idea: Reservations can be made up to two years ahead of time, and it really pays to book early! Tables are assigned in the order in which reservations are made and, since there is seating on two levels, reserving early helps ensure seating on the main floor, rather than in the balcony. Shows can sell out during busy times of the year, like around the holidays. Be sure to request any special requirements at time of booking, but you'll need to reconfirm a day or two before your show.

Other Special Needs Considerations: If you use a wheelchair/ECV remember to request the special seating area at the time you make your reservations. Also, if you are shy or afraid of strangers, you may be uncomfortable with the amount of attention the servers and performers pay to you—they try to get everyone to participate.

How to Get There: Fort Wilderness guests board the internal bus to the Settlement Depot. You can also drive (and then transfer to an internal bus), take the boat from Contemporary, Wilderness Lodge, or the Magic Kingdom, or take a bus from the Transportation and Ticket Center or any park.

Spirit of Aloha (Polynesian Luau)

Aloha! Presented nightly in Luau Cove, an open theater on the Seven Seas Lagoon, the Spirit of Aloha dinner show is everything that you'd expect from a **traditional luau**—women in "grass" skirts, men in face paint, fire dancers, traditional music, and a little bit of Elvis, as they all relate the modern Hawaii seen in Lilo and Stitch. Your hostess for the evening, Auntie Wini, invites you for a celebration of the cultures of Tahiti, Samoa, Tonga, New Zealand, and Hawaii, while you dine on a feast inspired by the flavors of Polynesia. Before the night is over, you'll learn all about their traditional values, including 'ohana (family).

Upon arrival, guests are presented with a complimentary lei and entertained in the garden before dinner. While you wait for the show, you can buy drinks and souvenirs and have a family photo taken. Guests are seated at long, wooden tables that fan out from the stage, all under shelter in the event of rain. The tables are long, so you may be seated with diners from another party. The **all-you-care-to-eat meal**, served family-style for your party, includes salad, fresh pineapple, roasted chicken, bbq ribs, rice, and sautéed vegetables, with a special "volcano dessert" (the name is the most exciting part). Included with your meal is your choice of unlimited soda, coffee, iced tea, milk, beer, and wine. Specialty drinks are extra. The show begins after dinner with Hawaiian music and plenty of South Seas dancing by both men and women. Children are quite welcome at the Luau. Although it's not as kid-friendly as the long-departed Mickey's Tropical Luau, the Lilo and Stitch tie-in helps, and the young ones will be invited on stage for a special dance number. Photos can be picked up after the show. Shows are held at 5:15 pm and 8:00 pm, Tuesdays through Saturdays. We prefer the later seating as the darkness adds to the mystique and romance of the show. Annual passholders may get a discount on the late show (ask when you call). In the cooler months, the late show may be cancelled. We highly recommend you make your reservations as early as possible—the best tables near the stage go to those who reserve first. Travel directions are detailed on the next page.

Planning · Your Special Need · Getting There · Staying in Style · Touring · Dining · Resources · Index

Special Meals (continued)

Special Diets: The Spirit of Aloha show will accommodate your special dietary requests (vegetarian, diabetic, etc.) if you call at least 24 hours in advance. Make your requests at 407-824-2803. When you call, be prepared to answer questions about what you want as your meal. Unlike other special requests (which will just alert the restaurant to be prepared for you to show up), this show generally wants to

Spirit of Aloha
© MediaMarx, Inc.

offer you suggestions and have you pick your substitutions on the spot. If you are calling for someone else, be sure you know exactly what they would prefer.

Ticket prices include tax and gratuity (as of June 2005): $50.22/adults; $25.43/children 3-9. Discounts are sometimes available, usually for annual passholders. Be sure to ask when you call. Call 407-WDW-3463 to make reservations. Note that your credit card will be charged at the time the reservation is made. There is a 48-hour cancellation policy.

Reader Tip: "Be sure to make your reservations for the Hoop Dee Doo Revue and the Spirit of Aloha shows as far in advance as possible, and have any accessibility needs noted on your reservation. There are no elevators at the Hoop Dee Doo for upstairs seating, but there is a special entrance for wheelchairs/ECVs at both shows."—contributed by peer reviewer Chet McDoniel

How to get there: To get to the Polynesian Luau, you can drive directly to the Polynesian Resort. From the Magic Kingdom, take the resort monorail. From other parks, bus to the Polynesian. From other resorts, bus to the Magic Kingdom and take the monorail (daytime) or bus (evening) to Downtown Disney and transfer to a Polynesian bus. Once inside the resort, follow signs to Luau Cove. Allow plenty of time for travel, especially from another resort.

House of Blues Gospel Brunch

If you're looking for something other than the run-of-the-mill Sunday brunch, head on over to the House of Blues at Downtown Disney's West Side. Twice each Sunday (at 10:30 am and 1:00 pm), this casual eatery, famous for its live entertainment, serves up 90 minutes of **grub and gospel revue**. You get about 45 minutes to sample the buffet, which consists of many of the usual brunch suspects mixed with some more Southern-inspired fare: pastries, breads, sausage, bacon, grits, prawns with cocktail sauce, smoked catfish, assorted salads, barbecued chicken, and chicken jambalaya, as well as roasted meats, made-to-order omelets, and desserts. After brunch, you're treated to 45 minutes of uplifting music and entertainment from a rotating cadre of gospel performers.

Special Needs Considerations: Seating in the front section nearest the stage is at long communal tables, on hard, narrow, wooden folding chairs. There is not much room to move, and once the show begins, with folks getting up and sitting down, it is fairly awkward. Seating around the back and sides of the restaurant and up in the balcony are at tables or booths, with some cocktail tables and stools. Lighting in the restaurant is very dim. Special diets can be accommodated with at least 72 hours' notice.

Ticket prices, as of May 2005: $30/adults; $15 children 3-9; under 2 free. There are sometimes discounts for Annual Passholders or Disney Vacation Club members—be sure to inquire. For reservations, call 407-934-BLUE (2583).

How to get there: Follow the directions for getting to Downtown Disney in chapter 5 on page 291.

Looking for information on dining on the Disney Cruise Line? See pages 178–191.

Dining Tips and Stories

We return to Disney every year because of their ability to adapt to dietary restrictions and make it seem like it's the most natural thing in the world and not a special request.

—contributed by Jennifer Aist

We make up some "tofu jerky" for our visit to the parks—this is just seasoned tofu, baked to dry it out, and then kept in plastic bags. It keeps for a long time without refrigeration and is very tasty. We also pack containers of peanut butter and vegan crackers. That gives us reliable sources of protein. The big pretzels are also vegan and make a good snack.

—contributed by Teresa Pitman

My wife Roz and I have found Disney chefs always willing to accommodate us, whether it is broiling our fish without butter at Cinderella's Royal Table, or getting plain steamed vegetables. The "sleeper" restaurant is The Plaza in the Magic Kingdom, where I always get a roasted veggie sandwich with hummus on multi-grain bread with German potato salad on the side. Mmmmmmm, my mouth is watering as I remember these epicurean delights! Thank you, Disney chefs, for your accommodations!

—contributed by Ricke Zeidman

I always carried a small soft side cooler for quick snacks as backup, just in case (Frigo cheese sticks, Hillshire Farms lunch meat, carrots, blueberries, strawberries, Glutino pretzels, and GF chocolate chip cookies). It also came in handy when my son, John, was served such large portions in the sit-down restaurants; we were able to take the leftovers with us for a quick meal later on. Take lots of extra baggies just for this reason.

—contributed by anonymous

Counter-service places offer some unique salads and they are always happy to omit meat and cheese, as well as supply dressing on the side.

—contributed by peer reviewer Kitty Smith

Low-carb diners, bring with you a few simple items, mostly so you are not ambushed by the bagel chips on the plane or in case of late-night cravings. Some suggestions are: macadamias, walnuts, or pecans in zipper-top bags—do not bring peanuts on a plane, as many people are allergic; pork rinds, if you like them; beef or other jerky; Atkins or other protein bars; fiber crackers. Should you have a refrigerator in your hotel room or suite, you might make a stop and purchase strawberries or sliced melon, whole-milk cottage cheese, cream for coffee (not dairy creamer or half-and-half), whole-milk plain yogurt (difficult to obtain in the World).

—contributed by Erica Freeman

Don't let special dietary needs of any kind deter you! Plan ahead, and don't be shy about telling cast members what you need. Then your biggest gastric concern will be those thirteen-story drops on Tower of Terror!

—contributed by anonymous

Your Dining Tips and Stories
(continued)

In the past, I've been embarrassed by my many allergies. However, a friend recently pointed out that at Walt Disney World, it's actually like an additional "attraction"—the Disney Meet the Chef attraction. And it's a good point. It's an excellent opportunity to meet some wonderful people and learn about them while they learn about you and your concerns. Besides, while most people may get a photo of the family and Mickey or Pooh, how many people have the opportunity to have a photo with Chef Amber (at the Liberty Tree Tavern) or Eddie (at Boma)?

—contributed by peer reviewer Beth Shorten

When dining with a vegetarian, it is easy to fall into the french fries/salad pattern. While nearly every Disney restaurant will offer at least one veggie option, or will make one up, that *one* option may not be to your liking. One of the best restaurants is Boma. There are always many options to choose from! Upon arrival, our host asked if we had special needs. Even though the restaurant was busy, the chef (and his assistant) came out to personally show us which dishes were vegetarian. Wow! We were made to feel like special guests, instead of outsiders.

—contributed by Lorraine Ivester

I am allergic to wheat. I mentioned this to the hostess at Liberty Tree Tavern and within a few minutes, the chef was by my side and asking questions that made it obvious that the man understands allergies. He told me which items on the normal menu that I could eat and what I should avoid. Then, he offered to make me special dinner rolls, gravy, and macaroni and cheese. I passed on the macaroni and cheese, but when they brought me the dinner rolls, I felt like I had gone to heaven. It's been six months since I've had bread and I don't actively miss it, but having it was an incredible treat. For dessert, I was brought a beautiful fruit tray with sorbet. The restaurant was very busy and crowded, but the entire staff made me feel very special. There wasn't a moment when I was allowed to feel as if I was a bother or an inconvenience.

—contributed by Tracy Arabian

While at Walt Disney World, I do not need to worry where or whether my child can eat. One particular magical moment stands out for me. We went to the Trail's End Restaurant, and Chef Gary came out with a huge plate of fried chicken (and green beans and corn) made especially for my son (he cannot eat gluten or dairy). The magic Chef Gary bestowed upon us cannot be measured. My son could not normally eat fried chicken because I could never get a gluten-free, dairy-free recipe right. My son wrote Chef Gary a thank you note, which he signed, "Love, Alex."

—contributed by peer reviewer Susan Koppel

My husband and I have both had the lapband surgery, so we spoke to a manager when we last ate at Boma and were charged the children's price. We left a tip on the regular adult amount, though.

—contributed by peer reviewer Melanie Emmons

Finding Pixie Dust and Resources

We've told you the whos, whats, whens, wheres, hows, and even the whys about staying at Walt Disney World and cruising aboard the Disney Cruise Line, but would you believe there's still more we could tell? We've been on countless Disney vacations, and there's still more to do each time we go. In this chapter, we've added a few things that are sort of the "icing on the cake"—a little pixie dust that adds to the magic of a Disney vacation.

Is a member of your group celebrating a birthday or anniversary? We tell you what you can do to ring in your special day in grand style! Are you hoping to tie the knot? We'll point you in the right direction for planning a wedding or even a vow renewal. Looking for a night out without the kids? We explain various child care options, including alternatives for families traveling with special needs children. Planning to attend (or maybe avoid) a special Disney event? We provide you with a calendar of Disney's upcoming festivals, holiday celebrations, and other special activities.

Even if you don't have a special event to celebrate, you can enhance your trip by trying some of the other ideas you'll find in this chapter. If you have a special needs traveler who gets bored easily or doesn't tolerate standing in lines well, searching for the Hidden Mickeys or coin press machines we discuss here will keep their active minds (and bodies) busy. Hunting for and finding the Disney characters can be another adventure, while collecting autographs and/or photographs is a special activity in and of itself. Use or adapt the suggestions we've made in this chapter to your benefit ... and let us know what others you come up with!

Finally, even a book of this size may leave you with some unanswered questions. We've compiled a list of resources that we think will be helpful to special needs travelers—they certainly came in handy for us as we developed this book! In addition, we've added numerous other special needs resources—Web sites, magazines, and other programs—contributed by our expert peer reviewers. These are tried-and-true resources that have proven valuable to travelers with a variety of special needs. We hope you'll find them useful as well.

Making Pixie Dust

Time to Celebrate

There are plenty of ways to make a birthday special at Walt Disney World. Stop at Guest Relations in any of the theme parks and ask for a **"Today's My Birthday" button** for the birthday boy or girl to wear. You'll be surprised at the special treatment you get! (On a recent trip, Deb Wills encouraged a group of her friends to sing Happy Birthday to a girl she spotted wearing the button in Epcot!) Even if you're too shy to wear the button, dial "O" from a Disney resort phone and ask to hear the special birthday message. Oh, and be sure to mention the birthday to restaurant servers, too!

Authors Deb and Deb show off their special birthday dessert at Narcoossee's

If you want a **birthday party** for your child, there are a number of alternatives. For kids 4–12, contact one of the child care clubs (see next page). For other parties or birthday cruises on Walt Disney World's waterways, contact Disney directly at 407-WDW-PLAY (407-939-7529).

Another idea is to have an outside outfit, such as Gifts of a Lifetime, **decorate your hotel room** while you're at a park or create a special birthday treasure hunt or anniversary vow renewal event. For details, visit http://www.giftsofalifetime.com.

Celebrating a birthday onboard

On the **Disney Cruise Line**, mention your birthday or anniversary at the time you reserve your cruise, and remind your servers again when you board. Cruisers celebrating birthdays and anniversaries get a special cake at dinner and a serenade from their dining room servers. You can also bring or purchase decorations for your stateroom! Consider decorating your stateroom while the birthday boy or girl is eating lunch on embarkation day; then when the room is seen for the first time, it'll be all decked out for the special event!

Planning

Your Special Need

Getting There

Staying in Style

Touring

Dining

Resources

Index

Grown-ups Need a Night Out ... Alone!

Taking a night out on the town without the kids may be a bit difficult for families with a special needs child. Several Disney resorts offer child care clubs, but they will only accept children 4–12 who are potty-trained. In addition, these child care clubs won't accept children who require specialized one-on-one attention. If, however, your child will be fine on his/her own, you can make arrangements at 407-WDW-DINE (407-939-3463) in advance.

Important Note: There have been reports that occasionally, Disney's child care club will take a special needs child, providing parents with a beeper so they can be called on to change diapers or assist the child with toileting. Be honest when you make your child care club reservation regarding the child's needs. The cast members at the child care club will make the final determination.

Here's a list of **Disney's child care clubs**:

✔ Camp Dolphin (Dolphin hotel)
✔ Simba's Cubhouse (Animal Kingdom Lodge)
✔ Mouseketeer Club (Grand Floridian)

✔ Cub's Den (Wilderness Lodge)
✔ Never Land Club (Polynesian)
✔ Sandcastle Club (Yacht & Beach Club)

Rates are about $10/hour per child, and some clubs have a minimum stay. Parents are given pagers so they can be reached if there's a problem.

If your child has special needs, **in-room babysitting** is another option. Kids Nite Out (407-828-0920) offers Disney-sanctioned, private babysitting 24 hours a day. Two other independent child care agencies, Fairy Godmothers (407-275-7326) and All About Kids (407-812-9300), offer similar services. With advance notice, the professional sitters will watch infants and children with some special needs. The sitters are bonded, insured, and well-trained and come equipped with games and activities. Rates vary, depending on the age and number of the children.

If your child requires **other medical care** that the babysitters are unable to provide, such as help with gastric feeding tubes (g-tubes), you may want to contact the Visiting Nurse Association at Orlando Regional Health Care Systems at 407-854-3100 for additional options.

Will You Marry Me?

Some people come to Walt Disney World to get engaged; others come for their anniversaries or honeymoons, still others come for the Big Event—the wedding itself! In fact, Disney's Fairy Tale Weddings department will plan your special occasion, whether it's a wedding or a vow renewal, from intimate to blow-out celebration. For details, call 407-824-3400 or visit http://www.disneyweddings.com.

© MediaMarx, Inc.

A Disney wedding

Making Pixie Dust (continued)

What's a Hidden Mickey?

They can take many forms, but the traditional two circles (ears) on top of a larger circle (Mickey's head), make a Hidden Mickey. Sometimes you'll even find Mickey's profile or his whole body! Once an inside joke for Imagineers and cast members, Hidden Mickeys are now popular with guests. There are hundreds scattered throughout Walt Disney World and the Disney Cruise Line, and trying to spot them can be a great diversion for an antsy child (or adult). You can find them everywhere: your resort bedspread, designed into furniture, on the wall of an attraction—you never know where they will turn up. To help get you started, check out the "Hidden Mickeys" guide by Steven M. Barrett (Intrepid Traveler), available in bookstores, many stores around Disney, and on the PassPorter Web site. He also has a Web site at http://www.hiddenmickeysguide.com.

© MediaMarx, Inc.

Two Hidden Mickeys appear in this small section of bedspread at Port Orleans French Quarter

Press a Penny

Looking for an inexpensive souvenir? Make a pressed coin. The machines can be found all over the parks and resorts. For 51 cents (pressed penny) or $1.25 (pressed quarter), you get a flattened coin that sports designs of Disney characters, the attractions, and a variety of Disney logos.

Bright Idea: Use shiny pennies from 1985 or earlier, as they have less zinc in them. When they are pressed, they make a more uniform copper-colored penny.

Take a Tour

Disney offers guided tours and behind-the-scenes peeks—see page 305.

Meet a Character

For kids young and old, being at Disney is all about seeing the characters. And we've heard from many relatives of special needs Disney-goers that spending time with the characters has done them a world of good, from simply boosting their spirits to even encouraging them to try new words. So how do you find the characters? They're all around the Disney theme parks and on the cruise ships. The best way to find them is to check with Guest Relations when you first get to the park. If you have a specific character that you simply *must* see, ask a cast member—they have a special phone number they can call to find out such information. You can also consult the theme park's times guide (or cruise's Navigator) to find out the times and locations of meet and greet spots. Be sure to arrive early—lines form fast. If you're after an autograph, be sure to have a thicker pen and your autograph book at the ready. If you're hoping for a photograph, too, keep your camera handy.

Special Events

Every month of the year there is **something special happening** at Walt Disney World. Just about every holiday has a special event, and Christmas and Halloween even have their own special "parties" at the Magic Kingdom. Here's just a sampling of what you can expect . For more information on these events, visit http://www.allearsnet.com or look at our PassPorter Walt Disney World guidebooks.

From now through December 2006—**The Happiest Celebration on Earth**: Disney theme parks all around the world are celebrating Disneyland's 50th Anniversary! There are special shows and new attractions at each Disney park plus some new perks, like Disney's Magical Express (see page 98).

January–March: Run, walk fast, or wheel fast in the **Walt Disney World Marathon** and Half Marathon in January (http://www.disneysports.com). Celebrate Mardi Gras, Valentine's Day, and St. Patrick's Day with special activities at Pleasure Island, and in March, watch the Atlanta Braves work out the kinks in spring training at Disney's Wide World of Sports.

April–June: Epcot leads the way with the six-week **International Flower & Garden Festival** and Flower Power Concert series. The Disney-MGM Studios hosts Star Wars Weekends, Grad Nights take over the Magic Kingdom for several evenings, and then there's Mother's Day!

July–August: The summer heats up with amazing fireworks displays celebrating **Independence Day**. Professional football's Tampa Bay Buccaneers hold training camp at Disney's Wide World of Sports.

September–December: **Nights of Joy** in September bring some of the biggest talents in Christian rock. **Epcot's International Food & Wine Festival** offers free and ticketed seminars and dining events, as well as a smorgasbord of ethnic cuisines in food booths located around the World Showcase Lagoon. Mickey's Not So Scary Halloween Party brings happy haunts to the Magic Kingdom on selected nights. Sports fans will enjoy the **Funai Classic** golf tournament. **ABC Super Soap Weekend** features your favorite daytime TV stars for a few days of autographs and fun. And the December holidays are observed in style with a variety of annual events: The Candlelight Processional is a moving show filled with music and the narration of the Christmas story. The Osborne Family Spectacle of Lights dominates the Studios. Mickey's Very Merry Christmas Party is held on certain nights in the Magic Kingdom, complete with hot cocoa and "snow" on Main Street, U.S.A. And what better place to celebrate New Year's Eve than Walt Disney World?

Resources

Our research journey for this guidebook introduced us to many informative resources. And our expert peer reviewers submitted their favorite sites to help special needs travelers, too. These resources range from those specifically about an individual special need to those that arrange for rental equipment or actual vacations for special needs travelers. We hope that you will find some of these sites useful, too.

General Information

Deb's Unofficial Walt Disney World Information Guide:
http://www.allearsnet.com

Walt Disney World Disabilities Guide:
http://disneyworld.disney.go.com/wdw/common/Plain?id=PlainHomePage

National Institutes of Health:
http://health.nih.gov

Council for Exceptional Children:
http://www.cec.sped.org

Access Florida helps you find which facilities and establishments are accessible, for a variety of special needs, all over Florida:
http://www.accessflorida.org

ABLEDATA provides information on assistive technology and rehabilitation equipment for consumers, organizations, professionals, and caregivers:
http://www.abledata.com
8630 Fenton Street, Suite 930, Silver Spring, MD 20910
800-227-0216 or 301-608-8998; TTY: 301-608-8912

Special Message Boards or Areas

Our own PassPorter Forum for Vacationing With Special Needs:
http://www.passporterboards.com/ubb/postlist.php?Board=UBB34

DIS Boards disABILITIES forum:
http://www.disboards.com/forumdisplay.php?forumid=20

MousePlanet.com Theme Park Access Guide for Disneyland:
http://mousepad.mouseplanet.com/forumdisplay.php?f=16

Special Needs Sites

ADHD *[A]*
ADHD/ADD and related disorders (they also have a magazine):
http://www.additudemag.com

CHADD—Children and Adults With Attention-Deficit/Hyperactivity Disorder:
http://www.chadd.org/

Answers to your questions about ADD:
http://addvance.com

Addiction Recovery *[R]*
Addiction Recovery Guide:
http://www.addictionrecoveryguide.org

Alcoholics Anonymous:
http://www.alcoholics-anonymous.org

Alcoholics Anonymous Orange County, FL meetings:
http://aaorlandointergroup.aa_site_80/800(index).html

Alcoholics Anonymous Osceola County, FL meetings:
http://osceolaintergroup.org

Gamblers Anonymous:
http://www.gamblersanonymous.org

Narcotics Anonymous:
http://www.na.org

Overeaters Anonymous:
http://www.oa.org

Allergies/Asthma *[G]*
Local pollen reports and forecasts (Walt Disney World's ZIP code is 32830):
http://www.pollen.com

Asthma and vacations
http://www.asthma-education.com/info16.html

Allergy and Asthma Network Mothers of Asthmatics:
http://www.breatherville.org

Asthma resources for parents:
http://www.keepkidshealthy.com/asthma

Planning

Your Special Need

Getting There

Staying in Style

Touring

Dining

Resources

Index

Resources (continued)

Autism Spectrum Disorders *[U]*
Autism Society of America:
http://www.autism-society.org

Autism One Radio, a web-based broadcast:
http://www.autismone.org

Autism Research Institute:
http://www.autism.com/ari

Asperger Syndrome:
http://www.udel.edu/bkirby/asperger

Center for the Study of Autism:
http://www.autism.org

Autism Speaks:
http://www.autismspeaks.org

Chronic Fatigue Syndrome and Fibromyalgia *[C]*
Chronic Fatigue Syndrome:
http://www.niaid.nih.gov/factsheets/cfs.htm

Chronic Fatigue and Immune Dysfunction Syndrome (CFIDS) Association of America:
http://www.cfids.org

National Fibromyalgia Association:
http://fmaware.org/index.html

National Fibromyalgia Research Association:
http://www.nfra.net

Diet *[D]*
The Food Allergy and Anaphylaxis Network:
http://www.foodallergy.org (English and Spanish)

Celiac Disease and Eating Gluten-Free:
http://www.celiac.com

Gluten-Free Casein-Free Diet (Parent Support Group):
http://www.gfcfdiet.com

Gluten Intolerance Group of North America:
http://gluten.net

Diet [D] *(continued)*
Vegetarian/vegan message board:
http://www.veggieboards.com/boards/index.php

Vegetarian- and vegan-friendly restaurants, resorts, and shops:
http://vegetarianusa.com

National Institutes of Health—Food Allergies:
http://www.niaid.nih.gov/factsheets/food.htm

Food and Drug Administration: Information about food allergies:
http://www.cfsan.fda.gov/~dms/wh-alrgy.html

Peanut Allergy—information and discussion boards:
http://www.peanutallergy.com

Vegan and vegetarian articles, recipes, message boards:
http://www.vegsource.com

Vegetarian Resource Group:
http://www.vrg.org

Down Syndrome, Fragile X, and Other Cognitive Disabilities [I]
National Fragile X Foundation:
http://www.nfxf.org

The Fragile X Research Foundation:
http://www.fraxa.org

Fears [F]
National Library of Medicine Phobias/Anxiety:
http://www.nlm.nih.gov/medlineplus/phobias.html

Teens Health—Fears and Phobias:
http://kidshealth.org/teen/your_mind/mental_health/phobias.html

Foreign Language [Ö]
USA Tourist: French, Spanish, German, Japanese:
http://usatourist.com

Shirato's Walt Disney World in Japanese:
http://www2s.biglobe.ne.jp/~n-shira/index.html

Universal Currency Converters:
http://www.xe.net/ucc
http://content.virgin.net/uk.vnetuk/travel/travelcurrency.htm

Planning

Your Special Need

Getting There

Staying in Style

Touring

Dining

Resources

Index

Resources (continued)

Hearing [H]
Forums for the deaf and hearing impaired:
http://www.alldeaf.com

Able Access Travel—TTY numbers:
http://www.access-able.com/relay.html

Heart Health [♥]
Traveling with heart disease:
http://www.swedish.org/17276.cfm

Infants [B]
Centers for Disease Control: Traveling with infants and children:
http://www.cdc.gov/travel/children_gen_info.htm

Medical Treatment [T]
Epilepsy and seizure information for patients and health professionals:
http://www.epilepsy.com

Epilepsy Foundation (travel tips):
http://www.epilepsyfoundation.org/epilepsyusa/travel.cfm

American Diabetes Association:
http://www.diabetes.org

American Sleep Apnea Association:
http://www.sleepapnea.org

Spina Bifida Association:
http://www.sbaa.org

Juvenile Diabetes Research Foundation International (traveling):
http://www.jdf.org/index.cfm?page_id=102705

"The Diabetes Travel Guide" published by the ADA:
http://www.diabetesnet.com/dtravl.php

Traveling with Diabetes:
http://www.acrn.com.au/factsheets/Travel.pdf

Companies that rent medical equipment (in addition to renting wheelchairs/ ECVs as mentioned in chapter 5, Wheels section):

Apria Healthcare (407-291-2229):
http://www.apria.com

CARE Medical (800-741-2282):
http://www.caremedicalequipment.com

Medical Treatment [T] (continued)
Dialysisfinder (dialysis center locator service)—Walt Disney World's ZIP code is 32830:
http://www.dialysisfinder.com

Medical Travel, Inc.:
http://www.medicaltravel.org

Medical Travel, Inc. caters to patients with special medical needs and can arrange vacations for dialysis patients, wheelchair users, those requiring oxygen, and others. They also can arrange wheelchair-accessible villa rentals just four miles from Walt Disney World. 5184 Majorca Club Drive, Boca Raton, FL 33486. 800-778-7953

TravelMed:
http://www.travelmedintl.com

TravelMed arranges for service providers to come to your hotel room for a fee. Their services range from physical therapists to oxygen service, wheelchairs and electric scooters, and mobile x-ray/EKG/MRI. 800-878-3627, 888-878-3627

Mental Health [T]
Child & Adolescent Bipolar Foundation—For families of children and adolescents with bipolar disorder and professionals who serve them:
http://www.bpkids.org

National Mental Health Association:
http://www.nmha.org

NAMI (formerly National Alliance for the Mentally Ill):
http://www.nami.org

Healthyplace.com:
http://www.healthyplace.com

A parent's guide to helping kids with learning difficulties:
http://www.schwablearning.org

Tourette Syndrome Online:
http://www.tourette-syndrome.com

Tourette Syndrome Association, Inc.:
http://www.tsa-usa.org

Planning

Your Special Need

Getting There

Staying in Style

Touring

Dining

Resources

Index

Resources (continued)

Mobility *[M]*
Cerebral Palsy:
http://www.ucpa.org

The Neuropathy Association:
http://www.neuropathy.org

Reflex Sympathetic Dystrophy Syndrome:
http://www.rsds.org

Motion Sensitivity *[Q]*
American Academy of Otolaryngology (Head and Neck Surgery) Dizziness and Motion Sickness:
http://www.entnet.org/healthinfo/balance/dizziness.cfm

Physical Therapy *[P]*
American Physical Therapy Association:
http://www.apta.org/Consumer

Physical Therapy and the Alexander Technique Homepage:
www.physicaltherapy.org/links

Pregnancy/Fertility *[E]*
Centers for Disease Control: Pregnancy, Breastfeeding, and Travel
http://www.cdc.gov/travel/pregnant.htm

Religion *[W]*
Kosher travel:
http://www.kashrut.com/travel

Kosher restaurant database:
http://shamash.org

First Baptist Church of Kissimmee:
http://www.fbckiss.org

Mary, Queen of the Universe Roman Catholic Shrine:
http://www.maryqueenoftheuniverse.org

Celebration Presbyterian Church:
http://www.commpres.org/connect.html

Islamic Society of Central Florida:
http://www.iscf.org

Celebration Jewish Congregation:
http://www.jrf.org/cjc/index.htm

Seniors [S]

Association for Advancement of Retired Persons (AARP):
http://www.aarp.com

Service Animals [H][M][V]

Commonly asked questions about service animals:
http://www.usdoj.gov/crt/ada/animal.htm

International Association of Assistance Dog Partners:
http://www.iaadp.org

Americans with Disabilities Act as it relates to service animals:
http://www.sitstay.com/store/clothing/svcdog/Brief_Service_Animals.htm

Human-Animal Health Connection:
http://www.deltasociety.org/default.html

Size [L]

Size Wise—Your World Your Size:
http://www.sizewise.com

AmpleStuff (travel products for people of size):
http://amplestuff.safeshopper.com/21/cat21.htm?68

National Association to Advance Fat Acceptance:
http://www.naafa.org/

Vision [V]

Blind Children's Resource Center:
http://www.blindchildren.org

Sensory Processing Disorder Community Network:
http://www.sinetwork.org

Travel tips for people who are blind or visually impaired:
http://www.access-able.com/tips/braille.htm

Center for the Partially Sighted:
http://www.low-vision.org/helping.html

Planning

Your Special Need

Getting There

Staying in Style

Touring

Dining

Resources

Index

Resources (continued)

Magazines

ABILITY Magazine (949-854-8700):
http://www.abilitymagazine.com

Emerging Horizons: Accessible Travel Information (209-599-9409):
http://www.emerginghorizons.com

Exceptional Parent Magazine (800-EPARENT or 800-372-7368):
http://www.eparent.com

Living Without Magazine (food allergies/preferences, 847-480-8810):
http://www.livingwithout.com

ADDitude (888-762-8475):
http://www.additudemag.com

Travel Sites

Centers for Disease Control's Traveler's Health:
http://www.cdc.gov/travel/index.htm

FAA information for passengers with disabilities:
http://www.faa.gov/arp/disab.htm

Guide to airline seating (covers most airlines)
http://www.seatguru.com

Canadian Transportation Agency:
http://www.cta-otc.gc.ca

MossRehab Resources Net:
http://www.mossresourcenet.org

Society for Accessible Travel and Hospitality:
http://www.sath.org

Medically Escorted Cruises and Tours
915 East Cypress Creek Road, Fort Lauderdale, FL 33334
877-226-3218 or 954-491-2223

Choice Travel
800-494-3999 or 818-367-4693; e-mail: choicetrav@aol.com

Travel Sites *(continued)*
Gimp on the Go—Wide range of special needs covered:
http://www.gimponthego.com

Freewheelin' Travel—Peer reviewer Chet McDoniel organizes group trips to
Walt Disney World and the Disney Cruise Line for folks using wheelchairs:
http://www.freewheelintravel.com

Special Programs

If your special needs traveler is a severely or terminally ill child, you may
also want to contact the following:

Make a Wish Foundation (800-722-WISH or 800-722-9474):
http://www.wish.org

Dream Factory (800-456-7556):
http://www.dreamfactoryinc.org

Give Kids the World (800-998-KIDS):
http://www.gktw.org

Orlando Area Facilities

If your special need requires a hospital facility—say you need periodic
dialysis—you'll need to make arrangements in advance. Your best bet is
to contact a local hospital. Here is a list of several local medical facilities
that should be able to arrange a variety of services and therapies for
you (contact numbers current as of May 2005). For additional details on
medical emergencies, see the sidebar on page 60.

Celebration Hospital is the closest hospital to the Walt Disney World
Resort. It accepts all medical plans for emergency care.
Phone: 407-303-4000

Florida Hospital Medical Center
601 E. Rollins Street, Orlando, FL 32803
Phone: 407-897-1985 or 407-303-6611

Florida Kidney Center
4301 Vineland Road South, Suite E-17, Orlando, FL 32811
Phone: 407-425-4415

Orlando Regional Medical Center
1414 Kuhl Ave., Orlando, FL; Phone: 407-896-6611 or 407 841-5111

Planning

Your Special Need

Getting There

Staying in Style

Touring

Dining

Resources

Index

Resources (continued)

Florida Children's Hospital:
Phone: 407-553-KIDS (407-553-5437) or toll-free 800-553-KIDS

Arnold Palmer Hospital for Children:
92 West Miller Street, Orlando, FL 32806; Phone: 407-841-5111

Ask-a-Nurse for doctor referrals or general information:
Phone: 407-303-1700

Centra Care In-Room Services:
Phone: 407-238-2000

Doctors on Call Service (DOCS):
Phone: 407-399-3627

EastCoast Medical—Call Center staffed by Registered Nurses and medical
ancillary staff 24 hours a day:
Phone: 407-648-5252

Celebration Dental Group—For dental emergencies:
Phone: 407-566-2222

If you need to get a prescription refilled, Turner Pharmacy (407-828-8125)
on S.R. 535, in the Centra Care Building, is open 8:00 am to midnight
Monday–Friday and 8:00 am to 8:00 pm weekends. Delivery is available
to resort guests for $5. Orders are left with the Lobby Concierge and are
charged to your account. Turner Pharmacy will not bill your insurance—you
must pay full price. The price can be charged to your resort account or
you can provide your credit card number and have it charged directly to
your credit card. If you have a vehicle, you can get prescriptions refilled
at Orlando-area discount stores, such as Walgreens, Wal-Mart, Target,
or Costco. Consult the phone book or Web site (see below) for locations.

Area grocers and/or pharmacies (visit the Web sites for store locations):
Albertson's: http://www.albertsons.com
Costco: http://www.costco.com
CVS: http://www.cvs.com
Goodings: http://www.goodings.com
K-Mart: http://www.bluelight.com
Kash n' Karry: http://www.kashnkarry.com
Publix: http://www.publix.com
Sam's Club: http://www.samsclub.com
Target: http://www.target.com
Walgreens: http://www.walgreens.com
Wal-Mart: http://www.walmart.com
Winn Dixie: http://www.winndixie.com

Your Resources

Note here the helpful resources and phone numbers you discover to keep your information in the same place.

Resource	Site Address/Phone Number

Readers' Tips and Stories

It is fun to celebrate special occasions at Walt Disney World. My husband and I have done birthdays there as seniors and had a great time. Our birthdays are only a day apart, so we both get special attention from one trip! Also, it has become a tradition for us to celebrate our wedding anniversary at the Brown Derby. The server recognizes the event with champagne, special dessert, and/or a phone call from Goofy with the phone brought right to the table.

—contributed by peer reviewer Jean Miller

Another great way to add a little bit of pixie dust to a vacation and get a little more individualized attention might be to go on one of the many guided tours they offer at the parks. For an animal lover who needs a little slower pace, the Backstage Safari at Disney's Animal Kingdom or the Dolphins in Depth program at Epcot is a really good way to view the parks. Kids with Autism Spectrum Disorders, particularly Asperger's, who are fascinated with animals, would be thrilled to see animals up close, get in-depth information on how Disney takes care of them, etc. Also, I know a child with Asperger's who has memorized just about everything there is to know about boats; a child with a similar love of trains would probably be happy to go on the train tour in the Magic Kingdom. It costs a little extra to do these things, but depending on the person, they could turn out to be priceless experiences and memories.   —contributed by peer reviewer Joshua Olive

We have been going to Disney World since Patrick was 5. Each time we did the Jungle Cruise, I tried to interpret some of the spiel, but as a mom and not a qualified ASL interpreter, I really wasn't that good. Patrick would usually tell me, "It's OK, don't bother," and he would just take in the sights. When the Sign Language Interpreter services were offered, Patrick was 9 and on his fourth Disney trip. Well, the first place we went was the Jungle Cruise and Patrick laughed hysterically throughout the whole cruise! It was so heartwarming when he turned to me at the end and signed, "I didn't know that this was funny!" All in all, it was the most magical trip we have had in more than 20 trips.

—contributed by peer reviewer Cathy McConnell

Our daughter Rachel has a variety of special needs, but her love of Disney keeps us going back many times. She has been to Walt Disney World four times and sailed the Disney cruise once. She knows practically everything there is to know about all things Disney! Rachel does not really enjoy the rides—what she wants to see are the characters! We have solved this by different means. First, we schedule a character breakfast or lunch almost every day. This is a calmer setting where she can withstand the "wait" and get plenty of personal time with the characters. Second, we make sure that we are in Toontown when it opens! There are lots of characters around and the crowds are sparse. She also likes the Downtown Disney shopping area—she takes pictures with the fiberglass characters. Also, the campfire at Fort Wilderness was not crowded and she got a few minutes with Chip and Dale. By far, the best character experiences were on the Disney cruise. The detailed character schedule is posted in the lobby so that we could plan our day around it. There are also characters in the shows and roaming around the ship which was pure heaven for her.

—contributed by Michelle Rigney

Index

Planning
Your Special Needs
Getting There
Staying in Style
Touring
Dining
Resources
Index

Planning

Your Special Need

Getting There

Staying in Style

Touring

Dining

Resources

Index

Planning
Your Special Need
Getting There
Staying in Style
Touring
Dining
Resources
Index

Planning

Your Special Need

Getting There

Staying in Style

Touring

Dining

Resources

Index

Your Special Need

Getting There

Staying in Style

Touring

Dining

Resources

Index

Planning

Your Special Need

Getting There

Staying in Style

Touring

Dining

Resources

Planning
Your Special Need
Getting There
Staying in Style
Touring
Dining
Resources
Index

Register Your PassPorter

We are <u>very</u> interested to learn how your vacation went and what you think of the PassPorter, how it worked (or didn't work) for you, and your opinion on how we could improve it! We encourage you to register your copy of PassPorter with us—in return for your feedback, we'll send you **two valuable coupons** good for discounts on PassPorters and PassHolder pouches when purchased directly from us. You can register your copy of PassPorter at http://www.passporter.com/register.htm, or you can send us a postcard or letter to P.O. Box 3880, Ann Arbor, Michigan 48106.

Report a Correction or Change

Keeping up with the changes at Walt Disney World is virtually impossible without your help. When you notice something is different from what is printed in PassPorter or you just come across something you'd like to see us cover, please let us know! You can report your news, updates, changes, and corrections at http://www.passporter.com/wdw/report.htm.

Contribute to the Next Edition of PassPorter

You can become an important part of our next edition of PassPorter's Walt Disney World For Your Special Needs! The easiest way is to rate the resorts, rides, and/or restaurants at http://www.passporter.com/wdw/rate.htm. Your ratings and comments become part of our reader ratings throughout the book and help future readers make travel decisions. Want to get more involved? Send us a vacation tip or story—if we use it in a future edition of PassPorter, we'll credit you by name in the guidebook and send you a free copy! Visit http://www.passporter.com/wdw/specialneeds/tips.htm.

Get Your Questions Answered

We love to hear from you! Alas, due to the thousands of e-mails and hundreds of phone calls we receive each week, we cannot offer personalized advice to all our readers. But there's a great way to get your questions answered: Ask your fellow readers! Visit our message boards at http://www.passporterboards.com, join for free, and post your question. In most cases, fellow readers and Disney fans will offer their ideas and experiences! Our message boards also function as an ultimate list of frequently asked questions. Just browsing through to see the answers to other readers' questions will reap untold benefit! This is also a great way to make friends and have fun while planning your vacation. But be careful—our message boards can be addictive!

PassPorter® Online

A wonderful way to get the most from your PassPorter is to visit our active Web site at http://www.passporter.com. We serve up valuable PassPorter updates, plus useful Disney and general information and advice we couldn't jam into our book. You can swap tales (that's t-a-l-e-s, Mickey!) with fellow Disney fans, play contests and games, find links to other sites, get plenty of details, and ask us questions. You can also order PassPorters and shop for PassPorter accessories and travel gear! The latest information on new PassPorters to other destinations is available on our Web site as well. To go directly to our latest list of page-by-page PassPorter updates, visit http://www.passporter.com/customs/bookupdates.htm.

PassPorter Web Sites	Address (URL)
Main Page: PassPorter Online	http://www.passporter.com
Special Needs Section	http://www.passporter.com/wdw/specialneeds
PassPorter Message Boards	http://www.passporterboards.com
Book Updates	http://www.passporter.com/customs/bookupdates.htm
Luggage Log and Tag Maker	http://www.passporter.com/wdw/luggagelog.htm
Rate the Rides, Resorts, Restaurants	http://www.passporter.com/wdw/rate.htm
Register Your PassPorter	http://www.passporter.com/register.htm

AllEarsNet.com®

AllEarsNet.com® is one of the Web's most popular Disney-related sites, consistently drawing hundreds of thousands of visitors each month to its unique blend of up-to-the-minute news and detailed information about Walt Disney World in Orlando, Florida. The Wall Street Journal, The Unofficial Guide to Walt Disney World, and even Disney's own Disney Magazine have all singled out AllEarsNet.com® as a top resource for vacation planners, and countless individuals on Internet discussion forums recommend the site for all kinds of Disney vacation information.

AllEarsNet.com® is as comprehensive as possible, with information that is relevant to not only the traditional family, but to singles, couples, travel professionals, first-timers, seasoned Walt Disney World veterans, those with special touring or dietary needs, and international travelers.

AllEarsNet.com® also encompasses the free electronic newsletter ALL EARS®, which is sent via e-mail to more than 60,000 subscribers weekly. The newsletter, which is entering its seventh year of publication, provides entertaining features, current news, reader-submitted tips, and commentary, all about Walt Disney World, with a dose of information on Disneyland and the Disney Cruise Line thrown for good measure.

Visit AllEarsNet.com® at http://www.allearsnet.com.

AllEarsNet.com and ALL EARS® are owned and operated by RYI Enterprises, LLC (Deb Wills, president).

PassPorter Goodies

PassPorter was born out of the necessity for more planning, organization, and a way to preserve the memories of a great vacation! Along the way we've found other things that either help us use the PassPorter better, appreciate our vacation more, or just make our journey a little more comfortable. Others have asked us about them, so we thought we'd share them with you. Order online at http://www.passporterstore.com, call us toll-free 877-929-3273, or use a photocopy of the order form below.

✂ ....

PassPorter® PassHolder is a small, lightweight nylon pouch that holds passes, ID cards, passports, money, and pens. Wear it around your neck for hands-free touring and for easy access at the airport. The front features a clear compartment, a zippered pocket, and a velcro pocket; the back has a small pocket (perfect size for FASTPASS) and two pen slots. Adjustable cord. Royal blue. 4 $^7/_8$" x 6 $^1/_2$"	**Quantity:** ____ x $7.95
PassPorter® Badge personalized with your name! Go around the "World" in style with our lemon yellow oval pin. Price includes personalization with your name, shipping, and handling. Please indicate pin name(s) with your order.	**Quantity:** ___ x $4.00 Name(s): _____
PassPorter® Pin is our collectible, cloissone pin. Our 2005 version (shown at left) depicts the colorful PassPorter logo, and we anticipate a new pin design for 2006. Watch for new pins to be introduced each year!	**Quantity:** ___ x $6.00

Please ship my PassPorter Goodies to:	
Name	Sub-Total:
Address	Tax*:
City, State, Zip	Shipping**:
Daytime Phone...	**Total:**
Payment: ❑ check (to "MediaMarx") ❑ charge card ❑ MasterCard ❑ Visa ❑ American Express ❑ Discover Card number ....Exp. Date. .... Signature	* Please include sales tax if you live in Michigan. **Shipping costs are: $5 for totals up to $9 $6 for totals up to $19 $7 for totals up to $29 $8 for totals up to $39 Delivery takes 1–2 weeks.

Send your order form to P.O. Box 3880, Ann Arbor, MI 48106, call us toll-free at 877-WAYFARER (877-929-3273), or order online http://www.passporterstore.com.

.... ➤

More PassPorters

You've asked for more PassPorters—we've listened! We're adding three brand-new PassPorter titles in 2005, all designed to make your Disney vacation the best it can be. And we also have our best-selling, award-winning general purpose guidebooks to both the Walt Disney World Resort (see below) and the Disney Cruise Line (see right). To learn about these and other PassPorters, visit http://www.passporter.com.

PassPorter Walt Disney World Spiral Edition

It all started with Walt Disney World (and a mouse)! Our general Walt Disney World guidebook covers everything you need to plan a practically perfect vacation, including fold-

out park maps; resort room layout diagrams; KidTips; descriptions, reviews, and ratings for the resorts, parks, attractions, and restaurants; and much more! This edition also includes 14 organizer pockets you can use to plan your trip before you go, hold papers while you're there, and record your memories for when you return. Learn more and order at http://www.passporter.com/wdw, or get a copy at your favorite bookstore. Our Walt Disney World guide is available in a spiral-bound edition (2005 edition ISBN: 158771020X or 2006 edition ISBN: 1587710277) and a Deluxe Edition (see below)—both have 14 PassPockets.

PassPorter Walt Disney World Deluxe Edition

Design first-class vacations with this loose-leaf ring binder edition. The Deluxe Edition features the same great content as the general PassPorter Walt Disney World spiral guide. Special features of the Deluxe Edition include ten interior storage slots in the binder to hold guidemaps, ID cards, and a pen (we even include a pen). The Deluxe binder makes it really easy to add, remove, and rearrange pages ... you can even download, print, and add updates and supplemental pages from our Web site, and refills are available for purchase. Learn more at http://www.passporter.com/wdw/deluxe.htm. The Deluxe Edition is available through bookstores by special order—just give your bookstore the ISBN for the 2005 Deluxe Edition (1587710218) or our 2006 Deluxe Edition (1587710285).

Wondering why PassPorter's Walt Disney World For Your Special Needs isn't available in a deluxe edition? The answer is simple—it's just too big to fit in the deluxe binder! If you must have a binder, consider getting a binder with just PassPockets (available on our Web site) and use both the binder and this book to plan your vacation!

Even More PassPorters

PassPorter's Field Guide to the Disney Cruise Line and Its Ports of Call—Third Edition

Completely updated for 2005! Includes complete itinerary and port-of-call descriptions for the Disney Magic's 2005 West Coast and Panama Canal itineraries. Get your cruise plans in shipshape with our updated field guide! Authors Jennifer and Dave Marx cover

the Disney Cruise Line in incredible detail, including deck plans, stateroom floor plans, original photos, menus, entertainment guides, port/shore excursion details, and plenty of worksheets to help you budget, plan, and record your cruise information. Now in its third edition, this is the original and most comprehensive guidebook devoted to the Disney Cruise Line! Learn more and order your copy at http://www.passporter.com/dcl or get a copy at your favorite bookstore (paperback, no PassPockets: ISBN: 1587710226). Also available in a Deluxe Edition with organizer PassPockets (ISBN:

(February 2005) 1587710234).

PassPorter Disneyland Resort and Southern California Attractions—First Edition

New for 2005! PassPorter tours the park that started it all, just in time for Disneyland's 50th anniversary. California's Disneyland, Disney's California Adventure, and Downtown Disney get PassPorter's expert treatment, and we throw in Hollywood and Downtown Los Angeles, San Diego, SeaWorld, the San Diego Zoo and Wild Animal Park, Legoland, and Six Flags Magic Mountain. All this, and PassPorter's famous PassPockets and planning features. Whether you're making the pilgrimage to Disneyland for the big celebration or planning a classic Southern California family vacation, you can't miss. Learn more and order a copy at http://www.passporter.com/dl, or pick it up at your favorite bookstore (ISBN: 1587710048). Also available as a Deluxe Edition in a padded, six-ring binder (ISBN: 1587710056).

PassPorter's Treasure Hunts at Walt Disney World

New for 2005! Have even more fun at Walt Disney World! Jennifer and Dave's treasure hunts have long been a favorite part of PassPorter reader gatherings at Walt Disney World, and now you can join in the fun. Gain a whole new appreciation of Disney's fabulous attention to detail as you search through the parks and resorts for the little (and big) things that you may never have noticed before. Great for individuals, families, and groups, with hunts for people of all ages and levels of Disney knowledge. Special, "secure" answer pages make sure nobody can cheat. Prepared with plenty of help from Jen Carter, famous for her all-day, all-parks scavenger hunts. Learn more about this fun new book and order at http://www.passporter.com/wdw/hunts or get a copy at your favorite bookstore (ISBN: 1587710269).

To order any of our guidebooks, visit http://www.passporterstore.com or call toll-free 877-929-3273. PassPorter guidebooks are also available in your local bookstore. If you don't see them on the shelf, just ask!

Note: The ISBN codes above apply to our 2005 editions. For the latest edition, ask your bookstore to search their database for "PassPorter."

Planning

Your Special Need

Getting There

Staying in Style

Touring

Dining

Resources

Index

Vacation at a Glance

You have our permission to make a copy of the chart below and create an itinerary overview. You can then make copies of it and give one to everyone in your traveling party, as well as to those who stay behind.

Name(s):	
Departing on:	Time: #:
Arriving at:	
Staying at:	Phone:

Date:	Date:
Park/Activity:	Park/Activity:
Breakfast:	Breakfast:
Lunch:	Lunch:
Dinner:	Dinner:
Other:	Other:

Date:	Date:
Park/Activity:	Park/Activity:
Breakfast:	Breakfast:
Lunch:	Lunch:
Dinner:	Dinner:
Other:	Other:

Date:	Date:
Park/Activity:	Park/Activity:
Breakfast:	Breakfast:
Lunch:	Lunch:
Dinner:	Dinner:
Other:	Other:

Date:	Date:
Park/Activity:	Park/Activity:
Breakfast:	Breakfast:
Lunch:	Lunch:
Dinner:	Dinner:
Other:	Other:

Date:	Date:
Park/Activity:	Park/Activity:
Breakfast:	Breakfast:
Lunch:	Lunch:
Dinner:	Dinner:
Other:	Other:

Departing on:	Time: #:
Returning at:	